ANNUAL EDITIONS

Social Problems 10/11

Thirty-Seventh Edition

EDITOR

Kurt Finsterbusch
University of Maryland, College Park

Kurt Finsterbusch received a bachelor's degree in history from Princeton University in 1957 and a bachelor of divinity degree from Grace Theological Seminary in 1960. His PhD in sociology, from Columbia University, was conferred in 1969. Dr. Finsterbusch is the author of several books, including *Understanding Social Impacts* (Sage Publications, 1980), *Social Research for Policy Decisions* (Wadsworth Publishing, 1980, with Annabelle Bender Motz), and *Organizational Change as a Development Strategy* (Lynne Rienner Publishers, 1987, with Jerald Hage). He is currently teaching at the University of Maryland, College Park, and, in addition to serving as editor for *Annual Editions: Social Problems,* he is also editor of *Annual Editions: Sociology,* McGraw-Hill/CLS's *Taking Sides: Clashing Views on Controversial Social Issues,* and *Sources: Notable Selections in Sociology.*

The McGraw·Hill Companies

Mc Graw Hill Connect Learn Succeed™

ANNUAL EDITIONS: SOCIAL PROBLEMS, THIRTY-SEVENTH EDITION

Annual Editions is published by the **Contemporary Learning Series** group within The McGraw-Hill Higher Education division.

1 2 3 4 5 6 7 8 9 0 WDQ/WDQ 1 0 9 8 7 6 5 4 3 2 1 0

ISBN 978–0–07–805056–5
MHID 0–07–805056–1
ISSN 1093–278X

Managing Editor: *Larry Loeppke*
Developmental Editor: *Debra Henricks*
Editorial Coordinator: *Mary Foust*
Editorial Assistant: *Cindy Hedley*
Production Service Assistant: *Rita Hingtgen*
Permissions Coordinator: *Lenny J. Behnke*
Senior Marketing Manager: *Julie Keck*
Senior Marketing Communications Specialist: *Mary Klein*
Marketing Coordinator: *Alice Link*
Director Specialized Production: *Faye Schilling*
Senior Project Manager: *Joyce Watters*
Design Specialist: *Margarite Reynolds*
Senior Production Supervisor: *Laura Fuller*
Cover Graphics: *Kristine Jubeck*

Compositor: Laserwords Private Limited
Cover Image: © Patrick Sheandell/Photo Alto (inset); © Getty Images/RF (background)

Library in Congress Cataloging-in-Publication Data
Main entry under title: Annual Editions: Social Problems. 2010/2011.
 1. Social Problems—Periodicals. I. Finsterbusch, Kurt, *comp*. II. Title: Social Problems.
658'.05

Editors/Academic Advisory Board

Members of the Academic Advisory Board are instrumental in the final selection of articles for each edition of ANNUAL EDITIONS. Their review of articles for content, level, and appropriateness provides critical direction to the editors and staff. We think that you will find their careful consideration well reflected in this volume.

ANNUAL EDITIONS: Social Problems 10/11
37th Edition

EDITOR

Kurt Finsterbusch
University of Maryland, College Park

ACADEMIC ADVISORY BOARD MEMBERS

Preface

In publishing ANNUAL EDITIONS we recognize the enormous role played by the magazines, newspapers, and journals of the public press in providing current, first-rate educational information in a broad spectrum of interest areas. Many of these articles are appropriate for students, researchers, and professionals seeking accurate, current material to help bridge the gap between principles and theories and the real world. These articles, however, become more useful for study when those of lasting value are carefully collected, organized, indexed, and reproduced in a low-cost format, which provides easy and permanent access when the material is needed. That is the role played by ANNUAL EDITIONS.

The reason we study social problems is so that we can do something about them. Corrective action, however, is not taken until the situation is seen as a problem and the fire of concern is kindled in a number of citizens. A democratic country gives those citizens means for legally trying to change things, and this freedom and opportunity is a great pride for our country. In fact, most college students have already given time or money to some cause in which they believe. This is necessary as each generation will face struggles for rights and justice. Daily forces operate to corrupt, distort, bias, exploit, and defraud as individuals and groups seek their own advantage at the expense of others and the public interest. Those dedicated to a good society, therefore, constantly struggle against these forces. Furthermore, the struggle is often complex and confusing. Not always are the defenders of the status quo wrong and the champions of change right. Important values will be championed by both sides. Today there is much debate about the best way to improve education. Opposing spokespersons think that they are serving the good of the children and of the United States. In a similar manner, conscientious students in the same college class and reading the same material will hotly disagree. Therefore, solving problems is usually not a peaceful process. First, it requires information and an understanding of the problem, and we can expect disagreements on both the facts and the interpretations. Second, it requires discussion, compromise, and a plan with majority support, or at least the support of the powerful groups. Third, it requires action. In a democratic society this process should involve tolerance and even goodwill toward one's opponents as long as they act honestly, fairly, and democratically. Class discussions should involve respect for each others' opinions.

In some ways the study of social problems is easy and in some ways it is hard. The easy aspect is that most people know quite a lot about the problems that this book addresses; the hard part is that solving those problems is very difficult. If the solutions were easy, the problems would have been solved by now, and we would not be studying these particular issues. It may be easy to plan solutions, but it is hard to implement them. In general, however, Americans are optimistic and believe in progress; we learn by our mistakes and keep trying until conditions are acceptable. For instance, the members of Common Cause, including myself, have worked for campaign finance reform since 1970. Our efforts failed until Watergate created a huge public demand for it, and both campaign finance reform and public-right-to-know laws were passed. The reform, however, led to the formation of PACs (Political Action Committees) to get around the law and buy influence legally. Recently, new campaign finance reform laws were passed.

Nevertheless, I would speculate that while they will somewhat reduce the influence of money on politics, sooner or later moneyed interests will find a way to continue to have inordinate influence on policy decisions and eventually precipitate yet another reform effort. It could be that at the end of the twenty-first century, Americans will still be struggling with many of the same problems as today. But it is reasonable to believe that things will be somewhat better at that point because throughout this century people will mobilize again and again to improve our society; some will even do this at considerable cost to themselves.

The articles presented here were selected for their attention to important issues, the value of the information and ideas they present, and/or their ability to move the reader to concern and possibly even action toward correcting social problems. This edition of *Annual Editions: Social Problems 10/11* begins in Unit 1 by defining social problems and presenting a general critique of U.S. society. In Unit 2 it examines some big issues in the political and economic systems that have society-wide impacts. Next, Unit 3 examines issues of inequality and injustice that challenge basic American values. Unit 4 considers how well the various institutions of society work. Most institutions are being heavily criticized. These articles help to explain why. Then, Unit 5 studies the traditional problem of crime and law enforcement. Fortunately, there is some good news here. Finally, Unit 6 focuses on the future and problems of population, environment, technology, globalization, community, and long-term change.

To assist the reader in identifying issues covered in the articles, the topic guide lists the topics in alphabetical order and the articles in which they are discussed. A reader doing research on a specific topic is advised to check this guide first. A valuable resource for users of this book is the Internet References that can be used to further explore article topics.

Annual Editions: Social Problems 10/11 depends upon the readers' responses to these articles. You are encouraged to return the postpaid article rating form at the back of the book with your opinions about existing articles, recommendations of articles for subsequent editions, and advice on how the anthology can be made more useful as a teaching and learning tool.

Kurt Finsterbusch

Kurt Finsterbusch
Editor
Dedicated to the many heros and heroines who are trying to fix the various social problems addressed here.

Contents

Preface   iv
Correlation Guide   xii
Topic Guide   xiii
Internet References   xvi

UNIT 1
Introduction: The Nature of Social Problems and General Critiques of American Society

Unit Overview   xviii

1. **Social Problems: Definitions, Theories, and Analysis,** Harold A. Widdison and H. Richard Delaney, *Social Problems: Definitions, Theories, and Analysis,* 1995
This essay, written specifically for this volume, explores the complexities associated with defining, studying, and attempting to resolve "social" problems. The three major theoretical approaches—**symbolic interactionism, functionalism,** and **conflict**—are summarized.   2

2. **The Fragmentation of Social Life: Some Critical Societal Concerns for the New Millennium,** D. Stanley Eitzen, *Vital Speeches of the Day,* July 1, 2000
Social interaction "is the basic building block of intimate relationships, small groups, formal organizations, communities, and societies." Therefore, Stanley Eitzen is concerned about numerous social trends, which he reports "that hinder or even eliminate social interaction, and that indicate a growing isolation as individuals become increasingly separated from their neighbors, their co-workers, and even their family members."   9

3. **Spent,** Amitai Etzioni, *New Republic,* June 17, 2009
Amitai Etzioni's title "Spent" Is short for **"consumerism,"** which is the value system that is undermining the moral life of the United States. The consequences are bad for America because laws and law enforcement by themselves are very limited in their ability to limit immoral behavior. The **moral system** and consciences of individuals are the first line of defense against immoral and illegal behavior. Morals must remain strong and Etzioni proposes ways that they can be strengthened.   13

UNIT 2
Problems of the Political Economy

Unit Overview   16

Part A.   The Polity

4. **Who Rules America?: Power, Politics, and Social Change,** G. William Domhoff, *Who Rules America? Power and Politics, and Social Change,* 2006
G. William Domhoff is the leading proponent of the **power elite** view of U.S. politics, which is explained in this article as it applies to **political influence** in the United States today.   18

5. **Inside the Hidden World of Earmarks,** Eamon Javers, *BusinessWeek,* September 17, 2007
The main criticism of the U.S. government is that it is not fair. The rich and large corporations get much of what they want and the general public gets little of what it wants. One of the processes that achieve these results is **earmarks.** Eamon Javers explains this process and its impacts and calls for its reform.   22

The concepts in bold italics are developed in the article. For further expansion, please refer to the Topic Guide.

6. **Foresight for Government,** David M. Walker, *The Futurist,* March/April 2007

Today's governments must govern in terms of long-term challenges. They must prepare for the future. David M. Walker, the past comptroller general of the United States, is responsible for making the **Government Accountability Office** an anticipatory agency and discusses some of greatest future challenges that our government must face.   **26**

Part B. The Economy

7. **A Smarter Planet,** Samuel J. Palmisano, *Vital Speeches of the Day,* January 2009

Globalization involves the international integration of **economic activity.** Samuel J. Palmisano presents a new view of globalization because he identifies how it is rapidly changing the **corporate world.** The multinational corporation is being replaced by a new kind of corporation that is being redesigned around **technologies** of interconnectedness, embedded sensors, and complex intelligence systems.   **30**

8. **Reversal of Fortune,** Bill McKibben, *Mother Jones,* March 2007

Bill McKibben raises the age-old question **"Does money buy happiness?"** in a new way, i.e., "Is more better?" The data indicate that economic "growth no longer makes us happier." In fact, the things that contribute most to happiness are under stress in modern life.   **32**

9. **Born to Buy: Interview with Juliet Schor,** James Woolman, *Dollars & Sense,* September/October 2004

The literature on the consumption side of the economy is quite dynamic today, and Juliet Schor discusses some of its major findings in this article, including the fact that the **materialism** that undergirds the consumer society "undermines well-being in lots of different ways. . . . People who are more materialistic are more depressed, they're more anxious, they have less vitality, they connect less-well with people, they have more stomachaches and headaches."   **41**

Part C. Problems of Place

10. **Why Aren't U.S. Cities Burning?,** Michael B. Katz, *Dissent Magazine,* Summer 2007

Sociologists should be surprised that U.S. cities are peaceful. Most of the conditions that produced nearly 150 riots in 1967 have continued, and some, like **racial segregation,** have worsened. Michael B. Katz tries to solve this paradox.   **44**

11. **Who We Are Now,** Jon Meacham, *Newsweek,* January 26, 2009

Since Johnson's Immigration Act of 1965, cumulative immigration flows along with brave civil rights activism have changed the United States and made the inauguration of America's first black president possible. Immigration has made our country better, which is encouraging, since by mid-century, the United States is expected to have a majority of minorities.   **49**

12. **The Invisible Ones,** Rebecca Clarren, *Ms.,* Summer 2007

Rebecca Clarren reports on the **slavery** that currently exists in America. Many people, usually foreigners, are held against their will and forced to work in factories under terrible conditions. Many others are forced into sex slavery. The public does not know about these slavery operations. Hopefully, this will change and the evil will be stopped.   **52**

UNIT 3
Problems of Poverty and Inequality

Unit Overview   **56**

Part A. Inequality and the Poor

13. **How Stratification Works: The American Stratification System,** Douglas S. Massey, *Categorically Unequal,* 2007

In this article Douglas S. Massey explains how **stratification** works and reviews its history. The two basic mechanisms that stratify societies are **exploitation** and **opportunity hoarding.** The latter involves a socially defined process of exclusion. All stratification systems are unfair, but some are much worse than others.   **58**

The concepts in bold italics are developed in the article. For further expansion, please refer to the Topic Guide.

14. **Goodbye, Horatio Alger: Moving up Economically Is Now Impossible for Many, If Not Most, Americans,** Jeff Madrick, *The Nation,* February 5, 2007

One of the prized characteristics of America has been the opportunity to go from rags to riches. Unfortunately, moving up economically is now impossible for most Americans. *Income mobility* has declined dramatically in the last three decades in America, and now several European countries have more income mobility than the United States.   **63**

15. **The Myth of the "Culture of Poverty",** Paul Gorski, *Educational Leadership,* April 2008

The *culture of poverty myth* accuses the poor of having beliefs, values, and behaviors that prevent them from achieving. Thus their failure is their fault. This myth must be challenged. Most poor people do have the work ethic, value education, and other characteristics that contradict the culture of poverty myth. Opportunity structures play a big role in poverty.   **67**

16. **Can Extreme Poverty Be Eliminated?,** Jeffrey D. Sachs, *Scientific American,* September 2005

Jeffrey D. Sachs argues that *world poverty* can be eliminated. The market and globalization have and will lift most people out of extreme poverty, but the elimination of extreme poverty would require the proper use of a $160 billion-a-year donation by the rich nations (0.5% of their GNP).   **71**

Part B.   Welfare and Welfare Reform

17. **A Work in Progress,** Ann Pomeroy, *HR Magazine,* February 2000

The *welfare reform of 1996* moved many people from welfare to work. Ann Pomeroy tells the stories of several women who made this transition and identifies some of the difficulties and perverse incentives that remain to limit the benefits of the program.   **76**

18. **Brave New Welfare,** Stephanie Mencimer, *Mother Jones,* January/February 2009

Stephanie Mencimer shows how many *welfare agencies* withhold a great deal of help that welfare recipients should receive. She tells some painful stories about welfare workers lying to or mistreating welfare applicants. Welfare is run by the states, and many states want to minimize their welfare expenses at the expense of their welfare clients.   **80**

Part C.   Racial and Ethnic Inequality and Issues

19. **Inequalities That Endure?: Racial Ideology, American Politics, and the Peculiar Role of the Social Sciences,** Lawrence D. Bobo, from *The Changing Terrain of Race and Ethnicity,* 2004

One way to understand the continuing *racism* in the U.S. is to see that the past attitudes, behaviors, and institutions recreate themselves in the present. Change occurs, but change is also resisted by those who fail to perceive the workings of the persisting *inequalities* in the United States.   **84**

20. **Why We Hate,** Margo Monteith and Jeffrey Winters, *Psychology Today,* May/June 2002

The authors demonstrate the prevalence of *prejudice and hatred* in the United States and explain this in terms of *social identity theory.* Whenever people are divided into groups, negative attitudes develop toward the out-group.   **88**

21. **American Dreamers,** Lisa Miller, *Newsweek,* July 30, 2007

A major cultural issue today is the place of *Muslim Americans* in the United States. They have been good citizens relative to other groups and think strongly of themselves as Americans. Now their situation is changing. Other Americans are becoming more suspicious of them, and, according to a government study, radicalism is growing among Muslims in the West.   **91**

Part D.   Gender Inequalities and Issues

22. **Great Expectations,** Judith M. Havemann, *The Wilson Quarterly,* Summer 2007

Women have taken tremendous strides toward *equality in the corporate world* and now hold half of all management and professional jobs. Their leadership style is superior to that of men. However, they rarely hold top management positions. Why? Several explanations are discussed.   **95**

The concepts in bold italics are developed in the article. For further expansion, please refer to the Topic Guide.

23. **Human Rights, Sex Trafficking, and Prostitution,** Alice Leuchtag,
The Humanist, January/February 2003
One of the evil plagues haunting the world today is **sex slavery,** and it is getting worse. It is the product of extreme poverty and the considerable profits it generates. The exploitation involved is horrendous. Human rights groups are trying to stop the practice. Alice Leuchtag covers many aspects of this issue.   **100**

24. **Answers to Questions about Marriage Equality,** Human Rights Campaign, 2009, *Washington Monthly,* March/April 2009
The **Human Rights Campaign** is an advocacy organization for gay and lesbian rights, and this article is their current statement advocating **same-sex marriage.** Although this is a totally biased statement, it is important to understand this viewpoint.   **105**

25. **(Rethinking) Gender,** Debra Rosenberg, *Newsweek,* May 21, 2007
Debra Rosenberg opens the window on **people who are born one gender but feel that they are the other gender.** Some use surgery and/or hormones to bring their bodies into compliance with their identity. Their stories are riveting, and their lives raise questions about what gender really is.   **108**

UNIT 4
Institutional Problems

Unit Overview   **112**

Part A. The Family

26. **The Frayed Knot,** *The Economist,* May 26, 2007
The thesis that marriage is in trouble is a half truth. It is true for the lower class and not for college educated class. Thus there is a **marriage gap,** and it contributes to the income gap.   **114**

27. **The Opt-Out Myth,** E. J. Graff, *Columbia Journalism Review,* March/April 2007
E. J. Graff explains why media reports of **upper-class women opting out of the labor market to raise children** in substantial numbers is a myth. The proportion of women, even mothers, in the labor force is increasing, not decreasing. The consequences and policy implications of the truth are immense.   **118**

28. **Good Parents, Bad Results,** Nancy Shute, *U.S. News & World Report,* June 23, 2008
Nancy Shute claims that research has determined what motivates children and exactly what **discipline methods** work and what don't: Parents must set limits; avoid micromanaging; not nag, lecture, or yell; and praise less and love more.   **122**

29. **Overworked, Time Poor, and Abandoned by Uncle Sam: Why Don't American Parents Protest?,** Janet C. Gornick, *Dissent Magazine,* Summer 2005
According to Janet C. Gornick the above title describes the **American parent,** especially the mother. Yes, parents are under considerable stress, but appropriate **public policies** would greatly help them.   **126**

30. **Peer Marriage,** Pepper Schwartz, *The Communitarian Reader: Beyond the Essentials,* 2004
Pepper Schwartz celebrates the widespread diffusion of **peer marriages** in which spouses regard each other as full **social equals,** both have careers, share family decision making, and more equally share child-rearing responsibilities. She argues that peer marriages generally result in **stronger families** and greater satisfaction.   **129**

The concepts in bold italics are developed in the article. For further expansion, please refer to the Topic Guide.

Part B.   Education

31. **Against School: How Public Education Cripples Our Kids, and Why,**
John Taylor Gatto, *Harper's Magazine,* September 2003
John Taylor Gatto attacks the **U.S. school system** for being boring and preventing
children from growing up. He suspects that this result is exactly what those who control
the school system want schools to be. In arguing his radical thesis he presents a very
provocative history of the evolution of the U.S. school system.   **134**

32. **Can the Center Find a Solution That Will Hold?: The High School
Experience: Proposals for Improvement,** Chester E. Finn, Jr.,
Education Next, Winter 2006
American high schools are failing, and Washington is not going to fix them. Chester
E. Finn, Jr. describes six major problems and proposes six solutions.   **138**

Part C.   Health

33. **Fixing Hospitals,** Robert Langreth, *Forbes Magazine,* June 20, 2005
Robert Langreth accepts the report that **medical errors** kill 100,000 Americans every
year and then proposes reforms that will dramatically reduce this number.   **142**

34. **The Medical Mafia,** Katherine Eban, *Fortune,* August 31, 2009
Katherine Eban tells the story of a **medical scam** and reveals a great deal about the
medical system, the legal system, and the **reforms** or regulations that are needed to
make these systems work as they should.   **146**

UNIT 5
Crime, Violence, and Law Enforcement

Unit Overview   **152**

Part A.   Crime

35. **Fighting Crime: An Economist's View,** John J. Donohue,
Milken Institute Review, First Quarter, 2005
It is amazing what conclusions we would come to about **crime and punishment** if we
used **economic logic,** as John J. Donohue shows in this article. We would stop building
prisons, abolish the death penalty, expand the police force, adopt sensible gun controls,
and legalize drugs, among other things.   **154**

36. **The Aggregate Burden of Crime,** David A. Anderson, *Journal of Law
and Economics,* October 1999
David A. Anderson makes a valiant effort to compute the **annual costs of major types
of crime** and the net annual total costs of all crime, which he claims annually exceeds
$1 trillion or over $4000 per capita. Fraud and cheating on taxes costs Americans over
20 times the costs of theft, burglary, and robbery.   **159**

37. **The Globalization of Crime,** Stephen Aguilar-Millan et al., *The Futurist,*
November/December 2008
The authors examine the ways in which crime has become globalized and reorganized.
In just 20 years globalization has restructured crime from vertical and horizontal industrialized forms to a large number of loosely connected networks spanning the globe. Their
major activities include **drugs, counterfeiting, the modern slave trade, and white
collar crime** (intellectual property crime, cybercrime, payment card fraud, computer
virus attacks, identity theft, and cyberterrorism).   **163**

Part B.   Law Enforcement

38. **Causes and Consequences of Wrongful Convictions,** Hugo Adam Bedau,
Current, March/April 2003
Recently much light has been shed on the **injustices of the criminal justice system.** Hugo
Adam Bedau has spent several decades researching **wrongful convictions** and lays out
the evidence for its prevalence and suggests reforms that should greatly reduce them.   **170**

The concepts in bold italics are developed in the article. For further expansion, please refer to the Topic Guide.

39. Reforming Juvenile Justice, Barry Krisberg, *The American Prospect,* September 2005

Juvenile justice needs to be reformed. Barry Krisberg reviews the history of the oscillation between punitive and rehabilitation phases in juvenile justice. Science supports the **rehabilitation model,** and public fears support the punitive model, which is in force today. But rehabilitation of children often occurs, and society gains from it.   **174**

40. America Incarcerated: Crime, Punishment, and the Question of Race, Glenn C. Loury, *Utne Reader,* November/December 2007

Glenn C. Loury reports that **the United States** houses 25% of the world's inmates while having only 5% of the world's population. We have the **highest incarceration rate** in the world. This is related to a widespread public attitude of punitiveness and underlying racial attitudes. Other countries have much better records of rehabilitation.   **177**

Part C.   Terrorism

41. Defeating Terrorism: Is It Possible? Is It Probable?, Marvin J. Cetron, *The Futurist,* May/June 2007

One of the leading futurists, Marvin Cetron, directed the most extensive projects forecasting the **future of terrorism** and reports its findings here.   **182**

42. Nightmare in Manhattan, Bruce Goldman, *New Scientist Magazine,* March 2006

America's biggest fear is **nuclear terrorism.** Bruce Goldman describes the impact on Manhattan of a terrorist nuclear bomb.   **187**

UNIT 6
Problems of Population, Environment, Technology, and the Future

Unit Overview   **190**

Part A.   Population and Environment Issues

43. Enough Already, Paul Ehrlich and Anne Ehrlich, *New Scientist Magazine,* September 30, 2006

Paul and Anne Ehrlich counter those who fear negative consequences of **stable or declining population.** The worriers fail to notice the benefits of stable population, and the population decline thesis is overblown. The population of developed countries with healthy economies is likely to grow through immigration. Stable or declining population countries will have to change some of their retirement policies and make other adaptations, but adjustments need not be very severe.   **192**

44. The World's New Numbers, Martin Walker, *Wilson Quarterly,* Spring 2009

The world's **birthrates** are changing in unexpected ways. In general, birthrates are falling in the developing countries and increasing in Europe and North America. The major exception is Africa, where birthrates remain high. Martin Walker also analyzes **world immigration trends.**   **196**

45. Plan B 3.0: Mobilizing to Save Civilization, Lester R. Brown, From *Plan B 3.0: Mobilizing to Save Civilization,* 2008

Lester R. Brown has been reporting on **environmental problems** for four decades and provides a synopsis of all the major environmental problems in this article. These problems must be addressed immediately because some of them might cross **ecosystem** thresholds and overcome equilibrating mechanisms with devastating results.   **200**

46. The Science of Climate Change, Anna da Costa, *The Ecologist,* January 2007

Climate change may be the major long-term trend affecting humanity. Anna da Costa explains what generates our climate, what is causing climate change, what are the expected impacts, and what can be done to prevent much of the predicted climate change and negative impacts.   **204**

The concepts in bold italics are developed in the article. For further expansion, please refer to the Topic Guide.

Part B. Technological Issues

47. **Who's Afraid of Human Enhancement?: A Reason Debate on the Promise, Perils, and Ethics of Human Biotechnology,** Nick Gillespie et al., *Reason Magazine,* January 2006

A major cultural debate of this century is how society will deal with **biotechnology.** The potential for reducing diseases, disabilities, and abnormalities, and enhancing performance is great. Eventually, children can be "designed." The **ethics** of human biotechnology is debated by four involved thinkers from different perspectives who ask, "What should biotechnology be allowed to do?"   **209**

48. **The Secret Nuclear War,** Eduardo Goncalves, *The Ecologist,* April 2001

An extremely consequential technology is nuclear. The energy it produces has greatly benefited mankind, but at what price? Eduardo Goncalves reports on all the **nuclear accidents, testings, experiments, leaks, production, cover-ups, and storage and reuse of nuclear materials** that he can find out about. The death toll could be as high as 175 million, and the shameful behavior of countless agencies that he reports on is shocking.   **217**

Part C. The World and the Future

49. **Update on the State of the Future,** Jerome C. Glenn and Theodore J. Gordon, *The Futurist,* January/February 2006

In this article two leading **futurists** provide a wide range of trends and predictions on the future. Jerome C. Glenn's and Theodore J. Gordon's **environmental predictions** are particularly frightening, but they do point to an increasing awareness of the problems and support for measures that favor **sustainability.**   **223**

50. **A User's Guide to the Century,** Jeffrey Sachs, *The National Interest,* July/August 2008

Jeffrey Sachs attempts to identify, briefly describe, and assess the consequences of the major developments of the twenty-first century. The world is converging technologically and economically, **economic and population growth** are threatening the **environment,** and vast inequalities in income and power between and within nations are destabilizing and increasing **conflicts.**   **227**

51. **The Rise of the Rest,** Fareed Zakaria, *Newsweek,* May 12, 2008

Fareed Zakaria argues that a great **power shift** is now occurring. For the last two decades America's superpower status in every realm has been largely unchallenged. Globalization and rapid economic growth in Asia have changed the world. America is still the unipolar power militarily but not in industrial, financial, social, cultural dimensions where the distribution of power is shifting, moving away from U.S. dominance to a situation defined and directed from many places and by many peoples.   **231**

Test-Your-Knowledge Form   **236**
Article Rating Form   **237**

The concepts in bold italics are developed in the article. For further expansion, please refer to the Topic Guide.

Correlation Guide

The *Annual Editions* series provides students with convenient, inexpensive access to current, carefully selected articles from the public press. **Annual Editions: Social Problems 10/11** is an easy-to-use reader that presents articles on important topics such as *poverty and inequality, the family, crime, law enforcement, terrorism,* and many more. For more information on *Annual Editions* and other *McGraw-Hill Contemporary Learning Series* titles, visit www.mhhe.com/cls.

This convenient guide matches the units in **Annual Editions: Social Problems 10/11** with the corresponding chapters in one of our best-selling McGraw-Hill Social Problems textbooks by Lauer/Lauer.

Annual Editions: Social Problems 10/11	Social Problems and the Quality of Life, 12/e by Lauer/Lauer
Unit 1: The Nature of Social Problems and Calls for Transforming Society	**Chapter 1:** Understanding Social Problems **Chapter 5:** Sexual Deviance
Unit 2: Problems of the Political Economy	**Chapter 9:** Government and Politics **Chapter 10:** Work and the Economy
Unit 3: Problems of Poverty and Inequality	**Chapter 6:** Poverty **Chapter 7:** Gender and Sexual Orientation **Chapter 8:** Race, Ethnic Groups, and Racism
Unit 4: Institutional Problems	**Chapter 11:** Education **Chapter 12:** Family Problems **Chapter 13:** Health Care and Illness: Physical and Mental
Unit 5: Crime, Violence, and Law Enforcement	**Chapter 2:** Alcohol and Other Drugs **Chapter 3:** Crime and Delinquency **Chapter 4:** Violence **Chapter 14:** War and Terrorism
Unit 6: Problems of Population, Environment, Resources, and the Future	**Chapter 15:** The Environment

Topic Guide

This topic guide suggests how the selections in this book relate to the subjects covered in your course. You may want to use the topics listed on these pages to search the Web more easily.

On the following pages a number of websites have been gathered specifically for this book. They are arranged to reflect the units of this Annual Editions reader. You can link to these sites by going to *http://www.mhhe.com/cls*.

All the articles that relate to each topic are listed below the bold-faced term.

Abuse
23. Human Rights, Sex Trafficking, and Prostitution

Aggression
20. Why We Hate

Assimilation
21. American Dreamers

Business and the market
3. Spent
5. Inside the Hidden World of Earmarks
7. A Smarter Planet
8. Reversal of Fortune
9. Born to Buy: Interview with Juliet Schor
33. Fixing Hospitals
50. A User's Guide to the Century

Capitalism
3. Spent
8. Reversal of Fortune
9. Born to Buy: Interview with Juliet Schor
19. Inequalities That Endure?: Racial Ideology, American Politics, and the Peculiar Role of the Social Sciences
50. A User's Guide to the Century

Children and childhood
26. The Frayed Knot
31. Against School: How Public Education Cripples Our Kids, and Why
39. Reforming Juvenile Justice

Cities
10. Why Aren't U.S. Cities Burning?

Civil rights
12. The Invisible Ones
23. Human Rights, Sex Trafficking, and Prostitution
24. Answers to Questions about Marriage Equality

Community
2. The Fragmentation of Social Life: Some Critical Societal Concerns for the New Millennium
10. Why Aren't U.S. Cities Burning?

Conflict
1. Social Problems: Definitions, Theories, and Analysis
10. Why Aren't U.S. Cities Burning?
20. Why We Hate
23. Human Rights, Sex Trafficking, and Prostitution

Crime
23. Human Rights, Sex Trafficking, and Prostitution
34. The Medial Mafia
36. The Aggregate Burden of Crime

37. The Globalization of Crime
38. Causes and Consequences of Wrongful Convictions
40. America Incarcerated: Crime, Punishment, and the Question of Race

Culture
2. The Fragmentation of Social Life: Some Critical Societal Concerns for the New Millennium
3. Spent
8. Reversal of Fortune
11. Who We Are Now
15. The Myth of the "Culture of Poverty"
21. American Dreamers
29. Overworked, Time Poor, and Abandoned by Uncle Sam: Why Don't American Parents Protest?
30. Peer Marriage
31. Against School: How Public Education Cripples Our Kids, and Why
51. The Rise of the Rest

Demography
43. Enough Already

Discrimination
10. Why Aren't U.S. Cities Burning?
20. Why We Hate
21. American Dreamers
23. Human Rights, Sex Trafficking, and Prostitution
24. Answers to Questions about Marriage Equality

Ecology and environment
44. The World's New Numbers
45. Plan B 3.0: Mobilizing to Save Civilization
46. The Science of Climate Change
50. A User's Guide to the Century

Economy
3. Spent
7. A Smarter Planet
8. Reversal of Fortune
9. Born to Buy: Interview with Juliet Schor
14. Goodbye, Horatio Alger: Moving up Economically Is Now Impossible for Many, If Not Most, Americans
17. A Work in Progress
19. Inequalities That Endure?: Racial Ideology, American Politics, and the Peculiar Role of the Social Sciences
50. A User's Guide to the Century
51. The Rise of the Rest

Education
31. Against School: How Public Education Cripples Our Kids, and Why
32. Can the Center Find a Solution That Will Hold?: The High School Experience: Proposals for Improvement

Family
26. The Frayed Knot
27. The Opt-Out Myth
28. Good Parents, Bad Results

Future

6. Foresight for Government
7. A Smarter Planet
16. Can Extreme Poverty Be Eliminated?
49. Update on the State of the Future
50. A User's Guide to the Century
51. The Rise of the Rest

Gender roles

24. Answers to Questions about Marriage Equality
25. (Rethinking) Gender
27. The Opt-Out Myth
29. Overworked, Time Poor, and Abandoned by Uncle Sam: Why Don't American Parents Protest?
30. Peer Marriage

Globalization

7. A Smarter Planet
37. The Globalization of Crime
50. A User's Guide to the Century
51. The Rise of the Rest

Government

5. Inside the Hidden World of Earmarks
6. Foresight for Government
17. A Work in Progress
18. Brave New Welfare
19. Inequalities That Endure?: Racial Ideology, American Politics, and the Peculiar Role of the Social Sciences
38. Causes and Consequences of Wrongful Convictions
48. The Secret Nuclear War
51. The Rise of the Rest

Health, Health Care, Medicine

33. Fixing Hospitals
34. The Medial Mafia

Iimmigration

11. Who We Are Now

Law enforcement

23. Human Rights, Sex Trafficking, and Prostitution
35. Fighting Crime: An Economist's View
36. The Aggregate Burden of Crime
37. The Globalization of Crime
38. Causes and Consequences of Wrongful Convictions
39. Reforming Juvenile Justice
40. America Incarcerated: Crime, Punishment, and the Question of Race

Lifestyles

3. Spent
8. Reversal of Fortune
9. Born to Buy: Interview with Juliet Schor
11. Who We Are Now
15. The Myth of the "Culture of Poverty"
24. Answers to Questions about Marriage Equality
29. Overworked, Time Poor, and Abandoned by Uncle Sam: Why Don't American Parents Protest?
45. Plan B 3.0: Mobilizing to Save Civilization
51. The Rise of the Rest

Lower class

12. The Invisible Ones
16. Can Extreme Poverty Be Eliminated?
18. Brave New Welfare
19. Inequalities That Endure?: Racial Ideology, American Politics, and the Peculiar Role of the Social Sciences

Marriage and divorce

24. Answers to Questions about Marriage Equality
26. The Frayed Knot

29. Overworked, Time Poor, and Abandoned by Uncle Sam: Why Don't American Parents Protest?
30. Peer Marriage

Multiculturalism

10. Why Aren't U.S. Cities Burning?
11. Who We Are Now
15. The Myth of the "Culture of Poverty"
20. Why We Hate

Politics

4. Who Rules America?: Power, Politics, and Social Change
6. Foresight for Government
7. A Smarter Planet
18. Brave New Welfare
19. Inequalities That Endure?: Racial Ideology, American Politics, and the Peculiar Role of the Social Sciences
23. Human Rights, Sex Trafficking, and Prostitution
24. Answers to Questions about Marriage Equality
48. The Secret Nuclear War
50. A User's Guide to the Century
51. The Rise of the Rest

Population

44. The World's New Numbers
45. Plan B 3.0: Mobilizing to Save Civilization

Poverty

15. The Myth of the "Culture of Poverty"
16. Can Extreme Poverty Be Eliminated?
17. A Work in Progress
24. Human Rights, Sex Trafficking, and Prostitution

Race and ethnic relations

10. Why Aren't U.S. Cities Burning?
11. Who We Are Now
20. Why We Hate
21. American Dreamers
40. America Incarcerated: Crime, Punishment, and the Question of Race

Sexism

23. Human Rights, Sex Trafficking, and Prostitution

Social change

2. The Fragmentation of Social Life: Some Critical Societal Concerns for the New Millennium
3. Spent
4. Who Rules America?: Power, Politics, and Social Change
7. A Smarter Planet
9. Born to Buy: Interview with Juliet Schor
10. Why Aren't U.S. Cities Burning?
24. Answers to Questions about Marriage Equality
29. Overworked, Time Poor, and Abandoned by Uncle Sam: Why Don't American Parents Protest?
30. Peer Marriage
50. A User's Guide to the Century
51. The Rise of the Rest

Social control

20. Why We Hate
36. The Aggregate Burden of Crime

Social relationships

2. The Fragmentation of Social Life: Some Critical Societal Concerns for the New Millennium
20. Why We Hate
24. Answers to Questions about Marriage Equality
28. Good Parents, Bad Results
29. Overworked, Time Poor, and Abandoned by Uncle Sam: Why Don't American Parents Protest?
30. Peer Marriage

Social stratification and inequality

5. Inside the Hidden World of Earmarks
11. Who We Are Now
12. The Invisible Ones
13. How Stratification Works: The American Stratification System
15. The Myth of the "Culture of Poverty"
16. Can Extreme Poverty Be Eliminated?
18. Brave New Welfare
19. Inequalities That Endure?: Racial Ideology, American Politics, and the Peculiar Role of the Social Sciences
23. Human Rights, Sex Trafficking, and Prostitution
30. Peer Marriage
50. A User's Guide to the Century

Social theory

1. Social Problems: Definitions, Theories, and Analysis

Technology

7. A Smarter Planet
47. Who's Afraid of Human Enhancement?: A Reason Debate on the Promise, Perils, and Ethics of Human Biotechnology
48. The Secret Nuclear War
50. A User's Guide to the Century

Terrorism

20. Why We Hate
41. Defeating Terrorism: Is It Possible? Is It Probable?
42. Nightmare in Manhattan

Upper class

4. Who Rules America?: Power, Politics, and Social Change
5. Inside the Hidden World of Earmarks
19. Inequalities That Endure?: Racial Ideology, American Politics, and the Peculiar Role of the Social Sciences
27. The Opt-Out Myth

29. Overworked, Time Poor, and Abandoned by Uncle Sam: Why Don't American Parents Protest?
30. Peer Marriage

Violence

36. The Aggregate Burden of Crime
48. The Secret Nuclear War

Wealth

3. Spent

Welfare

8. Reversal of Fortune
15. The Myth of the "Culture of Poverty"
17. A Work in Progress
18. Brave New Welfare

Women

22. Great Expectations
23. Human Rights, Sex Trafficking, and Prostitution
27. The Opt-Out Myth
29. Overworked, Time Poor, and Abandoned by Uncle Sam: Why Don't American Parents Protest?

Work and employment

12. The Invisible Ones
17. A Work in Progress
18. Brave New Welfare
19. Inequalities That Endure?: Racial Ideology, American Politics, and the Peculiar Role of the Social Sciences
27. The Opt-Out Myth
29. Overworked, Time Poor, and Abandoned by Uncle Sam: Why Don't American Parents Protest?
50. A User's Guide to the Century

Internet References

The following Internet sites have been selected to support the articles found in this reader. These sites were available at the time of publication. However, because websites often change their structure and content, the information listed may no longer be available. We invite you to visit http://www.mhhe.com/cls for easy access to these sites.

Annual Editions: Social Problems 10/11

General Sources

The Gallup Organization
http://www.gallup.com

Open this Gallup Organization home page for links to an extensive archive of public opinion poll results and special reports on a huge variety of topics related to U.S. society.

Library of Congress
http://www.loc.gov

Examine this extensive website to learn about resource tools, library services/resources, exhibitions, and databases in many different fields related to social problems.

National Geographic Society
http://www.nationalgeographic.com

This site provides links to National Geographic's huge archive of maps, articles, and other documents. There is a great deal of material related to social and cultural topics that will be of great value to those interested in the study of cultural pluralism.

UNIT 1: Introduction: The Nature of Social Problems and General Critiques of American Society

The American Studies Web
http://lamp.georgetown.edu/asw

This site functions as a search engine for resources in American Studies.

Anthropology Resources Page
http://www.usd.edu/anth

Many cultural topics can be accessed at this site from the University of South Dakota. Click on the links to find information about differences and similarities in values and lifestyles among the world's peoples.

Social Science Information Gateway
http://sosig.esrc.bris.ac.uk

This site provides access to online resources that have been evaluated and selected by subject specialists in the social sciences.

UNIT 2: Problems of the Political Economy

National Center for Policy Analysis
http://www.ncpa.org

Through this site, you can reach links that provide discussions of an array of topics that are of major interest in the study of American politics and government from a sociological perspective, including regulatory policy, affirmative action, and income.

Penn Library: Sociology
http://www.library.upenn.edu

This site allows you to research subjects and collections at the University of Pennsylvania's Penn Libraries.

UNIT 3: Problems of Poverty and Inequality

grass-roots.org
http://www.grass-roots.org

This site describes innovative grassroots programs in the U.S. that have helped people better their communities.

Immigration Facts
http://www.immigrationforum.org

Visit this site for press releases, facts on immigration and immigration reform, advocacy materials, and links to immigration reform resources.

Joint Center for Poverty Research
http://www.jcpr.org

Finding research information related to poverty is possible at this site. It provides working papers, answers to FAQs, and facts about who is poor in America. Welfare reform is also addressed.

SocioSite
http://www.pscw.uva.nl/sociosite/TOPICS/Women.html

Open this enormous sociology site of the University of Amsterdam's Sociological Institute to gain insights into a number of issues that affect both men and women. It provides biographies of women through history, an international network for women in the workplace, links to gay studies, affirmative action, family and children's issues, and much more. Return to the site's home page for many other sociological links.

William Davidson Institute
http://www.wdi.bus.umich.edu

The William Davidson Institute at the University of Michigan Business School is dedicated to the understanding and promotion of economic transition. Consult this site for discussion of topics related to the changing global economy and the effects of globalization in general.

WWW Virtual Library: Demography & Population Studies
http://demography.anu.edu.au/VirtualLibrary

Valuable information of interest to researchers in the field of Demography can be found through the Demography Program at Australian National University. Visit this site for more information and links to various resources.

UNIT 4: Institutional Problems

The Center for Education Reform
http://edreform.com/school_choice

Visit this site to learn how the Center for Education Reform combines education policy with grassroots advocacy, working in over 40 states to better education for America's communities.

Go Ask Alice!
http://www.goaskalice.columbia.edu

Columbia University's *Go Ask Alice!* is a web resource that answers questions about relationships, sexuality, sexual health, emotional health, fitness, nutrition, alcohol, nicotine and other drugs, and general health.

Internet References

The National Academy for Child Development (NACD)
http://www.nacd.org

Peruse this site to see how NACD partners with parents to help children reach their full potential through activities, tasks, and training sessions.

National Council on Family Relations (NCFR)
http://www.ncfr.com

This site provides a forum for family researchers, educators, and practitioners to share knowledge about families and their relationships as well as establish professional standards in order to promote family well-being.

National Institute on Aging (NIA)
http://www.nih.gov/nia

Browse this site to see how NIA provides leadership in aging research, training, health information dissemination, and other programs relevant to aging and the elderly.

National Institute on Drug Abuse (NIDA)
www.nida.nih.gov

This site provides information and research results in an effort to improve the treatment, policy, and prevention of drug abuse and addiction.

National Institutes of Health (NIH)
http://www.nih.gov

Consult this site for links to extensive health information and scientific resources of interest to sociologists from the NIH, one of eight health agencies of the Public Health Service.

Parenting and Families
http://www.cyfc.umn.edu/features/index.html

This site describes how the University of Minnesota and Minnesota communities use research, influence policy, and enhance practice in order to improve the well-being of Minnesota's children, youth, and families.

World Health Organization (WHO)
http://www.who.int/home-page

Access this site to see how the WHO provides leadership as well as monitors and assesses global health matters.

UNIT 5: Crime, Law Enforcement, and Terrorism

ACLU Criminal Justice Home Page
www.aclu.org/crimjustice/index.html

View this site to see how the ACLU is working to preserve all of the protections and guarantees of the Constitution.

Terrorism Research Center
http://www.terrorism.com

The Terrorism Research Center features definitions and original research on terrorism, counterterrorism documents, a comprehensive list of Web links, and monthly profiles of terrorist and counterterrorist groups.

UNIT 6: Problems of Population, Environment, Technology, and the Future

Human Rights and Humanitarian Assistance
http://www.etown.edu/vl/humrts.html

This site provides links to sites and search engines associated with human rights and humanitarian assistance.

The Hunger Project
http://www.thp.org

Browse through this nonprofit organization's site to explore how it tries to achieve its goal: the end to global hunger through leadership at all levels of society. The Hunger Project contends that the persistence of hunger is at the heart of the major security issues threatening our planet.

UNIT 1

Introduction: The Nature of Social Problems and General Critiques of American Society

Unit Selections

1. **Social Problems: Definitions, Theories, and Analysis,** Harold A. Widdison and H. Richard Delaney
2. **The Fragmentation of Social Life: Some Critical Societal Concerns for the New Millennium,** D. Stanley Eitzen
3. **Spent,** Amitai Etzioni

Key Points to Consider

• What do you think are the five major social problems in America? In what ways does your list seem to reflect one of the three major approaches to social problems?

• How much distance do you feel from people with very different interests, values, lifestyles, and of different religion, race or ethnicity, and class? What kinds of bonds do you feel with them?

• What signs of moral decay in America do you observe? What signs of moral strength do you observe?

• What aspects of modern life interfere with deep relationships and what aspects facilitate them?

Student Website

www.mhhe.com/cls

Internet References

The American Studies Web
   www.lamp.georgetown.edu/asw
Anthropology Resources Page
   http://www.usd.edu/anth
Social Science Information Gateway
   http://sosig.esrc.bris.ac.uk

What is a social problem? There are several different definitions of social problems and many different lists of serious social problems today. As editor of the 10/11 edition of *Annual Editions: Social Problems,* I have tried to provide valuable articles on all of the topics that are covered in most social problems textbooks. Three articles are included in this introductory unit. The first deals with the issue of the definition of "social problems" and the major approaches to understanding these problems in a larger theoretical framework. The second selection provides a thoroughgoing broad critique of American society. It does not address one social problem but presents the author's view of what is wrong with America in general. Its main theme is that social life in America is extremely fragmented, so individual well-being suffers. The third piece accepts the moral decline thesis and analyzes how America could re-moralize.

Harold Widdison and H. Richard Delaney, in the first article, introduce the reader to sociology's three dominant theoretical positions and give examples of how those espousing each theory would look at specific issues. The three theories—symbolic interactionism, functionalism, and conflict theory—represent three radically different approaches to the study of social problems and their implications for individuals and societies. The perceived etiology of problems and their possible resolutions reflect the specific orientations of those studying them. As you read the subsequent articles, try to determine which of the three theoretical positions the various authors seem to be utilizing. Widdison and Delaney conclude by suggesting several approaches that students may wish to consider in defining conditions as "social" problems and how they can and should be analyzed.

In the second selection, D. Stanley Eitzen analyzes a basic general problem of modern social life, i.e., that social life is atrophying. He identifies many social trends that hinder social interaction and increasingly isolate individuals from neighbors, fellow workers, and even family members. These trends include the frequency of relocation and separation from neighbors, immigration and separation from relatives in the home country, divorce and family breakups, and the substantial increase in the percent of people living alone. Technological changes have contributed enormously to isolation, including entertainment technology that provides individuals with a wide array of entertainment choices that can be enjoyed alone. What about the new communication technologies? Eitzen says that "the current communications

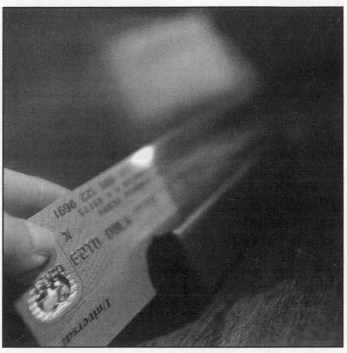

© Adam Crowley/Getty Images

revolution increases interaction while reducing intimacy." He also spells out the adverse consequences of these trends for society.

In the third selection, Amitai Etzioni examines the moral life of America. His analysis begins with the observation that laws, monitoring, and law enforcement are quite limited in their capacity to regulate and limit immoral behavior. People's consciences and the moral values they live by are the first line of defense against immoral and illegal behavior. The strength of these values has weakened over the past century, and the extremely destructive immoral behavior in business and more generally are the results. The major culprit, he claims, is consumerism. The answer is a cultural shift from consumerism to communitarianism, which "refers to investing time and energy in relations with the other, including family, friends, and members of one's community."

Social Problems: Definitions, Theories, and Analysis

Harold A. Widdison and H. Richard Delaney

Introduction and Overview

When asked, "What are the major social problems facing humanity today?" college students' responses tend to mirror those highlighted by the mass media—particularly AIDS, child abuse, poverty, war, famine, racism, sexism, crime, riots, the state of the economy, the environment, abortion, euthanasia, homosexuality, and affirmative action. These are all valid subjects for study in a social problems class, but some give rise to very great differences of opinion and even controversy. Dr. Jack Kevorkian in Michigan and his killing machine is one example that comes to mind. To some he evokes images of Nazi Germany with its policy of murdering the infirm and helpless. Others see Kevorkian's work as a merciful alternative to the slow and agonizing death of individuals with terminal illnesses. In the latter light, Kevorkian is not symbolic of a potentially devastating social issue, but of a solution to an escalating social problem.

The same controversy exists at the other end of life—specifically, what obligations do pregnant women have to themselves as opposed to the unborn? Some individuals see abortion as a solution to the problems of population, child abuse, disruption of careers, dangers to the physical and emotional health of women, as well as the prevention of the birth of damaged fetuses, and they regard it as a right to self-determination. Others look at abortion as attacking the sanctity of life, abrogating the rights of a whole category of people, and violating every sense of moral and ethical responsibility.

Affirmative action is another issue that can be viewed as both a problem and a solution. As a solution, affirmative action attempts to reverse the effects of hundreds of years of discrimination. Doors that have been closed to specific categories of people for many generations are, it is hoped, forced open; individuals, regardless of race, ethnicity, and gender, are able to get into professional schools, and secure good jobs, with the assurance of promotion. On the other hand, affirmative action forces employers, recruiting officers, and housing officials to give certain categories of individuals a preferred status. While affirmative action is promoted by some as a necessary policy to compensate for centuries of exclusion and discrimination, others claim that it is discrimination simply disguised under a new label but with different groups being discriminated against. If race, sex, age, ethnicity, or any other characteristic other than merit is used as the primary criterion for selection or promotion, then discrimination is

occurring. Discrimination hurts both sides. William Wilson, an African American social scientist, argues that it is very damaging to the self-esteem of black individuals to know that the primary reason they were hired was to fill quotas.

Both sides to the debate of whether these issues themselves reflect a social problem or are solutions to a larger societal problem have valid facts and use societal-level values to support their claims. Robin William Jr. in 1970 identified a list of 15 dominant value orientations that represent the concept of the good life to many Americans:

1. Achievement and success as major personal goals.
2. Activity and work favored above leisure and laziness.
3. Moral orientation—that is, absolute judgments of good/bad, right/wrong.
4. Humanitarian motives as shown in charity and crisis aid.
5. Efficiency and practicality: a preference for the quickest and shortest way to achieve a goal at the least cost.
6. Process and progress: a belief that technology can solve all problems and that the future will be better than the past.
7. Material comfort as the "American dream."
8. Equality as an abstract ideal.
9. Freedom as a person's right against the state.
10. External conformity: the ideal of going along, joining, and not rocking the boat.
11. Science and rationality as the means of mastering the environment and securing more material comforts.
12. Nationalism: a belief that American values and institutions represent the best on earth.
13. Democracy based on personal equality and freedom.
14. Individualism, emphasizing personal rights and responsibilities.
15. Racism and group-superiority themes that periodically lead to prejudice and discrimination against those who are racially, religiously, and culturally different from the white northern Europeans who first settled the continent.

This list combines some political, economic, and personal traits that actually conflict with one another. This coexistence of opposing values helps explain why individuals hold contradictory views of the same behavior and why some issues generate such intensity of feelings. It is the intent of this article and the readings included in this book to attempt to help students see the complex nature of a social problem and the impact that various values, beliefs, and actions can have on them.

In the next segment of this article, the authors will look at specific examples of values in conflict and the problems created by this conflict. Subsequently the authors will look at the three major theoretical positions that sociologists use to study social problems. The article will conclude with an examination of various strategies and techniques used to identify, understand, and resolve various types of social problems and their implications for those involved.

As noted above, contemporary American society is typified by values that both complement and contradict each other. For example, the capitalistic free enterprise system of the United States stresses rugged individualism, self-actualization, individual rights, and self-expression. This economic philosophy meshes well with Christian theology, particularly that typified by many Protestant denominations. This fact was the basis of German sociologist Max Weber's "The Protestant Ethic and the Spirit of Capitalism" (1864). He showed that the concepts of grace (salvation is a gift—not something you can earn), predestination (the fact that some people have this gift while others do not), and a desire to know if the individual has grace gave rise to a new idea of what constitutes success. Whereas, with the communitarian emphasis of Catholicism where material success was seen as leading to selfishness and spiritual condemnation, Protestantism viewed material success as a sign of grace. In addition, it was each individual's efforts that resulted in both the economic success and the spiritual salvation of the individual. This religious philosophy also implied that the poor are poor because they lack the proper motivation, values, and beliefs (what is known as the "culture of poverty") and are therefore reaping the results of their own inadequacies. Attempts to reduce poverty have frequently included taking children from "impoverished" cultural environments and placing them in "enriched" environments to minimize the potentially negative effects parents and a bad environment could have on their children. These enrichment programs attempt to produce attitudes and behaviors that assure success in the world but, in the process, cut children off from their parents. Children are forced to abandon the culture of their parents if they are to "succeed." Examples of this practice include the nurseries of the kibbutz in Israel and the Head Start programs in America. This practice is seen by some social scientists as a type of "cultural genocide." Entire cultures were targeted (sometimes explicitly, although often not intentionally) for extinction in this way.

This fact upsets a number of social scientists. They feel it is desirable to establish a pluralistic society where ethnic, racial, and cultural diversity exist and flourish. To them attempts to "Americanize" everyone are indicative of racism, bigotry, and prejudice. Others point to the lack of strong ethnic or racial identities as the unifying strength of the American system. When immigrants came to America, they put ethnic differences behind them, they learned the English language and democratic values, and they were assimilated into American life. In nations where immigrants have maintained their ethnic identities and held to unique cultural beliefs, their first loyalty is to their ethnic group. Examples of the destructive impact of strong ethnic loyalties can be seen in the conflict and fragmentation now occurring in the former Soviet Union, Czechoslovakia, and Yugoslavia.

James Q. Wilson (1994:54–55) noted in this regard:

We have always been a nation of immigrants, but now the level of immigration has reached the point where we have become acutely conscious, to a degree not seen, I think, since the turn of the century, that we are a nation of many cultures. I believe that the vast majority of those who have come to this country came because they, too, want to share in the American Dream. But their presence here, and the unavoidable tensions that attend upon even well-intentioned efforts at mutual coexistence, makes some people—and alas, especially some intellectuals in our universities—question the American Dream, challenge the legitimacy of Western standards of life and politics, and demand that everybody be defined in terms of his or her group membership. The motto of this nation—*E pluribus unum,* out of the many, one—is in danger of being rewritten to read, *Ex uno plures*—out of the one, many.

Theoretical Explanations: Symbolic Interaction, Functionalism, Conflict

In their attempts to understand social phenomena, researchers look for recurring patterns, relationships between observable acts, and unifying themes. The particular way in which researchers look at the world reflects not only their personal views and experiences, but their professional perspective as well. Sociologists focus on interactions between individuals, between individuals and groups, between groups, and between groups and the larger society in which they are located. They try to identify those things that facilitate or hinder interaction, and the consequences of each. But not all sociologists agree as to the most effective/appropriate approach to take, and they tend to divide into three major theoretical camps: symbolic interactionism, functionalism, and conflict theory. These three approaches are not mutually exclusive, but they do represent radically different perspectives of the nature of social reality and how it should be studied.

Symbolic Interaction

This theoretical perspective argues that no social condition, however unbearable it may seem to some, is inherently or objectively a social problem until a significant number of politically powerful people agree that it is contrary to the public good. Scientists, social philosophers, religious leaders, and medical people may "know" that a specific action or condition has or will eventually have a devastating effect on society or a specific group in society, but until they can convince those who are in a position to control and perhaps correct the condition, it is not considered a social problem. Therefore it is not the social condition, but how the condition is defined and by whom, that determines if it is or will become a social problem. The social process whereby a specific condition moves from the level of an individual concern to a societal-level issue can be long and arduous or very short. An example of the latter occurred in the 1960s when some physicians noticed a significant increase in infants born with severe physical deformities. Medical researchers looking into the cause made a connection between the deformities and the drug thalidomide. Pregnant women suffering from severe nausea and health-threatening dehydration were prescribed this drug, which dramatically eliminated the nausea and appeared to have no bad side effects. But their babies were born with terrible deformities. Once the medical researchers discovered the connection, they presented their findings to their colleagues. When the data were reviewed and found to be scientifically valid, the drug was banned immediately. Thus a small group's assessment of an issue as a serious problem quickly was legitimized by those in power as a societal-level social problem and measures were taken to eliminate it.

Most situations are not this clear-cut. In the mid-1960s various individuals began to question the real reason(s) why the United States was involved in the war in Southeast Asia. They discovered data indicating that the war was not about protecting the democratic rights of the Vietnamese. Those in power either ignored or rejected such claims as politically motivated and as militarily naive. Reports from the Vietcong about purported U.S. military atrocities were collected and used as supportive evidence. These claims were summarily dismissed by American authorities as Communistic propaganda. Convinced of the validity and importance of their cause, the protesters regrouped and collected still more evidence including data collected by the French government. This new information was difficult for the U.S. government to ignore. Nevertheless, these new claims were rejected as being somewhat self-serving since the Vietcong had defeated the French in Indochina and presumably the French government could justify its own failure if the United States also failed.

Over the years the amount of data continued to accumulate augmented by new information collected from disenchanted veterans. This growing pool of evidence began to bother legislators who demanded an accounting from the U.S. government and the Department of Defense, but none was forthcoming. More and more students joined the antiwar movement, but their protests were seen as unpatriotic and self-serving—that is, an attempt to avoid military service. The increasing numbers of protesters caused some legislators to look more closely at the claims of the antiwar faction. As the magnitude of the war and the numbers of American servicemen involved grew, the numbers of people affected by the war grew as well. Returning veterans' reports of the state of the war, questionable military practices (such as the wholesale destruction of entire villages), complaints of incompetent leadership in the military, and corrupt Vietnamese politicians gave greater credibility to the antiwar movement's earlier claims and convinced additional senators and representatives to support the stop-the-war movement, even though those in power still refused to acknowledge the legitimacy of the movement.

Unable to work within the system and convinced of the legitimacy of their cause, protesters resorted to unconventional and often illegal actions, such as burning their draft cards, refusing to register for the draft, seeking refuge in other countries, attacking ROTC (Reserve Officers' Training Corps) buildings on college campuses, and even bombing military research facilities. These actions were initially interpreted by government officials as criminal activities of self-serving individuals or activities inspired by those sympathetic with the Communist cause. The government engaged in increasingly repressive efforts to contain the movement. But public disaffection with the war was fueled by rising American casualties; this, coupled with the discontent within the ranks of the military, eventually forced those in power to acquiesce and accept the claims that the war was the problem and not the solution to the problem. Reaching this point took nearly 15 years.

For the symbolic interactionist, the fact that socially harmful conditions are thought to exist is not the criterion for what constitutes a social problem. Rather the real issue is to understand what goes into the assessment of a specific condition as being a social problem. To the symbolic interactionist, the appropriate questions are, (a) How is it that some conditions become defined as a social problem while others do not? (b) Who, in any society, can legitimate the designation of a condition as a social problem? (c) What solutions evolve and how do they evolve for specific social problems? (d) What factors exist in any specific society that inhibit or facilitate resolution of social problems?

In summary, symbolic interactionists stress that social problems do not exist independently of how people define their world. Social problems are socially constructed as people debate whether or not some social condition is a social problem and decide what to do about it. The focus is on the meanings the problem has for those who are affected by it and not on the impact it is having on them.

Functionalism

A second major theory sociologists use to study social problems is functionalism. Functionalists argue that society is a social system consisting of various integrated parts. Each of these parts fulfills a specific role that contributes to the overall functioning of society. In well-integrated systems, each part contributes to the stability of the whole. Functionalists examine each part in an attempt to determine the role it plays in the operation of the system as a whole. When any part fails, this creates a problem for the whole. These failures (dysfunctions) upset the equilibrium of the system and become social problems. To functionalists, anything that impedes the system's ability to achieve its goals is, by definition, a social problem. Unlike the symbolic interactionists, the functionalists argue that for itself that must necessarily be at the expense of other groups. It is this consistent conflict over limited resources that threatens societal peace and order.

Whereas the functionalists try to understand how different positions of power came into existence (Davis & Moore 1945), the conflictists show how those in power attempt to stay in power (Mills 1956). The conflict theorists see social problems as the natural and inevitable consequences of groups in society struggling to survive and gain control over those things that can affect their ability to survive. Those groups that are successful then attempt to use whatever means they must to control their environment and consolidate their position, thus increasing their chances of surviving. According to conflict theorists, those in power exploit their position and create poverty, discrimination, oppression, and crime in the process. The impact of these conditions on the exploited produces other pathological conditions such as alienation, alcoholism, drug abuse, mental illness, stress, health problems, and suicide. On occasions, such as that which occurred in Los Angeles in the summer of 1991 when policemen were found innocent of the use of excessive force in the beating of Rodney King, the feelings of helplessness and hopelessness can erupt as rage against the system in the form of violence and riots or as in Eastern Europe as rebellion and revolution against repressive governments.

The conflict theorists argue that drug abuse, mental illness, various criminal behaviors, and suicide are symptoms of a much larger societal malaise. To understand and eliminate these problems, society needs to understand the basic conflicts that are producing them. The real problems stem from the implications of being exploited. Being manipulated by the powerful and denied a sense of control tends (a) to produce a loss of control over one's life (powerlessness), (b) to lead to an inability to place one's productive efforts into some meaningful context (meaningless), (c) not to being involved in the process of change but only in experiencing the impact resulting from the changes (normlessness), and (d) to cause one to find oneself isolated from one's colleagues on the job (self-isolation). Conflictists see all of these problems as the product of a capitalistic system that alienates the worker from himself and from his or her fellow workers (Seeman 1959).

To protect their positions of power, privilege, prestige, and possessions, those in power use their wealth and influence to control organizations. For example, they manipulate the system to get key individuals into positions where they can influence legislation and decisions that are designed to protect their power and possessions. They might serve on or appoint others to school boards to assure that the skills and values needed by the economy are taught. They also assure that the laws are enforced internally (the police) or externally (the military) to protect their holdings. The war in the Persian Gulf is seen by many conflict theorists as having been fought for oil rather than for Kuwait's liberation. When the exploited attempt to do something about their condition by organizing, protesting, and rebelling, they threaten those in power. For example, they may go on a strike that might disrupt the entire nation. Under the pretext that it is for the best good of society, the government may step in and stop the strike. Examples are the air-traffic-controllers strike of 1987 and the railroad strike in 1991. In retaliation the workers may engage in work slow-down, stoppage, and even sabotage. They may stage protests and public demonstrations and cast protest votes at the ballot boxes. If these do not work, rebellions and revolutions may result. Those in power can respond very repressively as was the case in Tiananmen Square in China in 1989, threaten military force as the Soviet Union did with the Baltic countries in 1990, or back down completely as when the Berlin Wall came down. Thus reactions to exploitation may produce change but inevitably lead to other social problems. In Eastern Europe and the former Soviet Union, democracy has resulted in massive unemployment, spiraling inflation, hunger, crime, and homelessness.

Sometimes those in power make concessions to maintain power. Conflict theorists look for concessions and how they placate the poor while still protecting the privileged and powerful. The rich are viewed as sharing power only if forced to do so and only to the extent absolutely necessary.

Robert Michels (1949), a French social philosopher, looked at the inevitable process whereby the members of any group voluntarily give their rights, prerogatives, and power to a select few who then dominate the group. It may not be the conscious decision of those who end up in positions of power to dominate the group, but, in time, conscious decisions may be made to do whatever is necessary to stay in control of the group. The power, privilege, and wealth they acquire as part of the position alter their self-images. To give up the position would necessitate a complete revision of who they are, what they can do, and with whom they associate. Their "selves" have become fused/confused with the position they occupy, and in an attempt to protect their "selves," they resist efforts designed to undermine their control. They consider threats to themselves as threats to the organization and therefore feel justified in their vigorous resistance. According to Michels, no matter how democratic an organization starts out to be it will always become dominated and controlled by a few. The process

whereby this occurs he labeled the "Iron Law of Oligarchy." For example, hospitals that were created to save lives, cure the sick, and provide for the chronically ill, now use the threat of closure to justify rate increases. The hospital gets its rate increase, the cost of health goes up, and the number of individuals able to afford health care declines, with the ultimate result being an increase in health problems for the community. Although not explicitly stated, the survival of the organization (and its administrators) becomes more important than the health of the community.

In summary, the conflict theoretical model stresses the fact that key resources such as power and privilege are limited and distributed unequally among the members/groups in a society. Conflict is therefore a natural and inevitable result of various groups pursuing their interests and values. To study the basis of social problems, researchers must look at the distribution of power and privilege because these two factors are always at the center of conflicting interests and values. Moreover, whenever social change occurs, social problems inevitably follow.

Conflict and Functionalism: A Synthesis

While conflict theorists' and functionalists' explanations of what constitutes the roots of social problems appear to be completely contradictory, Dahrendorf (1959) sees them as complementary. "Functionalism explains how highly talented people are motivated to spend twenty-five years of study to become surgeons; conflict theory explains how surgeons utilize their monopoly on their vital skills to obtain rewards that greatly exceed that necessary to ensure an adequate supply of talent." (See also Ossowski 1963; van de Berghe 1963; Williams 1966; Horowitz 1962; and Lenski 1966 for other attempts at a synthesis between these two theoretical models.)

Social Problems: Definition and Analysis
Value Conflicts

It is convenient to characterize a social problem as a conflict of values, a conflict of values and duties, a conflict of rights (Hook, 1974), or a social condition that leads to or is thought to lead to harmful consequences. Harm may be defined as (a) the loss to a group, community, or society of something to which it is thought to be entitled, (b) an offense perceived to be an affront to our moral sensibilities, or (c) an impoverishment of the collective good or welfare. It is also convenient to define values as individual or collective desires that become attached to social objects. Private property, for example, is a valued social object for some while others disavow or reject its desirability; because of the public disagreement over its value, it presents a conflict of values. A conflict of values is also found in the current controversy surrounding abortion. Where pro-life supporters tend to see life itself as the ultimate value, supporters of pro-choice may, as some have, invoke the Fourteenth Amendment's right-to-privacy clause as the compelling value.

Values-versus-Duties Conflicts

A second format that students should be aware of in the analysis of social problems is the conflict between values and obligations or duties. This approach calls our attention to those situations in which a person, group, or community must pursue or realize a certain duty even though those participating may be convinced that doing so will not achieve the greater good. For example, educators, policemen, bureaucrats, and environmentalists may occupy organizational or social roles in which they are required to formulate policies and follow rules that, according to their understanding, will not contribute to the greater good of students, citizens, or the likelihood of a clean environment. On the other hand, there are situations in which we, as individuals, groups, or communities, do things that would not seem to be right in our pursuit of what we consider to be the higher value. Here students of social problems are faced with the familiar problem of using questionable, illogical, or immoral means to achieve what is perhaps generally recognized as a value of a higher order. Police officers, for example, are sometimes accused of employing questionable, immoral, or deceptive means (stings, scams, undercover operations) to achieve what are thought to be socially helpful ends and values such as removing a drug pusher from the streets. Familiar questions for this particular format are, Do the ends justify the means? Should ends be chosen according to the means available for their realization? What are the social processes by which means themselves become ends? These are questions to which students of social problems and social policy analysis should give attention since immoral, illegal, or deceptive means can themselves lead to harmful social consequences.

Max Weber anticipated and was quite skeptical of those modern bureaucratic processes whereby means are transformed into organizational ends and members of the bureaucracy become self-serving and lose sight of their original and earlier mission. The efforts of the Central Intelligence Agency (CIA) to maintain U.S. interests in Third World countries led to tolerance of various nations' involvement in illicit drugs. Thus the CIA actually contributed to the drug problem the police struggle to control. A second example is that of the American Association of Retired Persons (AARP). To help the elderly obtain affordable health care, life insurance, drugs, and so forth, the AARP established various organizations to provide or contract for services. But now the AARP seems to be more concerned about its corporate holdings than it is about the welfare of its elderly members.

Rights in Conflict

Finally, students of social problems should become aware of right-versus-right moral conflicts. With this particular format, one's attention is directed to the conflict of moral duties and obligations, the conflict of rights and, not least, the serious moral issue of divided loyalties. In divorce proceedings, for example, spouses must try to balance their personal lives and careers against the obligations and duties to each other and their children. Even those who sincerely want to meet their full obligations to both family and career often find this is not possible because of the real limits of time and means.

Wilson (1994:39, 54) observes that from the era of "Enlightenment" and its associated freedoms arose the potential for significant social problems. We are seeing all about us in the entire Western world the working out of the defining experience of the West, the Enlightenment. The Age of Enlightenment was the extraordinary period in the eighteenth century when individuals were emancipated from old tyrannies—from dead custom, hereditary monarchs, religious persecution, and ancient superstition. It is the period that gave us science

and human rights, that attacked human slavery and political absolutism, that made possible capitalism and progress. The principal figures of the Enlightenment remain icons of social reform: Adam Smith, David Hume, Thomas Jefferson, Immanuel Kant, Isaac Newton, James Madison. The Enlightenment defined the West and set it apart from all of the other great cultures of the world. But in culture as in economics, there is no such thing as a free lunch. If you liberate a person from ancient tyrannies, you may also liberate him or her from familiar controls. If you enhance his or her freedom to create, you will enhance his or her freedom to destroy. If you cast out the dead hand of useless custom, you may also cast out the living hand of essential tradition. If you give an individual freedom of expression, he or she may write *The Marriage of Figaro* or he or she may sing "gangsta rap." If you enlarge the number of rights one has, you may shrink the number of responsibilities one feels.

There is a complex interaction between the rights an individual has and the consequences of exercising specific rights. For example, if an individual elects to exercise his or her right to consume alcoholic beverages, this act then nullifies many subsequent rights because of the potential harm that can occur. The right to drive, to engage in athletic events, or to work, is jeopardized by the debilitating effects of alcohol. Every citizen has rights assured him or her by membership in society. At the same time, rights can only be exercised to the degree to which they do not trample on the rights of other members of the group. If a woman elects to have a baby, must she abrogate her right to consume alcohol, smoke, consume caffeine, or take drugs? Because the effects of these substances on the developing fetus are potentially devastating, is it not reasonable to conclude that the rights of the child to a healthy body and mind are being threatened if the mother refuses to abstain during pregnancy? Fetal alcohol effect/syndrome, for instance, is the number-one cause of preventable mental retardation in the United States, and it could be completely eliminated if pregnant women never took an alcoholic drink. Caring for individuals with fetal alcohol effect/syndrome is taking increasingly greater resources that could well be directed toward other pressing issues.

Rights cannot be responsibly exercised without individuals' weighing their potential consequences. Thus a hierarchy of rights, consequences, and harms exists and the personal benefits resulting from any act must be weighed against the personal and social harms that could follow. The decision to use tobacco should be weighed against the possible consequences of a wide variety of harms such as personal health problems and the stress it places on society's resources to care for tobacco-related diseases. Tobacco-related diseases often have catastrophic consequences for their users that cannot be paid for by the individual, so the burden of payment is placed on society. Millions of dollars and countless health care personnel must be diverted away from other patients to care for these individuals with self-inflicted tobacco-related diseases. In addition to the costs in money, personnel, and medical resources, these diseases take tremendous emotional tolls on those closest to the diseased individuals. To focus only on one's rights without consideration of the consequences associated with those rights often deprives other individuals from exercising their rights.

The Constitution of the United States guarantees individuals rights without clearly specifying what the rights really entail. Logically one cannot have rights without others having corresponding obligations. But what obligations does each right assure and what limitations do these obligations and/or rights require? Rights for the collectivity are protected by limitations placed on each individual, but limits of collective rights are also mandated by laws assuring that individual rights are not infringed upon. Therefore, we have rights as a whole that often differ from those we have as individual members of that whole. For example, the right to free speech may impinge in a number of ways on a specific community. To the members of a small Catholic community, having non-Catholic missionaries preaching on street corners and proselytizing door-to-door could be viewed as a social problem. Attempts to control their actions such as the enactment and enforcements of "Green River" ordinances (laws against active solicitation), could eliminate the community's problem but in so doing would trample on the individual's constitutional rights or religious expression. To protect individual rights, the community may have to put up with individuals pushing their personal theological ideas in public places. From the perspective of the Catholic community, aggressive non-Catholic missionaries are not only a nuisance but a social problem that should be banned. To the proselytizing churches, restrictions on their actions are violations of their civil rights and hence a serious social problem.

Currently another conflict of interests/rights is dividing many communities, and that is cigarette smoking. Smokers argue that their rights are being seriously threatened by aggressive legislation restricting smoking. They argue that society should not and cannot legislate morality. Smokers point out how attempts to legislate alcohol consumption during the Prohibition of the 1920s and 1930s was an abject failure and, in fact, created more problems than it eliminated. They believe that the exact same process is being attempted today and will prove to be just as unsuccessful. Those who smoke then go on to say that smoking is protected by the Constitution's freedom of expression and that no one has the right to force others to adhere to his or her personal health policies, which are individual choices. They assert that if the "radicals" get away with imposing smoking restrictions, they can and will move on to other health-related behaviors such as overeating. Therefore, by protecting the constitutional rights of smokers, society is protecting the constitutional rights of everyone.

On the other hand, nonsmokers argue that their rights are being violated by smokers. They point to an increasing body of research data that shows that secondhand smoke leads to numerous health problems such as emphysema, heart disease, and throat and lung cancer. Not only do nonsmokers have a right not to have to breathe smoke-contaminated air, but society has an obligation to protect the health and well-being of its members from the known dangers of breathing smoke.

These are only a few examples of areas where rights come into conflict. Others include environmental issues, endangered species, forest management, enforcement of specific laws, homosexuality, mental illness, national health insurance, taxes, balance of trade, food labeling and packaging, genetic engineering, rape, sexual deviation, political corruption, riots, public protests, zero population growth, the state of the economy, and on and on. It is notable that the degree to which any of these issues achieves widespread concern varies over time. Often, specific problems are given much fanfare by politicians and special interests groups for a time, and the media try to convince us that specific activities or behaviors have the greatest urgency and demand a total national commitment for a solution. However, after being in the limelight for a while, the importance of the problem seems to fade and new problems move into prominence. If you look back over previous editions of this

book, you can see this trend. It would be useful to speculate why, in American society, some problems remain a national concern while others come and go.

The Consequences of Harm

To this point it had been argued that social problems can be defined and analyzed as (a) conflicts between values, (b) conflicts between values and duties, and (c) conflicts between rights. Consistent with the aims of this article, social problems can be further characterized and interpreted as social conditions that lead, or are generally thought to lead, to harmful consequences for the person, group, community, or society.

Harm—and here we follow Hyman Gross's (1979) conceptualization of the term—can be classified as (a) a loss, usually permanent, that deprives the person or group of a valued object or condition it is entitled to have, (b) offenses to sensibility—that is, harm that contributes to unpleasant experiences in the form of repugnance, embarrassment, disgust, alarm, or fear, and (c) impairment of the collective welfare—that is, violations of those values possessed by the group or society.

Harm can also be ranked as to the potential for good. Physicians, to help their patients, often have to harm them. The question they must ask is, "Will this specific procedure, drug, or operation, produce more good than the pain and suffering it causes?" For instance, will the additional time it affords the cancer patient be worth all the suffering associated with the chemotherapy? In Somalia, health care personnel are forced to make much harder decisions. They are surrounded by starvation, sickness, and death. If they treat one person, another cannot be treated and will die. They find themselves forced to allocate their time and resources, not according to who needs it the most, but according to who has the greatest chance of survival.

Judges must also balance the harms they are about to inflict on those they must sentence against the public good and the extent to which the sentence might help the individual reform. Justice must be served in that people must pay for their crimes, yet most judges also realize that prison time often does more harm than good. In times of recession employers must weigh harm when they are forced to cut back their workforce: Where should the cuts occur? Should they keep employees of long standing and cut those most recently hired (many of which are nonwhites hired through affirmative action programs)? Should they keep those with the most productive records, or those with the greatest need for employment? No matter what employers elect to do, harm will result to some. The harm produced by the need to reduce the workforce must be balanced by the potential good of the company's surviving and sustaining employment for the rest of the employees.

The notion of harm also figures into the public and social dialogue between those who are pro-choice and those who are pro-life. Most pro-lifers are inclined to see the greatest harm of abortion to be loss of life, while most pro-choicers argue that the compelling personal and social harm is the taking away of a value (the right to privacy) that everyone is entitled to. Further harmful consequences of abortion for most pro-lifers are that the value of life will be cheapened, the moral fabric of society will be weakened, and the taking of life could be extended to the elderly and disabled, for example. Most of those who are pro-choice, on the other hand, are inclined to argue that the necessary consequence of their position is that of keeping government out of their private lives and bedrooms. In a similar way this "conflict of values" format can be used to analyze, clarify, and enlarge our understanding of the competing values, harms, and consequences surrounding other social problems. We can, and should, search for the competing values underlying such social problems as, for example, income distribution, homelessness, divorce, education, and the environment.

Loss, then, as a societal harm consists in a rejection or violation of what a person or group feels entitled to have. American citizens, for example, tend to view life, freedom, equality, property, and physical security as ultimate values. Any rejection or violation of these values is thought to constitute a serious social problem since such a loss diminishes one's sense of personhood. Murder, violence, AIDS, homelessness, environmental degradation, the failure to provide adequate health care, and abortion can be conveniently classified as social problems within this class of harms.

Offenses to our sensibilities constitute a class of harm that, when serious enough, becomes a problem affecting moral issues and the common good of the members of a society. Issues surrounding pornography, prostitution, and the so-called victimless crimes are examples of behaviors that belong to this class of harm. Moreover some would argue that environmental degradation, the widening gap between the very rich and the very poor, and the condition of the homeless also should be considered within this class of harm.

A third class of harm—namely impairments to the collective welfare—is explained, in part, by Gross (1979:120) as follows:

> Social life, particularly in the complex forms of civilized societies, creates many dependencies among members of a community. The welfare of each member depends upon the exercise of restraint and precaution by others in the pursuit of their legitimate activities, as well as upon cooperation toward certain common objectives. These matters of collective welfare involve many kinds of interests that may be said to be possessed by the community.

In a pluralistic society, such as American society, matters of collective welfare are sometimes problematic in that there can be considerable conflict of values and rights between various segments of the society. There is likely to remain, however, a great deal of agreement that those social problems whose harmful consequences would involve impairments to the collective welfare would include poverty, poor education, mistreatment of the young and elderly, excessive disparities in income distribution, discrimination against ethnic and other minorities, drug abuse, health and medical care, the state of the economy, and environmental concerns.

Bibliography

Dahrendorf, R. (1959). *Class and class conflict in industrial society.* Stanford, CA: Stanford University Press.

Davis, Kingsley, & Moore, Wilbert E. (1945). Some principles of stratification. *American Sociological Review, 10,* 242–249.

Gans, Herbert J. (1971). The uses of poverty: The poor pay all. *Social Policy.* New York: Social Policy Corporation.

Gross, Hyman. (1979). *A theory of criminal justice.* New York: Oxford University Press.

Hook, Sidney. (1974). *Pragmatism and the tragic sense of life.* New York: Basic Books.

Horowitz, M. A. (1962). Consensus, conflict, and cooperation. *Social Forces, 41,* 177–188.

Lenski, G. (1966). *Power and privilege.* New York: McGraw-Hill.

Michels, Robert. (1949). *Political parties: A sociological study of the oligarchical tendencies of modern democracy.* New York: Free Press.

Mills, C. Wright. (1956). *The power elite.* New York: Oxford University Press.

Ossowski, S. (1963). *Class structure in the social consciousness.* Translated by Sheila Patterson. New York: The Free Press.

Seeman, Melvin. (1959). On the meaning of alienation. *American Sociological Review, 24,* 783–791.

Van den Berghe, P. (1963). Dialectic and functionalism: Toward a theoretical synthesis. *American Sociological Review, 28,* 695–705.

Weber, Max. (1964). *The protestant ethic and the spirit of capitalism.* Translated by Talcott Parson. New York: Scribner's.

William, Robin, Jr. (1970). *American society: A sociological interpretation,* 3rd. ed. New York: Alfred A. Knopf.

Williams, Robin. (1966). Some further comments on chronic controversies. *American Journal of Sociology, 71,* 717–721.

Wilson, James Q. (1994, August). The moral life. *Brigham Young Magazine,* pp. 37–55.

Wilson, William. (1978). *The declining significance of race.* Chicago: University of Chicago Press.

The Fragmentation of Social Life
Some Critical Societal Concerns for the New Millennium

D. STANLEY EITZEN

For many observers of American society this is the best of times. The current economic expansion is the longest in U.S. history. Unemployment is the lowest in three decades. Inflation is low and under control. The stock market has risen from 3500 to over 11,000 in eight years. The number of millionaires has more than doubled in the past five years to 7.1 million. The Cold War is over. The United States is the dominant player in the world both militarily and economically. Our society, obviously, is in good shape.

But every silver lining has a cloud. While basking in unprecedented wealth and economic growth, the U.S. has serious domestic problems. Personal bankruptcies are at a record level. The U.S. has the highest poverty rate and the highest child poverty rate in the Western world. We do not have a proper safety net for the disadvantaged that other countries take for granted. Hunger and homelessness are on the rise. Among the Western nations, the U.S. has the highest murder rate as well as the highest incarceration rate. Also, we are the only Western nation without a universal health care system, leaving 44 million Americans without health insurance.

I want to address another crucial problem that our society faces—the fragmentation of social life. Throughout U.S. history, despite a civil war, and actions separating people by religion, class, and race, the nation has somehow held together. Will society continue to cohere or will new crises pull us apart? That is the question of the morning. While there are many indicators of reduced societal cohesion, I will limit my discussion to four: (1) excessive individualism; (2) heightened personal isolation; (3) the widening income and wealth gap; and (4) the deepening racial/ethnic/religious/sexuality divide.

Excessive Individualism

We Americans celebrate individualism. It fits with our economic system of capitalism. We are self-reliant and responsible for our actions. We value individual freedom, including the right to choose our vocations, our mates, when and where to travel, and how to spend our money. At its extreme, the individualistic credo says that it is our duty to be selfish and in doing so, according to Adam Smith's notion of an "invisible hand," society

benefits. Conservative radio commentator Rush Limbaugh said as much in his response to an initiative by President Clinton to encourage citizen volunteerism: "Citizen service is a repudiation of the principles upon which our country was based. We are here for ourselves."

While Rush Limbaugh may view rugged individualism as virtuous, I do not. It promotes inequality; it promotes the tolerance of inferior housing, schools, and services for "others"; and it encourages public policies that are punitive to the disadvantaged. For example, this emphasis on the individual has meant that, as a society, the United States has the lowest federal income tax rates in the Western world. Our politicians, especially Republicans, want to lower the rates even more so that individuals will have more and governments, with their presumed interest in the common good, will have less. As a result, the United States devotes relatively few resources to help the disadvantaged and this minimal redistribution system is shrinking.

In effect, our emphasis on individualism keeps us from feeling obligated to others.

Consider the way that we finance schools. Schools are financed primarily by the states through income taxes and local school districts through property taxes. This means that wealthy states and wealthy districts have more money to educate their children than the less advantaged states and districts. The prevailing view is that if my community or state is well-off, why should my taxes go to help children from other communities and other states?

The flaw in the individualistic credo is that we cannot go it alone—our fate depends on others. Paradoxically, it is in our individual interest to have a collective interest. We deny this at our peril for if we disregard those unlike ourselves, in fact doing violence to them, then we invite their hostility and violence, and, ultimately, a fractured society.

Heightened Personal Isolation

There are some disturbing trends that indicate a growing isolation as individuals become increasingly isolated from their neighbors, their co-workers, and even their family members.

To begin, because of computers and telecommunications there is a growing trend for workers to work at home. While home-based work allows flexibility and independence not found in most jobs, these workers are separated from social networks. Aside from not realizing the social benefits of personal interaction with colleagues, working from home means being cut off from pooled information and the collective power that might result in higher pay and better fringe benefits.

Our neighborhoods, too, are changing in ways that promote isolation. A recent study indicates that one in three Americans has never spent an evening with a neighbor. This isolation from neighbors is exacerbated in the suburbs. Not only do some people live in gated communities to physically wall themselves off from "others" but they wall themselves off from their neighbors behaviorally and symbolically within gated and nongated neighborhoods alike. Some people exercise on motorized treadmills and other home exercise equipment instead of running through their neighborhoods. Rather than walking to the corner grocery or nearby shop and visiting with the clerks and neighbors, suburbanites have to drive somewhere away from their immediate neighborhood to shop among strangers. Or they may not leave their home at all, shopping and banking by computer. Sociologist Philip Slater says that "a community life exists when one can go daily to a given location at a given time and see many of the people one knows." Suburban neighborhoods in particular are devoid of such meeting places for adults and children. For suburban teenagers almost everything is away—practice fields, music lessons, friends, jobs, school, and the malls. Thus, a disconnect from those nearby. For adults many go through their routines without sharing stories, gossip, and analyses of events with friends on a regular basis at a coffee shop, neighborhood tavern, or at the local grain elevator.

Technology also encourages isolation. There was a major shift toward isolation with the advent of television as people spent more and more time within their homes rather than socializing with friends and neighbors. Now, we are undergoing a communications revolution that creates the illusion of intimacy but the reality is much different. Curt Suplee, science and technology writer for the *Washington Post,* says that we have seen "tenfold increases in 'communication' by electronic means, and tenfold reductions in person-to-person contact." In effect, as we are increasingly isolated before a computer screen, we risk what Warren Christopher has called "social malnutrition." John L. Locke, a professor [of] communications argues in *The De-Voicing of Society* that e-mail, voice mail, fax machines, beepers, and Internet chat rooms are robbing us of ordinary social talking. Talking, he says, like the grooming of apes and monkeys, is the way we build and maintain social relationships. In his view, it is only through intimate conversation that we can know others well enough to trust them and work with them harmoniously. In effect, Locke argues that we are becoming an autistic society, communicating messages electronically but without really connecting. Paradoxically, then, these incredible communication devices that combine to connect us in so many dazzling ways also separate us increasingly from intimate relationships.

Fragmentation is also occurring within many families, where the members are increasingly disconnected from each other. Many parents are either absent altogether or too self-absorbed to pay very much attention to their children or each other. On average, parents today spend 22 fewer hours a week with their children than parents did in the 1960s. Although living in the same house, parents or children may tune out each other by engaging in solitary activities. A survey by the Kaiser Family Foundation found that the average child between 2 and 18, spends 5 and one-half hours a day alone watching television, at a computer, playing video games, on the Internet, or reading. Many families rarely eat together in an actual sit-down meal. All too often material things are substituted for love and attention. Some children even have their own rooms equipped with a telephone, television, VCR, microwave, refrigerator, and computer, which while convenient, isolates them from other family members. Such homes may be full of people but they are really empty.

The consequences of this accelerating isolation of individuals are dire. More and more individuals are lonely, bitter, alienated, anomic, and disconnected. This situation is conducive to alcohol and drug abuse, depression, anxiety, and violence. The lonely and disaffected are ripe candidates for membership in cults, gangs, and militias where they find a sense of belonging and a cause to believe in but in the process they may become more paranoid and, perhaps, even become willing terrorists. At a less extreme level, the alienated will disengage from society by shunning voluntary associations, by home schooling their children, and by not participating in elections. In short, they will become increasingly individualistic, which compounds their problem and society's problem with unity.

The Widening Inequality Gap

There is an increasing gap between the rich and the rest of us, especially between the rich and the poor. Data from 1998 show that there were at least 268 billionaires in the United States, while 35 million were below the government official poverty line.

Timothy Koogle, CEO of Yahoo made $4.7 million a day in 1999, while the median household income in that year was $110 a day. Bill Gates, CEO of Microsoft is richer than Koogle by far. He is worth, depending on [the] stock market on a given day, around $90 billion or so. Together, eight Americans—Microsoft billionaires Bill Gates, Paul Allen, and Steve Ballmer plus the five Wal-Mart heirs—have a net worth of $233 billion, which is more than the gross domestic product of the very prosperous nation of Sweden. The Congressional Budget Office reports that in 1999, the richest 2.7 million Americans, the top 1 percent of the population, had as many aftertax dollars to spend as the bottom 100 million put together.

Compared to the other developed nations, the chasm between the rich and the poor in the U.S. is the widest and it is increasing. In 1979, average family income in the top 5 percent of the earnings distribution was 10 times that in the bottom 20 percent. Ten years later it had increased to 16:1, and in 1999 it was 19:1, the biggest gap since the Census Bureau began keeping track in 1947.

The average salary of a CEO in 1999 was 419 times the pay of a typical factory worker. In 1980, the difference was only 42 times as much. This inequality gap in the United States, as measured by the difference in pay between CEOs and workers, is by far the highest in the industrialized world. While ours stands at 419 to 1, the ratio in Japan is 25 to 1, and in France and Germany it is 35 to 1.

At the bottom end of wealth and income, about 35 million Americans live below the government's official poverty line. One out of four of those in poverty are children under the age of 18. Poor Americans are worse off than the poor in other western democracies. The safety net here is weak and getting weaker. We do not have universal health insurance. Funds for Head Start are so inadequate that only one in three poor children who are eligible actually are enrolled in the program. Welfare for single mothers is being abolished, resulting in many impoverished but working mothers being less well-off because their low-wage work is not enough to pay for child care, health care, housing costs, and other living expenses. Although the economy is soaring, a survey of 26 cities released by the U.S. Conference on Mayors shows that the numbers of homeless and hungry in the cities have risen for 15 consecutive years. The demand for emergency food is the highest since 1992 and the demand for emergency shelter is the largest since 1994. According to the U.S. Department of Agriculture, there were about 36 million, including 14 million children living in households afflicted with what they call "food insecurity," which is a euphemism for hunger.

Of the many reasons for the increase in homelessness and hunger amidst increasing affluence, three are crucial. First, the government's welfare system has been shrinking since the Reagan administration with the support of both Republicans and Democrats. Second, the cost of housing has risen dramatically causing many of the poor to spend over 50 percent of their meager incomes for rent. And, third, charitable giving has not filled the void, with less than 10 percent of contributions actually going to programs that help the poor. In effect, 90 percent of philanthropy is funneled to support the institutions of the already advantaged—churches (some of which trickles down to the poor), hospitals, colleges, museums, libraries, orchestras, and the arts.

The data on inequality show clearly, I believe, that we are moving toward a two-tiered society. Rather than "a rising tide lifting all boats," the justification for capitalism as postulated by President John Kennedy, the evidence is that "a rising tide lifts only the yachts." The increasing gap between the haves and the have-nots has crucial implications for our society. First, it divides people into the "deserving" and the "undeserving." If people are undeserving, then we are justified in not providing them with a safety net. As economist James K. Galbraith says: "A high degree of inequality causes the comfortable to disavow the needy. It increases the psychological distance separating these groups, making it easier to imagine that defects of character or differences of culture, rather than an unpleasant turn in the larger schemes of economic history, lie behind the separation." Since politicians represent the monied interests, the wealthy get

their way as seen in the continuing decline in welfare programs for the poor and the demise of affirmative action. Most telling, the inequality gap is not part of the political debate in this, or any other, election cycle.

A second implication is that the larger the gap, the more destabilized society becomes.

In this regard economist Lester Thurow asks: "How much inequality can a democracy take? The income gap in America is eroding the social contract. If the promise of a higher standard of living is limited to a few at the top, the rest of the citizenry, as history shows, is likely to grow disaffected, or worse." Former Secretary of Labor, Robert Reich, has put it this way: "At some point, if the trends are not reversed, we cease being a society at all. The stability of the country eventually is threatened. No country can endure a massive gap between people at the top and people at the bottom." Or, as economist Galbraith puts it: "[Equality] is now so wide it threatens, as it did in the Great Depression, the social stability of the country. It has come to undermine our sense of ourselves as a nation of equals. Economic inequality, in this way, challenges the essential unifying myth of American national life."

The Deepening Racial/Ethnic/ Religious/Sexuality Divide

The United States has always struggled with diversity. American history is stained by the enslavement of Africans and later the segregated and unequal "Jim Crow" south, the aggression toward native peoples based on the belief in "Manifest Destiny," the internment of Japanese Americans during World War II, episodes of intolerance against religious minorities, gays and lesbians, and immigrants. In each instance, the majority was not only intolerant of those labeled as "others," but they also used the law, religious doctrine, and other institutional forms of discrimination to keep minorities separate and unequal. Despite these ongoing societal wrongs against minorities, there has been progress culminating in the civil rights battles and victories of the 1950s, 1960s, and early 1970s.

But the civil rights gains of the previous generation are in jeopardy as U.S. society becomes more diverse. Currently, the racial composition of the U.S. is 72 percent white and 28 percent nonwhite. In 50 years it will be 50 percent nonwhite. The racial landscape is being transformed as approximately 1 million immigrants annually set up permanent residence in the United States and another 300,000 enter illegally and stay. These new residents are primarily Latino and Asian, not European as was the case of earlier waves of immigration. This "browning of America" has important implications including increased division.

An indicator of fragmentation along racial lines is the "White flight" from high immigration areas, which may lead to what demographer William Frey has called the "Balkanization of America." The trends toward gated neighborhoods, the rise of private schools and home schooling are manifestations of exclusiveness rather than inclusiveness and perhaps they are precursors to this "Balkanization."

Recent state and federal legislation has been aimed at reducing or limiting the civil rights gains of the 1970s. For example, in 1994 California passed Proposition 187 by a 3- to 2-popular vote margin, thereby denying public welfare to undocumented immigrants. Congress in 1996 voted to deny most federal benefits to legal immigrants who were not citizens. A number of states have made English the official state language. In 1997 California passed Proposition 209, which eliminated affirmative action (a policy aimed at leveling the playing field so that minorities would have a fair chance to succeed). Across the nation, Congress and various state legislatures, most recently Florida, have taken measures to weaken or eliminate affirmative action programs.

Without question racial and ethnic minorities in the U.S. are the targets of personal prejudicial acts as well as pervasive institutional racism. What will the situation be like by 2050 when the numbers of Latinos triple from their present population of 31.4 million, and the Asian population more than triples from the current 10.9 million, and the African American population increases 70 percent from their base of 34.9 million now?

Along with increasing racial and ethnic diversity, there is a greater variety of religious belief. Although Christians are the clear majority in the United States, there are also about 7 million Jews, 6 million Muslims (there are more Muslims than Presbyterians), and millions of other non-Christians, including Buddhists, and Hindus, as well as atheists.

While religion often promotes group integration, it also divides. Religious groups tend to emphasize separateness and superiority, thereby defining "others" as infidels, heathens, heretics, or nonbelievers. Strongly held religious ideas sometimes split groups within a denomination or congregation. Progressives and fundamentalists within the same religious tradition have difficulty finding common ground on various issues, resulting in division. This has always been the case to some degree, but this tendency seems to be accelerating now. Not only are there clashes within local congregations and denominational conferences but they spill out into political debates in legislatures and in local elections, most notably school board elections, as religious factions often push their narrow, divisive sectarian policies. These challenges to religious pluralism are increasing, thus promoting fragmentation rather than unity.

There is also widespread intolerance of and discrimination toward those whose sexual orientation differs from the majority. The behaviors of gay men and lesbian women are defined and stigmatized by many members of society as sinful; their activities are judged by the courts as illegal; and their jobs and advancement within those jobs are often restricted because of their being different sexually. As more and more homosexuals become public with their sexuality, their presence and their political agenda are viewed as ever more threatening and must be stopped.

My point is this: diversity and ever increasing diversity are facts of life in our society. If we do not find ways to accept the differences among us, we will fragment into class, race, ethnic, and sexual enclaves.

Two social scientists, John A. Hall and Charles Lindholm, in a recent book entitled *Is America Breaking Apart?* argue that throughout American history there has been remarkable societal unity because of its historically conditioned institutional patterns and shared cultural values. Columnist George Will picked up on this theme in a *Newsweek* essay, postulating that while the U.S. has pockets of problems, "American society is an amazing machine for homogenizing people." That has been the case but will this machine continue to pull us together? I believe, to the contrary, that while the U.S. historically has overcome great obstacles, a number of trends in contemporary society have enormous potential for pulling us apart. Our society is moving toward a two-tiered society with the gap between the haves and the have-nots, a withering bond among those of different social classes, and a growing racial, ethnic, and sexuality divide. The critical question is whether the integrative societal mechanisms that have served us well in the past will save us again or whether we will continue to fragment?

The challenge facing U.S. society as we enter the new millennium is to shift from building walls to building bridges. As our society is becoming more and more diverse, will Americans feel empathy for, and make sacrifices on behalf of, a wide variety of people who they define as different? The answer to this crucial question is negative at the present time. Social justice seems to be an outmoded concept in our individualistic society.

I shall close with a moral argument posed by one of the greatest social thinkers and social activists of the 20th century, the late Michael Harrington. Harrington, borrowing from philosopher John Rawls, provides an intuitive definition of a justice. A just society is when I describe it to you and you accept it even if you do not know your place in it. Harrington then asks (I'm paraphrasing here): would you accept a society of 275 million where 44 million people do not have health insurance, where 35 million live in poverty including one-fifth of all children? Would you accept a society as just where discrimination against minorities is commonplace, even by the normal way society works? Would you accept a society where a sizable number of people live blighted lives in neighborhoods with a high concentration of poverty, with inferior schools, with too few good jobs? You'd be crazy to accept such a society but that is what we have. Harrington concludes: "If in your mind you could not accept a society in which we do unto you as we do unto them, then isn't it time for us to change the way we are acting towards them who are a part of us?" If, however, we accept an unjust society, then our society will move inexorably toward a divided and fortress society.

Spent

Amitai Etzioni

America after Consumerism

Much of the debate over how to address the economic crisis has focused on a single word: regulation. And it's easy to understand why. Bad behavior by a variety of businesses landed us in this mess—so it seems rather obvious that the way to avoid future economic meltdowns is to create, and vigorously enforce, new rules proscribing such behavior. But the truth is quite a bit more complicated. The world economy consists of billions of transactions every day. There can never be enough inspectors, accountants, customs officers, and police to ensure that all or even most of these transactions are properly carried out. Moreover, those charged with enforcing regulations are themselves not immune to corruption, and, hence, they too must be supervised and held accountable to others—who also have to be somehow regulated. The upshot is that regulation cannot be the linchpin of attempts to reform our economy. What is needed instead is something far more sweeping: for people to internalize a different sense of how one ought to behave, and act on it because they believe it is right.

That may sound far-fetched. It is commonly believed that people conduct themselves in a moral manner mainly because they fear the punishment that will be meted out if they engage in antisocial behavior. But this position does not stand up to close inspection. Most areas of behavior are extralegal; we frequently do what is expected because we care or love. This is evident in the ways we attend to our children (beyond a very low requirement set by law), treat our spouses, do volunteer work, and participate in public life. What's more, in many of those areas that are covered by law, the likelihood of being caught is actually quite low, and the penalties are often surprisingly mild. For instance, only about one in 100 tax returns gets audited, and most cheaters are merely asked to pay back what they "missed," plus some interest. Nevertheless, most Americans pay the taxes due. Alan Lewis's classic study, *The Psychology of Taxation,* concluded that people don't just pay taxes because they fear the government; they do it because they consider the burden fairly shared and the monies legitimately spent. In short, the normative values of a culture matter. Regulation is needed when culture fails, but it cannot alone serve as the mainstay of good conduct.

So what kind of transformation in our normative culture is called for? What needs to be eradicated, or at least greatly tempered, is consumerism: the obsession with acquisition that has become the organizing principle of American life. This is not the same thing as capitalism, nor is it the same thing as consumption. To explain the difference, it is useful to draw on Abraham Maslow's hierarchy of human needs. At the bottom of this hierarchy are basic creature comforts; once these are sated, more satisfaction is drawn from affection, self-esteem, and, finally, self-actualization. As long as consumption is focused on satisfying basic human needs—safety, shelter, food, clothing, health care, education—it is not consumerism. But, when the acquisition of goods and services is used to satisfy the higher needs, consumption turns into consumerism—and consumerism becomes a social disease.

The link to the economic crisis should be obvious. A culture in which the urge to consume dominates the psychology of citizens is a culture in which people will do most anything to acquire the means to consume—working slavish hours, behaving rapaciously in their business pursuits, and even bending the rules in order to maximize their earnings. They will also buy homes beyond their means and think nothing of running up credit-card debt. It therefore seems safe to say that consumerism is, as much as anything else, responsible for the current economic mess. But it is not enough to establish that which people ought not to do, to end the obsession with making and consuming evermore than the next person. Consumerism will not just magically disappear from its central place in our culture. It needs to be supplanted by something.

A shift away from consumerism, and toward this something else, would obviously be a dramatic change for American society. But such grand cultural changes are far from unprecedented. Profound transformations in the definition of "the good life" have occurred throughout human history. Before the spirit of capitalism swept across much of the world, neither work nor commerce were highly valued pursuits—indeed, they were often delegated to scorned minorities such as Jews. For centuries in aristocratic Europe and Japan, making war was a highly admired profession. In China, philosophy, poetry, and brush painting were respected during the heyday of the literati. Religion was once the dominant source of normative culture; then, following the Enlightenment, secular humanism was viewed in some parts of the world as the foundation of society. In recent years, there has been a significant increase in the influence of religious values in places like Russia and, of course, the Middle East. (Details can be found in John Micklethwait and Adrian Wooldridge's new book, *God Is Back*—although, for many, he never left.) It is true that not all these changes have elevated the human condition. The point is merely that such change, especially during times of crisis, is possible.

To accomplish this kind of radical change, it is neither necessary nor desirable to imitate devotees of the 1960s counterculture, early socialists, or followers of ascetic religious orders, all of whom have resisted consumerism by rejecting the whole capitalist project. On the contrary, capitalism should be allowed to thrive, albeit within clear and well-enforced limits. This position does not call for a life of sackcloth and ashes, nor of altruism. And it does not call on poor people or poor nations to be content with their fate and learn to love their misery; clearly, the capitalist economy must be strong enough to provide for the basic creature comforts of all people. But it does call for a new balance between consumption and other human pursuits.

There is strong evidence that when consumption is used to try to address higher needs—that is, needs beyond basic creature comforts—it is ultimately Sisyphean. Several studies have shown that, across many nations with annual incomes above $20,000, there is no correlation between increased income and increased happiness. In the United States since World War II, per capita income has tripled, but levels of life satisfaction remain about the same, while the people of Japan, despite experiencing a sixfold increase in income since 1958, have seen their levels of contentment stay largely stagnant. Studies also indicate that many members of capitalist societies feel unsatisfied, if not outright deprived, however much they earn and consume, because others make and spend even more: Relative rather than absolute deprivation is what counts. This is a problem since, by definition, most people cannot consume more than most others. True, it is sometimes hard to tell a basic good from a status good, and a status good can turn into a basic one (air conditioning, for instance). However, it is not a matter of cultural snobbery to note that no one needs inflatable Santas or plastic flamingos on their front lawn or, for that matter, lawns that are strikingly green even in the scorching heat of summer. No one needs a flat-screen television, not to mention diamonds as a token of love or a master's painting as a source of self-esteem.

Consumerism, it must be noted, afflicts not merely the upper class in affluent societies but also the middle class and many in the working class. Large numbers of people across society believe that they work merely to make ends meet, but an examination of their shopping lists and closets reveals that they spend good parts of their income on status goods such as brand-name clothing, the "right" kind of car, and other assorted items that they don't really need.

This mentality may seem so integral to American culture that resisting it is doomed to futility. But the current economic downturn may provide an opening of sorts. The crisis has caused people to spend less on luxury goods, such as diamonds and flashy cars; scale back on lavish celebrations for holidays, birthdays, weddings, and bar mitzvahs; and agree to caps on executive compensation. Some workers have accepted fewer hours, lower salaries, and unpaid furloughs.

So far, much of this scaling-back has been involuntary, the result of economic necessity. What is needed next is to help people realize that limiting consumption is not a reflection of failure. Rather, it represents liberation from an obsession—a chance to abandon consumerism and focus on . . . well, what exactly? What should replace the worship of consumer goods?

The kind of culture that would best serve a Maslowian hierarchy of needs is hardly one that would kill the goose that lays the golden eggs—the economy that can provide the goods needed for basic creature comforts. Nor one that merely mocks the use of consumer goods to respond to higher needs. It must be a culture that extols sources of human flourishing besides acquisition. The two most obvious candidates to fill this role are communitarian pursuits and transcendental ones.

Communitarianism refers to investing time and energy in relations with the other, including family, friends, and members of one's community. The term also encompasses service to the common good, such as volunteering, national service, and politics. Communitarian life is not centered around altruism but around mutuality, in the sense that deeper and thicker involvement with the other is rewarding to both the recipient and the giver. Indeed, numerous studies show that communitarian pursuits breed deep contentment. A study of 50-year-old men shows that those with friendships are far less likely to experience heart disease. Another shows that life satisfaction in older adults is higher for those who participate in community service.

Transcendental pursuits refer to spiritual activities broadly understood, including religious, contemplative, and artistic ones. The lifestyle of the Chinese literati, centered around poetry, philosophy, and brush painting, was a case in point, but a limited one because this lifestyle was practiced by an elite social stratum and based in part on exploitation of other groups. In modern society, transcendental pursuits have often been emphasized by bohemians, beginning artists, and others involved in lifelong learning who consume modestly. Here again, however, these people make up only a small fraction of society. Clearly, for a culture to buy out of consumerism and move to satisfying higher human needs with transcendental projects, the option to participate in these pursuits must be available on a wider scale.

All this may seem abstract, not to mention utopian. But one can see a precedent of sorts for a society that emphasizes communitarian and transcendental pursuits among retired people, who spend the final decades of their lives painting not for a market or galleries but as a form of self-expression, socializing with each other, volunteering, and, in some cases, taking classes. Of course, these citizens already put in the work that enables them to lead this kind of life. For other ages to participate before retirement, they will have to shorten their workweek and workday, refuse to take work home, turn off their BlackBerries, and otherwise downgrade the centrality of labor to their lives. This is, in effect, what the French, with their 35-hour workweeks, tried to do, as did other countries in "old" Europe. Mainstream American economists—who argue that a modern economy cannot survive unless people consume evermore and hence produce and work evermore—have long scoffed at these societies and urged them to modernize. To some extent, they did, especially the Brits. Now it seems that maybe these countries were onto something after all.

A society that downplayed consumerism in favor of other organizing principles would not just limit the threat of economic meltdown and feature a generally happier populace; it would have other advantages as well. Such a society would, for example, use fewer material resources and, therefore, be much more compatible with protecting the environment. It would also exhibit higher levels of social justice.

Social justice entails redistribution of wealth, taking from those disproportionally endowed and giving to those who are underprivileged through no fault of their own—for reasons ranging from past injustices and their lingering contemporary effects to technological changes to globalization to genetic differences. The reason these redistributions have been surprisingly limited in free societies is that those who command the "extra" assets tend also to be those who are politically powerful. Promoting social justice by organizing those with less and forcing those in power to yield has had limited success in democratic countries and led to massive bloodshed in others. So the question arises: Are there other ways to reduce the resistance of elites to redistribution?

The answer is found when elites derive their main source of contentment not from acquiring more goods and services, but from activities that are neither labor nor capital intensive and, hence, do not require great amounts of money. Communitarian activities require social skills and communication skills as well as time and personal energy—but, as a rule, minimal material or financial outlays. The same holds for transcendental activities such as prayer, meditation, music, art, sports, adult education, and so on. True, consumerism has turned many of these pursuits into expensive endeavors. But one can break out of this mentality and find that it is possible to engage in most transcendental activities quite profoundly using minimal goods and services. One does not need designer clothes to enjoy the sunset or shoes with fancy labels to benefit from a hike. Chess played with plastic pieces is the same game as the one played with carved mahogany or marble pieces. And I'm quite sure that the Lord does not listen better to prayers read from a leatherbound Bible than those read from a plain one, printed on recycled paper. (Among several books that depict how this kind of culture can flourish is *Seven Pleasures* by Willard Spiegelman.) In short, those who embrace this lifestyle will find that they can achieve a high level of contentment even if they give up a considerable segment of the surplus wealth they command.

As for actually putting this vision into practice: The main way societies will determine whether the current crisis will serve as an event that leads to cultural transformation or merely constitute an interlude in the consumerism project is through a process I call "moral megalogues." Societies are constantly engaged in mass dialogues over what is right and wrong. Typically, only one or two topics dominate these megalogues at any given time. Key recent issues have included the legitimacy of the 2003 invasion of Iraq and whether gay couples should be allowed to marry. In earlier decades, women's rights and minority rights were topics of such discussions. Megalogues involve millions of members of a society exchanging views with one another at workplaces, during family gatherings, in the media, and at public events. They are often contentious and passionate, and, while they have no clear beginning or endpoint, they tend to lead to changes in a society's culture and its members' behavior.

The megalogue about the relationship between consumerism and human flourishing is now flickering but has yet to become a leading topic—like regulation. Public intellectuals, pundits, and politicians are those best-positioned to focus a megalogue on this subject and, above all, to set the proper scope for the discussion. The main challenge is not to pass some laws, but, rather, to ask people to reconsider what a good life entails.

Having a national conversation about this admittedly abstract question is merely a start, though. If a new shared understanding surrounding consumption is to evolve, education will have a crucial role to play. Schools, which often claim to focus solely on academics, are actually major avenues through which changes in societal values are fostered. For instance, many schools deeply impress on young children that they ought to respect the environment, not discriminate on racial or ethnic grounds, and resolve differences in a peaceful manner. There is no reason these schools cannot push back against consumerism while promoting communitarian and transcendental values as well. School uniforms (to counter conspicuous consumption) and an emphasis on community service are just two ways to work these ideas into the culture of public education.

For adults, changes in the workplace could go a long way toward promoting these values. Limits on overtime, except under special conditions (such as natural disasters); shorter workweeks; more part- and flex-time jobs; increased freedom to work from home; allowing employees to dress down and thereby avoid squandering money on suits and other expensive clothes—all these relatively small initiatives would encourage Americans to spend more time on things besides work.

Finally, legislation has a role to play. Taxes can discourage the purchase of ever-larger houses, cause people to favor public transportation over cars, and encourage the use of commercial aviation rather than private jets. Government could also strike a blow against consumerism by instituting caps on executive pay.

Is all this an idle, abstract hypothesis? Not necessarily. Plenty of religious Americans have already embraced versions of these values to some extent or other. And those whose secular beliefs lead them to community service are in the same boat. One such idealist named Barack Obama chose to be a community organizer in Chicago rather than pursue a more lucrative career.

I certainly do not expect that most people will move away from a consumerist mindset overnight. Some may keep one foot in the old value system even as they test the waters of the new one, just like those who wear a blazer with jeans. Still others may merely cut back on conspicuous consumption without guilt or fear of social censure. Societies shift direction gradually. All that is needed is for more and more people to turn the current economic crisis into a liberation from the obsession with consumer goods and the überwork it requires—and, bit by bit, begin to rethink their definition of what it means to live a good life.

AMITAI ETZIONI served as president of the American Sociological Association and is the author of *The Active Society*.

UNIT 2

Problems of the Political Economy

Unit Selections

4. **Who Rules America?: Power, Politics, and Social Change,** G. William Domhoff
5. **Inside the Hidden World of Earmarks,** Eamon Javers
6. **Foresight for Government,** David M. Walker
7. **A Smarter Planet,** Samuel J. Palmisano
8. **Reversal of Fortune,** Bill McKibben
9. **Born to Buy: Interview with Juliet Schor,** James Woolman
10. **Why Aren't U.S. Cities Burning?,** Michael B. Katz
11. **Who We Are Now,** Jon Meacham
12. **The Invisible Ones,** Rebecca Clarren

Key Points to Consider

- How could the political decision-making process be made more fair and democratic? How can the influence of money on politics be reduced?

- How can our government prepare our society for the future?

- What are the strengths and weaknesses of American capitalism? What are some of the major problems that now face American businesses and workers, and how can they be solved?

- What are the problems with American consumer behavior?

- Why are American cities calm?

- What are the pros and cons of immigration today? What should our immigration policy be?

- In what ways does slavery still exist?

Student Website

www.mhhe.com/cls

Internet References

National Center for Policy Analysis
   http://www.ncpa.org
Penn Library: Sociology
   http://www.library.upenn.edu

Since the political system and the economy interpenetrate each other to a high degree, it is now common to study them together under the label political economy. The political economy is the most basic aspect of society, and it should be studied first. The way it functions affects how problems in other areas can or cannot be addressed. Here we encounter issues of power, control, and influence. It is in this arena that society acts corporately to address the problems that are of public concern. It is important, therefore, to ascertain the degree to which the economic elite control the political system. The answer determines how democratic America is. Next, we want to know how effective the American political economy is. Can government agencies be effective? Can government regulations be effective? Can the economy be effective? Can the economy make everyone, and not just the owners and top administrators, prosper and be happy?

The first subsection of Unit 2 includes three articles on the political system. In the first article G. William Domhoff presents his power elite theory. Owners and top administrators in large corporations have overwhelming influence over the government on matters that concern them and this influence results in losses for most Americans. The next article by Eamon Javers exposes one method that powerful groups use to get special benefits: earmarks. Some earmarks may support projects that truly benefit society as a whole, but most of them greatly benefit just a few at the expense of the public. In the third selection, the past comptroller general of the United States under George Bush, David M. Walker, argues that the federal government must develop greater capacity to forecast the near future and to prepare for it. He worked to have his agency, the Government Accountability Office, become more anticipatory. Walker argues that the government as a whole must become more proactive given the challenges that it faces.

The second subsection deals with major problems and issues of the economy. The first article deals with the impact of globalization on multinational corporations. Samuel J. Palmisano discusses how global economic integration is rapidly changing the corporate world. He sees the development of a new kind of corporation that is replacing the multinational corporation. The new globally integrated enterprise is the product of a new interconnected and intelligent world. Cell phone subscribers are approaching four billion. Sensors are embedded everywhere. Intelligence is exploding. The world is getting smarter with many important consequences. Everywhere we see inefficiencies, waste, and failure. That will change as the smarter world will transform all of these problems.

The next two articles focus on economic growth, consumption, lifestyles, and culture. First, Bill McKibben examines the core objective of American society, which is more economic growth, and asks whether it is good. Does it make us happy? The answer is no, and the drivers of growth seem to be undermining the things that really do contribute to happiness. The next piece focuses on consumption and reports similar findings. It explains how consumption and the materialistic values that undergird it have some serious negative effects on us without increasing our happiness.

© Getty Images/Digital Vision

The last subsection of Unit 2 looks at cities and communities. The first article tries to explain a paradox. Current conditions are bad enough to stimulate urban unrest and occasional riots, but the cities have been calm. Unfortunately, the reason is not that substantial progress on the worst problems has been made, but that cities have manipulatively managed the marginalized. In the second article Jon Meacham uses the inauguration of America's first black president to explain how our country got to this place. Immigration policies and immigration since 1965 are the main reasons both for the crumbling of traditional barriers of race, ethnicity, and gender and the election of Obama. In fact, by mid-century, the United States is expected to have a majority of minorities. Meanwhile, the young are the carriers of the spirit of the new America and will change America further. In the third article, Rebecca Clarren reports on the painful story of slavery currently existing in the United States. Not only does it involve sex trafficking but also coerced industrial or domestic labor. This slavery involves coercion, psychological abuse, fear, torture, and/or rape.

Who Rules America?
Power, Politics, and Social Change

G. William Domhoff

Introduction

Using a wide range of systematic empirical findings, this book shows how the owners and top-level managers in large companies work together to maintain themselves as the core of the dominant power group. Their corporations, banks, and agribusinesses form a *corporate community* that shapes the federal government on the policy issues of interest to it, issues that have a major impact on the income, job security, and well-being of most other Americans. At the same time, there is competition within the corporate community for profit opportunities, which can lead to highly visible policy conflicts among rival corporate leaders that are sometimes fought out in Congress. Yet the corporate community is cohesive on the policy issues that affect its general welfare, which is often at stake when political challenges are made by organized workers, liberals, or strong environmentalists. The book therefore deals with another seeming paradox: How can a highly competitive group of corporate leaders cooperate enough to work their common will in the political and policy arenas?

Partly because the owners and high-level managers within the corporate community share great wealth and common economic interests, but also due to political opposition to their interests, they band together to develop their own social institutions—gated neighborhoods, private schools, exclusive social clubs, debutante balls, and secluded summer resorts. These social institutions create social cohesion and a sense of group belonging, a "we" feeling, and thereby mold wealthy people into a *social upper class*. In addition, the owners and managers supplement their small numbers by financing and directing a wide variety of nonprofit organizations—e.g., tax-free foundations, think tanks, and policy-discussion groups—to aid them in developing policy alternatives that serve ther interests. The highest-ranking employees in these nonprofit organizations become part of a general leadership group for the corporate community and the upper class, called the *power elite*.

Corporate owners and their top executives enter into the electoral arena as the leaders of a *corporate-conservative coalition,* which they shape through large campaign contributions, the advocacy of policy options developed by their hired experts, and easy access to the mass media. They are aided by a wide variety of middle-class patriotic, antitax, and single-issue organizations that celebrate the status quo and warn against "big government." These opinion-shaping organizations are funded in good part by the corporate community, but they have some degree of independence due to direct-mail appeals and modest donations by a large number of middle-class conservatives. The corporate leaders play a large role in both of the major political parties at the presidential level and succeeded in electing a pro-corporate majority to Congress throughout the twentieth century. Historically, this majority in Congress consisted of Northern Republicans and Southern Democrats, but that arrangement changed gradually after the Voting Rights Act of 1965 made it possible for a coalition of African-Americans and white liberals to push the most conservative Southern Democrats into the Republican Party.

Since the last quarter of the twentieth century, the corporate-conservative coalition has been joined by the Christian Right, which consists of a wide range of middle-class religious groups concerned with a variety of social issues, including abortion, prayer in schools, teenage sexual behavior, homosexuality, gay marriage, and pornography. The alliance is sometimes an uneasy one because the corporate community and the Christian Right do not have quite the same priorities, yet they work together because of their common mistrust of government power.

The corporate community's ability to transform its economic power into policy influence and political access, along with its capacity to enter into a coalition with middle-class social and religious conservatives, makes it the most important influence in the federal government. Its key leaders are appointed to top positions in the executive branch and the policy recommendations of its experts are listened to carefully by its allies in Congress. This combination of economic power, policy expertise, and continuing political success makes the corporate owners and executives a *dominant class,* not in the sense of complete and absolute power, but in the sense that they have the power to shape the economic and political frameworks within which other groups and classes must operate. They therefore win far more often than they lose on the issues of concern to them.

Who Wins?

There are many issues over which the corporate-conservative and liberal-labor coalitions disagree, including taxation, unionization, business regulation, foreign trade, the outsourcing of jobs, and the funding of Social Security. Power can be inferred on the basis of these issue conflicts by determining who successfully initiates, modifies, or vetoes policy alternatives. This indicator, by focusing on relationships between the two rival coalitions, comes closest to approximating the process of power contained in the formal definition. It is the indicator preferred by most social scientists. For many reasons, however, it is also the most difficult to use in an accurate way. Aspects of a decision process may remain hidden, some informants may exaggerate or downplay their roles, and people's memories about who did what often become cloudy shortly after the event. Worse, the key concerns of the corporate community may never arise as issues for public discussion because it has the power to keep them off the agenda through a variety of means that are explained throughout later chapters.

Despite the difficulties in using the *Who wins?* indicator of power, it is possible to provide a theoretical framework for analyzing governmental decision-making that mitigates many of them. This framework encompasses the various means by which the corporate community attempts to influence both the government and the general population in a conscious and planned manner, thereby making it possible to assess its degree of success very directly. More specifically, there are four relatively distinct, but overlapping processes (discovered by means of membership network analysis) through which the corporate community controls the public agenda and then wins on most issues that appear on it. These four power networks, which are discussed in detail in later chapters, are as follows:

1. The *special-interest process* deals with the narrow and short-run policy concerns of wealthy families, specific corporations, and specific business sectors. It operates primarily through lobbyists, company lawyers, and trade associations, with a focus on congressional committees, departments of the executive branch, and regulatory agencies.

2. The *policy-planning process* formulates the general interests of the corporate community. It operates through a policy-planning network of foundations, think tanks, and policy-discussion groups, with a focus on the White House, relevant congressional committees, and the high-status newspapers and opinion magazines published in New York and Washington.

3. The *candidate-selection process* is concerned with the election of candidates who are sympathetic to the agenda put forth in the special-interest and policy-planning processes. It operates through large campaign donations and hired political consultants, with a focus on the presidential campaigns of both major political parties and the congressional campaigns of the Republican Party.

4. The *opinion-shaping process* attempts to influence public opinion and keep some issues off the public agenda.

Often drawing on policy positions, rationales, and statements developed within the policy-planning process, it operates through the public relations departments of large corporations, general public relations firms, and many small opinion-shaping organizations, with a focus on middle-class voluntary organizations, educational institutions, and the mass media.

Taken together, the people and organizations that operate in these four networks constitute the political-action arm of the corporate community and upper class.

How the Power Elite Dominate Government

The power elite build on their structural economic power, their storehouse of policy expertise, and their success in the electoral arena to dominate the federal government on the issues about which they care. Lobbyists from corporations, law firms, and trade associations play a key role in shaping government on narrow issues of concern to specific corporations or business sectors, and the policy-planning network supplies new policy directions on major issues, along with top-level governmental appointees to implement those policies.

However, victories within government are far from automatic. As is the case in the competition for public opinion and electoral success, the power elite face opposition from a minority of elected officials and their supporters in labor unions and liberal advocacy groups. These liberal opponents are sometimes successful in blocking the social initiatives put forth by the Christian Right, but the corporate-conservative coalition itself seldom loses when it is united.

Appointees to Government

The first way to see how the power elite shapes the federal government is to look at the social and occupational backgrounds of the people who are appointed to manage the major departments of the executive branch, such as state, treasury, defense, and justice. If the power elite are as important as this book claims, they should come disproportionately from the upper class, the corporate community, and the policy-planning network.

There have been numerous studies of major governmental appointees under both Republican and Democratic administrations, usually focusing on the top appointees in the departments that are represented in the president's cabinet. These studies are unanimous in their conclusion that most top appointees in both Republican and Democratic administrations are corporate executives and corporate lawyers, and hence members of the power elite. Moreover, they are often part of the policy-planning network as well, supporting the claim that the network plays a central role in preparing members of the power elite for government service.

The Special-Interest Process

The special-interest process consists of the many and varied means by which specific corporations and business sectors gain the favors, tax breaks, regulatory rulings, and other governmental assistance they need to realize their narrow and short-run interests. The process is carried out by people with a wide range of experiences: former elected officials, experts who once served on congressional staffs or in regulatory agencies, employees of trade associations, corporate executives whose explicit function is government liaison, and an assortment of lawyers and public-relations specialists. The process is based on a great amount of personal contact, but its most important ingredients are the information and financial support that the lobbyists have to offer. Much of the time this information comes from grassroots pressure generated by the lobbyists to show that voting for a given measure will or will not hurt a particular politician.

Corporations spend far more money on lobbying than their officers give to PACs, by a margin of ten to one. In 2000, for example, the tobacco industry, facing lawsuits and regulatory threats, spent $44 million on lobbyists and $17 million on the Tobacco Institute, an industry public relations arm, but gave only $8.4 million to political campaigns through PACs. More generally, a study of the top 20 defense contractors showed that they spent $400 million on lobbying between 1997 and 2003, but only $46 million on campaign contributions.

The trend toward increasingly large tax breaks continued from 2001 to 2003, with the effective tax rate on corporations declining from 21.7 percent during the last years of the Clinton Administration to 17.2 percent in 2003. Forty-six of 275 major companies studied for 2003 paid no federal income taxes, a considerable increase from a similar study in the late 1990s. A new tax bill in October 2004 added another $137 billion in tax breaks for manufacturing and energy companies, with General Electric, which spent $17 million in lobbying fees in 2003, once again the biggest beneficiary. At the same time, other legal loopholes have allowed multinational corporations to increase the sheltering of profits in foreign tax havens by tens of billions of dollars.

Special interests also work through Congress to try to hamstring regulatory agencies or reverse military purchasing decisions they do not like. When the Federal Communications Commission tried to issue licenses for over 1,000 low-power FM stations for schools and community groups, Congress blocked the initiative at the behest of big broadcasting companies, setting standards that will restrict new licenses to a small number of stations in the least populated parts of the country. When the Food and Drug Administration tried to regulate tobacco, Congress refused authorization in 2000 in deference to the tobacco industry. The FDA is now so lax with pharmaceutical companies that one-third of its scientific employees have less than full confidence that it tests new drugs adequately, and two-thirds expressed a lack of complete confidence in its monitoring of the safety of drugs once they are on the market.

The special-interest process often is used to create loopholes in legislation that is accepted by the corporate community in principle. "I spent the last seven years fighting the Clean Air Act," said a corporate lobbyist in charge of PAC donations, who then went on to explain why he gave money to elected officials even though they voted for the strengthening of the Clean Air Act in 1990:

"How a person votes on the final piece of legislation is not representative of what they have done. Somebody will do a lot of things during the process. How many guys voted against the Clean Air Act? But during the process some of them were very sympathetic to some of our concerns."

Translated, this means there are forty pages of exceptions, extensions, and other loopholes in the 1990 version of the act after a thirteen-year standoff between the Business Roundtable's Clean Air Working Group and the liberal-labor coalition's National Clean Air Coalition. For example, the steel industry has thirty years to bring twenty-six large coke ovens into compliance with the new standards. Once the bill passed, lobbyists went to work on the Environmental Protection Agency to win the most lax regulations possible for implementing the legislation. As of 1998, after twenty-eight years of argument and delay, the agency had been able to issue standards for less than ten of the many hazardous chemicals emitted into the air.

The Big Picture

This book began with two seeming paradoxes. How can the owners and managers of highly competitive corporations develop the policy unity to shape government policies? How can large corporations have such great power in a democratic country? The step-by-step argument and evidence presented in previous chapters provide the foundation for a theory that can explain these paradoxes—a *class-domination theory of power* in the United States.

Domination means that the commands of a group or class are carried out with relatively little resistance, which is possible because that group or class has been able to establish the rules and customs through which everyday life is conducted. Domination, in other words, is the institutionalized outcome of great distributive power. The upper class of owners and high-level executives, based in the corporate community, is a dominant class in terms of this definition because the cumulative effect of its various distributive powers leads to a situation where its policies are generally accepted by most Americans. The routinized ways of acting in the United States follow from the rules and regulations needed by the corporate community to continue to grow and make profits.

The overall distributive power of the dominant class is first of all based in its structural economic power, which falls to it by virtue of its members being owners and high-level executives in corporations that sell goods and services for a profit in a market economy. The power to invest or not invest, and to hire and fire employees, leads to a political context where elected officials try to do as much as they can to create a favorable investment climate to avoid being voted out of office in the event of an economic downturn. This structural power is augmented by the ability to create new policies through a complex policy-planning network, which the upper class has been able to institutionalize because common economic interests and social cohesion have given the corporate community enough unity to sustain such an endeavor over many decades.

But even these powers might not have been enough to generate a system of extreme class domination if the bargains and compromises embodied in the Constitution had not led unexpectedly to a two-party system in which one party was controlled by the Northern rich and the other by the Southern rich. This in turn created a personality-oriented candidate-selection process that is heavily dependent on large campaign donations—now and in the past as well. The system of party primaries is the one adaptation to this constrictive two-party system that has provided some openings for insurgent liberals and trade unionists.

Structural economic power and control of the two parties, along with the elaboration of an opinion-shaping network, results in a polity where there is little or no organized public opinion independent of the limits set by debates within the power elite itself. There is no organizational base from which to construct an alternative public opinion, and there have been until recently no openings within the political system that could carry an alternative message to government.

Finally, the fragmented and constrained system of government carefully crafted by the Founding Fathers led to a relatively small federal government that is easily entered and influenced by wealthy and well-organized private citizens, whether through Congress, the separate departments of the executive branch, or a myriad of regulatory agencies. The net result is that the owners and managers of large income-producing properties score very high on all three power indicators: who

benefits, who governs, and who wins. They have a greater proportion of wealth and income than their counterparts in any other capitalist democracy, and through the power elite they are vastly overrepresented in key government positions and decision-making groups. They win far more often than they lose on those issues that make it to the government for legislative consideration, although their lack of unity in the face of worker militancy in the 1930s made it possible for organized workers to have far more independence, income, and power than they ever had in the past.

Many Americans feel a sense of empowerment because they have religious freedom, free speech, and a belief that they can strike it rich or rise in the system if they try hard enough. Those with educational credentials and/or secure employment experience a degree of dignity and respect because there is no tradition of public degradation for those of average or low incomes. Liberals and leftists can retain hope because in recent decades they have had success in helping to expand individual rights and freedom—for women, for people of color, and most recently for gays and lesbians. But individual rights and freedoms do not necessarily add up to distributive power. In the same time period, when individual rights and freedoms expanded, corporate power also became greater because unions were decimated and the liberal-labor coalition splintered. This analysis suggests there is class domination in spite of a widening of individual freedoms and an expansion of the right to vote.

Inside the Hidden World of Earmarks

A *BusinessWeek* investigation reveals how company spending on lobbyists can pay off.

EAMON JAVERS

I n March, 2004, not long after the U.S. Navy had shipped off its official budget request for the next fiscal year, Admiral Vernon E. Clark, then Chief of Naval Operations, went shopping for more. Spending limits had forced the Navy to cut back on plenty of goodies it wanted, including a top-of-the-line Gulfstream jet. So Clark, the Navy's top-ranking officer, signed off on another, far less formal budget request, this one listing many projects that hadn't been funded. Soon that list began circulating among defense industry lobbyists, including those working for Gulfstream Aerospace Corp. and its parent, General Dynamics Corp. They hit the halls of Congress, and by the time the 2005 defense budget passed four months later, the Navy got its new Gulfstream, courtesy of a special funding request known as an earmark.

The Navy wasn't the only one happy with the behind-the-scenes deal. That one earmark alone was worth $53 million to Gulfstream, and it was just one of 29 earmarks valued at $169 million given to General Dynamics or its subsidiaries that year—quite a payout, especially considering that the company spent only $5.7 million on lobbying in 2004. Put another way, for every dollar it shelled out to lobbyists, it got almost $30 back in earmarks from Uncle Sam.

The Army and Navy quietly seek extra funds after signing off on official budgets.

One of Washington's great mysteries is exactly how much money companies rake in from their lobbying efforts on Capitol Hill. Sure, companies have to disclose how much they spend on the hired guns or in-house government affairs staffers who press their interests before regulators and Congress. And the population of lobbyists has clearly exploded—which suggests that their clients, at least, think they're getting a good deal. But no one outside the lobbying firms and corporate boardrooms has ever known just how much all those lobbyists bring in.

But now, thanks to disclosures prompted by recent scandals over congressional earmarks—those specially targeted spending measures that members of Congress slip into legislation to send money to favored companies and organizations—it's possible for the first time to shed light on at least that corner of the lobbying world. To do that, *BusinessWeek* teamed up with Columbia Books, a Washington publisher of lobbying and trade association directories and operator of a lobbying data Web site. Together we examined the nearly 2,000 earmarks that went to companies in fiscal 2005, the only year for which the government has released complete data. We then compared the earmark funding each company received with the amount it spent on lobbying the prior year.

The results suggest a startling conclusion: On average, companies generated roughly $28 in earmark revenue for every dollar they spent lobbying. And those at the very top did far better than the average: More than 20 companies pulled in $100 or more for every dollar spent. By any standard, that's a hefty ratio. The companies in the Standard & Poor's 500-stock index brought in just $17.52 in revenues for every dollar of capital expenditure in 2006. Or look at the results in direct marketing, where an extremely successful campaign might bring in $5 in revenue for every dollar spent. "If mainstream American businesses got a 28-to-1 ratio in sales, they'd be ecstatic," says Steve Zammarchi, president and CEO of Wunderman New York, a sales and marketing firm.

Of course, not every company emerges from the process a winner. Some end up without any earmarks despite extensive lobbying. Some secured earmarks even though they didn't pay out a dime to lobbyists that year. And since companies are not required to disclose how much of their lobbying goes toward earmarks vs. more general lobbying, it is impossible to know exactly how their spending is allocated. Many also lobby for policy changes, tax breaks, or money for projects in the regular budget, all of which can bring in revenues that can run into the hundreds of millions or more. So for many companies, particularly those in sectors like defense that depend heavily on government contracts, the true return on their lobbying dollars is probably far higher than stated here.

But if gauging the value of lobbying based on earmarks is by necessity an imprecise measure, it's also obvious that on that basis alone it can be highly lucrative. Take a look at just who got the most out of the earmarking process. In sheer dollar value, the defense industry is the uncontested winner. Of the top 50 earmark recipients in 2005, the vast majority were military contractors such as Raytheon Co. and Lockheed Martin Corp. The few nondefense companies among the top 50, such as Cummins Inc. and Caterpillar Inc., won their earmarks selling trucks or other equipment to the military. A rare exception to the military rule: the Alaska Railroad Corp., which got $43 million to finance everything from the development of a transportation facility in downtown Anchorage to routine rail maintenance, thanks to five earmarks sponsored by Senator Ted Stevens (R-Alaska) and the two others in the state's congressional delegation.

In many cases, companies won a dozen or more earmarks from different spending bills. Boeing Co., by far the biggest earmark recipient in 2005, got a total of $456 million through 29 separate earmarks to purchase everything from missile technology to helicopters. The prior year, the aerospace giant spent just $8.5 million on lobbying. That works out to $54 in earmark revenues alone for every lobbying dollar spent. Boeing does not disclose how much it spent on lobbying for earmarks vs. the many other projects it has pending with the federal government. Earmarks were just a small slice of the $28 billion the company booked that year in government contracts.

Like many other companies on the receiving end of earmarks, Boeing declined to answer questions about how they were granted or the lobbying involved. Those that did speak generally defend their awards as legitimate congressional spending on needed projects that were somehow overlooked by the bureaucracy. That argument has found an increasingly receptive audience on Capitol Hill over the years. As recently as 1987, President Ronald Reagan famously vetoed a highway bill because it included 157 earmarks valued at about $1 billion. But by 2006, Congress O.K.'d a breathtaking 13,000 earmarks overall worth $67 billion.

Critics counter that Congress is spending all that money for the wrong reasons. In the normal budget process, federal agencies and the Administration go through an extensive procedure to set spending priorities among competing projects, and contracts generally are only awarded following competitive bidding. With earmarks, that rarely happens. Members of Congress have wide discretion to target funding to pet projects, and they can direct the spending to a particular company or organization without taking any rival bids. Says Keith Ashdown, chief investigator for the watchdog group Taxpayers for Common Sense: "The lion's share of these projects is about politics and jobs, rather than real needs."

Proliferating Scandals

The sad history of earmarks features a long list of abuses: earmarks used by congressional leaders to buy votes on other legislation, earmarks sent to political donors, and earmarks used in outright bribery. Such issues continue to arise: As recently as July 30, the FBI raided the home of Senator Stevens in a probe into potential earmark-related corruption. Senator Stevens, who has not been charged with any wrongdoing, will not comment until the investigation is complete. In the face of recent earmark scandals, Congress in early August passed a reform bill aimed at reducing abuses by opening up the highly secretive process. Whether those efforts succeed won't be clear until year-end.

One indication will come from whether the defense sector continues to pocket such a large chunk of earmark dollars. Take the way Gulfstream Aerospace landed that order for a top-of-the-line jet in 2005. After Admiral Clark finished negotiating with Administration officials over the Navy's official budget for the year, he sent a letter known as an "unfunded request list" to key congressional leaders in charge of appropriations. At that, the Navy isn't alone—the U.S. Army and the other services all quietly circulate similar lists asking for more funding after signing off on their official budgets.

Tastes Like Pork

Think of them as essentially wish lists that each service puts out to cover all the extra stuff it wants but can't afford once their annual budgets are set. As those lists circulate, lobbyists scour them for their clients' products, then work with the companies to hit up the home state legislators where the goods will be manufactured. Lawmakers who want credit for generating jobs back home are only too eager to agree to an earmark.

That year, Clark's list included 61 items, including a request for a "C-37." That's the military designation for a Gulfstream G550 jet—the same civilian aircraft used by globe-trotting CEOs everywhere. Clark's list began circulating among defense industry lobbyists, including those working for Gulfstream Aerospace and General Dynamics. Soon, those lobbyists were talking with the Navy, whose officials told them the service needed the plane for the Pacific fleet, where officers have to travel great distances, says a person familiar with the situation. All of General Dynamics' lobbyists—both its hired guns and its in-house staff—began working Congress to try to win an earmark for the plane. They started with the Georgia congressional delegation, since Gulfstreams are built in that state. The tactic worked: The final defense bill that year included a $53 million earmark to fund the plane. In a press release, Saxby Chambliss (R-Ga.) took credit for the earmark as just one of "$147 million in new projects for Georgia that will help our troops win the war on terror." A spokeswoman for Chambliss says the senator is proud of the work he does to bring jobs to the state. Gulfstream referred calls to General Dynamics, where lobbyist Kendell Pease, a former rear admiral, said the earmark made sense for

Pentagon Players

Which companies pocket the most in earmarks? Defense contractors dominate the Top 20 recipients.

Recipient	2005 Earmark Amount (Millions)
Boeing	$456
Northrop Grumman	$198
General Dynamics	$169
Lockheed Martin	$167
Raytheon	$158
Bae Systems	$138
L-3 Communications	$109
Alliant Techsystems	$100
Saic	$ 95
Concurrent Technologies	$ 80
General Atomics	$ 78
Cummins	$ 63
Textron	$ 59
Drs Technologies	$ 51
Alaska Railroad	$ 44
Motorola	$ 32
Trex Enterprises	$ 31
Oshkosh Truck	$ 31
Argon St	$ 31
Intergraph	$ 29

the Navy, since the G550 fit the service's requirements for a long-range jet.

But that brand-new C-37 never made it to the Pacific. After taking possession of the plane, which came with a special oxygen atmosphere system designed to keep passengers fresh and alert on long trips, the Navy decided to keep it at Andrews Air Force Base near Washington, D.C., and designated it for use by two top officials: the Navy Secretary and the Chief of Naval Operations—the very same office that had requested the earmark in the first place. Told that the Navy had not sent the airplane to the Pacific, Pease lets out a chuckle. "Imagine that," he says. "They kept the new one."

Clark retired in July, 2005, before the Gulfstream was delivered. Now a director at Raytheon, he declined to comment. The earmarked Gulfstream is used today by Clark's successor, Admiral Michael Mullen, and Navy Secretary Donald C. Winter. A Navy spokesman says the service kept the Gulfstream in Washington so it could send an older plane to the Pacific. That plane was the same model as others used in the region, making upkeep easier.

If the big defense contractors dominate the list in total dollars awarded, even relatively small companies do well when measured by the ratio of lobbying spending to earmarks received. By that yardstick, the most successful company of

all is a little-known defense contractor based in Atlanta called Scientific Research Corp. The maker of classified intelligence technology spent just $60,000 on lobbying in 2004 and in fiscal 2005 got nine earmarks worth more than $20 million to develop covert radios for soldiers and threat simulation software, among other projects. For each lobbying dollar it spent, $344 in earmark funding flowed back its way. David Chapman, the company's vice-president for business development, says the contracts fulfilled "validated military needs," adding that in the congressional earmark process, "being a small company with small dollars, you can get some pretty high ratios."

It helps, of course, to hire the right lobbyist. The company hired just one in 2004: Hurt, Norton & Associates. That firm is run by Robert H. Hurt, a longtime staffer to Sam Nunn, the former Democratic Senator from Georgia who used to chair the Senate Armed Services Committee. The tie helps ensure the contacts and the access—not to mention the technical and budgetary know-how—to present their clients' projects to current congressional staffers in charge of defense spending.

Hurt declined to speak publicly about his role in lobbying for earmarks, but hiring such former Hill aides to pitch their old colleagues is clearly key. The list of lobbyists working for the most successful earmark-wrangling companies is replete with former Hill aides who served with the money-spending appropriations committees, and even a member of Congress or two. And as the number of dollars available on Capitol Hill has surged, earmark lobbying itself has become a cottage industry. In 1998, 1,447 entities hired lobbyists to work on budget and appropriations issues, according to Taxpayers for Common Sense. By 2006, that number had swelled to 4,516 lobbying clients.

It's not just the clients that have grown: From virtually nothing a decade ago, roughly a dozen firms specialize in garnering earmarks today. One such firm, PMA Group, founded in 1989 by former defense appropriations staffer Paul Magliochetti, represented at least 15 of the top 50 corporate earmark winners in 2005, including Lockheed Martin, General Dynamics, and Boeing. Others well known for delivering federal money include Van Scoyoc Associates, Alcalde & Fay, and Cassidy & Associates. In this quietly lucrative world, many say they don't advertise for clients—companies find them. "The people who want results come to me," says one prominent earmark lobbyist. "The smart ones figure out who can deliver."

Will the recent wave of reform efforts bring an end to such practices? Both President George W. Bush and House Speaker Nancy Pelosi (D-Calif.) have called for earmarks to be slashed in half this year. In early August, Congress passed extensive new disclosure requirements. New Internet databases will also make it easier for the press and the public to follow the money. That appears to be having an impact: From a peak of 2,657 earmarks worth $11.6 billion in the 2005 defense spending bill, earmarks in the fiscal 2008 defense spending bill are down significantly. The House version of the still incomplete bill includes 1,337 earmarks worth less than $4 billion, according to Taxpayers for Common Sense.

How Much Bang for the Buck?

On average, companies in fiscal 2005 got earmarks worth $28 for every dollar they spent on lobbying. But for some, earmarks were far more lucrative. Below, the Top 20 earmark recipients, ranked by the amount they received in earmarks for each dollar they paid their lobbyists.

Recipient	2004 Lobbying Spending (Thousands)	2005 Earmark Amount (Millions)	Earmarks For Every $1 Spent Lobbying	Recipient	2004 Lobbying Spending (Thousands)	2005 Earmark Amount (Millions)	Earmarks For Every $1 Spent Lobbying
Scientific Research	$ 60	$ 21	$344	Advanced Acoustic	$100	$ 14	$140
Concurrent Technologies	$300	$ 80	$268	Day & Zimmermann	$140	$ 19	$134
Argon St	$120	$ 31	$256	Prologic	$180	$ 24	$133
Chenega	$ 80	$ 18	$223	Trident Microsystems	$100	$ 13	$127
Isothermal Systems	$ 80	$ 18	$221	Alliant Techsystems	$860	$100	$116
Intergraph	$140	$ 29	$207	Trex Enterprises	$270	$ 31	$116
Alaska Railroad	$260	$ 44	$168	Miltec	$200	$ 22	$112
Saic	$660	$ 95	$144	L-3 Communications	$980	$109	$111
Arinc	$100	$ 14	$143	Apogen Technologies	$120	$ 13	$108
Anteon	$120	$ 17	$141	Israel Military Industries	$160	$ 17	$106

DATA: *BusinessWeek*/Columbia Books analysis of data from the Office of Management & Budget and the Senate Office of Public Records.

Still, many earmarks typically don't get added to the budget until the final days of budget negotiations, which will likely take place late this fall. And some old habits die hard. This year, the Navy trimmed its unfunded request list to just 20 items. But the dollar value of the earmarks is $5.6 billion—more than twice the $2.7 billion it requested for the 61 items on its 2005 wish list.

Privately, many lobbyists predict earmark totals will bounce back once the spotlight fades. "Ever since budgets were invented, man has figured out ways to get around them," says H. Stewart Van Scoyoc, president of Van Scoyoc Associates. "A lot of what we do in this town is gamesmanship of budgets."

And why not? With $28 in earmarks coming in for every dollar in lobbying, it's a great business.

Foresight for Government

The comptroller general of the United States examines the most significant long-term challenges facing the world community and outlines the steps that accountability agencies should take to help position their governments for the future.

DAVID M. WALKER

Nearly a century ago, one of my favorite U.S. presidents, Theodore Roosevelt, said, "We have to, as a nation, exercise foresight . . . and if we do not exercise that foresight, dark will be the future." These words resonate with me. But unfortunately, much of our world, including the United States, is consumed with the here and now. Far too little thought is given to what's come before or what lies ahead.

- Too many individuals tend to focus on their next paycheck.
- Too many company executives focus on the next quarterly earnings report.
- Too many politicians focus on the next election cycle rather than the next generation.
- And too many countries focus on their current position in the world while forgetting that we're all inhabitants of Planet Earth.

But whether we're talking about a government, a not-for-profit entity, or a for-profit company, it's vital for an organization to understand the big picture, to learn from the past and from others, and to prepare for the future. With change comes both opportunities and risks. Furthermore, change is inevitable and essential for innovation. However, it's also important to understand how organizations and others can manage change.

Myopia, or shortsightedness, can undermine a nation's willingness and ability to act. In the case of the United States, strong economic growth, modest inflation levels, relatively low interest rates, and our current superpower status have given many policy makers and the American public a false sense of security about our nation's current position and future prospects. Despite the impending retirement of the babyboom generation, America continues to party on and pile up record levels of debt.

On the other hand, recent history shows that some nations have begun to act on their long-term challenges. For example, two nations—Australia and New Zealand—chose to face their fiscal facts and made difficult decisions that caused some short-term pain in the interest of long-term gain. Like the United States, Australia and New Zealand have aging populations. However, unlike the United States, these two countries stepped up to the plate and took steps to deal with their long-range fiscal imbalances, including their overburdened and underfunded public entitlement programs. Australia and New Zealand are works in progress, but at least their leaders have addressed this large, known, and growing challenge.

When it comes to fiscal and other public policy issues, Supreme Audit Institutions (SAI) can help focus attention on what lies ahead. Most governments have an SAI. In the case of the United States, it's my agency, the U.S. Government Accountability Office (GAO). In Canada, for example, it's the Office of the Auditor General, headed by Sheila Fraser.

Over the years, government auditors have earned a reputation for independence and professionalism. We're known for putting the facts on the table and providing policy makers with timely, reliable, and objective information. Not everyone may like what we have to say, but we have an important role to play in promoting transparency, improving performance, ensuring accountability, and speaking truth to power. The truth is that sound policy choices are more likely when policy makers are equipped with solid facts and nonpartisan analyses rather than ideological arguments and partisan political spin.

SAIs have traditionally been in the oversight business. As government watchdogs, we scrutinize how taxpayer dollars are spent and advise policy makers on ways to make government work better. Many SAIs, including GAO, also undertake a range of insight activities designed to improve government effectiveness. These activities include performance and value-for-money audits and benchmarking and best-practices studies.

I believe that, in addition to providing oversight and insight work, SAIs can and should alert public officials to key emerging challenges and opportunities. They can provide policy makers with valuable foresight. SAIs have several traditional tools that can help bring a sharper focus to long-term policy issues, been introduced in 1898 to help pay for the Spanish-American War—a war that lasted only a few months.

Congress and the president need to decide which federal programs and policies remain priorities, which should be overhauled, and which have simply outlived their usefulness. I'm sure many other countries could also benefit from this kind of "spring cleaning."

Some Hopeful Signs

So, what's been the reaction of policy makers to our "21st Century Challenges" report? I'm pleased to say we're seeing some hopeful signs in several areas that GAO has highlighted. For example, our government is taking seriously the need to plan ahead for the possibility of a global influenza pandemic similar to the one in 1918, which killed millions worldwide.

The U.S. Congress is also keeping a closer eye on new trends on the nation's highways, particularly the growing role that high-tech driver distractions, like cell phones, are playing in traffic fatalities. We're also finally starting to see greater concern about our long-range fiscal imbalance and other key sustainability challenges, such as energy, health care, and the environment. Furthermore, recently proposed legislation would convene a commission of leaders to study entitlement and tax reform issues and recommend changes.

To better meet Congress's information need on these emerging issues, GAO has developed an approach we call "grounded foresight." We believe that, to be credible, foresight work must have a strong factual and conceptual basis. Such work needs to ground all trends in evidence. At the same time, such work also needs to clearly convey the uncertainty that's inherent in foresight analysis.

Several key tools are available to encourage a forward focus. These tools include strategic planning, key national indicators, and scenario planning. Unfortunately, not all governments, including my own, have taken full advantage of these tools.

The value of a strategic plan is probably obvious to futurists. By thinking more comprehensively, learning from the past and others, and focusing on the future, governments can better set priorities, target their efforts, add value, reduce risks, manage change, and capitalize on new opportunities. After all, if you don't have a plan, you don't have a prayer of maximizing value and mitigating risk.

In our case, GAO's strategic plan defines our agency's mission, goals, and objectives. GAO's strategic plan also includes our agency's core values. These values represent our institutional beliefs and boundaries that are designed to be timeless in nature. Furthermore, our plan also includes a range of key public policy trends and challenges that warrant attention from lawmakers and our agency. Because these trends and challenges lack geopolitical and sectoral boundaries, they are also relevant for many other nations.

Acknowledging and understanding these trends have improved the contextual sophistication of our current work while helping us to maintain a focus on the future. These trends have also encouraged knowledge sharing both domestically and internationally. In turn, this has led to greater cooperation

GAO's Mission

The Government Accountability Office, the investigative arm of Congress, exists to support Congress in meeting its constitutional responsibilities and to help improve the performance and accountability of the federal government for the American people. GAO examines the use of public funds; evaluates federal programs and policies; and provides analyses, recommendations, and other assistance to help Congress make informed oversight, policy, and funding decisions. GAO's commitment to good government is reflected in its core values of accountability, integrity, and reliability.

For more information, visit www.gao.gov.

including strategic planning. But SAIs should also take advantage of other valuable methods, such as long-term modeling and scenario planning.

More than ever, SAIs have an opportunity to encourage early action on a range of important issues—before they reach crisis proportions and while they're still manageable. Today, GAO is working hard to help members of Congress better understand the trends and challenges facing the United States and its position in the world. We're also trying to help lawmakers grasp the long-term implications of current policy choices.

Our goal is for Congress to expand its horizon and its peripheral vision. We want policy makers to better understand where we are, how we may look 30 or even 40 years out, and the collateral or ripple effects of various policies and programs.

For example, New Zealand and other countries have adopted fiscal sustainability reporting and various other measures that ensure a long-term focus. If they can do it, then the United States and other countries can and should do so as well.

In this spirit and in an effort to lead by example, GAO has published an unprecedented report called "21st Century Challenges" that asks a series of probing, sometimes provocative, questions about current government policies, programs, and operational practices. The report brings home how much of the U.S. government reflects organizational models, labor markets, life expectancies, transportation systems, security strategies, and other conditions that are rooted in the past. Clearly, the U.S. government isn't alone in this respect. In this report, we've also sought to communicate important foresight concepts in language used and understood by policy makers.

At the same time, the U.S. federal government, like many others, continues to expand, with new projects and initiatives added every year. Our Congress and the White House rarely seem to question the wisdom of existing federal activities. As former President Ronald Reagan once said, "The nearest thing to eternal life we'll ever see on this earth is a government program."

The same goes for many tax policies. For example, just last summer, the U.S. government announced it will stop collecting a 3% tax on long-distance telephone calls. This doesn't seem particularly startling until you realize that the tax had on a range of shared sustainability challenges, including fiscal, energy, environmental, and other key issues.

Prioritizing Policy Efforts

Perhaps the most urgent issue is America's worsening financial condition and growing long-term fiscal imbalance. Long-term fiscal analyses by GAO and our sister agency in the legislative branch, the Congressional Budget Office, show that federal deficits will grow to unsustainable levels in as little as two decades. At that point, without significant policy changes, federal deficits could reach 10% or more of our economy. States and local governments face increasing future fiscal pressures as well. Largely because of our aging population, rising healthcare costs, and relatively low revenues as a percentage of the economy, America faces decades of red ink.

Clearly, a crunch is coming, and eventually all of government will feel its impact. If America continues on its current course, it's only a matter of time before our ship of state hits the rocks. To put us on a more prudent and sustainable long-term path, the federal government must begin to make tough choices in connection with budget systems, legislative processes, entitlement programs, spending patterns, and tax policies. There's no way we will grow our way out of our fiscal hole. The sooner we begin to act, the better, because we are the world's largest debtor nation, and time is working against us.

The fact is that many other nations also face long-term fiscal risks. For example, a 2005 European Union report warned of unsustainable public finances in about half of the European Union member states, primarily because of the growing old-age dependency ratio.

As a citizen, a senior government official, and a father and grandfather, I take America's fiscal imbalance very seriously. It's not just a matter of numbers, it's also about values. It's easy to forget that deficits eventually have real-life consequences for real people, including our own children and grandchildren. As a result, I've been speaking out on this issue with increasing frequency and urgency in recent years. Raising public awareness, whether through audit reports, congressional testimony, speeches, radio commentaries, or opinion pieces, is an important part of GAO's and my foresight role.

Some members of Congress seem to be getting the message, but it's going to take years of sustained effort to get America's fiscal problems under control. It's important that we do so, not just for our own sakes but also for the sake of the global economy. After all, as the old saying goes, when America catches a cold, the rest of the world may catch the flu.

Beyond America's staggering fiscal challenge, GAO is keeping a close watch on several other long-term trends, many of which have no geopolitical boundaries. These trends include changing security threats, globalization of trade and financial markets, changing economic models, growing gaps between the haves and the have-nots, demographic changes, immigration patterns, energy supply and security issues, environmental concerns such as climate change and sustainable development, health-care challenges, education needs, rapidly

evolving science and technology, changing governance structures, and a range of other issues.

Transforming Governance Structures

Transforming existing governance structures is a theme that's especially important to GAO and worth elaborating on. As the pace of change accelerates in every aspect of life, national governments face new and more complex challenges that they cannot address alone. If we're to meet the public's wants and needs in light of these long-term trends, governance systems in America and most other countries must be revised.

In the twenty-first century, an effective governance structure recognizes that more and more policy challenges require multilateral action. We're also going to need greater coordination among various levels of government and the private and citizen sectors, both domestically and internationally. The plain but simple truth is that no nation in today's world, including the United States, can or should go it alone.

Beyond changing our governance approaches, we also need to consider how we keep score. In my view, key national and outcome-based indicators can help policy makers better assess a nation's status, its progress over time, and its position relative to other nations on issues like public safety, health care, housing, education, and the environment. Such indicators can help guide strategic planning, facilitate foresight, inform agenda setting, enhance performance and accountability reporting, and encourage more informed decision making and oversight, including much-needed and long-overdue efforts to reengineer the base of our federal government.

Key indicator systems are now used by various supranational and international entities, including the European Union, the Organization for Economic Co-operation and Development (OECD), and the United Nations. For years now, several countries, including Australia, Canada, and the United Kingdom, and even some U.S. states and localities, have used indicators to prioritize and target public resources. It's time the U.S. government did so as well. However, rather than a strictly federal initiative, this needs to be a national effort enlisting all levels of government, businesses, think tanks, nonprofit groups, and others.

We at GAO are working with the National Academies of Sciences, the OECD, and others to help make key national indicators a reality in the United States and elsewhere. Furthermore, the International Organization of Supreme Audit Institutions (INTOSAI), which serves as the umbrella organization for national audit offices worldwide, has adopted key national indicators as one of the two main themes for its 2007 Global Congress in Mexico City. Representatives from over 150 countries will address this topic and long-range fiscal challenges and related public debt issues.

U.S. civilian agencies, including GAO, have started using another foresight tool long familiar to our defense agencies: scenario planning. For years, this technique has played an important role in GAO's work on America's long-range fiscal imbalance. More recently, we've used scenario planning concepts to assess our nation's preparedness for natural disasters like Hurricane Katrina. We've found that using a range of realistic scenarios helps agencies responsible for emergency preparedness to identify and address various risks and possible gaps in capabilities—before a catastrophe hits. These scenarios can also help to identify redundancies and conflicts that need to be addressed.

Partnering for Progress

Tools like strategic plans, key indicators, and scenario planning aren't enough. The truth is, with the range of complicated problems I've just described, nations, institutions, and individuals are going to need to change the way they think and act. Among other things, they will need to join forces and partner for progress. By applying our collective expertise and experience to shared challenges, we can vastly increase our chances for success while avoiding common mistakes.

Politicians and civil servants must be willing to reach across institutional and geopolitical lines to share knowledge. Partnerships can be forged not only among various government agencies, but also with businesses and nonprofit groups. This approach can and should be used domestically as well as internationally.

Fortunately, more countries are recognizing the need to partner for progress. As never before, Europe is working together and making strides on a range of issues of mutual interest and concern. So far, we've seen important reforms in areas like public finance, immigration, and the capital markets.

The accountability profession, in which GAO is a leader, is also taking steps to focus on the future and partner for progress. For example, GAO led efforts to develop the first-ever strategic plan for INTOSAI. INTOSAI's members have enthusiastically embraced the plan, and it will undoubtedly help to raise the organization and its members to new heights in the years ahead.

If we expect to successfully tackle these tough issues, we'll need more leaders in the United States and elsewhere with four key attributes: courage, integrity, creativity, and stewardship.

By courage, I mean people who state the facts, speak the truth, and do the right thing, even if it isn't easy or popular.

By integrity, I mean people who practice what they preach and lead by example. People who understand that the law and professional standards represent the floor of acceptable behavior. People who set their sights higher and strive to do what's right.

By creativity, I mean people who can think outside the box and see new ways to address old problems. Individuals who have foresight and can help others see the way forward.

Finally, by stewardship, I mean people who don't just generate positive results today but who also leave things better positioned for the future when they depart their jobs and this earth. That's what real stewardship is all about, and we don't have enough of it today.

Focusing on foresight is an important but often a thankless job. Frankly, it's a subject with too few constituents. Consumed with the everyday demands of work and family, the average citizen in most countries probably doesn't give foresight a lot of thought, much less demand their elected representatives adopt a forward focus.

It's time for our leaders in all sectors of society to learn from the past and from others while preparing for the future. It's in our collective best interests, as well as the interests of our countries, our children, and our grandchildren, for them to do so.

David M. Walker is comptroller general of the United States. This article draws from his presentation "Focusing on Foresight" at the World Future Society's conference, WorldFuture 2006: Creating a Global Strategy for Humanity's Future.

A Smarter Planet

SAMUEL J. PALMISANO

The Next Leadership Agenda Delivered to the Council on Foreign Relations, New York City, New York, November 6, 2008. Thank you, Bob. And thank you, Richard. It is a pleasure and an honor to be here today in this distinguished assembly, and at this extraordinary moment: a major political transition in the United States, the global economy in flux, our financial markets restructuring themselves—and an acutely felt need for leadership.

Our political leaders aren't the only ones who've been handed a mandate for change. Leaders of businesses and institutions everywhere confront a unique opportunity to transform the way the world works.

We have this chance for reasons no one wished. The crisis in our financial markets has jolted us awake to the realities and dangers of highly complex global systems. But in truth, the first decade of the 21st century has been a series of wake-up calls with a single subject: the reality of global integration.

Two years ago, I published an essay in *Foreign Affairs* that described the changing structure of the corporation, which I felt had been largely left out of the discussion on globalization. I described the emergence of a new kind of corporation—the globally integrated enterprise, which was replacing the multinational.

Today there is growing consensus that global integration is changing the corporate model and the nature of work itself. But we now see that the movement of information, work, and capital across developed and developing nations—as profound as those are—constitute just one aspect of global integration.

In the last few years, our eyes have been opened to global climate change, and to the environmental and geopolitical issues surrounding energy. We have been made aware of global supply chains for food and medicine. And, of course, we entered the new century with the shock to our sense of security delivered by the attacks on 9/11.

These collective realizations have reminded us that we are all now connected—economically, technically, and socially. But we're also learning that being connected is not sufficient. Yes, the world continues to get "flatter." And yes, it continues to get smaller and more interconnected. But something is happening that holds even greater potential. In a word, our planet is becoming smarter.

This isn't just a metaphor. I mean infusing intelligence into the way the world literally works—the systems and processes that enable physical goods to be developed, manufactured, bought, and sold . . . services to be delivered . . . everything from people and money to oil, water, and electrons to move . . . and billions of people to work and live.

What's making this possible?

First, our world is becoming instrumented: The transistor, invented 60 years ago, is the basic building block of the digital age. Now, consider a world in which there are a billion transistors per human, each one costing one ten-millionth of a cent. We'll have that by 2010. There will likely be 4 billion mobile phone subscribers by the end of this year . . . and 30 billion Radio Frequency Identification tags produced globally within two years. Sensors are being embedded across entire ecosystems—supply-chains, healthcare networks, cities . . . even natural systems like rivers.

Second, our world is becoming interconnected: Very soon there will be 2 billion people on the Internet. But in an instrumented world, systems and objects can now "speak" to one another, too. Think about the prospect of a trillion connected and intelligent things—cars, appliances, cameras, roadways, pipelines . . . even pharmaceuticals and livestock. The amount of information produced by the interaction of all those things will be unprecedented.

Third, all things are becoming intelligent: New computing models can handle the proliferation of end-user devices, sensors, and actuators and connect them with back-end systems. Combined with advanced analytics, those supercomputers can turn mountains of data into intelligence that can be translated into action, making our systems, processes, and infrastructures more efficient, more productive, and responsive—in a word, smarter.

What this means is that the digital and physical infrastructures of the world are converging. Computational power is being put into things we wouldn't recognize as computers. Indeed, almost anything—any person, any object, any process, or any service, for any organization, large or small—can become digitally aware and networked.

With so much technology and networking abundantly available at such low cost, what wouldn't you enhance? What service wouldn't you provide a customer, citizen, student, or patient? What wouldn't you connect? What information wouldn't you mine for insight?

The answer is, you or your competitor—another company, or another city or nation—will do all of that. You will do it because you can—the technology is available and affordable.

But there is another reason we will make our companies, institutions, and industries smarter. Because we must. Not just at moments of widespread shock, but integrated into our day-to-day operations. These mundane processes of business, government, and life—which are ultimately the source of those "surprising" crises—are not smart enough to be sustainable.

Consider:

- How much energy we waste: According to published reports, the losses of electrical energy because grid systems are not "smart" range as high as 40 to 70 percent around the world.
- How gridlocked our cities are: Congested roadways in the U.S. cost $78 billion annually, in the form of 4.2 billion lost hours and 2.9 billion gallons of wasted gas—and that's not even counting the impact on our air quality.
- How inefficient our supply chains are: Consumer product and retail industries lose about $40 billion annually, or 3.5 percent of their sales, due to supply chain inefficiencies.

- How antiquated our healthcare system is: In truth, it isn't a "system" at all. It doesn't link from diagnosis, to drug discovery, to healthcare deliverers, to insurers, to employers. Meanwhile, personal expenditures on health now push more than 100 million people worldwide below the poverty line each year.
- How our planet's water supply is drying up: Global water usage has increased six-fold since the 1900s, twice the rate of human population growth. According to the Asian Development Bank, one in five people living today lacks access to safe drinking water, and half the world's population does not have adequate sanitation.
- And, of course, the crisis in our financial markets: This will be analyzed for decades, but one thing is already clear. Financial institutions spread risk but weren't able to track risk—and that uncertainty, that lack of knowing with precision, undermined confidence.

It's obvious, when you consider the trajectories of development driving the planet today, that we're going to have to run a lot smarter and more efficiently—especially as we seek the next areas of investment to drive economic growth and to move large parts of the global economy out of recession.

Fortunately, we now can. We see this in how companies and institutions are rethinking their systems and applying technology in new ways.

Stockholm's smart traffic system has resulted in 20 percent less traffic, a 12 percent drop in emissions and a reported 40,000 additional daily users of public transport. Smart traffic systems are strengthening the competitive positions of cities from London to Brisbane to Singapore—with many more being planned.

Intelligent oil field technologies can increase both pump performance and well productivity—in a business where only 20–30 percent of available reserves are currently extracted.

Smart food systems—such as one now running in the Nordics—can use RFID technology to trace meat and poultry from the farm through the supply chain to supermarket shelves.

Smart healthcare can lower the cost of therapy by as much as 90 percent—as ActiveCare Network is doing for more than 2 million patients in 38 states, whom it monitors for the proper delivery of their injections and vaccines.

There are many other examples I could cite. Smart systems are transforming energy grids, supply chains, and water management. They are ensuring the authenticity of pharmaceuticals and the security of currency exchanges. And they are changing everything from organizations' business models to how they enable their employees to collaborate and innovate.

And remember, the opportunity to become smarter applies not just to large enterprises, but to smaller and mid-sized companies—the engines of economic growth everywhere. When we think about systems like supply chains, healthcare delivery, and food systems, we're really talking about the interactions of hundreds, even thousands of companies, most of them small.

This opportunity also applies beyond business. Smart infrastructure is becoming the basis of competition between nations, regions, and cities.

In a globally integrated economy, investment and work flow not only to the places in the world that offer cost advantages, skills, and expertise. It is flowing to countries, regions, and cities that offer smart infrastructure—everything from efficient transportation systems, modern airports, and secure trade lanes . . . to reliable energy grids, transparent and trusted markets, and enhanced quality of life.

Certainly, as you travel the world, you see countries everywhere leapfrogging—not only to the latest technology and to digital infrastructures, but to the most modern business designs, processes, and models. Ultimately, this is about competitiveness in a globally integrated economy.

The importance of this moment, I believe, is that the key precondition for real change now exists: People want it. But this moment will not last forever.

Isn't it true that the hardest part of driving any kind of change is whether the individual—the employee, the citizen—feels the need to change at a deeply personal level? And in hindsight, when the circumstances that cry out for change are gone, when things have returned to "normal"—don't we always wish we had been bolder, more ambitious, gone faster, gone further?

Well, today, from the boardroom to the kitchen table, people everywhere are ready, eager for a new way of doing things.

That's why a period of discontinuity is, for those with courage and vision, a period of opportunity. Over the next couple of years, there will be winners, and there will be losers. And though it may not be easy to see now, I believe we will see new leaders emerge who win not by surviving the storm, but by changing the game.

To do that, they will practice forms of leadership that are very different from the models of the past.

Think about the way the world today actually works: Very few of our systems are the responsibility of a single entity or decision-maker. So leaders will need to hone their collaboration skills, because we will need leadership that pulls across systems. We will need to bring together stakeholders and experts from across business, government, and academia, and all of them will need to move outside their traditional comfort zones. This is something on which the Council on Foreign Relations has been showing the way for many years.

There is much serious work ahead of us, as leaders and as citizens. Together, we have to consciously infuse intelligence into our decision-making and management systems . . . not just infuse our processes with more speed and capacity.

But I think one thing is clear: The world will continue to become smaller, flatter . . . and smarter. We are moving into the age of the globally integrated and intelligent economy, society, and planet. The question is, what will we do with that?

The world now beckoning us is one of enormous promise. And I believe it is one that we can build—if we open our minds and let ourselves think about all that a smarter planet could be.

Thank you.

Reversal of Fortune

The formula for human well-being used to be simple: Make money, get happy. So why is the old axiom suddenly turning on us?

BILL MCKIBBEN

For most of human history, the two birds More and Better roosted on the same branch. You could toss one stone and hope to hit them both. That's why the centuries since Adam Smith launched modern economics with his book *The Wealth of Nations* have been so single-mindedly devoted to the dogged pursuit of maximum economic production. Smith's core ideas—that individuals pursuing their own interests in a market society end up making each other richer; and that increasing efficiency, usually by increasing scale, is the key to increasing wealth—have indisputably worked. They've produced more More than he could ever have imagined. They've built the unprecedented prosperity and ease that distinguish the lives of most of the people reading these words. It is no wonder and no accident that Smith's ideas still dominate our politics, our outlook, even our personalities.

But the distinguishing feature of our moment is this: Better has flown a few trees over to make her nest. And that changes everything. Now, with the stone of your life or your society gripped in your hand, you have to choose. It's More or Better.

Which means, according to new research emerging from many quarters, that our continued devotion to growth above all is, on balance, making our lives worse, both collectively and individually. Growth no longer makes most people wealthier, but instead generates inequality and insecurity. Growth is bumping up against physical limits so profound—like climate change and peak oil—that trying to keep expanding the economy may be not just impossible but also dangerous. And perhaps most surprisingly, growth no longer makes us happier. Given our current dogma, that's as bizarre an idea as proposing that gravity pushes apples skyward. But then, even Newtonian physics eventually shifted to acknowledge Einstein's more complicated universe.

[I] "We Can Do It If We Believe It": FDR, LBJ, and the Invention of Growth

It was the great economist John Maynard Keynes who pointed out that until very recently, "there was no very great change in the standard of life of the average man living in the civilized centers of the earth." At the utmost, Keynes calculated, the standard of living roughly doubled between 2000 B.C. and the dawn of the 18th century—four millennia during which we basically didn't learn to do much of anything new. Before history began, we had already figured out fire, language, cattle, the wheel, the plow, the sail, the pot. We had banks and governments and mathematics and religion.

And then, something new finally did happen. In 1712, a British inventor named Thomas Newcomen created the first practical steam engine. Over the centuries that followed, fossil fuels helped create everything we consider normal and obvious about the modern world, from electricity to steel to fertilizer; now, a 100 percent jump in the standard of living could suddenly be accomplished in a few decades, not a few millennia.

In some ways, the invention of the idea of economic growth was almost as significant as the invention of fossil-fuel power. But it took a little longer to take hold. During the Depression, even FDR routinely spoke of America's economy as mature, with no further expansion anticipated. Then came World War II and the postwar boom—by the time Lyndon Johnson moved into the White House in 1963, he said things like: "I'm sick of all the people who talk about the things we can't do. Hell, we're the richest country in the world, the most powerful. We can do it all. . . . We can do it if we believe it." He wasn't alone in thinking this way. From Moscow, Nikita Khrushchev thundered, "Growth of industrial and agricultural production is the battering ram with which we shall smash the capitalist system."

Yet the bad news was already apparent, if you cared to look. Burning rivers and smoggy cities demonstrated the dark side of industrial expansion. In 1972, a trio of MIT researchers released a series of computer forecasts they called "limits to growth," which showed that unbridled expansion would eventually deplete our resource base. A year later the British economist E. F. Schumacher wrote the best-selling *Small Is Beautiful*. (Soon after, when Schumacher came to the United States on a speaking tour, Jimmy Carter actually received him at the White House—imagine the current president making time for any economist.) By 1979, the sociologist Amitai Etzioni reported to President Carter that only 30 percent of Americans were "progrowth," 31 percent were "anti-growth," and 39 percent were "highly uncertain."

Such ambivalence, Etzioni predicted, "is too stressful for societies to endure," and Ronald Reagan proved his point. He convinced us it was "Morning in America"—out with limits, in with Trump. Today, mainstream liberals and conservatives compete mainly on the question of who can flog the economy harder. Larry Summers, who served as Bill Clinton's secretary of the treasury, at one point declared that the Clinton administration "cannot and will not accept any 'speed limit' on American economic growth. It is the task of economic policy to grow the economy as rapidly, sustainably, and inclusively as possible." It's the economy, stupid.

[2] Oil Bingeing, Chinese Cars, and the End of the Easy Fix

Except there are three small things. The first I'll mention mostly in passing: Even though the economy continues to grow, most of us are no longer getting wealthier. The average wage in the United States is less now, in real dollars, than it was 30 years ago. Even for those with college degrees, and although productivity was growing faster than it had for decades, between 2000 and 2004 earnings fell 5.2 percent when adjusted for inflation, according to the most recent data from White House economists. Much the same thing has happened across most of the globe. More than 60 countries around the world, in fact, have seen incomes per capita fall in the past decade.

For the second point, it's useful to remember what Thomas Newcomen was up to when he helped launch the Industrial Revolution—burning coal to pump water out of a coal mine. This revolution both depended on, and revolved around, fossil fuels. "Before coal," writes the economist Jeffrey Sachs, "economic production was limited by energy inputs, almost all of which depended on the production of biomass: food for humans and farm animals, and fuel wood for heating and certain industrial processes." That is, energy depended on how much you could grow. But fossil energy depended on how much had grown eons before—all those billions of tons of ancient biology squashed by the weight of time till they'd turned into strata and pools and seams of hydrocarbons, waiting for us to discover them.

To understand how valuable, and irreplaceable, that lake of fuel was, consider a few other forms of creating usable energy. Ethanol can perfectly well replace gasoline in a tank; like petroleum, it's a way of using biology to create energy, and right now it's a hot commodity, backed with billions of dollars of government subsidies. But ethanol relies on plants that grow anew each year, most often corn; by the time you've driven your tractor to tend the fields, and your truck to carry the crop to the refinery, and powered your refinery, the best-case "energy output-to-input ratio" is something like 1.34-to-1. You've spent 100 Btu of fossil energy to get 134 Btu. Perhaps that's worth doing, but as Kamyar Enshayan of the University of Northern Iowa points out, "it's not impressive" compared to the ratio for oil, which ranges from 30-to-1 to 200-to-1, depending on where you drill it. To go from our fossil-fuel world to a biomass world would be a little like leaving the Garden of Eden for the land where bread must be earned by "the sweat of your brow."

And east of Eden is precisely where we may be headed. As everyone knows, the past three years have seen a spate of reports and books and documentaries suggesting that humanity may have neared or passed its oil peak—that is, the point at which those pools of primeval plankton are half used up, where each new year brings us closer to the bottom of the barrel. The major oil companies report that they can't find enough new wells most years to offset the depletion in the old ones; rumors circulate that the giant Saudi fields are dwindling faster than expected; and, of course, all this is reflected in the cost of oil.

The doctrinaire economist's answer is that no particular commodity matters all that much, because if we run short of something, it will pay for someone to develop a substitute. In general this has proved true in the past: Run short of nice big sawlogs and someone invents plywood. But it's far from clear that the same precept applies to coal, oil, and natural gas. This time, there is no easy substitute: I like the solar panels on my roof, but they're collecting diffuse daily energy, not using up eons of accumulated power. Fossil fuel was an exception to the rule, a one-time gift that underwrote a one-time binge of growth.

This brings us to the third point: If we do try to keep going, with the entire world aiming for an economy structured like America's, it won't be just oil that we'll run short of. Here are the numbers we have to contend with: Given current rates of growth in the Chinese economy, the 1.3 billion residents of that nation alone will, by 2031, be about as rich as we are. If they then eat meat, milk, and eggs at the rate that we do, calculates ecostatistician Lester Brown, they will consume 1,352 million tons of grain each year—equal to two-thirds of the world's entire 2004 grain harvest. They will use 99 million barrels of oil a day, 15 million more than the entire world consumes at present. They will use more steel than all the West combined, double the world's production of paper, and drive 1.1 billion cars—1.5 times as many as the current world total. And that's just China; by then, India will have a bigger population, and its economy is growing almost as fast. And then there's the rest of the world.

Trying to meet that kind of demand will stress the earth past its breaking point in an almost endless number of ways, but let's take just one. When Thomas Newcomen fired up his pump on that morning in 1712, the atmosphere contained 275 parts per million of carbon dioxide. We're now up to 380 parts per million, a level higher than the earth has seen for many millions of years, and climate change has only just begun. The median predictions of the world's climatologists—by no means the worst-case scenario—show that unless we take truly enormous steps to rein in our use of fossil fuels, we can expect average temperatures to rise another four or five degrees before the century is out, making the globe warmer than it's been since long before primates appeared. We might as well stop calling it earth and have a contest to pick some new name, because it will be a different planet. Humans have never done anything more profound, not even when we invented nuclear weapons.

How does this tie in with economic growth? Clearly, getting rich means getting dirty—that's why, when I was in Beijing recently, I could stare straight at the sun (once I actually figured out where in the smoggy sky it was). But eventually, getting rich also means wanting the "luxury" of clean air and finding the technological means to achieve it. Which is why you can once again see the mountains around Los Angeles; why more of our rivers are swimmable every year. And economists have figured out clever ways to speed this renewal: Creating markets for trading pollution credits, for instance, helped cut those sulfur and nitrogen clouds more rapidly and cheaply than almost anyone had imagined.

But getting richer doesn't lead to producing less carbon dioxide in the same way that it does to less smog—in fact, so far it's mostly the reverse. Environmental destruction of the old-fashioned kind—dirty air, dirty water—results from something going wrong. You haven't bothered to stick the necessary filter on your pipes, and so the crud washes into the stream; a little regulation, and a little money, and the problem disappears. But the second, deeper form of environmental degradation comes from things operating exactly as they're supposed to, just too much so. Carbon dioxide is an inevitable byproduct of burning coal or gas or oil—not something going wrong. Researchers are struggling to figure out costly and complicated methods to trap some CO_2 and inject it into underground mines—but for all practical purposes, the vast majority of the world's cars and factories and furnaces will keep belching more and more of it into the atmosphere as long as we burn more and more fossil fuels.

True, as companies and countries get richer, they can afford more efficient machinery that makes better use of fossil fuel, like the hybrid Honda Civic I drive. But if your appliances have gotten more efficient, there are also far more of them: The furnace is better than it used to be, but the average size of the house it heats has doubled since 1950. The 60-inch TV? The always-on cable modem? No need for you to do the math—the electric company does it for you, every month. Between 1990 and 2003, precisely the years in which we learned about the peril presented by global warming, the United States' annual carbon dioxide emissions increased by 16 percent. And the momentum to keep going in that direction is enormous. For most of us, growth has become synonymous with the economy's "health," which in turn seems far more palpable than the health of the planet. Think of the terms we use—the economy, whose temperature we take at every newscast via the Dow Jones average, is "ailing" or it's "on the mend." It's "slumping" or it's "in recovery." We cosset and succor its every sniffle with enormous devotion, even as we more or less ignore the increasingly urgent fever that the globe is now running. The ecological economists have an enormous task ahead of them—a nearly insurmountable task, if it were "merely" the environment that is in peril. But here is where things get really interesting. It turns out that the economics of environmental destruction are closely linked to another set of leading indicators—ones that most humans happen to care a great deal about.

[3] "It Seems That Well-Being Is a Real Phenomenon": Economists Discover Hedonics

Traditionally, happiness and satisfaction are the sort of notions that economists wave aside as poetic irrelevance, the kind of questions that occupy people with no head for numbers who had to major in liberal arts. An orthodox economist has a simple happiness formula: If you buy a Ford Expedition, then ipso facto a Ford Expedition is what makes you happy. That's all we need to know. The economist would call this idea "utility maximization," and in the words of the economic historian Gordon Bigelow, "the theory holds that every time a person buys something, sells something, quits a job, or invests, he is making a rational decision about what will . . . provide him 'maximum utility.' If you bought a Ginsu knife at 3 A.M. a neoclassical economist will tell you that, at that time, you calculated that this purchase would optimize your resources." The beauty of this principle lies in its simplicity. It is perhaps the central assumption of the world we live in: You can tell who I really am by what I buy.

Yet economists have long known that people's brains don't work quite the way the model suggests. When Bob Costanza, one of the fathers of ecological economics and now head of the Gund Institute at the University of Vermont, was first edging into economics in the early 1980s, he had a fellowship to study "social traps"—the nuclear arms race, say—in which "short-term behavior can get out of kilter with longer broad-term goals."

It didn't take long for Costanza to demonstrate, as others had before him, that, if you set up an auction in a certain way, people will end up bidding $1.50 to take home a dollar. Other economists have shown that people give too much weight to "sunk costs"—that they're too willing to throw good money after bad, or that they value items more highly if they already own them than if they are considering acquiring them. Building on such insights, a school of "behavioral economics" has emerged in recent years and begun plumbing how we really behave.

The wonder is that it took so long. We all know in our own lives how irrationally we are capable of acting, and how unconnected those actions are to any real sense of joy. (I mean, there you are at 3 A.M. thinking about the Ginsu knife.) But until fairly recently, we had no alternatives to relying on Ginsu knife and Ford Expedition purchases as the sole measures of our satisfaction. How else would we know what made people happy?

That's where things are now changing dramatically: Researchers from a wide variety of disciplines have started to figure out how to assess satisfaction, and economists have begun to explore the implications. In 2002 Princeton's Daniel Kahneman won the Nobel Prize in economics even though he is trained as a psychologist. In the book *Well-Being,* he and a pair of coauthors announce a new field called "hedonics," defined as "the study of what makes experiences and life pleasant or unpleasant. . . . It is also concerned with the whole range of circumstances, from the biological to the societal, that occasion suffering and enjoyment." If you are worried that there might be something altogether too airy about this, be reassured—Kahneman thinks like an economist. In the book's very first chapter, "Objective Happiness," he describes an experiment that compares "records of the pain reported by two patients undergoing colonoscopy,"

wherein every 60 seconds he insists they rate their pain on a scale of 1 to 10 and eventually forces them to make "a hypothetical choice between a repeat colonoscopy and a barium enema." Dismal science indeed.

As more scientists have turned their attention to the field, researchers have studied everything from "biases in recall of menstrual symptoms" to "fearlessness and courage in novice paratroopers." Subjects have had to choose between getting an "attractive candy bar" and learning the answers to geography questions; they've been made to wear devices that measured their blood pressure at regular intervals; their brains have been scanned. And by now that's been enough to convince most observers that saying "I'm happy" is more than just a subjective statement. In the words of the economist Richard Layard, "We now know that what people say about how they feel corresponds closely to the actual levels of activity in different parts of the brain, which can be measured in standard scientific ways." Indeed, people who call themselves happy, or who have relatively high levels of electrical activity in the left prefrontal region of the brain, are also "more likely to be rated as happy by friends," "more likely to respond to requests for help," "less likely to be involved in disputes at work," and even "less likely to die prematurely." In other words, conceded one economist, "it seems that what the psychologists call subjective well-being is a real phenomenon. The various empirical measures of it have high consistency, reliability, and validity."

The idea that there is a state called happiness, and that we can dependably figure out what it feels like and how to measure it, is extremely subversive. It allows economists to start thinking about life in richer (indeed) terms, to stop asking "What did you buy?" and to start asking "Is your life good?" And if you can ask someone "Is your life good?" and count on the answer to mean something, then you'll be able to move to the real heart of the matter, the question haunting our moment on the earth: Is more better?

[4] If We're So Rich, How Come We're So Damn Miserable?

In some sense, you could say that the years since World War II in America have been a loosely controlled experiment designed to answer this very question. The environmentalist Alan Durning found that in 1991 the average American family owned twice as many cars as it did in 1950, drove 2.5 times as far, used 21 times as much plastic, and traveled 25 times farther by air. Gross national product per capita tripled during that period. Our houses are bigger than ever and stuffed to the rafters with belongings (which is why the storage-locker industry has doubled in size in the past decade). We have all sorts of other new delights and powers—we can send email from our cars, watch 200 channels, consume food from every corner of the world. Some people have taken much more than their share, but on average, all of us in the West are living lives materially more abundant than most people a generation ago.

What's odd is, none of it appears to have made us happier. Throughout the postwar years, even as the GNP curve has steadily climbed, the "life satisfaction" index has stayed exactly the same. Since 1972, the National Opinion Research Center has surveyed Americans on the question: "Taking all things together, how would you say things are these days—would you say that you are very happy, pretty happy, or not too happy?" (This must be a somewhat unsettling interview.) The "very happy" number peaked at 38 percent in the 1974 poll, amid oil shock and economic malaise; it now hovers right around 33 percent.

And it's not that we're simply recalibrating our sense of what happiness means—we are actively experiencing life as grimmer. In the winter of 2006 the National Opinion Research Center published data about "negative life events" comparing 1991 and 2004, two data points bracketing an economic boom. "The anticipation would have been that problems would have been down," the study's author said. Instead it showed a rise in problems—for instance, the percentage who reported breaking up with a steady partner almost doubled. As one reporter summarized the findings, "There's more misery in people's lives today."

This decline in the happiness index is not confined to the United States; as other nations have followed us into mass affluence, their experiences have begun to yield similar results. In the United Kingdom, real gross domestic product per capita grew two-thirds between 1973 and 2001, but people's satisfaction with their lives changed not one whit. Japan saw a fourfold increase in real income per capita between 1958 and 1986 without any reported increase in satisfaction. In one place after another, rates of alcoholism, suicide, and depression have gone up dramatically, even as we keep accumulating more stuff. Indeed, one report in 2000 found that the average American child reported higher levels of anxiety than the average child under psychiatric care in the 1950s—our new normal is the old disturbed.

If happiness was our goal, then the unbelievable amount of effort and resources expended in its pursuit since 1950 has been largely a waste. One study of life satisfaction and mental health by Emory University professor Corey Keyes found just 17 percent of Americans "flourishing," in mental health terms, and 26 percent either "languishing" or out-and-out depressed.

[5] Danes (and Mexicans, the Amish, and the Masai) Just Want to Have Fun

How is it, then, that we became so totally, and apparently wrongly, fixated on the idea that our main goal, as individuals and as nations, should be the accumulation of more wealth? The answer is interesting for what it says about human nature. Up to a certain point, more really does equal better. Imagine briefly your life as a poor person in a poor society—say, a peasant farmer in China. (China has one-fourth of the world's farmers, but one-fourteenth of its arable land; the average farm in the southern part of the country is about half an acre, or barely more than the standard lot for a new American home.) You likely have the benefits of a close and connected family, and a village environment where your place is clear. But you lack any modicum of security for when you get sick or old or your back simply gives out. Your diet is unvaried and nutritionally lacking; you're almost always cold in winter.

In a world like that, a boost in income delivers tangible benefits. In general, researchers report that money consistently buys happiness right up to about $10,000 income per capita. That's a useful number to keep in the back of your head—it's like the freezing point of water, one of those random figures that just happens to define a crucial phenomenon on our planet. "As poor countries like India, Mexico, the Philippines, Brazil, and South Korea have experienced economic growth, there is some evidence that their average happiness has risen," the economist Layard reports. Past $10,000 (per capita, mind you—that is, the average for each man, woman, and child), there's a complete scattering: When the Irish were making two-thirds as much as Americans they were reporting higher levels of satisfaction, as were the Swedes, the Danes, the Dutch. Mexicans score higher than the Japanese; the French are about as satisfied with their lives as the Venezuelans. In fact, once basic needs are met, the "satisfaction" data scrambles in mind-bending ways. A sampling of *Forbes* magazine's "richest Americans" have identical happiness scores with Pennsylvania Amish, and are only a whisker above Swedes taken as a whole, not to mention the Masai. The "life satisfaction" of pavement dwellers—homeless people—in Calcutta is among the lowest recorded, but it almost doubles when they move into a slum, at which point they are basically as satisfied with their lives as a sample of college students drawn from 47 nations. And so on.

On the list of major mistakes we've made as a species, this one seems pretty high up. Our single-minded focus on increasing wealth has succeeded in driving the planet's ecological systems to the brink of failure, even as it's failed to make us happier. How did we screw up?

The answer is pretty obvious—we kept doing something past the point that it worked. Since happiness had increased with income in the past, we assumed it would inevitably do so in the nature. We make these kinds of mistakes regularly: Two beers made me feel good, so ten will make me feel five times better. But this case was particularly extreme—in part because as a species, we've spent so much time simply trying to survive. As the researchers Ed Diener and Martin Seligman—both psychologists—observe, "At the time of Adam Smith, a concern with economic issues was understandably primary. Meeting simple human needs for food, shelter and clothing was not assured, and satisfying these needs moved in lockstep with better economics." Freeing people to build a more dynamic economy was radical and altruistic.

Consider Americans in 1820, two generations after Adam Smith. The average citizen earned, in current dollars, less than $1,500 a year, which is somewhere near the current average for all of Africa. As the economist Deirdre McCloskey explains in a 2004 article in the magazine *Christian Century*, "Your great-great-great-grandmother had one dress for church and one for the week, if she were not in rags. Her children did not attend school, and probably could not read. She and her husband worked eighty hours a week for a diet of bread and milk—they were four inches shorter than you." Even in 1900, the average American lived in a house the size of today's typical garage. Is it any wonder that we built up considerable velocity trying to escape the gravitational pull of that kind of poverty? An object in motion stays in motion, and our economy—with the built-up individual expectations that drive it—is a mighty object indeed.

You could call it, I think, the Laura Ingalls Wilder effect. I grew up reading her books—*Little House on the Prairie, Little House in the Big Woods*—and my daughter grew up listening to me read them to her, and no doubt she will read them to her children. They are the ur-American story. And what do they tell? Of a life rich in family, rich in connection to the natural world, rich in adventure—but materially deprived. That one dress, that same bland dinner. At Christmastime, a penny—a penny! And a stick of candy, and the awful deliberation about whether to stretch it out with tiny licks or devour it in an orgy of happy greed. A rag doll was the zenith of aspiration. My daughter likes dolls too, but her bedroom boasts a density of Beanie Babies that mimics the manic biodiversity of the deep rainforest. Another one? Really, so what? Its marginal utility, as an economist might say, is low. And so it is with all of us. We just haven't figured that out because the momentum of the past is still with us—we still imagine we're in that little house on the big prairie.

[6] This Year's Model Home: "Good for the Dysfunctional Family"

That great momentum has carried us away from something valuable, something priceless: It has allowed us to become (very nearly forced us to become) more thoroughly individualistic than we really wanted to be. We left behind hundreds of thousands of years of human community for the excitement, and the isolation, of "making something of ourselves," an idea that would not have made sense for 99.9 percent of human history. Adam Smith's insight was that the interests of each of our individual selves could add up, almost in spite of themselves, to social good—to longer lives, fuller tables, warmer houses. Suddenly the community was no longer necessary to provide these things; they would happen as if by magic. And they did happen. And in many ways it was good.

But this process of liberation seems to have come close to running its course. Study after study shows Americans spending less time with friends and family, either working longer hours, or hunched over their computers at night. And each year, as our population grows by 1 percent we manage to spread ourselves out over 6 to 8 percent more land. Simple mathematics says that we're less and less likely to bump into the other inhabitants of our neighborhood, or indeed of our own homes. As the *Wall Street Journal* reported recently, "Major builders and top architects are walling people off. They're touting one-person 'Internet alcoves,' locked-door 'away rooms,' and his-and-her offices on opposite ends of the house. The new floor plans offer so much seclusion, they're 'good for the dysfunctional family,' says Gopal Ahluwahlia, director of research for the National Association of Home Builders." At the building industry's annual Las Vegas trade show, the "showcase 'Ultimate Family Home' hardly had a family room," noted the *Journal*. Instead, the boy's personal playroom had its own 42-inch plasma TV, and the girl's bedroom had a secret mirrored door leading to a "hideaway karaoke room." "We call this the ultimate home for families who don't want anything to do with one another," said Mike McGee, chief executive of Pardee Homes of Los Angeles, builder of the model.

This transition from individualism to hyper-individualism also made its presence felt in politics. In the 1980s, British prime minister Margaret Thatcher asked, "Who is society? There is no such thing. There are individual men and women, and there are families." Talk about everything solid melting into air—Thatcher's maxim would have spooked Adam Smith himself. The "public realm"—things like parks and schools and Social Security, the last reminders of the communities from which we came—is under steady and increasing attack. Instead of contributing to the shared risk of health insurance, Americans are encouraged to go it alone with "health savings accounts." Hell, even the nation's most collectivist institution, the U.S. military, until recently recruited under the slogan an "Army of One." No wonder the show that changed television more than any other in the past decade was Survivor, where the goal is to end up alone on the island, to manipulate and scheme until everyone is banished and leaves you by yourself with your money.

It's not so hard, then, to figure out why happiness has declined here even as wealth has grown. During the same decades when our lives grew busier and more isolated, we've gone from having three confidants on average to only two, and the number of people saying they have no one to discuss important matters with has nearly tripled. Between 1974 and 1994, the percentage of Americans who said they visited with their neighbors at least once a month fell from almost two-thirds to less than half, a number that has continued to fall in the past decade. We simply worked too many hours earning, we commuted too far to our too-isolated homes, and there was always the blue glow of the tube shining through the curtains.

[7] New Friend or New Coffeemaker? Pick One

Because traditional economists think of human beings primarily as individuals and not as members of a community, they miss out on a major part of the satisfaction index. Economists lay it out almost as a mathematical equation: Overall, "evidence shows that companionship . . . contributes more to well-being than does income," writes Robert E. Lane, a Yale political science professor who is the author of *The Loss of Happiness in Market Democracies.* But there is a notable difference between poor and wealthy countries: When people have lots of companionship but not much money, income "makes more of a contribution to subjective well-being." By contrast, "where money is relatively plentiful and companionship relatively scarce, companionship will add more to subjective well-being." If you are a poor person in China, you have plenty of friends and family around all the time—perhaps there are four other people living in your room. Adding a sixth doesn't make you happier. But adding enough money so that all five of you can eat some meat from time to time pleases you greatly. By contrast, if you live in a suburban American home, buying another coffeemaker adds very little to your quantity of happiness—trying to figure out where to store it, or wondering if you picked the perfect model, may in fact decrease your total pleasure. But a new friend, a new connection, is a big deal. We have a surplus of individualism and a deficit of companionship, and so the second becomes more valuable.

Indeed, we seem to be genetically wired for community. As biologist Edward O. Wilson found, most primates live in groups and get sad when they're separated—"an isolated individual will repeatedly pull a lever with no reward other than the glimpse of another monkey." Why do people so often look back on their college days as the best years of their lives? Because their classes were so fascinating? Or because in college, we live more closely and intensely with a community than most of us ever do before or after? Every measure of psychological health points to the same conclusion: People who "are married, who have good friends, and who are close to their families are happier than those who are not," says Swarthmore psychologist Barry Schwartz. "People who participate in religious communities are happier than those who do not." Which is striking, Schwartz adds, because social ties "actually decrease freedom of choice"—being a good friend involves sacrifice.

Do we just think we're happier in communities? Is it merely some sentimental good-night-John-Boy affectation? No—our bodies react in measurable ways. According to research cited by Harvard professor Robert Putnam in his classic book *Bowling Alone,* if you do not belong to any group at present, joining a club or a society of some kind cuts in half the risk that you will die in the next year. Check this out: When researchers at Carnegie Mellon (somewhat disgustingly) dropped samples of cold virus directly into subjects' nostrils, those with rich social networks were four times less likely to get sick. An economy that produces only individualism undermines us in the most basic ways.

Here's another statistic worth keeping in mind: Consumers have 10 times as many conversations at farmers' markets as they do at supermarkets—an order of magnitude difference. By itself, that's hardly life-changing, but it points at something that could be: living in an economy where you are participant as well as consumer, where you have a sense of who's in your universe and how it fits together. At the same time, some studies show local agriculture using less energy (also by an order of magnitude) than the "it's always summer somewhere" system we operate on now. Those are big numbers, and it's worth thinking about what they suggest—especially since, between peak oil and climate change, there's no longer really a question that we'll have to wean ourselves of the current model.

So as a mental experiment, imagine how we might shift to a more sustainable kind of economy. You could use government policy to nudge the change—remove subsidies from agribusiness and use them instead to promote farmer-entrepreneurs; underwrite the cost of windmills with even a fraction of the money that's now going to protect oil flows. You could put tariffs on goods that travel long distances, shift highway spending to projects that make it easier to live near where you work (and, by cutting down on commutes, leave some time to see the kids). And, of course, you can exploit the Net to connect a lot of this highly localized stuff into something larger. By way of example, a few of us are coordinating the first nationwide global warming demonstration—but instead of marching on Washington, we're rallying in our local areas, and then fusing our efforts, via the website stepitup07.org, into a national message.

It's easy to dismiss such ideas as sentimental or nostalgic. In fact, economies can be localized as easily in cities and suburbs as rural villages (maybe more easily), and in ways that look as much to the future as the past, that rely more on the solar panel and the Internet than the white picket fence. In fact, given the trendlines for phenomena such as global warming and oil supply, what's nostalgic and sentimental is to keep doing what we're doing simply because it's familiar.

[8] The Oil-For-People Paradox: Why Small Farms Produce More Food

To understand the importance of this last point, consider the book *American Mania* by the neuroscientist Peter Whybrow. Whybrow argues that many of us in this country are predisposed to a kind of dynamic individualism— our gene pool includes an inordinate number of people who risked everything to start over. This served us well in settling a continent and building our prosperity. But it never got completely out of control, says Whybrow, because "the marketplace has always had its natural constraints. For the first two centuries of the nation's existence, even the most insatiable American citizen was significantly leashed by the checks and balances inherent in a closely knit community, by geography, by the elements of weather, or, in some cases, by religious practice." You lived in a society—a habitat—that kept your impulses in some kind of check. But that changed in the past few decades as the economy nationalized and then globalized. As we met fewer actual neighbors in the course of a day, those checks and balances fell away. "Operating in a world of instant communication with minimal social tethers," Whybrow observes, "America's engines of commerce and desire became turbocharged."

Adam Smith himself had worried that too much envy and avarice would destroy "the empathic feeling and neighborly concerns that are essential to his economic model," says Whybrow, but he "took comfort in the fellowship and social constraint that he considered inherent in the tightly knit communities characteristic of the 18th century." Businesses were built on local capital investment, and "to be solicitous of one's neighbor was prudent insurance against future personal need." For the most part, people felt a little constrained about showing off wealth; indeed, until fairly recently in American history, someone who was making tons of money was often viewed with mixed emotions, at least if he wasn't giving back to the community. "For the rich," Whybrow notes, "the reward system would be balanced between the pleasure of self-gain and the civic pride of serving others. By these mechanisms the most powerful citizens would be limited in their greed."

Once economies grow past a certain point, however, "the behavioral contingencies essential to promoting social stability in a market-regulated society—close personal relationships, tightly knit communities, local capital investment, and so on—are quickly eroded." So re-localizing economies offers one possible way around the gross inequalities that have come to mark our societies. Instead of aiming for growth at all costs and hoping it will trickle down, we may be better off living in enough contact with each other for the affluent to once again feel some sense of responsibility for their neighbors. This doesn't mean relying on noblesse oblige; it means taking seriously the idea that people, and their politics, can be changed by their experiences. It's a hopeful sign that more and more local and state governments across the country have enacted "living wage" laws. It's harder to pretend that the people you see around you every day should live and die by the dictates of the market.

Right around this time, an obvious question is doubtless occurring to you. Is it foolish to propose that a modern global economy of 6 (soon to be 9) billion people should rely on more localized economies? To put it more bluntly, since for most people "the economy" is just a fancy way of saying "What's for dinner?" and "Am I having any?," doesn't our survival depend on economies that function on a massive scale—such as highly industrialized agriculture? Turns out the answer is no—and the reasons why offer a template for rethinking the rest of the economy as well.

We assume, because it makes a certain kind of intuitive sense, that industrialized farming is the most productive farming. A vast Midwestern field filled with high-tech equipment ought to produce more food than someone with a hoe in a small garden. Yet the opposite is true. If you are after getting the greatest yield from the land, then smaller farms in fact produce more food.

If you are one guy on a tractor responsible for thousands of acres, you grow your corn and that's all you can do—make pass after pass with the gargantuan machine across a sea of crop. But if you're working 10 acres, then you have time to really know the land, and to make it work harder. You can intercrop all kinds of plants—their roots will go to different depths, or they'll thrive in each other's shade, or they'll make use of different nutrients in the soil. You can also walk your fields, over and over, noticing. According to the government's most recent agricultural census, smaller farms produce far more food per acre, whether you measure in tons, calories, or dollars. In the process, they use land, water, and oil much more efficiently; if they have animals, the manure is a gift, not a threat to public health. To feed the world, we may actually need lots more small farms.

But if this is true, then why do we have large farms? Why the relentless consolidation? There are many reasons, including the way farm subsidies have been structured, the easier access to bank loans (and politicians) for the big guys, and the convenience for food-processing companies of dealing with a few big suppliers. But the basic reason is this: We substituted oil for people. Tractors and synthetic fertilizer instead of farmers and animals. Could we take away the fossil fuel, put people back on the land in larger numbers, and have enough to eat?

The best data to answer that question comes from an English agronomist named Jules Pretty, who has studied nearly 300 sustainable agriculture projects in 57 countries around the world. They might not pass the U.S. standards for organic certification, but they're all what he calls "low-input." Pretty found that over the past decade, almost 12 million farmers had begun using sustainable practices on about 90 million acres. Even more remarkably, sustainable agriculture increased food production by 79 percent per acre. These were not tiny isolated demonstration farms—Pretty studied 14 projects where 146,000 farmers across a broad swath of the developing world were raising potatoes, sweet potatoes, and cassava, and he found that practices such as cover-cropping and fighting pests with natural adversaries had increased production 150 percent—17 tons per household. With 4.5 million small Asian grain farmers, average yields rose 73 percent. When Indonesian rice farmers got rid of pesticides, their yields stayed the same but their costs fell sharply.

"I acknowledge," says Pretty, "that all this may sound too good to be true for those who would disbelieve these advances. Many still believe that food production and nature must be separated, that 'agroecological' approaches offer only marginal opportunities to increase food production, and that industrialized approaches represent the best, and perhaps only, way forward. However, prevailing views have changed substantially in just the last decade."

And they will change just as profoundly in the decades to come across a wide range of other commodities. Already I've seen dozens of people and communities working on regional-scale sustainable timber projects, on building energy networks that work like the Internet by connecting solar rooftops and backyard windmills in robust mini-grids. That such things can begin to emerge even in the face of the political power of our reigning economic model is remarkable; as we confront significant change in the climate, they could speed along the same kind of learning curve as Pretty's rice farmers and wheat growers. And they would not only use less energy; they'd create more community. They'd start to reverse the very, trends I've been describing, and in so doing rebuild the kind of scale at which Adam Smith's economics would help instead of hurt.

In the 20th century, two completely different models of how to run an economy battled for supremacy. Ours won, and not only because it produced more goods than socialized state economies. It also produced far more freedom, far less horror. But now that victory is starting to look Pyrrhic; in our overheated and underhappy state, we need some new ideas.

We've gone too far down the road we're traveling. The time has come to search the map, to strike off in new directions. Inertia is a powerful force; marriages and corporations and nations continue in motion until something big diverts them. But in our new world we have much to fear, and also much to desire, and together they can set us on a new, more promising course.

Born to Buy
Interview with Juliet Schor

JAMES WOOLMAN

Americans love to shop. We own roughly one TV per person and acquire an average of 48 new pieces of apparel a year. We also work longer hours than people in any other industrial country, and 1.5 million U.S. households declare bankruptcy every year. Economist Juliet B. Schor has studied the work-and-spend phenomenon in her popular books *The Overworked American* and *The Overspent American*. In her new book, *Born to Buy: The Commercialized Child and the New Consumer Culture*, Schor looks at how corporations enlist schools, cultural institutions, and even other kids to transform children into consumers.

—James Woolman

Dollars & Sense: In *The Overworked American* you found that Americans are working more than they used to. Could you describe what you found and what's behind those trends?

Juliet Schor: I began *The Overworked American* from a theoretical point of view, which was that in a capitalist economy there are structural biases in the way the labor market and the firm operate that lead to using productivity growth to produce more output rather than to give people more free time. Because with productivity growth, you always have the option of either producing the same amount with fewer hours of work or keeping work hours constant and producing more. What I found was that beginning with the 1970s, you start to see a small increase in the annual hours of work, particularly once you correct for a simultaneous growth in structural underemployment and unemployment. So you had one group of people not getting enough work, either no job at all or working part-year or part-time, and another group, the majority, working more and more hours, more than they wanted to. This trend, which is very modest in the 70s, picks up steam in the 80s and 90s, so what you have is a long-term trajectory of growing hours of work.

> **"You could be invited to a friend's slumber party and it could turn out to be a marketing opportunity. Most parents have no idea that this kind of stuff is going on."**

I came to think of those changes as very analogous to the first industrial revolution, which was a period of rapid technical change, but which also saw very big increases in hours of work. Employers want workers to work more hours, because those technical innovations, which are theoretically labor-saving innovations, represent a possibility for increased productivity, but they need to harness the labor to them. My view is that we're going through something like a second industrial revolution in terms of the demand of the market economy for more and more hours and also more people working those long hours. So the message of the first book was, why aren't we getting the benefits of increased productivity in the form of shorter hours of work, which is what everybody thought would happen.

D&S: How does this relate to your study of consumer culture in *The Overspent American?*

JS: The second book took up a question that was raised in the first one. In the first book, I developed what I called the "cycle of work and spend," which was about how workers don't have the option to reduce their hours of work. Typically they would get higher incomes, and then spend those incomes and get locked into that spending. The second book is an attempt to understand why it is that people spend rising levels of income. Of course not everyone's getting increased incomes. Particularly over the 80s and 90s you start to see that dramatic worsening of the income distribution. But with the rising work effort of women, you see family incomes growing. So *The Overspent American* is about the social pressures to spend, and the ways in which consumption is really a very social process, and Americans have basically been in a situation where the pressures to ratchet up spending have become extremely intense.

D&S: What effect has this increase in consumerism and consumption had on people's well-being?

JS: What happens is you have the majority of the population, which in relative terms is doing worse because you've got this worsening income distribution. Twenty percent are doing better—they're setting the standards. Part of my argument was that the consumption patterns of the top 20% became the norm that people throughout the society are trying to emulate. For the other 80% of households who are trying to keep up, it becomes harder and harder because the norms are rising faster than their purchasing power. So they end up adding more workers to the labor force to keep up, their savings diminish, you have record levels of consumer debt, record levels of bankruptcy, high levels of stress as people feel they're running harder and harder to stay in place because there is a gap between what you need to keep up and the purchasing power that the system is delivering to you. Plus, now there is lots of research showing that materialism as a value system undermines well-being in lots of different ways. It undermines physical well-being, it undermines your emotional and social well-being. People who are more materialistic are more depressed, they're more anxious, they have less vitality, they connect less well with people, they have more stomach aches and headaches.

D&S: Why did you decide to write a book about children and marketing?

JS: Well, when I started working on *The Overspent American* in the early 90s, one of the things I started seeing was that a lot of the "action" in consumer markets was happening in youth consumer markets. Youth marketing was being transformed from a relative backwater to something where a lot of cutting-edge trends were happening. It was also the case that youth were being targeted increasingly for what had historically been adult products, so that you get the influence of youth in cars, and hotels, tourist destinations, a whole range of products that parents and adults are buying, not kids. Why are they advertising these products on Nickelodeon? The other important thing for me was that I had my first child at the time that I started working on consumer issues, so I was interested in this as a parent—my kids were being born into a childhood culture that was increasingly commercialized, and I didn't like it.

D&S: How have marketing and products directed at children changed, and what makes marketing directed at children today so different from what it used to be?

JS: Some of it is similar to what went on in the 1950s, for example, Saturday morning television: there are still sugared cereal commercials, and toy commercials for boys with lots of crashes, and toy commercials for girls that are all pink and sweet. The marketing people want to keep our attention focused on that, because that's where they can say, well, there's nothing new.

I found that the kids who are more involved in consumer culture are much worse off psychologically. They're more depressed, they're more anxious, they have less self-esteem.

What's different is, number one, the quantity of advertising. You've had very rapid increases. There's now about $15 billion a year in child-directed advertising. When I started doing this

work about ten years ago, the estimates that I was seeing were more on the order of $1 to $2 billion.

There's been a big increase in the number of places where kids are advertised to. TV turns out to be just the tip of the iceberg now. Kids are advertised to almost everywhere. Schools have become a huge area of advertising. You have coercive advertising in schools, such as Channel One, which gives schools televisions if they play their programs. If you're in a Channel One school, you have to watch a 10-minute broadcast every day, which is two minutes of advertising and eight minutes of so-called news that also has a lot of advertising in it. Channel One is in 12,000 schools, so 8 million middle and high school students are forced to watch ads for junk food, movies, even military recruiting. There is a lot of other advertising going on in schools: curriculum being written by corporations and a lot of freebie, give-away advertising, book covers and so forth.

You see advertising in cultural institutions like museums and zoos. There's a lot of what's called peer-to-peer advertising in which companies are enlisting kids to market to their friends. You could be invited to a slumber party by a friend, if you're an 11-year-old girl, and it could turn out to be a marketing opportunity. Most parents have no idea that this kind of stuff is going on.

D&S: Has the content of advertising changed?

JS: The messages that are used are different now, and there's a wider range of messages. The marketers have figured out peer dynamics. As kids move through elementary school and then especially into middle and high school, the peer dynamics are so important. And they've figured out how to insinuate themselves into that and to make products a really central part of a kid's social experiences. Kids today have access to more money, and they are much more status conscious than they used to be. Brands have become more important to kids than function. Marketers tap into this on purpose. The number one theme that's marketed to kids now is "cool," which is really about inequality, exclusion, having something others don't have or can't afford.

D&S: Why should we be concerned about the growth in marketing to children, or the trends in children's consumption?

JS: The literature on children and consumer culture has focused on two things. One is whether advertising to kids is inherently unfair, because kids can't resist advertising. We need a lot more research, but the old research at least showed that kids have a hard time resisting advertising.

The second question is the kinds of products that are being advertised to kids. A lot of them are not healthy. The number one product that is marketed to kids is junk food. And of course we've seen a huge increase in obesity and obesity-related diseases. You also have cigarette advertising, alcohol advertising, other kinds of drug advertising, advertising of violent products. So most of the products being sold by consumer culture aren't things that are good for kids.

The third aspect of it, which the study I did for my book addresses, is that advertising is getting kids more and more involved in consumer culture, in the values of consumer culture, in the practices, in the aspirations. Does that have an impact on kids' well-being? I studied a sample of mostly fifth and sixth graders and interviewed a smaller sample of their parents, and what I found was that the kids who are more involved in consumer culture, who care more about the stuff, who care more about money, and labels, and collecting, and all of those things are much worse off psychologically. They're more depressed, they're more anxious, they have less self-esteem. In some cases they had worse relations with their parents, they had worse peer self-esteem, they were more likely to have stomach aches and headaches, to feel bored. There's just a wide range of bad outcomes associated with being heavily involved in consumer culture.

D&S: What specific policies or actions can be taken to combat the child marketing industry and child consumerism?

JS: There are different types of things. Just today, I believe, Tom Harkin introduced a bill into the Senate that would restore to the FTC its ability to regulate children's advertising. That ability was stripped from the FTC in 1980, I believe, when they came close to advocating a ban on advertising sugared cereals and sugared foods. It's very early, but there is a growing coalition of activists who are trying to push for federal legislation, on a variety of things, whether it's disclosing of product placement; disclosing the authorship of ads, so that people and agencies will have to take more responsibility for their messages; getting commercial marketing out of schools. There's been a lot on the soft drinks in schools, vending machines, and other kinds of junk food within schools. A really good source, reproduced in an appendix to my book, is something called the "Parents' Bill of Rights," which is a series of proposed legislation put together by a group called Commercial Alert. They advocate things like banning advertising to kids younger

than 12, keeping advertising out of schools, and requiring labeling of fast food content.

I advocate a tax on advertising to children which could be deployed to create publicly-owned, child-controlled media, where kids could write and produce their own shows. I think one of the big challenges is to change the kind of media that kids have, and to make it much more child-friendly, oriented not to making money off kids but to actually doing well by kids. We need to genuinely empower kids to gain more control over their environment, whether we're talking about the media environment or their actual spatial environment. One of the reasons that corporate-dominated childhood has come to pass is that kids have been restricted to the indoors, and electronic media has supplanted outdoor play. It is important that we give kids the ability to play outside safely with other kids, and not only in adult-supervised environments. The third key area we need to change is food, replacing the junk food culture that kids live in with really healthy food that kids are excited about and participate in growing, cooking, and eating. These are the really broad scale sort of cultural changes in childhood that I think are necessary to move away from corporate childhood.

James Woolman is a member of the *Dollars & Sense* collective. **Juliet Schor** is professor of sociology at Boston College. She is the author of *The Overworked American: The Unexpected Decline of Leisure* and *The Overspent American: Why We Want What We Don't Need*. She co-edited *The Golden Age of Capitalism: Reinterpreting the Postwar Experience, The Consumer Society Reader*, and *Sustainable Planet: Solutions for the 21st Century*. Her new book, *Born to Buy: The Commercialized Child and the New Consumer Culture*, was published in September by Scribner.

Why Aren't U.S. Cities Burning?

Michael B. Katz

The summer of 2007 marks the fortieth anniversary of America's worst season of urban disorder. The most famous riots happened in Newark and Detroit. But "nearly 150 cities reported disorders in Negro—and in some instances Puerto Rican—neighborhoods," reported the 1968 National Advisory Commission on Civil Disorders. Today, the most intriguing question is not why the riots occurred but why they have not recurred. With the exception of Liberty City, Miami, in 1980, and South-central Los Angeles in 1992, American cities have not burned since the early 1970s. Even the botched response to Hurricane Katrina did not provoke civil violence.

The question becomes all the more intriguing in light of October 2005, when riots erupted in at least three hundred cities and towns across France. They were the worst France had experienced since 1968. Mass joblessness, isolation in ethnic ghettos, and cultural discrimination fueled anger at the police, which erupted after two teenagers of North African and Malian origins were electrocuted as they climbed a fence to escape what they believed to be police pursuit.

As in France, immigrants are transforming U.S. cities, which, already highly segregated by race, contain zones of exclusion characterized by poverty and joblessness. But American cities do not burn. Urban violence has not disappeared; it has been transformed. Anger and frustration turn inward, exploding in gang warfare, homicide, and random killing in drive-by shootings. But civil violence—burning, looting, sniping at police—actions aimed largely at symbols and agents of exclusion and exploitation remain part of urban history, not live possibilities in the urban present. What accounts for the absence of civil violence on American streets?

The question is puzzling because many of the conditions thought to have precipitated the eruption of civil violence in the 1960s either persist or have grown worse. Nationally, after the Second World War, income inequality decreased until 1973, when it swung upward. Even worse, the proportion of African American men out of the regular labor force rose sharply. The number of incarcerated skyrocketed. On any given day, one of three black men age twenty to twenty-nine was either in jail or on probation or parole. Nor did allegations of police violence disappear. Police departments professionalized, waves of reform swept across urban schools, job training programs proliferated, new government incentives promised to recreate markets in inner cities. But city schools by and large continued to fail; the homeless haunted city streets; most public housing, when it was available, was awful; the police were still problematic; chronic joblessness increased; and inner cities remained bleak.

Other conditions that had contributed to the 1960s' civil violence also worsened. Racial segregation increased until the 1990s, reaching historic highs. Although African American poverty rates declined, within cities the spatial concentration of poverty intensified as whites moved to the suburbs. Ethnic transition added to urban tensions as immigration, primarily from Asia and Latin America, soared after 1980, accounting for one-third of population growth in the 1990s. Recent immigrants settled mainly in cities.

Cities confronted the problems that resulted from poverty, inequality, segregation, and ethnic transformation with fewer resources than in the 1960s and early 1970s. The federal government slashed direct aid to cities; other programs—such as public assistance—took major hits; the real value of the minimum wage spiraled downward. The safety net created in the Great Society years frayed, heightening vulnerability and insecurity.

Poverty, inequality, chronic joblessness, segregation, police violence, ethnic transition, a frayed safety net: surely, these composed a combustible ensemble of elements, which a reasonable observer might have expected to ignite. Why did no one light the match?

No single reason explains why American cities did not burn. Rather, the relative absence of civil violence resulted from the interplay of factors that fall under three broad headings: the ecology of power, the management of marginalization, and the incorporation and control of immigrants.

The Ecology of Power

Throughout the history of American cities, challenges to established geographic boundaries have often precipitated civil violence—when, for example, African Americans tried to breach racial segregation in Detroit in the 1920s and in Chicago in the 1940s. The Great Migration of African Americans northward after the Second World War was the greatest challenge yet to ethnic boundaries within predominantly white cities. To preserve existing boundaries, whites often turned to violence. The civil violence of the 1960s erupted at the height of urban boundary challenge, when huge numbers of African Americans had moved in and whites had not yet moved out. In the years following the Great Migration, whites left central cities for suburbs, where they found ways to erect new and effective borders, and many cities became majority or near-majority minority. By 2000, only 21 percent of whites remained in central cities. As a result, boundary challenges receded, and the ecology of urban power was rearranged.

As they decamped for the suburbs, whites ceded effective political control of cities to African Americans, retaining only a hold on commerce and finance and gentrified pockets of downtown. Between 1970 and 2001, the number of African American county and municipal officials rose 960 percent and 619 percent respectively. African Americans also made inroads into the police, the most visible and, often, hated agents of the local state. The irony, of course, is that African Americans inherited city governments at the moment when de-industrialization, cuts in federal aid, and white flight were decimating tax bases and job opportunities while fueling homelessness, street crime, and poverty. Newly African American-led city governments confronted escalating demands for services and the repair of crumbling infrastructures with shrinking resources and power curtailed by often hostile state governments. This kind of governmental power was truly, as a political scientist wrote in 1969, a "hollow prize." Nonetheless, with so many whites gone, boundaries became less contentious, eroding one major source of civil violence.

In the 1980s, massive immigration from Latin America and Asia reignited urban boundary conflicts, particularly in the gateway cities where most immigrants entered. The civil violence that exploded in South-central Los Angeles in 1992 marked the first major boundary conflict since the 1960s. Despite widespread fear, however, events in Los Angeles did not light a long fuse stretching across urban America. Why did it prove so hard to ignite civil violence throughout the nation? The answer lies partly in a set of mechanisms that complemented the new ecology of urban power. Collectively, these mechanisms deflected civil violence by managing marginalization.

Management of Marginalization

Usually, civil violence in American history has involved marginalized populations who have served both as objects of attack (in lynchings) and as active participants (in Watts in 1965, for example). By marginalized, I mean groups largely excluded from the prerogatives and rewards that accompany full citizenship, including employment, housing, consumption, social benefits, and equal justice. Before the 1950s or 1960s, nearly all African Americans remained marginalized in one way or another and far too many, along with Puerto Ricans and many immigrants, still do. Since the 1960s, however, deprivation rarely has translated into civil violence. Americans have learned to manage marginalization. Five mechanisms have proved crucial: selective incorporation; ostensible, or mimetic, reform; indirect rule; consumption; and repression and surveillance. Together, they set in motion a process of de-politicization that undercuts the capacity for collective action.

In recent decades, gateways to better education, jobs, income, and housing have opened to a significant fraction of African Americans and other minorities. This is what I mean by selective incorporation. As a result, African American social structure resembles the social structure of white America, albeit with a smaller middle class and fewer wealthy. This incorporation resulted primarily from government and private-sector sponsorship and depended heavily on public or quasi-public employment (that is, in private agencies largely dependent on public funds).

For the most part, selective incorporation constructed limited ladders of social mobility. African American men entering the professions, for example, clustered largely in the human services, not in law, medicine, or the top ranks of corporate America. African American women professionals worked disproportionately as technicians, the lowest rung on the professional ladder. Nonetheless, this limited mobility proved very important, fracturing African American communities along lines of class and gender (women fared far better than men) and eroding the potential for collective protest by holding out the promise of economic and occupational achievement and spreading a modest prosperity more widely than ever before—a prosperity that was extremely fragile because it depended so heavily on public sector jobs.

Ostensible, or mimetic, reform also dampened the potential for collective violence. By mimetic reform, I mean measures that respond to insurgent demands without transferring real power or redistributing significant resources. Such reform cools out insurgencies; it does not resolve the problems that underlie them. One example is provided by Ira Katznelson's account of how in New York City in the late 1960s the Lindsay administration redirected demands for community control of schools in northern Manhattan to conservative ends. Another is Rebuild L.A., which promised to reconstruct South-central Los Angeles after the 1992 civil violence but delivered very little.

White abandonment, selective incorporation, and mimetic reform resulted in indirect rule. Like colonial British imperialists, who kept order through the exercise of authority by indigenous leaders, powerful white Americans retained authority over cities through their influence on minorities elected to political office, appointed to public and social service bureaucracies, and hired in larger numbers by police forces. Despite African American ascension to public office, real power lay elsewhere. By law, cities are creatures of state governments, and states exercise control over cities in many ways—most obviously by retaining effective control of city finances. Corporations also limited the autonomy of city governments by threatening to leave, taking with them needed jobs. City leaders remained trapped between constituents who elected them and the state, national, and corporate authorities who supplied funds for their campaigns and circumscribed their actions. But indirect rule meant that civil violence or other claims on city government increasingly would be directed toward African American elected officials, public bureaucrats, and police.

In the 1960s, corporate America discovered the newly urbanized black consumer. Corporations recognized a new market and quickly responded with massive advertising campaigns and new media ventures targeted at both adults and youths. With these strategies, the private sector helped dampen the potential for civil violence by incorporating potential insurgents into America's Consumers' Republic—in Lizabeth Cohen's definition an "economy, culture, and politics built around the promises of mass consumption, both in terms of the material life and the more idealistic goals of freedom, democracy, and equality." With more spare cash than ever before, targeted by advertising, many African Americans were able to purchase the material symbols of the good life. By 1993, for instance, the black consumer electronics market had reached $2.5 billion. In the late twentieth century, African American spending patterns did not differ very much from whites (although blacks did spend less per capita on alcoholic beverages).

African Americans' entrance into the Consumers' Republic is full of irony. Consumption demands—equal access to public accommodation, entertainment, shopping, and transportation—were key goals in the civil rights movement. They also helped precipitate the civil disorders of the 1960s. The national welfare rights movement made full membership in the Consumers' Republic a major demand. But the Consumers' Republic also undermined black protest by shifting the focus of black demands to public accommodation and market access, thereby linking African American goals to mainstream American aspirations and subordinating alternatives based on black nationalism or social democratic visions of economic justice. Among both black and white Americans consumption masked widening inequality, environmental degradation, and heightened insecurity with a blanket of inexpensive goods available to nearly everyone through the magic of credit. The result was consumer debt and bankruptcy that reached previously unimagined heights, rather than mobilization expressed through politics or other forms of collective action.

By facilitating the rise of the Consumers' Republic, the private sector developed an indirect mechanism for deflecting the potential for civil violence. Public authorities also deployed more direct mechanisms. In 1968, Congress passed the Omnibus Crime Control and Safe Streets Act, which created the Law Enforcement Assistance Administration (LEAA). The LEAA, according to one historian, "provided a law-and-order alternative to the social, cultural, and economic perspective of the Kerner Commission." Operating mainly through block grants to states, the LEAA gave money to police forces and other parts of the criminal justice system. The legislation specified that no more than one-third of federal grants go to personnel—a requirement that excluded manpower-intensive programs, including those that focused on community relations and social service. But the police easily fulfilled the law's mandate by purchasing hardware such as antiriot tools, helicopters, and vehicles. Thus, until its abolition in 1980, much LEAA money supplied technologies of repression and control.

Despite the LEAA, state and local governments bore most of the responsibility and expense for law enforcement. Like the federal government, in the aftermath of the civil violence of the 1960s, they also ramped up spending, often on equipment and practices associated more with the military than with civil police. Although local governments paid most of the cost of police, state governments picked up the largest share of the escalating cost of incarceration, which, after the mid-1970s, became America's principal strategy for fighting crime.

What impact did increased funding and militarized policing have on crime? Most analyses claim that the LEAA failed to reduce crime. As for incarceration, even optimistic accounts show a meager return for massive public investment. Indeed, crime rates, which had been increasing during the early 1960s, soared *after* the episodes of civil violence. Nonetheless, with few exceptions, the civil violence of the 1960s did not recur. Did the militarization of policing and mass incarceration help authorities break up potential insurgencies, respond more effectively to ones that occurred, and prevent them from spreading to other cities? And, if they did, at what cost?

In Los Angeles, Mike Davis contends, police repression of black power undermined a promising gang truce, while the decimation of the Black Panthers resulted in a revival of black gangs, now permeated by a culture of violence and domination. In the early 1990s, public authorities again dismissed gang truces and summits, failing to capitalize on their moves toward conventional politics and requests for job training and other economic benefits. Were disillusionment, depoliticization, and a renewal of criminal violence one result?

Fewer black men, in fact, could participate in politics, even if they wanted to—because they were felons. Felony disenfranchisement laws had long been on the books in most states, but their consequences became more severe as aggressive law enforcement, including draconian drug laws, created unprecedented numbers of felons, who were disproportionately black. Together, the combination of incarcerated felons and former inmates barred from voting means that about 1.4 million, or 13 percent, of African American men are effectively disenfranchised, a rate seven times the national average. Looking ahead to younger men, the situation appears even bleaker. If the current rate of incarceration continues, at some point in their lives 30 percent of the next generation of black men (according to The Sentencing Project) will face disenfranchisement, a fraction that rises to a possible stunning 40 percent of black men who live in states that permanently bar ex-offenders from voting. Many black men, moreover, evading warrants or just fearful of potential arrest, avoid the institutions and agents of the state, thereby eliminating themselves from participation in political action.

That public authorities contributed to the depoliticization of young African Americans and the surge in criminal violence remains a hypothesis—intriguing, explosive in its implications, and in need of much research. Indeed, the lack of research on the question, and on the social history of policing post-1960, remains stunning and surprising. Clearly, though, the turn from politics also reflected other influences, of which disillusionment with the achievements of civil rights liberalism and black power were among the most important, as Matthew J. Countryman points out in his history of civil rights and black power in Philadelphia. Similarly, in his ethnography of the informal economy in a Chicago neighborhood, Sudhir Alladi Venkatesh shows how, even at the height of the administration of Chicago's first black mayor (Harold Washington), poor Southside Chicagoans found their political influence and patronage cut off by an administration that depended increasingly on a coalition of black middle- and upper-class supporters. The result was the "gradual withdrawal of grassroots persons from the mainstream black political scene."

In the 1970s and 1980s, as the spread of black poverty turned vast areas of cities into reservations for the black poor, as fewer black men found work in the regular labor market, as mass incarceration locked unprecedented numbers of them away, young African Americans had reason to look with skepticism at civil rights liberalism, black power, and politics in general.

Other factors already discussed—the Consumers' Republic, selective incorporation, mimetic reform, and indirect rule—also facilitated depoliticization, without which the management of marginalization would have proved far more difficult. In the 1960s, African Americans lacked channels through which to make effective claims on the state. They were underrepresented in Congress, state legislatures, city councils, police forces, and in influential positions in private corporations. Other than through collective action, whether sit-ins or violence, they had few ways to force their grievances onto public attention or persuade authorities to respond. This changed as the new demography of urban politics, the victories of the civil rights movement, and affirmative action combined to open new channels of access. As selective incorporation bifurcated the African American social structure, unprecedented numbers of African Americans became public officials, bureaucrats, and administrators of social service agencies. People who once might have led protests now held positions from which they could argue that civil violence was both unnecessary and counterproductive. Others remained in America's inner cities, struggling to get by, disenfranchised, wary of the state, disillusioned with politicians, lacking leadership or a vision strong enough to mobilize them once again to make claims on the state.

Co-Opting and Controlling Immigrants

I have been asking why the explosions that rocked African American ghettos in the 1960s failed to recur despite the persistence, in some instances the intensification, of the joblessness, racial segregation, unequal justice, and institutional failure that had helped fuel them. But these factors, important as they are, fit the past better than the present and future, are myopic in an international context, and are only partially helpful in contrasting American with European experience. For the civil violence that rocked Paris and frightens other Europeans is a product of recent immigration, not of the grievances and frustrations of historically marginalized citizens.

Both European and American cities have experienced recent massive immigration. Both have had to cope with infusions of low-skilled workers from different cultural traditions. But there the parallels cease as immigrant incorporation and control take different routes. The results have important implications for the turn toward civil violence.

Two events framed the 2005–2006 academic year. In October, immigrants concentrated in Parisian *banlieues* and the working-class suburbs of other cities took to the streets for two weeks of collective violence. In April and May, immigrants across the United States, outraged by proposed federal legislation that would turn illegal immigrants into felons and criminalize efforts to assist them, also took to the streets—but their protests were coordinated, massive, and completely peaceful. On May 1, more than one million marched in protest rallies in cities across the United States. Most of the four hundred thousand marchers in Los Angeles waved American flags.

The two events—civil violence in France, peaceful protest in the United States—highlight divergent relations of immigrants to the state and economy. U.S. immigrants sought redress through government. Their protests assumed that they could realize their goals through the nation's political institutions. They approached government as a potential ally, not an enemy, wanting nothing so much as the rights of American citizens. Their faith in the ameliorative capacity of American government marked their assimilation more effectively than their ability to speak English or whether they sang the "Star Spangled Banner" in Spanish—an important point lost on opponents who relentlessly prophesied the submersion of American nationality in an alien sea. They were also largely employed. Labor force detachment, by and large, has been an African American, not an immigrant problem. Paradoxically, the most exploited immigrants, the undocumented, have been the most closely attached to work. They risked crossing the border—too often at the cost of their lives—to work at jobs for which they had been recruited or that they knew were waiting, even though those jobs paid poorly and offered no benefits or protections.

In Paris, immigrants showed no such faith in the state, and the labor market lacked places for them. In the United States, distrust of the police did not automatically reinforce suspicion of the national state. In fact, with policing decentralized, insurgents tried to enlist the federal government as an agent of police reform. In France, conversely, where policing remained highly centralized, antagonism toward the police reinforced distrust of the national government. Many immigrants to France and their descendants were former colonial subjects with bitter memories of anticolonial wars, exploitation, and discrimination. The state, moreover, pursued a relentless policy of nationalization, rejecting even benign symbols of their culture, such as wearing head scarves in school—a prohibition unthinkable in the United States. Their protests, neither planned nor coordinated, reflected frustration, rage, alienation, and a lack of confidence in or access to official political channels. In this, they resembled African Americans in the 1960s more than immigrants to the United States late in the twentieth century.

The protests in France in the fall and the United States in the spring underlined differences in national immigrant incorporation. In the United States, protest also highlighted the split between immigrant incorporation and control. In the United

States, references to the second generation contained a hyphen that joined an ethnic designation to "American," as in Mexican-American. In Europe, Mark Leon Goldberg has pointed out, even though born in Europe, members of the second generation are called immigrants. "The term 'immigrant' connotes different things in continental Europe than in the United States. Generally speaking, in Europe it refers not just to emigrants from foreign countries, but to their children and in some cases grandchildren as well." The United States, by contrast, takes some justifiable pride in its history of diversity and celebrates the contribution of its immigrants. The astonishing ascendance of immigration as a national political issue in the spring of 2006 centered on immigrants who had entered the nation illegally, not on the desirability of immigration itself, to which even xenophobic public commentators paid rhetorical homage.

Naturalization laws both reflected and reinforced divergent paths to immigrant incorporation. These differences in requirements for citizenship show up in naturalization rates, which are much lower in France. For individuals over the age of eighteen, the annual rate of naturalization is about 2.75 percent in France compared to 4.8 percent in the United States. After fifteen to nineteen years of residence, naturalization rates are twenty percentage points lower in France than in the United States, and, after twenty-five years, they are thirty points lower.

In the United States, however, not all immigrants are on a fast track to citizenship. For the huge numbers of the undocumented, the road to economic and civic incorporation is difficult, if not impossible to reach. As is well known, U.S. immigration policy is schizophrenic. Large segments of the economy run on cheap immigrant labor, as they once did on cheap black labor. Business interests demand and abet the flow of undocumented immigrants across borders. Undocumented immigrants are, after all, an ideal work force—hardworking,

terrified, and exploitable. At the same time, public anger at undocumented immigration, long simmering, has exploded with stunning velocity, demanding still more border militarization and punitive policies toward immigrants themselves and those who employ, house, or assist them. The result, of course, undercuts potential immigrant protest. Threats of deportation and unemployment constitute an effective mechanism of social control that dampens the potential for both civil violence and peaceful protest—an outcome reinforced by U.S. Immigration and Customs Enforcement (ICE) raids on undocumented immigrants this past spring.

Thus, discussions of the potential for collective violence, or its absence, in American cities must move beyond a black-white frame to include immigrants. Both European nations and the United States have experienced massive immigration, but they have responded differently, with immense consequences for the integration of newcomers. The argument about immigration needs to include both the positive elements that dampen the possibility of violence by facilitating incorporation and the darker story in which civil peace results from schizoid public policies that promote the vulnerability of a large fraction of the nation's newcomers.

The nation's avoidance of civil violence in its segregated ghettos has one other lesson for Europeans concerned about urban unrest. It is that in modern techniques for managing marginalization—for keeping the peace in the face of persistent, and growing, inequality—the United States is a world leader.

MICHAEL B. KATZ is Walter H. Annenberg Professor of History at the University of Pennsylvania. His most recent book, co-authored with Mark J. Stern, is *One Nation Divisible: What America Was and What It Is Becoming* (Russell Sage Foundation, 2006). This article is based on the author's presidential address to the Urban History Association in January 2007. A much longer and fully documented version will appear in the *Journal of Urban History* (January 2008).

Originally published in *Dissent Magazine*, Summer 2007, pp. 23–29. Copyright © 2007 by Foundation for Study of Independent Ideas, Inc. Reprinted by permission. www.dissentmagazine.org

Who We Are Now

**We have a new president. But he, too, has a new nation to
lead, one that's changing almost beyond recognition.**

Jon Meacham

The message seemed mixed. It was 3 o'clock on the afternoon of Sunday, Oct. 3, 1965, and President Lyndon B.
Johnson had come to the foot of the Statue of Liberty
in New York Harbor to sign the unsexily named Immigration
and Nationality Act. It was a grand and sentimental stage for
Johnson, who loved the grand and the sentimental. There he
was, less than a year into a term he'd won in the greatest of
landslides over Barry Goldwater, at the mythic gateway to
America, Robert and Ted Kennedy in the audience, the eyes
of the press fixed on him in the shadows of the nation's most
fabled icon of freedom. "Our beautiful America was built by
a nation of strangers," Johnson said, reaching for political
poetry. "From a hundred different places or more they have
poured forth into an empty land, joining and blending in one
mighty and irresistible tide."

But the president was openly ambivalent, too. "The bill that
we sign today is not a revolutionary bill," he said, defensively,
almost as though to reassure white Americans that they had
nothing to fear. "It does not affect the lives of millions. It will
not reshape the structure of our daily lives, or really add importantly to either our wealth or our power."

To borrow an old line about Winston Churchill, when Lyndon
Johnson was right, he was right, but when he was wrong, well,
my God. (See, for example, War, Vietnam.) On reflection, the
bill LBJ signed on that October day was one of the most significant of his momentous presidency, and the virtually forgotten
legislation played a key role in creating the America that made
this week's inauguration of Barack Obama possible.

Why exhume the long-dead Johnson on the occasion of one
of the most engaging inaugurals since George Washington took
the oath at Federal Hall in New York City in 1789? Because who
we are now—a country in which traditional barriers of race
and age and gender are crumbling—flows in many ways from
what LBJ did then. His conflicting language on that October
day, meanwhile, underscores the nation's occasionally wary view
of the changes wrought by immigration. We like to say we love
the new, but the familiar, come to think of it, is awfully comfortable, too. So which will it be in the coming years: the America
of the melting pot, or the America of resentments? The America

of Lincoln's better angels, or the America of Nixon's Silent
Majority?

"We" is getting ever trickier to define in terms of race, ethnicity and religion.

The answer is almost certainly that we will be one or another
of these Americas at different times depending on different circumstances. One reason to think that we might find ourselves
with Lincoln more often than with Nixon, though, is that the
"we" is getting ever trickier to define quickly and easily in terms
of race, ethnicity and religion. We the People of 2009 are not
the We the People of 1959 or 1969 or even 1979. And that is
because of Lyndon Johnson.

There is something quintessentially American about a lum-
bering white man from Texas—a complex, gifted and ultimately
tragic politician—transforming, however inadvertently, a largely
Anglo-Saxon nation into a country which, in roughly the same
amount of time that separates us from John F. Kennedy's inauguration, will have more people of color than whites. (The short-
hand for this milestone, projected to take place in about 2050, is
the arrival of a "majority-minority" country, but if the minorities
are actually the majorities, we should probably find a cleaner
linguistic way to talk about the coming reality.)

Stories about demography tend to be prospective and general, and it is all too easy to exaggerate this turn in the statistics
or that tick in the projections. But this much is clear and certain:
The nation over which Obama will preside is changing, rapidly,
and history is likely to connect his political rise to the shifting
nature of a country that was largely one thing in the wake of
World War II and through the Cold War and into the opening
years of the 21st century, and quite another as the Obama era
began.

In the understandable thrill of the inaugural season, all eyes
are turned to this single man, all ears attuned to his voice. Whatever your politics, the election of the 44th president represents
a kind of redemption from the long and tragic history of blacks

in America since the first slaves arrived in Jamestown, Va., in 1619. Ever since, as the biographer Taylor Branch once wrote, color has defined American life as it defines vision itself.

Yet the Obama victory is about more than Obama, and about more than black and white. In a democratic republic like ours (a product, in large part, of Madison's insight, Jackson's energy and Lincoln's genius), the president is both a maker and a mirror of the manners and morals of the electorate that has invested him with ultimate authority. We have not reached the promised land in which race and ethnicity no longer matter; history tells us that racism, tribalism and nativism will be always with us. The America of 2009, though, is not the America that Johnson felt coming into being the year before he spoke at the Statue of Liberty. After signing the Civil Rights Act of 1964, he told an aide he had just handed the South to the Republicans for a generation. (If you count a generation as roughly 21 years, he was off the mark, since the racially inspired backlash shaped politics for more than 40 years.)

For the moment—and it could be a very brief moment—the division of voters into us and them along racial and ethnic lines is at once more difficult and less effective. As the electorate changes, voters themselves are more likely to come from diverse backgrounds or live in a world in which diversity is the rule, not the exception. Not every part of the country is like the Bronx, where there is a 90 percent chance that any two people chosen at random will be of a different race or ethnicity. But there are now Hispanics, for instance—the country's fastest-growing population—living in practically every county in the country.

We have not reached the promised land. Racism will always be with us.

The roots of this new America—for it is quite new—can be traced to our long-running debate over immigration, a debate Johnson was trying to shape. Immigration boomed in the first decade of the 20th century, too. Waves came from Italy (1.9 million), Russia (1.5 million) and Austria-Hungary, which included Poland (2 million). All told, by 1910 there were about 13.5 million foreign-born people in the United States, according to the U.S. Census, and 87.4 percent of them were European.

Nativist Americans, though, thought many of the Europeans who were being admitted were inferior, and the Immigration Restriction League was formed to argue against the undesirables, most of whom were Southern and Eastern Europeans. In 1909, Sen. Henry Cabot Lodge proposed a literacy test to restrict the influx of "Italians, Russians, Poles, Hungarians, Greeks, and Asiatics." (Lodge liked "English-speaking [immigrants] . . . Germans, Scandinavians, and French.") The test, along with other restrictions, passed in 1917. In the 1920s, amid difficult economic times and fears of communism in the wake of the Russian Revolution, America passed quotas that favored Lodge's preferred region of Europe. Jews and Asians were particular targets.

Then, in 1952, Congress passed the McCarran-Walter Act, which essentially made naturalization colorblind. In other words, anyone admitted as an immigrant could apply for citizenship. "By eliminating racial discrimination in naturalization, it helped change the whole pattern after that," says Roger Daniels, professor emeritus of history at the University of Cincinnati and author of several authoritative books on immigration. "Not a lot of Europeans came immediately after the 1952 act, but many recent immigrants, especially Asians who had not been able to naturalize, were able to become citizens."

The 1965 bill was intended to reward the Southern and Eastern Europeans (chiefly the Italians and the Poles) who had been loyal Democrats. It completely abolished national quotas and allowed naturalized citizens to send for relatives—thus rewarding initiative and family stability. "Johnson thought that he was getting payback for the things that had been done to the new immigrants of 1920, the Italians and the Poles, and he thought this would take care of them," says Daniels. "If this had passed soon after World War II, when Europe was a mess, maybe that would have been true. And if it had not been for the Iron Curtain, it would have been something else. But in 1965, immigration from Europe was down to 10 percent." Asians, Mexicans and other Latin Americans began flowing in. Four decades on, Census data estimate that of the nearly 40 million foreign-born people in the United States, the largest percentages come from Mexico, China, the Philippines, India and Vietnam.

Acceptance of interracial marriage is up: 54 percent in 1995 vs. 80 percent today.

The tension between assimilation and separation is eternal, but there is no doubt that this flood of immigration and the breaking down of barriers between previously estranged groups within the country has created a much more fluid culture than previous generations might have thought possible.

The new reality is reflected in the *Newsweek* Poll. Sixteen years ago, in the wake of the recession of 1991–92, anti-immigrant sentiment ran high, with 60 percent of Americans saying that they thought current immigration to the United States was a bad thing on the whole, and only 29 percent saying it was a good thing. Now the public is evenly divided, 44 percent to 44 percent. The percentage saying there are too many people coming to America from Africa has dropped from 47 percent in 1992 to 21 percent. Closer to home, public approval of interracial marriages (like the one between Obama's parents) has risen significantly in the past decade, from 54 percent in 1995 to 80 percent today. The percentage of Americans who say they know a mixed-race couple has risen from 58 to 79 percent since 1995, and more than a third (34 percent) say they or a close family member have married or live with someone of another race or who has a very different racial, ethnic or religious background, including a quarter (24 percent) who say it is specifically an interracial marriage or live-in relationship.

By and large, the younger you are, the more assimilated you are in this new tapestry of daily life. The key cohort is the 75 million-strong generation known as the millennials (those born roughly between 1980 and 2000). To state the obvious, the experiences of the younger generation—now voting and beginning their adult lives—are not the experiences of their parents or of their grandparents. Vietnam seems as distant as Saratoga;

Roe v. Wade as far off as Dred Scott. That much is self-evident, and perennial. (Every generation is shaped by unique forces; that is part of what makes them a generation, aside from the accident of a birth date.) What was less than clear until the election of 2008 was whether the experience of younger Americans would produce a shift in political attitudes, and would such a shift be felt beyond Facebook and Starbucks? Could Obama count on them to show up?

Yes, he could. The disparity between older and younger voters was greater in 2008 than at any other time since exit polling began in 1972, according to the Pew Research Center. Obama won 66 percent of the 18- to 29-year-old vote, 12 points more than John Kerry attracted in 2004. The younger cohort is more diverse than the general population, more female, more secular, less socially conservative and more willing to describe themselves as liberals. Note to the ghost of LBJ: 20 percent of this crucial group are children of immigrants.

The disparity between older and younger voters in 2008 was the widest ever recorded.

And 2009 is only the beginning of the story. According to Pew, if current trends continue, the U.S. population will rise from 296 million in 2005 to 438 million in 2050. Eighty-two percent—let me repeat that: 82 percent—of the increase will be attributable to immigrants arriving after 2005 and to their descendants. By that point, whites may make up only 47 percent of the country, ending centuries of a majority-white America.

Will the journey be smooth? That is doubtful. Politics can quickly turn mean. In hard economic times there is often a search for an "other" on which to blame the problems of life. In the wake of a possible terrorist attack, fear could easily lead to tension, resentment and discord. The good news about America, though, is that for all of our nativist fevers and periodic witch hunts, we tend, often after having exhausted every other option, to do what is right.

Johnson closed his remarks in October 1965 by alluding to nearby Ellis Island, "whose vacant corridors echo today the joyous sound of long-ago voices." The voices of the new America, of Obama's America, are just beginning to be heard.

With Pat Wingert, Marc Bain and Daniel Stone.

The Invisible Ones

Ms. undertook an investigation into the shadow world of sex and labor trafficking in the United States, and learned not just the dimensions of the problem but the startling inadequacy of the federal response.

Rebecca Clarren

We like to think of slavery in America as something consigned to history books, a dark chapter set in Southern cotton plantations and the hulls of ships set sail from Africa. Florencia Molina wishes this were true.

For part of the year in 2002, Molina, a 30-year-old Mexican, was held against her will and forced to work in a factory in Southern California, making dresses from 5:30 in the morning until 11 at night, seven days a week. She was not allowed to take a shower or leave the factory, at night sharing a small bed with another woman. She received one meal of beans and rice a day. If she didn't sew fast enough, her boss would pull her hair, pinch and slap her. Though she often worked 17 hours a day, her time card only gave credit for three.

Molina wasn't physically chained to her sewing machine; she wasn't shackled to the floor of the factory. Even so, she says she was in bondage. The factory doors were locked during the day and at night a watchman prevented her from leaving.

"If we wouldn't do what she [her boss] said, she told us somebody who we love would pay the consequences," says Molina, a small woman with steady dark eyes and black hair that falls below her waist. "She told me she could kill me and no one would ask her for me. She told me dogs have more rights than I have in this country."

Molina is one of the estimated tens of thousands of people trafficked into the U.S. from other countries and forced to work against their will. Large numbers are from El Salvador, Mexico, Korea, Vietnam and China, but in any country where people are desperate for jobs, they're prey to the allure of a mythic, prosperous U.S. It's hard to find an incontrovertible estimate of the numbers, because trafficking operates in a shadow world, but the CIA estimated in 1999 that as many as 50,000 women and children were trafficked into the U.S. each year. More recent estimates by the Bush administration have lowered this figure— to between 14,500 and 17,500. Polaris Project, an international anti-trafficking group, thinks there are likely more than 100,000 trafficking victims currently enslaved in the U.S., and those include, unbelievably, an undetermined number of enslaved U.S. residents as well.

Whatever the tally of victims, all modern-day slavery, or human trafficking, operates on coercion, fear, psychological abuse, torture or rape. About 80 percent of those enslaved are women and girls, pawns in the fastest-growing and one of the largest criminal industries in the world, second only to the drug trade, and tied with the arms trade. With an estimated 800,000 people trafficked across all international borders each year, the shadow industry is estimated to generate $31.6 billion in profits annually.

Molina's story is not unusual. Desperate times had prompted her to leave Mexico, after her ex-husband kicked her and their young children out of the house. She seized a chance to work in a U.S. factory owned by a woman from her town, planning to return to Mexico in six months with enough money to open her own sewing shop.

However, when she arrived in Southern California, the boss confiscated her birth certificate and ID and told her that if she tried to run away and go to the police, she would be jailed. Without knowing English, and with a fear of police based on the corrupt law enforcement of her hometown, Molina believed her.

"When I came to this country, I came with a lot of dreams," she says. "But when I arrived I realized that my dreams were dead. I was in the darkness with no hope and no light."

There is a perception, propagated in large part by mainstream media, that slavery in the U.S. occurs mostly in the guise of forced prostitution. But sex trafficking constitutes only about half of slavery in the U.S., according to a report by the Berkeley Human Rights Center and the nonprofit Free the Slaves based on surveys of trafficking service providers, newspaper articles and government reports.

The majority of trafficking victims are people who may be sewing our clothes, picking our crops, washing dishes in our restaurants, cleaning our motel rooms and building our homes and office buildings. They may be enslaved as domestic servants in our neighbors' homes. And they're everywhere in the U.S. While trafficking victims are most prevalent in New York,

Texas, Florida and California, investigations have been opened in 48 states and all U.S. territories.

Due in large part to the efforts of feminist groups, in 2000 Congress passed the Trafficking Victims Protection Act (TVPA), which created a special "T visa" that enables victims of sex and labor trafficking to remain temporarily in the United States—if they agree to assist in the investigation or prosecution of their traffickers and if they would suffer severe harm if removed from the U.S. After three years, the attorney general can admit them for permanent residency—though a process for doing so has yet to be worked out. Previously, trafficking victims were often deported as "illegal" aliens.

Under the TVPA, trafficking victims also become eligible to receive federally and state-funded services just as if they were refugees. These include cash assistance, housing, food stamps, health care, and educational and job services.

According to President George W. Bush, human trafficking is an issue that his administration cares about deeply. "We're beginning to make good, substantial progress," said Bush in 2004. "The message is getting out: We're serious. And when we catch you, you'll find out we're serious. We're staying on the hunt."

But, in fact, seven years after the passage of what was hailed as a very innovative law that created powerful new tools to prosecute and punish traffickers, the Bush administration has failed to fund and implement its provisions in a truly meaningful way. There has been a shocking lack of trafficking investigations—just 639 were opened by the Department of Justice between fiscal years 2001 and 2006. Only 360 defendants have been charged, resulting in 238 convictions. And, as of January, the federal government has provided refugee-type benefits to just over 1,100 people who had been trafficked.

"Here we have this crime that is often rape plus torture plus assault, and yet we have very little enforcement," says Kevin Bales, president of the Washington, D.C.-based Free the Slaves, which works to end slavery worldwide. "Think of it this way: Roughly 17,000 people were murdered in America last year—about the same number as the State Department claims were trafficked. Imagine if we only prosecuted, as we do with slavery, a little over 100 of those cases. People would freak out; it would be on the cover of *Time*. So far we've heard plenty of talk and [had] very little walk."

Furthermore, the regulations that the federal government was supposed to write enabling victims of trafficking to gain permanent residency status have yet to be completed, so those who have been released from enslavement are left in limbo. A spokesperson for the Department of Homeland Security says that the rules remain in draft form and there is no pending date for their release.

Hope for victims of trafficking has an address; it's just very hard to find. In Los Angeles, off a busy street near apartment buildings and convenience stores, hidden away behind oodles of security, is a confidential shelter. In the backyard, bright flowers and fruit trees line a vegetable garden where survivors of trafficking plant not only vegetables and herbs, but also the seeds of their own recovery.

"Our clients planted this garden as a place of refuge and meditation to help them start to take control of their lives again. It's about trying to re-create a normal life," says Kay Buck, executive director of the Coalition to Abolish Slavery & Trafficking (CAST), a nonprofit that runs the shelter and provides other social services for trafficking victims.

> ## "Here we have this crime that is often rape plus torture plus assault, yet we have very little enforcement."
>
> —Kevin Bales

In the entire U.S., there are only a handful of shelters devoted entirely to victims of trafficking, and the situation is unlikely to improve in the near future. CAST has seen its budget sliced by over 50 percent since the federal Office of Refugee Resettlement, under the Department of Health and Human Services, restructured its funding stream in 2006. Now, over half the federal money available for victim services no longer goes directly to nonprofit service providers, but instead is given to intermediaries, primarily the U.S. Conference of Catholic Bishops' Migration and Refugee Services. The Conference, which receives up to $6 million per year under a five-year contract, then subcontracts with individual groups like CAST, reimbursing groups on a per-victim basis—at an initial maximum of $600 per victim per month—to pay for such needs as food, rent and health care. The groups are only guaranteed these funds, individual by individual, for a few months at a time before they must reapply, thus hindering long-term service plans. The U.S. Conference of Catholic Bishops also requires that service providers stipulate that they won't hand out condoms or provide referral for abortion.

"We are being nickeled and dimed to the point where we do not have time to provide much-needed services to trafficked individuals," says Joy Zarembka, director of Break the Chain Campaign, a Washington, D.C.-based group that helps victims of domestic servitude. "Because organizations have no way of knowing how many cases they will have or how much money they will receive, they cannot guarantee that there is funding for staff. How can you predict a budget that is predicated on the amount of trafficked individuals who may escape in your jurisdiction over the course of a year? This is not what the Trafficking Act intended."

For women like Eyam (not her real name), 37, a former slave of an Indonesian family living in Beverly Hills, this failure to create a process for permanent residency has prevented her from feeling truly free. Enslaved for 17 years, Eyam was beaten with hangers, raped and often fed only noodles or rice. She was paid nothing to clean, cook and wait on the family 24 hours a day.

"I was living in a hell," she says in her heavily accented voice. "They make me really hurt in my life. I don't trust any more with men. Only thing they didn't do to me was to take my spirit out of my body."

Eyam escaped in 2000, using a knife to open a lock while her captors were out of town. She is worried that she will not receive permanent residency and will be forced to return to Indonesia. Returning to Indonesia permanently, where her U.S. captor has many connections and where she fears retaliation for cooperating with U.S. law-enforcement authorities, isn't an option. Eyam is desperate to visit her family—poor farmers in rural Indonesia—but immigration attorneys warn her and others not to travel outside the U.S. until their permanent residency status is approved.

The requirement that trafficking victims must cooperate with law enforcement to prosecute their traffickers in order to receive a T visa can put women or their families at tremendous risk, says Kamala D. Harris, district attorney of San Francisco. Harris was one of the driving forces behind state legislation to make human trafficking a felony in California and to provide additional funds for trafficking survivors to receive social services.

"We have to do everything we can to make sure women and girls don't face retaliation, even death, for testifying," she says. "First and foremost our guiding approach should be protecting victims. Then, in the process, if victims want to come forward and lend their voices, that's all the better."

Trafficked women don't easily trust law enforcement anyway, according to Mario Estrada, a 32-year veteran with the Los Angeles County Sheriff's Department. As he passes through Hacienda Heights, a middle-class community east of the city of Los Angeles, he recalls a raid at an ordinary-looking beige house six months before. There, behind the boarded-up windows, seven Korean women, the youngest aged 15, were forced to work as prostitutes.

"The girls kept saying they were OK," says Estrada. "They're so afraid of law enforcement, they won't help us, they won't open up. It's the hardest thing to convince them that [they're] not suspects, [they're] victims."

While Estrada suspects there could be over 100 similar operations in Los Angeles County, he isn't optimistic about uncovering too many of them. There are 9,000 law enforcement officers in the Sheriff's Department, but only Estrada and three others have experience and training in human trafficking. In the past year, they've busted just five human trafficking operations.

And Los Angeles—where county sheriff's department and city police personnel are now being educated on human trafficking—is better at dealing with trafficking than most jurisdictions. While 34 states have passed some form of anti-trafficking law, only California and a few other states mandate that law enforcement be trained in recognizing and apprehending traffickers. On the federal level, as of May the U.S. Department of Justice had given only 42 grants to cities and states to train local law enforcement. That means that while agents at the FBI and at Immigration and Customs Enforcement offices throughout the country may understand human trafficking, many local law enforcement officers—who are most likely to be the first to come in contact with trafficking victims—remain clueless.

"In the absence of training, the concern is that trafficking cases may be misdiagnosed," says Katherine Chon, executive

director of Polaris Project, a Washington, D.C.-based nonprofit. "For example, in the Asian massage-parlor network, women are transported to the parlor by taxis that are controlled by traffickers. An untrained observer might assume that the woman was free to walk to a street corner and hail a cab, not realizing she was a trafficking victim."

Aside from federal and local law enforcement identifying trafficking victims, the federal Department of Labor (DOL) also plays a role, as it's charged with monitoring labor conditions to ensure that slavery doesn't occur. The DOL's already under-staffed Wage and Hour Division, which interfaces with victims of trafficking in farm fields and factories, saw its staff cut further between 2001 and 2005. And it shows. At the DOL office in Fort Myers, Fla., for example, which serves an estimated 100,000 Spanish-speaking migrant workers, there is no full-time staff and the office is open just a half-day a week.

Within the next year, Congress will very likely re-authorize the Trafficking Victims Protection Act for the next two years. It's an opportunity, say advocates, to reform the law. Aside from trying to untangle T visas from the requirement that victims cooperate with law enforcement, a coalition of antitrafficking advocates wants U.S. and international agencies to establish a database on patterns of trafficking.

At the state level, says Jessica Neuwirth, founder of the international human-rights-for-women organization Equality Now, the need remains for anti-trafficking legislation to authorize local prosecutions and provide more money for shelters, victim services and law-enforcement training. Neuwirth helped draft stronger anti-trafficking legislation for New York—which passed this June—to separate sex and labor trafficking into separate categories, placing sex-trafficking crimes under the existing laws against prostitution and pimping. The law also works to stop sex trafficking at the demand end by increasing penalties for johns.

"We have to shift the burden of responsibility to the people who go out and buy a woman for sex," says Neuwirth. "Hopefully other states will use the New York law as a model."

Clearly, better training for law enforcement will be a key to victim identification. Groups such as the National Center for Women & Policing (NCWP), a Washington, D.C.-based division of the Feminist Majority Foundation (publisher of *Ms.*), have brokered meetings between nonprofit social service providers and federal law enforcement authorities to increase outreach and education about trafficking. In addition, NCWP has brought together law-enforcement officials from various foreign embassies to share their country's experiences with trafficking and attempt to coordinate international responses to trafficking. More models such as this are needed, says Margie Moore, director of the NCWP.

Ultimately ending labor slavery will take more than good laws and trained law enforcement. Corporations that profit from cheap labor must be held accountable, says Julie A. Su, co-founder of Sweatshop Watch in Los Angeles and litigation director of the Asian Pacific American Legal Center. Those corporations often subcontract labor, then claim ignorance of worker enslavement by their subcontractors. That's no excuse, says Su: "If they claim they don't know the conditions in which workers labor, they're willfully ignorant. A primary reason trafficking exists is the demand by companies for the cheapest, most vulnerable workers."

While Su and others have filed lawsuits over the past several years to ensure that companies pay legal wages, she suggests the situation won't improve greatly until the public becomes aware and outraged by the conditions under which a pair of pants was sewn, or produce was picked. Laws that require "sweatshop free" labeling in garments and on food products would increase consumer awareness and pressure for change.

Trafficking survivors such as Molina and Eyam are instigating change, and reclaiming their lives. They have joined a 10-member advisory caucus created by CAST to advocate for local and national policy, empower other survivors and become leaders in the fight to end modern-day slavery.

Today, Eyam lives in her own apartment, and cooks and cleans at a local homeless shelter. When she talks about her job, her face breaks into a wide smile, exposing brand-new braces on her teeth.

Molina works as a security guard in Los Angeles; she's completed English classes and is working toward her GED. But she has not yet been able to bring her sons from Mexico to the U.S.

> **"If [corporations] claim they don't know the conditions in which workers labor, they're willfully ignorant. A primary reason for trafficking is demand for the cheapest workers."**
>
> —Julie Su

"Not being with my children is the hardest part. I know some days they might have pain and feel sad and I'm not there to console them," she says, tears streaking her cheeks. Then she swallows hard and talks about her hopes: She wants to become a sheriff to help other victims of trafficking.

"I want to be for my children somebody who can inspire them to be a good person. I want to be a voice for those who are in fear, who don't have the power or the courage to come forward. There were a lot of people who helped me; I call them my angels. I want to be one of them for someone else."

REBECCA CLARREN writes about labor issues for a variety of national magazines. She lives in Portland, Ore. *Ms.* research associate Jennifer Hahn contributed to this article. For ways to help stop trafficking, see www.msmagazine.com.

UNIT 3

Problems of Poverty and Inequality

Unit Selections

13. **How Stratification Works,** Douglas S. Massey
14. **Goodbye, Horatio Alger: Moving up Economically Is Now Impossible for Many, If Not Most, Americans, Horatio Alger,** Jeff Madrick
15. **The Myth of the "Culture of Poverty",** Paul Gorski
16. **Can Extreme Poverty Be Eliminated?,** Jeffrey D. Sachs
17. **A Work in Progress,** Ann Pomeroy
18. **Brave New Welfare,** Stephanie Mencimer
19. **Inequalities That Endure?: Racial Ideology, American Politics, and the Peculiar Role of the Social Sciences,** Lawrence D. Bobo
20. **Why We Hate,** Margo Monteith and Jeffrey Winters
21. **American Dreamers,** Lisa Miller
22. **Great Expectations,** Judith M. Havemann
23. **Human Rights, Sex Trafficking, and Prostitution,** Alice Leuchtag
24. **Answers to Questions about Marriage Equality,** Human Rights Campaign, 2009
25. **(Rethinking) Gender,** Debra Rosenberg

Key Points to Consider

- Why has inequality increased over the past three decades? How might increased inequality adversely impact American society?

- How would you compare the lives of people at the bottom rung of the social ladder with the people at the top?

- Are people poor because they lack ambition and willingness to work or because their opportunities are very constrained?

- Is America still the land of opportunity?

- Can extreme poverty be eliminated in poor countries or is the problem of extreme poverty practically insoluble?

- How well are welfare agencies run? How helpful are they?

- How extensive is discrimination between racial and ethnic groups in the U.S. today?

- How different is the world of men from the world of women in American society today? Compare the treatment of women in America with their treatment around the world.

- Americans believe in tolerance, but what should be tolerated and what should not be tolerated? Explain.

- What is your view on gay marriage? Should it be legalized?

Student Website

www.mhhe.com/cls

Internet References

grass-roots.org
   http://www.grass-roots.org
Immigration Facts
   http://www.immigrationforum.org
Joint Center for Poverty Research
   http://www.jcpr.org

SocioSite
   http://www.pscw.uva.nl/sociosite/TOPICS/Women.html
William Davidson Institute
   http://www.wdi.bus.umich.edu
WWW Virtual Library: Demography & Population Studies
   http://demography.anu.edu.au/VirtualLibrary

America is famous as the land of opportunity, and people from around the world have come to its shores in pursuit of the American dream. But how is America living up to this dream today? It is still a place for people to get rich, but it is also a place where people are trapped in poverty. This unit tells a number of stories of Americans dealing with advantages and disadvantages, opportunities and barriers, power and powerlessness.

The first subsection of this unit deals with income inequality and the hardships of the poor. In the first article, Douglas S. Massey explains how stratification works and how frequently it involves unjust processes such as exploitation, restriction of opportunities, socially defined processes of exclusion, intimidation, victimization, segregation, prejudice, violence, and coercion. Massey emphasizes that the boundaries between advantaged and disadvantaged groups are constantly being contested as the disadvantaged group resists the unfavorable framing by the advantaged group. The next article demonstrates that the reputation of the United States as the land of opportunity is outdated. Now America has less social mobility than most industrialized countries. Next, Paul Gorski attacks the culture of poverty myth that the poverty of the poor is their own fault because they have the wrong values, beliefs, and behaviors. The truth is that most of the poor want to work, value education, and are willing to try. The main problem is their lack of real opportunities. Next, Jeffrey D. Sachs maintains that extreme poverty can be eliminated throughout the world at the modest price of $160 billion a year for a couple of decades. This is a paltry sum (0.5% of GNP) for the rich countries of the world, which have a combined GNP of over $3 trillion. For this to be successful, the money would have to be invested carefully in ways that he suggests are right.

The next subsection examines welfare and welfare reform. Everyone acknowledges that the 1996 Welfare Reform succeeded in reducing welfare roles and getting many welfare recipients into the labor force. Nevertheless, problems of the administration of welfare remain and the following two articles address these problems. First, Ann Pomeroy tells how welfare recipients made the transition from welfare to work. Supporting programs like job training and child care help played crucial roles in aiding the transition in several of the stories. Next, Stephanie Mencimer tells some painful stories about how welfare agencies lied to or mistreated welfare applicants. The states run the welfare programs, and many states want to minimize their welfare expenses at the expense of the welfare clients.

The three articles in the next subsection present various aspects of inter-group conflicts, including the cultural and attitudinal foundations of negative racial and ethnic relations. The most poignant inequality in America is the gap between blacks and whites as discussed in the article by Lawrence D. Bobo. He tries to explain why inequalities endure so long after strong civil rights legislation was passed. He argues that a subtle racism is the root of the problem. Blatant prejudice and discrimination has changed for the better, but unconscious prejudice and discrimination has not. In the next article, the authors

© Jack Star/PhotoLink/Getty Images

demonstrate the prevalence of prejudice in America and how quickly hatred toward a group can evolve. Since September 11, 2001, hatred toward Muslims has erupted despite calls for tolerance by President George W. Bush and other public leaders. One explanation of hatred and prejudice against entire groups is the social identity theory. There is a powerful drive to classify people into groups, identify with one group, and develop negative views on some of the out-groups. Fortunately, "people who are concerned about their prejudices have the power to correct them." Meanwhile, as the next article points out, the above theory of hate is being played out today in the increasing prejudice toward Arab Americans despite the fact that they have had an exemplary record as good, patriotic, and successful Americans.

The final subsection focuses on gender inequality and related issues. Its first article documents the great progress women have made in the corporate world. Women now hold more than half of all management and professional jobs, but rarely do they hold the top management positions. Women have the degrees, the talent, and the ambition to reach the highest levels of the corporate world, but the "glass ceiling" persists. Next, Alice Leuchtag describes one of the great evils that haunts the world today: sex slavery. The sex trade system grows out of poverty and profits—extreme poverty forces parents to sell their girls into servitude, often not knowing that they will become sex slaves. Considerable profits drive the system. The exploitation involved is horrendous, making this a painful worldwide human rights issue. Next, the Human Rights Campaign provides its advocacy statement on behalf of same-sex marriage. It would be conducted by the state and not require any participation by religious groups. It argues that it would not negatively impact heterosexual marriages. Finally, Debra Rosenberg turns the spotlight on a social paradox. Some people contradict the basic social category of gender. They are born one gender but feel they are the other gender and use surgery or hormones to make their bodies comply with their identities.

How Stratification Works
The American Stratification System

Douglas S. Massey

All human societies have a social structure that divides people into categories based on a combination of achieved and ascribed traits. Achieved characteristics are those acquired in the course of living, whereas ascribed characteristics are set at birth. The categories defined within a social structure may be nominal or graduated—that is, they may assign labels to people on the basis of shared qualitative attributes, or they may rank people along some quantitative continuum (see Blau 1977). Ascribed social categories include nominal groupings such as gender, in which people are labeled male or female on the basis of inherited physical traits (ultimately, the possession of one versus two X chromosomes), as well as graduated categories such as age, in which people are classified according to the amount of time elapsed since birth. Achieved statuses may also be nominal—being a member of a fraternal lodge such as the Moose or Elks—or graduated—being a member of an income class.

Stratification refers to the unequal distribution of people across social categories that are characterized by differential access to scarce resources. The resources may be material, such as income and wealth; they may be symbolic, such as prestige and social standing; or they may be emotional, such as love, affection, and, of course, sex. The term "stratification" comes from the Latin *stratum,* which in the geological sense refers to an identifiable layer of sediment or material in the ground. Over time, changing environmental conditions produce identifiable layers within the earth's crust, known as strata, which are distinctive in composition and can be associated temporally with different geological eras. In an analogous manner, societies may be conceptualized as having social strata, different layers that are distinctive in composition and characterized by more or less access to material, symbolic, and emotional resources.

Stratification systems order people vertically in a social structure characterized by a distinct top and bottom. The distance from the top to the bottom of any society is indicated by the size of the gap in access to resources between those in the uppermost and lowermost social categories. As the distance between the top and the bottom of a social structure increases, and as the distribution of people across social categories shifts toward the extremes, a society is said to become more stratified—literally having more socially defined layers with more people distributed among them at greater distances from one another. The degree of social stratification is often measured in terms of inequality, which assesses the degree of variability in the dispersion of people among ranked social categories.

Human societies differ greatly with respect to their degree of social inequality. In general, small foraging societies in which people hunt and gather for a living tend to be quite egalitarian (Kelly 1995). Social categories are defined mainly on the basis of gender, age, and kinship, categorical perceptions that appear to be hardwired into human social cognition (Macrae and Bodenhausen 2000). Among hunters and gatherers there is little inequality in access to material resources. The stratification that does exist is mainly expressed as unequal access to symbolic or emotional resources. Among men, prestige and sexual access derive not simply from skill at hunting and successful food provision but also from generosity and sharing within the group. Selfishness and hoarding are discouraged through a variety of informal leveling mechanisms that involve ridicule, shaming, and humor, which are often enforced through prescribed rituals (Gamble 1999).

The most common form of stratification in foraging societies occurs on the basis of gender. Stratification between males and females derives primarily from the amount of time that men spend alone together, typically on a hunt, and is thus determined by local ecology (Massey 2005a). Societies where men spend large amounts of time away from women hunting large game tend to be more gender-stratified. During the time they are away on their own, males reinforce male predispositions and tendencies to become more aggressive and domineering (Macoby 1998). At the same time, females left by themselves reinforce female predispositions and tendencies to become more caring and nurturing. The end result is a divergence in gender-specific attitudes and behaviors that works to the detriment of females once the two sexes reunite (Macoby 1998; Sanday 1981). Compared with foraging societies built around the hunting of large mammals, societies that rely on aquatic resources, gathering and scavenging, or the pursuit of small game tend to be much lower in gender inequality.

Sedentary agrarian societies are more stratified than foraging societies (Sjoberg 1960). The domestication of plants and animals around ten thousand years ago enabled farmers to produce more food than they themselves consumed, and thus a very small number of people could stop toiling each day to procure the calories needed for survival. Instead, these fortunate few pursued other, non-food-producing activities such as trade, manufacturing, politics, religion, and soldiering (Chant and Goodman 1999).

Given a pre-industrial agrarian technology, the food surplus was necessarily meager, and to support even a small class of non-food-producing specialists, crops had to be collected over a large area and assembled at a fixed location for redistribution to people who had no direct role in their cultivation; these fixed locations were the first cities (Chandler and Fox 1974). Since peasant households do not willingly hand over the fruits of their labor to others, social structures came into existence to effect and legitimate the confiscation, leading to the formation of ruling and working classes in addition to peasant farmers (Sjoberg 1960). Noble and priestly families based in cities enjoyed favored access to material, symbolic, and emotional resources; workers, tradesmen, and artisans made do with whatever the ruling classes granted them; and peasants were heavily taxed to support both sets of urban dwellers.

Although the distance between the top and bottom rungs of society was large compared with foraging societies and mobility between classes was minimal, the total amount of inequality was constrained by the small size of the food surplus produced with a pre-industrial technology (Massey 2005a). In the world of agrarian urbanism, which prevailed from 8000 B.C. to around 1800 A.D., no more than 5 percent of the inhabitants within any society ever lived in cities, and among urban dwellers only a tiny fraction belonged to the ruling elite. The typical member of a pre-industrial agrarian society was an illiterate peasant whose access to resources was the same as that of most of the rest of the population. Despite the existence of privileged classes, total inequality was actually quite modest by contemporary standards.

Beginning around 1800, however, the industrial revolution breached the technological cap that had limited inequality for millennia. Mechanization enabled a dramatic increase in agricultural productivity so that for the first time fewer than 5 percent of humans could produce enough food for everyone else (Berry 1973). Industrial societies urbanized, and the vast majority of people came to inhabit cities and work in non-agricultural occupations. As the share of workers employed in manufacturing and services grew, the number and range of occupations expanded rapidly to produce new social forms of differentiation. In the United States, for example, the variance in the distribution of people across occupational categories increased by a factor of four between 1850 and 1950 (Massey 2005a).

Industrialization also enabled an unprecedented increase in material well-being, dramatically widening the absolute distance between the top and the bottom of human social structures. Between 1850 and 1950, the total value of goods and services produced in the global economy rose from $939 trillion to $5,336 trillion (Maddison 2003), and the largest private fortune in the United States rose from $1 million to $1.6 billion (Phillips 2002). This increased distance between the top and bottom of the social hierarchy and the proliferation of categories in between made possible a new burst of stratification and inequality that lasted well into the twentieth century (Williamson 1980).

In the United States, the restructuring of the political economy in the wake of the Great Depression and the Second World War compressed the distribution of earnings and substantially reduced levels of inequality, beginning in the 1930s (Goldin and Margo 1992). From 1945 to 1975, under structural arrangements implemented during the New Deal, poverty rates steadily fell, median incomes consistently rose, and inequality progressively dropped as a rising economic tide lifted all boats (see Burtless and Smeeding 2001; Danziger and Gottschalk 1995; Freeman 2001; Levy 1998; Smeeding, O'Higgins, and Rainwater 1990).

During the 1970s, however, a new *post-industrial* economy arose, one based on the creation of knowledge and manipulation of information rather than the production of goods and services or the cultivation of food (Devine and Waters 2004; Svallfors 2005). Once again occupational differentiation increased and the distance between the top and the bottom of the social hierarchy grew. Whereas the largest private fortune in the United States stood at $3.6 billion in 1968, by 1999 it had reached $85 billion, raising the distance between the top and bottom of the social structure by a factor of 24 in just thirty years (Phillips 2002). Likewise, from 1975 to 2000 wealth inequality increased by 11 percent while income inequality rose by 23 percent (Keister 2000; Massey 2005a). At century's end, the richest 1 percent of Americans controlled 40 percent of the nation's total wealth.

Categorical Inequality

Despite the radical transformation of human societies over time—from foraging societies through agrarian urbanism into industrial urbanism and on to our current post-industrial world—the fundamental mechanisms producing stratification have not changed much. Although the number and range of categories in the social structure may have risen dramatically, and the stock of material resources may have accumulated to new heights, the basic means by which people are granted more or less access to scarce material, emotional, and symbolic resources have remained remarkably similar through the ages. Indeed, all stratification processes boil down to a combination of two simple but powerful mechanisms: the allocation of people to social categories, and the institutionalization of practices that allocate resources unequally across these categories. Together, these two social processes produce what Charles Tilly (1998) calls "categorical inequality"—a pattern of social stratification that is remarkably "durable" in the sense that it is reproduced across time and between generations.

The Basic Mechanisms of Stratification

Given socially defined categories and people being distributed among them, inequality is generated and perpetuated by two basic mechanisms: exploitation and opportunity hoarding (Tilly 1998). *Exploitation* occurs when people in one social group expropriate a resource produced by members of another social group and prevent them from realizing the full value of their effort in producing it. *Opportunity hoarding* occurs when one social group restricts access to a scarce resource, either through outright denial or by exercising monopoly control that requires out-group members to pay rent in return for access. Either way, opportunity hoarding is enabled through a *socially defined process of exclusion*.

The most extreme form of categorical inequality ever invented by human beings is slavery, wherein the labor of one socially defined group is expropriated in its entirety by another, whose members simultaneously and drastically restrict the access of the enslaved to material, symbolic, and emotional resources. The Jim Crow social system that replaced slavery in the American South after 1876 used sharecropping as a new institutional means of exploitation and carrying out exclusion and opportunity hoarding (Foner 1988). Until quite recently, racial stratification in the southern United States was extreme and social mobility for African Americans was limited.

Within any social structure, exploitation and opportunity hoarding are, in turn, reinforced by two other social processes that work over time to institutionalize categorical distinctions and lock them into place (Tilly 1998). The first is *emulation,* whereby one group of people copies a set of social distinctions and interrelationships from another group or transfers the distinctions and interrelationships from one social setting to another. The second is *adaptation:* social relations and day-to-day behaviors at the microsocial level become oriented toward ranked categories, so that decisions about who to befriend, who to help, who to share with, who to live near, who to court, and who to marry are made in ways that assume the existence and importance of asymmetric social categories. In the words of Tilly (1998, 10): "Exploitation and opportunity hoarding favor the installation of categorical inequality, while emulation and adaptation generalize its influence."

In the Jim Crow South, for example, if legislation to enforce racial segregation that was invented in one southern state was successful, it would be imitated by other southern states, such that by 1920 all the states of the former Confederacy came to have remarkably similar legal codes on the issue of race (Packard 2002; Woodward 1955; Wormser 2003). At the same time, faced with violence and coercion, blacks came to "know their place" in the southern social order and adapted to it in ways that reinforced their subjugation. Whites throughout the South likewise adapted their behaviors according to the formal and informal rules of Jim Crow, which allowed them to intimidate, victimize, and punish African Americans with impunity. As a result, racial segregation was enforced not only formally in public settings but also informally in private practice through a racial etiquette negotiated daily by black and white southerners. . . .

The Creation of Capital

The position of a group within the social space defined by warmth and competence is not fixed but malleable, varying across time, space, and culture (Leslie, Constantine, and Fiske 2006). Although social categories are ultimately constructed and maintained by individuals within their own minds, the process by which boundaries are expressed is ultimately social. Group identities and boundaries are negotiated through repeated interactions that establish working definitions of the categories in question, including both objective and subjective content, a process that sociologists have labeled *boundary work* (Gieryn 1983; Lamont and Molnar 2002). When social actors succeed in establishing the limits and content of various social categories in the minds of others, psychologists refer to the process as *framing* (Kahneman and Tversky 2000). In essence, boundary work involves defining categories in the social structure, and framing involves defining them in human cognition.

People naturally favor boundaries and framings that grant them greater access to material, symbolic, and emotional resources, and they seek to convince others to accept their favored version of social reality (Lakoff 2002; Lakoff and Johnson 2003). In general, social actors who control more resources in society—those toward the top of the stratification system—have the upper hand in framing and boundary work. Whites historically have perpetuated negative stereotypes of African Americans as unintelligent, violent, hypersexual, and shiftless, and rich people likewise have promoted a view of the poor as lazy, unmotivated, undisciplined, and undeserving. To the extent that such stereotypes become a part of everyday social cognition, individual members of the stereotyped out-group tend to experience discrimination and exclusion.

Nonetheless, exclusionary social distinctions and demeaning framings are always contested by people on the receiving end (Barth 1969). Those subject to exploitation by a particular framing of social reality work to oppose it and substitute an alternative framing more amenable to their interests. Likewise, when they encounter categorical boundaries that prevent them from accessing a desired resource, people work actively to resist and subvert the social definitions as best they can. Members of subjugated groups have their own expectations about how they should be perceived and treated, and even if they outwardly adapt to the social preconceptions of more powerful others, they generally work inwardly to undermine the dominant conceptual and social order in small and large ways.

Through such two-way interactions, however asymmetric they may be, people on both sides of a stratified social divide actively participate in the construction of the boundaries and identities that define a system of stratification. No matter what their position in the system, people seek to define for themselves the content and meaning of social categories, embracing some elements ascribed to them by the dominant society and rejecting others, simultaneously accepting and resisting the constraints and opportunities associated with their particular social status. Through daily interactions with individuals and institutions, people construct an understanding of the lines between specific social groups (Barth 1981).

The reification of group boundaries within human social structures creates two important resources that are widely deployed in the process of social stratification: social capital and cultural capital (Bourdieu 1986). In classical economics, of course, capital refers to anything that can be used in the production of other resources, is human-made, and is not fully consumed in the process of production (Ricardo 1996). Common examples are *financial capital,* which can be invested to generate income, and *physical capital,* which can be applied in production to increase output. Economists later generalized the concept by defining *human capital* as the skills and abilities embodied in people, notably through education and training (Schultz 1963). By investing in education, parents and societies thus create human capital in their children, and when individuals forgo income and incur costs to gain additional training, they invest in their own human capital. Individuals recoup this investment through higher lifetime earnings; societies recoup it through higher taxes and enhanced productivity; and parents recoup it by enjoying the economic independence and financial security of their adult children (Becker 1975).

Sociologists have broadened the concept of capital to embrace resources derived from social ties to people and institutions (Bourdieu 1986; Coleman 1988). *Social capital* comes into existence whenever a social connection to another person or membership in a social organization yields tangible benefits with respect to material, symbolic, or emotional resources, such as getting a job that offers higher income, greater prestige, and more access to attractive sexual partners. Most "good" jobs are not found through formal mechanisms such as paid advertisements but through informal connections with other social actors who provide information and leads (Granovetter 1974). Because ties to friends and family do not extend very far and mostly yield redundant information, weak ties to casual acquaintances are generally more important in getting a job than close relationships to close friends or kin (Granovetter 1973).

The use of framing and boundary work to construct an advantaged social group with privileged access to resources and power creates the potential for social capital formation. Having a tie to a member of a privileged elite increases the odds of being able to access resources and power oneself. Elites implicitly recognize this fact and generally take steps to restrict social ties to other members of the elite. Marriage outside the group is discouraged; friendships are turned inward through exclusive organizations such as clubs, fraternities, and lodges; and rules of inheritance conserve elite status along family lines. To the extent that group members are successful in confining social ties to other group members, they achieve *social closure*. Outsiders trying to break into elite circles are labeled bounders or interlopers, and they are derided for acting "uppity" or "above their station."

Social closure within elite networks and institutions also creates the potential for another valuable resource known as *cultural capital* (Bourdieu 1986). In contrast to human capital, which includes knowledge, skills, and abilities that make people directly productive as individuals, cultural capital consists of knowledge and manners that do not make individuals more productive in and of themselves, but that permit them to be more effective as actors within a particular social context—in this case, elite settings. Because members of an elite tend to go to the same schools, read the same books, peruse the same periodicals, learn the same stylized manners, follow the same fashions, and develop the same accents and speech patterns, they are easily able to acquire a common set of socially defined markers that designate "good taste" and "high class," so that elite members are quickly recognizable to one another and to the masses.

The possession of cultural capital makes an individual more productive not because he or she can perform a given operation better or faster, but because he or she can navigate structures of power with greater ease, feeling relaxed and comfortable in the social settings they define and thus interacting with other persons of influence to get things done. Cultural capital represents a symbolic resource that privileged groups can manipulate through opportunity hoarding to perpetuate stratification and increase inequality. . . .

To this point, I have argued that stratification stems from a social process wherein individuals form categorical mental representations of in-groups and out-groups through framing; translate these representations into social categories through boundary work; and then establish institutional structures for exploitation and opportunity hoarding that correspond to categorical boundaries, thereby generating unequal access to resources such as financial capital, human capital, social capital, and cultural capital. . . .

Markets and Stratification

The mechanisms of stratification described so far do not presuppose any particular economic system. They can function in a command economy, where property is owned by the state and decisions about production and consumption are made by central planners, or in a capitalist economy, where property is privately held and decisions about production and consumption are made by free and autonomous agents working through markets. Stratification and inequality are not created by capitalism, and the existence of markets does not guarantee inequality; nor does their absence preclude it. Markets are a human invention, and until recently most transactions occurred outside the market. Stratification has been with us, however, for millennia (Massey 2005a).

Markets are basically competitions between people that occur within socially constructed arenas according to socially defined rules using a socially accepted medium of exchange (Massey 2005b). By building the competitive arenas, defining the rules of play, and defining the media of exchange, societies bring markets into existence to facilitate the production, consumption, and distribution of goods and services. If markets are socially constructed by actors within the societies in which they are embedded, then there is no inherently correct number, distribution, or nature of markets. As societies change socially, demographically, and culturally, as new technologies emerge, and as new knowledge is created, the nature and number of markets change.

For transactions to occur, buyers and sellers must come together within a mutually accepted arena. Sometimes the arena is delimited physically (such as the trading pit in the New York Stock Exchange), and at other times it is geographically diffuse (as with NASDAQ, where securities are traded electronically in hyperspace). But competitive arenas are always defined *socially* by mutually agreed-upon rules, both formal and informal, that govern transactions. As markets have evolved and expanded, the rules have increasingly shifted from the informal to the formal realm (Carruthers and Babb 2000).

Formal rules are laws and regulations that are written down by political authorities to recognize private property, define the rights of buyers and sellers, establish a basis for the execution and enforcement of contracts, and define acceptable behaviors within a competitive arena. Informal rules are unwritten codes of conduct and practice that are implicitly understood by market participants and reinforced through mechanisms of enforceable trust such as ridicule, gossip, shaming, exclusion, and ostracism. Whereas some markets are predominantly formal (such as U.S. mortgage markets), others remain highly informal (for example, the global diamond trade). Most markets, however, remain mixtures of formal and informal mechanisms (jobs and hiring).

In addition to being supported by a social infrastructure of laws, regulations, expectations, and conventions, competitive arenas often require a physical infrastructure (Massey 2005b). The necessary infrastructure may be erected by public or private efforts, but it is generally achieved by a mixture of the two. Whereas private interests may finance the construction of factories to produce consumer goods, for example, the public builds highways and ports and subsidizes air and rail travel, which enables producers to bring the goods to market. A core responsibility of the state is to make sure, by some combination of public and private means, that the physical and social infrastructure necessary for markets is created and maintained.

The final task of the state is to establish a secure medium of exchange (Massey 2005b). The invention of something called "money" is not inherent in the logic of the market. Rather, the idea of money was invented independently and then imposed on markets through a long series of trials and errors that only gradually revealed the most effective course of action (Davies 2002). . . .

Markets came into existence because human beings created social structures, innovated cultural understandings, built competitive arenas, defined formal and informal rules of competition, and specified media of exchange to allow for the production, distribution, and consumption of goods and services. Because markets are always embedded within a particular constellation of social institutions and cultural conventions (Granovetter 1985; Swedberg 2003), there is no single way to create a functioning market society and no unique architecture for successful market relations (Fligstein 2001; Hall and Soskice 2002; Whitley 1999). It all depends on the institutional context within which a market is working (Massey, Sanchez, and Behrman 2006).

From the viewpoint of stratification, the competitive arenas, rules of competition, and media of exchange may be structured by social actors so as to produce more or less inequality—either to maximize the opportunities for exploitation and opportunity hoarding or to minimize them. Whatever their institutional foundations, however, markets enhance the *potential* for stratification by increasing the total stock of material resources and multiplying the number of social categories across which they are distributed. Having more resources spread across a larger number of social categories yields greater inequality, and history has clearly shown that markets produce more wealth and income than other economic systems, other things equal.

Although economic growth under market mechanisms may increase the potential for stratification and inequality by accelerating income accumulation, wealth creation, and social differentiation relative to other economic systems, *how* the resulting wealth is distributed across categories within the underlying social structure is not predetermined. The distribution of material resources depends very much on choices made by social actors in creating the institutions and practices that underlie the market. Exploitation and opportunity hoarding may be built into the way a market functions if they are embedded within the institutional matrix that contains the market (Massey 2005b).

Categorical inequality results whenever those in power enact policies and practices to give certain groups more access to markets than others; offer competitive advantages to certain classes of people within markets; protect certain groups from market failures more often than others; invest more in the human capital of certain groups than others; and systematically channel social and cultural capital to certain categories of people. Historically, many social groups in the United States were excluded from markets as a matter of both formal policy and informal practice. . . .

Before people can compete effectively in markets, of course, they must be prepared for competition through the deliberate cultivation of human, social, and cultural capital. Human capabilities are generally created through some mixture of public and private auspices. The private institution most fundamentally and universally involved in producing capable human beings is the family (Folbre 2001). Within families, children are born, fed, housed, clothed, and taught. Within the confines of the family, people learn to walk, speak, behave, and think. As a result of structured instruction and unstructured emulation, children learn to value and follow certain patterns of thought and action and to devalue and shun others.

As the size and complexity of human populations have increased, however, other social institutions have assumed larger roles in the creation and enhancement of human capabilities, and in the last quarter of the twentieth century the importance of nonfamily institutions increased dramatically (Massey 2005a). Industrialization created new needs for literate workers and led governments to require and provide primary and secondary schooling to citizens on a mass basis. The recent shift to a knowledge-based information economy has further accelerated the rate of investment in post-graduate education, research, and lifetime training. In advanced market societies, a critical responsibility of government is to ensure levels of education and training that not only will permit citizens to participate effectively in a growing array of complex markets but also will promote the sustained growth of income and the continued creation of wealth in a competitive global economy. . . .

Finally, markets can never achieve all the goals that citizens would like to see accomplished, nor are they foolproof mechanisms for the seamless production, distribution, and consumption of resources. The history of capitalism is replete with examples of failed, missing, and ineffective markets. Although improvements in institutions and technology have reduced the depth and frequency of market failures, the hazard can never be eliminated entirely from a capitalist economy. In response, most developed nations have erected social "safety nets"—aid programs such as unemployment insurance, welfare payments, medical insurance, old-age benefits, and food subsidies—to prevent citizens from falling too far down the economic ladder. Once again, however, the eligibility rules and regulations for social benefits in the United States were historically written to exclude certain social groups and favor others. In enacting most of the social welfare provisions of the New Deal, for example, laws were written in such a way as to minimize participation by African Americans (Katznelson 2005; Quadagno 1994).

Massey, Douglas S. *Categorically Unequal*. © 2007 Russell Sage Foundation, 112 East 64th Street, New York, NY 10021. Reprinted with permission.

Goodbye, Horatio Alger

Moving up Economically Is Now Impossible for Many, If Not Most, Americans

JEFF MADRICK

The Democratic pragmatists in Congress are so wedded to their middle-of-the-road attitudes about government social programs, which some of them insist won them victory in November, that they seem incapable of seeing the economic state of the nation for what it has sadly become. To put it simply, the Democratic majority that took control of Congress in January is inheriting a class society. Today in America, one's birth largely determines one's future.

We may quibble about the exact threshold over which a nation must pass to be described as a class society, but the latest research on income mobility is startling. As economists Isabel Sawhill and Sara McLanahan state in the fall volume of the journal they edit, *The Future of Children,* the American ideal of a classless society "is one in which all children have a roughly equal chance of success regardless of the economic status of the family into which they were born." In sum, they write, "the association between one's parents' income and one's own should be small."

But that is not the case in America. Only a couple of decades ago, economists thought that in the land of Horatio Alger, only 20 percent of one's future income was determined by one's father's income, a conclusion that University of Chicago economic Nobelist Gary Becker, among others, hailed as proof of the fairness and health of the American economic model. More sophisticated research in the 1990s, however, suggested that the relationship between incomes of fathers and their sons was closer to 40 percent—disheartening if true. Some relationship between intergenerational incomes is to be expected through biological inheritance, cultural privilege and the passing on of social norms, but at 40 percent, the Chicago school argument took a serious blow.

Now, based on new data gathered in the past few years, some economists, led by Bhashkar Mazumder of the Federal Reserve Bank of Chicago, argue that 60 percent of a son's income is determined by the level of income of the father. For women, it is roughly the same. Sixty percent is a shocking number, and some economists want to await further research, but Mazumder's methodology is persuasive. At the least, the estimate of a 40 percent correlation is likely too low.

Still, has mobility declined in recent decades? Mazumder and others think it has. Their research finds that the correlation of income between generations rose markedly in the 1980s and '90s. Again, not all economists agree, but most of those doing research in the area do concede that income mobility today is greater in many European countries than it is in America. My guess is that few in Congress, or in the media for that matter, believe that yet. Reality dawns slowly on unwilling eyes.

The findings would not be as disturbing, of course, if incomes had been growing about equally for all levels of Americans over the past quarter-century. But income inequality has risen since the 1970s to the levels of the Roaring Twenties. For example, the income of the top fifth of American households after inflation has risen by 50 percent since the late 1970s, the next fifth by only about 20 percent and the middle fifth by only 10 percent or so. A gain of 10 or even 20 percent over roughly a quarter-century is close to trivial, and the income of those in the bottom fifth did not increase at all over this period. By contrast, throughout American industrial history, incomes grew 30 to 50 percent or more every quarter-century, and in the quarter-century after World War II, gains reached more than 100 percent for all income categories. Since the late 1970s, only the top 1 percent of households increased their income by 100 percent.

Thus, an American worker in the 1950s and '60s could improve his or her standard of living significantly even without rising in the hierarchy, because incomes increased handsomely for all levels of earners. To do well now, you've got to climb the pyramid, as conservatives until recently could insist Americans did. It is now clear that many, probably most, cannot.

What's going on? First, the nature of the economy changed beginning in the 1970s, and median wages, for a variety of reasons, largely stagnated. For men alone, they declined.

Second, to make it to the middle class—or stay there—a college degree increasingly became a requirement. College was a new and expensive cost for those climbing into the middle class.

And third, as the economy changed and society evolved, government essentially sat it out. The influence of a neoliberal ideology of minimal government was effectively promulgated by Ronald Reagan and economists led by Milton Friedman. Generally slow economic growth since the early 1970s also meant lower federal tax revenues, which the Reagan and Bush tax cuts reduced even further. The Republicans did not succeed in cutting the absolute size of government, largely because entitlement programs like Medicare and Medicaid grew, but both Republicans and Democrats were party to what amounted to a sharp reversal of the progressive history in America, in which government since 1900 had been an active, constructive force to help people adapt to changing and difficult economic circumstances.

No doubt, government programs by the 1970s and '80s required reform, pruning and some serious rethinking. But the government activism that started with Teddy Roosevelt did not dampen prosperity, and effective and concerned government policy would not have done so in the past quarter-century either. To the contrary, during the progressive first three-quarters of the twentieth century, the nation grew faster than it has since the Reagan revolution. Americans swallowed such laissez-faire illusions before, notably in the late 1800s and the 1920s, and the promises turned out as empty then as they are today.

Today the United States is two nations, but not so much divided between rich and poor, as former Senator John Edwards puts it, as between the well-educated and the rest. A college degree is not a guarantee of a middle-class life, but it has become pretty close to a necessity. And a college degree is expensive, even for those who attend public institutions. The demand for ever more education is not new in our history. But when Americans first needed a good primary education in the mid-1800s, state and local governments provided it, and made sure it was also available in poorer communities. Along with the distribution of land, free primary schooling was among the first income redistribution programs in the nation. In the early 1900s, when Americans needed high schools, state and local governments built thousands across the land, and graduation rates soared. In the second half of the nineteenth century, the federal government also actively supported new land-grant colleges, which became the basis of a state university system. The federal and state governments never went as far as they did with high school, however, and today the nation still treats higher education as if it is a privilege. There is federal and state aid, but increasingly it comes in the form of loans, leaving graduates even of state and community institutions burdened with record levels of debt. And tuition and room and board at private universities has risen considerably faster than has aid, even in the form of loans.

Economists Timothy Smeeding and Robert Haveman report in an essay in *The Future of Children* that the median income of workers with a bachelor's degree or higher is about double the income for those with only a high school diploma, and that more than 40 percent of all new jobs now require a college degree. The Census Bureau figures college graduates will earn about $2.5 million over their lifetimes in today's dollars, compared with $1.5 million for high school graduates. Those with advanced degrees will earn a lot more.

The differences are especially stark for men. Male high school graduates have weathered a sharp fall of about 15 percent in their median wages since the 1970s. Median wages of men with college degrees have risen some 14 percent—nothing to crow about, frankly, but nevertheless leaving a wide gap between them and their high school graduate peers.

It would be comforting if economists fully understood why this is happening, because it might help us understand what social policies to adopt. One of the obvious causes is deindustrialization—the loss of manufacturing jobs in particular, which once paid high school graduates well, provided good benefits and pensions, and often turned out to be jobs for life. But why has deindustrialization occurred? Globalization, including foreign competition from low-wage nations like China, the offshoring of good jobs to nations like India and the rapid flow of capital to good investment opportunities in foreign lands, certainly contributes to the education wage gap. But the loss of middle-class jobs for high school graduates started long before trade and offshoring became so influential.

Today the United States is two nations, but not so much divided between rich and poor as between the well-educated and the rest.

Most economists, in fact, ascribe the shift in the demand for college graduates to changing technologies, as Information Age businesses require sophisticated workers with better educations. But the case for "skill bias technology" is suspiciously fashionable and oversimplified. A more mundane and convincing variant of the hypothesis is that America has become an office economy of white-collar workers, whose growth industries include finance, marketing, consulting, public relations, healthcare and the media, all of which generally require workers with college educations, and the social skills often acquired there (or required to gain admission). A final argument too often neglected is also credible: Federal policies have restrained growth and kept unemployment too high on average for a generation, resulting in an excess supply of labor that has enabled employers to pick and choose workers with the best qualifications, even when workers with those qualifications are not needed. High rates of unemployment also helped business and its allies in the government win the battle against union power. Meanwhile, those without a college degree are often consigned to low-wage jobs, especially punishing over a generation in which the government refused to raise the minimum wage to keep up with inflation.

Whatever the reasons, some could argue that this transformation to a college-based labor market is in fact pretty terrific. College can indeed be the great equalizer: Be disciplined, study and go to college, and you will be just fine. And Americans did respond. About 26 percent of all Americans over 25 have a bachelor's or more today, compared to 14 percent in 1975. About 40 percent of all those between 25 and 34 have a college degree or higher.

But because of high expenses and inadequate aid, among other causes, the march toward ever higher college graduation rates has stalled in America over the past two decades, and other nations are catching up or even surpassing American levels. Among those aged 25 to 34, Canada, Japan, Finland and Korea boast higher college graduation rates, with another handful of nations just behind the United States and gaining fast.

More important, fewer middle-income and poor kids go to college, get into a good college or finish college than better-off kids. To put it simply, going to college also depends on who your parents are. Had the nation adequately enrolled its lower-income students in solid four-year programs, the nation's college graduation rate would still lead the world by a handsome margin. But to the contrary, college attendance has not enabled lower-income Americans to escape their class in the way promised. Rather, the process reinforces class disparities.

For example, four out of five high school graduates from the top-income quintile enroll in college after they graduate from high school, compared with only two in five from the bottom quintile. Even when lower-income children have the same test scores, go to similar schools and have the same class rankings, they are significantly less likely to go to college. Poorer students tend to cluster in two-year community colleges, and when they do go to four-year colleges, they finish less frequently than better-off students.

As for going to a good college, family background is even more important. One study ranked colleges into four tiers and broke families into quarters according to their socioeconomic status (family income, occupation and parental education). Only 3 percent of those students in the lowest quarter of families attended a tier-one school, while 74 percent of those from the top quarter of families did. By contrast, 21 percent of those in the bottom quarter attended a community college.

The issue is not merely how much it costs to go to college. Researchers point out that the well-off have more money to spend on developing their children's abilities and interests, and on prepping them for college entrance exams; they expose them to more books and other intellectual stimuli at an early age; they are more aware of how the college admissions process works; and they can afford to send their children to better primary and secondary schools.

Reform, then, is not just a matter of making college more affordable. Evidence that high-quality preschool programs work to improve children's educational capacities is now overwhelming. Thus, policies to make high-quality pre-K education universally available should be a high priority in America. K–12 education generally requires serious improvements, especially in poorer neighborhoods. There can also be many useful reforms of college subsidization without increasing federal funds. Smeeding and Haveman propose a number of such reforms, including funneling state assistance directly to low-income students rather than to the institutions themselves.

I n sum, the dirty little secret is that the central role of college in getting a good job is now probably reinforcing a class society, not leveling it. Add to this the disparity in educational quality for pre-K and K–12, and we are getting to the heart of the matter. This is essentially why Bhashkar Mazumder and his colleagues are probably right when they argue statistically that mobility has declined in modern America. As Smeeding and Haveman summarize, "Though college attendance rates are rising, college graduation rates are growing slowly, if at all, and changes in the composition of the college-eligible and college graduating populations appear to perpetuate existing class differences."

I am not saying that improving access to good education is alone the answer to America's class disparities. But it is the central one. In the nation today, a college education provides access to a decent job. And the way the nation has organized itself, adequate health insurance and a decent retirement income also depend on the quality and duration of one's job. Nearly 24 percent of American workers with only a high school diploma, for example, have no health insurance, compared with less than 10 percent of those with college degrees. For high school graduates who have just entered the job market, both healthcare and pension coverage have plunged since the 1970s.

Again, let me emphasize that college is not a panacea. Healthcare and pension coverage have also declined for college graduates, though not as dramatically. And incomes are by no means rising rapidly for typical college graduates, especially men. Moreover, even for them, incomes are growing in a highly unequal way, and American economic life has become less secure. But college graduates are the ones who have a reasonable chance to make it through to a full and decent life. And to produce more college graduates, improvements must begin with early childhood and, arguably, even with prenatal care, and move up the ladder, including K–12.

Despite the anti-Republican rhetoric of some of the Democratic leadership, little in the agenda of the new Democratic majority so far will change these prospects. The strategy of the new majority may admittedly be a sensible one: Make a few broadly acceptable policy reforms, such as raising the minimum wage, modestly raising college subsidies and getting some drug costs down. Then, win the presidency in 2008, and at last begin to address the enormous challenges left to the nation by twenty-five years of substantial neglect.

That of course is the optimistic view of well-meaning legislators. And some are talking seriously about bolder programs down the road. Senator Edward Kennedy, now chair of the Senate Committee on Health, Education, Labor and Pensions, has proposed forgiving all college loans after ten years if graduates enter public service professions, for example. John Edwards, now running for President, has made universal healthcare a centerpiece of his campaign. Kennedy has proposed a Medicare-for-all universal healthcare program in his book *America Back on Track* (I worked on the book with him). Several states, now possibly including California, are taking the lead in providing universal healthcare to residents.

But the federal programs needed are decidedly on the legislative back burner. It seems that too many Democrats, arguably

the most influential of them, are themselves sincerely skeptical of government and are unwilling to raise the tax money to
do the job properly. Even if they see clearly how the state of
the nation has decayed, many simply believe it is politically
unwise to bring the issues out of the shadows. Meantime, the
American promise is being betrayed, and no one knows the
level of cynicism this will generate over time in a large portion of the population. We may expect a blithe and even san-
guine attitude toward the true state of the economy from the
old Republican majority. But too many Democrats neglect the
urgency of the nation's challenges. Class war? If it is necessary to make America a just and equal society again, yes.
You bet.

JEFF MADRICK, editor of *Challenge* magazine and director of policy research at the Schwartz Center for Economic Policy Analysis at
the New School, is writing a history of the American economy since
1970.

The Myth of the "Culture of Poverty"

Instead of accepting myths that harm low-income students, we need to eradicate the systemwide inequities that stand in their way.

PAUL GORSKI

As the students file out of Janet's classroom, I sit in the back corner, scribbling a few final notes. Defeat in her eyes, Janet drops into a seat next to me with a sigh.

"I love these kids," she declares, as if trying to convince me. "I adore them. But my hope is fading."

"Why's that?" I ask, stuffing my notes into a folder.

"They're smart. I know they're smart, but . . . "

And then the deficit floodgates open: "They don't care about school. They're unmotivated. And their parents—I'm lucky if two or three of them show up for conferences. No wonder the kids are unprepared to learn."

At Janet's invitation, I spent dozens of hours in her classroom, meeting her students, observing her teaching, helping her navigate the complexities of an urban midwestern elementary classroom with a growing percentage of students in poverty. I observed powerful moments of teaching and learning, caring and support. And I witnessed moments of internal conflict in Janet, when what she wanted to believe about her students collided with her prejudices.

Like most educators, Janet is determined to create an environment in which each student reaches his or her full potential. And like many of us, despite overflowing with good intentions, Janet has bought into the most common and dangerous myths about poverty.

Chief among these is the "culture of poverty" myth—the idea that poor people share more or less monolithic and predictable beliefs, values, and behaviors. For educators like Janet to be the best teachers they can be for all students, they need to challenge this myth and reach a deeper understanding of class and poverty.

Roots of the Culture of Poverty Concept

Oscar Lewis coined the term *culture of poverty* in his 1961 book *The Children of Sanchez*. Lewis based his thesis on his ethnographic studies of small Mexican communities. His studies uncovered approximately 50 attributes shared within these communities: frequent violence, a lack of a sense of history, a neglect of planning for the future, and so on. Despite studying very small communities, Lewis extrapolated his findings to suggest a universal culture of poverty. More than 45 years later, the premise of the culture of poverty paradigm remains the same: that people in poverty share a consistent and observable "culture."

Lewis ignited a debate about the nature of poverty that continues today. But just as important—especially in the age of data-driven decision making—he inspired a flood of research. Researchers around the world tested the culture of poverty concept empirically (see Billings, 1974; Carmon, 1985; Jones & Luo, 1999). Others analyzed the overall body of evidence regarding the culture of poverty paradigm (see Abell & Lyon, 1979; Ortiz & Briggs, 2003; Rodman, 1977).

These studies raise a variety of questions and come to a variety of conclusions about poverty. But on this they all agree: *There is no such thing as a culture of poverty.* Differences in values and behaviors among poor people are just as great as those between poor and wealthy people.

In actuality, the culture of poverty concept is constructed from a collection of smaller stereotypes which, however false, seem to have crept into mainstream thinking as unquestioned fact. Let's look at some examples.

Myth: Poor people are unmotivated and have weak work ethics.

The Reality: Poor people do not have weaker work ethics or lower levels of motivation than wealthier people (Iversen & Farber, 1996; Wilson, 1997). Although poor people are often stereotyped as lazy, 83 percent of children from low-income families have at least one employed parent; close to 60 percent have at least one parent who works full-time and year-round (National Center for Children in Poverty, 2004). In fact, the severe shortage of living-wage jobs means that many poor adults must work two, three, or four jobs. According to the Economic Policy Institute (2002), poor working adults spend more hours working each week than their wealthier counterparts.

Myth: Poor parents are uninvolved in their children's learning, largely because they do not value education.

The Reality: Low-income parents hold the same attitudes about education that wealthy parents do (Compton-Lilly, 2003; Lareau & Horvat, 1999; Leichter, 1978). Low-income parents are less likely to attend school functions or volunteer in their children's classrooms (National Center for Education Statistics, 2005)—not because they care less about education, but because they have less access to school involvement than their wealthier peers. They are more likely to work multiple jobs, to work evenings, to have jobs without paid leave, and to be unable to afford child care and public transportation. It might be said more accurately that schools that fail to take these considerations into account do not value the involvement of poor families as much as they value the involvement of other families.

Myth: Poor people are linguistically deficient.

The Reality: All people, regardless of the languages and language varieties they speak, use a full continuum of language registers (Bomer, Dworin, May, & Semingson, 2008). What's more, linguists have known for decades that all language varieties are highly structured with complex grammatical rules (Gee, 2004; Hess, 1974; Miller, Cho, & Bracey, 2005). What often are assumed to be *deficient* varieties of English—Appalachian varieties, perhaps, or what some refer to as Black English Vernacular—are no less sophisticated than so-called "standard English."

Myth: Poor people tend to abuse drugs and alcohol.

The Reality: Poor people are no more likely than their wealthier counterparts to abuse alcohol or drugs. Although drug sales are more visible in poor neighborhoods, drug use is equally distributed across poor, middle class, and wealthy communities (Saxe, Kadushin, Tighe, Rindskopf, & Beveridge, 2001). Chen, Sheth, Krejci, and Wallace (2003) found that alcohol consumption is significantly higher among upper middle class white high school students than among poor black high school students. Their finding supports a history of research showing that alcohol abuse is far more prevalent among wealthy people than among poor people (Diala, Muntaner, & Walrath, 2004; Galea, Ahern, Tracy, & Vlahov, 2007). In other words, considering alcohol and illicit drugs together, wealthy people are more likely than poor people to be substance abusers.

The Culture of Classism

The myth of a "culture of poverty" distracts us from a dangerous culture that does exist—the culture of classism. This culture continues to harden in our schools today. It leads the most well intentioned of us, like my friend Janet, into low expectations for low-income students. It makes teachers fear their most powerless pupils. And, worst of all, it diverts attention from what people in poverty *do* have in common: inequitable access to basic human rights.

The most destructive tool of the culture of classism is deficit theory. In education, we often talk about the deficit perspective—defining students by their weaknesses rather than their strengths. Deficit theory takes this attitude a step further, suggesting that poor people are poor because of their own moral and intellectual deficiencies (Collins, 1988). Deficit theorists use two strategies for propagating this world view: (1) drawing on well-established stereotypes, and (2) ignoring systemic conditions, such as inequitable access to high-quality schooling, that support the cycle of poverty.

The implications of deficit theory reach far beyond individual bias. If we convince ourselves that poverty results not from gross inequities (in which we might be complicit) but from poor people's own deficiencies, we are much less likely to support authentic antipoverty policy and programs. Further, if we believe, however wrongly, that poor people don't value education, then we dodge any responsibility to redress the gross education inequities with which they contend. This application of deficit theory establishes the idea of what Gans (1995) calls the *undeserving poor*—a segment of our society that simply does not deserve a fair shake.

If the goal of deficit theory is to justify a system that privileges economically advantaged students at the expense of working-class and poor students, then it appears to be working marvelously. In our determination to "fix" the mythical culture of poor students, we ignore the ways in which our society cheats them out of opportunities that their wealthier peers take for granted. We ignore the fact that poor people suffer disproportionately the effects of nearly every major social ill. They lack access to health care, living-wage jobs, safe and affordable housing, clean air and water, and so on (Books, 2004)—conditions that limit their abilities to achieve to their full potential.

Perhaps most of us, as educators, feel powerless to address these bigger issues. But the question is this: Are we willing, at the very least, to tackle the classism in our own schools and classrooms?

The myth of a "culture of poverty" distracts us from a dangerous culture that does exist—the culture of classism.

This classism is plentiful and well documented (Kozol, 1992). For example, compared with their wealthier peers, poor students are more likely to attend schools that have less funding (Carey, 2005); lower teacher salaries (Karoly, 2001); more limited computer and Internet access (Gorski, 2003); larger class sizes; higher student-to-teacher ratios; a less-rigorous curriculum; and fewer experienced teachers (Barton, 2004). The National Commission on Teaching and America's Future (2004) also found that low-income schools were more likely to suffer from cockroach or rat infestation, dirty or inoperative student bathrooms, large numbers of teacher vacancies and substitute teachers, more teachers who are not licensed in their subject areas, insufficient or outdated classroom materials, and inadequate or nonexistent learning facilities, such as science labs.

Here in Minnesota, several school districts offer universal half-day kindergarten but allow those families that can afford to do so to pay for full-day services. Our poor students scarcely make it out of early childhood without paying the price for our culture of classism. Deficit theory requires us to ignore these inequities—or worse, to see them as normal and justified.

What does this mean? Regardless of how much students in poverty value education, they must overcome tremendous inequities to learn. Perhaps the greatest myth of all is the one that dubs education the "great equalizer." Without considerable change, it cannot be anything of the sort.

What Can We Do?

The socioeconomic opportunity gap can be eliminated only when we stop trying to "fix" poor students and start addressing the ways in which our schools perpetuate classism. This includes destroying the inequities listed above as well as abolishing such practices as tracking and ability grouping, segregational redistricting, and the privatization of public schools. We must demand the best possible education for all students—higher-order pedagogies, innovative learning materials, and holistic teaching and learning. But first, we must demand basic human rights for all people: adequate housing and health care, living-wage jobs, and so on.

Of course, we ought not tell students who suffer today that, if they can wait for this education revolution, everything will fall into place. So as we prepare ourselves for bigger changes, we must

- Educate ourselves about class and poverty.
- Reject deficit theory and help students and colleagues unlearn misperceptions about poverty.
- Make school involvement accessible to all families.
- Follow Janet's lead, inviting colleagues to observe our teaching for signs of class bias.
- Continue reaching out to low-income families even when they appear unresponsive (and without assuming, if they are unresponsive, that we know why).
- Respond when colleagues stereotype poor students or parents.
- Never assume that all students have equitable access to such learning resources as computers and the Internet, and never assign work requiring this access without providing in-school time to complete it.
- Ensure that learning materials do not stereotype poor people.
- Fight to keep low-income students from being assigned unjustly to special education or low academic tracks.
- Make curriculum relevant to poor students, drawing on and validating their experiences and intelligences.
- Teach about issues related to class and poverty—including consumer culture, the dissolution of labor unions, and environmental injustice—and about movements for class equity.
- Teach about the antipoverty work of Martin Luther King Jr., Helen Keller, the Black Panthers, César Chávez,

and other U.S. icons—and about why this dimension of their legacies has been erased from our national consciousness.
- Fight to ensure that school meal programs offer healthy options.
- Examine proposed corporate-school partnerships, rejecting those that require the adoption of specific curriculums or pedagogies.

Most important, we must consider how our own class biases affect our interactions with and expectations of our students. And then we must ask ourselves, Where, in reality, does the deficit lie? Does it lie in poor people, the most disenfranchised people among us? Does it lie in the education system itself—in, as Jonathan Kozol says, the savage inequalities of our schools? Or does it lie in us—educators with unquestionably good intentions who too often fall to the temptation of the quick fix, the easily digestible framework that never requires us to consider how we comply with the culture of classism.

References

Abell, T., & Lyon, L. (1979). Do the differences make a difference? An empirical evaluation of the culture of poverty in the United States. *American Anthropologist, 6*(3), 602–621.

Barton, R. E. (2004). Why does the gap persist? *Educational Leadership, 62*(3), 8–13.

Billings, D. (1974). Culture and poverty in Appalachia: A theoretical discussion and empirical analysis. *Social Forces, 53*(2), 315–323.

Bomer, R., Dworin, J. E., May, L., & Semingson, R. (2008). Miseducating teachers about the poor: A critical analysis of Ruby Payne's claims about poverty. *Teachers College Record,* 110(11). Available: www.tcrecord.org/PrintContent.asp?ContentID=14591

Books, S. (2004). *Poverty and schooling in the U.S.: Contexts and consequences.* Mahway, NJ: Erlbaum.

Carey, K. (2005). *The funding gap 2004: Many states still shortchange low-income and minority students.* Washington, DC: Education Trust.

Carmon, N. (1985). Poverty and culture. *Sociological Perspectives, 28*(4), 403–418.

Chen, K., Sheth, A., Krejci, J., & Wallace, J. (2003, August). *Understanding differences in alcohol use among high school students in two different communities.* Paper presented at the annual meeting of the American Sociological Association, Atlanta, GA.

Collins, J. (1988). Language and class in minority education. *Anthropology and Education Quarterly, 19*(4), 299–326.

Compton-Lilly, C. (2003). *Reading families: The literate lives of urban children.* New York: Teachers College Press.

Diala, C. C., Muntaner, C., & Walrath, C. (2004). Gender, occupational, and socioeconomic correlates of alcohol and drug abuse among U.S. rural, metropolitan, and urban residents. *American Journal of Drug and Alcohol Abuse, 30*(2), 409–428.

Economic Policy Institute. (2002). *The state of working class America* 2002–03. Washington, DC: Author.

Galea, S., Ahern, J., Tracy, M., & Vlahov, D. (2007). Neighborhood income and income distribution and the use of cigarettes, alcohol, and marijuana. *American Journal of Preventive Medicine, 32*(6), 195–202.

Gans, H. J. (1995). *The war against the poor: The underclass and antipoverty policy.* New York: BasicBooks.

Gee, J. R (2004). *Situated language and learning: A critique of traditional schooling.* New York: Routledge.

Gorski, R. C. (2003). Privilege and repression in the digital era: Rethinking the sociopolitics of the digital divide. *Race, Gender and Class,* 10(4), 145–176.

Hess, K. M. (1974). The nonstandard speakers in our schools: What should be done? *The Elementary School Journal,* 74(5), 280–290.

Iversen, R. R., & Farber, N. (1996). Transmission of family values, work, and welfare among poor urban black women. *Work and Occupations,* 23(4), 437–460.

Jones, R. K., & Luo, Y. (1999). The culture of poverty and African-American culture: An empirical assessment. *Sociological Perspectives,* 42(3), 439–458.

Karoly, L. A. (2001). Investing in the future: Reducing poverty through human capital investments. In S. Danzinger & R. Haveman (Eds.), *Undemanding poverty* (pp. 314–356). New York: Russell Sage Foundation.

Kozol, J. (1992). *Savage inequalities. Children in America's schools.* New York: Harper-Collins.

Lareau, A., & Horvat, E. (1999). Moments of social inclusion and exclusion: Race, class, and cultural capital in family-school relationships. *Sociology of Education,* 72, 37–53.

Leichter, H. J. (Ed.). (1978). *Families and communities as educators.* New York: Teachers College Press.

Lewis, O. (1961). *The children of Sanchez: Autobiography of a Mexican family.* New York: Random House.

Miller, R. J., Cho, G. E., & Bracey, J. R. (2005). Working-class children's experience through the prism of personal story-telling. *Human Development,* 48, 115–135.

National Center for Children in Poverty. (2004). *Parental employment in low-income families.* New York: Author.

National Center for Education Statistics. (2005). *Parent and family involvement in education:* 2002–03. Washington, DC: Author.

National Commission on Teaching and America's Future. (2004). *Fifty years after* Brown v. Board of Education: *A two-tiered education system.* Washington, DC: Author.

Ortiz, A. T., & Briggs, L. (2003). The culture of poverty, crack babies, and welfare cheats: The making of the "healthy white baby crisis." *Social Text,* 21(3), 39–57.

Rodman, R. (1977). Culture of poverty: The rise and fall of a concept. *Sociological Review,* 25(4), 867–876.

Saxe, L., Kadushin, C., Tighe, E., Rindskopf, D., & Beveridge, A. (2001). *National evaluation of the fighting back program: General population surveys, 1995–1999.* New York: City University of New York Graduate Center.

Wilson, W. J. (1997). *When work disappears.* New York: Random House.

PAUL GORSKI is Assistant Professor in the Graduate School of Education, Hamline University, St. Paul, Minnesota, and the founder of EdChange (www.edchange.org).

Can Extreme Poverty Be Eliminated?

Market economics and globalization are lifting the bulk of humanity out of extreme poverty, but special measures are needed to help the poorest of the poor.

JEFFREY D. SACHS

Almost everyone who ever lived was wretchedly poor. Famine, death from childbirth, infectious disease and countless other hazards were the norm for most of history. Humanity's sad plight started to change with the Industrial Revolution, beginning around 1750. New scientific insights and technological innovations enabled a growing proportion of the global population to break free of extreme poverty.

Two and a half centuries later more than five billion of the world's 6.5 billion people can reliably meet their basic living needs and thus can be said to have escaped from the precarious conditions that once governed everyday life. One out of six inhabitants of this planet, however, still struggles daily to meet some or all of such critical requirements as adequate nutrition, uncontaminated drinking water, safe shelter and sanitation as well as access to basic health care. These people get by on $1 a day or less and are overlooked by public services for health, education and infrastructure. Every day more than 20,000 die of dire poverty, for want of food, safe drinking water, medicine or other essential needs.

For the first time in history, global economic prosperity, brought on by continuing scientific and technological progress and the self-reinforcing accumulation of wealth, has placed the world within reach of eliminating extreme poverty altogether. This prospect will seem fanciful to some, but the dramatic economic progress made by China, India and other low-income parts of Asia over the past 25 years demonstrates that it is realistic. Moreover, the predicted stabilization of the world's population toward the middle of this century will help by easing pressures on Earth's climate, ecosystems and natural resources—pressures that might otherwise undo economic gains.

EXTREME POVERTY could become a thing of the past in a few decades if the affluent countries of the world pony up a small percentage of their wealth to help the planet's 1.1 billion indigent population out of conditions of dire poverty.

Although economic growth has shown a remarkable capacity to lift vast numbers of people out of extreme poverty, progress is neither automatic nor inevitable. Market forces and free trade are not enough. Many of the poorest regions are ensnared in a poverty trap: they lack the financial means to make the necessary investments in infrastructure, education, health care systems and other vital needs. Yet the end of such poverty is feasible if a concerted global effort is undertaken, as the nations of the world promised when they adopted the Millennium Development Goals at the United Nations Millennium Summit in 2000. A dedicated cadre of development agencies, international financial institutions, nongovernmental organizations and communities throughout the developing world already constitute a global network of expertise and goodwill to help achieve this objective.

This past January my colleagues and I on the U.N. Millennium Project published a plan to halve the rate of extreme poverty by 2015 (compared with 1990) and to achieve other quantitative targets for reducing hunger, disease and environmental degradation. In my recent book, *The End of Poverty,* I argue that a large-scale and targeted public investment effort could in fact eliminate this problem by 2025, much as smallpox was eradicated globally. This hypothesis is controversial, so I am pleased to have the opportunity to clarify its main arguments and to respond to various concerns that have been raised about it.

Beyond Business as Usual

Economists have learned a great deal during the past few years about how countries develop and what roadblocks can stand in their way. A new kind of development economics needs to emerge, one that is better grounded in science—a "clinical economics" akin to modern medicine. Today's medical professionals understand that disease results from a vast array of interacting factors and conditions: pathogens, nutrition, environment, aging, individual and population genetics, lifestyle. They also know that one key to proper treatment is the ability to make an individualized diagnosis of the source of illness. Likewise, development economists need better diagnostic skills

Crossroads for Poverty

The Problem:

- Much of humankind has succeeded in dragging itself out of severe poverty since the onset of the Industrial Revolution in the mid-18th century, but about 1.1 billion out of today's 6.5 billion global inhabitants are utterly destitute in a world of plenty.
- These unfortunates, who get by on less than $1 a day, have little access to adequate nutrition, safe drinking water and shelter, as well as basic sanitation and health care services. What can the developed world do to lift this huge segment of the human population out of extreme poverty?

The Plan:

- Doubling affluent nations' international poverty assistance to about $160 billion a year would go a long way toward ameliorating the terrible predicament faced by one in six humans. This figure would constitute about 0.5 percent of the gross national product (GNP) of the planet's rich countries. Because these investments do not include other categories of aid, such as spending on major infrastructure projects, climate change mitigation or post conflict reconstruction, donors should commit to reaching the long standing target of 0.7 percent of GNP by 2015.
- These donations, often provided to local groups, would need to be closely monitored and audited to ensure that they are correctly targeted toward those truly in need.

to recognize that economic pathologies have a wide variety of causes, including many outside the traditional ken of economic practice.

Public opinion in affluent countries often attributes extreme poverty to faults with the poor themselves—or at least with their governments. Race was once thought the deciding factor. Then it was culture: religious divisions and taboos, caste systems, a lack of entrepreneurship, gender inequities. Such theories have waned as societies of an ever widening range of religions and cultures have achieved relative prosperity. Moreover, certain supposedly immutable aspects of culture (such as fertility choices and gender and caste roles) in fact change, often dramatically, as societies become urban and develop economically.

Most recently, commentators have zeroed in on "poor governance," often code words for corruption. They argue that extreme poverty persists because governments fail to open up their markets, provide public services and clamp down on bribe taking. It is said that if these regimes cleaned up their acts, they, too, would flourish. Development assistance efforts have become largely a series of good governance lectures.

The availability of cross-country and time-series data now allows experts to make much more systematic analyses.

Although debate continues, the weight of the evidence indicates that governance makes a difference but is not the sole determinant of economic growth. According to surveys conducted by Transparency International, business leaders actually perceive many fast-growing Asian countries to be more corrupt than some slow-growing African ones.

Geography—including natural resources, climate, topography, and proximity to trade routes and major markets—is at least as important as good governance. As early as 1776, Adam Smith argued that high transport costs inhibited development in the inland areas of Africa and Asia. Other geographic features, such as the heavy disease burden of the tropics, also interfere. One recent study by my Columbia University colleague Xavier Sala-i-Martin demonstrated once again that tropical countries saddled with malaria have experienced slower growth than those free from the disease. The good news is that geographic factors shape, but do not decide, a country's economic fate. Technology can offset them: drought can be fought with irrigation systems, isolation with roads and mobile telephones, diseases with preventive and therapeutic measures.

The other major insight is that although the most powerful mechanism for reducing extreme poverty is to encourage overall economic growth, a rising tide does not necessarily lift all boats. Average income can rise, but if the income is distributed unevenly the poor may benefit little, and pockets of extreme poverty may persist (especially in geographically disadvantaged regions). Moreover, growth is not simply a free-market phenomenon. It requires basic government services: infrastructure, health, education, and scientific and technological innovation. Thus, many of the recommendations of the past two decades emanating from Washington—that governments in low-income countries should cut back on their spending to make room for the private sector—miss the point. Government spending, directed at investment in critical areas, is itself a vital spur to growth, especially if its effects are to reach the poorest of the poor.

The Poverty Trap

So what do these insights tell us about the region most afflicted by poverty today, Africa? Fifty years ago tropical Africa was roughly as rich as subtropical and tropical Asia. As Asia boomed, Africa stagnated. Special geographic factors have played a crucial role.

Foremost among these is the existence of the Himalaya Mountains, which produce southern Asia's monsoon climate and vast river systems. Well-watered farmlands served as the starting points for Asia's rapid escape from extreme poverty during the past five decades. The Green Revolution of the 1960s and 1970s introduced high-yield grains, irrigation and fertilizers, which ended the cycle of famine, disease and despair.

It also freed a significant proportion of the labor force to seek manufacturing jobs in the cities. Urbanization, in turn, spurred growth, not only by providing a home for industry and innovation but also by prompting greater investment in a healthy and skilled labor force. Urban residents cut their fertility rates

Globalization, Poverty and Foreign Aid

Average citizens in affluent nations often have many questions about the effects of economic globalization on rich and poor nations and about how developing countries spend the aid they receive. Here are a few brief answers:

Is Globalization Making the Rich Richer and the Poor Poorer?

Generally, the answer is no. Economic globalization is supporting very rapid advances of many impoverished economies, notably in Asia. International trade and foreign investment inflows have been major factors in China's remarkable economic growth during the past quarter century and in India's fast economic growth since the early 1990s. The poorest of the poor, notably in sub-Saharan Africa, are not held back by globalization; they are largely bypassed by it.

Is Poverty the Result of Exploitation of the Poor by the Rich?

Affluent nations have repeatedly plundered and exploited poor countries through slavery, colonial rule and unfair trade practices. Yet it is perhaps more accurate to say that exploitation is the result of poverty (which leaves impoverished countries vulnerable to abuse) rather than the cause of it. Poverty is generally the result of low productivity per worker, which reflects poor health, lack of job-market skills, patchiness of infrastructure (roads, power plants, utility lines, shipping ports), chronic malnutrition and the like. Exploitation has played a role in producing some of these conditions, but deeper factors [geographic isolation, endemic disease, ecological destruction, challenging conditions for food production] have tended to be more important and difficult to overcome without external help.

Will Higher Incomes in Poor Countries Mean Lower Incomes in Rich Countries?

By and large, economic development is a positive-sum process, meaning that all can partake in it without causing some to suffer. In the past 200 years, the world as a whole has achieved a massive increase in economic output rather than a shift in economic output to one region at the expense of another. To be sure, global environmental constraints are already starting to impose themselves. As today's poor countries develop, the climate, fisheries and forests are coming under increased strain. Overall global economic growth is compatible with sustainable management of the ecosystems on which all humans depend—indeed, wealth can be good for the environment—but only if public policy and technologies encourage sound practices and the necessary investments are made in environmental sustainability.

Do U.S. Private Contributions Make Up for the Low Levels of U.S. Official Aid?

Some have claimed that while the U.S. government budget provides relatively little assistance to the poorest countries, the private sector makes up the gap. In fact, the Organization for Economic Cooperation and Development has estimated that private foundations and nongovernmental organizations give roughly $6 billion a year in international assistance, or 0.05 percent of U.S. gross national product (GNP). In that case, total U.S. international aid is around 0.21 percent of GNP—still among the lowest ratios of all donor nations.

—J.D.S.

and thus were able to spend more for the health, nutrition and education of each child. City kids went to school at a higher rate than their rural cousins. And with the emergence of urban infrastructure and public health systems, city populations became less disease-prone than their counterparts in the countryside, where people typically lack safe drinking water, modern sanitation, professional health care and protection from vector-borne ailments such as malaria.

Africa did not experience a green revolution. Tropical Africa lacks the massive floodplains that facilitate the large-scale and low-cost irrigation found in Asia. Also, its rainfall is highly variable, and impoverished farmers have been unable to purchase fertilizer. The initial Green Revolution research featured crops, especially paddy rice and wheat, not widely grown in Africa (high-yield varieties suitable for it have been developed in recent years, but they have not yet been disseminated sufficiently). The continent's food production per person has actually been falling, and Africans' caloric intake is the lowest in the world; food insecurity is rampant. Its labor force has remained tethered to subsistence agriculture.

Compounding its agricultural woes, Africa bears an overwhelming burden of tropical diseases. Because of climate and the endemic mosquito species, malaria is more intensively transmitted in Africa than anywhere else. And high transport costs isolate Africa economically. In East Africa, for example, the rainfall is greatest in the interior of the continent, so most people live there, far from ports and international trade routes.

Much the same situation applies to other impoverished parts of the world, notably the Andean and Central American highlands and the landlocked countries of Central Asia. Being economically isolated, they are unable to attract much foreign investment (other than for the extraction of oil, gas and precious minerals). Investors tend to be dissuaded by the high transport costs associated with the interior regions. Rural areas therefore remain stuck in a vicious cycle of poverty, hunger, illness and illiteracy. Impoverished areas lack adequate internal savings to make the needed investments because most households live hand to mouth. The few high-income families, who do accumulate savings, park them overseas rather than at home. This capital flight includes not only financial capital but also the human variety, in the form of skilled workers—doctors, nurses, scientists and engineers, who frequently leave in search of improved economic opportunities abroad. The poorest countries are often, perversely, net exporters of capital.

Put Money Where Mouths Are

The Technology to overcome these handicaps and jump-start economic development exists. Malaria can be controlled using bed nets, indoor pesticide spraying and improved medicines. Drought-prone countries in Africa with nutrient depleted soils can benefit enormously from drip irrigation and greater use of fertilizers. Landlocked countries can be connected by paved highway networks, airports and fiber-optic cables. All these projects cost money, of course.

Many larger countries, such as China, have prosperous regions that can help support their own lagging areas. Coastal eastern China, for instance, is now financing massive public investments in western China. Most of today's successfully developing countries, especially smaller ones, received at least some backing from external donors at crucial times. The critical scientific innovations that formed the underpinnings of the Green Revolution were bankrolled by the Rockefeller Foundation, and the spread of these technologies in India and elsewhere in Asia was funded by the U.S. and other donor governments and international development institutions.

We in the U.N. Millennium Project have listed the investments required to help today's impoverished regions cover basic needs in health, education, water, sanitation, food production, roads and other key areas. We have put an approximate price tag on that assistance and estimated how much could be financed by poor households themselves and by domestic institutions. The remaining cost is the "financing gap" that international donors need to make up.

For tropical Africa, the total investment comes to $110 per person a year. To place this into context, the average income in this part of the world is $350 per annum, most or all of which is required just to stay alive. The full cost of the total investment is clearly beyond the funding reach of these countries. Of the $110, perhaps $40 could be financed domestically, so that $70 per capita would be required in the form of international aid.

Adding it all up, the total requirement for assistance across the globe is around $160 billion a year, double the current rich-country aid budget of $80 billion. This figure amounts to approximately 0.5 percent of the combined gross national product (GNP) of the affluent donor nations. It does not include other humanitarian projects such as postwar Iraqi reconstruction or Indian Ocean tsunami relief. To meet these needs as well, a reasonable figure would be 0.7 percent of GNP, which is what all donor countries have long promised but few have fulfilled. Other organizations, including the International Monetary Fund, the World Bank and the British government, have reached much the same conclusion.

When polled, Americans greatly overestimate how much foreign aid the U.S. gives—by as much as 30 times.

We believe these investments would enable the poorest countries to cut poverty by half by 2015 and, if continued, to

Foreign Aid: How Should the Money Be Spent?

Here is a breakdown of the needed investment for three typical low-income African countries to help them achieve the Millennium Development Goals. For all nations given aid, the average total annual assistance per person would come to around $110 a year. These investments would be financed by both foreign aid and the countries themselves.

Investment Area	Average per Year between 2005–2015 ($ per capita)		
	Ghana	Tanzania	Uganda
Hunger	7	8	6
Education	19	14	5
Gender equality	3	3	3
Health	25	35	34
Water supply and sanitation	8	7	5
Improving slum conditions	2	3	2
Energy	15	16	12
Roads	10	22	20
Other	10	10	10
Total	100	117	106

Calculated from data from *Investing in Development* [U.N. Millennium Project, Earthscan Publications, 2005]. Numbers do not sum to totals because of rounding.

eliminate it altogether by 2025. They would not be "welfare payments" from rich to poor but instead something far more important and durable. People living above mere subsistence levels would be able to save for their futures; they could join the virtuous cycle of rising incomes, savings and technological inflows. We would be giving a billion people a hand up instead of a handout.

If rich nations fail to make these investments, they will be called on to provide emergency assistance more or less indefinitely. They will face famine, epidemics, regional conflicts and the spread of terrorist havens. And they will condemn not only the impoverished countries but themselves as well to chronic political instability, humanitarian emergencies and security risks.

The debate is now shifting from the basic diagnosis of extreme poverty and the calculations of financing needs to the practical matter of how assistance can best be delivered. Many people believe that aid efforts failed in the past and that care is needed to avoid the repetition of failure. Some of these concerns are well grounded, but others are fueled by misunderstandings.

When pollsters ask Americans how much foreign aid they think the U.S. gives, they greatly overestimate the amount by as much as 30 times. Believing that so much money has been donated and so little has been done with it, the public concludes that these programs have "failed." The reality is rather different. U.S. official assistance to sub-Saharan Africa has been running at $2 billion to $4 billion a year, or roughly $3 to $6 for every African. Most of this aid has come in the form of "technical cooperation" (which goes into the pockets of consultants), food contributions for famine victims and the cancellation of unpaid debts. Little of this support has come in a form that can be invested in systems that improve health, nutrition, food production and transport. We should give foreign aid a fair chance before deciding whether it works or not.

A second common misunderstanding concerns the extent to which corruption is likely to eat up the donated money. Some foreign aid in the past has indeed ended up in the equivalent of Swiss bank accounts. That happened when the funds were provided for geopolitical reasons rather than development; a good example was U.S. support for the corrupt regime of Mobutu Sese Seko of Zaire (now the Democratic Republic of the Congo) during part of the cold war. When assistance has been targeted at development rather than political goals, the outcomes have been favorable, ranging from the Green Revolution to the eradication of smallpox and the recent near-eradication of polio.

The aid package we advocate would be directed toward those countries with a reasonable degree of good governance and operational transparency. In Africa, these countries include Ethiopia, Ghana, Mali, Mozambique, Senegal and Tanzania. The money would not be merely thrown at them. It would be provided according to a detailed and monitored plan, and new rounds of financing would be delivered only as the work actually got done. Much of the funds would be given directly to villages and towns to minimize the chances of their getting diverted by central governments. All these programs should be closely audited.

Western society tends to think of foreign aid as money lost. But if supplied properly, it is an investment that will one day yield huge returns, much as U.S. assistance to western Europe and East Asia after World War II did. By prospering, today's impoverished countries will wean themselves from endless charity. They will contribute to the international advance of science, technology and trade. They will escape political instability, which leaves many of them vulnerable to violence, narcotics trafficking, civil war and even terrorist takeover. Our own security will be bolstered as well. As U.N. Secretary-General Kofi Annan wrote earlier this year: "There will be no development without security, and no security without development."

The author, **JEFFREY D. SACHS**, directs the Earth Institute at Columbia University and the United Nations Millennium Project. An economist, Sachs is well known for advising governments in Latin America, eastern Europe, the former Soviet Union, Asia and Africa on economic reforms and for his work with international agencies to promote poverty reduction, disease control and debt reduction in poor countries. A native of Detroit, he received his BA, MA and PhD degrees from Harvard University.

A Work in Progress

In 1996, legislators sought to 'end welfare as we know it.' More than a decade after reform, the program serves as a conduit to employment.

ANN POMEROY

"If you're on welfare, we think we know all about you" says Julie Kirksick, executive director of the New Hope Project in Milwaukee, a nonprofit organization that helps welfare-to-work participants and other hard-to-place workers find jobs.

Welfare myths tend to have a long life. In the 1980s, President Reagan told a story about a "welfare queen driving her welfare Cadillac." According to the president, she was a Chicago woman who had ripped off $150,000 from the government using 80 aliases, 30 addresses, a dozen Social Security cards and four fictional dead husbands. When reporters tried to find the woman, however, they discovered that the story was apocryphal.

Decades later, this 1980s image still haunts the public mind, says Deborah Schlick, executive director of the Affirmative Options Coalition, a Minnesota policy advocacy organization that promotes state and federal welfare policies to help low-wage Minnesota workers.

Yet the U.S. welfare system has undergone significant changes since President Reagan's time. The most dramatic changes went into effect on Aug. 22, 1996, when President Clinton signed the Personal Responsibility and Work Opportunity Reconciliation Act, the first major overhaul of the welfare system since the New Deal era of the 1930s. The lofty goal of bipartisan welfare reform was to "end welfare as we know it" by requiring work in exchange for time-limited assistance.

Moving off welfare proves to be a complex, erratic process, but an increasing number of employers have discovered business advantages in providing training, flexible work arrangements and other assistance to such employees. Companies of all sizes now work with federal, state and local employee-placement groups to identify and develop highly motivated workers. Here are their stories.

Falling on Hard Times

Julia Doyle says she "fell on hard times" after overwhelming life events.

In 1990, her mother was killed by a drunk driver. Doyle, who had two children at the time, was working at Marquette University in Milwaukee. Determined to bring the driver to trial, Doyle began missing work. Eventually, she lost the job she had held for 10 years.

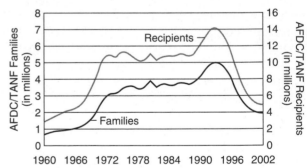

Recipients of Federal Cash Assistance

The national caseload for the federal Temporary Assistance to Needy Families (TANF) program fell slightly during fiscal 2003, the latest year for which official figures are available, continuing long-term decline since the program's creation. Federal officials say the reduction that began in 1994 continues today. The graph shows the average monthly number of families and recipients receiving Aid to Families with Dependent Children (AFDC) benefits or TANF assistance from 1960 through 2002.

Source: TANF Seventh Annual Report to Congress, U.S. Department of Health and Human Services' Office of Family Assistance.

In 1991–92, Doyle gave birth to two more children. Her last child was born prematurely on the day the driver who killed her mother came to trial. With little financial help from the children's fathers, Doyle wound up on welfare.

Doyle admits that she used drugs during this period. Then, one day when she was buying "my week's stash," she discovered that her son had witnessed the transaction. "I realized then that children are videotaping your life," she says. It was the wake-up call she needed to begin turning her life around.

A neighbor told Doyle about the New Hope Project's welfare-to-work research program, and she applied. "I won the lottery," she says, when she was randomly selected as a participant.

Kirksick says the goal of the three-year program was to help low-wage workers get out of poverty through work. " 'If you work, you should not be poor' was our guiding principle," she says.

The New Hope Project was open to adults 18 or older in Milwaukee's poorest neighborhoods. Following the program model that continues today, participants were required to work 30 or more hours each week; New Hope subsidized temporary community-service jobs for those unable to find work on their own after eight weeks. They received cash supplements that raised their incomes above the poverty level while they continued to search for permanent employment. New Hope also subsidized child and health care.

Doyle credits the program with making it possible for her to "get back on track." Today, she is a full-time administrator and has worked for the same employer since 1997. She also served on the New Hope board for several years.

With her youngest children doing well in private school and her daughter a freshman at Marquette University, Doyle's back in school, too, working toward a degree in leadership and development at Marquette.

The 'Long-Term Detached'

Although Doyle went through some hard times, she was able to care for her children and rejoin the workforce with help. For some long-unemployed people, however, the situation can be more intractable, says Toby Herr, founder and director of Project Match in Chicago.

The nonprofit organization matches employers and employees and has helped many of Chicago's poorest people find jobs since 1985. Project Match began operations in the notorious Cabrini-Green neighborhood, a public housing complex where drugs and gangs flourished. In 2003, the Chicago Housing Authority began tearing down the neighborhood's Henry Horner Homes and building mixed-income housing.

Herr's clients include the 'long-term detached:' She says "the work ethic is missing" for many. Some may have grown up on welfare; others are unable to work because of serious disabilities, including psychological problems. Project Match operates today on Chicago's Near West Side in West Haven, and continues to act as an intermediary between employers and clients attempting to make the often-difficult transition into the full-time workforce.

Herr has tracked Project Match's efforts with hard data (see the online sidebar "A Welfare-to-Work Track Record" at www .shrm.org/hrmagazine). Dedicated to her work, she says helping people progress toward full-time employment requires "starting where they are and building gradually," and measuring progress "by the distance traveled" rather than by the final outcome.

Warrine Pace, director of services at the West Haven center, is equally passionate about the value of this work and serenely competent as she prepares clients for job interviews. In addition to helping each candidate with resume preparation, interview practice, and advice about appropriate clothing and behavior, Pace and her staff conduct a complete background check, including criminal convictions, on each participant.

'Do You Want to Change Your Life?'

Joyce Bailey, one of Project Match's first participants, was an early success. She spotted a sign one day at her neighborhood health center. The sign offered a question: "Do you want to change your life?"

At the time—the mid-1980s—Bailey was on welfare. She had dropped out of high school in 1976 when her first child was born and then had a second child. Her husband was unable to provide much financial support.

Bailey went to the Project Match service center to learn more. "Toby and Warrine have been my friends ever since," she says.

Pace takes a step-by-step, "crawl before you walk" approach that breaks seemingly insurmountable tasks into manageable chunks. "It's a process," she told Bailey as she guided her through moving off welfare. First, finish high school, either by going back to her old school or by passing the high-school equivalency exam.

Bailey chose the exam, but was dismayed when she failed. She tried again, though, and passed on the second try. That hurdle cleared, she began volunteering at the health center, and that led to part-time paid work. Ultimately, she moved into a full-time job as a school health aide and case manager.

By then, Bailey had four children. With Pace's encouragement, however, she went back to school part time while working and caring for the children. "It was so hard," she says. "I kept saying, 'I can't do this,' but Warrine and Toby kept saying, 'Yes. You can do it.' "

And she did—first earning an associate's degree and then a bachelor's degree in sociology and criminal justice. Bailey says the women at Project Match were so encouraging that she didn't want to let them down. She's thinking about going back to school for a master's degree.

Regina Allen came to Project Match in 2000. Her job history was erratic. Like Bailey, Allen had dropped out of high school. She gave birth to her first child at 19, followed quickly by four more, and spent seven years on welfare before taking a series of low-wage temporary jobs.

With help from Project Match, Allen became interested in security work and completed a 20-hour security training course. In October 2007, she was hired as a security officer. Now she's looking ahead to weapons training that would prepare her for more-lucrative positions as an armed security officer.

Employers Count on Pace

Pace has developed strong relationships with Chicago area employers, including Silverhawk Security where Elaine Crossman handles human resource functions.

"Warrine sends me all good people," says Crossman, who hires about a dozen Project Match clients each year. Many of these employees receive some government assistance.

Crossman knows that Project Match-trained candidates have passed criminal background checks—essential for security jobs. She knows, too, that they will have up-to-date resumes and be well-prepared for their interviews.

Crossman understands the difficulties faced by single mothers with few job skills and little money, because she was in that

For CVS, a Recruiting Resource

In 1997, President Clinton created a public-private Welfare to Work Partnership to encourage employers to commit to hiring welfare-to-work participants. Several large corporations, including retail drug giant CVS/pharmacy, responded. According to Steve Wing, director of government programs, CVS has hired more than 60,000 low-wage and welfare-to-work participants since that time.

One of its early hires was Deb Autry, a part-time clerk at the Ohio pharmacy group Revco when it was acquired by CVS in 1996. Autry saw a sign in the store window one day about a training class for employees who wanted to become pharmacy technicians. With her supervisor's encouragement, she applied and was accepted, becoming one of six members of the first CVS welfare-to-work training class.

Autry was a single mother of a daughter and twin sons. With no financial help from their father, she depended on welfare until her sons reached 14.

At CVS, Autry moved into a full-time job after she completed training. Today, she enjoys her work as a certified lead technician at a store in Akron, Ohio. She's one of four members of that class still working for CVS.

The twins are 22 and her daughter 30, but Autry still remembers the day she came home with her first paycheck. The children greeted her excitedly, eager to "go to the store with mom and watch her pay with cash."

Wing says these training programs have been highly successful for CVS. It partners with several agencies working directly with welfare-to-work clients. These organizations function "like an arm of the HR department," he says, and they recruit for 6,200 CVS stores in 38 states.

Wing and members of his department plan and administer employee training, including a two-year pharmacy apprenticeship that prepares employees to enter a college pharmacy program. Participants also qualify for tuition reimbursement.

The "Pathways to Pharmacy" program is staffed by retired pharmacists who visit primary and secondary schools to encourage students to consider pharmacy as a career. More than 2,000 students completed internships in all kinds of jobs at CVS stores during summer 2007.

Programs that help employees advance are a boon for the company, says Wing. Along with other drug retailers, CVS faces stiff competition from "big box" stores such as Wal-Mart and Target for a dwindling supply of qualified pharmacists and technicians.

"For CVS, these programs are a good business decision," he says.

—Ann Pomeroy

situation. Crossman had two children while still in her teens and received food stamps when they were young. Like Allen, she started as a security officer at Silverhawk; she points out that Silverhawk's beginning security officers have the same opportunities to advance as she did.

Nathan Thomas, a branch manager at Andy Services, tells a similar story. His company is one of an increasing number of security firms in Chicago since the Sept. 11, 2001, terrorist attacks. Like Crossman, Thomas began as a security officer and relies on Project Match for qualified candidates. Today, he mulls the possibility of starting his own business.

The End of Welfare as We Know It?

Schlick assesses the results of welfare reform this way: "We did not really end welfare as we know it. We took the basic architecture of the program and redecorated it." She points out that the federal Temporary Assistance to Needy Families (TANF) program of cash assistance for very poor mothers with children—the replacement for Aid to Families with Dependent Children (AFDC)—is still delivered through county or State welfare offices. As a result, "All the stigma the public associated with the AFDC program, it continued to associate with the welfare-to-work programs that replaced it."

But Schlick says valuable lessons were learned from reform. First, the general economic climate has a major impact on welfare reforms success. People will work if jobs are available. If the jobs don't pay well, however, work won't get them out of poverty, she says. For example, the parent of a family of three working 37 hours a week for the minimum wage earns well below the Minnesota poverty level of $16,000 each year; nevertheless, that parent loses all cash welfare assistance.

The size of welfare cash grants matters, Schlick continues. That same family of three receives $532 a month as a TANF payment in Minnesota, an amount that has not increased since 1986. That's well below the rent for a two-bedroom apartment in a metropolitan area, she adds, thereby refuting the myth of living high on welfare.

Discouragingly, "We have not figured out how to help those who most inspired welfare reform—the relatively few families who use welfare for long periods of time," Schlick adds. "We thought we were dealing with character and motivation issues. Instead, we are dealing primarily with disabilities [often psychological ones]."

Ellen S. Alberding, president of the nonprofit Joyce Foundation, a funding source for research by groups in the Great Lakes area such as Project Match and the New Hope Project, says Congress' reauthorization of the welfare reform law in 2006 "largely sidesteps" these concerns.

Nevertheless, says Douglas Besharov, a professor at the University of Maryland's School of Public Policy, "it's great news that a lot of people have left welfare since 1996. The big surprise of the last 10 or 15 years is how many low-skilled, low-income women have been able to enter the workforce." Besharov directs the Welfare Reform Academy, helping managers and planners decipher the intricacies of the federal block grant system for states.

In fact, the welfare rolls have been cut in half since the reform act went into effect. In its *TANF Seventh Annual Report to Congress* in December 2006, the U.S. Department of Health and Human Services' Office of Family Assistance reported a decrease of 54.4 percentage points in families receiving AFDC or TANF aid from August 1996 to September 2003 (see previous line graph and table following).

However, many former TANF recipients have moved off welfare and into the ranks of the working poor whose incomes remain below the poverty level. According to the U.S. Census

Bureau, 12.2 percent of all U.S. families were living below the poverty level in 1996; by 2002, the latest year for which figures are available, that percentage had decreased by less than 2 percentage points, to 10.4 percent.

The percentages are much higher for families headed by single females. In 1996, 35.8 percent of these families lived in poverty; in 2002, the figure was 28.8 percent.

Elizabeth Lower-Basch, a senior policy analyst at the Center for Law and Social Policy in Washington, D.C., agrees that there has been a "huge increase" in single moms working now that cash assistance is less available. But "about 40 percent of low-wage workers have no sick leave or family leave," she points out. "The question we should be asking now is what do [these workers] need to succeed?"

She maintains that health insurance, education, training and child care remain most pressing. Recent changes to the Deficit Reduction Act of 2005 that make the requirements for receiving cash assistance increasingly restrictive are "a step in the wrong direction," she says. For example, as of Oct. 1, 2006, state welfare-to-work programs are required to meet a minimum of 50 percent work participation by single-parent TANF families.

That creates a "vicious cycle" that puts even greater pressure on single parents to participate in welfare-to-work programs without providing them with the basic tools to make success possible, says Lower-Basch.

"The middle class has work/life problems, too, but their situations are usually not as fragile as those of low-wage workers."

A Step in the Right Direction

There are "two worldviews" about what causes people to stay on welfare, says Kirksick: Some blame the person, while others blame structural problems within the welfare system. "I think it's some of both," she says.

Kirksick agrees with Schlick that the lack of affordable health care and child care represent stumbling blocks for many, who "cycle in and out of jobs without finding traction." She also agrees that the Deficit Reduction Act's stringent requirements push single parents to participate in welfare-to-work programs, while the low-wage jobs they qualify for seldom provide the essential benefits that would allow them to succeed. But she has high praise for the earned income tax credit (EITC) that reduces tax payments for low-wage workers. "It's the U.S government's greatest single anti-poverty program," according to Kirksick.

That sentiment was echoed recently by members of the American Economic Association. In a survey released in July 2007, 70 percent of these labor economists responded that expanding the EITC would be the most effective tool for fighting poverty; 64 percent said it would lead to gains in employment.

Overall, many sources agree with Herr's assessment of the 1996 overhaul as "one of the government's most successful public welfare programs." Writing in *Beyond Barriers to Work: A Workforce Attachment Approach That Addresses Unpredictability, Halting Progress and Human Nature* (Project Match-Families in Transition Association, February 2007), Herr notes that critics of the 1996 reform "have called the legislation a

Recipients of Temporary Assistance to Needy Families

Percent net change since 1994 TANF enactment, by state

State	%	State	%
Alabama	-53.1%	Montana	46.0
Alaska	-59.6	Nebraska	-23.5
Arizona	-17.7	Nevada	-30.4
Arkansas	-51.3	New Hampshire	33.2
California	-49.0	New Jersey	-57.1
Colorado	-58.8	New Mexico	47.8
Connecticut	-63.4	New York	65.2
Delaware	-46.2	North Carolina	64.4
District of Columbia	33.6	North Dakota	-30.1
Florida	-70.9	Ohio	-58.4
Georgia	-54.2	Oklahoma	-57.9
Guam	-37.0	Oregon	39.5
Hawaii	-57.2	Pennsylvania	-54.8
Idaho	-79.9	Puerto Rico	-62.7
Illinois	-84.3	Rhode Island	-37.3
Indiana	-0.5	South Carolina	-51.9
Iowa	-36.2	South Dakota	-53.9
Kansas	-33.3	Tennessee	-25.6
Kentucky	-50.5	Texas	-51.7
Louisiana	-65.8	Utah	-37.1
Maine	-54.7	Vermont	-45.1
Maryland	63.7	Virgin Islands	-61.6
Massachusetts	-39.9	Virginia	-86.7
Michigan	-53.8	Washington	-45.1
Minnesota	-37.5	West Virginia	-55.7
Mississippi	57.5	Wisconsin	-58.2
Missouri	48.2	Wyoming	-91.0

Source: U.S. Department of Health and Human Services' Office of Family Assistance TANF Seventh Annual Report to Congress.

failure, since . . . many of the families that left welfare for work are still poor. But what were these families' earnings before welfare reform? For many, zero."

From a human-development perspective, the progress of clients like hers is dramatic, says Herr. "Considering where these families started and where they are now, their progress as workers is significant, and not just in terms of changes in earnings." The changes in "attitudes, behaviors, self-identity, relationships with friends and family, and status in the community" are even more impressive and heartening, she notes.

Steve Wing, director of government programs for retail drug company CVS/pharmacy, concurs. He regards the welfare-to-work participants CVS hires as a "pot of gold, a valuable untapped resource." (See box "For CVS, a Recruiting Resource") Although the 1996 reform hasn't solved all problems, it's a step in the right direction, he says. "Welfare reform has made a major difference, and the story needs to get out.

ANN POMEROY is senior writer for *HR Magazine*.

Brave New Welfare

STEPHANIE MENCIMER

Georgia officials lied to Gabby's mom to keep her from getting a $100 monthly check. From red tape to dirty tricks and outright abuse, here's what awaits if your luck runs out.

I n 2006, Letorrea Clark was 22 years old, unemployed, and living with her boyfriend in Homerville, a tiny town near the Okefenokee Swamp in southern Georgia, when she discovered she was pregnant. The timing wasn't ideal. Her boyfriend's job at the local can-manufacturing plant supported them both, but his largesse came at a price. The man was controlling, unfaithful, and jealous, a problem only enhanced by the wide array of drugs that filled his freezer. Clark had hit the stash, too, but the pregnancy pushed her to get clean and get out. She slept on a park bench until a friend helped her secure a place to stay.

Two-year-old Gabby and her mother are among thousands eligible for welfare who have been denied benefits as states push to trim the rolls.

Desperate, with her due date fast approaching, Clark decided to apply for Temporary Assistance for Needy Families (TANF), better known as welfare. But when she went to the local Division of Family and Children Services office, a caseworker told her—wrongly—that she couldn't apply until after the baby was born. "They basically said, 'Go get a job,'" says Clark. "I was eight months pregnant."

Gabby arrived by C-section a month later, and Clark brought the chubby newborn home to a sweltering trailer with a busted fridge, no air conditioning, and no running water. (Her ex had reneged on promises to get the water turned on.) Clark got by with help from her church and her landlord, who let her stay for free until she was able to move. Later, she found a job in a day care. But the center docked her paycheck for Gabby's care, an expense the state would have picked up had she been able to get on TANF. Sometimes she'd go home with just $20 at the end of the week.

Clark patched things together with food stamps and $256 a month in child support. But after nine months, Gabby's father stopped paying just long enough for Clark to get evicted. She went back to the welfare office, where caseworkers turned her away, saying—falsely again—that because she'd been getting child support she was ineligible for TANF.

What Clark didn't know was that Georgia, like many other states, was in the midst of an aggressive push to get thousands of eligible mothers like her off TANF, often by duplicitous means, to use the savings elsewhere in the state budget. Fewer than 2,500 Georgia adults now receive benefits, down from 28,000 in 2004—a 90 percent decline. Louisiana, Texas, and Illinois have each dropped 80 percent of adult recipients since January 2001. Nationally, the number of TANF recipients fell more than 40 percent between then and June 2008, the most recent month for which data are available. In Georgia last year, only 18 percent of children living below 50 percent of the poverty line—that is, on less than $733 a month for a family of three—were receiving TANF.

Plunging welfare rolls were big news in the wake of Bill Clinton's 1996 welfare reform, which limited benefits and required recipients to engage in "work-related" activities. Those declines coincided with record numbers of poor single mothers heading into the workplace and a significant drop in child poverty—proof, supporters said, that the new policy was a success. But the reform took effect at a time when unemployment was at a historic low—there were actually jobs for welfare moms to go to. In recent years, by contrast, TANF caseloads have been falling even as unemployment has soared and other poverty programs have experienced explosive growth. (Nearly 11 million more people received food stamps last year than did in 2000.) With the economy settling into a prolonged slump, this trend could be devastating.

Welfare is the only cash safety-net program for single moms and their kids, notes Rebecca Blank, an economist at the Brookings Institution and one of the nation's leading experts on poverty. "One has to worry, with a recession, about the number of women who, if they get unemployed, are not going to have anywhere to turn."

No longer the polarizing, racially tinged political issue it was when Ronald Reagan attacked "welfare queens," the welfare system today is dying a quiet death, neatly chronicled in the pages of academic and policy journals, largely unnoticed by the rest of us. Yet its demise carries significant implications. Among the most serious: the rise of what academics call the "disconnected," people who live well below the poverty line and are neither working nor receiving cash benefits like Social Security disability or TANF. Estimates put this group at roughly 2 million women caring for 4 million children, many dealing with a host of challenges from mental illness to domestic violence. "We don't really know how they survive," says Blank.

Women turned away from TANF lose more than a check. TANF is a gateway to education, drug rehab or mental health care, child care, even transportation and disability benefits—tools for upward mobility. Without those options, some women are driven to more desperate measures. In one of the towns in Georgia where I traveled to research this story, arrests of women for prostitution and petty crime went up as more and more families were pushed off welfare. And women are increasingly vulnerable to sexual assault and exploitation—sometimes, as I discovered, from the very officials or caseworkers who are supposed to help them. In the worst cases, they are losing custody of their children, precisely what TANF was designed to prevent. "I worry a lot about the kids in these families," Blank says. "We don't know where the kids are going."

One good thing did come from Letorrea Clark's final attempt to get on TANF. Federal law requires caseworkers to ask applicants about domestic violence, and when Clark mentioned that Gabby's father was stalking her, a concerned caseworker sent her to a shelter in another city. When the ex found Clark there, she was transferred to a shelter an hour away in Albany, a midsize town nestled among some of the nation's most impoverished rural counties.

The shelter staff did for Clark what the TANF office would not: extended her a lifeline. With their help, Clark and Gabby moved to a dingy one-room apartment in a low-slung brick complex filled with ex-cons and drug addicts, clients of the nonprofit group that runs the building. This is where I found them during several visits over the summer. Mother and daughter slept on a donated mattress; crates set inside an oversize, listing four-poster frame served as the box spring. Free rent made the roaches tolerable, but there were other liabilities. Upon Clark's arrival, the nonprofit group's caseworker asked her for sex. "He said, 'You ain't got nothing; you might as well,'" she said.

As we spoke in July, Clark sat in an overstuffed chair holding Gabby, a vivacious toddler whose head sprouted with braids. Clark was worried. She needed to get a job so she could keep food in the house; she was haunted by the possibility of losing Gabby if she didn't. But there were serious obstacles. She's been diagnosed with bipolar disorder and ADHD; "I don't like to be around a lot of people," she said. She can't drive and fears the bus because "I suffer from paranoia. I always think I'm going to fall off those seats."

Born in Hattiesburg, Mississippi, one of six children, Clark barely knows her father. She suspects both her mother and grandmother suffer from mental illness. One day when she was five, she told me, her mother whipped her back with an extension cord and then made her stand in a corner all night long. In kindergarten the next day, a concerned teacher lifted up her shirt and fell to her knees at the sight of so much blood. Social workers investigated, but didn't take Clark away from her mother for another six years of crushing abuse.

In school, she languished in special education classes; her behavior turned violent. At 11, the state finally put her into foster care, and later, when foster families wouldn't have her, a mental hospital. Eventually she was returned to her mother, who coveted her monthly disability check. "When I turned 18, my mom wanted me to stay home to live off my tit," she says. Instead, "I saw an ad on TV for Job Corps and thought that was my ticket out." After she got her GED and became certified as a nursing assistant, Job Corps helped her find work in a nursing home, but the death of a woman she cared for left her rattled. She quit and was soon homeless. Somewhere along the way, she lost the disability benefits she'd received since she was a child. After she was raped in a crack house, Clark sought refuge in the only safe place she could think of—jail. "I hadn't ate in like two weeks," she says, so she went to Wal-Mart and started taking things off the shelves—a sandwich, soda, candy. "I knew I was going to get caught, but I just kept eating. I kept thinking that if I went to jail I could sleep."

After her sojourn in lockup, she met Gabby's father and moved in with him. While her pregnancy was unplanned, Clark believes that Gabby saved her life. "If I didn't have her, I'd have probably lost my mind," says Clark. "She's my pride and joy."

In his 1903 book *The Souls of Black Folk*, W.E.B. Du Bois described Albany as the capital of Georgia's "Black Belt." At the time, the area was home to 2,000 white people and 10,000 blacks; the cotton trade had collapsed, and Albany was a landscape of decaying one-room slave cabins occupied by tenant farmers eking out a meager existence from the depleted soil.

Things have improved since then, but only slightly. Despite the addition of an aquarium and civic center, the downtown looks much as it must have when Martin Luther King Jr. was jailed here after a civil rights protest in 1961. The main drags offer gas stations, dollar stores, and an outfit advertising $99 headstones. More than one-fifth of Albany families live below the poverty line—nearly twice the national average. About one in three adults is illiterate. Nearly 16 percent are unemployed. Eighty percent of children born here in 2007 had single mothers, many of them teenagers.

Despite those dismal demographics, in July 2006, only 143 adults in the 14 surrounding counties—some of whose demographics make Albany look downright prosperous—were receiving TANF benefits. The number had fallen 96 percent from 2002, according to the Georgia Budget and Policy Institute, though not because poverty was on the retreat: During the same period, unemployment in the area shot up 15 percent and food stamp use increased 24 percent.

After interviewing dozens of clients of Liberty House, the Albany domestic violence shelter where Clark sought refuge, I discovered that getting TANF in Albany is virtually impossible. While most of the women were eligible for benefits under state rules, many had been turned away for some reason or another. A caseworker incorrectly told one woman that she didn't qualify because her three kids—all under 15—were too old. Another, a 30-year-old with six kids between the ages of 2 and 12, had been in the shelter for a month after the district attorney from her hometown drove her there from the hospital. ("The guy that I was dating tried to kill me," she explained matter-of-factly.) She'd applied for TANF to get subsidized child care and go back to work. But a four-hour visit to the welfare office produced nothing but a promise that she'd receive a letter with an appointment date. A month later, she still hadn't gotten the letter. She says the county offered her three weeks of child care with the warning—false—that if she didn't find a job during that time, she wouldn't be eligible for TANF. "But if I find a job, I don't need TANF," she said with a laugh.

In 2006, the Georgia Coalition Against Domestic Violence conducted a survey to figure out why so many women were suddenly failing to get TANF benefits. They discovered that caseworkers were actively talking women out of applying, often using inaccurate information. (Lying to applicants to deny them benefits is a violation of federal law, but the 1996 welfare reform legislation largely stripped the Department of Health and Human Services of its power to punish states for doing it. Meanwhile, county officials have tried to head off lawyers who might take up the issue by pressing applicants to sign waivers saying they voluntarily turned down benefits.) Allison Smith, the economic justice coordinator at the coalition, says the group has gotten reports of caseworkers telling TANF applicants they have to be surgically sterilized before they can apply. Disabled women have been told they can't apply because they can't meet the work requirement. Others have been warned that the state could take their children if they get benefits. Makita Perry, a 23-year-old mother of four who did manage to get on TANF for a year, told me caseworkers "ask you all sorts of personal questions, like when the last time you had sex was and with who." Elsewhere, women are being told to get a letter proving they've visited a family-planning doctor.

Simply landing an appointment with a caseworker is an ordeal that can take 45 days, according to some of the women I interviewed—and applicants must clear numerous other hurdles, including conducting a job search, before being approved. Few complete the process. One study found that in April 2006, caseworkers in Georgia green-lighted only 20 percent of TANF applications, down from 40 percent in 2004. The lucky few who are accepted must often work full time in "volunteer" jobs in exchange for their benefits, which max out at $280 a month for a family of three.

Even as it blocks potential applicants, Georgia is also pushing current TANF recipients off the rolls at a rapid clip. Sandy Bamford runs a federally funded family literacy program in Albany where single mothers can get their GEDs. TANF allows recipients to attend school, but Bamford says officials routinely tell her clients otherwise: In a single month, one caseworker informed three of her students (incorrectly) that because they had turned 20, they could no longer receive benefits while completing their degrees. One was about to become the first in her family to graduate from high school. She quit and took a job as a dishwasher. Students as young as 16 have been told they must go to work full time or lose benefits. The employee who threatened to drop the students, says Bamford, became "caseworker of the month" for getting so many people off TANF.

As welfare officials go, B.J. Walker is something of a rock star. Appointed commissioner of Georgia's Department of Human Resources in 2004, Walker quickly became famous for her push to get virtually every adult off the state's public assistance rolls. By 2006, the state claimed Walker's agency had produced an astounding increase in the work participation rate of its TANF recipients, which in four years had jumped from 8 percent to nearly 70 percent.

Those numbers caught the attention of the Bush administration, which was in the midst of writing strict new regulations to require states to put 50 percent of their TANF caseloads into work activities, a target that only a handful of states had ever met. To unveil the new regs, administration officials brought Walker to Washington for a photo op and declared Georgia a model for other states.

To researchers, though, Georgia's rosy statistics looked too good to be true—especially given that Walker's own agency had found that the collapse of Georgia's textile industry and other manufacturing sectors left former TANF clients with far fewer job opportunities. In fact, even as the number of TANF recipients fell nearly 90 percent between January 2002 and November 2007, unemployment jumped 30 percent.

So how did Georgia put all those welfare moms to work? It didn't. As the Center on Budget and Policy Priorities' Liz Schott explained in a 2007 paper, "the increased work participation rate is primarily a factor of fewer families receiving assistance."

As for that "work participation," Stacy Haire, an outreach worker at Liberty House, says it's unlikely to help recipients find actual jobs. "They will put you at a police department. You'll be cleaning up behind toilets, picking up trash," she says. The TANF office once sent a client of hers to see a local government official about a job. The official told her he'd be glad to help out if she'd have sex with him. The woman filed a police report, but the man was never prosecuted. "That's what they can do in these towns," Haire says. "I see some sickening stuff."

Georgia isn't the only state that's found that dropping people from TANF is the easiest and cheapest way to meet federal work requirements. Texas reduced its caseloads by outsourcing applications to a call center, which wrongfully denied some families and lost others' applications altogether. In Florida, one innovative region started requiring TANF applicants to attend 40 hours of classes before they could even apply. Clients trying to restore lost benefits had once been able to straighten out paperwork with the help of caseworkers. In 2005, officials assigned all such work to a single employee, available two hours a week. The area's TANF caseload fell by half in a year.

Walker admits that Georgia has actively discouraged people from getting on TANF, primarily by emphasizing how meager the benefits are. "Two hundred eighty dollars a month does not make for a very good life," she told me. "This is really in the best interest of the children."

Walker acknowledges that some people struggle. "A lot of the people we see on TANF have made a mistake in choosing to have children," she offers. "We meet them at the front door and try to make sure that from day one they're engaged in some sort of productive activity." As for people like Clark who can't seem to get and keep a full-time job, Walker responds simply, "Can't? Won't."

Whatever their philosophical convictions, officials have another incentive for paring the TANF rolls: money. That's because the Clinton-era welfare reform turned what had been an entitlement program like Social Security—the more people needed help, the more money was spent—into a block grant, a fixed amount of money given to the states, regardless of need. The money, $16.5 billion a year, came mostly unencumbered by regulation. States could divert the funds to any program vaguely related to serving the needy.

Not only did the block grant doom the program to a slow death by inflation (by 2010, it will have lost 27 percent of its value), it also encouraged states to deny benefits to families, since they'd get the same amount of federal funds regardless of how many people received assistance. Georgia's share of the federal grant is nearly $370 million a year. "Even if caseloads go to zero, they get the same amount of money," notes Robert Welsh of the Georgia Budget and Policy Institute.

Some states have used surplus TANF money to expand child care, job training, and transportation to help recipients find jobs. But Georgia didn't use the bulk of its money for those programs—instead, it cut spending on child care and put the money into child protective services in the wake of a lawsuit against the state over the mistreatment of children in foster care. "The feds are just fine with that," Walker insists. "We use our block grant to support other vulnerable families. That was the intent of the block grant."

Georgia is not alone in shifting its TANF money to other areas. The Government Accountability Office found in 2006 that many states were moving federal welfare funds away from cash assistance to the poor, or even "work supports" like child care, to plug holes in state budgets. Yet over the past 12 years, federal regulators have cited states only 11 times for misusing their TANF block grant, and only two suffered any financial penalty, according to Ken Wolfe, a spokesman for the Administration for Children and Families, which oversees the program. "As far as the federal government's concerned, it's not a big problem," he says.

On the run from an abusive boyfriend, Letorrea Clark struggles to keep food in the house for her daughter.

Terrell county, population 10,260, covers a rural corner of southwest Georgia not far from Jimmy Carter's boyhood peanut farm. Forty percent of the children here live below the poverty line; since the civil rights era the place has been known as "Terrible Terrell" because of the racial violence that erupted in the area. When I visited the Martin Luther King Jr. public housing project in the town of Dawson, a cluster of postwar-era brick buildings in the shadow of the Golden Peanut factory, three women sat in folding chairs drinking Miller Lites under a big oak tree, bird-dogging the gaggle of children darting through the shirts flapping on laundry lines. One of them was a sturdy 30-year-old in a yellow T-shirt with three children, 13, 11, and 10, no husband, and no job.

The woman, who did not want her name used, had her first baby at 17, dropped out, and moved into the three-bedroom apartment where she's been ever since. For a decade, she had help from her children's father, who worked at the peanut factory. But three years ago they broke up, and he hasn't been heard from since. Not long ago, she got a letter from the state saying it had seized $900 from his tax refund for child support, but rather than sending it to his kids, the state would keep it as "back pay" for TANF checks she received years ago. She long ago exhausted her TANF benefits, which Georgia limits to 48 months over the course of a lifetime. She and the kids get $542 a month in food stamps; her electric bill alone runs $265 a month when the air conditioning's on.

So, as some women have always done in desperate times, she gets help from men. "Shit like that happens," she says. "If it was me, I probably wouldn't do stuff like that, but I got three babies to care for." She has held down jobs in the past, at Dawson Manufacturing, which made auto parts, and the Tyson chicken plant. But Dawson closed in 2007. Tyson won't rehire her because she had too many write-ups on the job. The only other major employer in town is Golden Peanut, right next door, but applying requires a trip to a temp agency in Sylvester, 45 miles away with no bus connection, which might as well be outer Mongolia for someone with no car and no money for gas. "I get on my knees and pray to that man above to make things change," she says.

In the meantime, she's getting by with help from her mom, and the man who slips in and out of her house when the kids aren't home. "I keep it on the down low from them," she explains. When she has bills due, her friend will give her $200 or $250, just about what she used to get in TANF benefits. "If he wants some and I need some money to keep the lights on, he hands out a pretty good penny," she says with a laugh.

Her experience isn't especially unusual. Toni Grebel, a relief worker at the Lord's Pantry, an Albany food bank, says she's heard many similar stories from her clients, who, at one time, were virtually all receiving TANF. Stacy Haire, the domestic violence outreach worker, says, "A lot of my clients, they're resorting to favors from men to get money." Albany police data show a sharp jump in arrests for prostitution and other crimes committed by women in 2005—shortly after the state began dumping its TANF caseloads.

Other women are turning to various illicit schemes: trading food stamps for cash to buy diapers; selling their kids' Social Security numbers to people with jobs, who use them to collect the Earned Income Tax Credit. One woman told me she got $800 each for her children's Social Security numbers, which she used to buy her kids summer clothes and new beds. "That money comes in handy. If you're not using it, why not help someone else?" she said.

One afternoon last fall, Letorrea Clark's caseworker from Liberty House, Ellen Folmar, stopped in to give her a ride to the post office. For a while, Clark had landed a job as a nanny, but that ended when school started. A Legal Aid lawyer helped her try to regain her lost disability benefits, but the appeal had recently been denied. Now, she'd lost her food stamp card. For the past few weeks, Gabby had subsisted on little but eggs and rice, and Clark was frantic.

Clark's life is a string of these sorts of crises. Mental illness wreaks havoc with her organizational skills. Medicaid doesn't pay for all her drugs, so when her child support money runs out, she doesn't always take the medication that keeps her stable. Finding no food stamp card at the post office, Clark fell apart. She was such a pathetic sight that a woman handed her $40. A weepy Clark got back in the van, consoled only after Folmar rounded up some emergency food from the shelter to tide the family over. "I got gravy!" Clark exclaimed with delight as she examined her bounty.

Back home later that week, Clark was happily entertaining a fellow Jehovah's Witness, who had a daughter Gabby's age. Gabby danced around the tiny space in her princess nightgown while Clark made the girls a brunch of eggs, bologna slices, tortilla chips, and apple juice cut with water to make it last longer. She put the paper plates on a plastic crate serving as a table. Clark was hoping her friend would get a job so that she could babysit her daughter. "Even in high school I worked with kids. That's my niche," she said. "That's the only thing that makes me happy. If it paid better, I'd be real happy."

As she talked, Clark stuck some donated chicken nuggets into the oven. She joked that her ADD was showing as she burned the first batch. As she started over, the two women swapped stories about ringing doorbells for the Lord. "I get a better response rate with Gabby," Clark said with a laugh. The Witnesses' generosity was on display in her apartment—a donated microwave, the TV, curtains, toys. Clark had piles of religious tracts in the apartment, some in Spanish, a language she was trying to learn from CDs, "so I can find me a Spanish husband," she joked.

The happy scene was but a temporary respite. Gabby's father had found Clark again. Two weeks later, her nonprofit landlord would tell her she had to move, citing budget woes. Shelter workers would search frantically to find her somewhere else to go. (They eventually found a place in yet another town.) Right now, though, Clark was focused on the chicken nuggets, and on Gabby, who climbed up, kissed her mother, and erupted into giggles. "I'm doing a good job with her," Clark said.

Inequalities That Endure?

Racial Ideology, American Politics, and the Peculiar Role of the Social Sciences

Lawrence D. Bobo

As part of research on the intersection of poverty, crime, and race, I conducted two focus groups in a major eastern city in early September 2001, just prior to the tragic events of September 11. The dynamics of the two groups, one with nine white participants and another with nine black participants, drove home for me very powerfully just how deep but also just how sophisticated, elusive, and enduring a race problem the United States still confronts. An example from each group begins to make the point that the very nature of this problem and our vocabularies for discussing it have grown very slippery, very difficult to grasp, and therefore extremely difficult to name and to fight.

First let's consider the white focus group. In response to the moderator's early question, "What's the biggest problem facing your community?" a young working-class white male eagerly and immediately chimed in, "Section 8 housing." "It's a terrible system," he said. The racial implications hung heavy in the room until a middle-aged white bartender tried to leaven things a bit by saying:

> All right. If you have people of a very low economic group who have a low standard of living who cannot properly feed and clothe their children, whose speech patterns are not as good as ours [and] are [therefore] looked down upon as a low class. Where I live most of those people happen to be black. So it's generally perceived that blacks are inferior to whites for that reason.

The bartender went on to explain: "It's not that way at all. It's a class issue, which in many ways is economically driven. From my perspective, it's not a racial issue at all. I'm a bartender. I'll serve anybody if they're a class [act]." At this, the group erupted in laughter, but the young working-class male was not finished. He asserted, a bit more vigorously:

> Why should somebody get to live in my neighborhood that hasn't earned that right? I'd like to live [in a more affluent area], but I can't afford to live there so I don't. . . . So why should somebody get put in there by the government that didn't earn that right?

And then the underlying hostility and stereotyping came out more directly when he said: "And most of the people on that program are trashy, and they don't know how to behave in a working neighborhood. It's not fair. I call it unfair housing laws."

Toward the end of the session, when discussing why the jails are so disproportionately filled with blacks and Hispanics, this same young man said: "Blacks and Hispanics are more violent than white people. I think they are more likely to shoot somebody over a fender bender than a couple of white guys are. They have shorter fuses, and they are more emotional than white people."

In fairness, some members of the white group criticized antiblack prejudice. Some members of the group tried to point out misdeeds done by whites as well. But even the most liberal of the white participants never pushed the point, rarely moved beyond abstract observations or declarations against prejudice, and sometimes validated the racial stereotypes more overtly embraced by others. In an era when everyone supposedly knows what to say and what not to say and is artful about avoiding overt bigotry, this group discussion still quickly turned to racial topics and quickly elicited unabashed negative stereotyping and antiblack hostility.

When asked the same question about the "biggest problem facing your community," the black group almost in unison said, "Crime and drugs," and a few voices chimed in, "Racism." One middle-aged black woman reported: "I was thinking more so on the lines of myself because my house was burglarized three times. Twice while I was at work and one time when I returned from church, I caught the person in there."

The racial thread to her story became clearer when she later explained exactly what happened in terms of general police behavior in her community:

> The first two robberies that I had, the elderly couple that lived next door to me, they called the police. I was at work when the first two robberies occurred. They called the police two or three times. The police never even showed up. When I came in from work, I had to go . . . file a police

report. My neighbors went with me, and they had called the police several times and they never came. Now, on that Sunday when I returned from church and caught him in my house, and the guy that I caught in my house lives around the corner, he has a case history, he has been in trouble since doomsday. When I told [the police] I had knocked him unconscious, oh yeah, they were there in a hurry. Guns drawn. And I didn't have a weapon except for the baseball bat, [and] I wound up face down on my living room floor, and they placed handcuffs on me.

The moderator, incredulous, asked: "Well, excuse me, but they locked you and him up?" "They locked me up and took him to the hospital."

Indeed, the situation was so dire, the woman explained, that had a black police officer who lived in the neighborhood not shown up to help after the patrol car arrived with sirens blaring, she felt certain the two white police officers who arrived, guns drawn, would probably have shot her. As it was, she was arrested for assault, spent two days in jail, and now has a lawsuit pending against the city. Somehow I doubt that a single, middle-aged, churchgoing white woman in an all-white neighborhood who had called the police to report that she apprehended a burglar in her home would end up handcuffed, arrested, and in jail alongside the burglar. At least, I am not uncomfortable assuming that the police would not have entered a home in a white community with the same degree of apprehension, fear, preparedness for violence, and ultimate disregard for a law-abiding citizen as they did in this case. But it can happen in black communities in America today.

To say that the problem of race endures, however, is not to say that it remains fundamentally the same and essentially unchanged. I share the view articulated by historians such as Barbara Fields and Thomas Holt that race is both socially constructed and historically contingent. As such, it is not enough to declare that race matters or that racism endures. *The much more demanding challenge is to account for how and why such a social construction comes to be reconstituted, refreshed, and enacted anew in very different times and places.* How is it that in 2001 we can find a working-class white man who is convinced that many blacks are "trashy people" controlled by emotions and clearly more susceptible to violence? How is it that a black woman defending herself and her home against a burglar ends up apprehended as if she were one of the "usual suspects"? Or cast more broadly, how do we have a milestone like the *Brown* decision and pass a Civil Rights Act, a Voting Rights Act, a Fair Housing Act, and numerous acts of enforcement and amendments to all of these, including the pursuit of affirmative action policies, and yet still continue to face a significant racial divide in America?

The answer I sketch here is but a partial one, focusing on three key observations. First, as I have argued elsewhere and elaborate in important ways here, I believe that we are witnessing the crystallization of a new racial ideology here in the United States. This ideology I refer to as laissez-faire racism. We once confronted a slave labor economy with its inchoate ideology of racism and then watched it evolve in response to war

and other social, economic, and cultural trends into an explicit Jim Crow racism of the de jure segregation era. We have more recently seen the biological and openly segregationist thrust of twentieth-century Jim Crow racism change into the more cultural, free-market, and ostensibly color-blind thrust of laissez-faire racism in the new millennium. But make no mistake—the current social structure and attendant ideology reproduce, sustain, and rationalize enormous black-white inequality.

Second, race and racism remain powerful levers in American national politics. These levers can animate the electorate, constrain and shape political discourse and campaigns, and help direct the fate of major social policies. From the persistently contested efforts at affirmative action through a historic expansion of the penal system and the recent disbanding of "welfare as we know it," the racial divide has often decisively prefigured and channeled core features of our domestic politics.

Third, social science has played a peculiar role in the problem of race. And here I wish to identify an intellectual and scholarly failure to come to grips with the interrelated phenomena of white privilege and black agency. This failure may present itself differently depending on the ideological leanings of scholars. I critique one line of analysis on the left and one on the right. On the left, the problem typically presents as a failure of sociological imagination. It manifests itself in arguments that seek to reduce racialized social dynamics to some ontologically more fundamental nonracialized factor. On the right, the problem is typically the failure of explicit victim-blaming. It manifests itself in a rejection of social structural roots or causation of racialized social conditions. I want to suggest that both tactics—the left's search for some structural force more basic than race (such as class or skill levels or child-rearing practices) and the right's search for completely volitional factors (cultural or individual dispositions) as final causes of "race" differences—reflect a deep misunderstanding of the dynamics of race and racism. Race is not just a set of categories, and racism is not just a collection of individual-level anti-minority group attitudes. Race and racism are more fundamentally about sets of intertwined power relations, group interests and identities, and the ideas that justify and make sense out of (or challenge and delegitimate) the organized racial ordering of society. The latter analytic posture and theory of race in society is embodied in the theory of laissez-faire racism.

On Laissez-Faire Racism

There are those who doubt that we should be talking about racism at all. The journalist Jim Sleeper denounces continued talk of racism and racial bias as mainly so much polarizing "liberal racism." The political scientists Paul Sniderman and Edward Carmines write of the small and diminishing effects of racism in white public opinion and call for us to "reach beyond race." And the linguist John McWhorter writes of a terrible "culture of victimology" that afflicts the nation and ultimately works as a form of self-sabotage among black Americans. Even less overtly ideological writers talk of the growing victory of our Myrdalian "American Creed" over the legacy of racism. Some prominent black intellectuals, such as the legal scholar Randall Kennedy, while not as insensitive to the evidence of real and persistent inequality and discrimination, raise profound questions about race-based claims on the polity.

These analysts, I believe, are wrong. They advance a mistaken and counterproductive analysis of where we are today, how we got here, and the paths that we as a nation might best follow in the future. In many respects, these analysts are so patently wrong that it is easy to dismiss them.

Let's be clear first on what I mean by "racism." Attempts at definition abound in the scholarly literature. William Julius Wilson offers a particularly cogent specification when he argues that racism is "an ideology of racial domination or exploitation that (1) incorporates belief in a particular race's cultural and/or inherent biological inferiority and (2) uses such beliefs to justify and prescribe inferior or unequal treatment for that group." I show here that there remains a profound tendency in the United States to blame racial inequality on the group culture and active choices of African Americans. This is abundantly clear in public opinion data, and it is exemplified by more than a few intellectual tracts, including McWhorter's *Losing the Race.* Closely attendant to this pattern is the profound tendency to downplay, ignore, or minimize the contemporary potency of racial discrimination. Again, this tendency is clear in public opinion and finds expression in the scholarly realm in the Thernstroms' book *America in Black and White.* These building blocks become part of the foundation for rejecting social policy that is race-targeted and aims to reduce or eliminate racial inequality. In effect, these attitudes facilitate and rationalize continued African American disadvantage and subordinated status. Our current circumstances, then, both as social structure and ideology, warrant description and analysis as a racist regime. Yet it is a different, less rigid, more delimited, and more permeable regime as well.

Laissez-faire racism involves persistent negative stereotyping of African Americans, a tendency to blame blacks themselves for the black-white gap in socioeconomic status, and resistance to meaningful policy efforts to ameliorate U.S. racist social conditions and institutions. It represents a critical new stage in American racism. As structures of racial oppression became less formal, as the power resources available to black communities grew and were effectively deployed, as other cultural trends paved the way for an assault on notions of biologically ranked "races," the stage was set for displacing Jim Crow racism and erecting something different in its place.

I have taken up a more complete development of the historical argument and the contemporary structural argument elsewhere. What is worth emphasizing here is, first, the explicit social groundedness and historical foundation of our theoretical logic—something that sets this theory of racial attitudes apart from notions like symbolic racism. Although not directly inspired by his work, our theoretical logic is a direct reflection of ideas articulated by the historian Thomas Holt. As he explains: "Racial phenomena and their meaning do change with time, with history, and with the conceptual and institutional spaces that history unfolds. More specifically they are responsive to major shifts in a political economy and to the cultural systems allied with that political economy."

The second point to emphasize here is that this is an argument about general patterns of group relations and ideology—not merely about variation in views among individuals from a single racial or ethnic category. As such, our primary concern is with the central tendency of attitudes and beliefs within and between racial groups and the social system as such, not within and between individuals. It is the collective dimensions of social experience that I most intend to convey with the notion of laissez-faire racism—not a singular attitude held to a greater or lesser degree by particular individuals. The intellectual case for such a perspective has been most forcefully articulated by the sociologist Mary R. Jackman. We should focus an analysis of attitudes and ideology on group-level comparisons, she writes, because doing so

> draws attention to the structural conditions that encase an intergroup relationship and it underscores the point that individual actors are not free agents but caught in an aggregate relationship. Unless we assume that the individual is socially atomized, her personal experiences constitute only one source of information that is evaluated against the backdrop of her manifold observations of the aggregated experiences (both historical and contemporaneous) of the group as a whole.

The focus is thus more on the larger and enduring patterns and tendencies that distinguish groups than on the individual sources of variation.

With this in mind, I want to focus on three pieces of data, the first of which concerns the persistence of negative stereotypes of African Americans [in a survey he conducted]. . . . Several patterns stand out. It is easier for both blacks and whites to endorse the positive traits when expressing views about the characteristics of blacks than the negative traits. However, African Americans are always more favorable and less negative in their views than whites. Some of the differences are quite large. For instance, there is a thirty-percentage-point difference between white and black perceptions on the trait of intelligence and a thirty-three-percentage-point difference on the "hardworking" trait. . . .

Negative stereotypes of African Americans are common, though not uniform, and to a distressing degree they exist among both blacks and whites and presumably influence perceptions and behaviors for both groups. However, there is a sharp difference in central tendency within each group, in predictable directions. One cannot escape the conclusion that most whites have different and decidedly lesser views of the basic behavioral characteristics of blacks than do blacks themselves. And that generally these patterns indicate that African Americans remain a culturally dishonored and debased group in the American psyche. . . .

On American Politics

As a historic fact and experience as well as a contemporary political condition, racial prejudice has profoundly affected American politics. A wide body of evidence is accumulating to show that racial prejudice still affects politics. Black candidates for office typically encounter a severe degree of difficulties securing white votes, partly owing to racial prejudice. There is some evidence, to be sure, that the potency of racial prejudice varies with the racial composition of electoral districts and the salience of race issues in the immediate political context.

Moreover, political candidates can use covert racial appeals to mobilize a segment of the white voting public under some circumstances. For example, the deployment of the infamous Willie Horton political ad during the 1988 presidential campaign heightened the voting public's concern over race issues. It also accentuated the impact of racial prejudice on electoral choices and did so in a way that did not increase concern with crime per se. That is, what appears to give a figure like Willie Horton such efficacy as a political symbol is not his violent criminal behavior per se, but rather his being a violent black man whose actions upset a racial order that should privilege and protect whites.

Major social policy decisions may also be driven by substantially racial considerations. The political psychologists David Sears and Jack Citrin make a strong case that antiblack prejudice proved to be a powerful source of voting in favor of California's historic property tax reduction initiative (Proposition 13), a change in law that fundamentally altered the resources available to government agencies.

On an even larger stage, the very design and early implementation of core features of the American welfare state were heavily shaped by racial considerations. Robert Lieberman has shown that the programs that became Social Security, Aid to Families with Dependent Children (AFDC), and unemployment insurance were initially designed to either exclude the great bulk of the black population or leave the judgment of qualification and delivery of benefits to local officials. The latter design feature of AFDC (originally ADC) had the effect in most southern states of drastically curtailing the share of social provision that went to African Americans. . . .

There are good reasons to believe that the push to "end welfare as we know it"—which began as a liberal reform effort but was hijacked by the political right and became, literally, the end of welfare as we had known it—was just as surely impelled by heavily racial considerations. The political sociologist Martin Gilens (1999) has carefully analyzed white opinion on the welfare state in the United States. Some features of the welfare state, he finds, lack an overtone of black dependency (such as Social Security) and enjoy high consensus support. Other programs (AFDC, food stamps, general relief) are heavily racialized, with much of the white voting public regarding these programs as helping lazy and undeserving blacks.

Indeed, the fundamental alignment of the U.S. national political panics has been centrally driven by a racial dynamic. Over the past thirty-five years we have witnessed a fundamental transformation in the Democratic and Republican party system, a transformation that political scientists call realignment. The more the Democratic Party was seen as advancing a civil rights agenda and black interests—in a manner that clearly set them apart from the Republican Party—the more race issues and race itself became central to party affiliations, political thinking, and voting in the mass white public. What was once a solid white Democrat-controlled South has thus shifted to a substantially white Republican-controlled South.

The end result of all of these patterns, simply put, is that African Americans do not enjoy a full range of voice, representation, and participation in politics. Black candidates, particularly if they are identified with the black community, are unlikely to be viable in majority white electoral districts. Even white candidates who come to be strongly associated with black interests run the risk of losing many white voters. As a consequence, party leaders on both sides have worked to organize the agenda and claims of African Americans out of national politics. In particular, the national Democratic Party, which should arguably reward its most loyal constituents in the black community, instead has often led the way in pushing black issues off the stage. As the political scientist Paul Frymer has explained, party leaders do so because they are at risk of losing coveted white "swing voters" in national elections if they come to be perceived as catering to black interests. Thus is the elite discourse around many domestic social policies, and their ultimate fate, bound up in racial considerations.

Against this backdrop it becomes difficult, if not counterproductive, to accept the widely shared view that American democracy is on an inexorable path toward ever-greater inclusivity and fuller realization of its democratic potential. In the context of such enduring and powerful racialization of American politics, such an assumption is naive at best.

There is an even more incisive point to be made. The presumption of ever-expanding American liberalism is mistaken. For example, the Pulitzer Prize winning–historian Joseph Ellis writes of the terrible "silence" on the subject of slavery and race that the "founding fathers" *deliberately* adopted. They waged a Revolutionary War for freedom, declared themselves the founders of a new nation, and in very nearly the same moment *knowingly* wedded democracy to slave-based racism. The philosopher Charles Mills extends the reach of this observation by showing the deep bias of Enlightenment thinkers toward a view of those on the European continent—whites—as the only real signatories to the "social contract." Others, particularly blacks, were never genuinely envisioned or embraced as fully human and thus were never intended to be covered by the reach of the social contract.

Considerations of this kind led the political theorist Rogers Smith to suggest that the United States has not one but rather multiple political traditions. One tradition is indeed more democratic, universalistic, egalitarian, and expansive. But this tradition competes with and sometimes decisively loses out to a sharply hierarchical, patriarchal, and racist civic tradition. The ultimate collapse of Reconstruction following the Civil War and the subsequent gradual development of de jure segregation and the Jim Crow racist regime provide one powerful case in point.

Bobo, Lawrence D., Inequalities That Endure? Racial Ideology, American Politics, and the Peculiar Role of the Social Sciences. In *The Changing Terrain of Race and Ethnicity,* edited by Maria Krysan and Amanda E. Lewis. ©2004 Russell Sage Foundation, 112 East 64th Street, New York, NY 10021. Reprinted with permission.

Why We Hate

We may not admit it, but we are plagued with xenophobic tendencies. Our hidden prejudices run so deep, we are quick to judge, fear and even hate the unknown.

MARGO MONTEITH, PhD AND JEFFREY WINTERS

Balbir Singh Sodhi was shot to death on September 15 in Mesa, Arizona. His killer claimed to be exacting revenge for the terrorist attacks of September 11. Upon his arrest, the murderer shouted, "I stand for America all the way." Though Sodhi wore a turban and could trace his ancestry to South Asia, he shared neither ethnicity nor religion with the suicide hijackers. Sodhi—who was killed at the gas station where he worked—died just for being different in a nation gripped with fear.

For Arab and Muslim Americans, the months after the terrorist attacks have been trying. They have been harassed at work and their property has been vandalized. An Arab San Francisco shop owner recalled with anger that his five-year-old daughter was taunted by name-callers. Classmates would yell "terrorist" as she walked by.

Public leaders from President George W. Bush on down have called for tolerance. But the Center for American-Islamic Relations in Washington, D.C., has tallied some 1,700 incidents of abuse against Muslims in the five months following September 11. Despite our better nature, it seems, fear of foreigners or other strange-seeming people comes out when we are under stress. That fear, known as xenophobia, seems almost hardwired into the human psyche.

Researchers are discovering the extent to which xenophobia can be easily—even arbitrarily—turned on. In just hours, we can be conditioned to fear or discriminate against those who differ from ourselves by characteristics as superficial as eye color. Even ideas we believe are just common sense can have deep xenophobic underpinnings. Research conducted this winter at Harvard reveals that even among people who claim to have no bias, the more strongly one supports the ethnic profiling of Arabs at airport-security checkpoints, the more hidden prejudice one has against Muslims.

But other research shows that when it comes to whom we fear and how we react, we do have a choice. We can, it seems, choose not to give in to our xenophobic tendencies.

The Melting Pot

America prides itself on being a melting pot of cultures, but how we react to newcomers is often at odds with that self-image. A few years ago, psychologist Markus Kemmelmeier, PhD, now at the University of Nevada at Reno, stuck stamped letters under the windshield wipers of parked cars in a suburb of Detroit. Half were addressed to a fictitious Christian organization, half to a made-up Muslim group. Of all the letters, half had little stickers of the American flag.

Would the addresses and stickers affect the rate at which the letters would be mailed? Kemmelmeier wondered. Without the flag stickers, both sets of letters were mailed at the same rate, about 75 percent of the time. With the stickers, however, the rates changed: Almost all the Christian letters were forwarded, but only half of the Muslim letters were mailed. "The flag is seen as a sacred object," Kemmelmeier says. "And it made people think about what it means to be a good American."

In short, the Muslims didn't make the cut.

Not mailing a letter seems like a small slight. Yet in the last century, there have been shocking examples of xenophobia in our own back yard. Perhaps the most famous in American history was the fear of the Japanese during World War II. This particular wave of hysteria lead to the rise of slurs and bigoted depictions in the media, and more alarmingly, the mass internment of 120,000 people of Japanese ancestry beginning in 1942. The internments have become a national embarrassment: Most of the Japanese held were American citizens, and there is little evidence that the imprisonments had any real strategic impact.

Today the targets of xenophobia—derived from the Greek word for *stranger*—aren't the Japanese. Instead, they are Muslim immigrants. Or Mexicans. Or Chinese. Or whichever group we have come to fear.

Just how arbitrary are these xenophobic feelings? Two famous public-school experiments show how easy it is to turn one "group" against another. In the late 1960s, California high school history teacher Ron Jones recruited students to participate in an exclusive new cultural program called "the Wave." Within weeks, these students were separating themselves from others and aggressively intimidating critics. Eventually, Jones confronted the students with the reality that they were unwitting participants in an experiment demonstrating the power of nationalist movements.

"Am I fearful of Arab men in turbans? No, I am not. I was born and raised in India, and I am familiar with other races. I have learned to be attuned to different cultures. I find that there are always new, positive things to be learned from other people; it brings out the best in us."

—Sonam Wangmo

A few years later, a teacher in Iowa discovered how quickly group distinctions are made. The teacher, Jane Elliott, divided her class into two groups—those with blue eyes and those with brown or green eyes. The brown-eyed group received privileges and treats, while the blue-eyed students were denied rewards and told they were inferior. Within hours, the once-harmonious classroom became two camps, full of mutual fear and resentment. Yet, what is especially shocking is that the students were only in the third grade.

Social Identity

The drive to completely and quickly divide the world into "us" and "them" is so powerful that it must surely come from some deep-seated need. The exact identity of that need, however, has been subject to debate. In the 1970s, the late Henri Tajfel, PhD, of the University of Bristol in England, and John Turner, PhD, now of the Australian National University, devised a theory to explain the psychology behind a range of prejudices and biases, not just xenophobia. Their theory was based, in part, on the desire to think highly of oneself. One way to lift your self-esteem is to be part of a distinctive group, like a winning team; another is to play up the qualities of your own group and denigrate the attributes of others so that you feel your group is better.

"I am planning a trip to Florida, and I'm nervous about flying with my kids; I'm scared. If an Arab man sat next to me, I would feel nervous. I would wonder, 'Does he have explosives?' But then I feel ashamed to think this way. These poor people must get so scrutinized. It's wrong."

—Terry Kalish

Tajfel and Turner called their insight "social identity theory," which has proved valuable for understanding how prejudices develop. Given even the slenderest of criteria, we naturally split people into two groups—an "in-group" and an "out-group." The categories can be of geopolitical importance—nationality, religion, race, language—or they can be as seemingly inconsequential as handedness, hair color or even height.

Once the division is made, the inferences and projections begin to occur. For one, we tend to think more highly of people in the in-group than those in the out-group, a belief based only on group identity. Also, a person tends to feel that others in the in-group are similar to one's self in ways that—although stereotypical—may have little to do with the original criteria used to split the groups. Someone with glasses may believe that other people who wear glasses are more voracious readers—even more intelligent—than those who don't, in spite of the fact that all he really knows is that they don't see very well. On the other hand, people in the out-group are believed to be less distinct and less complex than are cohorts in the in-group.

Although Tajfel and Turner found that identity and categorization were the root cause of social bias, other researchers have tried to find evolutionary explanations for discrimination. After all, in the distant past, people who shared cultural similarities were found to be more genetically related than those who did not. Therefore, favoring the in-group was a way of helping perpetuate one's genes. Evolutionary explanations seem appealing, since they rely on the simplest biological urges to drive complicated behavior. But this fact also makes them hard to prove. Ironically, there is ample evidence backing up the "softer" science behind social identity theory.

Hidden Bias

Not many of us will admit to having strong racist or xenophobic biases. Even in cases where bias becomes public debate—such as the profiling of Arab Muslims at airport-security screenings—proponents of prejudice claim that they are merely promoting common sense. That reluctance to admit to bias makes the issue tricky to study.

To get around this problem, psychologists Anthony Greenwald, PhD, of the University of Washington in Seattle, and Mahzarin Banaji, PhD, of Harvard, developed the Implicit Association Test. The IAT is a simple test that measures reaction time: The subject sees various words or images projected on a screen, then classifies the images into one of two groups by pressing buttons. The words and images need not be racial or ethnic in nature—one group of researchers tested attitudes toward presidential candidates. The string of images is interspersed with words having either pleasant or unpleasant connotations, then the participant must group the words and images in various ways—Democrats are placed with unpleasant words, for instance.

"For the months following 9/11, I had to endure my daily walk to work along New York City's Sixth Avenue. It seemed that half the people stared at me with accusation. It became unbearable. Yet others showed tremendous empathy. Friends, co-workers and neighbors, even people I had never met, stopped to say, 'I hope your turban has not caused you any trouble.' At heart, this is a great country."

—Rangr

The differences in reaction time are small but telling. Again and again, researchers found that subjects readily tie in-group images with pleasant words and out-group images with unpleasant words. One study compares such groups as whites and blacks, Jews and Christians, and young people and old people. And researchers found that if you identify yourself in one group, it's easier to pair images of that group with pleasant words—and easier to pair the opposite group with unpleasant imagery. This reveals the underlying biases and enables us to study how quickly they can form.

Really though, we need to know very little about a person to discriminate against him. One of the authors of this story, psychologist Margo Monteith, PhD, performed an IAT experiment comparing attitudes toward two sets of made-up names; one set was supposedly "American," the other from the fictitious country of Marisat. Even though the subjects knew nothing about Marisat, they showed a consistent bias against it.

While this type of research may seem out in left field, other work may have more "real-world" applications. The Southern Poverty Law Center runs a Web version of the IAT that measures biases based on race, age and gender. Its survey has, for instance, found that respondents are far more likely to associate European faces, rather than Asian faces, with so-called American images. The implication being that Asians are seen as less "American" than Caucasians.

Similarly, Harvard's Banaji has studied the attitudes of people who favor the racial profiling of Arab Muslims to deter terrorism, and her results run contrary to the belief that such profiling is not driven by xenophobic fears. "We show that those who endorse racial profiling also score high on both explicit and implicit measures of prejudice toward Arab Muslims," Banaji says. "Endorsement of profiling is an indicator of level of prejudice."

Beyond Xenophobia

If categorization and bias come so easily, are people doomed to xenophobia and racism? It's pretty clear that we are susceptible to prejudice and that there is an unconscious desire to divide the world into "us" and "them." Fortunately, however, new research also shows that prejudices are fluid and that when we become conscious of our biases we can take active—and successful—steps to combat them.

Researchers have long known that when observing racially mixed groups, people are more likely to confuse the identity of two black individuals or two white ones, rather than a white with a black. But Leda Cosmides, PhD, and John Tooby, PhD, of the Center for Evolutionary Psychology at the University of California at Santa Barbara, and anthropologist Robert Kurzban, PhD, of the University of California at Los Angeles, wanted to test whether this was innate or whether it was just an artifact of how society groups individuals by race.

To do this, Cosmides and her colleagues made a video of two racially integrated basketball teams locked in conversation, then they showed it to study participants. As reported in the *Proceedings of the National Academy of Sciences,* the researchers discovered that subjects were more likely to confuse two players on the same team, regardless of race, rather than two players of the same race on opposite teams.

Cosmides says that this points to one way of attacking racism and xenophobia: changing the way society imposes group labels. American society divides people by race and by ethnicity; that's how lines of prejudice form. But simple steps, such as integrating the basketball teams, can reset mental divisions, rendering race and ethnicity less important.

This finding supports earlier research by psychologists Samuel Gaertner, PhD, of the University of Delaware in Newark, and John Dovidio, PhD, of Colgate University in Hamilton, New York. Gaertner and Dovidio have studied how bias changes when members of racially mixed groups must cooperate to accomplish shared goals. In situations where team members had to work together, bias could be reduced by significant amounts.

Monteith has also found that people who are concerned about their prejudices have the power to correct them. In experiments, she told subjects that they had performed poorly on tests that measured belief in stereotypes. She discovered that the worse a subject felt about her performance, the better she scored on subsequent tests. The guilt behind learning about their own prejudices made the subjects try harder not to be biased.

This suggests that the guilt of mistaking individuals for their group stereotype—such as falsely believing an Arab is a terrorist—can lead to the breakdown of the belief in that stereotype. Unfortunately, such stereotypes are reinforced so often that they can become ingrained. It is difficult to escape conventional wisdom and treat all people as individuals, rather than members of a group. But that seems to be the best way to avoid the trap of dividing the world in two—and discriminating against one part of humanity.

Read More About It

Nobody Left to Hate: Teaching Compassion After Columbine, Elliot Aronson (W.H. Freeman and Company, 2000)

The Racist Mind: Portraits of American Neo-Nazis and Klansmen, Madonna Kolbenschlag (Penguin Books, 1996)

MARGO MONTEITH, PhD, is an associate professor of psychology at the University of Kentucky. JEFFREY WINTERS is a New York-based science writer.

American Dreamers

**Muslim Americans are one of this country's greatest strengths.
But they're vulnerable as never before.**

LISA MILLER

Fareed Siddiq is a successful businessman and a father of two. He lives in Chagrin Falls, Ohio—a 19th-century mill town built on a river and known for its scenic waterfalls and dams—in a five-bedroom house he recently paid for, in cash, with his savings. Prominent in local civic and religious organizations, including the Red Cross and the chamber of commerce, Siddiq was invited to the InterContinental Hotel in downtown Cleveland earlier this month along with about 400 other business leaders to hear President George W. Bush speak.

He was moved to ask his president a question: "What," he asked, hauling his 6-foot-5, 245-pound frame to the microphone, "are we doing with public diplomacy to change the hearts and minds of a billion and a half Muslims around the world?" What should he tell his friends and relatives in Pakistan about why he continues to live in the United States?

"Great question," answered the president. "I'm confident your answer is, 'I love living in America, the land of the free and the home of the brave, the country where you can come and ask the president a question and a country where—' Are you a Muslim?"

"Yes," answered Siddiq.

"Where you can worship your religion freely. It's a great country where you can do that."

It was a good answer, says Siddiq, but not enough for him—not when he, a financial adviser at a major investment bank, is afraid to use the bathroom on flights because he doesn't want to frighten his fellow passengers as he walks down the aisle. He thinks anti-Muslim sentiment in the country is getting worse, not better. "I'm not so much worried about myself," he adds. "It's the young people I'm concerned with. Those are the people we need to try—not only as Muslims but as Americans—to make them feel part of America. If you alienate the Muslim young people from America, that is dangerous."

Nearly six years after 9/11, the story of Muslims in America is one of overwhelming success. The National Intelligence Estimate released last week warned that Osama bin Laden and Al Qaeda continue to have their sights set on an attack within the United States. The report also notes a growing radicalism among Muslims in the West. But at a press briefing, intelligence officials were particularly concerned about the threat of homegrown terror cells within Europe's Muslim communities. America, the officials said, has so far provided relatively infertile ground for the growing and grooming of Muslim extremists. "Most Muslims in America think of themselves as Americans," says Charlie Allen, intelligence chief at the Homeland Security Department.

In fact, Muslim Americans represent the most affluent, integrated, politically engaged Muslim community in the Western world. According to a major survey done by the Pew Research Center and released last spring, Muslims in America earn about the same as their neighbors, and their educational levels are about the same. An overwhelming number—71 percent—agree that in America, you can "get ahead with hard work." In stark contrast, Muslims in France, Germany and England are about 20 percent more likely to live in poverty.

The alleged terror plots uncovered since 9/11 are a sign that this success cannot be taken for granted. Ire among Muslim Americans at U.S. policies in Iraq, Afghanistan and the Palestinian territories is at a peak, and thanks to satellite news channels like Al-Jazeera and the Internet, that dissatisfaction can spread like fire. As the Muslim community expands and becomes more established, tensions within the community are also growing—between young and old, immigrant and native-born. Across the country, second- and third-generation Muslims are visibly grappling with how to be Muslim and American at once, while their parents look on with pride—and, like Siddiq, concern.

There are 2.35 million Muslims in America according to Pew, though many estimates put that number much higher, and 65 percent of them are foreign-born. These Muslims began coming here in large waves after 1965, when U.S. law changed to allow increased immigration from countries beyond Western Europe. Over the past four decades they have come from South Asia (Pakistan, India and most recently Bangladesh), the Arab world (the Palestinian territories, Lebanon, Egypt, Iran), as well as Europe and Africa. They came for education and advancement, but also to follow family, and—as in the case of the 35,000 Somalis who began arriving in the 1990s—to flee war and oppression in their home countries. The pull of the American dream remains strong. "The U.S. is founded on the idea that we're all connected to a set of ideas, not a set of histories," says Keith Ellison, the Democrat from Minnesota who is Congress's first Muslim. "For all our criticisms, the idea of America is an amazing thing—a society organized around a set of principles instead of around racial or cultural identity."

Most of the Muslims who were born here are African-American converts and descendants of converts. But a fast-growing number are the children of immigrants, and this last group is extremely young; nearly half are between 18 and 29. In this melting pot, no one group is significantly bigger or more powerful than any of the others—it is, Muslim Americans like to say, the most diverse group of Muslims anywhere except in Mecca during the annual pilgrimage, or hajj.

This profound diversity and relative affluence sets the Muslim community here dramatically apart from those in Europe, where Muslims came from their native countries as many as four generations ago largely as factory workers or laborers. "The Moroccans, the Turks, they were recruited for their illiteracy, for their strong hands and good teeth," says the provocative Dutch singer Raja el-Mouhandiz, whose parents were from North Africa. When the factory jobs went away, Europe's Muslims continued to live in ethnic ghettos, isolated from the larger society—a society that tended to be white, homogenous and, on some basic level, impenetrable. In most European countries, Muslim employment is 15 to 40 percent below the population at large.

Significantly, one of the more notable cases in America—the young men from upstate New York, dubbed the Lackawanna Six, who were arrested in 2002 and pleaded guilty to having trained with Al Qaeda in Afghanistan—grew up in an environment somewhat analogous to that of Europe. Yemenites migrated to Lackawanna in the 1930s for jobs in the steel mills. Those jobs disappeared, but the Yemenite population, now fully American, grew and stayed, and the young people there continue to struggle with drugs, crime and unemployment. In the Yemenite neighborhoods of Lackawanna, about a third live below the poverty line.

An equally critical but perhaps less obvious benefit to U.S. Muslims is the religiosity of the American people. Even if a religious practice is regarded with suspicion in America, it is generally treated with respect. In a *Newsweek* poll, 69 percent of Americans said they thought Muslim American students should be allowed to wear headscarves in class. (The devout prime minister of Turkey, a Muslim country with a tradition of militant secularism, actually sent his daughters to America for college so they could continue wearing their scarves.) "When I say to an evangelical Christian, 'It's prayer time,' they might question the way I pray, but they understand viscerally the importance of prayer," says Eboo Patel, founder of the Interfaith Youth Core in Chicago. "When I lived in England"—which Patel did from 1998 to 2001—"and I said, 'It's prayer time,' people looked at me as if I was an alien."

It wouldn't be too much of an exaggeration to say that on September 10, 2001, the Muslim American universe was largely invisible. The only Muslims most people here knew by name

were Malcolm X, Louis Farrakhan and Muhammad Ali. If their doctor or accountant was Muslim, the average American probably didn't give it much thought.

The Muslim community itself was partially responsible for this isolation—like the Italian, Irish and Jewish immigrants before them, many hunkered down in ethnic enclaves. They strove to fit in, but quietly. For decades, the Islamic Center of New England, in Quincy, Mass., was home to a growing group of Lebanese immigrants who came to America for work in the shipyards. It was a cozy place, where people with similar backgrounds came to meet, pray and gossip. The imam, a Lebanese man named Talal Eid, was a perfect fit—he understood the community's values and he shared their interest in becoming American. "I have a woman with a head cover and a Muslim woman without a head cover," he says of his congregation at the time. "I'm not here to judge which is good and which is bad. I am here to serve them all equally." (In the past decade, however, his congregation changed as new immigrants arrived from Algeria, Morocco, Egypt and Pakistan; Eid was ousted in favor of a more conservative imam in 2005.)

The relative peace that came with invisibility disappeared after 9/11. When Muslims became objects of fear, "people who had never recognized and seen themselves as Muslims had no choice but to see themselves as Muslim," says Muzaffar Chisti, director of the Migration Policy Institute at the New York University School of Law. Young women who had never before worn the traditional Islamic head covering—and whose mothers saw it as a symbol of the backwardness they had left at home—put on the veil. According to a 2002 study from Hamilton College, more than a third of Muslim American women now wear the veil every day.

The first thing Razi Mohiuddin and his wife, Tahseen, did after 9/11 was to host an open house for the larger community at their mosque, the Muslim Community Association in Silicon Valley. More than a thousand non-Muslims showed up. The next thing they did was take their children out of their elite private school and install them in the school at the mosque. Before the attacks, the Mohiuddins lived the lives of busy, successful professionals: he launched start-ups; she was a pre-K teacher. Their own religious observance, the backbone of their family life, was private.

After the attacks "our responsibilities changed," says Mohiuddin, who emigrated from India when he was 17. "It forced people to say, 'Where do I stand? Either I walk away from the faith or I become more involved in defending the faith, which [is] under assault'." His children, he thought, needed to know they were Muslim and feel proud. Hindsight has given Mohiuddin more reason to feel glad of this decision; the boys are teenagers now, and Mohiuddin is thankful that they have more than a passing knowledge of the restraint required of an observant Muslim.

To combat the discrimination many were feeling, many Muslim Americans turned, in classic American fashion, to the courts. The Council on American Islamic Relations, an advocacy group, counted nearly 2,500 civil-rights complaints by Muslim Americans in 2006, a dramatic increase over the previous year. These are the kinds of stories that make news—women who sue for the right to wear the *hijab* in their driver's license photo—and Muslim Americans say they show how invested they are in the American system. This is important: history suggests that thriving civil societies tend to smooth the sharper edges of faith. Religious convictions are no less firm or real, but they are less likely to fuel the kind of extremism that can lead to violence. The six imams who were pulled off a US Airways flight last fall after praying openly at a Minneapolis airport gate have sued the airline and the airport commission for civil-rights violations. "I believe in justice in the United States, and that's why we've taken this case to court," says Didmar Faja, one of the imams.

For younger Muslims the attention of the world means they have to grapple in a very conscious way with what they call their hyphenated identity. The result has been an open embrace of their religion, but in a manner suited to the community's diversity. According to Pew, 60 percent of Muslims age 18 to 29 think of themselves as "Muslim first," compared with 40 percent of people older than 30, and they are much more likely than their parents to go to mosque every week. At the same time, they tend to be blind to ethnic and racial differences, and they dismiss Islamic customs about gender roles as so much cultural baggage. Sakina Al-Amin, a student at the University of Michigan at Ann Arbor who is active in the Muslim Students' Association there, says that sometimes "parents are too into culture, and then the child tries to find ways out of it." When a parent objects, for example, to an inter-ethnic marriage, Al-Amin says the children may argue that Islam does not prevent such a union. Idil Jama Farah, a 21-year-old Somali student at the University of Minnesota, is a case in point. She recently married a white Muslim convert from Boston, in spite of her mother's initial disapproval. "I don't think culture is very important. I think religion is important," she says.

In Muslim intellectual circles, imagining ways to accommodate these young people is topic A, but the reality is somewhat grimmer. There are so few homegrown Muslim clerics in America today—and almost no institutions for training them—that prayer in most mosques is led by a scholar fresh off the plane from Lebanon, say, or Saudi Arabia, someone with no connection to America and no affinity for its culture. The foreign-born imams "are at a disconnect with our new generation," says Maher Hathout, an Egyptian-born cardiologist and senior adviser to the Muslim Public Affairs Council in Los Angeles. "If you get the best scholar in Islamics, but he cannot connect with my child or my grandchild, it's a waste. It's the opposite of what we want."

More unsettling is the question of what these foreign-born imams preach. According to unofficial estimates by government investigators, at least 50 percent of American mosques may receive some funding from foreign governments or institutions, mostly Saudi Arabia. The danger is obvious: if Saudi Arabia is exporting its Wahhabi Islam to this country via imams, pamphlets, Qur'ans and buildings, how long before a warped version of this extremist ideology intersects with a vulnerable group of teenagers? So far, connections between Saudi influence and the handful of suspected terror plots hatched here since 9/11 have been tenuous, according to the public record. However, Hathout deems such gifts risky enough that the bylaws of his mosque mandate against them. Foreign money, he says, is "problematic to the point of being dangerous. It creates a dependence."

Whatever its source, fundamentalist Islamic ideology is readily available on the Internet as well as in U.S. mosques. In one poor neighborhood in Trenton, N.J., at the Masjid As-Saffat, which for more than 20 years had served a mixed community of Muslims from Afghanistan, Egypt, Somalia and the Palestinian territories, the presiding imam several years ago suddenly and inexplicably had an ideological change of heart. Whereas once people worshiped together in a communal, almost relaxed way, imam Sabur Abdul Hakim began applying rigid standards to prayer and worship. Last year he closed the mosque school, saying it wasn't sufficiently Islamic, congregants say. He began to preach a Salafi ideology, invoking the purity of the earliest Muslims and disapproving of any variation. In a perfectly American response, a group of Hakim's opponents sued him, demanding that he and his supporters be removed from the board of directors, that they turn over the mosque's accounting books and records and that elections be held to instate new trustees. The case is in mediation; Hakim and his lawyer declined to comment.

While the schism within the mosque is on the surface ideological, it is also at least partly racial and ethnic. The majority of the congregation is foreign-born. Hakim and most of his supporters are African-American. And while the community lived and worshiped together peacefully for almost two decades, Hakim's new stance elicited powerful, dormant feelings about whose Islam is authentic. Gulgai Masuod, a 62-year-old immigrant from Afghanistan, had been close to Hakim for years, but strongly disapproves of his changes. Hakim and his cohorts, says Masuod, "have no knowledge of Islam . . . My father and great-grandfathers have been Muslim for 1,400 years. You are not telling me how to practice Islam."

African-American Muslims say such reactions are common. Growing up African-American and Muslim in Chicago, Ismail Mitchel says he never fit in. Black Muslims are in a "no man's land," says Mitchel, a 21-year-old student at the University of Illinois at Urbana-Champaign. "We get flak from Arabs and we get flak from other black people." Neither group, he says, wants to embrace him. "It's like we're the black sheep of the whole community, literally."

Muslim American advocates have critiqued the press coverage of the Pew study, saying it focused too much on the bad news and not enough on the good. The bad news, however, bears repeating: 26 percent of Muslims age 18 to 29 believe that suicide bombing can be justified. Thirty-eight percent of that group believe that Arabs did not carry out the 9/11 attacks. These data, combined with the rising religious conservatism of young Muslim Americans, have led some experts to argue that differences between Europe and America have been overblown, that affluence and education do not inoculate a society against radicalization. "This idea that all those who are middle class are exempted from extremism has always been false," says Geneive Abdo, author of "Mecca and Main Street." "The leadership of the extremist movements have always been highly educated Muslims."

It's impossible to underestimate the emotional nature of anti-Israel sentiment among Arab-American youth, argues Ismael Ahmed, executive director of the Arab Community Center for Economic and Social Services in Detroit. "I think the poll miscaptures what's being said," he says. "There is such a thing as legitimate resistance to oppression, and there is terrorism on both sides. It's wrong, but there's also the right to resist." The poll numbers, in his view, don't point to a threat of homegrown suicide bombers, but to a passionate defense of a resistance movement—the way, 30 years ago, an Irish-American teenager would have supported the IRA.

The deeper problem is a growing sense of alienation among young Muslims, a sense that they don't feel part of the American story. According to Pew, 39 percent of Muslim Americans age 18 to 29 believe that newly arrived Muslims should remain distinct from society at large, compared with 17 percent of Muslims older than 55. Ferdous Sajedeen arrived here from Bangladesh in 1975 and built a successful pharmacy business in Queens. For years, Sajedeen imagined that he would eventually return to Bangladesh, but after visiting Dhaka several years ago, he realized how impossible that was; he didn't understand the jokes anymore, he didn't feel part of the culture. "I don't deny my roots," he says. "I am proud to be a Bangladeshi, but at the same time the reality is I am a Bangladeshi-American." September 11, he says, was "one of the saddest stories anywhere in the world."

His son Autri, who at 21 is in his fourth year of pharmacy school and lives at home with his parents, does not feel his father's patriotism. "When we grew up, nobody ever looked at us like we were Americans," he says. On 9/11, "it sounds bad to say, but I remember thinking that I didn't care that it happened. A lot of my friends didn't care. I think it's because we're Muslim." For him, the bombing of Afghanistan that followed was much more tragic and painful. Fundamentalists are "crazy," he adds emphatically. He would never condone terrorism.

This sense of alienation can be seen most clearly in places like Lackawanna, home of the six convicted young men. Earlier this year the Lackawanna varsity and junior-varsity soccer teams were suspended from the local league for rough play. The varsity team, which is predominantly Yemenite, accuses some of the referees and fans of being racist. (Fans called them "terrorists" and "camel jockeys" during games, players say.) At the same time, the players broke the rules of good behavior: after losing a critical game, 3-2, they swore at and allegedly spit on the other players, and in one case allegedly shoved a referee. In a town with high unemployment and the constant risk of losing kids to drugs and crime, soccer was a wholesome, if occasionally rough, way to pass the time. The team played "all night, all day," says star varsity forward Hamud Alasri, 17. Alasri was hoping to get a soccer scholarship to the University of Buffalo, but with the team's suspension, that opportunity has passed.

Kathy Ahmed, 37, refused to let her son, Jamil, now 20, join the soccer team; she didn't like the racist environment of the public high school or the league play. Asked if she's worried that the young men in her community are at risk of becoming terrorists, Ahmed says no: the Lackawanna Six were vulnerable boys seduced by a charismatic radical. "I'm not worried about [boys in Lackawanna] becoming terrorists. I worry that they'll lose their spirituality. There are so many things calling them. I see them as lost." Losing Jamil Ahmed and Autri Sajedeen would be the worst thing in the world—not just for them, but for all of us.

With Roya Wolverson in Lackawanna, Sanhita Sen in Queens, Karen Breslau and Robina Riccitiello in Silicon Valley, Julie Scelfo in Trenton, Arian Campo-Flores in Boston, Hilary Shenfeld in Chicago, Roqaya Ashmawey in Ann Arbor, Aisha Eady in Minneapolis, Christopher Dickey in Paris, Mark Hosenball, Daren Briscoe and Abby Dalton in Washington and Owen Matthews in Istanbul.

Great Expectations

**Women now hold half of all management jobs in America.
Business books and magazines tout their superior leadership
style. What's really changing in the country's corner offices?**

JUDITH M. HAVEMANN

On July 17, 1975, less than a year after President Richard M. Nixon resigned in the Watergate scandal, *Washington Post* publisher Katharine Graham threw open the doors of her Georgetown mansion for one of her trademark dinners, with strolling violinists and elegant cuisine. Along the right-hand wall of the foyer, a wheel of tiny envelopes held the table numbers of the 58 guests. On the terrace, Graham, in a pink hostess outfit, greeted people from five different levels of the paper's management by name, introducing each newcomer flawlessly. Then everybody sat down for a gourmet dinner served on her mother's hand-painted china.

It was a virtuoso performance by one of the masters of gracious entertaining. But Graham was applying her formidable social skills to a different arena: her company's business. Although the *Post* was then at the height of its influence and glamour, several of its 13 unions were fighting for their lives. Union contracts were up for negotiation, and Graham, who had become an instant corporate president 12 years earlier on the suicide of her husband, was preparing for trouble. She fretted that the newspaper's managers, on whom she would have to rely to publish the paper in the event of strikes, didn't think of themselves as a team. She wanted her staff to work together and get along. So on a hot July night, Katharine Graham did a stereotypically female thing: She threw a party.

Today her management method is called "transformational" or cooperative—as opposed to the "transactional," or authoritarian, manner then supposedly employed by the men who ran America's biggest companies. But her style was just that—a style. When it came to making decisions, Graham was as tough as any man. She fired former secretary of the Navy Paul Ignatius when he disappointed her as president of the company, hustled his successor upstairs, and ousted a subsequent replacement. When the pressmen's union went on strike in the middle of the night three months after her garden party, she got the paper out with a crew of managers and volunteers. When the pressmen turned down her contract offer, she replaced them with non-union workers.

True, she talked stirringly about women's issues—sensitized by a friendship with Gloria Steinem, no less. But the *Post* implemented little of the feminist's agenda. It had no daycare center and offered only a bare-bones maternity leave. Part-time schedules to accommodate child rearing were a rare privilege, and part-time employees were ineligible for raises. Although the paper was often generous in family tragedies, it had to issue checks to its female news employees to settle an Equal Employment Opportunity Commission sex discrimination suit over hiring, pay, promotions, and leave. Graham was sympathetic to women, but the pay, benefits, and day-to-day operations of the nation's most famous female-led company broke no feminist ground. Today, Graham's longtime executive editor, Ben Bradlee, cannot think of a single decision that she made because she was a woman.

The corporate world of Graham's era was a men's club, by and large, staffed with female worker bees. Little had changed since William H. Whyte wrote his classic midcentury dissection of corporate conformity and bureaucratic culture, *The Organization Man* (1956). Whyte's index includes a single entry for women: "slenderness progression." But under pressure from a growing women's movement and the federal government, by the 1970s businesses were promoting a few women, although it wasn't at all clear how they would fare when they took charge. At the beginning of the decade, Dr. Edgar Berman, a Democratic national committeeman and close confidante of Vice President Hubert Humphrey, created a minor uproar when he opined that "raging hormonal imbalance" rendered women too unstable to hold top jobs, such as president of the United States.

But Berman's view was not all that unusual, at least among men. Women held only a tiny fraction of supervisory jobs, a category that included management of secretarial pools and other ghettoized occupations. They were simply excluded from elite downtown clubs, golf courses, and other institutions.

Leading companies ran advertising campaigns portraying women as playthings—and they worked. The National Organization for Women was outraged by the 1971 "I'm Cheryl, Fly Me" ads for National Airlines, but the number of passengers grew 23 percent in the first year of the campaign.

Today's corporations are as different from their predecessors as 45-rpm records are from iPods. Women hold half of all management, professional, and related jobs in the United States, and—although some of their companies are small—nearly one-quarter of all CEO positions: Between 1997 and 2002 women started an average of 424 new ventures each day, and by 2004 about 6.7 million privately held businesses were majority owned by women, says *The Journal of Small Business Management*. At the very top of the corporate heap, among the country's Fortune 500 companies, women hold 15.6 percent of corporate officer positions (defined as board elected or board appointed), according to Catalyst, a business research institute in New York. They occupy 14.6 percent of the seats on boards of directors. And they run 13 of the corporations.

That's not the revolution many had hoped for, but it's a significant change. The leadership positions held by women are not only in the corporate world but in the nonprofit sector, the military, higher education, and other fields. They sit on boards and campaign for public office. One of them even stands a good chance of making Edgar Berman's worst nightmare come true. In fact, now the shoe is sometimes on the other foot. A handful of management gurus in the business world are proclaiming that possessing a pair of X-chromosomes equips a person to be a superior leader.

In books such as *Enlightened Power* (2005), *Why the Best Man for the Job Is a Woman* (2000), and *The Female Advantage: Women's Ways of Leadership* (1990), to say nothing of *Secrets of Millionaire Moms* (2007), writers are advancing what some call the "great woman school of leadership." Magazines now assure women that their feminine style will give them an edge in the new "transformational" corporation. *BusinessWeek* has declared that women have the "right stuff" and, even more sensationally, that a "new gender gap" might leave men as "losers in a global economy that values mental powers over might."

After several decades of experience and enough studies to fall a sizable hard drive, there ought to be answers to some basic questions about women's leadership: Does difference make a difference? Are women more effective leaders, producing more successful companies? Are female-led firms better places to work?

Increasingly, research shows that women—surprise!—are indeed different from men. They do a better job, on average, of collaborating, coaching, teaching, and inspiring others to be creative. Yet it is far from clear that gender in the corner office makes a momentous difference. Evidence that female-led organizations produce superior results is scant. A leadership style that works well in certain fields may bomb in others. And as people climb closer to the top of an organization, gender-related styles of management seem to matter less than other factors in determining who wins the race and what they do as leaders.

Alice H. Eagly, chair of the department of psychology at Northwestern University and perhaps the most commonly cited scholar on gender-based leadership differences, finds in a recent overview of many studies in the field that superiors, peers, and subordinates generally rate women better leaders than men. Women are more "interpersonally oriented," a key ingredient in the transformational leadership style, now the *modus du jour* in the American corporation. Transformational leaders lead by example, empower their subordinates, and focus on the future. They stress cooperation, mentoring, and collaboration rather than a top-down, authoritarian structure. Many of these attributes are exactly the traits associated with women, even if not all women exhibit them.

In male-dominated occupations, from the military to auto sales, women are still judged less effective than men.

But there are wrinkles. Leaders face expectations that they must meet to persuade others to get behind them, and what peers and subordinates look for can vary according to circumstance. "Neither men nor women are better," Eagly says. "Effectiveness is contextual." Women are ranked higher as leaders in fields such as education, government, and social services, where there is more focus on interaction and—some say—less on the bottom line. And since women are already more numerous in the upper ranks of these fields, those on the way up have an easier time persuading others to accept them as leaders. But in male-dominated occupations, from the military to auto sales, women are still judged less effective than men.

In many industries, stereotypes about leaders are ripped from the playbook of men, and women are at a disadvantage because they don't look "usual or natural" in a leader role, Eagly says. "Women in highly masculine domains often have to contend with expectations and criticisms that they lack the toughness and competitiveness needed to succeed." When they do show grit, they are accused of being unfeminine. Just ask Hillary Clinton, who is criticized for being both too steady and controlled and not emotional *enough*.

Recalling her stint as the head of the troubled computer giant Hewlett-Packard, Carly Fiorina said in a recent interview that her enemies in the corporate and tech worlds routinely referred to her "as either a bimbo—too soft, or a bitch—too hard." She shook up the entire company, eventually laying off 36,000 people and attracting almost as much media attention as the executives who bankrupted Enron and went to jail. "It broke my heart every time we had to do it," she says of the layoffs. "It was tearing what people thought was the heart of the company. But it had to be done to save more jobs. Once I was fired, they said I didn't do enough of it." Hewlett-Packard has since gone from being a laggard to a leader, but Fiorina's successor, rightly or wrongly, has reaped much of the credit.

Barbara Krumsiek, CEO and president of the Calvert Group, a $14 billion mutual fund company, said in an interview that advancement after a certain point "is not a matter of competence, it is how you are perceived." After her first daughter was born, Krumsiek, then still climbing the corporate ladder, began hearing

Women at the Top

Women CEOs by Industry

Nonprofit	29.6%
Health Care	22.1%
Law Firms & Legal Services	17.7%
Finance	9.6%
Real Estate	9.1%
Insurance	8.9%
Pharmaceutical	8.3%
Construction	7.4%
Software	7.3%
Manufacturing	5.2%
Aerospace	4.5%
Automotive	4.2%
Semiconductor	3.1%

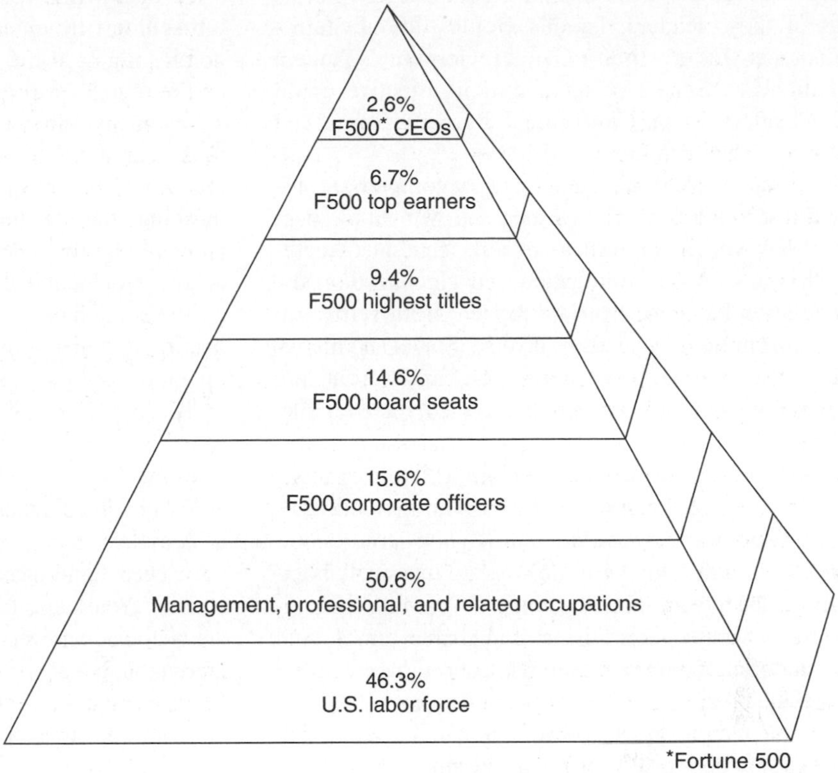
2.6%
F500* CEOs
6.7%
F500 top earners
9.4%
F500 highest titles
14.6%
F500 board seats
15.6%
F500 corporate officers
50.6%
Management, professional, and related occupations
46.3%
U.S. labor force
*Fortune 500

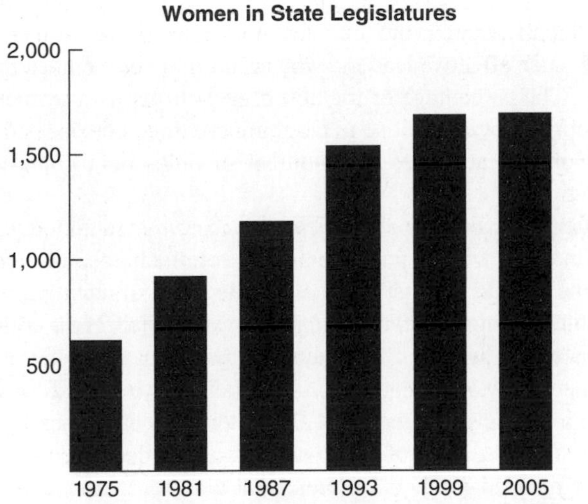
Women in State Legislatures
2,000
1,500
1,000
500
1975
1981
1987
1993
1999
2005

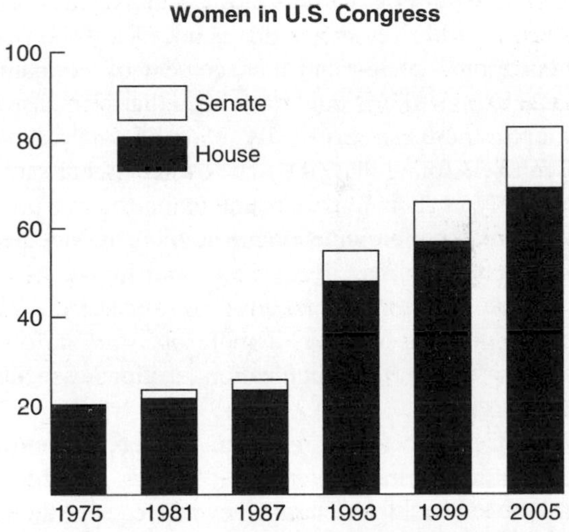
Women in U.S. Congress
100
80
60
40
20
Senate
House
1975
1981
1987
1993
1999
2005

Moving up: Women tend to be judged as more effective in industries where there are more of them. Female state legislators have increased five-fold since 1971, with Democrats outnumbering Republicans by more than two to one. In Congress, the party ratio is roughly the same.

Sources: (top left) *ZoomInfo Inside Report: Gender in the Executive Suite—A Quantitative View of Gender Roles in Business Leadership,* May 2007; (top right) Catalyst Research. *The Catalyst Pyramid: U.S. Women in Business,* 2007; (both bottom charts) Center for American Women and Politics, Eagleton Institute of Politics, Rutgers, The State University of New Jersey.

comments suggesting that she should step aside. A colleague flat out told her, "Women who really love their children stay home with them." Feeling that she had to produce still more signs of her commitment to work, she hired an executive coach and became active in professional organizations. Her climb resumed.

While perceptions matter a great deal, the problem with research such as Eagly's is that it only goes so far. It is one thing to ask people whether the female bosses they know are good leaders, another to find hard evidence that female leadership produces results that are better. Scholars have been able to provide correlations, but no proof. The research group Catalyst, for example, divided the Fortune 500 companies into quartiles based on the share of top management jobs held by women, and found that the companies in the top quartile performed 35 percent better (judged by return on equity) than those in the bottom quartile. But the study didn't show that women were responsible for that success. It may be, for example, that successful companies tend to hire more women.

It is hardly surprising that scholars have not been able to identify a precise "female difference." Just consider the political agendas of these leaders: Israel's Golda Meir, Britain's Margaret Thatcher, India's Indira Gandhi, Germany's Angela Merkel. In the U.S. Senate, what common adjective could describe the leadership of California's Barbara Boxer and North Carolina's Elizabeth Dole?

In the Darwinian world of the contemporary corporation, survival of the fittest requires ambitious men and women to adapt whatever methods work, even if they are soft, "feminine" methods. Under the pressure of competition and globalization, the modern corporation has gone from fat to lean, from vertical to horizontal, and from homogeneous to diverse. Status and hierarchies are out, team building, "open innovation," and learning are in. The corporation's work force is better educated, more mobile, and more demanding than it was only a few decades ago. In this new world, the top-down leadership paradigm of the past looks only a little less outdated than a watch fob. The new mantras, propounded in books such as *Leading at a Higher Level* (2006), *Wikinomics* (2006), and *True North* (2007), are mass collaboration, "authentic" leadership, and becoming a "learning" organization through communication, vision, and shared power. And who's better at collaboration and communication than women? Well, sometimes men are, or at least they are no worse.

Analyzing the results of 50-to-80-minute interviews with male and female owners of 229 firms in the mid-1990s, management scholars Jennifer E. Cliff, Nancy Langton, and Howard E. Aldrich found striking evidence that gender had "no effect" on the organizational design and management of companies. The traditional explanation would have been that women were forced to adopt a more stereotypically masculine approach. In fact, the researchers found that "the male owners in our sample were just as likely as their female counterparts to have implemented archetypically feminine organizational arrangements and practices in their firms." Both male- and female-headed firms, for example, had reduced the levels of hierarchy and cut back on formal policies in favor of more open and informal procedures and modes of communication—actions associated with women leaders.

What was different between men and women, the authors wrote in 2005 in the journal *Organization Studies,* was the way they *talked* about leadership. Men said they wanted to be thought of "as God . . . as capable . . . as the captain of the ship who calls the shots." Women wanted to be thought of as "someone who's here to work for my employees . . . as a resource . . . [as having] their well-being at heart." But despite these contrasting self-evaluations, the management methods men and women adopted were, on the whole, "indistinguishable."

Female business leaders interviewed recently tended to stress that while gender bias often posed special challenges every step of the way, the leadership qualities needed near the top transcended gender. "We don't have a real meritocracy in this country, although we have made great progress," Fiorina says. "Women face barriers and have to work harder to get ahead. Men and women have different styles, and people focus on the style of women and the substance of men. But the fundamentals of leadership are not gender specific."

Ginger Graham, a former Arkansas state rodeo queen with a Harvard MBA, has had an unusual career. She got her first job selling herbicides to local farmers as an agricultural economics major at the University of Arkansas, rose at Eli Lilly, and eventually was named CEO of Amylin, a biopharmaceutical company. When Graham (no relation to Katharine Graham) took over at Amylin in 2003, she adopted a management style that would be unusual, perhaps inconceivable, for a man. The morning after the company's diabetes drug, Symlin, was finally approved by the federal government after 18 years of research and development, she arrived in the office in a Sleeping Beauty costume and handed out copies of the fairy tale. She wanted to inspire a company that now needed to set up a manufacturing operation and hire a sales force almost overnight. When a second drug was approved six weeks later, Graham jumped into the fountain at corporate headquarters. She punctuated company sales meetings with shouts of "whoo-hoo!"

By the time Graham stepped down, this past March, the price of Amylin's stock had nearly doubled. But while her style may have been flamboyant at times, her management moves were classic. "You stand alone in these jobs," she says. "Obviously they are well paid and very fulfilling. They call for an element of collaboration, but at some point you must make the transition from being a collaborator to a decision maker. You have to transform empathy and engagement to accountability and decisiveness."

F inally, there is the touchiest question of all: If women are such effective leaders, why aren't more of them leading? The percentage of the 500 biggest firms with women at the helm is not even close to cracking the three percent barrier, and women's advances in a number of fields have come to a standstill.

After Betty Friedan's *The Feminine Mystique* reignited feminism in 1963, women poured into politics, medicine, the clergy, and the military. Most all-male college enrollment policies crumbled within a decade. Today, more than half of all college graduates are women. They are a majority in many fields of graduate study. Affirmative action policies have helped women move into many occupations. But after early increases in the 1970s and '80s, some of the advances have stalled. The percentage of married mothers of preschool children who are in the labor force has dropped four points since 1997.

In politics, despite the emergence of stars such as Hillary Clinton, Condoleezza Rice, and Nancy Pelosi, gains are uneven. Female representation in state legislatures hasn't budged much since topping 22 percent of legislative seats in 2001. Even some advances are colored by puzzling setbacks. While young women's level of participation in college sports has soared, thanks in part to federal Title IX legislation, the number of female coaches has dropped. Coaches often travel three or four days a week and must go on many recruiting trips during the off-season, a schedule that particularly puts off women who have, or want to have, a family, according to *The Chronicle of Higher Education.*

Anxiety over this stalled progress may explain the firestorm touched off by Princeton graduate Lisa Belkin's 2003 article in *The New York Times Magazine* describing what she called an "opt-out" generation of highly educated women like herself who said, "The heck with it, I'd rather stay at home with my kids."

At first dismissed by some as a luxury confined to elite wives with well-paid husbands, the "opt-out" phenomenon has found some support in statistical evidence, notably the data that show a dip in employment among women at every income level who have younger children. (Sixty percent of these women are now in the labor force.)

"Women naturally don't like this hard-driving competitive atmosphere that is part of business and law firms," argues Phyllis Schlafly, president of the conservative Eagle Forum and a lawyer who played a prominent role in the defeat of the Equal Rights Amendment. It isn't really motherhood that makes women drop out, she says; "they just get tired of it."

Belkin's passionate critics scoff that the moms-go-home theme has been "discovered" at least four times in the last half-century by *The New York Times* alone. They say it's no surprise that women in jobs with no flexibility, forced to choose between feeling they aren't good mothers or aren't good workers, elect to stay home. "If women feel undervalued and stalled in their jobs, no wonder they opt out," says Sally J. Kenney, director of the Center on Women and Public Policy at the University of Minnesota. At the same time, many advocates surely worry that the opt-out phenomenon will reinforce the negative expectation that women won't go the distance, harming the prospects of those who remain in the race.

Increasingly the question of whether women get to the top of the heap hinges on their own choices and actions.

For more than a hundred years, women have explained their lack of power by citing barriers: laws that bar women from certain jobs, prejudice, a pay gap that saps the incentive to keep working, the unequally shared burden of child care and housework, the "mommy track." In addition to the "glass ceiling," British writers have identified a "glass cliff"—the overrepresentation of women in nearly impossible high-level jobs in which the risk of failure is high. It is said that women

are denied plum assignments because they're thought likely to opt out. They choke in emergencies. (Now making the rounds is a study of professional tennis—whose methodology has been vehemently assaulted—showing that women make more unforced errors on crucial points than on others, a difference absent in men.) They won't work as many hours as men. (A recent *Harvard Business Review* survey of "extreme jobs" found that women in these high-pressure white-collar occupations "are not matching the hours logged by their male colleagues.")

Many barriers still exist in some form, but increasingly the question of whether women get to the top of the heap hinges on their own choices and actions. It's possible that the ascension of more women will produce a tipping point, dramatically easing the way for future female leaders in every field. Perhaps the continuing transformation of the corporation and other institutions will make them more female friendly and humane. Maybe Americans three decades from now will look back on our present-day conundrums with the same disbelief with which we view "fly me" advertisements.

Yet a consistent message from women who have reached the heights is that gender does not make a big difference in conducting the essential business of leadership. Katharine Graham had to fire executives and crush unions. It was her son and successor, Donald, who added female-friendly benefits such as family leave, tax-deferred accounts for dependent care, and part-time schedules when they were needed to attract and retain talented people. For mother and son alike, the task was the same: Keep their company healthy and growing.

Just when women have the greatest opportunities in history, top jobs have become more demanding than ever. The pace of change has quickened, the rigors of competition have increased, and the scrutiny of leaders has grown more intense. The route to the top may remain even more difficult than it is for men, but the decision that women face now is whether they want to enter—and perhaps hope to alter—the demolition derby.

JUDITH M. HAVEMANN is senior editor of *The Wilson Quarterly.* She was a reporter and editor during a long career at *The Washington Post.*

From *The Wilson Quarterly,* Summer 2007, pp. 46–53. Copyright © 2007 by Wilson Quarterly. Reprinted by permission.

Human Rights, Sex Trafficking, and Prostitution

ALICE LEUCHTAG

Despite laws against slavery in practically every country, an estimated twenty-seven million people live as slaves. Kevin Bales, in his book *Disposable People: New Slavery in the Global Economy* (University of California Press, Berkeley, 1999), describes those who endure modern forms of slavery. These include indentured servants, persons held in hereditary bondage, child slaves who pick plantation crops, child soldiers, and adults and children trafficked and sold into sex slavery.

A Life Narrative

Of all forms of slavery, sex slavery is one of the most exploitative and lucrative with some 200,000 sex slaves worldwide bringing their slaveholders an annual profit of $10.5 billion. Although the great preponderance of sex slaves are women and girls, a smaller but significant number of males—both adult and children—are enslaved for homosexual prostitution.

The life narrative of a Thai girl named Siri, as told to Bales, illustrates how sex slavery happens to vulnerable girls and women. Siri is born in northeastern Thailand to a poor family that farms a small plot of land, barely eking out a living. Economic policies of structural adjustment pursued by the Thai government under the aegis of the World Bank and the International Monetary Fund have taken former government subsidies away from rice farmers, leaving them to compete against imported, subsidized rice that keeps the market price artificially depressed.

Siri attends four years of school, then is kept at home to help care for her three younger siblings. When Siri is fourteen, a well-dressed woman visits her village. She offers to find Siri a "good job," advancing her parents $2,000 against future earnings. This represents at least a year's income for the family. In a town in another province the woman, a trafficker, "sells" Siri to a brothel for $4,000. Owned by an "investment club" whose members are business and professional men—government bureaucrats and local politicians—the brothel is extremely profitable. In a typical thirty-day period it nets its investors $88,000.

To maintain the appearance that their hands are clean, members of the club's board of directors leave the management of the brothel to a pimp and a bookkeeper. Siri is initiated into prostitution by the pimp who rapes her. After being abused by her first "customer," Siri escapes, but a policeman—who gets a percentage of the brothel profits—brings her back, whereupon the pimp beats her up. As further punishment, her "debt" is doubled from $4,000 to $8,000. She must now repay this, along with her monthly rent and food, all from her earnings of $4 per customer. She will have to have sex with three hundred men a month just to pay her rent. Realizing she will never be able to get out of debt, Siri tries to build a relationship with the pimp simply in order to survive.

The pimp uses culture and religion to reinforce his control over Siri. He tells her she must have committed terrible sins in a past life to have been born a female; she must have accumulated a karmic debt to deserve the enslavement and abuse to which she must reconcile herself. Gradually Siri begins to see herself from the point of view of the slaveholder—as someone unworthy and deserving of punishment. By age fifteen she no longer protests or runs away. Her physical enslavement has become psychological as well, a common occurrence in chronic abuse.

Siri is administered regular injections of the contraceptive drug Depo-Provera for which she is charged. As the same needle is used for all the girls, there is a high risk of HIV and other sexual diseases from the injections. Siri knows that a serious illness threatens her and she prays to Buddha at the little shrine in her room, hoping to earn merit so he will protect her from dreaded disease. Once a month she and the others, at their own expense, are tested for HIV. So far Siri's tests have been negative. When Siri tries to get the male customers to wear condoms—distributed free to brothels by the Thai Ministry of Health—some resist wearing them and she can't make them do so.

As one of an estimated 35,000 women working as brothel slaves in Thailand—a country where 500,000 to one million prostituted women and girls work in conditions of degradation and exploitation short of brothel slavery—Siri faces at least a 40 percent chance of contracting the HIV virus. If she is lucky, she can look forward to live more years before she becomes too ill to work and is pushed out into the street.

Thailand's Sex Tourism

Though the Thai government denies it, the World Health Organization finds that HIV is epidemic in Thailand, with the largest segment of new cases among wives and girlfriends of men who buy prostitute sex. Viewing its women as a cash crop to be exploited, and depending on sex tourism for foreign exchange dollars to help pay interest on the foreign debt, the Thai government can't acknowledge the epidemic without contradicting the continued promotion of sex tourism and prostitution.

By encouraging investment in the sex industry, sex tourism creates a business climate conducive to the trafficking and enslavement of vulnerable girls such as Siri. In 1996 nearly five million sex tourists from the United States, Western Europe, Australia, and Japan visited Thailand. These transactions brought in about $26.2 billion—thirteen times more than Thailand earned by building and exporting computers.

In her 1999 report *Pimps and Predators on the Internet: Globalizing the Sexual Exploitation of Women and Children,* published by the Coalition Against Trafficking in Women (CATW), Donna Hughes quotes from postings on an Internet site where sex tourists share experiences and advise one another. The following is one man's description of having sex with a fourteen-year-old prostituted girl in Bangkok:

> "Even though I've had a lot of better massages . . . after fifteen minutes, I was much more relaxed. . . . Then I asked for a condom and I fucked her for another thirty minutes. Her face looked like she was feeling a lot of pain. . . . She blocked my way when I wanted to leave the room and she asked for a tip. I gave her 600 bath. Altogether, not a good experience."

Hughes says, "To the men who buy sex, a 'bad experience' evidently means not getting their money's worth, or that the prostituted woman or girl didn't keep up the act of enjoying what she had to do . . . one glimpses the humiliation and physical pain most girls and women in prostitution endure."

Nor are the men oblivious to the existence of sexual slavery. One customer states, "Girls in Bangkok virtually get sold by their families into the industry; they work against their will." His knowledge of their sexual slavery and lack of sensitivity thereof is evident in that he then names the hotels in which girls are kept and describes how much they cost!

As Hughes observes, sex tourists apparently feel they have a right to prostitute sex, perceiving prostitution only from a self-interested perspective in which they commodify and objectify women of other cultures, nationalities, and ethnic groups. Their awareness of racism, colonialism, global economic inequalities, and sexism seems limited to the way these realities benefit them as sex consumers.

Sex Traffickers Cast Their Nets

According to the *Guide to the New UN Trafficking Protocol* by Janice Raymond, published by the CATW in 2001, the United Nations estimates that sex trafficking in human beings is a $5 billion to $7 billion operation annually. Four million persons are moved illegally from one country to another and within countries each year, a large proportion of them women and girls being trafficked into prostitution. The United Nations International Children's Emergency Fund (UNICEF) estimates that some 30 percent of women being trafficked are minors, many under age thirteen. The International Organization on Migration estimates that some 500,000 women per year are trafficked into Western Europe from poorer regions of the world. According to *Sex Trafficking of Women in the United States: International and Domestic Trends,* also published by the CATW in 2001, some 50,000 women and children are trafficked into the United States each year, mainly from Asia and Latin America.

Because prostitution as a system of organized sexual exploitation depends on a continuous supply of new "recruits," trafficking is essential to its continued existence. When the pool of available women and girls dries up, new women must be procured. Traffickers cast their nets ever wide and become ever more sophisticated. The Italian Camorra, Chinese Triads, Russian Mafia, and Japanese Yakuza are powerful criminal syndicates consisting of traffickers, pimps, brothel keepers, forced labor lords, and gangs which operate globally.

After the breakdown of the Soviet Union, an estimated five thousand criminal groups formed the Russian Mafia, which operates in thirty countries. The Russian Mafia traffics women from African countries, the Ukraine, the Russian Federation, and Eastern Europe into Western Europe, the United States, and Israel. The Triads traffick women from China, Korea, Thailand, and other Southeast Asian countries into the United States and Europe. The Camorra traffics women from Latin America into Europe. The Yakuza traffics women from the Philipines, Thailand, Burma, Cambodia, Korea, Nepal, and Laos into Japan.

A Global Problem Meets a Global Response

Despite these appalling facts, until recently no generally agreed upon definition of trafficking in human beings was written into international law. In Vienna, Austria, during 1999 and 2000, 120 countries participated in debates over a definition of trafficking. A few nongovernmental organizations (NGOs) and a minority of governments—including Australia, Canada, Denmark, Germany, Ireland, Japan, the Netherlands, Spain, Switzerland, Thailand, and the United Kingdom—wanted to separate issues of trafficking from issues of prostitution. They argued that persons being trafficked should be divided into those who are forced and those who give their consent, with the burden of proof being placed on persons being trafficked. They also urged that the less explicit means of control over trafficked persons—such as abuse of a victim's vulnerability—not be included in the definition of trafficking and that the word *exploitation* not be used. Generally supporters of this position were wealthier countries where large numbers of women were being trafficked and countries in which prostitution was legalized or sex tourism encouraged.

> **People being trafficked shouldn't be divided into those who are forced and those who give their consent because trafficked persons are in no position to give meaningful consent.**

The CATW—140 other NGOs that make up the International Human Rights Network plus many governments (including those of Algeria, Bangladesh, Belgium, China, Columbia, Cuba, Egypt, Finland, France, India, Mexico, Norway, Pakistan, the Philippines, Sweden, Syria, Venezuela, and Vietnam)—maintains that trafficking can't be separated from prostitution. Persons being trafficked shouldn't be divided into those who are forced and those who give their consent because trafficked persons are in no position to give meaningful consent. The subtler methods used by traffickers, such as abuse of a victim's vulnerability, should be included in the definition of trafficking and the word *exploitation* be an essential part of the definition. Generally supporters of this majority view were poorer countries from which large numbers of women were being trafficked or countries in which strong feminist, anti-colonialist, or socialist influences existed. The United States, though initially critical of the majority position, agreed to support a definition of trafficking that would be agreed upon by consensus.

The struggle—led by the CATW to create a definition of trafficking that would penalize traffickers while ensuring that all victims of trafficking would be protected—succeeded when a compromise proposal by Sweden was agreed to. A strongly worded and inclusive *UN Protocol to Prevent, Suppress, and Punish Trafficking in Persons*—especially women and children—was drafted by an ad hoc committee of the UN as a supplement to the Convention Against Transnational Organized Crime. The UN protocol specifically addresses the trade in human beings for purposes of prostitution and other forms of sexual exploitation, forced labor or services, slavery or practices similar to slavery, servitude, and the removal of organs. The protocol defines trafficking as:

> The recruitment, transportation, transfer, harboring or receipt of persons, by means of the threat or use of force or other forms of coercion, of abduction, of fraud, of deception, of the abuse of power or of a position of vulnerability or of the giving or receiving of payments or benefits to achieve the consent of a person having control over another person, for the purpose of exploitation.

While recognizing that the largest amount of trafficking involves women and children, the wording of the UN protocol clearly is gender and age neutral, inclusive of trafficking in both males and females, adults and children.

In 2000 the UN General Assembly adopted this convention and its supplementary protocol; 121 countries signed the convention and eighty countries signed the protocol. For the convention and protocol to become international law, forty countries must ratify them.

Highlights

Some highlights of the new convention and protocol are:

For the first time there is an accepted international definition of trafficking and an agreed-upon set of prosecution, protection, and prevention mechanisms on which countries can base their national legislation.

- The various criminal means by which trafficking takes place, including indirect and subtle forms of coercion, are covered.
- Trafficked persons, especially women in prostitution and child laborers, are no longer viewed as illegal migrants but as victims of a crime.

> **For the first time there is an accepted international definition of trafficking and an agreed-upon set of prosecution, protection, and prevention mechanisms on which countries can base their national legislation.**

- The convention doesn't limit its scope to criminal syndicates but defines an organized criminal group as "any structured group of three or more persons which engages in criminal activities such as trafficking and pimping."
- All victims of trafficking in persons are protected, not just those who can prove that force was used against them.
- The consent of a victim of trafficking is meaningless and irrelevant.
- Victims of trafficking won't have to bear the burden of proof.
- Trafficking and sexual exploitation are intrinsically connected and not to be separated.
- Because women trafficked domestically into local sex industries suffer harmful effects similar to those experienced by women trafficked transnationally, these women also come under the protections of the protocol.
- The key element in trafficking is the exploitative purpose rather than the movement across a border.

The protocol is the first UN instrument to address the demand for prostitution sex, a demand that results in the human rights abuses of women and children being trafficked. The protocol recognizes an urgent need for governments to put the buyers of prostitution sex on their policy and legislative agendas, and it calls upon countries to take or strengthen legislative or other measures to discourage demand, which fosters all the forms of sexual exploitation of women and children.

As Raymond says in the *Guide to the New UN Trafficking Protocol:*

"The least discussed part of the prostitution and trafficking chain has been the men who buy women for sexual exploitation in prostitution. . . . If we are to find a permanent path to ending these human rights abuses, then we cannot just shrug our shoulders and say, "men are like this," or "boys will be boys," or "prostitution has always been around." Or tell women and girls in prostitution that they must continue to do what they do because prostitution is inevitable. Rather, our responsibility is to make men change their behavior, by all means available—educational, cultural and legal."

Two U.S. feminist, human rights organizations—Captive Daughters and Equality Now—have been working toward that goal. Surita Sandosham of Equality Now says that when her organization asked women's groups in Thailand and the Philippines how it could assist them, the answer came back, "Do something about the demand." Since then the two organizations have legally challenged sex tours originating in the United States and have succeeded in closing down at least one operation.

Refugees, Not Illegal Aliens

In October 2000 the U.S. Congress passed a bill, the Victims of Trafficking and Violence Protection Act of 2000, introduced by New Jersey republican representative Chris Smith. Under this law penalties for traffickers are raised and protections for victims increased. Reasoning that desperate women are unable to give meaningful consent to their own sexual exploitation, the law adopts a broad definition of sex trafficking so as not to exclude so-called consensual prostitution or trafficking that occurs solely within the United States. In these respects the new federal law conforms to the UN protocol.

Two features of the law are particularly noteworthy:

- In order to pressure other countries to end sex trafficking, the U.S. State Department is to make a yearly assessment of other countries' anti-trafficking efforts and to rank them according to how well they discourage trafficking. After two years of failing to meet even minimal standards, countries are subject to sanctions, although not sanctions on humanitarian aid. "Tier 3" countries—those failing to meet even minimal standards—include Greece, Indonesia, Israel, Pakistan, Russia, Saudi Arabia, South Korea, and Thailand.
- Among persons being trafficked into the United States, special T-visas will be provided to those who meet the criteria for having suffered the most serious trafficking abuses. These visas will protect them from deportation so they can testify against their traffickers. T-non immigrant status allows eligible aliens to remain in the United States temporarily and grants specific non-immigrant benefits. Those acquiring T-1 non-immigrant status will be able to remain for a period of three years

and will be eligible to receive certain kinds of public assistance—to the same extent as refugees. They will also be issued employment authorization to "assist them in finding safe, legal employment while they attempt to retake control of their lives."

A Debate Rages

A worldwide debate rages about legalization of prostitution fueled by a 1998 International Labor Organization (ILO) report entitled *The Sex Sector: The Economic and Social Bases of Prostitution in Southeast Asia.* The report follows years of lobbying by the sex industry for recognition of prostitution as "sex work." Citing the sex industry's unrecognized contribution to the gross domestic product of four countries in Southeast Asia, the ILO urges governments to officially recognize the "sex sector" and "extend taxation nets to cover many of the lucrative activities connected with it." Though the ILO report says it stops short of calling for legalization of prostitution, official recognition of the sex industry would be impossible without it.

Raymond points out that the ILO's push to redefine prostitution as sex work ignores legislation demonstrating that countries can reduce organized sexual exploitation rather than capitulate to it. For example, Sweden prohibits the purchase of sexual services with punishments of still fines or imprisonment, thus declaring that prostitution isn't a desirable economic and labor sector. The government also helps women getting out of prostitution to rebuild their lives. Venezuela's Ministry of Labor has ruled that prostitution can't be considered work because it lacks the basic elements of dignity and social justice. The Socialist Republic of Vietnam punishes pimps, traffickers, brothel owners, and buyers—sometimes publishing buyer's names in the mass media. For women in prostitution, the government finances medical, educational, and economic rehabilitation.

> **Instead of transforming the male buyer into a legitmate customer, the ILO should give thought to innovative programs that make the buyer accountable for his sexual exploitation.**

Raymond suggests that instead of transforming the male buyer into a legitimate customer, the ILO should give thought to innovative programs that make the buyer accountable for his sexual exploitation. She cites the Sage Project, Inc. (SAGE) program in San Francisco, California, which educates men arrested for soliciting women in prostitution about the risks and impacts of their behavior.

Legalization advocates argue that the violence, exploitation, and health effects suffered by women in prostitution aren't inherent to prostitution but simply result from the random behaviors of bad pimps or buyers, and that if prostitution were regulated by the state these harms would diminish. But examples show these arguments to be false.

Prostituted women are even more marginalized and tightly locked into the system of organized sexual exploitation while the state, now an official party to the exploitation, has become the biggest pimp of all.

In the pamphlet entitled *Legalizing Prostitution Is Not the Answer: The Example of Victoria, Australia,* published by the CATW in 2001, Mary Sullivan and Sheila Jeffreys describe the way legalization in Australia has perpetuated and strengthened the culture of violence and exploitation inherent in prostitution. Under legalization, legal and illegal brothels have proliferated, and trafficking in women has accelerated to meet the increased demand. Pimps, having even more power, continue threatening and brutalizing the women they control. Buyers continue to abuse women, refuse to wear condoms, and spread the HIV virus—and other sexually transmitted diseases—to their wives and girlfriends. Stigmatized by identity cards and medial inspections, prostituted women are even more marginalized and tightly locked into the system of organized sexual exploitation while the state, now an official party to the exploitation, has become the biggest pimp of all.

The government of the Netherlands has legalized prostitution, doesn't enforce laws against pimping, and virtually lives off taxes from the earnings of prostituted women. In the book *Making the Harm Visible* (published by the CATW in 1999), Marie-Victoire Louis describes the effects on prostituted women of municipal regulation of brothels in Amsterdam and other Dutch cities. Her article entitled "Legalizing Pimping, Dutch Style" explains the way immigration policies in the Netherlands are shaped to fit the needs of the prostitution industry so that traffickers are seldom prosecuted and a continuous supply of women is guaranteed. In Amsterdam's 250 officially listed brothels, 80 percent of the prostitutes have been trafficked in from other countries and 70 percent possess no legal papers. Without money, papers, or contact with the outside world, these immigrant women live in terror instead of being protected by the regulations governing brothels, prostituted women are frequently beaten up and raped by pimps. These "prostitution managers" have practically been given a free hand by the state and by buyers who, as "consumers of prostitution," feel themselves entitled to abuse the women they buy. Sadly and ironically the "Amsterdam model" of legalization and regulation is touted by the Netherlands and Germany as "self-determination and empowerment for women." In reality it simply legitimizes the "right" to buy, sexually use, and profit from the sexual exploitation of someone else's body.

A Human Rights Approach

As part of a system of organized sexual exploitation, prostitution can be visualized along a continuum of abuse with brothel slavery at the furthest extreme. All along the continuum, fine lines divide the degrees of harm done to those caught up in the system. At the core lies a great social injustice no cosmetic reforms can right: the setting aside of a segment of people whose bodies can be purchased for sexual use by others. When this basic injustice is legitimized and regulated by the state and when the state profits from it, that injustice is compounded.

In her book *The Prostitution of Sexuality* (New York University Press, 1995), Kathleen Barry details a feminist human rights approach to prostitution that points the way to the future. Ethically it recognizes prostitution, sex trafficking, and the globalized industrialization of sex as massive violations of women's human rights. Sociologically it considers how and to what extent prostitution promotes sex discrimination against individual women, against different racial categories of women, and against women as a group. Politically it calls for decriminalizing prostitutes while penalizing pimps, traffickers, brothel owners, and buyers.

Understanding that human rights and restorative justice go hand in hand, the feminist human rights approach to prostitution addresses the harm and the need to repair the damage. As Barry says:

"Legal proposals to criminalize customers, based on the recognition that prostitution violates and harms women, must ... include social-service, health and counseling and job retraining programs. Where states would be closing down brothels if customers were criminalized, the economic resources poured into the former prostitution areas could be turned toward producing gainful employment for women."

With the help of women's projects in many countries—such as Buklod in the Philippines and the Council for Prostitution Alternatives in the United States—some women have begun to confront their condition by leaving prostitution, speaking out against it, revealing their experiences, and helping other women leave the sex industry.

Ending the sexual exploitation of trafficking and prostitution will mean the beginning of a new chapter in building a humanist future—a more peaceful and just future in which men and women can join together in love and respect, recognizing one another's essential dignity and humanity. Humanity's sexuality then will no longer be hijacked and distorted.

Freelance writer **ALICE LEUCHTAG** has worked as a social worker, counselor, college instructor, and researcher. Active in the civil rights, peace, socialist, feminist, and humanist movements, she has helped organize women in Houston to oppose sex trafficking.

Answers to Questions about Marriage Equality

HUMAN RIGHTS CAMPAIGN, 2009

10 Facts

1. Same-sex couples live in 99.3 percent of all counties nationwide.
2. There are an estimated 3.1 million people living together in same-sex relationships in the United States.
3. Fifteen percent of these same-sex couples live in rural settings.
4. One out of three lesbian couples is raising children. One out of five gay, male couples is raising children.
5. Between 1 million and 9 million children are being raised by lesbian, gay, and bisexual parents in the United States today.
6. At least one same-sex couple is raising children in 96 percent of all counties nationwide.
7. The highest percentages of same-sex couples raising children live in the South.
8. Nearly one in four same-sex couples includes a partner 55 years old or older, and nearly one in five same-sex couples is composed of two people 55 or older.
9. More than one in 10 same-sex couples include a partner 65 years old or older, and nearly one in 10 same-sex couples is composed of two people 65 or older.
10. The states with the highest numbers of same-sex senior couples are also the most popular for straight senior couples: California, New York, and Florida.

These facts are based on analyses of the 2000 Census conducted by the Urban Institute and the Human Rights Campaign. The estimated number of people in same-sex relationships has been adjusted by 62 percent to compensate for the widely reported undercount in the Census. (See "Gay and Lesbian Families in the United States: Same-Sex Unmarried Partner Households" at www.hrc.org.)

Why Same-Sex Couples Want to Marry

Many same-sex couples want the right to legally marry because they are in love—many, in fact, have spent the last 10, 20, or 50 years with that person—and they want to honor their relationship in the greatest way our society has to offer, by making a public commitment to stand together in good times and bad, through all the joys and challenges family life brings.

Many parents want the right to marry because they know it offers children a vital safety net and guarantees protections that unmarried parents cannot provide. And still other people—both gay and straight—are fighting for the right of same-sex couples to marry because they recognize that it is simply not fair to deny some families the protections all other families are eligible to enjoy.

Currently in the United States, same-sex couples in long-term, committed relationships pay higher taxes and are denied basic protections and rights granted to married straight couples. Among them:

- **Hospital visitation.** Married couples have the automatic right to visit each other in the hospital and make medical decisions. Same-sex couples can be denied the right to visit a sick or injured loved one in the hospital.
- **Social Security benefits.** Married people receive Social Security payments upon the death of a spouse. Despite paying payroll taxes, gay and lesbian partners receive no Social Security survivor benefits—resulting in an average annual income loss of $5,528 upon the death of a partner.
- **Immigration.** Americans in bi-national relationships are not permitted to petition for their same-sex partners to immigrate. As a result, they are often forced to separate or move to another country.
- **Health insurance.** Many public and private employers provide medical coverage to the spouses of their employees, but most employers do not provide coverage to the life partners of gay and lesbian employees. Gay and lesbian employees who do receive health coverage for their partners must pay federal income taxes on the value of the insurance.
- **Estate taxes.** A married person automatically inherits all the property of his or her deceased spouse without paying estate taxes. A gay or lesbian taxpayer is forced to pay estate taxes on property inherited from a deceased partner.

- **Family leave.** Married workers are legally entitled to unpaid leave from their jobs to care for an ill spouse. Gay and lesbian workers are not entitled to family leave to care for their partners.
- **Nursing homes.** Married couples have a legal right to live together in nursing homes. The rights of elderly gay or lesbian couples are an uneven patchwork of state laws.
- **Home protection.** Laws protect married seniors from being forced to sell their homes to pay high nursing home bills; gay and lesbian seniors have no such protection.
- **Pensions.** After the death of a worker, most pension plans pay survivor benefits only to a legal spouse of the participant. Gay and lesbian partners are excluded from such pension benefits.

Why Civil Unions Aren't Enough

Comparing marriage to civil unions is a bit like comparing diamonds to rhinestones. One is, quite simply, the real deal; the other is not. Consider:

- Opposite-sex couples who are eligible to marry may have their marriage performed in any state and have it recognized in every other state in the nation and every country in the world.
- Couples who are joined in a civil union, for example in Vermont, New Jersey, or New Hampshire, have no guarantee that its protections will travel with them to other states.

Moreover, even couples who have a civil union and remain in Vermont, New Jersey, or New Hampshire receive only second-class protections in comparison to their married friends and neighbors. While they receive state-level protections, they do not receive any of the more than 1,100 federal benefits and protections of marriage.

In short, civil unions are not separate but equal—they are separate and unequal. And our society has tried separate before. It just doesn't work.

Marriage:
- State grants marriage licenses to couples.
- Religious institutions are not required to perform marriage ceremonies.

Civil unions:
- State would grant civil union licenses to couples.
- Couples receive legal protections and rights under state law only.
- Civil unions are not necessarily recognized by other states or the federal government.
- Religious institutions are not required to perform civil union ceremonies.

Answers to Questions People Are Asking
Answers to Questions about Marriage Equality

"I believe God meant marriage for men and women. How can I support marriage for same-sex couples?"

Many people who believe in God—as well as fairness and justice for all—ask this question. They feel a tension between religious beliefs and democratic values that has been experienced in many different ways throughout our nation's history. That is why the framers of our Constitution established the principle of separation of church and state.

That principle applies no less to the marriage issue than it does to any other. Indeed, the answer to the apparent dilemma between religious beliefs and support for equal protections for all families lies in recognizing that marriage has a significant religious meaning for many people, but that it is also a legal contract. And it is strictly the legal—not the religious—dimension of marriage that is being debated now.

Granting marriage rights to same-sex couples would not require leaders of Christian, Jewish, Islamic, or any other religious leaders to perform these marriages. It would not require religious institutions to permit these ceremonies to be held on their grounds. It would not even require that religious communities discuss the issue. People of faith would remain free to make their own judgments about what makes a marriage in the eyes of God—just as they are today.

Consider, for example, the difference in how the Roman Catholic Church and the U.S. government view couples who have divorced and remarried. Because church tenets do not sanction divorce, the second marriage is not valid in the church's view. The government, however, recognizes the marriage by extending to the remarried couple the same rights and protections as those granted to every other married couple in America. In this situation—as would be the case in marriage for same-sex couples—the church remains free to establish its own teachings on the religious dimension of marriage while the government upholds equality under law.

A growing number of religious communities bless same-sex unions, including Reform Judaism, the Unitarian Universalist Association, and the Metropolitan Community Church. The Presbyterian Church (USA) allows ceremonies to be performed but they're not considered the same as marriage. The Episcopal Church, United Church of Christ, and the United Synagogue of Conservative Judaism allow individual congregations to set their own policies on same-sex unions.

"This is different from interracial marriage. Sexual orientation is a choice."

"We cannot keep turning our backs on gay and lesbian Americans. I have fought too hard and too long against discrimination based on race and color not to stand up against discrimination based on sexual orientation. I've heard the reasons for opposing civil marriage for same-sex couples. Cut through the distractions, and they stink of the same fear, hatred, and intolerance I have known in racism and in bigotry."

—Rep. John Lewis, D-Ga., a leader of the black civil rights movement, writing in the *Boston Globe,* Nov. 25, 2003

Decades of research all point to the fact that sexual orientation is not a choice, and that a person's sexual orientation cannot be changed. To whom one is drawn is a fundamental aspect of who we are.

In this way, the struggle for marriage equality for same-sex couples is just as basic as the successful fight for interracial marriage. It recognizes that Americans should not be coerced into false and unhappy marriages but should be free to marry the person they love—thereby building marriage on a true and stable foundation.

"I strongly believe children need a mother and a father."

Many of us grew up believing that everyone needs a mother and father, regardless of whether we ourselves happened to have two parents, or two good parents.

But as families have grown more diverse in recent decades, and researchers have studied how these different family relationships affect children, it has become clear that the quality of a family's relationship is more important than the particular structure of families that exist today.

In other words, the qualities that help children grow into good and responsible adults—learning how to learn, to have compassion for others, to contribute to society and be respectful of others and their differences—do not depend on the sexual orientation of their parents but on their parents' ability to provide a loving, stable and happy home, something no class of Americans has an exclusive hold on.

That is why research studies have consistently shown that children raised by gay and lesbian parents do just as well as children raised by straight parents in all conventional measures of child development, such as academic achievement, psychological well-being and social abilities.

That is also why the nation's leading child welfare organizations, including the American Academy of Pediatrics, the American Academy of Family Physicians and others, have issued statements that dismiss assertions that only straight couples can be good parents—and declare that the focus should now be on providing greater protections for the 1 million to 9 million children being raised by gay and lesbian parents in the United States today.

"Can't same-sex couples go to a lawyer to secure all the rights they need?"

Not by a long shot. When a gay or lesbian person gets seriously ill, there is no legal document that can make their[sic] partner eligible to take leave from work under the federal Family and Medical Leave Act to provide care—because that law applies only to married couples.

When gay or lesbian people grow old and in need of nursing home care, there is no legal document that can give them the right to Medicaid coverage without potentially causing their partner to be forced from their home—because the federal Medicaid law only permits married spouses to keep their home without becoming ineligible for benefits.

And when a gay or lesbian person dies, there is no legal document that can extend Social Security survivor benefits or the right to inherit a retirement plan without severe tax burdens that stem from being "unmarried" in the eyes of the law.

These are only a few examples of the critical protections that are granted through more than 1,100 federal laws that protect only married couples.

In the absence of the right to marry, same-sex couples can only put in place a handful of the most basic arrangements, such as naming each other in a will or a power of attorney. And even these documents remain vulnerable to challenges in court by disgruntled family members.

(Rethinking) Gender

A growing number of Americans are taking their private struggles with their identities into the public realm. How those who believe they were born with the wrong bodies are forcing us to re-examine what it means to be male and female.

DEBRA ROSENBERG

Growing up in Corinth, Miss., J. T. Hayes had a legacy to attend to. His dad was a well-known race-car driver and Hayes spent much of his childhood tinkering in the family's greasy garage, learning how to design and build cars. By the age of 10, he had started racing in his own right. Eventually Hayes won more than 500 regional and national championships in go-kart, midget and sprint racing, even making it to the NASCAR Winston Cup in the early '90s. But behind the trophies and the swagger of the racing circuit, Hayes was harboring a painful secret: he had always believed he was a woman. He had feminine features and a slight frame—at 5 feet 6 and 118 pounds he was downright dainty—and had always felt, psychologically, like a girl. Only his anatomy got in the way. Since childhood he'd wrestled with what to do about it. He'd slip on "girl clothes" he hid under the mattress and try his hand with makeup. But he knew he'd find little support in his conservative hometown.

In 1991, Hayes had a moment of truth. He was driving a sprint car on a dirt track in Little Rock when the car flipped end over end. "I was trapped upside down, engine throttle stuck, fuel running all over the racetrack and me," Hayes recalls. "The accident didn't scare me, but the thought that I hadn't lived life to its full potential just ran chill bumps up and down my body." That night he vowed to complete the transition to womanhood. Hayes kept racing while he sought therapy and started hormone treatments, hiding his growing breasts under an Ace bandage and baggy T shirts.

Finally, in 1994, at 30, Hayes raced on a Saturday night in Memphis, then drove to Colorado the next day for sex-reassignment surgery, selling his prized race car to pay the tab. Hayes chose the name Terri O'Connell and began a new life as a woman who figured her racing days were over. But she had no idea what else to do. Eventually, O'Connell got a job at the mall selling women's handbags for $8 an hour. O'Connell still hopes to race again, but she knows the odds are long: "Transgendered and professional motor sports just don't go together."

To most of us, gender comes as naturally as breathing. We have no quarrel with the "M" or the "F" on our birth certificates. And, crash diets aside, we've made peace with how we want the world to see us—pants or skirt, boa or blazer, spiky heels or sneakers. But to those who consider themselves transgender, there's a disconnect between the sex they were assigned at birth and the way they see or express themselves. Though their numbers are relatively few—the most generous estimate from the National Center for Transgender Equality is between 750,000 and 3 million Americans (fewer than 1 percent)—many of them are taking their intimate struggles public for the first time. In April, *L.A. Times* sportswriter Mike Penner announced in his column that when he returned from vacation, he would do so as a woman, Christine Daniels. Nine states plus Washington, D.C., have enacted antidiscrimination laws that protect transgender people—and an additional three states have legislation pending, according to the Human Rights Campaign. And this month the U.S. House of Representatives passed a hate-crimes prevention bill that included "gender identity." Today's transgender Americans go far beyond the old stereotypes (think "Rocky Horror Picture Show"). They are soccer moms, ministers, teachers, politicians, even young children. Their push for tolerance and acceptance is reshaping businesses, sports, schools and families. It's also raising new questions about just what makes us male or female.

Born female, he feels male. 'I challenge the idea that all men were born with male bodies.'

—Mykell Miller, age 20

What is gender anyway? It is certainly more than the physical details of what's between our legs. History and science suggest that gender is more subtle and more complicated than anatomy. (It's separate from sexual orientation, too, which determines which sex we're attracted to.) Gender helps us organize the world into two boxes, his and hers, and gives us a way of quickly sizing up every person we see on the street. "Gender is a way of making the world secure," says feminist scholar Judith Butler, a rhetoric professor at University of California, Berkeley. Though some scholars like Butler consider gender largely a social construct, others increasingly see it as a complex interplay of biology, genes, hormones and culture.

She kept her job as a high-school teacher. 'Most people don't get this fortunate kind of ending.'

—Karen Kopriva, age 49

Genesis set up the initial dichotomy: "Male and female he created them." And historically, the differences between men and women in this country were thought to be distinct. Men, fueled by testosterone, were the providers, the fighters, the strong and silent types who brought home dinner. Women, hopped up on estrogen (not to mention the mothering hormone oxytocin), were the nurturers, the communicators, the soft, emotional ones who got that dinner on the table. But as society changed, the stereotypes faded. Now even discussing gender differences can be fraught. (Just ask former Harvard president Larry Summers, who unleashed a wave of criticism when he suggested, in 2005, that women might have less natural aptitude for math and science.) Still, even the most diehard feminist would likely agree that, even apart from genitalia, we are not exactly alike. In many cases, our habits, our posture, and even cultural identifiers like the way we dress set us apart.

Now, as transgender people become more visible and challenge the old boundaries, they've given voice to another debate—whether gender comes in just two flavors. "The old categories that everybody's either biologically male or female, that there are two distinct categories and there's no overlap, that's beginning to break down," says Michael Kimmel, a sociology professor at SUNY-Stony Brook. "All of those old categories seem to be more fluid." Just the terminology can get confusing. "Transsexual" is an older term that usually refers to someone who wants to use hormones or surgery to change their sex. "Transvestites," now more politely called "cross-dressers," occasionally wear clothes of the opposite sex. "Transgender" is an umbrella term that includes anyone whose gender identity or expression differs from the sex of their birth—whether they have surgery or not.

Gender identity first becomes an issue in early childhood, as any parent who's watched a toddler lunge for a truck or a doll can tell you. That's also when some kids may become aware that their bodies and brains don't quite match up. Jona Rose, a 6-year-old kindergartner in northern California, seems like a girl in nearly every way—she wears dresses, loves pink and purple, and bestowed female names on all her stuffed animals.

But Jona, who was born Jonah, also has a penis. When she was 4, her mom, Pam, offered to buy Jona a dress, and she was so excited she nearly hyperventilated. She began wearing dresses every day to preschool and no one seemed to mind. It wasn't easy at first. "We wrung our hands about this every night," says her dad, Joel. But finally he and Pam decided to let their son live as a girl. They chose a private kindergarten where Jona wouldn't have to hide the fact that he was born a boy, but could comfortably dress like a girl and even use the girls' bathroom. "She has been pretty adamant from the get-go: 'I am a girl,'" says Joel.

Male or female, we all start life looking pretty much the same. Genes determine whether a particular human embryo will develop as male or female. But each individual embryo is equipped to be either one—each possesses the Mullerian ducts that become the female reproductive system as well as the Wolffian ducts that become the male one. Around eight weeks of development, through a complex genetic relay race, the X and the male's Y chromosomes kick into gear, directing the structures to become testes or ovaries. (In most cases, the unneeded extra structures simply break down.) The ovaries and the testes are soon pumping out estrogen and testosterone, bathing the developing fetus in hormones. Meanwhile, the brain begins to form, complete with receptors—wired differently in men and women—that will later determine how both estrogen and testosterone are used in the body.

After birth, the changes keep coming. In many species, male newborns experience a hormone surge that may "organize" sexual and behavioral traits, says Nirao Shah, a neuroscientist at UCSF. In rats, testosterone given in the first week of life can cause female babies to behave more like males once they reach adulthood. "These changes are thought to be irreversible," says Shah. Between 1 and 5 months, male human babies also experience a hormone surge. It's still unclear exactly what effect that surge has on the human brain, but it happens just when parents are oohing and aahing over their new arrivals.

Here's where culture comes in. Studies have shown that parents treat boys and girls very differently—breast-feeding boys longer but talking more to girls. That's going on while the baby's brain is engaged in a massive growth spurt. "The brain doubles in size in the first five years after birth, and the connectivity between the cells goes up hundreds of orders of magnitude," says Anne Fausto-Sterling, a biologist and feminist at Brown University who is currently investigating whether subtle differences in parental behavior could influence gender identity in very young children. "The brain is interacting with culture from day one."

So what's different in transgender people? Scientists don't know for certain. Though their hormone levels seem to be the same as non-trans levels, some scientists speculate that their brains react differently to the hormones, just as men's differ from women's. But that could take decades of further research to prove. One 1997 study tantalizingly suggested structural differences between male, female and transsexual brains, but it has yet to be successfully replicated. Some transgender people blame the environment, citing studies that show pollutants have disrupted reproduction in frogs and other animals. But those links are so far not proved in humans. For now, transgender issues are classified as "Gender Identity Disorder" in the psychiatric manual DSM-IV. That's controversial, too—gay-rights activists spent years campaigning to have homosexuality removed from the manual.

Gender fluidity hasn't always seemed shocking. Cross-dressing was common in ancient Greece and Rome, as well as among Native Americans and many other indigenous societies, according to Deborah Rudacille, author of "The Riddle of Gender." Court records from the Jamestown settlement in 1629 describe the case of Thomas Hall, who claimed to be both a man and a woman. Of course, what's considered masculine or feminine has long been a moving target. Our Founding Fathers wouldn't be surprised to see men today with long hair or earrings, but they might be puzzled by women in pants.

Transgender opponents have often turned to the Bible for support. Deut. 22:5 says: "The woman shall not wear that which pertaineth unto a man, neither shall a man put on a woman's garment: for all that do so are abomination unto the Lord thy God." When word leaked in February that Steve Stanton, the Largo, Fla., city manager for 14 years, was planning to transition to life as a woman, the community erupted. At a public meeting over whether Stanton should be fired, one of many critics, Ron Sanders, pastor of the Lighthouse Baptist Church, insisted that Jesus would "want him terminated." (Stanton did lose his job and this week will appear as Susan Stanton on Capitol Hill to lobby for antidiscrimination laws.) Equating gender change with homosexuality, Sanders says that "it's an abomination, which means that it's utterly disgusting."

Not all people of faith would agree. Baptist minister John Nemecek, 56, was surfing the Web one weekend in 2003, when his wife was at a baby shower. Desperate for clues to his long-suppressed feelings of femininity, he stumbled across an article about gender-identity disorder on WebMD. The suggested remedy was sex-reassignment surgery—something Nemecek soon thought he had to do. Many families can be ripped apart by such drastic changes, but Nemecek's wife of 33 years stuck by him. His employer of 15 years, Spring Arbor University, a faith-based liberal-arts college in Michigan, did not. Nemecek says the school claimed that transgenderism violated its Christian principles, and when it renewed Nemecek's contract—by then she was taking hormones and using the name Julie—it barred her from dressing as a woman on campus or even wearing earrings. Her workload and pay were cut, too, she says. She filed a discrimination claim, which was later settled through mediation. (The university declined to comment on the case.) Nemecek says she has no trouble squaring her gender change and her faith. "Actively expressing the feminine in me has helped me grow closer to God," she says.

Others have had better luck transitioning. Karen Kopriva, now 49, kept her job teaching high school in Lake Forest, Ill., when she shaved her beard and made the switch from Ken. When Mark Stumpp, a vice president at Prudential Financial, returned to work as Margaret in 2002, she sent a memo to her colleagues (subject: Me) explaining the change. "We all joked about wearing panty hose and whether 'my condition' was contagious," she says. But "when the dust settled, everyone got back to work." Companies like IBM and Kodak now cover

trans-related medical care. And 125 Fortune 500 companies now protect transgender employees from job discrimination, up from three in 2000. Discrimination may not be the worst worry for transgender people: they are also at high risk of violence and hate crimes.

Perhaps no field has wrestled more with the issue of gender than sports. There have long been accusations about male athletes' trying to pass as women, or women's taking testosterone to gain a competitive edge. In the 1960s, would-be female Olympians were required to undergo gender-screening tests. Essentially, that meant baring all before a panel of doctors who could verify that an athlete had girl parts. That method was soon scrapped in favor of a genetic test. But that quickly led to confusion over a handful of genetic disorders that give typical-looking women chromosomes other than the usual XX. Finally, the International Olympic Committee ditched mandatory lab-based screening, too. "We found there is no scientifically sound lab-based technique that can differentiate between man and woman," says Arne Ljungqvist, chair of the IOC's medical commission.

The IOC recently waded into controversy again: in 2004 it issued regulations allowing transsexual athletes to compete in the Olympics if they've had sex-reassignment surgery and have taken hormones for two years. After convening a panel of experts, the IOC decided that the surgery and hormones would compensate for any hormonal or muscular advantage a male-to-female transsexual would have. (Female-to-male athletes would be allowed to take testosterone, but only at levels that wouldn't give them a boost.) So far, Ljungqvist doesn't know of any transsexual athletes who've competed. Ironically, Renee Richards, who won a lawsuit in 1977 for the right to play tennis as a woman after her own sex-reassignment surgery, questions the fairness of the IOC rule. She thinks decisions should be made on a case-by-case basis.

> ## 'We all joked about wearing panty hose and whether "condition" was contagious.'
> —Margaret Stumpp, age 54

Richards and other pioneers reflect the huge cultural shift over a generation of gender change. Now 70, Richards rejects the term transgender along with all the fluidity it conveys. "God didn't put us on this earth to have gender diversity," she says. "I don't like the kids that are experimenting. I didn't want to be something in between. I didn't want to be trans anything. I wanted to be a man or a woman."

But more young people are embracing something we would traditionally consider in between. Because of the expense, invasiveness and mixed results (especially for women becoming men), only 1,000 to 2,000 Americans each year get sex-reassignment surgery—a number that's on the rise, says Mara Keisling of the National Center for Transgender Equality. Mykell Miller, a Northwestern University student born female who now considers himself male, hides his breasts under a special compression vest. Though he one day wants to take hormones and get a mastectomy, he can't yet afford it. But that doesn't affect his self-image. "I challenge the idea that all men were born with male bodies," he says. "I don't go out of my way to be the biggest, strongest guy."

Nowhere is the issue more pressing at the moment than a place that helped give rise to feminist movement a generation ago: Smith College in Northampton, Mass. Though Smith was one of the original Seven Sisters women's colleges, its students have now taken to calling it a "mostly women's college," in part because of a growing number of "transmen" who decide to become male after they've enrolled. In 2004, students voted to remove pronouns from the student government constitution as a gesture to transgender students who no longer identified with "she" or "her." (Smith is also one of 70 schools that have antidiscrimination policies protecting transgender students.) For now, anyone who is enrolled at Smith may graduate, but in order to be admitted in the first place, you must have been born a female. Tobias Davis, class of '03, entered Smith as a woman, but graduated as a "transman." When he first told friends over dinner, "I think I might be a boy," they were instantly behind him, saying "Great! Have you picked a name yet?" Davis passed as male for his junior year abroad in Italy even without taking hormones; he had a mastectomy last fall. Now 25, Davis works at Smith and writes plays about the transgender experience. (His work "The Naked I: Monologues From Beyond the Binary" is a trans take on "The Vagina Monologues.")

As kids at ever-younger ages grapple with issues of gender variance, doctors, psychologists and parents are weighing how to balance immediate desires and long-term ones. Like Jona Rose, many kids begin questioning gender as toddlers, identifying with the other gender's toys and clothes. Five times as many boys as girls say their gender doesn't match their biological sex, says Dr. Edgardo Menvielle, a psychiatrist who heads a gender-variance outreach program at Children's National Medical Center. (Perhaps that's because it's easier for girls to blend in as tomboys.) Many of these children eventually move on and accept their biological sex, says Menvielle, often when they're exposed to a disapproving larger world or when they're influenced by the hormone surges of puberty. Only about 15 percent continue to show signs of gender-identity problems into adulthood, says Ken Zucker, who heads the Gender Identity Service at the Centre for Addiction and Mental Health in Toronto.

In the past, doctors often advised parents to direct their kids into more gender-appropriate clothing and behavior. Zucker still tells parents of unhappy boys to try more-neutral activities— say chess club instead of football. But now the thinking is that kids should lead the way. If a child persists in wanting to be the other gender, doctors may prescribe hormone "blockers" to keep puberty at bay. (Blockers have no permanent effects.) But they're also increasingly willing to take more lasting steps: Isaak Brown (who started life as Liza) began taking male hormones at 16; at 17 he had a mastectomy.

For parents like Colleen Vincente, 44, following a child's lead seems only natural. Her second child, M. (Vincente asked to use an initial to protect the child's privacy), was born female. But as soon as she could talk, she insisted on wearing boy's clothes. Though M. had plenty of dolls, she gravitated toward "the boy things" and soon wanted to shave off all her hair. "We went along with that," says Vincente. "We figured it was a phase." One day, when she was 2 ½, M. overheard her parents talking about her using female pronouns. "He said, 'No—I'm a him. You need to call me him,'" Vincente recalls. "We were shocked." In his California preschool, M. continued to insist he was a boy and decided to change his name. Vincente and her husband, John, consulted a therapist, who confirmed their instincts to let M. guide them. Now 9, M. lives as a boy and most people have no idea he was born otherwise. "The most important thing is to realize this is who your child is," Vincente says. That's a big step for a family, but could be an even bigger one for the rest of the world.

This story was written by **Debra Rosenberg,** with reporting from Lorraine Ali, Mary Carmichael, Samantha Henig, Raina Kelley, Matthew Philips, Julie Scelfo, Kurt Soller, Karen Springen and Lynn Waddell.

UNIT 4

Institutional Problems

Unit Selections

26. **The Frayed Knot,** *The Economist*
27. **The Opt-Out Myth,** E. J. Graff
28. **Good Parents, Bad Results,** Nancy Shute
29. **Overworked, Time Poor, and Abandoned by Uncle Sam: Why Don't American Parents Protest?,** Janet C. Gornick
30. **Peer Marriage,** Pepper Schwartz
31. **Against School: How Public Education Cripples Our Kids, and Why,** John Taylor Gatto
32. **Can the Center Find a Solution That Will Hold?: The High School Experience: Proposals for Improvement,** Chester E. Finn, Jr.
33. **Fixing Hospitals,** Robert Langreth
34. **The Medical Mafia,** Katherine Eban

Key Points to Consider

- What changes in the family in the past half century do you think are good, and what changes do you think are bad? What can be done about the bad changes?

- What are the forces behind high divorce rates? Will these forces decline or increase? Defend your answer.

- How are work life and careers affecting family life?

- What type of marriage relationship do you think is ideal?

- What are some major principles of good parenting?

- What is wrong with America's education system, and how can it be improved?

- What are some of the major problems with the health care system today?

Student Website
www.mhhe.com/cls

Internet References

The Center for Education Reform
http://edreform.com/school_choice

Go Ask Alice!
http://www.goaskalice.columbia.edu

The National Academy for Child Development (NACD)
http://www.nacd.org

National Council on Family Relations (NCFR)
http://www.ncfr.com

National Institute on Aging (NIA)
http://www.nih.gov/nia

National Institute on Drug Abuse (NIDA)
www.nida.nih.gov

National Institutes of Health (NIH)
http://www.nih.gov

Parenting and Families
http://www.cyfc.umn.edu/features/index.html

World Health Organization (WHO)
http://www.who.int/home-page

This unit looks at the problems in three institutional areas: family, education, and health care. The family is the basic institution in society. Politicians and preachers are earnestly preaching this message today as though most people need to be convinced, but everyone already agrees. Nevertheless, families are having real problems, and sociologists should be as concerned as are preachers. Unlike the preachers who blame the couples who divorce for shallow commitment, sociologists point to additional causes such as the numerous changes in society that have had an impact on the family. For example, women have to work because many men do not make enough income to support a family adequately. So, women are working not only to enjoy a career but also out of necessity. Working women are often less dependent on their husbands. As a result, divorce can be an option for badly treated wives.

In the first article, *The Economist* shows that the common complaints about the increasing problems of marriage are not true of the upper and middle classes but are overwhelmingly true of the lower class and contributes substantially to its poverty. Next, E. J. Graff attacks the media-reported myth that many upper-class women are opting out of work in order to raise children. The facts are that more than ever before, women, including mothers, are working in the labor force. The real story is the inflexibility of workplaces that give women with children only bad choices. Some women choose to stay home because better choices are not available. In the next article, Nancy Schute reports on the research findings about good and bad parenting practices. Some common parenting mistakes are overindulging children on the one hand and nagging or lecturing them on the other hand. Parents must set limits but not micromanage their children. Not surprisingly, research shows that loving them is essential to good parenting.

Next, Janet C. Gornick reports on the work/family time pressures on parents that are adversely affecting families. This is where government policies could be a big help, but the U.S. lags far behind other developed countries on such policies. In the following article, Pepper Schwartz claims that peer marriages have become quite common in just one generation. Old patriarchal norms have been challenged and no longer provide a sure normative guide to marriage patterns because they are out of step with modern culture, society, and economic conditions.

© Stockbyte/Getty Images

"Peer marriage offers a new formula for family and marital stability that may be . . . better adapted to the demands of contemporary culture."

The second subsection deals with education, a perennial problem area. John Taylor Gatto attacks the U.S. school system for slowing the maturation of students and for being boring. He suspects that this result is exactly what those who control the school system want schools to do. In arguing his radical thesis, Gatto presents a very provocative history of the evolution of the U.S. school system. A key issue for many parents and children is the quality of education, and the public's perception is rather negative. In the next article Chester E. Finn, Jr., addresses the failure of U.S. high schools. He identifies six major problems and offers his solutions for each.

The last subsection deals with health-care issues, and this sphere is also in turmoil and plagued with problems. Robert Langreth reveals that medical errors could be responsible for some 100,000 deaths a year. He proposes reforms to prevent many of these mistakes. Finally, Katherine Eban gives a thorough account of some doctors and lawyers defrauding health and car insurance companies for unnecessary health-care costs and damages for car accidents. They got caught but did not pay appropriately for their crimes. This maddening story shines light on some of the problems of the medical and legal systems in this country.

The Frayed Knot

As the divorce rate plummets at the top of American society and rises at the bottom, the widening "marriage gap" is breeding inequality.

The students at West Virginia University don't want you to think they take life too seriously. It is the third-best "party school" in America, according to the Princeton Review's annual ranking of such things, and comes a creditable fifth in the "lots of beer" category. Booze sometimes causes students' clothes to fall off. Those who wake up garmentless after a hook-up endure the "walk of shame," trudging back to their own dormitories in an obviously borrowed football shirt, stirring up gossip with every step.

And yet, for all their protestations of wildness, the students are a serious-minded bunch. Yes, they have pre-marital sex. "I don't see how it's a bad thing," says Ashley, an 18-year-old studying criminology. But they are careful not to fall pregnant. It would be "a major disaster," says Miss Hill. She has plans. She wants to finish her degree, go to the FBI academy in Virginia and then start a career as a "profiler" helping to catch dangerous criminals. She wants to get married when she is about 24, and have children perhaps at 26. She thinks having children out of wedlock is not wrong, but unwise.

A few blocks away, in a soup kitchen attached to a church, another 18-year-old balances a baby on her knee. Laura has a less planned approach to parenthood. "It just happened," she says. The father and she were "never really together," merely "friends with benefits, I guess." He is now gone. "I didn't want to put up with his stuff," she says. "Drugs and stuff," she adds, by way of explanation.

There is a widening gulf between how the best- and least-educated Americans approach marriage and child-rearing. Among the elite (excluding film stars), the nuclear family is holding up quite well. Only 4% of the children of mothers with college degrees are born out of wedlock. And the divorce rate among college-educated women has plummeted. Of those who first tied the knot between 1975 and 1979, 29% were divorced within ten years. Among those who first married between 1990 and 1994, only 16.5% were.

At the bottom of the education scale, the picture is reversed. Among high school dropouts, the divorce rate rose from 38% for those who first married in 1975–79 to 46% for those who first married in 1990–94. Among those with a high school diploma but no college, it rose from 35% to 38%. And these figures are only part of the story. Many mothers avoid divorce by never marrying in the first place. The out-of-wedlock birth rate among women who drop out of high school is 15%. Among African-Americans, it is a staggering 67%.

Does this matter? Kay Hymowitz of the Manhattan Institute, a conservative think-tank, says it does. In her book "Marriage and Caste in America," she argues that the "marriage gap" is the chief source of the country's notorious and widening inequality. Middle-class kids growing up with two biological parents are "socialised for success." They do better in school, get better jobs and go on to create intact families of their own. Children of single parents or broken families do worse in school, get worse jobs and go on to have children out of wedlock. This makes it more likely that those born near the top or the bottom will stay where they started. America, argues Ms Hymowitz, is turning into "a nation of separate and unequal families."

A large majority—92%—of children whose families make more than $75,000 a year live with two parents (including step-parents). At the bottom of the income scale—families earning less than $15,000—only 20% of children live with two parents. One might imagine that this gap arises simply because two breadwinners earn more than one. A single mother would have to be unusually talented and diligent to make as much as $75,000 while also raising children on her own. And it is impossible in America for two full-time, year-round workers to earn less than $15,000 between them, unless they are (illegally) paid less than the minimum wage.

But there is more to it than this. Marriage itself is "a wealth-generating institution," according to Barbara Dafoe Whitehead and David Popenoe, who run the National Marriage Project at Rutgers University. Those who marry "till death do us part" end up, on average, four times richer than those who never marry. This is partly because marriage provides economies of scale—two can live more cheaply than one—and because the kind of people who make more money—those who work hard, plan for the future and have good interpersonal skills—are more likely to marry and stay married. But it is also because marriage affects the way people behave.

American men, once married, tend to take their responsibilities seriously. Avner Ahituv of the University of Haifa and Robert Lerman of the Urban Institute found that "entering marriage raises hours worked quickly and substantially." Married men

More education, less divorce . . .

Marital dissolution rates*
By women's level of education, %

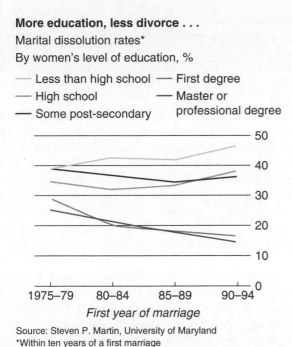

Source: Steven P. Martin, University of Maryland
*Within ten years of a first marriage

. . . and fewer single parents

Percentage of children raised by single mothers
By education of the mother

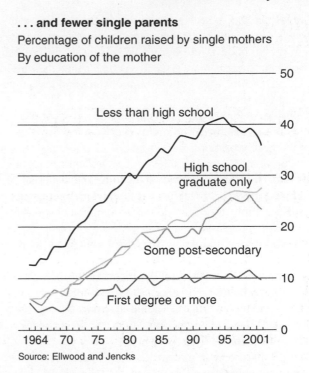

Source: Ellwood and Jencks

drink less, take fewer drugs and work harder, earning between 10% and 40% more than single men with similar schooling and job histories. And marriage encourages both spouses to save and invest more for the future. Each partner provides the other with a form of insurance against falling sick or losing a job.

Marriage also encourages the division of labour. Ms Dafoe Whitehead and Mr Popenoe put it like this: "Working as a couple, individuals can develop those skills in which they excel, leaving others to their partner." Mum handles the tax returns while Dad fixes the car. Or vice versa. As Adam Smith observed two centuries ago, when you specialise, you get better at what you do, and you produce more.

Perhaps the most convincing work showing that marriage is more than just a piece of paper was done by Mr Lerman of the Urban Institute. In "Married and Unmarried Parenthood and Economic Well-being," he addressed the "selection effect"—the question of whether married-couple families do better because of the kind of people who marry, or because of something about marriage itself.

Using data from a big annual survey, he looked at all the women who had become pregnant outside marriage. He estimated the likelihood that they would marry, using dozens of variables known to predict this, such as race, income and family background. He then found out whether they did in fact marry, and what followed.

His results were striking. Mothers who married ended up much better off than mothers with the same disadvantages who did not. So did their children. Among those in the bottom quartile of "propensity to marry," those who married before the baby was six months old were only half as likely to be raising their children in poverty five years later as those who did not (33% to 60%).

Changes in family structure thus have a large impact on the economy. One of the most-cited measures of prosperity, household income, is misleading over time because household

sizes have changed. In 1947, the average household contained 3.6 people. By 2006, that number had dwindled to 2.6. This partly reflects two happy facts: more young singles can afford to flee the nest and their parents are living longer after they go. But it also reflects the dismal trend towards family break-up. A study by Adam Thomas and Isabel Sawhill concluded that if the black family had not collapsed between 1960 and 1998, the black child-poverty rate would have been 28.4% rather than 45.6%. And if white families had stayed like they were in 1960, the white child poverty rate would have been 11.4% rather than 15.4%.

Children of the Sexual Revolution

Since the 1960s, the easy availability of reliable contraception has helped to spur a revolution in sexual mores. As opportunities for women opened up in the work-place, giving them an incentive to delay child-bearing, a little pill let them do just that without sacrificing sex. At the same time, better job opportunities for women changed the balance of power within marriage. Wives became less economically dependent on their husbands, so they found it easier to walk out of unhappy or abusive relationships.

As the sexual revolution gathered steam, the idea that a nuclear family was the only acceptable environment in which to raise a child crumbled. The social stigma around single motherhood, which was intense before the 1960s, has faded. But attitudes still vary by class.

College-educated women typically see single motherhood as a distant second-best to marriage. If they have babies out of wedlock, it is usually because they have not yet got round to marrying the man they are living with. Or because, finding themselves single and nearly 40, they decide they cannot wait for Mr Right and so seek a sperm donor. By contrast, many of America's least-educated women live in neighbourhoods where single motherhood is the norm. And when they have babies outside marriage, they are typically younger than their middle-class counterparts, in less stable relationships and less prepared for what will follow.

Consider the home life of Lisa Ballard, a 26-year-old single mother in Morgantown. She strains every nerve to give her children the best upbringing she can, while also looking for a job. Her four-year-old son Alex loves the Dr Seuss book "Green Eggs and Ham," so she reads it to him, and once put green food colouring in his breakfast eggs, which delighted him. But the sheer complexity of her domestic arrangements makes life "very challenging," she says.

She has four children by three different men. Two were planned, two were not. Two live with her; she has shared custody of one and no custody of another. One of the fathers was "a butthole" who hit her, she says, and is no longer around. The other two are "good fathers," in that they have steady jobs, pay maintenance, make their children laugh and do not spank them. But none of them still lives with her.

Miss Ballard now thinks that having children before getting married was "not a good idea." She says she would like to get married some day, though she finds the idea of long-term commitment scary. "You've got to definitely make sure it's the person you want to grow old with. You know, sitting on rocking chairs giggling at the comics. I want to find the right one. I ask God: 'What does he look like? Can you give me a little hint?'"

If she does find and wed the man of her dreams, Miss Ballard will encounter a problem. She has never seen her own father. Having never observed a stable marriage close-up, she will have to guess how to make one work. By contrast, Ashley, the criminology student at the nearby university, has never seen a divorce in her family. This makes it much more likely that, when the time is right, she will get married and stay that way. And that, in turn, makes it more likely that her children will follow her to college.

Most children in single-parent homes "grow up without serious problems," writes Mary Parke of the Centre for Law and Social Policy, a think-tank in Washington, DC. But they are more than five times as likely to be poor as those who live with two biological parents (26% against 5%). Children who do not live with both biological parents are also roughly twice as likely to drop out of high school and to have behavioural or psychological problems. Even after controlling for race, family background and IQ, children of single mothers do worse in school than children of married parents, says Ms Hymowitz.

Children whose father was never around face the toughest problems. For those whose parents split up, the picture is more nuanced. If parents detest each other and quarrel bitterly, their kids may actually benefit from a divorce. Paul Amato of Penn State University has found that 40% of American divorces leave the children better (or at least, no worse) off than the turbulent marriages that preceded them. In other cases, however, what is good for the parents may well harm the children. And two parents are likely to be better at child-rearing because they can devote more time and energy to it than one can.

Research also suggests that middle- and working-class parents approach child-rearing in different ways. Professional parents shuttle their kids from choir practice to baseball camp and check that they are doing their homework. They also talk to them more. One study found that a college professor's kids hear an average of 2,150 words per hour in the first years of life. Working-class children hear 1,250 and those in welfare families only 620.

Co-habiting couples have the same number of hands as married couples, so they ought to make equally good parents. Many do, but on average the children of co-habiting couples do worse by nearly every measure. One reason is that such relationships are less stable than marriages. In America, they last about two years on average. About half end in marriage. But those who live together before marriage are more likely to divorce.

Many people will find this surprising. A survey of teenagers by the University of Michigan found that 64% of boys and 57% of girls agreed that "it is usually a good idea for a couple to live together before getting married in order to find out whether they really get along." Research suggests otherwise. Two-thirds of American children born to co-habiting parents who later marry will see their parents split up by the time they are ten. Those born within wedlock face only half that risk.

The likeliest explanation is inertia, says Scott Stanley of the Centre for Marital and Family Studies at the University of Denver, Colorado. Couples start living together because it is more fun (and cheaper) than living apart. One partner may see this as a prelude to marriage. The other—usually the man—may see it as something more temporary. Since no explicit commitment is made, it is easier to drift into living together than it is to drift into a marriage. But once a couple is living together, it is harder to split up than if they were merely dating. So "many of these men end up married to women they would not have married if they hadn't been living together," says Mr Stanley, co-author of a paper called "Sliding versus deciding."

A Little Help from the Government

Most American politicians say they support marriage, but few do much about it, except perhaps to sound off about the illusory threat to it from gays. The public are divided. Few want to go back to the attitudes or divorce laws of the 1950s. But many at both ends of the political spectrum lament the fragility of American families and would change, at least, the way the tax code penalises many couples who marry. And some politicians want the state to draw attention to benefits of marriage, as it does to the perils of smoking. George Bush is one.

Since last year, his administration has been handing out grants to promote healthy marriages. This is a less preachy enterprise than you might expect. Sidonie Squier, the bureaucrat in charge, does not argue that divorce is wrong: "If you're being abused, you should get out." Nor does she think the government should take a view on whether people should have premarital sex.

Her budget for boosting marriage is tiny: $100m a year, or about what the Defence Department spends every two hours. Some of it funds research into what makes a relationship work well and whether outsiders can help. Most of the rest goes to groups that try to help couples get along better, some of which are religiously-inspired. The first 124 grants were disbursed only last September, so it is too early to say whether any of this will work. But certain approaches look hopeful.

One is "marriage education." This is not the same as marriage therapy or counselling. Rather than waiting till a couple is in trouble and then having them sit down with a specialist to catalogue each other's faults, the administration favours offering relationship tips to large classes.

The army already does this. About 35,000 soldiers this year will get a 12-hour course on how to communicate better with their partners, and how to resolve disputes without throwing plates. It costs about $300 per family. Given that it costs $50,000 to recruit and train a rifleman, and that marital problems are a big reason why soldiers quit, you don't have to save many marriages for this to be cost-effective, says Peter Frederich, the chaplain in charge.

Several studies have shown that such courses do indeed help couples communicate better and quarrel less bitterly. As to whether they prevent divorce, a meta-analysis by Jason Carroll and William Doherty concluded that the jury was still out. The National Institutes of Health is paying for a five-year study of Mr Frederich's soldiers to shed further light on the issue.

Americans expect a lot from marriage. Whereas most Italians say the main purpose of marriage is to have children, 70% of Americans think it is something else. They want their spouse to make them happy. Some go further and assume that if they are not happy, it must be because they picked the wrong person. Sometimes that is true, sometimes not. There is no such thing as a perfectly compatible couple, argues Diane Sollee, director of smart-marriages.com, a pro-marriage group. Every couple has disputes, she says. What matters most is how they resolve them.

At the end of the day, says Ms Squier, the government's influence over the culture of marriage will be marginal. Messages from movies, peers and parents matter far more. But she does not see why, for example, the government's only contact with an unmarried father should be to demand that he pay child support. By not even mentioning marriage, the state is implying that no one expects him to stick around. Is that a helpful message?

The Opt-Out Myth

E. J. GRAFF

On October 26, 2003, *The New York Times Magazine* jump-started a century-long debate about women who work. On the cover it featured "The Opt Out Revolution," Lisa Belkin's semipersonal essay, with this banner: Why don't more women get to the top? They choose not to. Inside, by telling stories about herself and eight other Princeton grads who no longer work full-time, Belkin concluded that women were just too smart to believe that ladder-climbing counted as real success.

But Belkin's "revolution"—the idea that well-educated women are fleeing their careers and choosing instead to stay home with their babies—has been touted many times before. As Joan C. Williams notes in her meticulously researched report, " 'Opt Out' or Pushed Out? How the Press Covers Work/Family Conflict," released in October 2006 by the University of California Hastings Center for WorkLife Law, where she is the director, *The New York Times* alone has highlighted this "trend" repeatedly over the last fifty years: in 1953 (Case History of an Ex-Working Mother), 1961 (Career Women Discover Satisfactions in the Home), 1980 (Many Young Women Now Say They'd Pick Family over Career), 1998 (The Stay-at-Home Mother), and 2005 (Many Women at Elite Colleges Set Career Path to Motherhood).

And yet during the same years, the U.S. has seen steady upticks in the numbers and percentages of women, including mothers, who work for wages. Economists agree that the increase in what they dryly call "women's participation in the waged workforce" has been critical to American prosperity, demonstrably pushing up our GDP. The vast majority of contemporary families cannot get by without women's income—especially now, when upwards of 70 percent of American families with children have all adults in the work force, when 51 percent of American women live without a husband, and when many women can expect to live into their eighties and beyond.

The moms-go-home story keeps coming back, in part, because it's based on some kernels of truth. Women *do* feel forced to choose between work and family. Women *do* face a sharp conflict between cultural expectations and economic realities. The workplace is still demonstrably more hostile to mothers than to fathers. Faced with the "choice" of feeling that they've failed to be *either* good mothers or good workers, many women wish they could—or worry that they should—abandon the struggle and stay home with the kids.

The problem is that the moms-go-home storyline presents all those issues as personal rather than public—and does so in misleading ways. The stories' statistics are selective, their anecdotes about upper-echelon white women are misleading, and their "counterintuitive" narrative line parrots conventional ideas about gender roles. Thus they erase most American families' real experiences and the resulting social policy needs from view.

Here's why that matters: if journalism repeatedly frames the wrong problem, then the folks who make public policy may very well deliver the wrong solution. If women are happily choosing to stay home with their babies, that's a private decision. But it's a public policy issue if most women (and men) need to work to support their families, and if the economy needs women's skills to remain competitive. It's a public policy issue if schools, jobs, and other American institutions are structured in ways that make it frustratingly difficult, and sometimes impossible, for parents to manage both their jobs and family responsibilities.

So how can this story be killed off, once and for all? Joan Williams attempts to chloroform the moms-go-home storyline with facts. "Opt Out or Pushed Out?" should be on every news, business, and feature editor's desk. It analyzes 119 representative newspaper articles, published between 1980 and 2006, that use the opt-out storyline to discuss women leaving the workplace. While business sections regularly offer more informed coverage of workplace issues, the "opt out" trend stories get more prominent placement, becoming "the chain reaction story that flashes from the *Times* to the columnists to the evening news to the cable shows," says Caryl Rivers, a Boston University journalism professor and the author of *Selling Anxiety: How the News Media Scare Women* (April 2007).

There are a number of problems with the moms-go-home storyline. First, such articles focus excessively on a tiny proportion of American women—white, highly educated, in well-paying professional/managerial jobs. Just 8 percent of American working women fit this demographic, writes Williams. The percentage is smaller still if you're dealing only with white women who graduated from the Ivies and are married to high-earning men, as Belkin's article does. Furthermore, only 4 percent of women in their mid-to late thirties with children have advanced degrees and are in a privileged income bracket like that of Belkin's fellow Princeton grads, according to Heather Boushey, a senior economist with the Center for Economic and Policy Research. That group is far more likely than average women to be married when they give birth (91 percent, as opposed to 73 percent of all women), and thus to have a second income on which to survive. But because journalists and editors increasingly come from and socialize in this class, their anecdotes loom large in our personal rearview mirrors—and in our most influential publications. Such women are chastised for working by Caitlin Flanagan (a woman rich enough to stay home and have a nanny!) in *The Atlantic,* and for lacking ambition by Linda Hirshman in *The American Prospect.* But such "my-friends-and-me" coverage is an irresponsible approach to major issues being wrestled with by every American family and employer.

The stories are misleading in a second important way. Williams's report points out that "opt-out stories invariably focus on women in one particular situation: after they have 'opted out' but before any of them divorce." The women in those articles often say their skills can be taken right back onto the job. It's a sweetly optimistic notion, but studies show that, on average, professional women who come back after time away—or even after working part-time, since U.S. women working part-time earn 21 percent less per hour worked than those who work full-time—take a hefty and sustained pay cut, and a severe cut in responsibility level. Meanwhile, nearly 50 percent of American marriages end in divorce, according to the latest census figures. While numbers are lower for marriages in the professional class, divorce remains a real possibility. Williams points to Terry Martin Hekker, one of the ur opt-out mothers, who in 1977 published an op-ed in *The New York Times* entitled, "The Satisfactions of Housewifery and Motherhood in 'An Age of Do-Your-Own-Thing.'" In 2006, Hekker wrote-again in the *Times,* but demoted to the Sunday Style section—about having been divorced and financially abandoned: "He got to take his girlfriend to Cancun, while I got to sell my engagement ring to pay the roofer."

In other words, interview these opt-out women fifteen years later—or forty years later, when they're trying to live on skimpy retirement incomes—and you might hear a more jaundiced view of their "choices."

The opt-out stories have a more subtle, but equally serious, flaw: their premise is entirely ahistorical. Their opening lines often suggest that a generation of women is flouting feminist expectations and heading back home. At the simplest factual level, that's false. Census numbers show no increase in mothers exiting the work force, and according to Heather Boushey, the maternity leaves women do take have gotten shorter. Furthermore, college-educated women are having their children later, in their thirties—after they've established themselves on the job, rather than before. Those maternity leaves thus come in mid-career, rather than pre-career. Calling that "opting out" is misleading. As Alice Kessler-Harris, a labor historian at Columbia University, put it, "I define that as redistributing household labor to adequately take care of one's family." She adds that even while at home, most married women keep bringing in family income, as women traditionally have. Today, women with children are selling real estate, answering phone banks, or doing office work at night when the kids are in bed. Early in the twentieth century, they might have done piecework, taken in laundry, or fed the boarders. Centuries earlier, they would have been the business partners who took goods to market, kept the shop's accounts, and oversaw the adolescent labor (once called housemaids and dairymaids, now called nannies and daycare workers).

Which brings us to an even deeper historical flaw: editors and reporters forget that Belkin's generation isn't post-feminism; it's mid-feminism. Women's entrance into the waged work force has been moving in fits and starts over the past century. Earlier generations of college-educated women picked either work *or* family, work *after* family, or family *after* work; those who graduated in the 1980s and 1990s—Belkin's cohort—are the first to expect to do both at the same time. And so these women are shocked to discover that, although 1970s feminists knocked down the barrier to entering the professions in large numbers, the workplace still isn't fixed. They are standing on today's feminist frontier: the bias against mothers that remains embedded on the job, in the culture, and at home.

Given that reality, here's the biggest problem with the moms-go-home storyline: it begins and ends with women saying they are *choosing* to go home, and ignores the contradictory data sandwiched in between.

Williams establishes that "choice" is emphasized in eighty-eight of the 119 articles she surveyed. But keep reading. Soon you find that staying home wasn't these women's first choice, or even their second. Rather, every other door slammed. For instance, Belkin's prime example of someone who "chose" to stay home, Katherine Brokaw, was a high-flying lawyer until she had a child. Soon after her maternity leave, she exhausted herself working around the clock to prepare for a trial—a trial that, at the last minute, was canceled so the judge could go fishing. After her firm refused even to consider giving her "part-time" hours—forty hours now being considered part-time for high-end lawyers—she "chose" to quit.

More than a third of the articles in Williams's report cite "workplace inflexibility" as a reason mothers leave their jobs. Nearly half mention how lonely and depressed those women get when they've been downgraded to full-time nannies. Never do such articles cite decades of social science research showing that women are happier when occupying several roles; that homemakers' well-being suffers compared to that of working women; or that young adults who grew up in dual-earner families would choose the same family model for their own kids. Rarely do such articles ask how husband and wife negotiated which one of them would sacrifice a career. Only by ignoring both the women's own stories and the larger context can the moms-go-home articles keep chirping on about choice and about how such women now have "the best job in the world."

Underlying all this is a genuinely new trend that the moms-go-home stories never mention: the all-or-nothing workplace. At every income level, Americans work longer hours today than fifty years ago. Mandatory overtime for blue- and pink-collar workers, and eighty-hour expectations for full-time professional workers, deprive everyone of a reasonable family life. Blue-collar and low-wage families increasingly work "tag-team" schedules so that someone's always home with the kids. In surveys done by the Boston College Sloan Work and Families Research Network and by the New York-based Families and Work Institute, among others, women and men increasingly say that they'd like to have more time with their families, and would give up money and advancement to do it—if doing so didn't mean sacrificing their careers entirely. Men, however, must face fierce cultural headwinds to choose such a path, while women are pushed in that direction at every turn.

Finally, the opt-out articles never acknowledge the widespread hostility toward working mothers. Researching the book I wrote for Evelyn Murphy in 2005, *Getting Even: Why Women Don't Get Paid Like Men—and What to Do About It,* I was startled by how many lawsuits were won because managers openly and publicly told women that they couldn't be hired because they were pregnant; or that having a child would hurt them; or that it was simply impossible for women to both work and raise kids. Many other women we talked with had the same experience, but chose not to ruin their lives by suing. One lawyer who'd been on the partner track told us that once she had her second child, her colleagues refused to give her work in her highly remunerative specialty, saying that she now had other priorities—even though she kept meeting her deadlines, albeit after the kids were asleep. She was denied partnership. A high-tech project manager told me that when she was pregnant in 2002, she was asked: Do you feel stupider? Her colleague wasn't being mean; he genuinely wanted to know if pregnancy's hormones had dumbed her down. Or consider the experience of Dr. Diane Fingold, an internist at Massachusetts General Hospital in Boston and an assistant professor at Harvard Medical School, where she won the 2002 Faculty Prize for Excellence in Teaching, the school's highest teaching award. Her credentials are outstanding, yet when she asked to work three-and-a-half fewer hours a week so that she could manage her family demands—"just a little flexibility for a short period in my life!"—her practice refused. She was enraged. "I thought hard about leaving medicine altogether," she said. Her husband is a successful venture capitalist whose "annual Christmas bonus is what I make in a year!"

Had Fingold left, in other words, she would have fit neatly with Belkin's hyperachievers. But she loves practicing and teaching medicine, and realized she couldn't reenter at the same level if she walked away entirely. So she moved to another practice that was willing to accommodate her part-time schedule until, in a few years, she can return to full-time. Had she chosen the Belkin course, would she have opted out—or been pushed out?

Experiences like Fingold's bear out what social scientists are finding: strong bias against mothers, especially white mothers, who work. (Recent research shows bias against African American mothers of any class who don't work, a subject that deserves an article of its own.) Consider the work being done by Shelley Correll, a Cornell sociology professor, described in an article in the March 2007 *American Journal of Sociology.* In one experiment, Correll and her colleagues asked participants to rate a management consultant. Everyone got a profile of an equally qualified consultant—except that the consultant was variously described as a woman with children, a woman without children, a man with children, and a man without children. When the consultant was a "mother," she was rated as less competent, less committed, less suitable for hiring, promotion, or training, and was offered a lower starting salary than the other three.

Here's what feminism hasn't yet changed: the American idea of mothering is left over from the 1950s, that odd moment in history when America's unrivaled economic power enabled a single breadwinner to support an entire family. Fifty years later we still have the idea that a mother, and not a father, should be available to her child at every moment. But if being a mom is a 24-hour-a-day job, and being a worker requires a similar commitment, then the two roles are mutually exclusive. A lawyer might be able to juggle the demands of many complex cases in various stages of research and negotiation, or a grocery manager might be able to juggle dozens of delivery deadlines and worker schedules—but should she have even a fleeting thought about a pediatrics appointment, she's treated as if her on-the-job reliability will evaporate. No one can escape that cultural idea, reinforced as it is by old sitcoms, movies, jokes—and by the moms-go-home storyline.

Still, if they were pushed out, why would smart, professional women insist that they chose to stay home? Because that's the most emotionally healthy course: wanting what you've got. "That's really one of the agreed-upon principles of human nature. People want their attitudes and behavior to be in sync," said Amy Cuddy, an assistant professor in the management and organizations department at Northwestern Kellogg School of Management. "People who've left promising careers to stay home with their kids aren't going to say, 'I was forced out. I really want to be there.' It gives people a sense of control that they may not actually have."

So yes, maybe some women "chose" to go home. But they didn't choose the restrictions and constrictions that made their work lives impossible. They didn't choose the cultural expectation that mothers, not fathers, are responsible for their children's doctor visits, birthday parties, piano lessons, and summer schedules. And they didn't choose the bias or earnings loss that they face if they work part-time or when they go back full time.

By offering a steady diet of common myths and ignoring the relevant facts, newspapers have helped maintain the cultural temperature for what Williams calls "the most family-hostile public policy in the Western world." On a variety of basic policies—including parental leave, family sick leave, early childhood education, national childcare standards, after school programs, and health care that's not tied to a single all-consuming job—the U.S. lags behind almost every developed nation. How far behind? Out of 168 countries surveyed by Jody Heymann, who teaches at both the Harvard School of Public Health and McGill University, the U.S. is one of only five without mandatory paid maternity leave—along with Lesotho, Liberia, Papua New Guinea, and Swaziland. And any parent could tell you that it makes no sense to keep running schools on nineteenth century agricultural schedules, taking kids in at 7 A.M. and letting them out at 3 P.M. to milk the cows, when their parents now work until 5 or 6 P.M. Why can't twenty-first century school schedules match the twenty-first century workday?

The moms-go-home story's personal focus makes as much sense, according to Caryl Rivers, as saying, "Okay, let's build a superhighway; everybody bring one paving stone. That's how we approach family policy. We don't look at systems, just at individuals. And that's ridiculous."

E. J. Graff is senior researcher at Brandeis University's Schuster Institute for Investigative Journalism. From "The opt-out myth: Most moms have to work to make ends meet. So why does the press write only about the elite few who don't?" *Columbia Journalism Review* 45.6 (March-April 2007): 51(4).

Good Parents, Bad Results

Science is providing proof of where Mom and Dad go wrong.

NANCY SHUTE

Does your 3-year-old throw a five-alarm tantrum every time you drop him off at day care? Does "you're so smart!" fail to inspire your 8-year-old to turn off *Grand Theft Auto IV* and tackle his math homework? Do the clothes remain glued to your teenager's bedroom floor, along with your antisocial teenager, no matter how much you nag or cajole? Being a parent has never been easy—just ask your own. But in this day of two-earner couples and single parents, when 9-year-olds have cellphones, 12-year-olds are binge drinking and having oral sex, and there is evidence that teens are more fearful and depressed than ever, the challenges of rearing competent and loving human beings are enough to make a parent seek help from Supernanny. Actually, there is something better: science.

Researchers have spent decades studying what motivates children to behave and can now say exactly what discipline methods work and what don't: Call it "evidence-based parenting." Alas, many of parents' favorite strategies are scientifically proven to fail. "It's intuitive to scream at your child to change their behavior, even though the research is unequivocal that it won't work," says Alan Kazdin, a psychologist who directs the Yale Parenting Center and Child Conduct Clinic. Other examples:

- Yelling and reasoning are equally ineffective; kids tune out both.
- Praise doesn't spoil a child; it's one of the most powerful tools that parents can use to influence a child's actions. But most parents squander praise by using it generically—"you're so smart" or "good job!"—or skimping.
- Spanking and other harsh punishments ("You're grounded for a month!") do stop bad behavior but only temporarily. Punishment works only if it's mild, and it is far outweighed by positive reinforcement of good behavior.

As yet, few of the bestselling books and videos that promise to turn surly brats into little buttercaps make use of this knowledge. That may be because the research goes on in academia—at Yale, at Vermost's Behavior Therapy and Psychotherapy Center, and at the University of Washington's Parenting Clinic, for example. Surprisingly, many family therapists and parenting educators aren't up to speed on the research, either, so that parents who seek professional help won't necessarily get the most proven advice. Case in point: Just 16 programs designed for treating kids with disruptive behavior have been proven "well established" in randomized clinical trials, according to a review led by Sheila Eyberg at the University of Florida and published in the January *Journal of Clinical Child and Adolescent Psychology*. Kazdin, who for years has pushed clinical psychologists to adopt evidence-based methods, published a book for parents earlier this year: *The Kazdin Method for Parenting the Defiant Child*. Other lab-tested tomes include *Parenting the Strong-Willed Child* by Rex Forehand and Nicholas Long and *The Incredible Years* by Carolyn Webster-Stratton.

These discipline programs are grounded in classical behavioral psychology—the positive reinforcement taught in Psych 101. Researchers have run randomized controlled trials on all the nuances of typical parent-child interactions and thus can say just how long a timeout should last to be effective or how to praise a 13-year-old so that he beams when he takes out the trash. Who knew that effectively praising a child in order to motivate her has three essential steps? They are: 1) Praise effusively, with the enthusiasm of a Powerball winner. 2) Say exactly what the child did right. 3) Finish with a touch or hug.

What else can parents learn from the science? Researchers say these are the biggest common boo-boos:

1. Parents Fail at Setting Limits

It would be hard to find a parent who doesn't agree that setting and enforcing rules are an essential part of the job description. Yet faced with whining, pouting, and tantrums, many parents cave. "The limited time you have with your kids, you want to make it ideal for them," says Forehand, a professor of psychology at the University of Vermont whose evidence-based program is outlined in his book. "As a result, we end up overindulging our kids."

But, paradoxically, not having limits has been proven to make children *more* defiant and rebellious, because they feel unsafe and push to see if parents will respond. Research since

A Good Parent's Dilemma: Is It Bad to Spank?

Plenty of People Argue for an Occasional Swat

Last year, the California Legislature considered criminalizing the spanking of toddlers. But at least half of parents, and according to some surveys as many as 94 percent, consider a swat on the bottom to be an appropriate form of discipline. "Spanking has worked very well for us," says Tim Holt, a 45-year-old insurance agent and the father of four children, ages 4 to 13, in Simpsonville, S.C., who notes that he and his wife spank very rarely. He recalls spanking his 7-year-old son, Scott, after Scott hit his brother in the head with a shoe and then lied to his father about it. "I pulled Scott aside. We discussed what he had done: Why is it wrong? What does God's law say? That we don't take our anger out on others." Then Holt put Scott over his knee and smacked him on his pants with a plastic glue stick. "It's something that gets his attention and provides a little bit of pain to his bottom."

Proponents include James Dobson, a psychologist and founder of Focus on the Family, who likens squeezing a child's shoulder or spanking his behind to discomfort that "works to shape behavior in the physical world." He writes in *The New Dare to Discipline:* "The minor pain that is associated with this deliberate misbehavior tends to inhibit it. . . . A boy or girl who knows love abounds at home will not resent a well-deserved spanking." But the subject generates more heat than just about any other child-rearing issue. Sweden banned spanking in 1979. The United Nations Committee on the Rights of the Child has been seeking a ban on corporal punishment worldwide since 1996.

The evidence. The debate roils academia, too. Murray Straus, a professor of sociology at the University of New Hampshire, says 110 studies have linked spanking to increased misbehavior in childhood as well as adult problems such as increased spousal abuse and depression. In February, Straus published research linking being spanked in childhood with an adult preference for sadomasochistic sex. Straus acknowledges that most of today's parents were themselves spanked as children but says that since spanking is no more effective than other discipline methods and can cause harm it's not worth the misery. Other researchers, including Diana Baumrind, a psychologist at the University of California-Berkeley, have found that children who were spanked occasionally had no more behavior problems than children who were never spanked. But Baumrind says regular reliance on physical punishment, as well as "impulsive and reactive spanking," causes harm to a child. The bottom line: Proponents of either position can come up with enough evidence to support their belief—but not enough to convince the other side.

Demonizing spanking may leave some parents feeling they must avoid *any* discipline that makes a child feel bad, says Lawrence Diller, a developmental pediatrician in Walnut Creek, Calif., who works with children with attention deficit hyperactivity disorder. He speculates that a more coherent disciplinary approach that includes an occasional well-timed swat can make the overall system more effective and could "make the difference in whether your child will be on Ritalin or not. You don't have to spank. But if you're using spanking as one of an array of tools to get control of your kid, you're not hurting them in the long term."

—N.S.

the 1960s on parenting styles has found that a child whose mom and dad are permissive is more likely to have problems in school and abuse drugs and alcohol as teenagers. "Parents ask their 1-year-olds what they want for dinner now," says Jean Twenge, an associate professor of psychology at San Diego State University and author of *Generation Me.* "No one ever said that a generation or two ago." Using surveys dating back to the 1930s. Twenge has found significant increases in reported symptoms of depression and anxiety among today's children and teenagers, compared with earlier generations. Suniya Luthar, a psychologist at Columbia University Teachers College, reported in 2003 that children who are showered with advantages are more likely to be depressed and anxious and to abuse drugs and alcohol than the norm. Luthar says that's probably because those children are under a lot of pressure to achieve at school and think that their parents value their achievements more than themselves. They also feel isolated from their parents.

Rule-setting works best when parents give simple, clear commands and discuss the family rules with kids well in advance of a conflict, according to Robert Hendren, a professor of psychiatry at the Medical Investigation of Neurodevelopmental Disorders Institute at the University of California—Davis and president of

the American Academy of Child and Adolescent Psychiatry. A common recommendation for parents who fear coming off as a meanie: Let the child choose between two options when either choice is acceptable to the parent. A half-hour of Nintendo right after school, then homework? All homework before game time?

Consistency is also key. "I have to be very strict with myself and go over and tell him the rules and walk away," says Lauren Jordan, a stay-at-home mom in Essex Junction, Vt., whose 4-year-old son, Peter, would scream and hit Jordan and her husband, Sean, then kick the wall during timeout. "It felt out of control." Jordan signed up with Vermont's Behavior Therapy and Psychotherapy Center to learn Forehand's five-week process.

The first week was spent just "attending" to Peter, watching him play and commenting without telling the pre-schooler what to do. "He *loved* it," says Jordan, whose older son has autism and has required an outsize share of her energy. "I realized at that point that he needs this one-on-one attention." Jordan then had to learn to ignore Peter's minor bad behavior (such as screaming for attention while Mom is on the phone) and to not rush in to scold him during a timeout. "Consistency is the key. It's not easy," Jordan says, "But it's made our home a much happier place."

2. They're Overprotective

Teachers, coaches, and psychotherapists alike have noticed that parents today can't stand to see their children struggle or suffer a setback. So they're stepping in to micromanage everything from playground quarrels to baseball team positions to grades. Even bosses aren't immune. One owner of a New York public relations firm says he has gotten e-mails from parents telling him that's he's making their child work too much. The child in questions is in his 20s.

"Many well-meaning parents jump in too quickly," says Robert Brooks, a clinical psychologist in Needham, Mass., and coauthor of *Raising Resilient Children*. "Resilient children realize that sometimes they will fail, make mistakes, have setbacks. They will attempt to learn from them." When parents intercede, Brooks says, "it communicates to the kid that 'I don't think you're capable of dealing with it.' We have to let kids experience the consequences of their behavior."

Otherwise, they may grow afraid to try. "I see a lot of kids who seem really unmotivated," says Kristen Gloff, 36, a clinical and school social worker in the Chicago area. "It's not that they're lazy. They don't want to fail."

3. They Nag. Lecture. Repeat. Then Yell

If one verbal nudge won't get a kid to come to dinner, 20 surely will. Right? In fact, there's abundant evidence that humans tune out repeated commands. "So many parents think they have to get very emotionally upset, yell, threaten, use sarcasm," says Lynn Clark, a professor emeritus of psychology at Western Kentucky University and author of *SOS Help for Parents*. "The child imitates that behavior, and you get sassy talk."

Nagging also gives children "negative reinforcement," or an *incentive*—parental attention—to keep misbehaving. "I was kind of ignoring the good behavior, and every time he did something wrong, I would step in and give him attention," says Nancy Ailes, a 46-year-old stay-at-home mom in East Haven, Conn. She was frustrated with her 9-year-old son, Nick, who would melt down and throw things if the day's schedule changed, drag his feet about cleaning his room or doing homework, and call her "bad Mommy" if she complained.

Parent management training this spring at the Yale Child Conduct Center taught Ailes and her husband how to use positive reinforcement instead—to praise Nick immediately and enthusiastically. Now, when Nick is picking up his toys in the family room, she sits down, watches, and says: "Wow, that looks really nice!"

Ailes and her husband, David, also learned how to set up a reward system with points that Nick can cash in for Yu-Gi-Oh cards and Game Boy time and to back up the system with timeouts for bad behavior. Within three weeks, Ailes says, Nick had made a complete turnaround. "Instead of doing things that make people unhappy," she says, "you do things that make them happy!"

4. They Praise Too Much— and Badly

It seems like a truism that praising children would make them feel good about themselves and motivate them to do better. But parents don't give children attaboys as often as they think, Kazdin says. And when they do, it's all too often either generic ("good job!") or centered on the person, not the task ("you're so smart!"). This kind of praise actually makes children less motivated and self-confident. In one experiment by Carol Dweck, a psychologist now at Stanford University, fifth graders who were praised for being intelligent, rather than making a good effort, actually made less of an effort on tests and had a harder time dealing with failure.

"It's so common now for parents to tell children that they're special," says Twenge. That fosters narcissism, she says, not self-esteem. Twenge thinks parents tell a child "You're special" when they really mean "You're special to me." Much better in every way, she says, to just say: "I love you."

5. They Punish Too Harshly

Although spanking has been deplored by child-development experts since the days of Dr. Spock in the 1940s, as many as 90 percent of parents think it's OK to spank young children, according to research by Murray Straus, a professor of sociology at the University of New Hampshire. Kazdin and other behavioral researchers say parents commonly punish far more harshly than they need to.

After all, it's not supposed to be about payback, though that's often what's going on, says Jamila Reid, codirector of the Parenting Clinic at the University of Washington. The clinic's "The Incredible Years" program has been found in seven studies to improve children's behavior. "Often parents come looking for bigger sticks. We tell parents the word discipline means 'teach.' It's something to teach a child that there's a better way to respond."

Consider the fine art of the timeout. Parents often sabotage timeouts by lecturing or by giving hugs, according to Sheila Eyberg, a professor of psychology at the University of Florida. Her Parent-Child Interaction Therapy is used in many mental health clinics. Forehand and other researchers have spent many hours observing the use of timeout as a disciplinary strategy to determine exactly what makes it effective. The key finding: Discipline works best when it's immediate, mild, and brief, because it's then associated with the transgression and doesn't breed more anger and resentment. A timeout should last for just a few minutes, usually one minute for each year of age of the child.

Teenagers who have outgrown timeouts shouldn't lose a privilege for more than a day. Beyond that, the child's attitude shifts from regretting bad behavior to resenting the parent. "The punishment business isn't just ineffective," Kazdin says. "It leads to avoidance and escape. It puts a little wedge in the relationship between parent and child." Long groundings also make it more likely that the parents will relent after a few days. Better, Kazdin says, to ask the child to practice good behavior, such as fixing something he damaged, in order to win privileges back.

6. They Tell Their Child How to Feel

Most parenting books focus on eradicating bad behavior. But in study after study, empathy for other people leads the list of qualities that people need to successfully handle relationships at school, at work, and in the family. Children need to think about how their own feelings will be affected by what they do, as well as the feelings of others, says Myrna Shure, a developmental psychologist at Drexel University and author of *Raising a Thinking Child.* "That is what will inhibit a child from hurting others, either physically or emotionally."

And parents, by telling children "you're fine" or "don't cry," deny children the chance to learn those lessons. "The child learns empathy through being empathized with," says Stanley Greenspan, a child psychiatrist in Chevy Chase, Md., whose most recent book, *Great Kids,* tells parents how to help their child develop 10 essential qualities for a happy life. Empathy, creativity, and logical thinking top the list. A simple "We're so sorry, we know how it feels" is enough.

"Modeling empathic behavior is really very important," says James Windell, a counselor with the juvenile court system in Oakland County, Mich., and author of *8 Weeks to a Well-Behaved Child,* "How you respond to your children's needs sets the stage. It's really easy to be a supportive parent when they bring home a straight-A report card. When they get a bad grade, that's when they really need our support."

7. They Put Grades and SATs Ahead of Creativity

An overemphasis on good grades can also distort the message about how and what children should learn. "We like kids to learn rules, and we want them to learn facts," says Greenspan. "We're impressed when they can read early or identify their shapes. It's much harder for us to inspire them to come up with a creative idea." Children who can think creatively are more likely to be able to bounce back if their first idea doesn't work. They also know it can take time and patience to come up with a good solution. The goal, says Greenspan, is not to have a child who knows how to answer questions but one who will grow up to ask the important questions.

Parents can help their children become independent thinkers by asking open-ended questions like: Can you think of another way to solve the problem with your teammate? Or ask a whining preschooler: Can you think of a different way to tell me what you want?

8. They Forget to Have Fun

"When I talk to families that aren't functioning so well, and I ask, how often do you laugh together, they say: We haven't laughed together for a long time." says Hendren. Those little signs of love and connection—a laugh, a song shared in the car—are, he says, signs of health.

Overworked, Time Poor, and Abandoned by Uncle Sam
Why Don't American Parents Protest?

JANET C. GORNICK

The story of the overworked American parent is by now well-known. Every day, millions of American parents—single and partnered, low-income and affluent—scramble to coordinate the demands of employment with their children's need for care and supervision. In the majority of families in the United States, all the adults are in the workforce, more often than not working full time. It is not surprising that the stressed-out working parent is now a staple in multiple venues, from social science research to newspaper opinion columns to TV-land.

As Kathleen Gerson pointed out in these pages last year ("The Morality of Time: Women and the Expanding Work Week," Fall 2004), the common wisdom in the United States generally lays the responsibility for the work-family time bind on individuals and lets American institutional realities off the hook. Conservatives typically focus on mothers, protesting that many (middle-class and well-off) women are choosing paid work over family, indulging themselves while leaving their children and husbands unattended. (Poor single mothers, of course, have long been exempted from this criticism, as they are expected to work for pay.) And many progressives, Gerson argues, have not helped matters, too often attributing Americans' notoriously long work hours to their ever-expanding desire for consumption or their preference for the effects-oriented workplace over the strains and uncertainties of life at home.

But, in fact, the American institutional landscape deserves much of the blame. Many workplaces are still designed for workers who have no competing responsibilities, and the paucity of public policies that support working families can hardly be overstated. As Marcia Meyers and I argue in our book—*Families That Work*—the American state provides much less to working parents than do many other countries, especially the high-income countries of northern and western Europe.

For starters, parents in several European countries have access to multiple forms of paid family leave and to high-quality affordable child care. In addition, working-time regulations limit the imposition of excessively long weekly work hours and effectively cap the number of days worked each year. Furthermore, public measures in all European Union member countries require pay and benefit parity for part-time workers—making shorter-hour work a more feasible option. And a growing number of countries grant full-time workers the right to temporarily downsize to part-time work and/or to alter the scheduling of their assigned hours. These so-called work-family reconciliation measures are, of course, embedded in larger social protection systems that provide universal health insurance, among

other crucial components. All told, these comprehensive policy packages allow parents ample latitude in deciding how to allocate their time between paid work and care. Public supports also indemnify families against substantial fluctuations in disposable income when parents temporarily diminish their time in paid work, or take a break altogether, to concentrate on caregiving.

In contrast, American public policy leaves the vast majority of working parents high and dry. The meager Family and Medical Leave Act of 1993 provides some parents limited rights to periods of unpaid leave to take care of infants and other family members. (Workers in small enterprises and without substantial work experience in the prior year are not eligible.) As for paid leave, only five states offer mothers any wage replacement following childbirth or adoption (through public temporary disability insurance laws) and only one (California) offers benefits for fathers. The standard work week remains set at forty hours, a level established more than six decades ago, and American working-time law is silent on equal treatment for part-time workers, on rights to part-time or flexible scheduling, and on the right to a minimum number of paid days off per year. The public child care system in the United States is among the least developed in the industrialized world.

In the absence of public supports, Americans are left with the market. With the exception of the poorest workers, parents turn to consumer markets to purchase child care—or they manage with informal arrangements. Workers who get family-friendly leave and working-time options generally get them in the labor market, sometimes as part of a standard employee benefit package, sometimes via individualized negotiation. While many workers—especially more highly educated, higher-earning workers—secure workplace benefits, many others do not. The weakness of unions in the United States, due in part to public policy, means that when American parents turn to their employers for work-family benefits, they commonly have a weak collective voice and little bargaining power.

The Problem of Private Solutions

What do American parents do in the absence of public supports? How do they manage the work-family crunch? As we argue in *Families That Work*, U.S. parents craft a range of private solutions to reconcile high rates of parental employment with their children's need for care. In many families, parents reduce the labor market attachment of one parent—in practice, overwhelmingly, the mother. Women with children often choose various forms of underemployment, opting for jobs that demand less of them than their skills would otherwise warrant; others are employed part time and/or intermittently. (The paucity of high-quality, remunerative work in the thirty-five- to thirty-nine-hour range leads many couples to end up with one long-hour worker and one part-time worker.) Other families choose a different route, opting for what Harriet Presser has dubbed "split-shift parenting." Split-shift parents—or any pair of caregivers, more generally—arrange employment schedules so that they work opposite hours; one leaves for the workplace as the other comes home. Yet another group of families makes extensive use of non-parental care, with many placing their children in child care starting in early infancy.

These private solutions are adaptive and work well for many individual families. But they also exacerbate long-standing problems of gender inequality and create new social and economic problems. The "one-parent-chooses-partial-employment" option cements gender divisions of labor, because it is mothers, and rarely fathers, who cut back on paid work to care for children. While split-shift parenting works well for some families, and may strengthen fathers' ties to their children, other social consequences are problematic—including disproportionately high rates of marital dissolution and negative effects on children's well-being. Likewise, intensive use of non-parental child care, even from early infancy, also works well for many families. But, for others, the out-of-pocket costs deplete family disposable income, and too many children end up in care of worrisome quality. And leaving child care to the market, especially with limited regulation, also means that many child care workers are very poorly paid, which places them and their own families at risk.

Finally, leaving work-family benefits to labor and consumer markets deepens inequalities. As Jody Heymann's work has demonstrated, market-based work-family benefits are not only limited in the United States, their distribution is extremely regressive. Although many highly educated, high-earning workers have ample workplace benefits—and excellent child care options—their less privileged counterparts typically have access to far less for themselves and their children. As Jason DeParle relates in heartbreaking detail in his book *American Dream,* many low-wage workers—especially those who are also solo parents—hold jobs with little in the way of workplace benefits, and high quality child care, especially for infants, remains largely out of reach.

How U.S. Parents and Children Fare

A mountain of research reveals that American working parents have a tougher job than their counterparts in other high-income countries. Among two-parent families, with two earners, U.S. couples spend just over eighty hours a week (jointly) working for pay. In a number of other rich countries—including France, Germany, and the United Kingdom—dual-earner couples with children average between seventy-three and seventy-eight hours a week, whereas Dutch and Swedish dual-earners average between sixty-five and sixty-eight hours a week, or the equivalent of nearly two fewer days per week, relative to U.S. couples. Even more remarkable, nearly two-thirds of U.S. couples work *more* than eighty hours each week jointly—a distribution that no European country even approaches.

How about gender equality in the labor market? With all that hard work, surely the United States must be the world's leader in women's engagement in paid labor. In fact, gender equality in the U.S. labor market is only fair-to-middling, relative to more than half of ten European comparison countries and Canada. Among parents with partners, U.S. mothers take home about 28 percent of total parental earnings—substantially less than the share commanded by mothers in Denmark, Sweden, Finland, Norway, France, and Belgium. And equality at home? Gender disparities in the American labor market spill over into the home: American working fathers spend forty-four minutes doing unpaid work at home for every hundred minutes invested by their working wives, a ratio that lags behind that reported in a handful of European countries.

Not surprisingly, more Americans than Europeans report dissatisfaction with their ability to balance work and family life. According to a recent national survey conducted by the Families and Work Institute, over half of American workers report that they experience conflict "in balancing work, personal life, and family life." In a recent survey, when EU parents were asked, "In general, do your working hours fit in with your family or social commitments outside work very well, fairly well, not very well or not at all well?," a remarkable 80 percent of parents responded that their work hours and private commitments fit "very well" or "fairly well."

Clearly many U.S. parents feel unbalanced, but how about our children? Does our hard work at least benefit America's children? Sadly, there is little evidence that it does—children in the United States are not doing especially well either. That is most evident at the bottom of the income distribution. Relative to many other rich countries, American children are much more likely to be poor—no matter what their family's structure and their parents' employment status. But average outcomes are none too great either. American children, on average, are also more likely to die in infancy or in young childhood, to perform poorly on international math and science tests during their adolescent years, and to conceive or bear children as teenagers. (American children also watch inordinate amounts of television, possibly because it serves as low-cost child care.) Although much research establishes that public policies have a powerful direct effect on parents' working hours, and even on gendered labor market outcomes, it is much harder to establish that the U.S. work-family policy configuration is the *cause* of our relatively poor child outcomes. Nevertheless, what we do know is that the "American model" for balancing work and family—essentially, leaving it to individuals and markets—is not associated with impressive outcomes for our children.

There Is Some Good News—Sort Of

Is there some good news? Yes, to some extent. While Americans' long work hours may produce deleterious results for many parents and children, we do earn a lot. The United States ranks first among the thirty OECD (Organization for Economic Cooperation and Development) member countries in per capita income, using purchasing-power-adjusted exchange rates. That means that, on average, Americans enjoy a relatively high standard of living—when standard of living is captured by this common measure—compared to our neighbors in other rich countries. Many argue that this result closes the case: despite some distributional concerns, it is argued, the American model, overall, remains the most economically advantageous. European workers may feel good about their generous benefit packages but, in the end, so goes the argument, they and their families pay a considerable price.

That's a powerful claim, but, at the same time, average per capita income needs a second look. First of all, it doesn't account for many forms of non-market income, such as education, health care, child care, and the like—forms of income that we know lag (and are regressively distributed) in the United States. Second, some scholars argue that it is misleading to measure "standard of living" solely in monetary terms, without taking into account time investments. As Lars Osberg, a Canadian economist has argued: " 'Quality of life' or 'economic well-being' may be hard to define precisely, but most would agree that they depend on both an individual's income level and the discretionary time they have in which to enjoy it."

So, American workers—on average—do take home a sizable chunk of income compared to average workers elsewhere, but for many American workers and their families, that economic payoff is compromised by the family time-poverty that enables it. It's also the case that Americans may work so hard that we are on the diminishing-returns portion of the productivity curve. While the United States leads the world in gross domestic product per worker, we are ranked eighth among the OECD countries in GDP per worker-hour. It is possible that, as a society, we could shift some hours from work to family *and* see a rise in our hourly output. What is clear is that the current work-family arrangement—with its weak protections and limited benefits for working parents—is problematic on many fronts, and that large numbers of American parents and their children are poorly served.

Why Don't U.S. Parents Protest?

Why do American working parents accept the paltry public supports? Why don't they object to the absence of paid family leave, the weak working-time protections, and the near total absence of public investment in child care? Even more starkly, where is the public outcry as the Bush administration chips away at the Family and Medical Leave Act and weakens the Fair Labor Standards Act? Why do large numbers of Americans tell pollsters that they *want* more help from government, specifically for working parents, and then fail to form an effective social movement calling for that help? Why was work-family policy nearly invisible in the last election cycle? Why did so many who claim to want help for American working families pull the other lever?

There are no easy answers. Although there is much to argue with in *What's the Matter With Kansas?*, Thomas Frank has surely awakened us to the larger possibility that a peculiar form of cultural alienation has pushed many Americans to vote against their own material interests. Speaking more broadly, Jeff Madrick tells us that, in contemporary America, supporting government—even with a policy agenda that promises economic growth—is simply against our "national character." "The American national character," Madrick writes in *Why Economies Grow*, "has prevented the nation from adopting a new social contract to lead it forward. We do not even speak in terms of the social contract anymore because, implicitly, we do not give government sufficient status to enter into a contract with the people. These days, as large as government is, in the public mind it is an appendage and a burden, not a partner."

In addition to these dispiriting—and largely persuasive—analyses I would point to two more barriers to work-family policy development that may ultimately be more malleable. First of all, many Americans envision well-being so narrowly as to be counter-productive. As an example, in a recent *New York Times* column (January 4, 2005) David Brooks laid out the same cross-national portrait of working hours that I present to illustrate the work-family time bind in the United States.

Brooks, however, told the mirror tale. He praised the fact that Americans work "50 percent more than Germans, French, and Italians." Because of our industriousness, he argued, "American GDP per capita is about 30 percent higher than Europe's and the gap, if anything, is getting wider." (Several of my progressive colleagues sent me that column, adding "Unfortunately, he's right, isn't he?") Long work hours may indeed produce a lot of output—and, of course, for many families, much-needed income—but they are also associated with an array of negative social consequences that aren't talked about enough, even on the left.

Second, Americans remain remarkably unaware that generous work-family reconciliation policies operate successfully—and with widespread political support—in many other rich countries. Unfortunately, it is not just conservatives, but often progressives as well, who have absorbed damaging misperceptions—in particular, that the European countries have cut work-family programs in recent years (not true), after concluding that these programs, along with the social safety net more generally, have negative macroeconomic consequences (also not true). In fact, a mounting body of research challenges the claim that social spending is harmful to economic growth. Peter Lindert's comprehensive new study on the impact of social spending, *Growing Public: Social Spending and Economic Growth Since the Eighteenth Century,* concludes, "Contrary to the intuition of many economists and the ideology of many politicians, social spending has contributed to, rather than inhibited, economic growth." (On top of that, Lindert argues, public investments in women's employment constitute a crucial pro-growth strategy.) Lawrence Mishel, Jared Bernstein, and Sylvia Allegretto concur that public social protections often bring macroeconomic benefits. Their own empirical results—presented in *The State of Working America 2004–2005*—lead them to conclude that "although the U.S. economy saw increased productivity in the last few years, it under-performed relative to other OECD economies for most of the past 20 years. . . . This suggests that those formulating policy may benefit from looking beyond the U.S. model."

Building a social consensus in the United States for more government support for working families will not be easy, but a few things are clear. If we want to spur change, we need a dramatically altered discourse about the role of government in the lives of American families. We need a new lexicon concerning "family values," one that includes the damaging consequences of time poverty, as well as income poverty, for American workers and their families. We need to recognize that we, as a nation, must invest in our children's care and education during the first five years of their lives—rather than waiting until they are old enough for kindergarten. We need to alert many more Americans to the extreme exceptionalism of U.S. family policy offerings relative to the other rich countries of the world—and, increasingly, from a global perspective as well. (The United States is one of five countries in the entire world without a national policy of paid maternity leave.) And, finally, we need to persuade Americans, on both the left and right, that a comprehensive package of work-family policies would be consistent with a more equitable distributional result—for women, for men, and for children—and with healthy macroeconomic outcomes as well.

JANET C. GORNICK is, with Marcia K. Meyers, coauthor of *Families That Work: Policies for Reconciling Parenthood and Employment*, published by the Russell Sage Foundation in 2003 and released in paperback in April 2005.

Originally published in *Dissent Magazine*, Summer 2005, pp. 65–69. Copyright © 2005 by Foundation for Study of Independent Ideas, Inc. Reprinted by permission. www.dissentmagazine.org

Peer Marriage

PEPPER SCHWARTZ

Our generation has been the first to witness the emergence of "partnership" or "peer" marriages on a large social scale. Such marriages differ from their traditional counterparts in at least four key respects: men and women in these relationships regard each other as full social equals; both pursue careers; partners share equal authority for financial and other decision making; and, not least important, husbands typically assume far greater responsibility for child-rearing than in the past. Many of us—including much of the feminist movement, of which I have been a part—tend to regard these marriages as a major social breakthrough, the culmination of an arduous, generation-long effort to redefine women's roles and to secure for women the same freedom and dignity that society has traditionally accorded to men.

Yet in recent years conservatives, particularly the adherents of the "pro-family" or "family values" movement, have increasingly called for a rejection of the peer marriage ideal and a return by society as a whole to the traditional role-differentiated model. Bolstering their case is a significant body of traditional social theory arguing for the superior stability of the role-differentiated marriage, in which the husband serves as sole provider and main figure of authority, and the wife bears the lion's share of responsibilities for child rearing and day-to-day household maintenance.

Contemporary concerns with marital and family stability are certainly warranted. In a society with a 50 percent divorce rate—in which a host of social pathologies can be traced directly to havoc in fatherless or broken homes—policymakers and theorists are right to place a high priority on measures aimed at keeping families intact. Yet it is far from self-evident that the road to greater marital stability lies in a return to tradition. Over the past generation, I would argue, broad changes in society—and in the expectations that men and women bring to the marital relationship—have undermined much of the original basis of the traditional model of marriage. In reality, as I will try to show here, peer marriage offers a new formula for family and marital stability that may be both more durable and better adapted to the demands of contemporary culture than the older form. New data from studies that I and others have conducted support the notion that peer marriages are at least as stable as traditional unions and may in the long run prove more resilient vis-à-vis the special social pressures that marriages confront today.

Marital Stability and Marital Satisfaction

There is a close connection between marital stability and happiness or satisfaction in marriage—in both practice and theory. Even the most hard-headed theorists of the traditional model—such as sociologist Talcott Parsons or economist Gary Becker—have invariably sought to reconcile their advocacy of gender-based role differentiation with the possibility of marital satisfaction. To justify the traditional division of labor in marriage purely on the basis of men's and women's different biological aptitudes, historical experience, or cultural training is, after all, not a difficult theoretical task. But to posit happiness and mutual satisfaction as the outcome of such a union is another matter.

This is not to say that happiness was or is impossible to achieve under the traditional marital regime. Many people, especially when the larger culture supports it, find happiness in holding up their part of the marital bargain: women who like to be in charge of the kitchen, and men who want to bring home the bacon but do not want to cook it. In the past, and even today, this contract has worked for many people. Increasingly, however, it does not work as well as it used to. It did not work for me as well as it worked for my mother, and it didn't work for her all the time, either. The gender-based division of labor, so automatic for so much of history, increasingly fails to bring the promised emotional fulfillment that was supposed to be a major part of its contribution to family satisfaction and stability—emotional fulfillment which is increasingly vital to marital stability today.

We may contrast the experience of my mother's generation with that of my own. Like so many women of her era, my mother traded *service* for *support,* a transaction with which she usually seemed content. She bore almost complete responsibility for raising her children and at the same time had full charge of household upkeep: cooking, cleaning, keeping my father's closets and drawers impeccably neat, and so forth. My father, not atypical of his generation, was a man who never packed his own suitcase for a trip. In return, he provided handsomely—beyond my mother's wildest dreams, since she had grown up in poverty and was forced to drop out of high school to support her ailing mother and her youngest sisters. Having met my father as a secretary in his fledgling law office, my mother was very grateful to have been pulled from destitution into a different social class. Later she could afford to finish high school and college, raise three children, and become a docent in an art museum. Her lifestyle with my father was something secure and in a sense wonderful, exceeding all her childhood expectations.

The arrangement worked well for my father also. He was not born to privilege. The eldest of five growing up on a farm in Indiana, he put himself through law school, transferring from the University of Chicago to night school at Loyola when times got rough. He scrambled to better himself and his family. He and his wife had the same goal: to achieve the means for the good life. They entertained clients and traveled.

But my father also expected my mother to do everything he told her to do. After all, his own father had been dictatorial; it was something a woman owed a man—even though, in my grandfather's case, his wife had purchased the farm for the family. No matter. Leadership at home was owed a man as part of his birthright. When my mother—an intense, intelligent woman—would occasionally resist an order or talk back, my father's response to her was scathing and uninhibited.

What was the bargain my mother willingly made? She had a husband who loved her, who created an increasingly luxurious environment, and who ordered her around and reminded her—almost incessantly—about how lucky she was to have him. Love and what my generation of women would call patriarchal control went hand in hand. On my mother's side, gratitude, deep resentment, and anger all came in a neat package. The marriage lasted 55 years, until my mother's death. Children were launched. The marriage could be declared a success. Nevertheless, under today's circumstances, I would expect such a marriage to survive ten years at best.

Today my mother would have had a chance at her own career, at which she had the talent to excel. She would have had a new identity as a human being with core rights and her own sense of entitlement. (Surely, she promoted mine.) She would have had a different standard of equality and different ideas about equity. She would probably not have thought it enough to have been rescued from poverty. She would have felt entitled to a different style of family decision making, and she would have had the options—and the cultural support—to demand more. But if my father had remained the same man he was when I was growing up, he would not have acquiesced. Under contemporary circumstances, the marriage most probably would have broken up—much to my own, my siblings', and probably my parents' disadvantage.

And that is one reason why I believe peer marriage—a marriage founded on the principle of equality and supported by shared roles and a greater chance of shared sensibilities—is an adaptation in the direction of greater family stability rather than instability. Indeed, in contemporary culture, a peer or partner relationship between spouses has become increasingly vital to keeping families intact. It also offers new advantages to children, to which I will return in a moment.

We must be clear, however, that the mere existence of separate careers does not guarantee a peer marriage. Such a marriage also requires a comprehensive reconceptualization of the partners' roles. Dual incomes alone are insufficient to guarantee stability.

Money and Work

Indeed, much empirical research, some of it my own, indicates that labor force participation and achievement of high income by women destabilizes marriage. A number of studies, including the well-known Income Maintenance Study done out of the University of Michigan, found that when one raised the income of low-income women—hoping to stabilize families by reducing poverty—divorce increased substantially. Theorists have deduced that, under such circumstances, growth in income simply opens a new option for women to leave the relationship, an option that many of them exercise. Moreover, many studies show high-earning women with higher breakup rates. It is unclear whether high earnings make women less willing to tolerate unwanted behaviors or other disappointments on the part of their spouses, or whether men find women who are ambitious or aggressive (or who possess other traits consonant with career success) unsatisfying to be with in the long run. At any rate, the correlation is real enough.

Nor do couples necessarily adapt smoothly to equalization of income and status between partners. In *American Couples*, a study of 6,000 married, cohabiting, and lesbian and gay couples, Phil Blumstein and I found that a partner's power rose in relation to his or her relative income as compared with that of the spouse or live-in lover, but not necessarily in the ways we would have predicted. Women's power rose and became equal to their partners' when they had equal income—but only if they had a supportive ideology that allowed them to claim equal power. And power did not necessarily increase proportionally to the income differential. For example, more power did not release women from as much housework as one might expect. Higher-income career women did less, but not equivalently less, and their partners did not do proportionately more. (Male partners of high-earning women *did* feel their partners were entitled to do less housework, but did not feel required to do more themselves!) Feminists may be inclined to despair: Are men so resistant to participation in household labor that nothing will induce them to pitch in appropriately?

Yet—and this is the key point—it remains to be seen whether the tensions we found are the permanent consequence of change or merely transitional pains that arise as couples, and society as a whole, grope for a new definition of the marital relationship. Many men are clearly uncomfortable with the weakening of the traditional male role as sole provider. And, notably, there has been little effort—outside a small and probably unrepresentative "men's movement"—to reconceptualize the husband's role under these new economic circumstances. However, several changes are conspiring to move society as a whole beyond this sometimes painful transitional phase: transformations in the economy, in the attitudes of younger men, and in the cultural definition of marriage itself.

In the first place, in the contemporary economy female income has become an important ingredient of family prosperity (even, in many cases, a necessity). Economists have long recognized that household income has maintained stability in the United States over the past decades only through large-scale entry of women into the work force. The two-income household, once an exception, is now increasingly the norm.

Furthermore, corporate restructuring and downsizing have tended to intensify the trend. Women's labor force participation has become increasingly vital to family stability in a society where job security is, for all but a few, a thing of the past. Men are now beginning to realize that their hold on continuous employment after age 40 is, to say the least, shaky. By age 55, less than half of all men are still fully employed. Women, having many of the skills necessary for a service-oriented society, stay employable longer and more steadily. Indeed, in our society, the nonworking wife is increasingly becoming a symbol of exceptional wealth or conspicuous consumption—or of a major ideological commitment either to the patriarchal family or to a vision of the female as the primary parent.

There are signs that these new economic realities are beginning to affect attitudes among men in their 20s. Young boys today are increasingly growing up in two-parent families where females are either the chief provider or an essential contributor to family income. Moreover, they understand their own economic futures as providers to be far from secure. Partly as a result, more and more young men are seeking in marriage someone to be part of an economic team rather than an exclusive parenting specialist. Just as women have in the past sought "a good provider," so, I predict, men will increasingly want to marry (and stay married to) a woman who can provide her share of economic stability.

But possibly the most important change has come in the subtle cultural redefinition of the marital relationship itself. In a society in which divorce is prevalent and the economic independence of both spouses is the rule, marital stability depends increasingly on factors of personal satisfaction and emotional fulfillment. The glue holding marriages together today is neither economic necessity nor cultural sanction, but emotion. Marital stability in contemporary society increasingly depends on sustaining the emotional satisfaction of *both* partners. It is here that peer marriage shows its special advantages.

Under these new economic and cultural circumstances, the ability of men and women to participate in each other's lives—to build companion status—becomes essential to marital survival. Equality is a crucial ingredient of this form of intimacy. When women have validation in the outside world through career, and when couples can operate as a team on both economic and home issues, partners become more similar to each other and achieve greater emotional compatibility—or so I would hypothesize on the basis of my research with peer couples. With more outside experiences to bring to the marital community, the woman becomes a more interesting companion for the long run. Moreover, whatever competition or tensions may result from this new arrangement, women today probably need some of these career-related personality traits simply to stay competitive with the women men increasingly meet in the workplace. This was less important in a society where home and family were sacrosanct and a mother and wife—no matter

how far she was from being a "soul mate"—was automatically protected from outside contenders for her spouse. However, that is not the society we live in any more, nor is it likely to return. And even though income creates independence and therefore opportunities for separation, the recognition that spouses would lose their mutually constructed lifestyle if the marriage ended has its own stabilizing effect, as I have found in my interviews with dozens of peer couples.

Love versus Money

Of course, even today, if one were to analyze marriage in purely economic terms, the traditional model can seem to offer certain advantages over the peer arrangement. Becker and others have contended that, at least during child-raising years, couples with the woman in a full-time mothering role tend to gain more income. And a few studies have shown that men with working wives have lower incomes than men with nonworking wives. Economically ambitious couples probably calculate correctly that one parent, usually the male, should be released from most parental duties to earn as much as he can; the payoff here will lie in enhanced family income and social status, in which both partners presumably will share.

But this approach fails to address the real problem at the base of today's shaky marital system—maintaining a high standard of emotional fulfillment. "Efficient" role allocation frequently leaves partners leading parallel and largely separate lives. Mom and Dad did that—each an expert in their separate spheres. It worked when there was less expectation that marriage should produce a soul mate, and when Mom's tolerance levels were higher for the habitual carping at dinner. While this system did and does work for some, it tends to diminish emotional partnership. People in such "parallel marriages," financially secure, look at each other ten years later and say, "Why you?"—and they divorce, often with children in primary grades.

Secrets of Peer Success

One key to the success of peer unions lies in *joint child rearing*—the creation of a male parenting niche in day-to-day family life. Indeed, I would go so far as to say that joint child rearing constitutes the secret of successful peer unions and a new pathway to marital and family stability in contemporary life. Joint child-rearing cements a new intimacy between husband and wife and, research shows, builds a critical and difficult-to-sever tie between the two parents and the children.

Some theorists in the past have actually argued *against* a model of significant daily paternal participation in parenting, on the grounds that male involvement will erode the natural dependence of men on women and that men, resenting the extra burden, will ultimately leave. Of course, a lot of men are leaving in any case. And certainly some studies, particularly among working-class men, show child care and household labor participation to be associated with lower marital satisfaction. Still, other researchers have found large numbers of men whose perception of shared participation correlates with greater marital satisfaction.

On the woman's side, moreover, the picture is not at all ambiguous. Shared labor has a *major* impact on women's satisfaction in marriage—and since more women than men leave relationships, this is a significant finding. A 1996 study by Nancy K. Grote and others showed that the more traditional the division of labor, the lower marital satisfaction was for women (though *not* for men). However, *both* men and women reported higher erotic satisfaction and friendship with one another when household labor, including parenting, was shared more equitably.

My studies and others show several other important benefits to joint child rearing: First, the more men participate, the more attached they are to their children. Second, the more they parent, the more grateful wives are. Third, under joint parenting, it becomes harder for either the husband or the wife to consider leaving. And finally, unless the men are manifestly awful parents, children benefit from their father's attention, skills, and additional perspective. This extra parenting and contact with the father can represent a real boon for children.

While my study draws from interviews with only about one hundred couples, some research based on large data sets reinforces my findings. In *Bitter Choices: Blue Collar Women In and Out of Work,* E. I. Rosin showed that a substantial number of working-class women interpreted the husband's help with children and housework as an expression of love and caring. A very interesting study by Diane Lye at the University of Washington found, among other things, that men who had the lowest divorce rates had the highest interaction with their sons around traditionally male games—football, baseball, etc. Interestingly, the same was true of men who participated in similar activities with their daughters. Other studies have found a lower divorce rate among men who attended prenatal classes.

Still, one may argue that we are talking here about atypical men. Only a certain kind of fellow will participate in a prenatal class: peer men are born, not made. Yet that is not what I found in my own research. Most men I interviewed in egalitarian marriages did not come to them by way of ideological motivation, nor were they married to women who described themselves as feminists. The usual road to peer marriage was happenstance. The four most common routes: (1) A serious desire on the part of the husband to father more, and more effectively, than he himself had been fathered (men in these situations were frequently wrestling with significant pain left over from paternal abuse, neglect, or abandonment). (2) A job that *required* shift work or role sharing and which, over time, greatly attached the father to the parenting role. (3) A strong-willed working partner who presumed egalitarian marriage; men in these cases were mostly prepared to structure the marriage any way their wives (often not declared feminists) preferred to have it. (4) The experience of an unsatisfactory, highly traditional first marriage in which the wife was perceived as too emotionally dependent during the marriage and too economically helpless after it was over; men in these cases consciously selected a different kind of spouse and marital bargain in the second marriage.

Were they happy with their new bargain? Most of these men expressed pride in themselves, their wives, and their home life.

Were these typical egalitarian marriages? it is impossible to say. But these marriages, while not invulnerable, looked more stable for their integration—in much the way traditional marriages often appear: integrated, independent, and satisfied.

"Near Peers"

Some of the most troubled contemporary marriages, I have found, are those, in essence, caught between the old and the new paradigm—marriages that are neither fully traditional nor fully peer. I called such couples "near peers," since they professed belief in equal participation but failed to achieve it in practice. I believe the experience of such "near peers" may lie behind some of the frustrations that lead conservatives and others today to declare, in effect, that "We have tried equality and it has failed." In reality, what many couples have tried is inequality under the label of equality—an experience which has given equality, in some quarters, a bad name.

In "near peer" marriages, the wife typically devoted vastly more energy to the children while holding down a job. Although the husband made certain contributions to child rearing and household upkeep, and professed an eagerness to do more, actual male performance fell short of the intended ideal, stirring the wife's resentment. In most cases, "near peer" men still controlled the finances and exercised veto power over the wife. The wife, performing a full-time job outside the home with little or not relief inside of it, was typically caught in a "slow burn" of inward anger. Paradoxically, such women did not long for more equality, since they assumed it would bring more of the same—increased responsibilities with no substantial male contribution. These women felt trapped and overwhelmed and many of them, I found, would have been happy to leave the work force if it were financially possible. Furthermore, all their power—and much of their pleasure—continued to reside in the mothering role. They loved their children, felt compromised at the inadequacy of parenting time, and, perhaps surprisingly, rarely considered that one answer might be greater paternal participation. In truth, many such women were unwilling to surrender hegemony at home.

In such marriages, each spouse typically clings to his or her traditional powers while simultaneously craving a more partnership-oriented relationship. The result is emotional disappointment and conflict. Women in such relationships tend to view egalitarian gender roles as oppressive—seeing more respect, security, and satisfaction in the role of full-time mother. Yet they simultaneously resent the husband's low participation and quasi-autocratic behavior, since they feel they have earned equality and crave it on an emotional level.

Roadblocks and Suggested Policy Reforms

While I have found that there are many different routes to a stable peer marriage, achievement of such a relationship is not automatic, as the experiences of the "near peers" attest. Several barriers stand in the way.

In the first place, it is often hard to avoid role differentiation, especially when partners have been strongly socialized to one or the other role. For example, it is simply not in the couple's best interests for the "bad cook" to prepare dinner while the good one does dishes. Even though cooking can be learned—quite easily, in fact—the startup costs (bad meals for a while) stop most couples in their tracks. The better the homemaker-parent and the more outstanding the provider, the less likely there is to be taste for change.

Other inhibitors to peer marriages include the gender-based organization of jobs in the outside world (which affect evaluations of each partner's career prospects), and the overall pull of the status quo. Yet in a sense, the biggest roadblock we face is our sense of the possible. Many women and men simply do not believe an egalitarian marriage is feasible—unless they happen to be in one. Even many who desire the peer model do not believe it can be achieved within ordinary working schedules. And most women expect significant male resistance and see a risk in asserting themselves, fearing that conflict with their husbands will lead to defeat and deeper resentment on their own part, or even divorce.

These are all reasonable cautions. The pleasure of sharing the day-to-day administration of home and family is not apparent to many men, especially those socialized to the older model. Nonetheless, today we find an increasing number of young men and remarried men actually yearning to be an involved parent. This represents a shift in ideology, a new view of "what is important in life."

However, women, too, need to change. Many women are used to being taken care of and are trained for submissive interaction with men. In effect, they set up during courtship many of the inequities they will complain about in marriage—and ultimately flee from. They want intimacy, yet they often establish conditions—such as maximization of male income—that subvert family time and marital closeness.

In addition, there are several public policy reforms that might assist in the formation of peer marriages and thereby help anchor families of the future. Such reforms might include classes on marriage and the family in high school, where young men and women can learn a model of partnership, equity, and friendship; more pressure on employers to offer flextime and on-site child care, so that individuals are not penalized for their parenting choices; and after-school care in the public schools (until 6 P.M.).

There also needs to be more cultural support from the larger society. Most parents do not want to see their sons in the role of primary parent, do not want their sons' careers compromised, and still view a woman's work—including care for children—as unmanly. Moreover, most women are not encouraged to think of themselves as potential providers; only recently have they come to imagine themselves as fully committed to careers. I know there is a great split of opinion over whether young mothers should work at all, much less be encouraged to be responsible for their own economic welfare. But I would suggest that too much specialization in parenting and insufficient equality of experience may be more injurious in the long run than the difficulties involved when both partners juggle work and home.

Conclusions

We must recognize that there is no one form of marital organization appropriate for all couples. But I believe the "pro-family" or "family values" movement has been needlessly antagonistic to feminist models of marriage. After all, the two sides in this dialogue share some important goals: we do not want marriages to break up unless they absolutely have to; we want children to be loved and cherished and brought to adulthood in an intact family if there is any way it can be accomplished without punishment to either the children or the parents; we want people to want to form lasting bonds that strengthen the extended family.

The big question is how best to accomplish this. I suggest that shared parenting and increased spousal satisfaction are the most effective routes to family stability. I think that newfound feelings about equity and emotional closeness are essential to modern marital durability. Peer relationships will be good for women, children, and families—and a great benefit for men as well. Peer marriage is not a feminist or elitist vision. It is a practical plan to lower the divorce rate. But in order to see how well it works, society needs to offer the cultural and structural support to permit both men and women to parent, to participate in each other's lives, and to have the time together that a strong relationship requires. Whether peer marriage will actually work better than traditional marriage is, at this point, a matter of conjecture. We do know, however, that traditional roles have failed to ensure stability. The new model is an experiment we can ill afford to ignore.

Against School
How Public Education Cripples Our Kids, and Why

JOHN TAYLOR GATTO

I taught for thirty years in some of the worst schools in Manhattan, and in some of the best, and during that time I became an expert in boredom. Boredom was everywhere in my world, and if you asked the kids, as I often did, *why* they felt so bored, they always gave the same answers: They said the work was stupid, that it made no sense, that they already knew it. They said they wanted to be doing something real, not just sitting around. They said teachers didn't seem to know much about their subjects and clearly weren't interested in learning more. And the kids were right: their teachers were every bit as bored as they were.

Boredom is the common condition of schoolteachers, and anyone who has spent time in a teachers' lounge can vouch for the low energy, the whining, the dispirited attitudes, to be found there. When asked why *they* feel bored, the teachers tend to blame the kids, as you might expect. Who wouldn't get bored teaching students who are rude and interested only in grades? If even that. Of course, teachers are themselves products of the same twelve-year compulsory school programs that so thoroughly bore their students, and as school personnel they are trapped inside structures even more rigid than those imposed upon the children. Who, then, is to blame?

We all are. My grandfather taught me that. One afternoon when I was seven I complained to him of boredom, and he batted me hard on the head. He told me that I was never to use that term in his presence again, that if I was bored it was my fault and no one else's. The obligation to amuse and instruct myself was entirely my own, and people who didn't know that were childish people, to be avoided if possible. Certainty not to be trusted. That episode cured me of boredom forever, and here and there over the years I was able to pass on the lesson to some remarkable student. For the most part, however, I found it futile to challenge the official notion that boredom and childishness were the natural state of affairs in the classroom. Often I had to defy custom, and even bend the law, to help kids break out of this trap.

The empire struck back, of course; childish adults regularly conflate opposition with disloyalty. I once returned from a medical leave to discover that all evidence of my having been granted the leave had been purposely destroyed, that my job had been terminated, and that I no longer possessed even a teaching license. After nine months of tormented effort I was able to retrieve the license when a school secretary testified to witnessing the plot unfold. In the meantime my family suffered more than I care to remember. By the time I finally retired in 1991, I had more than enough reason to think of our schools—with their long-term, cell-block-style, forced confinement of both students and teachers—as virtual factories of childishness. Yet I honestly could not see *why* they had to be that way. My own experience had revealed to me what many other teachers must learn along the way, too, yet keep to themselves for fear of reprisal: if we wanted to we could easily and inexpensively jettison the old, stupid structures and help kids *take* an education rather than merely *receive* a schooling. We could encourage the best qualities of youthfulness—curiosity, adventure, resilience, the capacity for surprising insight—simply by being more flexible about time, texts, and tests, by introducing kids to truly competent adults, and by giving each student what autonomy he or she needs in order to take a risk every now and then.

But we don't do that. And the more I asked why not, and persisted in thinking about the "problem" of schooling as an engineer might, the more I missed the point: What if there is no "problem" with our schools? What if they are the way they are, so expensively flying in the face of common sense and long experience in how children learn things, not because they are doing something wrong but because they are doing something right? Is it possible that George W. Bush accidentally spoke the truth when he said we would " leave no child behind"? Could it be that our schools are designed to make sure not one of them ever really grows up?

Do we really need school? Six classes a day, five days a week, nine months a year, for twelve years? Is this deadly routine really necessary?

Do we really need school? I don't mean education, just forced schooling: six classes a day, five days a week, nine months a year, for twelve years. Is this deadly routine really necessary? And if so, for what? Don't hide behind reading, writing, and arithmetic as a rationale, because 2 million happy homeschoolers have surely put that banal justification to rest. Even if they hadn't, a considerable number of well-known Americans never went through the twelve-year wringer our kids currently go through, and they turned out all right. George Washington, Benjamin Franklin, Thomas Jefferson, Abraham Lincoln? Someone taught them, to be sure, but they were not products of a school *system,* and not one of them was ever "graduated" from a secondary school. Throughout most of American history, kids generally didn't go to high school, yet the unschooled rose to be admirals, like Farragut; inventors, like Edison; captains of industry like Carnegie and Rockefeller; writers, like Melville and Twain and Conrad; and even scholars, like Margaret Mead. In fact, until pretty recently people who reached the age of thirteen weren't looked upon as children at all. Ariel Durant, who co-wrote an enormous, and very good, multivolume history of the world with her husband, Will, was happily married at fifteen, and who could reasonably claim that Ariel Durant was an uneducated person? Unschooled, perhaps, but not uneducated.

We have been taught (that is, schooled) in this country to think of "success" as synonymous with, or at least dependent upon, "schooling," but historically that isn't true in either an intellectual or a financial sense. And plenty of people throughout the world today find a way to educate themselves without resorting to a system of compulsory secondary schools that all too often resemble prisons. Why, then, do Americans confuse education with just such a system? What exactly is the purpose of our public schools?

In 1843, Horace Mann wrote a paean to the land of Frederick the Great and called for its schooling to be brought here.

Mass schooling of a compulsory nature really got its teeth into the United States between 1905 and 1915, though it was conceived of much earlier and pushed for throughout most of the nineteenth century. The reason given for this enormous upheaval of family life and cultural traditions was, roughly speaking, threefold:

1) To make good people.
2) To make good citizens.
3) To make each person his or her personal best.

These goals are still trotted out today on a regular basis, and most of us accept them in one form or another as a decent definition of public education's mission, however short schools actually fall in achieving them. But we are dead wrong. Compounding our error is the fact that the national literature holds numerous and surprisingly consistent statements of compulsory schooling's true purpose. We have, for example, the great H. L. Mencken, who wrote in *The American Mercury* for April 1924 that the aim of public education is not:

> to fill the young of the species with knowledge and awaken their intelligence. . . . Nothing could be further

from the truth. The aim . . . is simply to reduce as many individuals as possible to the same safe level, to breed and train a standardized citizenry, to put down dissent and originality. That is its aim in the United States . . . and that is its aim everywhere else.

Because of Mencken's reputation as a satirist, we might be tempted to dismiss this passage as a bit of hyperbolic sarcasm. His article, however, goes on to trace the template for our own educational system back to the now vanished, though never to be forgotten, military state of Prussia. And although he was certainly aware of the irony that we had recently been at war with Germany, the heir to Prussian thought and culture, Mencken was being perfectly serious here. Our educational system really is Prussian in origin, and that really is cause for concern.

The odd fact of a Prussian provenance for our schools pops up again and again once you know to look for it. William James alluded to it many times at the turn of the century. Orestes Brownson, the hero of Christopher Lasch's 1991 book, *The True and Only Heaven,* was publicly denouncing the Prussianization of American schools back in the 1840s. Horace Mann's "Seventh Annual Report" to the Massachusetts State Board of Education in 1843 is essentially a paean to the land of Frederick the Great and a call for its schooling to be brought here. That Prussian culture loomed large in America is hardly surprising, given our early association with that utopian state. A Prussian served as Washington's aide during the Revolutionary War, and so many German-speaking people had settled here by 1795 that Congress considered publishing a German-language edition of the federal laws. But what shocks is that we should so eagerly have adopted one of the very worst aspects of Prussian culture: an educational system deliberately designed to produce mediocre intellects, to hamstring the inner life, to deny students appreciable leadership skills, and to ensure docile and incomplete citizens—in order to render the populace "manageable."

Modern, industrialized, compulsory schooling was to make a surgical incision into the prospective unity of the underclasses.

It was from James Bryant Conant—president of Harvard for twenty years, WWI poison-gas specialist, WWII executive on the atomic-bomb project, high commissioner of the American zone in Germany after WWII, and truly one of the most influential figures of the twentieth century—that I first got wind of the real purposes of American schooling. Without Conant, we would probably not have the same style and degree of standardized testing that we enjoy today, nor would we be blessed with gargantuan high schools that warehouse 2,000 to 4,000 students at a time, like the famous Columbine High in Littleton, Colorado. Shortly after I retired from teaching I picked up Conant's 1959 book-length essay, *The Child the Parent and the State,* and was more than a little intrigued to see him mention in passing that the modern schools we attend were the result of a " revolution" engineered between 1905 and 1930. A revolution? He declines to elaborate, but he does direct the curious and the uninformed to Alexander Inglis's 1918 book, *Principles of Secondary Education,* in which "one saw this revolution through the eyes of a revolutionary."

Inglis, for whom a lecture in education at Harvard is named, makes it perfectly clear that compulsory schooling on this continent was intended to be just what it had been for Prussia in the 1820s: a fifth column into the burgeoning democratic movement that threatened to give the peasants and the proletarians a voice at the bargaining table. Modern, industrialized, compulsory schooling was to make a sort of surgical incision into the prospective unity of these underclasses. Divide children by subject, by age-grading, by constant rankings on tests, and by many other more subtle means, and it was unlikely that the ignorant mass of mankind, separated in childhood, would ever re-integrate into a dangerous whole.

Inglis breaks down the purpose—the *actual* purpose—of modern schooling into six basic functions, any one of which is enough to curl the hair of those innocent enough to believe the three traditional goals listed earlier:

1) The *adjustive* or *adaptive* function. Schools are to establish fixed habits of reaction to authority. This, of course, precludes critical judgment completely. It also pretty much destroys the idea that useful or interesting material should be taught, because you can't test for *reflexive* obedience until you know whether you can make kids learn, and do, foolish and boring things.

2) The *integrating* function. This might well be called "the conformity function," because its intention is to make children as alike as possible. People who conform are predictable, and this is of great use to those who wish to harness and manipulate a large labor force.

3) The *diagnostic* and *directive* function. School is meant to determine each student's proper social role. This is done by logging evidence mathematically and anecdotally on cumulative records. As in "your permanent record." Yes, you do have one.

4) The *differentiating* function. Once their social role has been " diagnosed," children are to be sorted by role and trained only so far as their destination in the social machine merits—and not one step further. So much for making kids their personal best.

School didn't have to train kids to think they should consume nonstop; it simply taught them not to think at all.

5) The *selective* function. This refers not to human choice at all but to Darwin's theory of natural selection as applied to what he called "the favored races." In short,

the idea is to help things along by consciously attempting to improve the breeding stock. Schools are meant to tag the unfit—with poor grades, remedial placement, and other punishments—clearly enough that their peers will accept them as inferior and effectively bar them from the reproductive sweepstakes. That's what all those little humiliations from first grade onward were intended to do: wash the dirt down the drain.

6) The *propaedeutic* function. The societal system implied by these rules will require an elite group of caretakers. To that end, a small fraction of the kids will quietly be taught how to manage this continuing project, how to watch over and control a population deliberately dumbed down and declawed in order that government might proceed unchallenged and corporations might never want for obedient labor.

That, unfortunately, is the purpose of mandatory public education in this country. And lest you take Inglis for an isolated crank with a rather too cynical take on the educational enterprise, you should know that he was hardly alone in championing these ideas. Conant himself, building on the ideas of Horace Mann and others, campaigned tirelessly for an American school system designed along the same lines. Men like George Peabody, who funded the cause of mandatory schooling throughout the South, surely understood that the Prussian system was useful in creating not only a harmless electorate and a servile labor force but also a virtual herd of mindless consumers. In time a great number of industrial titans came to recognize the enormous profits to be had by cultivating and tending just such a herd via public education, among them Andrew Carnegie and John D. Rockefeller.

There you have it. Now you know. We don't need Karl Marx's conception of a grand warfare between the classes to see that it is in the interest of complex management, economic or political, to dumb people down, to demoralize them, to divide them from one another, and to discard them if they don't conform. Class may frame the proposition, as when Woodrow Wilson, then president of Princeton University, said the following to the New York City School Teachers Association in 1909: "We want one class of persons to have a liberal education, and we want another class of persons, a very much larger class, of necessity, in every society, to forgo the privileges of a liberal education and fit themselves to perform specific difficult manual tasks." But the motives behind the disgusting decisions that bring about these ends need not be class-based at all. They can stem purely from fear, or from the by now familiar belief that "efficiency" is the paramount virtue, rather than love, liberty, laughter, or hope. Above all, they can stem from simple greed.

There were vast fortunes to be made, after all, in an economy based on mass production and organized to favor the large corporation rather than the small business or the family farm. But mass production required mass consumption, and at the turn of the twentieth century most Americans considered it both unnatural and unwise to buy things they didn't actually need.

Mandatory schooling was a godsend on that count. School didn't have to train kids in any direct sense to think they should consume nonstop, because it did something even better: it encouraged them not to think at all. And that left them sitting ducks for another great invention of the modern era—marketing.

Now, you needn't have studied marketing to know that there are two groups of people who can always be convinced to consume more than they need to: addicts and children. School has done a pretty good job of turning our children into addicts, but it has done a spectacular job of turning our children into children. Again, this is no accident. Theorists from Plato to Rousseau to our own Dr. Inglis knew that if children could be cloistered with other children, stripped of responsibility and independence, encouraged to develop only the trivializing emotions of greed, envy, jealousy, and fear, they would grow older but never truly grow up. In the 1934 edition of his once well-known book *Public Education in the United States,* Ellwood P. Cubberley detailed and praised the way the strategy of successive school enlargements had extended childhood by two to six years, and forced schooling was at that point still quite new. This same Cubberley—who was dean of Stanford's School of Education, a textbook editor at Houghton Mifflin, and Conant's friend and correspondent at Harvard—had written the following in the 1922 edition of his book *Public School Administration:* "Our schools are . . . factories in which the raw products (children) are to be shaped and fashioned. . . . And it is the business of the school to build its pupils according to the specifications laid down."

Mandatory schooling's purpose is to turn kids into servants. Don't let your own have their childhoods extended, not even for a day.

It's perfectly obvious from our society today what those specifications were. Maturity has by now been banished from nearly every aspect of our lives. Easy divorce laws have removed the need to work at relationships; easy credit has removed the need for fiscal self-control; easy entertainment has removed the need to learn to entertain oneself; easy answers have removed the need to ask questions. We have become a nation of children, happy to surrender our judgments and our wills to political exhortations and commercial blandishments that would insult actual adults. We buy televisions, and then we buy the things we see on the television. We buy computers, and then we buy the things we see on the computer. We buy $150 sneakers whether we need them or not, and when they fall apart too soon we buy another pair. We drive SUVs and

believe the lie that they constitute a kind of life insurance, even when we're upside-down in them. And, worst of all, we don't bat an eye when Ari Fleischer tells us to "be careful what you say," even if we remember having been told somewhere back in school that America is the land of the free. We simply buy that one too. Our schooling, as intended, has seen to it.

Now for the good news. Once you understand the logic behind modern schooling, its tricks and traps are fairly easy to avoid. School trains children to be employees and consumers; teach your own to be leaders and adventurers. School trains children to obey reflexively; teach your own to think critically and independently. Well-schooled kids have a low threshold for boredom; help your own to develop an inner life so that they'll never be bored. Urge them to take on the serious material, the *grown-up* material, in history, literature, philosophy, music, art, economics, theology—all the stuff schoolteachers know well enough to avoid. Challenge your kids with plenty of solitude so that they can learn to enjoy their own company, to conduct inner dialogues. Well-schooled people are conditioned to dread being alone, and they seek constant companionship through the TV, the computer, the cell phone, and through shallow friendships quickly acquired and quickly abandoned. Your children should have a more meaningful life, and they can.

First, though, we must wake up to what our schools really are: laboratories of experimentation on young minds, drill centers for the habits and attitudes that corporate society demands. Mandatory education serves children only incidentally; its real purpose is to turn them into servants. Don't let your own have their childhoods extended, not even for a day. If David Farragut could take command of a captured British warship as a preteen, if Thomas Edison could publish a broadsheet at the age of twelve, if Ben Franklin could apprentice himself to a printer at the same age (then put himself through a course of study that would choke a Yale senior today), there's no telling what your own kids could do. After a long life, and thirty years in the public school trenches, I've concluded that genius is as common as dirt. We suppress our genius only because we haven't yet figured out how to manage a population of educated men and women. The solution, I think, is simple and glorious. Let them manage themselves.

JOHN TAYLOR GATTO is a former New York State and New York City Teacher of the Year and the author, most recently, of *The Underground History of American Education.* He was a participant in the *Harper's Magazine* forum "School on a Hill," which appeared in the September 2001 issue.

Can the Center Find a Solution That Will Hold?

The High School Experience: Proposals for Improvement

CHESTER E. FINN, JR.

The year 2005 began with high schools taking center stage in Washington's continuing drama concerning education reform. President George W. Bush started things off in January, when he delivered a ringing address at a suburban D.C. high school about the urgency of reforming American high schools and offered a bold $1.5 billion plan for doing so. A month after the presidential call to arms for high-school reform, 45 governors and a host of education leaders and CEOs met in a downtown Washington, D.C., hotel for a summit devoted to the subject.

In his keynote address to that gathering, Microsoft chairman Bill Gates pronounced current U.S. high schools "obsolete" and said, "Even when they are working as designed, they cannot teach all our students what they need to know today." At the same conclave, the new secretary of education, Margaret Spellings, declared that America "must make a high-school diploma a ticket to success in the 21st century." The summit concluded by adopting a five-part state "action agenda": restoring value to the diploma; redesigning the high school as an institution; strengthening the quality of high-school teachers and principals; holding high schools accountable for their results; and streamlining "education governance."

With all these powerful people talking high-school reform, it seemed that the planets had aligned to make high schools, the lost child of public education, the featured attraction on the U.S. education-policy agenda. But the universe then began to shift and the planets were knocked out of alignment. First, House Education Committee chairman John Boehner, a Republican from Ohio and longtime proponent of education reform, expressed doubts about the federal government's role in leading the high-school reform effort. "The current system," Boehner remarked at a late-May committee hearing, "isn't getting the job done. But that doesn't necessarily mean the solution to the problem should be driven from Washington." Another senior member of that committee, former Delaware governor Michael Castle, also a Republican, was blunter. "Frankly," he said, "there's political opposition to it, and it's not just Democrats. It's within the Republican Party as well." And on the other side of the Capitol a spokesman for Senator Mike Enzi, chairman of the Senate

Education Committee, noted, "Senator Enzi has made several other education issues the first priority."

As if that weren't trouble enough, the president's $1.5 billion plan entailed shifting to his high-school reform plan funds traditionally spent on vocational education, a move that riled many members of Congress since "voc ed" remains popular back home.

What happened? Has the White House initiative been stopped at the starting gate? Is high-school reform a dead issue?

The Need Is Great, the Political Will Weak

As nearly everyone in education knows, something is wrong with our high schools. And, for the most part, the Bush administration's proposal seemed built on that consensus, much the same accord that brought us No Child Left Behind and the determination that schools need a regimen of standards, testing, and accountability.

"Out of a hundred 9th graders in our public schools," said Mr. Bush in his January speech, "only 68 will complete high school on time. Now, we live in a competitive world, and a 68 percent graduation rate for 9th graders is not good enough to be able to compete in this competitive world. In math and science, the problem is especially urgent. A recent study showed that American 15-year-olds ranked 27th out of 39 countries in math literacy. I don't know about you, but I want to be ranked first in the world, not 27th."

The president proposed a series of programs to help high-school students graduate with "skills necessary to succeed." The plan included money to identify at-risk 8th graders and intervene in their academic lives "before it's too late." But the centerpiece was a call for tests in reading and math in the 9th, 10th, and 11th grades. "Testing at high-school levels will help us to become more competitive as the years go by," said Bush. "Testing in high schools will make sure that our children are employable for the jobs of the 21st century. Testing will allow teachers to improve their classes. Testing will enable schools to track. Testing will make sure that a diploma is not merely a sign of endurance, but the mark of a young person ready to succeed."

The plan seemed sensible enough. And it is possible, of course, that parts of the president's plan could reemerge when No Child Left Behind is reauthorized. At present, though, Congress seems to think it has done plenty to make over K–12 education and is loath to extend NCLB's scope at the very time that the ambitious statute is facing so many implementation challenges as well as so much opposition from states and districts. Indeed, the controversies surrounding NCLB have at least delayed, if not doomed, both the administration's version of high-school reform and any other bold federal entry into that territory.

Maximum Feasible Myopia

The real question, then, though perhaps born of necessity, is whether it's such a bad thing that responsibility for revitalizing U.S. high schools has been thrust back on states and districts, private funders, and diverse reform architects. Could the federal government's failure to mount a political consensus open the way to useful experimentation with various potential solutions?

Indeed, much experimenting is already under way across the land. And remembering the warning of the French political commentator George Bernanos may enhance the chances of finding useful solutions: "The worst, the most corrupting of lies, are problems poorly stated." In other words, if a problem is misrepresented or its definition is disputed, any given solution is unlikely to solve it to everyone's satisfaction.

A vivid American example of this policy perplexity was embodied in a famous 1969 book, *Maximum Feasible Misunderstanding,* by the late senator Daniel Patrick Moynihan. The title was a play on a key phrase in the Economic Opportunity Act of 1964 (which launched LBJ's "war on poverty") calling for the "maximum feasible participation" of residents and groups affected by the legislation's centerpiece Community Action Program. Moynihan's point was that the program's architects didn't actually agree on what the problem was, so the legislation they created fell apart when the time came for its implementation. It was, if you will, a modern public-policy rendition of the tale of the blind men and the elephant, wherein each sightless man had a different notion of the essential nature of this beast depending on which part he was touching. Moynihan contended that the Community Action Program was doomed because the rush to legislate had led people to reach superficial agreement on the definition of the policy problem.

Trying to Define the Problem

As America embarks on high-school reform, it runs a similar risk. The nation is awash in different solutions to the high-school problem. But mostly we are still grappling with trying to define the problem. Sure, from 30,000 feet we can reach broad agreement as to what's wrong. Nearly everyone shares the concern of the president and the governors that U.S. high-school students are not learning enough; that they're being surpassed by their peers in other lands; that too many are bored to death; that too many drop out; that few of those who graduate are

well prepared for college and employment. And so on. From six miles up, we know we have a problem and can even reach a meeting of minds as to its most vivid manifestations.

Yes, there's a problem, several problems, in fact, and the rationale for high-school reform would seem compelling. But as we get closer to the ground, the picture loses focus. Is the problem with high school that it is not engaging students or that it is not academically challenging enough? Can we *simultaneously* reduce dropouts and beef up academic achievement? Will stiffer graduation requirements and more high-stakes testing cause even more young people to quit? Are these complementary goals, or are they trade-offs? Are these even the right questions?

One thing we do know is that if we get the answers wrong, we invite a new maximum feasible misunderstanding, and high-school reform will be declared a failure. Thus I sense that it's just as well Uncle Sam is not rushing in with a predetermined, nationwide strategy and that we're giving states, communities, and private organizations some leeway to work out different approaches. If we monitor and evaluate their efforts, we stand to learn more about what works for whom in what circumstances.

Knowing What's Wrong

How many options are there, really? Allowing for mixing and matching, I can identify at least six versions of the problem, each giving rise to different theories of action and strategies for solving it. The now-dormant White House proposals tapped into several of these, as did the summit communiqué released by the National Governors Association. At the end of the day, we will likely conclude that the high-school problem is actually a tangle of problems in need of a multipart solution. Well and good. First, though, all the blind men should come to understand the many-faceted nature of this particular beast.

Problem 1: Achievement Is Too Low

Solution. Extend standards-based reform to high schools by making them accountable for their students' achievement and completion rates. A number of states have begun to do this, and the Bush proposal is focused here, bringing high schools under the NCLB umbrella, primarily via testing and public accountability. This is a familiar, government-driven, top-down, standards-based, institution-centered approach, already fairly well established in the primary and middle schools.

Problem 2: Students Aren't Working Hard Enough, Taking the Right Courses, or Learning Enough

Solution. Since all they need do to get a diploma is go through the motions and rack up the course credits, no real reward follows from studying hard (save for the small fraction seeking entry to competitive colleges), and no unpleasantness results from taking it easy. We thus need to establish high-stakes graduation tests that students must pass to earn their diplomas. This, too, is a behaviorist, top-down, results-based, accountability-driven system, but this version bears down primarily on the kids rather than on their schools. About half the states have already put into place some form of statewide graduation test. Some also supply carrots along with the sticks via positive inducements such as college scholarships for those with B averages. The Bush administration suggested fatter Pell grants for those who complete a challenging curriculum.

Problem 3:
High School Is a Lockstep Bore, and Consequently Too Many Kids Turn Off, Tune Out, and Quit. If They Don't Stick Around (or Come Back), There's No Way They'll Learn

Solution. Prevent dropouts and maximize completions by making the high-school experience more appealing: individualize it, let students move at their own pace. This was the thrust of a recent task force report in Ohio titled "High-Quality High Schools"; it was the point of the president's proposed $200 million Performance Plan Fund (part of the $1.5 billion initiative); and it's the essence of any number of private-sector initiatives. With it, sometimes, comes the idea of creating new education options for out-of-school youth and dropout recovery programs for those who have fallen by the wayside. (Indeed, we could identify seven reform strategies rather than six by bisecting this one and distinguishing between prevention and retrieval schemes.) The underlying theory of action is that, if young people like school more (and, presumably, succeed at it), they'll hang in there. Well-conceived specialty schools and programs can reengage young people who have already had it with formal education.

Problem 4:
The Circa–1950s, One-Size-Fits-All, Comprehensive High School Is Itself Dysfunctional, an Inefficient, Outmoded Vehicle for Teaching Young People What They Need to Learn

Solution. Devise new institutional forms for delivering secondary education, using technology, modern organization theory, and outsourcing. Give young people choices among the formats: early-college high schools; smaller schools; schools within schools; charter schools; KIPP schools; high-tech high schools; virtual high schools; and more. Much has been tried on this front, and the innovations take many shapes, as do the schemes whereby young people and their parents can access the version that works best for them.

Problem 5:
The Courses Are Too Easy, Pointless, and Ill Matched to the Demands of the Real World

Solution. Beef up the curriculum. Broaden access to Advanced Placement courses and propagate the International Baccalaureate. Strengthen state standards. Revise the textbooks. Team up with colleges to create K–16 programs. Make college-prep the default curriculum. Blend higher-education's expectations with those of modern jobs, à la the American Diploma Project, and work backward through the K–12 grades.

Problem 6:
Academic Work and Intellectual Activity Are No Way to the Adolescent Heart

Solution. Since teenagers are animated by things with tangible rewards and sleeves-rolled-up engagement, we need to get practical. Focus on tech-prep programs, ventures that join high schools to community colleges, work-study, schedules that blend school with jobs, voluntarism and community service, and kindred ways of tapping into the "affective," pecuniary, and social sides of young people.

High School Is Different

To be sure, we could slice these strategies differently and combine them in any number of packages. And yes, with a bit of effort they can be loosely grouped under the two familiar headings that we know as standards-based and choice-based reform. But that may not be the most useful way to frame them. Indeed, it may invite people to slip into familiar ideological postures rather than to think closely about high schools.

The fact is that high schools pose challenges distinct from those of K–8. Their students don't really have to be there. Even where state compulsory attendance laws extend to age 17 or 18, our sky-high dropout rate proves those statutes are unenforceable. High schools are larger than elementary schools and there are fewer of them, which makes choice-based strategies harder. For every person who believes that the high school's mission is to supply all students with a solid liberal arts education, someone else is convinced that young people's differing tastes and aspirations should preclude uniformity of academic standards and curriculum. On a major national survey conducted in April 2005, for example, 76 percent of Americans opposed making college prep the universal high-school curriculum and instead favored "career/technical education to equip students who don't go to college with real-world skills." (Hence the continuing appeal of voc ed.) By the high-school years, moreover, achievement levels range widely: some students still need basic reading and arithmetic, while others crave university-level coursework and Intel science competitions.

Adult World Problems Not Addressed

Adolescents also have much on their minds besides school: money, sports, and socializing, for starters. More than a few have tangled with such adult-world problems as drugs, crime, and pregnancy. And many have scant use for authority (or even advice) proffered by grown-ups—their parents, teachers, or anybody else.

As if that did not present a sufficiently daunting picture for would-be reformers, lots of Americans don't really see a big problem with high schools in their present form, at least not with the schools they know best. Parents typically give high marks to their own children's high schools, institutions that also anchor many communities, provide Friday-night football games, and seem to be doing an adequate job of turning out graduates who go on to college, even if some must take remedial courses when they get there. The dropout rate means that the high schools' most acute failures largely vanish from sight. At the top, honors students fret not about boredom or weak achievement, but about the stress that attends all that cramming and homework as they compete for entry into high-status universities. And just about everyone who sticks it out can at least attend the local community college, join the military, or find an entry-level job of some sort. "What, exactly, is the problem with our high school?" ask the residents of River City, U.S.A.

Considering all the impediments to wholesale high-school reform and the absence of true consensus as to the nature and urgency of the problem, I conclude that diversity and experimentation are a reasonable way to proceed in mid-decade, rather than pressing for elusive agreement about a single national strategy. That doesn't mean I'm complacent about today's high schools. They are not, in fact, getting us where we need to go as a country. But neither are they going to be turned around from Washington, which lacks the political will to make this problem its own. Instead, let us welcome the mixing of strategies and matching of solutions, the combining of ideas and refining of programs. Let us try all six (or five or seven) of the aforementioned reform notions and any number of permutations and combinations of them and seek to determine what works best for whom in which circumstances. High-school reform may resemble welfare reform, where it was important that states had the freedom and incentive to try various approaches before the time was ripe for a national strategy.

Let us acknowledge, though, that a decentralized, piecemeal approach invites its own messy confusion, the more so if we have no common metrics by which to gauge progress, compare results, or define success from one place to another.

Multiple reform strategies cast the greatest light when they at least share measures of performance. For which purpose, let us return to 30,000 feet and suggest that the two essential sets of data for tracking America's progress or lack thereof in revitalizing the high school are objective test scores and graduation rates.

Neither, alas, is easy to come by nor itself the object of wide consensus.

Results Not Reported

Twelfth-grade scores on the National Assessment of Educational Progress (NAEP), aka the nation's report card, are not even reported by state, though 4th- and 8th-grade results are, and have long been shadowed by doubts as to their accuracy, considering that many high-school seniors don't take the exams seriously. They do not, after all, "count" for anything in the student's own life. Other national tests used for college entrance—SATs, ACTs, Advanced Placement—are taken only by a subset of juniors and seniors. And of course none is taken by the horde of young people who don't complete high school.

Though many states have instigated graduation tests, these often have low passing levels and, in any case, are not readily compared from one jurisdiction to the next.

International tests such as the Trends in International Mathematics and Science Study (TIMSS) are valuable for purposes of comparing U.S. student performance with their overseas counterparts, but these do not occur on a predictable cycle.

As for graduation and dropout rates, the National Center for Education Statistics has multiple definitions and measures; the Census Bureau counts "high-school equivalency" certificates along with actual, on-time graduates; and several independent analysts insist that the true graduation rate is far lower than federal data suggest, very different from state to state, often even different from what states think it is. (Fortunately, this may change over the next few years, as all but a handful of governors, declining to wait for Uncle Sam, announced in July 2005 that they would collaborate on a single, simplified graduation gauge.)

Thus it will be no small challenge even to monitor and evaluate U.S. high-school reform initiatives if we don't have measures that people agree on. And that's without resolving the policy paradox of whether achievement scores and graduation rates can realistically be raised at the same time, along with the level of student engagement, or whether those worthy goals tend to cancel one another.

At day's end, the multifaceted challenge of high-school reform seems to be a problem that needs to ripen before any comprehensive solution can drop from the policy tree. Americans hold disparate goals for high schools, conflicting priorities for strengthening them, and dissimilar yardsticks for tracking progress.

This is not to say the problem doesn't cry for a solution or that complacency rules the day. In a survey of high-school students released by the National Governors Association in July 2005, more than a third of respondents said their school had not done a good job of challenging them academically or preparing them for college; almost two-thirds said they would work harder if the courses were more demanding or interesting. A month earlier, the Educational Testing Service released a survey indicating that 51 percent of the general public think U.S. high schools need either "major changes" or a "complete overhaul," even if there's considerable dissonance as to what those changes should be. Furthermore, the imperative to make any changes may not extend to their own community high school.

That more and more people are discontented with today's high schools and their results is surely a good thing. This issue deserves to be on the national stage. But first it has to play in the provinces, in summer stock, and in off-off Broadway theaters, where actors, directors, investors, critics, and audiences alike can come to understand it.

CHESTER E. FINN, JR. is president of the Thomas B. Fordham Foundation, a senior fellow at the Hoover Institution, and senior editor of *Education Next*.

From *Education Next,* Winter 2006, pp. 27–32. Copyright © 2006 by Education Next. Reprinted by permission.

Fixing Hospitals

Medical errors kill 100,000 Americans every year. A new vanguard is out to fix the fatal flaws.

ROBERT LANGRETH

Josie King was a curious and precocious baby. At 18 months old she loved jumping on the trampoline and had recently learned to say "I love you." She toddled into the bathroom one day when no one was looking, slipped into the tub and turned scalding hot water on herself. After ten days in the pediatric intensive care unit at Johns Hopkins Children's Center in Baltimore, her burns were healing so fast that doctors moved her to an intermediate care ward with hopes of releasing her soon. Her three older siblings started planning a coming-home party.

Then things went terribly wrong. Her mother noticed that Josie started screaming for liquid every time she saw a drink. At one point the girl desperately sucked water out of a washcloth. But nurses told Josie's mom, Sorrel King, to resist giving her daughter any drinks as she had been vomiting. That evening Josie's eyes started rolling back in her head, but when Sorrel pointed this out she was told Josie's vital signs were fine. The next morning Sorrel persuaded doctors to let Josie drink, but then one doc ordered heavy-duty narcotics against another's instructions. A few minutes later Josie's heart stopped. She was taken off life support two days later, dying of dehydration and bad medicine in one of the nation's premier hospitals.

"It was such simple stuff that went wrong; it wasn't one doctor or one nurse or one decimal point. It was a huge systems breakdown," Sorrel King says. Johns Hopkins resolutely admitted its mistakes and cooperated with a Baltimore Sun series on the 2001 incident. The hospital paid the family an undisclosed settlement and agreed to work with King to fix the flaws, revamping its systems for a sharper focus on safe care. But the broader problem remains, King says. "The general public still doesn't get it that thousands and thousands and thousands of people are dying every year because of medical errors."

Shoddy quality control plagues American medicine, killing at least a hundred thousand people every year and running up an estimated $500 billion a year in avoidable medical costs, or 30% of all health care spending. The quality crisis fuels the litigation crisis: Medical malpractice costs hit $27 billion in 2003.

"American health care operates with levels of unreliability, injury, waste and just plain poor service that long ago became absolutely unacceptable in many other industries," says Donald Berwick, a Harvard pediatrician and a crusader for fixing flawed care.

Many of the needed fixes are surprisingly simple, and new technology has arrived to modernize the antiquated systems that make the medical industry one of the least wired businesses in the U.S. economy.

> **61%** of doctors wash their hands before examining a patient if they know someone is watching.
> **44%** wash their hands if they think no one is watching.
> *University of Geneva study; Annals of Internal Medicine.*

After Josie King died, Hopkins Children's added a multidisciplinary team to each floor—one unit is named after her—and started holding meetings twice a month to raise safety concerns. A new safety director visits nurses weekly to unearth impending problems. Some 145 issues have come up in two years, and more than 100 of them have been fixed. When it emerged recently that two asthma drugs came in vials so similar as to risk confusing them, the staff confiscated current stocks, and the hospital got a new contract for two drugs with dissimilar packaging.

Yet many hospitals are painfully slow to embrace a revamping. One of the biggest obstacles: American medicine's cult of the "doctor is God," says Harvard's Lucian Leape, an early researcher in doctor errors. Doctors, who typically are independent of a hospital's direct control and are free to prescribe drugs for uses that haven't been approved by regulators, resist any second-guessing and perceived threats to their autonomy. Trying to reform the system sparks turf wars and staunch resistance. Only 34% of doctors have participated in quality-improvement efforts, one study says; two-thirds of doctors in one recent survey oppose disclosing their track records to the public.

The doctor-as-God approach "doesn't work in the 21st century," says Dr. Leape, a professor at the Harvard School of Public Health, not with the proliferation of new drugs and tests and tools and surgical procedures. Hospital patients often take dozens of drugs simultaneously and undergo scores of procedures and tests every day. Doctors and nurses still try to keep track of it all using paper, pen and clipboard—just as they did 50 years ago. New tools and better vetting of doctor decisions are critical to fixing this flawed system. Leape calls it "a tectonic shift in the practice of medicine."

"There is a massive gap between where we are and where we could be," says Dr. Brent James, a vice president at Intermountain Health Care in Salt Lake City, a big hospital chain that was one of the first to focus on systemic quality improvements. Better quality control, says Dr. Kenneth Kizer, who heads the National Quality Forum, "has the potential to do more for health care than any foreseeable technology improvement—including a cure for cancer."

The good news: After years of an industry in denial, some pioneering doctors and hospital chains, including Intermountain, Ascension Health in St. Louis and OSF Healthcare System in Illinois, are finally taking action. A reform movement is gaining ground, aiming to pull off a radical overhaul of America's 5,764 hospitals. Some 2,000 hospitals have joined an initiative known as the "100,000 Lives" campaign led by Harvard's Berwick, chief of the nonprofit Institute for Healthcare Improvement in Cambridge, Mass. He got religion after seeing his wife hospitalized for an autoimmune condition in 1999 and learning that "errors were not rare, they were the norm," as he put it later in a controversial speech; one urgently needed drug took 60 hours to get to her room. Now Berwick's 80 employees scour the world for simple, proven remedies for medicine's reliability woes. They farm out recommendations to the collaborating hospitals on everything from better infection control to eliminating drug mix-ups.

There is a massive gap between where we are and where we could be.

In this new focus on error-free medicine, hospitals are dropping age-old assumptions that their doctors are doing a good job and instead are measuring performance and issuing report cards. They are standardizing basic procedures to help reduce errors and condensing long-winded practice guidelines that harried doctors don't read into simple checklists integrated into daily work flow. They are instituting teamwork training, encouraging physicians to swallow their egos and go on rounds with nurses and empowering nurses to challenge doctors when they spot potential goofs—an especially heretical act. They are pushing for the digitization of medical records, at long last, so that crucial test results and other vital records can be tracked and communicated. In one controversial move, reformers are pushing hospitals to release their performance results to the public.

Meanwhile, high-tech patient simulators, such as those at Brigham and Women's Hospital, are enabling doctors and nurses to hone their technical skills for difficult emergency procedures and boost teamwork under pressure. "Simulation is on a steep explosion curve," says Ron M. Walls, who chairs emergency medicine at Brigham.

It may be too much change too fast for some. "Doctors are wary of changes that reduce their ability to act autonomously," says Berwick. Standardization "seems to them double-edged." Many in medicine, however, say they have no other choice but to adopt big changes. "There are three parts to medicine: understanding disease, identifying effective therapies and then making sure the therapies are used safely and consistently. We have totally neglected the third part," says Dr. Peter Pronovost, an intensive care specialist and safety researcher at Johns Hopkins University. His father died in 1990 in excruciating pain from misdiagnosed cancer. "I was told that I had to accept it. I thought patients deserved more," he says.

The reform movement doesn't yet have definitive clinical results, but early results are promising. Innovative hospitals are showing they can drastically cut medication errors and all but eliminate some deadly hospital infections by consistently applying known steps. "We don't have any idea of how low we can go, because the benchmarks are all based on a broken system. But we are seeing performances that are unheard of," says Pronovost.

He works on one project aimed at reducing the death rate from sepsis, a leading killer, and says thousands of lives could be saved each year if every hospital implemented the measures used in the study. It involves a network of 20 intensive care units at Johns Hopkins and elsewhere; the overall rate of sepsis deaths has fallen from 26% of sepsis patients in late 2003 to 20% now. The rate fell thanks to the addition of systems to ensure the simple stuff—that every patient with the ailment is quickly identified and immediately gets all recommended treatments.

For decades doctors figured occasional mishaps were inevitable and that the only solution was to work harder. One of the first to investigate the issue more deeply was Harvard's Leape. In 1991 he was part of a group of researchers seeking to catalog medical errors; they reviewed 30,000 in-patient records from 51 New York hospitals and found that roughly 4% of patients had been seriously harmed by their care. Two-thirds of the injuries were caused by errors. This later was extrapolated to estimates of almost 100,000 deaths from errors nationwide, and since then studies around the world have echoed the New York results.

Curious, Leape went to Harvard's vast medical library to see what had been written about preventing medical error. To his astonishment he was unable to find a single journal article on the subject. No one had even considered the matter, so alien was the concept that bad systems, not just bad doctors, might be responsible for patient injuries. Leape did turn up extensive safety literature from cognitive psychology, aviation and nuclear power, gleaning lessons—reducing reliance on memory, standardizing processes, promoting teamwork—that might apply well to medicine. He wrote his ideas up for publication, likening medicine's injury problem to "three jumbo jet crashes every two days." The article, published in late 1994, didn't go over well with most of his colleagues. "The common response was 'You are making us look bad,'" he says. But some saw the wisdom and the patient safety movement began.

A decade later some hospitals are achieving miraculous results from rethinking the way they deliver and monitor care.

Getting Back to Basics

In Utah, Intermountain's LDS hospital was an early innovator in studying medical reliability. LDS researchers benefited from one of the country's first computerized medical record systems, in place by the early 1980s, which provided a trove of data to track real-time results and spot problems. One early focus was slashing postsurgical infections. In the mid-1980s LDS infectious disease specialist John Burke and colleagues found only 40% of surgery patients at LDS were getting antibiotics during the optimal time window, zero to two hours before an operation. The remainder had vastly higher infection rates. Later other studies confirmed the problem was prevalent. Today 99% of surgical patients at LDS get antibiotics within the correct window. The biggest changes were cultural, Burke says. "We only made progress when we got the team together and got them to commit to using a checklist, like in a 747 before takeoff."

Burke and colleague David Classen then turned their attention to drug reactions. They designed software that scans drug orders and lab tests in the hospital database and flags problems. It showed only 1 in 60 toxic drug reactions were being reported through normal channels; in most cases doctors hadn't even noticed the problem. Today the software is used at LDS to spot mismatches in real time.

For years fixes at LDS and other Intermountain hospitals were piecemeal. That changed when a new executive vice president, William Nelson, was appointed in 1995 (he became chief executive in 1999). An accountant, he realized that higher reliability would save lives and money. Nelson corralled quality director Brent James and pressed him to delve into the unglamorous nitty-gritty of changing the entire hospital chain.

The first step was to revamp Intermountain's database to better link patient records at its hospitals and clinics to track how well each patient was faring in various measures of care, such as whether heart patients were getting the right drugs. This task took 20 programmers and statisticians over a year.

The harder step was persuading physicians to buy in. Intermountain hired 21 respected doctors part-time and an equal number of full-time nurses to act as peer reviewers for doctors at Intermountain's far-flung operations. They issued monthly reports to the hospitals on how various departments were doing. When data showed that many expectant mothers at its hospitals were being induced two weeks or more early simply because it was more convenient, even though national studies hinted it is safer to wait until 39 weeks, Intermountain clamped down in 2001. Some obstetricians objected, resenting the intrusion. "They tried to sabotage it," says Dr. Bryan Oshiro, who led the program. "They said the studies are wrong. 'Our patients are different. This is just administrators trying to tell us what to do.'" Oshiro's team reanalyzed Intermountain's own data and showed that deliveries even a week early had higher complication rates. The critics faded.

Results have been rolling in. Annual deaths from congestive heart failure plummeted 22% by adding (and enforcing) a checklist to ensure all patients get the right medicines before they leave the hospital. A mandate to test all newborns for high bilirubin levels, which can lead to brain damage, slashed the number of infants requiring readmission by 24%. Various childbirth measures have helped reduce Intermountain's cost per delivery by $350 in four years, saving $10 million annually.

A new set of standing orders helps doctors select the most appropriate antibiotics for treating pneumonia, and this has reduced the associated death rate among severe cases from 14% to 11%, saving nearly 100 lives a year. Doctors went from prescribing the optimal drugs in only 22% of cases in 1995 to 87% of cases now. Postsurgical infections occur only in 1 in 200 patients at Intermountain versus 1 in 50 nationally, thanks to its on-time prophylactic antibiotic program.

"What we are doing is simple but had never been done because there was no process and no accountability," says Nelson, Intermountain's chief executive. General Electric's health IT unit is so impressed with Intermountain's algorithms that it is opening a center in Utah to adapt them for mass use.

Touting Teamwork

Intensive care units specialize in stopping gravely ill patients from slipping over the edge. But what happens to patients in other wards who deteriorate? All too often a coordinated response doesn't occur until the patient's heart stops—and by then the patient has only a 15% chance of surviving. Signs of distress, such as breathing difficulties, usually appear six to eight hours before cardiac arrest, but nurses and junior residents may lack the expertise to stabilize patients on their own, and it can take hours to get an experienced doctor's help. "You have a universal problem: People who get sicker in the hospital don't get urgent care quickly," says Rinaldo Bellomo, an intensive care specialist at the University of Melbourne in Australia.

The solution: 24-hour emergency response teams that nurses can call, bypassing the chain of command, when they perceive a patient is in trouble. The teams bring together up to eight doctors and nurses with expertise in critical care and resuscitation. Some 1,200 hospitals now work with Harvard's Institute for Healthcare Improvement to implement these teams.

The University of Pittsburgh Medical Center adopted the teams in the late 1990s and has seen unexpected deaths drop 30% since then, says Michael DeVita, a critical care specialist at the hospital. DeVita says he hears from nurses at other hospitals who say they tried to get emergency attention for deteriorating patients only to be lectured never to call the cardiac-arrest team until the patient arrests. "It is unbelievable, but it is true," he says. "This should be mandatory for all hospitals." Bellomo's Austin Hospital in Melbourne was among the first to study the impact of the roving teams. It started using them in November 2000, and soon cardiac-arrest alerts over the hospital's public address system, once routine, stopped happening for weeks at a time. In the four months after implementing the teams, cardiac arrests plummeted 65%.

Other hospitals are trying to avert breakdowns in information sharing. In medical mistakes "the same theme comes up time and time again: lack of communication and confusion among team members," says Harry C. Sax, chief of surgery at Miriam Hospital in Providence, R.I. In one published case, CT-scan results revealing possible tuberculosis in a 70-year-old patient somehow didn't reach the treating doctors. By the time the disease was diagnosed four months later, it was too late and the patient died. In another, a who's-on-first name mix-up resulted in the wrong woman getting an invasive heart procedure; at least five nurses and three doctors disregarded the woman's objections or failed to verify her identity.

To fix the situation researchers hope to borrow from aviation, running checklists before operations and doing simulator training to practice teamwork. Last October surgeons at the Michael E. DeBakey VA Medical Center in Houston started doing preoperative briefings with nurses and anesthesiologists to verify the plans for the surgery and make sure all necessary preoperative drugs have been given. The briefing requires doctors to arrive at the OR ten minutes earlier, and it already has caught mistakes, chief of surgery David Berger says. In one case a surgery was canceled when doctors going through a checklist found out from a patient that he had taken, against orders, anticlotting drugs that could have caused bleeding.

Taming Infection

Each year 2 million hospitalized Americans develop additional infections during their stays; 90,000 of them die, according to the Centers for Disease Control. "It is staggeringly outrageous that this problem is allowed to continue and proliferate," says patient advocate Michael Bennett of Baltimore. His 89-year-old father, hospitalized for a respiratory infection, died last June after contracting six bacterial infections in five hospitals over four months, including flesh-eating bacteria that claimed a leg and other strains that ravaged his heart, kidneys, throat, liver and bloodstream. Bennett plans to sue one hospital (he won't name it) and is pushing for laws requiring hospitals to make infection rates public. "I know that my dad would still be alive today if he hadn't gone to the hospital," Bennett says.

We don't have any idea of how low we can go, because the benchmarks are based on a broken system.

For years doctors have assumed that certain rates of infections were simply the cost of doing business. But now hospitals are finding they can slash rates of killer infections by 50% or more by changing how they do things. One big source of deadly infections is surgical wounds, which hit 2% of surgical patients. Another rampant problem is ventilator-associated pneumonia, which afflicts anywhere from 10% to 25% of patients on the machines. The longer you remain on a ventilator, the greater the odds that germ-laden gunk from the back of the throat will get sucked into the lungs. Some embarrassingly low-tech steps can make a difference, if only hospitals would make the effort to do them. One is tilting the bed to 30 degrees, so secretions are less likely to bubble into the lungs. Another is minimizing the time patients are on ventilators, removing sedation once a day in order to assess whether patients are ready to be weaned. When Baptist Memorial Hospital-DeSoto in Southaven, Miss. made these and other changes in its ICU in 2003, its ventilator-pneumonia rate plummeted; it hasn't had a case in 12 months.

The final killer is blood infections from central IV lines installed into veins near the heart; these finish off 28,000 patients a year. Installing a central line is a tricky procedure that is often done by inexperienced residents. Sterility guidelines, such as draping the patient in a sterile sheet and wearing a mask and gown, are often forgotten. To make it easier to do it right, some ICUs now gather all the equipment needed on a single cart ahead of time and give nurses

> **47** minutes Median time it takes hospitals to give heart attack patients clot-busting drugs
> **30** minutes National standard for giving heart attack patients clot busters
>
> *National Healthcare Quality Report.*

permission to halt a central line procedure if they see a doctor doing it wrong. When Johns Hopkins Hospital did this and took other steps in a surgical ICU, rates of catheter infections dropped to nearly zero.

Sidestepping Drug Toxicity

Patricia Unger had worked at Rogue Valley Medical Center in Medford, Ore. for 18 years before being diagnosed with lymphoma and undergoing treatment there. In a high-dose chemo regimen, caregivers allowed blood levels of the toxic chemo drug methotrexate to soar to a thousand times above the safe level when a doctor misread a lab test, says the late Unger's son, Mark Unger. Soon there was nothing left to do but watch her burn to death from the inside out.

"Bedding was dripping on the floor from all the fluid coming out of her. At one point I was holding her hand and her whole palm came off," he recalls. Unger settled a malpractice lawsuit against the hospital and doctor for an undisclosed amount. "There was no system to catch the error, no safety net at all," he says. The hospital says that it has added multiple new safety systems including processes to prevent overmedication.

Drug toxicity is the single most common threat, hitting 6.5% of hospitalized patients. Information technology can help prevent errors and catch drug interactions before they do much damage. Brigham and Women's Hospital has been a pioneer here. Computerized doctor order systems can reduce harmful errors by 55%, says one study by David Bates at Brigham, which introduced such a system in 1993. But the order systems are expensive to install and tricky to get right, involving a big change in work flow. "The verdict is still out," says Marlene Miller, director of safety for Johns Hopkins Children's Center, which plans to install a computerized ordering system this year and is spending months programming dosing rules for kids, which the software doesn't offer.

In the meantime Dr. Berwick and IHI are working with hospitals on simpler measures that can slash drug-related injuries. Many drug mix-ups occur when a patient is admitted, discharged or transferred; carefully reconciling a patient's drug list every time he is moved can avoid this problem. OSF Healthcare in Peoria, Ill. has reduced drug-related injuries by almost 75% since 2001 with this and other techniques.

The Medical Mafia

Prosecutors say a group of top Las Vegas lawyers and doctors conspired to collect millions in inflated damages by pushing accident victims into dubious surgery. The lawyers and doctors say they're legitimate— and so far they're winning.

KATHERINE EBAN

It began as the most ordinary of fender-benders. Cynthia Johnson, an office manager for a real estate company, was driving to work on Interstate 15 near the Las Vegas strip when a fellow commuter clipped the rear bumper of her Toyota Avalon, propelling it into the truck in front. No one seemed hurt, and the drivers exchanged information.

The accident, on June 12, 2002, might have been forgotten. But Johnson woke up the next day with back pain. She went to her regular doctor but was told that she'd have to pay all her treatment costs upfront, since a car accident could result in lawsuits and her health insurance might not cover her. Worried about the costs, she consulted a physician friend, who pledged to find someone to help her.

No more than 30 minutes later she got a call from a man named Howard Awand, who said he was in the business of handling such cases. Awand (pronounced AY-wand) managed to get her an appointment that night with one of the busiest spine surgeons in the country, Mark Kabins. After examining her, the surgeon referred her to several other doctors and said that Awand had also arranged for her to see one of the town's most prominent plaintiffs attorneys, Robert Vannah. All for a routine accident on the way to work. Johnson couldn't believe her luck.

Better still, she didn't have to pay any money upfront. On her first visit to Vannah's office, she signed a medical lien. Such agreements mean injured parties pay nothing unless they collect a settlement; if that happens, the person holding the lien (which could be a plaintiff's lawyer, a doctor, or a hospital) is then paid from the settlement. "Over the next six weeks, I had so many doctor's appointments that I couldn't keep up," recalls Johnson, who was grateful for the attention but also confused by a directive from Vannah's office: Don't mention Howard Awand's name to anybody.

As Johnson underwent cortisone injections and physical therapy, her pain began to ease. Yet each time she saw Kabins, she says, he urged her to undergo spinal surgery. The doctor asserted that if she didn't, her pain would be 20 times worse in 10 years, she recalls.

Meanwhile, her lawyer, Vannah, filed suit against the driver who hit Johnson, asking for a minimum of $200,000 in damages. Unbeknown to Vannah, the driver was a federal prosecutor who had been in his car on government business. This detail meant nothing to Johnson. But it would come to mean everything to her lawyer: Instead of facing a local defense attorney, Vannah was squaring off against Ruth Cohen, a seasoned lawyer in the U.S. attorney's civil division.

Almost immediately, Cohen sensed something strange. For a minor traffic accident, Johnson had seen no fewer than eight doctors and racked up more than $40,000 in medical bills. Working late one Friday night, Cohen called a former colleague, William Turner, who was then managing attorney for the Las Vegas office of Farmers Insurance. As she described the case and listed the doctors involved, Turner interrupted, saying, "They're all connected to Awand."

"Who?" Cohen asked. She had never heard of the man. But she had stumbled into the middle of what prosecutors would later allege was a massive conspiracy whose participants, witnesses told the FBI, dubbed themselves the "medical mafia."

Prosecutors charge that a group of top Las Vegas plaintiffs' lawyers and doctors, with the 64-year-old Awand at its center, conspired in an audacious fraud. The participants appeared to act independently but instead colluded. Unwitting accident victims were recruited as plaintiffs and then persuaded to undergo serious, sometimes needless, surgeries. The procedures, in turn, helped inflate the size of personal-injury claims. The result was multimillion-dollar insurance settlements, even for dubious cases, and lucrative fees for the doctors, the lawyers, and, of course, Howard Awand.

The alleged scheme began in 1999 and lasted for at least six years, prosecutors charge. Business and court records and local press reports suggest that the group—which numbered about 30—colluded in hundreds of suits that yielded hundreds of millions in settlements. According to government evidence, the group coordinated their testimony as expert witnesses, lied under oath, protected one another from malpractice lawsuits—even after the surgeries left a few patients paralyzed—and ate away at the plaintiffs' settlement money with kickbacks disguised as contingency fees.

For prosecutors, the alleged conspiracy was almost impossible to detect—and maddeningly difficult to prove beyond a reasonable doubt. After all, the process looked remarkably like American-style justice: crusading plaintiffs' lawyers forcing corporate deep pockets to pay big for injured clients.

So far Awand and his associates have thwarted prosecutors. After five years of FBI investigation, three indictments, a highly publicized trial, and testimony from two complicit surgeons given immunity, no one has been found guilty. A judge dismissed indictments against Awand and one plaintiff's lawyer because a key witness wouldn't testify. (The government is appealing the dismissal.) Though prosecutors have declined to share information not already public while their investigation continues, the saga's details were gleaned from interviews with 40 people—including two admitted participants—and a review of thousands of pages of trial testimony and evidence, as well as nonpublic government records.

For his part, Awand asserts his innocence and dismisses the medical mafia as "nonexistent." Kabins has also proclaimed his innocence, and Vannah, who has not been charged with anything by the government, says he has done nothing wrong. Vannah and others claim the real collusion in the case is between the prosecutors and the insurers.

Awand says he has proof that he has been railroaded by the government, but adds, "Basically my attorney has advised me not to say anything." The lawyer, Harland Braun, calls the case against Awand "totally phony" and asserts that his client did nothing wrong. What the government paints as "collusion," Braun says, was nothing more than cooperation among professionals. Because Awand was beating the insurance industry in court, the government concluded "it must be a conspiracy," says Braun. "What Awand did is level the playing field."

Needless to say, the insurers see it in starkly different terms. As one executive puts it, "This is a horror movie. In your wildest dreams you've never seen anything like this."

The Consultant

One month after Cynthia Johnson's accident, Howard Awand threw open his sprawling lakefront home in Big Bear, Calif., to Las Vegas' A-list professionals. Kabins and Vannah, the doctor and the lawyer in the Johnson case, were there, along with 200 other top doctors, lawyers, judges, and their spouses and kids. The event, including a buffet dinner of filet mignon and lobster, was a fundraiser for two Las Vegas judges who faced reelection; some $30,000 in checks piled up in two crystal bowls, several partygoers recall.

But it was also a showcase for Awand, who played the welcoming host. A self-proclaimed "medical consultant," he was short and bespectacled, with a slight mustache and a paunch. With his boastful patter, he projected a smug sense of power. Some guests would later tell the FBI they were afraid of him because they thought he had connections in the military and intelligence worlds. Awand fed that impression by alluding to high-level work on national-security matters he couldn't discuss. A framed case of military and intelligence medals reinforced this story. Other people at the party, though, thought he was a brain surgeon or a lawyer.

Awand's background was almost impossible to pin down, and the truth of it was considerably less glamorous than he let on to his guests. A former Army medic, he had bounced around from Alaska to Colorado assessing personal-injury claims for insurance companies before setting up shop in Las Vegas in the late 1980s.

Deeper into the house, though, was a clue that seemed to reveal the real Awand. A framed photograph depicted him jokingly cuddling with Kabins and Vannah. The message wasn't hard to decipher: They were all in bed together. (Like Vannah, the other two men in the photo have not been charged with any wrongdoing by prosecutors.)

Long before Awand's party, insurance defense lawyers in Las Vegas had noticed a worrying pattern: Claims that should have been minor were becoming major. Patients usually treated with a little physical therapy were undergoing drastic spine-fusion surgeries. Insurers sent in their top lawyers, only to see them mowed down in court. The plaintiffs' expert witnesses testified so seamlessly they were impossible to contradict. And in each questionable case, the name "Howard Awand" surfaced.

The insurance industry battles some $80 billion in fraud annually, from staged auto accidents to phantom patients and nonexistent clinics billing for procedures that never happen. In a typical scheme, a victim might collude with his lawyer to exaggerate his injuries a little. But in Las Vegas, the accident victims knew nothing of the alleged conspiracy. More important, at least from the insurers' point of view, cases they estimated would max out at $1 million were getting jury verdicts for seven times that amount. "Your first reaction is, 'It's not possible. It can't be that pervasive,'" says Nelson Cohen, an attorney for State Farm Insurance.

By 2002, insurance defense lawyers were so concerned they held an unusual meeting. More than a dozen attorneys for competing insurers met to compare notes. Some who had subpoenaed Awand described getting threatening calls from his associates warning that their business would dry up if they didn't back down, William Turner of Farmers Insurance recalls. The lawyers, he says, recounted tales of strange behavior or even intimidation. Expert witnesses, for example, suddenly and inexplicably changed their testimony; some doctors who refused to cooperate with Awand had been threatened with frivolous malpractice lawsuits. By meeting's end, the lawyers felt certain they were facing something bigger and more sinister than garden-variety fraud.

At some of Las Vegas' booming plaintiffs' law firms, Awand was hailed as a fixer with no equal. Before he arrived in town, it could be difficult to rope in prominent doctors to serve as expert witnesses in personal-injury cases; they didn't want to testify against fellow doctors and feared being sued themselves. But Awand had a "magic formula to make the dogs and cats work together," says John Thalgott, a spine surgeon and admitted former participant in the medical mafia who left the group and later was granted immunity as a government witness.

Awand offered the doctors protection, according to Thalgott and others. Because he held sway over key lawyers, he could virtually guarantee they would never sue his doctors for malpractice. In one e-mail to a physician, Awand described himself as a "fixer" and bragged of "saving my friends' butts from lawsuits."

With Awand's doctors freed from anxiety about litigation, and with almost every patient on medical liens—which severed them from any oversight or restriction their health insurance companies might impose—there were almost no limits. Awand's patients became perfect unwitting objects for almost any procedure imaginable.

The "Kabinsectomy"

Thalgott first glimpsed Awand around 2000. "This little fat guy starts showing up in the office carrying [patient] charts," the surgeon recalls. "I thought it was pretty intrusive." Awand was there to see Thalgott's junior partner Mark Kabins, whom colleagues describe as a socially awkward workaholic with impeccable medical credentials.

Thalgott had recruited Kabins and then temporarily handed over his practice to his colleague when Thalgott took a break after a divorce. Once he returned, he found Kabins making three times his own salary, up to a staggering $750,000 a month. There was only one notable difference between his practice and Kabins's: Howard Awand.

And so the senior surgeon signed on. "My greedy voice said, 'I'll do a few cases,'" Thalgott recalls.

Awand became a fixture in the office. Kabins installed a dedicated phone line for his use, and the two men spoke sometimes every 15 minutes. Awand even entered Kabins's exam rooms and scrubbed into the operating room.

By 2000, Kabins's practice had become a factory producing multimillion-dollar insurance settlements, according to witness statements and interviews. The volume was so great that Awand himself couldn't keep track. In June 2002 he wrote to Kabins, asking him to create a list of all the clients he'd sent: "We are reaching critical mass and both of us are losing money by my failure to keep up with the referrals."

Kabins became so infamous that insurance investigators coined a term—a "Kabinsectomy"—for a needless surgery in Vegas. He often worked 20 hours a day, seven days a week, with patients prepped for surgery from 6:30 in the morning until 10:30 at night, according to several former colleagues. Kabins would even take calls from lawyers and schedule depositions while in the operating room. By day's end, his hands would be shaking and his gown drenched in sweat, one of Kabins's former surgical assistants says.

When Kabins wasn't in surgery, he was often prepping for litigation. He and Thalgott, along with a constant stream of doctors and lawyers, would meet with Awand for hours at a time. Awand would "script" testimony, which the group would then rehearse; he liked to tell the story of a doctor who memorized his script so perfectly that on the stand he accidentally said, "Pause for effect," before correcting himself. Afterward, the group would drink champagne and smoke cigars.

The medical mafia distributed millions of dollars to its members, prosecutors have charged. Disbursements took place at fancy restaurants and parties, with lawyers handing Awand huge checks and doctors receiving envelopes of cash when their wives went to the ladies' room.

Some doctors received referral fees for sending patients into the network. Others took kickbacks when their cases settled for large sums, as Benjamin Venger, a neurosurgeon also given immunity, admitted under oath. He testified that he tried to conceal six-figure kickbacks by falsely claiming to have rented Awand his plane and to have consulted on starting an imaging-facility business.

Awand, meanwhile, earned consulting fees. He also found a second revenue stream: Almost all the patients were on medical liens, so prosecutors say he opened companies that bought liens from doctors at a reduced cost. Once the cases settled, he collected payment in full. All told, Awand's taxable income was rising above $2 million in some years, according to tax returns cited in a government filing.

With these profits, Awand became increasingly bellicose. In 2002, Rick Harris, a lawyer working with Awand, attempted to save a client about $15,000 by trying to negotiate a 50% discount from the company holding the liens on the client's medical bills. Unbeknown to Harris, the company was Awand's. Awand responded by writing a letter asserting that it "takes a lot of balls to cut someone's bill fifty percent (50%) without even giving them the courtesy of a kiss when you are done screwing them. It's obvious that you are never going to be able to handle big cases because you don't know how to deal with the people who make you money."

Says Harris, who subsequently became a government witness: "It was as if we had upset the Godfather."

Call Me Brother

Thalgott admits that he got into the network for ego, money, and legal protection. But it was the case of his patient Melodie Simon that made him want to get out. In August 2000 he performed a vertebrae fusion on Simon, a former Olympic volleyball player and high school softball coach. Then he went on a scheduled family vacation, leaving his partner Kabins in charge. Within days, Simon developed numbness and tingling in her legs, according to her trial testimony (she declined to be interviewed). A CT scan revealed that blood clots had formed in her spine.

Without immediate surgery, she faced the prospect of irreversible damage. But Kabins—who was having one of his periodic "clinic" days, where he typically saw 65 to 80 patients, according to a former assistant in his office—allegedly ignored her deteriorating condition for almost 24 hours. By the time he finally took her into surgery, it was too late, a medical expert later testified for the government. At age 41, she was permanently paralyzed from the chest down.

Simon turned to one of the town's top plaintiffs lawyers, Noel Gage, asking him, "What would you do if it was your sister?" Gage responded that she should call him "brother."

But Gage would show more allegiance to Awand than to his client, prosecutors contend. Awand arranged a secret meeting with Gage, Kabins, and Thalgott in which, according to prosecutors and Thalgott, the men agreed to pin the blame on another doctor altogether, the anesthesiologist who had drained Simon's spine. Gage agreed not to sue the surgeons in exchange for a lucrative case referral from Awand. (Kabins and Gage deny any deal; they have said the meeting was simply an opportunity to hear each side's position.)

The depositions and evidence that Awand coordinated implicated the anesthesiologist so perfectly that his insurer had no choice but to settle the suit. By secretly agreeing not to sue the two surgeons, prosecutors would later argue, Gage allowed a case potentially worth $10 million to settle for $2 million, netting Simon far less than she would need for a lifetime of treatment.

Awand's hold seemed unshakable. But on Jan. 6, 2005, a small item by the city's best-known investigative reporter, George Knapp, appeared in the *Las Vegas Mercury*. He mused about "doctors and lawyers, working together on a major, ongoing fraud scheme, but with help from hospital executives and a judge or two, and all centered on a shadowy, shady middleman." The FBI, he wrote, was "already asking questions."

Not What They're Supposed to Be

Cynthia Johnson entered the courtroom on July 21, 2005, for a routine procedural hearing. Though her case was the only one on the docket, she was surprised to see the courtroom packed with men in dark suits. Vannah seemed rattled, she says, and he complained to the judge that government lawyer Ruth Cohen had "leaked it all over the community that I'm being investigated by her and her cronies for criminal conduct." At the hearing's conclusion, a newspaper columnist rushed up to Johnson, asking, "Are you seeking to get compensation for injuries you don't really have?"

Johnson had no idea what was happening. After the hearing, Vannah screamed, "Things are not what they're supposed to be," as he rushed across the parking lot with an associate, she recalls. The bewildering scene made Johnson so uneasy that she told Kabins she would not undergo surgery.

Within a week, Vannah asked Johnson to come see him. He requested that she sign a document releasing him from her case. He claimed—incorrectly—that she'd failed to disclose previous visits to a chiropractor. If she signed, he continued, she'd owe him no attorney fees and would be responsible only for her medical costs, which had climbed into the many thousands.

As she resisted, he grew more agitated, screaming that if she didn't sign, she'd owe him vast sums. He stood, banging the table and yelling that she was under federal investigation and that "the government had killed people for lesser things than you're doing right now," she recalls.

Vannah denies any impropriety and says he isn't surprised that Johnson's accident received extra attention from the government, given that a government employee caused it. Vannah has not lost sleep over the protracted investigation, he says—even though he has been subpoenaed by government investigators, has been able to dodge an ethics complaint by a client over his payments to Awand, and has been secretly taped boasting "there are five or six judges that will do anything I want." Still, he notes, prosecutors have not charged him with anything.

Johnson left Vannah's office in tears that day, without signing the document. She had several chilling realizations. Her lawyer appeared to be under investigation, though she had no idea for what. He was panicking. And he'd just threatened her. She needed help from someone she could trust.

The next day, Johnson called every local attorney she could think of—and almost no one called back. Her case had become radioactive. Sleepless, depressed, and not knowing what else to do, she finally found a lawyer who steered her to Ruth Cohen, the government lawyer on the other side, who immediately called her back. Within days, Johnson was sitting down with the FBI.

Beating the Cavalry

In May 2007, federal prosecutors unveiled indictments against Awand and Gage that charged them with conspiracy, fraud, and (in Awand's case) witness tampering. The indictments referred to six other doctors, identified by letters only, who allegedly had also been involved. Gage and Awand pleaded not guilty.

That was just the beginning. Some 20 doctors and nearly a dozen personal-injury lawyers were in the government's cross hairs, the Las Vegas *Mercury's* Knapp reported at the time, and prosecutors suspected harm to hundreds of patients. "Stay tuned," an FBI agent told the media. It seemed the cavalry had finally arrived.

But for all the promise of the indictments, the prosecution began to run into difficulty almost immediately. In the run-up to Gage's trial in February 2008, for example, all 10 federal judges in Nevada recused themselves, one of them noting that "it's wise to stay away from cases that are local and involve attorneys." A U.S. district court judge from Washington State, Justin Quackenbush, was assigned and promptly threw out 13 of the 19 counts against Gage, including the core of the conspiracy charges. The jury ended up considering a far narrower case, dealing largely with Melodie Simon.

At trial, Gage's lawyers skewered the prosecution, arguing that the case boiled down to an accusation that Gage had netted his client only $1.3 million. Moreover, they charged, the star witnesses, Thalgott and Venger, were avowed liars. The local press corps shredded the two doctors. One columnist wrote that Venger needed a "reputation transplant." The trial ended with a hung jury.

Gage staunchly maintains his innocence: "I don't believe there is a medical mafia, and if there is, I am certainly not aligned with it." Calling government investigators "despicable, dishonest human beings," he says they have not proved "one scintilla of criminality."

Things turned from bad to worse for the prosecutors as the summer of 2008 began. With Gage's retrial looming, his lawyers argued that only Kabins could refute his former partner Thalgott's testimony. But Kabins wouldn't take the stand unless the government granted him immunity. Prosecutors refused, arguing that they'd already identified him as a target. Last June, Judge Quackenbush ruled that Gage's right to a fair trial would be violated without Kabins's testimony. The judge threw out the government's case.

Quackenbush then dismissed the conspiracy case against Awand, also citing the absence of Kabins's testimony. In October the government appealed to the Ninth Circuit Court of Appeals. Oral arguments were scheduled for Aug. 11.

Gone but Not Gone?

These days Howard Awand is no longer a "medical consultant." In 2007 he and his wife, Linda, moved to a historic, fog-shrouded town on the Ohio River in Vevay, Ind. There they restored a Victorian mansion, filled it with elegant antiques, and reinvented themselves as proprietors of a bed-and-breakfast called the Rosemont Inn.

Though Awand has been able to fend off the conspiracy case till now, he faces a second case: Awand and his wife were charged with four counts of misdemeanor tax evasion. They have pleaded not guilty and the trial is scheduled for September.

Despite Awand's departure, according to insurance lawyers, collusion continues among the members of the medical mafia. In their appeal in the Awand case, prosecutors allege the scheme is "ongoing." The doctors keep testifying, and the insurers keep losing. "They're cockier than ever," says Michael Hall, an insurance defense lawyer. Ruth Cohen, who has left the U.S. attorney's office and is now in private practice, wonders whether prosecutors arrived "too late" to change anything.

So far, the only person to receive punishment in the case is one of the doctors who admitted his role and cooperated with the prosecution. In May the Nevada medical board sanctioned the neurosurgeon Venger, giving him a year and a half of probation and over 800 hours of community service.

Thalgott, the other doctor who cooperated—who by most accounts was dramatically less involved than Venger—is also facing a threat to his medical license. The county and state medical boards have announced inquiries. Thalgott wonders whether he is being investigated for his lapses—or for talking about them openly. "I'm under an ethics investigation, and I'm the only ethical person in the whole mix," he says. "I fell on my sword for nothing." Thalgott, who paid the former Olympic volleyball player

Simon $1.5 million as part of his immunity deal, has taken steps to protect himself, spreading shotguns around his house. "These guys have a lot of money, and people are getting desperate," he says.

Meanwhile, the federal prosecutors continue to bring cases. In March a federal grand jury indicted Kabins on eight counts of conspiracy and fraud, all relating to the case of Simon. He pleaded not guilty. In response to detailed questions for this article, his lawyers David Chesnoff and Martin Weinberg write that Kabins "vigorously denied the allegations that have been lodged against him." They also state that he has never been sued for unnecessary surgeries, has never been found liable for medical malpractice, and has an "impeccable reputation in the medical community."

On advice from his lawyers, Kabins declined to be interviewed. But in a deposition for Cynthia Johnson's lawsuit he testified, "My integrity is everything; my outcomes of my patients are everything; I live and die with my patients; if they do well, I'm on top of the world. If they struggle, I struggle." He also denied pushing Johnson to have surgery, saying, "My recommendation is always, if you can live with it, live with it, because surgery has inherent risks. There's no guarantee surgery is going to make you better."

After entering his plea of not guilty at the courthouse in March, Kabins emerged flanked not only by his own defense attorneys but also by a number of the city's most prominent plaintiffs' lawyers. Kabins's lawyer Chesnoff says the gathering was an "outpouring of support" from family members, medical staff, and even a family rabbi.

They may have intended to protest what they view as the government's war on litigators. But marching grimly in a protective phalanx in their dark sunglasses and suits, some of them bullying the lone TV cameraman, the group seemed to resemble just the sort of cabal described by prosecutors: a gang of doctors and lawyers, with no intention of backing down.

UNIT 5

Crime, Law Enforcement, and Terrorism

Unit Selections

35. **Fighting Crime: An Economist's View,** John J. Donohue
36. **The Aggregate Burden of Crime,** David A. Anderson
37. **The Globalization of Crime,** Stephen Aguilar-Millan et al.
38. **Causes and Consequences of Wrongful Convictions,** Hugo Adam Bedau
39. **Reforming Juvenile Justice,** Barry Krisberg
40. **America Incarcerated: Crime, Punishment, and the Question of Race,** Glenn C. Loury
41. **Defeating Terrorism: Is It Possible? Is It Probable?,** Marvin J. Cetron
42. **Nightmare in Manhattan,** Bruce Goldman

Key Points to Consider

- What are some of the reasons for the high crime rate in America? Why has the crime rate dropped recently?

- What are some of the policy options for reducing crime?

- What are some of the major activities of globalized crime?

- What law enforcement policies are most heavily relied upon today? What do you think are the best policies and why?

- What are the costs of crime to society? What kinds of crimes are the most costly and why?

- Do you think that many innocent people are convicted of murder? How do you explain cases of the miscarriage of justice?

- How much of a threat is terrorism toward the United States? How can the public be protected from it?

Student Website
www.mhhe.com/cls

Internet References

ACLU Criminal Justice Home Page
   www.aclu.org/crimjustice/index.html
Terrorism Research Center
   http://www.terrorism.com

This unit deals with criminal behavior and its control by the law enforcement system. The first line of defense against crime is the socialization of the young to internalize norms against harmful and illegal behavior. Thus families, schools, religious institutions, and social pressure are the major crime fighters, but they do not do a perfect job, and the police have to handle their failures. Over the last half century until recently, crime has increased, signaling for some commentators a decline in morality. If the power of norms to control criminal behavior diminishes, the role of law enforcement must increase, and that is what has happened. The societal response to crime has been threefold: hire more police, build more prisons, and toughen penalties for crimes. These policies by themselves can have only limited success. For example, putting a drug dealer in prison just creates an opportunity for another person to become a drug dealer. Another approach is to give potential criminals alternatives to crime. The key factor in this approach is a healthy economy that provides many job opportunities for unemployed young men. To some extent, this has happened, and the crime rate has dropped. Programs that work with inner-city youth might also help, but budget-tight cities are not funding many programs like this. Amid the policy debates there is one thing we can agree upon: Crime has declined significantly in the past two decades (with a slight increase lately) after rising substantially for a half century.

The first subsection deals with crime; a major concern today because crime and violence seem to be out of control. In the first article, John J. Donohue analyzes crime using economic cost-benefit analysis. His research leads him to recommend that we expand police forces, adopt sensible gun control laws, legalize drugs, and stop building prisons. In the second article on crime, David A. Anderson uses a similar analytical methodology. He tries to put into monetary terms the impacts of various types of crimes in the United States. The results produce some surprises. First, when he includes many costs that are seldom taken into account, such as the costs of law enforcement, security measures, and lost time at work, the total crime bill is over $1 trillion, or over $4,000 per person. Another surprise is the relative costs of white-collar crime versus street crime. Fraud and cheating on taxes costs Americans over 20 times the costs of theft, burglary, and robbery. The next article reports on the major change in the organization and operation of crime in the last two decades—globalization and its consequences. Globalization has transformed organized crime from hierarchies to networks that span the world. Globalized crime continues the traffic in drugs, sex, slavery, and counterfeiting but also increasingly focus on fraud, identity theft, intellectual property, and cybercrime.

The next subsection deals with law enforcement. Hugo Adam Bedau examines a troubling aspect of the judicial system—wrongful convictions. He presents the fruit of decades

© Brand X Pictures

of research on miscarriages of justice. Some of the stories are shameful and shocking, and they justify calls for reform. Bedau identifies several major reform efforts, but few changes have been made to date. Next, Barry Krisberg provides a brief history of U.S. policies for treating juvenile offenders, which have oscillated between punitive and rehabilitative approaches. Public opinion supports the punitive approach, which is in force today. Science supports the rehabilitative approach in the case of juveniles, and both the children and society would gain from it. The next article discusses an exceptional characteristic of the United States: It has the highest incarceration rate in the world. Glenn C. Loury points out that "the United States—with 5 percent of the world's population—houses 25 percent of the world's inmates." To explain this sad fact, Loury explores public attitudes, the crime rate, institutions, and racism.

The final subsection deals with terrorism. The first article, by Marvin J. Cetron, reports on the study that his company did for the federal government on the future of terrorism. It predicts increasing terrorist events and carnage and a long war on terrorism without winning greater security. Muslim extremists will acquire nuclear weapons in the next ten years with the intent to use them on the United States. This thought sets the stage for the next article, which vividly describes the impact of a nuclear explosion in Manhattan. God help us.

Fighting Crime
An Economist's View

JOHN J. DONOHUE

Over the past 40 years, the number of motor vehicle fatalities per mile driven in the United States has dropped an astounding 70 percent. While some of the gains can be attributed to improvements in technology, public policy has made a big difference. The government followed the advice of researchers who had studied auto accidents, improving highway design and instituting a variety of regulations, including mandatory seat belt use and harsher penalties for drunken driving. By contrast, most types of street crime are still above the levels of 40 years ago, despite the impressive drops in the 1990s. A major reason for the difference, I would argue, is that the crime issue has been hijacked by ideologues and special interests, preventing the emergence of a policy consensus driven by research.

Why listen to an economist pontificate on what most people would call criminology? Economists bring a unique perspective to the table—a utilitarian view in which one assumes that behavior can be changed by altering incentives, that the costs of crime can be measured in terms of money and that public policy is best evaluated by comparing costs and benefits. It's hardly the only view, but I would argue that it is a view that provides exceptional insight into limiting the adverse consequences of antisocial behavior.

We know more today than ever how to reduce crime. If we could get past the barriers of ideology and special pleading, we could see reductions in crime rivaling the magnitude of the gains in automobile safety. What follows are a host of measures that would sharply reduce the $400 billion annual toll from street crime in the United States.

Stop the Building Boom in Prisons

Virtually everyone agrees that incarceration must remain a core element of any strategy to fight crime. Locking up more people reduces crime because more criminals are kept off the streets and/ or the prospect of time behind bars deters criminal behavior. But you can have too much of a "good" thing. Between 1933 and 1973, incarceration in the United States varied within a narrow band of roughly 100 to 120 prisoners per 100,000 population. Since then, this rate has been increasing by an average of 5 percent annually. As of June 2003, some two million individuals were imprisoned—a rate of almost 500 per 100,000.

Costs of Prison

To determine whether the current level of incarceration makes sense, one must ask whether the benefits at the margin in terms of less crime exceed the costs to society. On the benefit side, the research suggests that the "elasticity" of crime with respect to incarceration is somewhere between 0.1 and 0.4—that is, increasing the prison population by 10 percent reduces crime by 1 to 4 percent. On the other side of the equation, estimates of the cost of locking up another individual run between $32,000 and $57,000 annually.

The most rigorous study on the relevant elasticity was conducted by William Spelman of the University of Texas. He concluded that "we can be 90 percent confident that the true value is between 0.12 and 0.20, with a best single guess of 0.16." Since Spelman's estimates accounted for the incapacitation effect, but ignore any deterrence effect, I rely conservatively on somewhat larger elasticity of 0.2.

The most carefully constructed and comprehensive study on the costs of incarcerating a criminal was a 1990 report prepared for the National Institute of Justice, which produced the high-end estimate ($57,000 annually, in 2003 dollars). I adjust this figure downward (in part because the study probably overstates prison construction costs and exaggerates the social cost of welfare payments to the dependents of the incarcerated) to arrive at a figure of $46,000 per prisoner per year.

With an elasticity of crime with respect to incarceration of 0.2 and an annual cost of housing a prisoner of $46,000, the "optimal" level of incarceration would require imprisoning 300,000 fewer individuals. This is just a ballpark estimate, of course. But, at the very least, it implies that we cannot expect to get much more crime reduction at reasonable cost by increasing the numbers behind bars. It is time to stop making prison construction the major public works project of our day.

Abolish the Death Penalty

In recent years, the death penalty has been meted out an average of 80 times annually. These executions come at a high tangible cost. For while executing an individual does save the money that would have been used for a lifetime in prison, these savings are dwarfed by the costs of death-penalty trials and appeals. The most scholarly research on the topic, by Philip Cook and Donna Slawson Kuniholm of Duke, found that the State of North Carolina spent $2.16 million per execution more than what would be spent if the maximum penalty were life in prison.

Proponents of the death penalty usually justify these costs by invoking its deterrence effect. But Steve Levitt of the University of Chicago has noted that the risk of execution for those who commit murder is typically small compared with the risk of death that violence-prone criminals willingly face in daily life—and this certainly raises questions about the efficacy of threatening them with the death penalty. Currently, the likelihood of a murderer being executed is less than 1 in 200. By way of comparison, Levitt and his colleague Sudhir Venkatesh find 7 percent of street-level drug sellers die each year. Levitt concludes that "it is hard to believe the fear of execution would be a driving force in a rational criminal's calculus in modern America."

Nor is there direct evidence that the death penalty generates gains for society in terms of murders deterred. In an often-cited paper written in the early 1970s, Isaac Ehrlich (then a graduate student at the University of Chicago) estimated that one execution could save eight lives. But research since has showed that minor changes in the way the figure is estimated eliminate the deterrence effect. Indeed, Levitt, working with Lawrence Katz of Harvard and Ellen Shustorovich of the City University of New York, found that the death penalty might even add to the total number of murders. Thus, abolishing the death penalty would save American taxpayers more than $150 million a year at no apparent cost to society.

Expand the Police Force

In the 1990s, a variety of new policing strategies were introduced in New York City and other localities. New York increased enforcement of statutes on petty crimes like graffiti and marijuana possession and made better use of technology and statistics in identifying crime "hot spots." Boston adopted an innovative multi-agency collaboration that took aim at gang violence. And numerous cities, notably San Diego, introduced "community policing," in which police attempted to work as allies with communities, rather than just antagonists to criminals. The results seem impressive: from 1991 to 1998, the cities that experienced the largest decline in murder rates were San Diego (a 76 percent drop), New York City (71 percent) and Boston (69 percent).

Were better policing strategies responsible for these results, and would cities be wise to adopt or expand such programs? A study of Cincinnati found that a "community service model" of policing, in which cops become more familiar with the neighborhoods they served, did not significantly lower crime. Furthermore, community policing did not seem to affect attitudes toward police.

Two New York Factors

Note, too, that New York's experiments are inconclusive—cities without tough policies on minor crime experienced significant crime drops, too. Moreover, New York's substantial crime declines began before 1993, the year in which Mayor Giuliani took office and initiated the policing changes. Indeed, two other factors seem to explain all of the crime drop in New York City: increases in the total number of police officers and its high abortion rate many years earlier, which Levitt and I found to correlate with subsequent declines in crime because of the reduction in unwanted births of children most at risk of becoming criminals.

Another change in the 1990s—one that received far less press attention than changing policing strategies—was the substantial increase in the size of police forces. From 1994 through 1999, the number of police per capita in the United States grew by almost 10 percent. The expansion was even more pronounced in big cities with high crime rates. Much of this increase can be attributed to the Community Oriented Policing Services (COPS) program, which was signed into law by President Clinton in 1994 and is now in the process of being phased out by President Bush. A report commissioned by the Justice Department credits this program with adding more than 80,000 officers to the streets.

The effects of increases in police, as opposed to changes in policing strategies, have been widely studied, with most studies showing that the benefits have exceeded the costs. The most rigorous studies have found elasticities of crime with respect to police of between 0.30 and 0.79—that is, a 10 percent increase in police reduces crime between 3.0 and 7.9 percent. Using a conservative estimate for this elasticity (0.4) and a rather high estimate of the total annual cost of maintaining an extra police officer ($90,000) while assuming that crime costs $400 billion a year, the United States would have to hire 500,000 additional police officers to reach the optimal policing level. According to the FBI, there are some 665,000 police in the United States. So the optimal level is almost double the number we have today. Thus while adding hundreds of thousands of police officers is hardly a political priority these days, simply restoring financing for the COPS program would be a start.

Adopt Sensible Gun Control

In 2002, there were some 11,000 homicide deaths by firearms. The United States' per capita firearm homicide rate is more than eight times that of Canada, France, Germany, Japan, Spain and Britain. Much could be done to reduce gun-related crime. Most such initiatives are off the table, however, because conservatives have garnered enormous electoral benefits from fighting gun control.

What's more, the highly publicized work of the researcher John Lott has confirmed the views of many conservatives that gun control is already excessive—that allowing citizens to carry concealed handguns would drastically *reduce* violent crime. Lott reasons that the threat of these concealed weapons serves as a deterrent to crime. And his research has been cited by many politicians supporting laws allowing concealed weapons, which have been passed by some 30 states.

There are, however, serious flaws in Lott's research. The best guess based on all the empirical evidence is that these "shall issue" laws actually increase crime, albeit by a relatively modest amount. There are a number of possible explanations for this: the guns being carried are easier to steal (more than a million guns are stolen each year, which is a major source of supply to criminals), for one, while the threat of being shot in a confrontation may inspire criminals to shoot first. It is worth noting, moreover, that laws allowing for easier access to guns increase the threats of both accidental death and suicide.

One alternative to "shall issue" laws is "may issue" laws, which allow discretion in handing out permits, with an applicant having to prove a need for protection. These laws, which have been passed in 11 states, could have some of the deterrent benefits Lott speaks of without as many of the harmful effects that plague "shall issue" laws if the licensing discretion is used wisely.

Another much-debated gun law was President Clinton's 1994 assault-weapons ban, which was recently allowed to expire. This law prohibited a specific list of semiautomatic guns deemed useful for criminal purposes but unnecessary for sport or self-defense, and banned ammunition feeding devices that accept more than 10 rounds. According to plausible guesstimates, assault weapons were used in about 2 percent of pre-ban murders, and large-capacity magazines were used in about 20 percent. The secondary goal of the assault weapons ban was to reduce the harm from crime by forcing criminals to employ less dangerous weapons. Jeffrey Roth and Christopher Koper of the Urban Institute in Washington found that those murdered by assault weapons had, on average, more wounds than those killed with other guns. They also found that, in mass murders, those involving assault weapons included more victims.

Was the ban effective? Probably not very. The law was rife with loopholes. For one thing, the law grandfathered assault weapons produced before the ban, which led gun manufacturers to increase production before the law took effect. In addition, gun companies could—and did—produce potent legal guns with little change in performance. Admittedly, a true ban on assault weapons would not have a huge effect on homicide since most criminals would simply use less powerful guns if the desired weapons were unavailable. A strong ban on large capacity magazines, however, which are estimated to be used in 20 percent of homicides, could be very helpful.

David Hemenway, an economist and director of the Harvard Injury Control Research Center, has examined the evidence on the potential impact of other gun-related measures and identifies six that have shown some success in lowering crime:

- preventing police from selling confiscated guns.
- instituting one-gun-purchase-per-month laws.
- plugging secondary-market loopholes.
- tracing all guns used in crime.
- producing guns that can be fired only by their owners.
- registering all handguns.

None of these, alas, is an easy political sell in today's America.

Legalize Drugs

The most effective federal crime-fighting public initiative in American history was the lifting of alcohol prohibition in the early 1930s. Homicides fell by 14 percent in the two years after prohibition ended. In all likelihood, similar benefits would emerge if we ended drug prohibition, although obviously other steps would need to be taken to reduce the societal costs associated with drug use.

The logic behind drug legalization as a crime reducer is twofold. First, a significant number of homicides are caused by drug-related disputes. The FBI has classified about 5 percent of homicides as drug-related. And this number is very conservative since the FBI attributes only one cause to each murder. A fatal dispute about a drug deal may be characterized as an "argument over money" or a "gangland killing" rather than a drug homicide. Paul Goldstein of the University of Illinois at Chicago found that about 9 percent of homicides in New York City were caused by broader "systemic" drug issues.

The major reason so many drug disputes end in violence is the lack of institutional mechanisms to resolve them—buyers and sellers cannot seek redress in court, or complain to the Better Business Bureau. Legalization could also lower crime by freeing crime-fighters for other purposes. About $40 billion is spent annually on the war on drugs.

Decriminalizing drugs would also free space in prisons. Levitt found a substantial "crowding out" effect, meaning that increased incarceration of drug-related criminals decreases incarceration of other criminals. Currently, more than 400,000 individuals are in prison for nonviolent drug crimes, with about 50,000 of them imprisoned for violations involving only marijuana.

Of course, drug legalization is not without risks. Legalization would tend to increase drug consumption, lowering economic productivity and perhaps increasing behavior that is dangerous to nondrug users.

One simple way to restrain drug consumption after legalization would be through taxation. Gary Becker and Kevin Murphy of the University of Chicago along with Michael Grossman of the City University of New York construct a model in which the optimal equilibrium with legalization and taxation can actually lead to higher retail prices—and lower consumption—than the optimal system under prohibition. Such a policy would also raise additional money for the government, which could be used for any number of purposes. It would be substantially easier to enforce a tax on drugs than it is to enforce the current ban on drugs, since most individuals would pay a premium to purchase their drugs legally. Instead of turning the hundreds of thousands of workers in the illegal drug markets (and their customers) into criminals, we could focus law enforcement on the much smaller set of tax evaders to keep consumption no higher than the levels of today.

Given the highly controversial nature of this proposal, a prudent first step might be to adopt this legalization/taxation/demand control scheme for marijuana to illustrate the benefits of shrinking the size of illegal markets while establishing that an increase in drug usage can be avoided. A number of other measures should be adopted to limit demand. Strict age limits could be enforced, advertising could be banned, and some of the money raised by taxes on drugs could be used to market abstinence and treatment of addicts.

Expand Successful Social Programs

In accepting his party's nomination, John Kerry said, "I am determined that we stop being a nation content to spend $50,000 a year to keep a young person in prison for the rest of their life—when we could invest $10,000 to give them Head Start, Early Start, Smart Start, the best possible start in life." He was expressing a belief common on the center-left that early child-hood intervention can make children less likely to commit crime and actually save money down the road.

Is this view correct? Studies on Head Start have shown it to have lamentably little effect on participants' outcomes later in life, including their likelihood of committing crimes. Other programs, however, have shown tremendous potential in reducing crime (and enhancing other positive life outcomes), and resources should be shifted away from the unproductive programs toward the few that seem to work.

One of the most notable, the experimental Perry Preschool program, provided preschool classes to a sample of children in Michigan when they were 3 and 4 years old. This program attempted to involve the whole family by having the preschool teacher conduct weekly home visits. By age 19, Perry Preschool graduates were 40 percent less likely to be arrested than a control group, 50 percent less likely to be arrested more than twice, and far less likely to be arrested for major crimes.

While I would not expect a scaled-up program to perform as well as one implemented with a small group, even half the reduction in crime would be cost-effective. Estimates from studies of the program indicate that financial benefits to government, which came in the form of higher taxes from employment, lower welfare utilization and reduced crime, exceeded program costs by as much as seven to one.

Another cost-effective crime-fighting program is the Job Corps, which provides educational and vocational-skills training and counseling to at-risk youths. Each year, Job Corps enrolls some 60,000 kids at a cost of more than $1 billion. Unlike some similar teenage intervention programs, the Job Corps is residential. Like the Perry Preschool Program, Job Corps has proved to pay for itself, generating more revenue in the form of taxes and avoided welfare payments than the costs of training the at-risk teens. Job Corps has also proved effective in lowering crime: a randomized experiment conducted by the research corporation Mathematica estimates that Job Corps participants are 16 percent less likely to be arrested than their peers.

For programs like the Perry Preschool and Job Corps to be successful in lowering crime, they must be targeted at those most likely to commit crimes. Six percent of the population commits more than 50 percent of crimes. While there are moral and legal issues in targeting groups based on race, it should be possible to use such information to expand successful programs so that they cover more high-risk individuals.

Defend Roe v. Wade

One often overlooked variable in crime is the legal status of abortion. Levitt and I found that as much as half of the drop in crime in the 1990s can be explained by the legalization of abortion in the early 1970s. There are two reasons that legalized abortion lowers the crime rate. The first is obvious: more abortions mean fewer children, which in turn can mean fewer criminals when those who would have been born would have reached their high-crime years. The second is more important: abortion reduces the number of unwanted births, and unwanted children are at much greater risk of becoming criminals later on. The five states that legalized abortion before the rest of the country experienced significant drops in crime before other states did. What's more, the higher the rate of abortion in a state in the mid 1970s, the greater the drop in crime in the 1990s.

What would be the impact on crime if *Roe v. Wade* were overturned? If the Supreme Court restored the pre-1973 law allowing states to decide for themselves whether to legalize abortion, I suspect most of the blue states would keep abortion legal. Even in the red states, abortion would not disappear entirely because residents could still find safe, out-of-state abortions. But the number of abortions would fall sharply, particularly for poor women.

Suppose that abortion were outlawed in every state that voted for Bush in 2004 and that the abortion rate dropped by 75 percent in these states but remained the same in blue states. Our research suggests that violent crime would eventually increase by about 12 percent and property crime by about 10 percent over the baseline figure.

Reduce Teen Pregnancy

Keeping abortion legal would prevent crime increases, but we can use the insight from the casual link between abortion and crime reduction to achieve the same ends in a better way: reduce the number of unwanted and teen pregnancies. Take the Children's Aid Society-Carrera program, which aims to reduce births to teenagers by changing their incentives. The three-year after-school program for 13-year-olds includes a work component designed to assist participants to find decent jobs, an academic component including tutoring and homework help, an arts component, an individual sports component, and comprehensive family life and sexual education. Program participants have been 70 percent less likely to give birth in the three years after the program ended than members of a control group.

Again, the success of any social program designed to reduce crime requires targeting, in this case at those most likely to give birth in their teens. The groups with the highest rates of teen births are Hispanics, with a rate of 83 births per 1,000 women 15 to 19 years old, and non-Hispanic blacks, with a rate of 68 per thousand—both well above the national rate of 43. Suppose the program was expanded so that it covered half of all Hispanic and black females ages 13 to 15—some two million girls. With a per-person cost of $4,000, the annual outlay would be roughly $4 billion.

Again, one would not expect a large program to be able to replicate the substantial reductions seen in the smaller program. But an initiative only half as effective in reducing teen births would still lower the birth rates of the 15- to 19-year-old participants by 35 percent. Under these assumptions, the expanded program would lead to about 40,000 fewer teen births a year—a 9 percent reduction.

Recent work by Anindya Sen enables us to quantify the expected reduction in crime from this potential drop in teen births. Sen finds that a 1 percent drop in teen births is associated with a 0.589 percent drop in violent crime years later, when the individuals born to teenagers would have reached their high-crime ages. Thus, the 9 percent reduction in teen births would eventually cut violent crime by 5 percent. Assuming two-thirds of crime costs are attributable to violent crime, this 5 percent reduction would eventually save society more than $14 billion per year. In other words, the benefits would be three times greater than the cost.

Expand the DNA Database

While much of the attention on the use of DNA in criminal justice has focused on its potential for establishing the innocence of the wrongly accused, we have not yet tapped the potential of DNA testing to deter crime. Individuals whose DNA is on file with the government know that leaving even a single hair at the scene of a crime is likely to lead to their arrest and conviction, so a major expansion in the DNA database should generate substantial crime reduction benefits. While some are concerned that the government would get information about a person's medical history, the privacy problem can be minimized. It is possible to take someone's DNA and discard all information except for the unique identifying genetic marker.

Currently, every state requires violent criminals and sex offenders to submit to DNA testing. Most states require testing for all felons and juvenile convicts. If a person is found innocent, his or her DNA sample must be discarded. But the United States' DNA crime-fighting system can be expanded and improved. England tests anyone suspected of a "recordable" offense, with the profile remaining on file even if the person is cleared of the crime. This has allowed Britain to build a DNA database with some two million profiles. England's Forensic Science Service estimates that, in a typical year, matches are found linking suspects to 180 murders, 500 rapes and other sexual offenses, and 30,000 motor vehicle, property and drug crimes. In other words, DNA is used to solve fully 20 percent of murders and a significant fraction of other crimes.

A more drastic—and potentially effective—approach was endorsed by Rudolph Giuliani: recording the DNA of every newborn. One way to lower the costs of the project without eliminating much of the gains would be to test only males, who are far more likely to commit crimes.

To improve the effectiveness of the policy, however, it would be necessary to test every male—not just male babies. This would increase the start-up costs to $15 billion (although thought should be given to the appropriate age cutoff—say age 50—as a plausible cost-reduction measure). In every year thereafter, however, it would be necessary to test only newborns. In 2002, there were a little more than 2 million male births in the United States. So testing every male infant would cost about $200 million annually.

One particular crime-deterrent benefit of having the DNA of every male on file is it would be likely to drastically reduce rapes by strangers. Let's assume (conservatively) that half of all such rapes—half of 56,000 a year—would be deterred by the existence of a complete DNA database. Ted Miller, Mark Cohen and Shelli Rossman added the costs of medical bills, lost productivity, mental health trauma and quality of life changes, to estimate that the average rape costs $90,000. Hence, 28,000 of the rapes by strangers in 2002 cost society about $2.5 billion. While the costs of testing every male—$15 billion in the first year—would exceed the $2.5 billion in benefits in reduced rapes from such a plan, the total benefits from rape reduction alone would exceed the costs in roughly seven years (and perhaps less if the initial testing were limited with a judicious age cutoff). Note, moreover, that stranger rapes are only one of many classes of crimes that would see sharp declines with such expansive DNA testing.

What We Are Losing

Few of these proposals seem likely to be adopted any time soon. Former attorney general John Ashcroft stressed incarceration and the death penalty as principal crime-fighting tools, and President Bush's new attorney general, Alberto Gonzalez, appears wed to an even tougher line. Bush seems intent on shrinking the budget for police and early-intervention social programs. The NRA continues to have success in fighting even the most sensible gun control policies. And few in either political party are willing to discuss the legalization of drugs or a major expansion in the DNA database. The politicians in power thus seem stuck on anti-crime policies that guarantee that crime levels will be far higher than can be justified by any reasonable comparison of costs and benefits—let alone respect for life and property.

Adopting the policies set out above would reduce crime in the neighborhood of 50 percent, saving thousands of lives annually and avoiding crime victimization for millions more. Is anybody in Washington, or the state capitals, listening?

MR. DONOHUE teaches law and economics at the Yale Law School. From "Fighting Crime: An Economist's View," *The Milken Institute Review,* First Quarter 2005, pages 47–58.

The Aggregate Burden of Crime

DAVID A. ANDERSON

Introduction

Distinct from previous studies that have focused on selected crimes, regions, or outcomes, this study attempts an exhaustively broad estimation of the crime burden. . . .

Overt annual expenditures on crime in the United States include $47 billion for police protection, $36 billion for corrections, and $19 billion for the legal and judicial costs of state and local criminal cases. (Unless otherwise noted, all figures are adjusted to reflect 1997 dollars using the Consumer Price Index.) Crime victims suffer $876 million worth of lost workdays, and guns cost society $25 billion in medical bills and lost productivity in a typical year. Beyond the costs of the legal system, victim losses, and crime prevention agencies, the crime burden includes the costs of deterrence (locks, safety lighting and fencing, alarm systems and munitions), the costs of compliance enforcement (non-gendarme inspectors and regulators), implicit psychic and health costs (fear, agony, and the inability to behave as desired), and the opportunity costs of time spent preventing, carrying out, and serving prison terms for criminal activity.

This study estimates the impact of crime taking a comprehensive list of the repercussions of aberrant behavior into account. While the standard measures of criminal activity count crimes and direct costs, this study measures the impact of crimes and includes indirect costs as well. Further, the available data on which crime cost figures are typically based is imprecise. Problems with crime figures stem from the prevalence of unreported crimes, inconsistencies in recording procedures among law enforcement agencies, policies of recording only the most serious crime in events with multiple offenses, and a lack of distinction between attempted and completed crimes. This research does not eliminate these problems, but it includes critical crime-prevention and opportunity costs that are measured with relative precision, and thus places less emphasis on the imprecise figures used in most other measures of the impact of crime. . . .

Previous Studies

Several studies have estimated the impact of crime; however, none has been thorough in its assessment of the substantial indirect costs of crime and the crucial consideration of private crime prevention expenditures. The FBI Crime Index provides a measure of the level of crime by counting the acts of murder, rape, robbery, aggravated assault, burglary, larceny, motor vehicle theft, and arson each year. The FBI Index is purely a count of crimes and does not attempt to place weights on various criminal acts based on their severity. If the number of acts of burglary, larceny, motor vehicle theft, or arson decreases, society might be better off, but with no measure of the severity of the crimes, such a conclusion is necessarily tentative. From a societal standpoint what matters is the extent of damage inflicted by these crimes, which the FBI Index does not measure.

Over the past three decades, studies of the cost of crime have reported increasing crime burdens, perhaps more as a result of improved understanding and accounting for the broad repercussions of crime than due to the increase in the burden itself. Table 1 summarizes the findings of eight previous studies. . . .

The Effects of Crime

The effects of crime fall into several categories depending on whether they constitute the allocation of resources due to crime that could otherwise be used more productively, the production of ill-favored commodities, transfers from victims to criminals, opportunity costs, or implicit costs associated with risks to life and health. This section examines the meaning and ramifications of each of these categories of crime costs.

Crime-Induced Production

Crime can result in the allocation of resources towards products and activities that do not contribute to society except in their association with crime. Examples include the production of personal protection devices, the trafficking of drugs, and the operation of correctional facilities. In the absence of crime, the time, money, and material resources absorbed by the provision of these goods and services could be used for the creation of benefits rather than the avoidance of harm. The foregone benefits from these alternatives represent a real cost of crime to society. (Twenty dollars spent on a door lock is twenty dollars that cannot be spent on groceries.) Thus, expenditures on crime-related products are treated as a loss to society.

Crimes against property also create unnecessary production due to the destruction and expenditure of resources, and crimes against persons necessitate the use of medical and psychological care resources. In each of these cases, crime-related purchases bid-up prices for the associated items, resulting in higher prices for all consumers of the goods. In the absence of crime, the dollars currently spent to remedy and recover from crime would largely be spent in pursuit of other goals, bidding-up the prices of alternative categories of goods. For this reason, the *net* impact of price effects is assumed to be zero in the present research.

Table 1

Previous Study	Focus	Not Included	$ (billions)
Colins (1994)	General	Opportunity Costs, Miscellaneous Indirect Components	728
Cohen, Miller, and Wiersema (1995)	Victim Costs of Violent and Property Crimes	Prevention, Opportunity, and Indirect Costs	472
U.S. News (1974)	General	Opportunity Costs, Miscellaneous Indirect Components	288
Cohen, Miller, Rossman (1994)	Cost of Rape, Robbery, and Assault	Prevention, Opportunity, and Indirect Costs	183
Zedlewski (1985)	Firearms, Guard Dogs, Victim Losses, Commercial Security	Residential Security, Opportunity Costs, Indirect Costs	160
Cohen (1990)	Cost of Personal and Household Crime to Victims	Prevention, Opportunity, and Indirect Costs	113
President's Commission on Law Enforcement (1967)	General	Opportunity Costs, Miscellaneous Indirect Components	107
Klaus (1994)	National Crime and Victimization Survey Crimes	Prevention, Opportunity, and Indirect Costs	19

Opportunity Costs

As the number of incarcerated individuals increases steadily, society faces the large and growing loss of these potential workers' productivity.... Criminals are risk takers and instigators—characteristics that could make them contributors to society if their entrepreneurial talents were not misguided. Crimes also take time to conceive and carry out, and thus involve the opportunity cost of the criminals' time regardless of detection and incarceration. For many, crime is a full-time occupation. Society is deprived of the goods and services a criminal would have produced in the time consumed by crime and the production of "bads" if he or she were on the level. Additional opportunity costs arise due to victims' lost workdays, and time spent securing assets, looking for keys, purchasing and installing crime prevention devices, and patrolling neighborhood-watch areas.

The Value of Risks to Life and Health

The implicit costs of violent crime include the fear of being injured or killed, the anger associated with the inability to behave as desired, and the agony of being a crime victim. Costs associated with life and health risks are perhaps the most difficult to ascertain, although a considerable literature is devoted to their estimation. The implicit values of lost life and injury are included in the list of crime costs below; those not wishing to consider them can simply subtract these estimates from the aggregate figure.

Transfers

One result of fraud and theft is a transfer of assets from victim to criminal....

Numerical Findings
Crime-Induced Production

... Crime-induced production accounts for about $400 billion in expenditures annually. Table 2 presents the costs of goods and services that would not have to be produced in the absence of crime. Drug trafficking accounts for an estimated $161 billion in expenditure. With the $28 billion cost of prenatal drug exposure and almost $11 billion worth of federal, state, and local drug control efforts (including drug treatment, education, interdiction, research, and intelligence), the combined cost of drug-related activities is about $200 billion. Findings that over half of the arrestees in 24 cities tested positive for recent drug use and about one-third of offenders reported being under the influence of drugs at the time of their offense suggest that significant portions of the other crime-cost categories may result indirectly from drug use.

About 682,000 police and 17,000 federal, state, special (park, transit, or county) and local police agencies account for $47 billion in expenditures annually. Thirty-six billion dollars is dedicated each year to the 895 federal and state prisons, 3,019 jails, and 1,091 state, county, and local juvenile detention centers. Aside from guards in correctional institutions, private expenditure on guards amounts to more than $18 billion annually. Security guard agencies employ 55 percent of the 867,000 guards in the U.S.; the remainder are employed in-house. While guards are expected and identifiable at banks and military complexes, they have a less conspicuous presence at railroads, ports, golf courses, laboratories, factories, hospitals, retail stores, and other places of business. The figures in this paper do not include receptionists, who often play a duel role of monitoring unlawful entry into a building and providing information and assistance....

Opportunity Costs

In their study of the costs of murder, rape, robbery, and aggravated assault, Cohen, Miller, and Rossman estimate that the average incarcerated offender costs society $5,700 in lost productivity per year. Their estimate was based on the observation that many prisoners did not work in the legal market prior to their offense, and the opportunity cost of those prisoners' time can be considered to be zero. The current study uses a higher estimate of the opportunity cost of incarceration because unlike previous

Table 2

Crime-Induced Production	$ (millions)
Drug Trafficking	160,584
Police Protection	47,129
Corrections	35,879
Prenatal Exposure to Cocaine and Heroin	28,156
Federal Agencies	23,381
Judicial and Legal Services—State & Local	18,901
Guards	17,917
Drug Control	10,951
DUI Costs to Driver	10,302
Medical Care for Victims	8,990
Computer Viruses and Security	8,000
Alarm Systems	6,478
Passes for Business Access	4,659
Locks, Safes, and Vaults	4,359
Vandalism (except Arson)	2,317
Small Arms and Small Arms Ammunition	2,252
Replacements due to Arson	1,902
Surveillance Cameras	1,471
Safety Lighting	1,466
Protective Fences and Gates	1,159
Airport Security	448
Nonlethal weaponry, e.g., Mace	324
Elec. Retail Article Surveillance	149
Theft Insurance (less indemnity)	96
Guard Dogs	49
Mothers Against Drunk Driving	49
Library Theft Detection	28
Total	**397,395**

studies, it examines the relative savings from a *crime-free* society. It is likely that in the absence of crime including drug use, some criminals who are not presently employed in the legal workforce would be willing and able to find gainful employment. This assumption is supported by the fact that many criminals are, in a way, motivated entrepreneurs whose energy has taken an unfortunate focus. In the absence of more enticing underground activities, some of the same individuals could apply these skills successfully in the legal sector. . . .

The Value of Risks to Life and Health

Table 3 presents estimates of the implicit costs of violent crime. The value of life and injury estimates used here reflect the amounts individuals are willing to accept to enter a work environment in which their health state might change. The labor market estimates do not include losses covered by workers' compensation, namely health care costs (usually provided without dollar or time limits) and lost earnings (within modest bounds, victims or their spouses typically receive about two

Table 3

The Value of Risks to Life and Health	$ (millions)
Value of Lost Life	439,880
Value of Injuries	134,515
Total	**574,395**

thirds of lost earnings for life or the duration of the injury). The values do capture perceived risks of pain, suffering, and mental distress associated with the health losses. If the risk of involvement in violent crime evokes more mental distress than the risk of occupational injuries and fatalities, the labor market values represent conservative estimates of the corresponding costs of crime. Similar estimates have been used in previous studies of crime costs. . . .

The average of 27 previous estimates of the implicit value of human life as reported by W. Kip Viscusi is 7.1 million. Removing two outlying estimates of just under $20 million about which the authors express reservation, the average of the remaining studies is $6.1 million. Viscusi points out that the majority of the estimates fall between $3.7 and $8.6 million ($3 and $7 million in 1990 dollars), the average of which is again $6.1 million. The $6.1 million figure was multiplied by the 72,111 crime-related deaths to obtain the $440 billion estimate of the value of lives lost to crime. Similarly, the average of 15 studies of the implicit value of non-fatal injuries, $52,637, was multiplied by the 2,555,520 reported injuries resulting from drunk driving and boating, arson, rape, robbery, and assaults to find the $135 billion estimate for the implicit cost of crime-related injuries.

Transfers

More than $603 billion worth of transfers result from crime. After the $204 billion lost to occupational fraud and the $123 billion in unpaid taxes, the $109 billion lost to health insurance fraud represents the greatest transfer by more than a factor of two, and the associated costs amount to almost ten percent of the nations' health care expenditures. Robberies, perhaps the classic crime, ironically generate a smaller volume of transfers ($775 million) than any other category of crime. The transfers of goods and money resulting from fraud and theft do not necessarily impose a net burden on society, and may in fact increase social welfare to the extent that those on the receiving end value the goods more than those losing them. Nonetheless, as Table 4 illustrates, those on the losing side bear a $603 billion annual burden. . . .

There are additional cost categories that are not included here, largely because measures that are included absorb much of their impact. Nonetheless, several are worth noting. Thaler, Hellman and Naroff, and Rizzo estimate the erosion of property values per crime. An average of their figures, $2,024, can be multiplied by the total number of crimes reported in 1994, 13,992, to estimate an aggregate housing devaluation of $28 billion. Although this figure should reflect the inability to behave as desired in the presence of crime, it also includes psychic and monetary costs imposed by criminal behavior that are already included in this [article].

Table 4

Transfers	$ (millions)
Occupational Fraud	203,952
Unpaid Taxes	123,108
Health Insurance Fraud	108,610
Financial Institution Fraud	52,901
Mail Fraud	35,986
Property/Casualty Insurance Fraud	20,527
Telemarketing Fraud	16,609
Business Burglary	13,229
Motor Vehicle Theft	8,913
Shoplifting	7,185
Household Burglary	4,527
Personal Theft	3,909
Household Larceny	1,996
Coupon Fraud	912
Robbery	775
Total	**603,140**

Julie Berry Cullen and Stephen D. Levitt discuss urban flight resulting from crime. They report a nearly one-to-one relationship between serious crimes and individuals parting from major cities. The cost component of this is difficult to assess because higher commuting costs must be measured against lower property costs in rural areas, and the conveniences of city living must be compared with the amenities of suburbia. Several other categories of crime costs receive incomplete representation due to insufficient data, and therefore make the estimates here conservative. These include the costs of unreported crimes (although the National Crime Victimization Survey provides information beyond that reported to the police), lost taxes due to the underground economy, and restrictions of behavior due to crime.

When criminals' costs are estimated implicitly as the value of the assets they receive through crime, the gross cost of crime (including transfers) is estimated to exceed $2,269 billion each year, and the net cost is an estimated $1,666 billion. When criminals' costs are assumed to equal the value of time spent planning and committing crimes and in prison, the estimated annual gross and net costs of crime are $1,705 and $1,102 billion respectively. Table 5 presents the aggregate costs of crime based on the more conservative, time-based estimation method. The disaggregation of this and the previous tables facilitates the creation of customized estimates based on the reader's preferred assumptions. Each of the general studies summarized in Table 1 included transfers, so the appropriate comparison is to the gross cost estimate in the current study. As the result of

Table 5

The Aggregate Burden of Crime	$ (billions)
Crime-Induced Production	397
Opportunity Costs	130
Risks to Life and Health	574
Transfers	603
Gross Burden	**$1,705**
Net of Transfers	**$1,102**
Per Capita (in dollars)	**$4,118**

a more comprehensive treatment of repercussions, the cost of crime is now seen to be more than twice as large as previously recognized.

Conclusion

Previous studies of the burden of crime have counted crimes or concentrated on direct crime costs. This paper calculates the aggregate burden of crime rather than absolute numbers, includes indirect costs, and recognizes that transfers resulting from theft should not be included in the net burden of crime to society. The accuracy of society's perspective on crime costs will improve with the understanding that these costs extend beyond victims' losses and the cost of law enforcement to include the opportunity costs of criminals' and prisoners' time, our inability to behave as desired, and the private costs of crime deterrence.

As criminals acquire an estimated $603 billion dollars worth of assets from their victims, they generate an additional $1,102 billion worth of lost productivity, crime-related expenses, and diminished quality of life. The net losses represent an annual per capita burden of $4,118. Including transfers, the aggregate burden of crime is $1,705 billion. In the United States, this is of the same order of magnitude as life insurance purchases ($1,680 billion), the outstanding mortgage debt to commercial banks and savings institutions ($1,853 billion), and annual expenditures on health ($1,038 billion).

As the enormity of this negative-sum game comes to light, so, too, will the need for countervailing efforts to redefine legal policy and forge new ethical standards. Periodic estimates of the full cost of crime could speak to the success of national strategies to encourage decorum, including increased expenditures on law enforcement, new community strategic approaches, technological innovations, legal reform, education, and the development of ethics curricula. Economic theory dictates that resources should be devoted to moral enhancement until the benefits from marginal efforts are surpassed by their costs. Programs that decrease the burden of crime by more than the cost of implementation should be continued, while those associated with negligible or positive net increments in the cost of crime should be altered to better serve societal goals.

From *Journal of Law and Economics,* Vol. 42, October 1999, pp. 611–642. Copyright © 1999 by David A. Anderson. Reprinted by permission of the author.

The Globalization of Crime

A team of futurists examines the ways in which crime has become globalized and how the worlds of legitimate and illicit finance intertwine.

STEPHEN AGUILAR-MILLAN ET AL.

The nature of crime has changed significantly in a single generation. Just 20 years ago, crime was organized in a hierarchy of operations. It was "industrial" in that it contained the division of labor and the specialization of operations. This structure extended internationally, as organized crime mirrored the business world.

Then, just as it happened in the business world, the vertical and horizontal hierarchies of organized crime dissolved into a large number of loosely connected networks. Each node within a network would be involved in any number of licit and illicit operations. Networked systems spanned the globe. An event in one place might have a significant impact on the other side of the world. In short, crime became globalized.

Organized crime involves the illicit flow of goods and services in one direction and the flow of the proceeds of crime in the other. Just as the business world has benefited from globalization, so has organized crime.

Crime as a Globalized Activity: An Overview

In many ways, it is helpful to consider crime as a special form of business activity, affected by the same trends as other business activities.

Globalization—including the globalization of crime—can be said to have started with the fall of the Berlin Wall, the collapse of the Soviet Union, and the attempts by Western thinkers to offer economic prescriptions and organize international affairs along the lines of Western capitalism.

In practice, Western capitalism consisted of a belief in free markets for the allocation of resources, free flows of goods and services across international borders, and the free movement of labor and capital to harness the demand created by the free market. For globalization to take hold, two further revolutions were needed—the growth of low-cost mass-transit facilities and the growth of international telecommunications (i.e., the Internet).

The transportation revolution facilitated the mass movement of goods and people across the globe, and the Internet revolution has allowed the development of global service infrastructures, such as banking and financial services. It's also enabled global operations to be monitored and controlled remotely from anywhere in the world that has Internet access.

As these revolutions—the freeing of markets, the transportation revolution, and the Internet revolution—were taking place, the way in which the world works was also changing. In global business especially, the world shifted from being one of hierarchies to being one of networks. The rise of the networked organization laid the foundation for two features of modern life—outsourcing (where key roles are undertaken outside of the formal organizational structure) and offshoring (where, thanks to the transportation and Internet revolutions, key roles can be undertaken anywhere in the world). Needless to say, such encouragements of lawful trade proved to be a boon for illicit trade as well.

From a commercial perspective, the key to the flow of illicit goods—be they narcotics, people, counterfeit goods, or human transplant organs—is logistics: How do you move the goods from the point of origin to the point of consumption? The revolution in transportation lowered the cost of freight and increased the number of routes available. The need to secure these routes for illicit flows of goods has also led to the growth in the arms trade—especially of personal weapons of a relatively small caliber.

From the perspective of the law enforcement agencies, the problem with policing such activities is jurisdiction, which has led to the increase in cross-border police cooperation. The key to success in halting the flow of illicit goods is to have good intelligence, so law enforcement agencies (usually the police and customs agencies) are cooperating more closely with the military services (particularly military intelligence and the naval arm). In effect, law enforcement agencies have globalized in order to respond to the globalization of criminal gangs.

Meanwhile, some illicit activities have moved from the corporeal world to cyberspace. For example, the development of the Internet has allowed much pornographic activity to migrate to the virtual world. Initially, this was restricted to the transmission of images, but the development has taken on new forms with the rise of online worlds such as Second Life.

Global Crime Case: Drugs and the U.S.–Mexico Border

The border between the United States and Mexico is 1,954 miles long and the most heavily transited international border in the world. Mexico is the United States' second-largest trading partner and a party to the North American Free Trade Agreement. Yet, mixed among the legal trade and visitations are smuggled goods and the infiltration of illegal migrants.

Criminal enterprises are in business to make money. Most often, they do so through the smuggling of contraband. Along the U.S.–Mexico border, the contraband consists primarily of drugs and people. The criminal organizations present today are the products of a multi-decade evolutionary path that began with the Medellín and Cali cartels of Colombia.

In a continuing engagement of action and reaction, governments have pursued strategies that have shaped the contemporary organizations. During the *Miami Vice* days, drug contraband was shipped from Colombia to the United States through the Caribbean islands. As a result of successful enforcement actions by the United States, the drug cartels moved their transshipment avenues west. Successful aerial interdiction by the U.S. Customs Service made direct smuggling flights into the United States untenable. Consequently, Colombian traffickers began to contract with emerging organizations in northern Mexico.

Initially, these organizations specialized in border transshipment, taking custody of the client's narcotics in Mexico and delivering them to the client's agents in the United States. In the process, the locus of power shifted from the

Colombian cartels to the Mexican cartels. The Mexican cartels also developed sophisticated money-laundering operations to realize their profits.

The demise of the Colombian cartels precipitated a transition in the shape of organizations to less vertically integrated models; the new system offered a network of criminal organizations with various specialties.

Today, there are five Mexican cartels: Gulf, Sinaloa, Juarez, Tijuana, and Valencia. Three of the five—Sinaloa, Juarez, and Valencia—cooperate in an alliance called the Federation. The Gulf and Tijuana cartels have also partnered against the Juarez cartel. In the midst, affiliated coyote organizations have arisen to smuggle human beings into the United States. They provide services to an international clientele.

What can we expect in the future? Much depends on how powerful the cartels grow, whether the Mexican government can eradicate corruption and reestablish control over the largely lawless regions dominated by the cartels, and the development of U.S. policy along the border. Policy regimes that simply maintain enough pressure to force the cartels to evolve will likely result in more efficient and sophisticated criminal enterprises. Policy regimes that eliminate or substantially constrain the cartels may force human and narcotic trafficking across other borders. So long as demand for illegal drugs and illegal labor remain high, traffickers will adjust and find new ways to move contraband. And these flows are occurring on a global scale.

—Stephen Aguilar-Millan, Joan E. Foltz, John Jackson, and Amy Oberg

---

Online, the confusion of legal jurisdictions creates new problems. For example, in the case of online gambling, firms in the United Kingdom were engaged in the provision of gambling activities that were legal under European Union law but illegal in the United States. Alternatively, Second Life is alleged to host pedophile rings whose activities are contrary to EU law but take protection from the First Amendment in the United States. There has been some harmonization in legal codes, but this process is far from complete. What is needed is the globalization of legal codes to complete the process.

The flow of illicit goods in both the corporeal and the virtual worlds is aided by illicit services, particularly banking and financial services. The development of the Internet has greatly assisted global criminal networks in laundering their money. Preventing money laundering is likely to become even harder as new forms of money and financial instruments emerge. Just imagine a Rotterdam cocaine futures market!

The nature of banking is also changing. As we see with the development of payments through cellphone transfers, it will become harder for the monetary authorities to police the monetary system.

We can reasonably expect the flow of illicit goods to increase if the globalization trend continues. Some of the flows will be diverted from the corporeal world to the virtual world. New

crimes will develop within the virtual world as people exercise their inventiveness, and more illicit services will be invented to channel the proceeds of crime into lawful investment assets.

In the years ahead, national law enforcement agencies are likely to cooperate more, and there may also be greater involvement of military assets for law enforcement purposes. However, this is unlikely to be entirely successful without the political willingness to harmonize legal codes and to deploy international resources to where they have the greatest impact. This point is best demonstrated in the area of white-collar crime.

The High Stakes of White-Collar Crime

The profile of white-collar criminals is changing as the possibility of enormous payouts increases the high stakes of the game. The $1-trillion illicit trade market is being fueled not just by organized groups, but also by individuals who are lured by the opportunities rising from the globally integrated financial systems. The rapid advancement of wireless technology enables financial transactions in every region in the world, so opportunities for white-collar crimes are proliferating as fast as the criminal landscape is changing.

Global Crime Case: The Modern Slave Trade

Human slavery is alive and prospering hundreds of years after wars were fought to abolish it. It is a growing part of the larger global problem of human trafficking.

Human trafficking involves the involuntary movement of people across and within borders and typically involves coercion, deception, and violence. Behind drugs and guns, human trafficking is the third largest illicit global trade and reportedly the fastest growing. While exact numbers associated with human trafficking are hard to generate, the United Nations estimates that global trafficking involves at least 4 million people each year and generates estimated annual revenues of $7 billion–$10 billion. By some accounts, however, the UN estimate is quite low. China reportedly generates $1 billion–$3 billion annually via human trafficking activities, and Mexico, $6 billion–$9 billion.

Many trafficked victims fall into some form of human slavery—serving as sex, farm, factory, or domestic slaves. In many cases, the victims are young children who have been sold into slavery by family members desperately in need of money. Globally, it is estimated that some 27 million people are being held as slaves in an industry that may generate as much as $32 billion a year, according to International Labour Organization estimates.

Sex slavery, trafficking, and trade can be found all around the world: in China, Cambodia, Thailand, Russia and other former Soviet states, the Philippines, Colombia, Japan, Italy, the European Union, and the United States, to name just a few. Southeast Asia is one of the world's largest exporters of sex slaves and a sex hot spot. Thanks to devastating and widespread poverty, there is an abundant supply of recruits available to meet the demands of wealthy customers in Japan, China, Australia, Europe, and the United States. In 2006, Cambodia was one of the busiest spots in the world for human trafficking, with a majority of victims from Cambodia being delivered into the sex trade in Southeast Asia. An estimated 30,000 of those Cambodians exploited in the sex trade were children.

Employing their financial resources to bribe officials, international networks to arrange swift transport, and new technologies to generate false documents, traffickers can complete the process of abduction in one hot spot to delivery in another within a 48-hour to two-week time frame. Globalization has made human trafficking easier. Deregulation, open borders, entwined economies, and the ease of international banking have all facilitated the ability to market and traffic human beings. The complexity of networks, e-cash, and cross-border enforcement issues have also significantly decreased the risks associated with this illicit trade.

Governments had been trying to curb human trafficking, but much of the policing focus and funding has shifted from trafficking and other such crimes to terrorism, so action has become limited. Human trafficking is also an international issue, complicated by politics, morality, and gender biases that collectively have also limited government activities.

Nongovernmental organizations (NGOs) are not so burdened. They can more easily work across borders and across organizations than can official government agencies. While they have been making progress against human trafficking and slavery, they, too, have been limited. NGOs suffer from lack of funding, and efforts to raise funds have been difficult. The phenomenon of human trafficking and slavery is evidently so abhorrent that it is hard to find those who will acknowledge its existence and fund efforts against it.

—Stephen Aguilar-Millan, Joan E. Foltz, John Jackson, and Amy Oberg

---

Organized crime has long been involved in money laundering, fraud, and currency counterfeiting for self-benefit. More recently, governmental agencies are concerned about how the magnitude of those activities and other white-collar crimes could threaten national security and global financial markets. White-collar crime also includes intellectual property crime, payment card fraud, computer virus attacks, and cyberterrorism.

Corporate fraud has become a priority of the FBI, which has pursued cases involving more than $1 billion in losses to individuals, as well as securities and commodities fraud that amounts to approximately $40 billion worth of corporate losses per year.

The sophistication of the schemes is growing and the frequency of events is accelerating as improving technology eases the transfer of money across international borders and gives criminals access to more identities that may be stolen. With a growing amount of corporate and financial records, there is more potential opportunity for manipulation—and that threat has expanded to global proportions.

The spread of capitalism promotes open markets and aims to maximize opportunity but blurs the line between what is considered creative money management and what is considered criminal behavior. The increasing opportunities for white-collar crimes and their potential payoff is extremely enticing to individuals who do not fit the typical criminal profile.

Social attitudes toward money and finances are also changing worldwide, and as yet there is no accepted global definition of white-collar crime. Some cultures don't consider certain activities involving corruption, corporate malfeasance, and stock manipulation even to be criminal. White-collar crime is not always a clear-cut act of deviance and is often intermingled with legitimate behavior that is spread out over a number of incidents. Meeting the goals of capitalism requires tough competition, which promotes attitudes and behaviors that may blur ethical lines. What behaviors should be rewarded? What should be penalized?

Electronic funds transfer systems handle more than $6 trillion in wire transfers daily, and the growing speed and interconnectivity of those transactions adds to the difficulty of tracing money transfers, particularly across borders into regions where regulations are not enforced. To combat the problem, more countries will participate in international organizations to regulate and

Global Crime Case: Cybercrime and Counterfeiting

Much of the modern organized crimes are very similar to the old. The most significant transformation from the streets to cyberspace has enlarged the territory of individuals and organized groups. Enabled by the Internet, criminals can operate in cyberspace where less governance, a transnational stage, and a multitude of transactions to monitor complicate surveillance and enforcement.

From counterfeiting drugs and software to identity theft and credit-card fraud, illegal transactions are increasingly infiltrating legitimate businesses where counterfeited goods and money laundering are buried in the billions of legitimate computer transactions made daily around the globe.

Counterfeited products are rising through global distribution via Internet sites. According to the World Health Organization, 50% of the medicines sold online are counterfeit.

The expanse of international criminal activity has been followed with an increase in prosecution through cooperating international law enforcement agencies willing to join the fight against globalized crime.

The following sampling of the U.S. Department of Justice prosecutions in 2007 and 2008 shows that crimes that were once national or regional now commonly cross borders and have a transnational impact on businesses and victims.

- Members of an international organized crime group operating a "phishing" scheme in the United States, Canada, Pakistan, Portugal, and Romania obtained private information for credit-card fraud. Among the financial institutions affected were Citibank, Capital One, JPMorgan Chase, Comerica Bank, Wells Fargo, eBay, and PayPal.
- Hackers were arrested for infiltrating cash register terminals at Dave & Buster's restaurants in the United States to acquire credit-card information, which was resold to others for criminal purposes. The hackers were prosecuted with the cooperation of the Turkish and German governments.
- A Nigerian installed a spyware program on a NASA employee's computer to capture personal data, such as bank account numbers, Social Security number, driver's license information, home address, and passwords to various computer accounts, as well as to intercept private electronic communications.

- A Colombian computer fraud scheme captured data to access bank and brokerage accounts on more than 600 people in the United States through computers located in hotel business centers and Internet lounges around the world. Actual loss from the scheme was estimated at $1.4 million.
- An international enforcement initiative undertaken by the United States and Canada has resulted in more than 400 seizures of counterfeit Cisco network hardware and labels with an estimated retail value of more than $76 million.
- A Boeing engineer stole trade secrets related to aerospace programs, including the Space Shuttle, the C-17 military transport aircraft, and the Delta IV rocket, to sell to the People's Republic of China.
- A New Hampshire Company, Vee Excel Drugs & Pharmaceuticals Inc., was charged with trafficking counterfeit drugs and introducing misbranded drugs into the United States. The company conspired with an Indian corporation to ship counterfeit Cialis tablets into the United States in packages fraudulently identified as containing chlorine tablets.
- A global criminal ring smuggled counterfeit luxury goods into the United States from the People's Republic of China. Valued at more than $100 million, the counterfeit handbags, wallets, purses, and carry-on bags were labeled with such name brands as Nike, Burberry, Chanel, Polo Ralph Lauren, and Baby Phat. The defendants paid more than $500,000 in bribes to an undercover agent.
- Operation Phony Pharm investigated the illegal sale of anabolic steroids, human growth hormone, and other controlled substances over the Internet. Raw materials imported from China and manufactured in U.S., Canadian, and Mexican underground laboratories were distributed through a MySpace profile and a website. Collaboration with Operation Raw Deal has resulted in the seizure of 56 steroid labs across the United States. The U.S. operation took place in conjunction with enforcement operations in Mexico, Canada, China, Belgium, Australia, Germany, Denmark, Sweden, and Thailand.

—Joan E. Foltz

control fraudulent financial activity, perhaps spurred by the proliferation of money laundering of funds for terrorist activities. International agencies such as Interpol also work closely with technology providers to develop security controls for tracking and preventing financial and high-tech crimes. But even the most advanced security systems and coordinated enforcement cannot prevent targeted attacks on international financial systems.

Daily international transfers of $2 trillion via computer communications pass through conventional banks, Internet banking, mobile banking, and e-commerce transactions. Many transactions cross borders going not through financial institutions, but rather through professional services, such as real estate agents

and accountants facilitating transactions that exchange cash for purchases to mask ownership of originating funds. Offshore corporations and relatives also offer assistance transferring funds via mobile phones and Internet payment services such as PayPal.

The same technologies that make criminal activities possible—rapid financial transactions via mobile devices or the Internet, for instance—also make transborder e-commerce more transparent and secure. Authorities can more easily track investment transactions. However, rogue traders and terrorist groups may continue to manipulate currencies and stocks and threaten to infiltrate financial systems, so countries, companies,

Global Crime Case: Gangs Go Global

Criminal gangs are thriving in cities around the world, and they aren't going away anytime soon, criminal justice professor John M. Hagedorn asserts in his new book, *A World of Gangs.*

"Large areas within megacities have admittedly become unmanageable, and armed groups are stepping in to manage the unmanageable spaces," he explains. The equation, as he sees it, is quite simple: urbanization + poverty = gangs.

Already, the majority of the global population lives in densely packed urban areas, and by the year 2020, half of the world's urban population will live in poverty, according to UN estimates. Hagedorn places much of the blame squarely on globalization, claiming that the new global economy "has resulted in economic and social polarization in much of the world." He cites the gentrification of inner-city areas and the resulting displacement of the urban poor as one specific example. Whenever circumstances for basic survival become dire, gangs begin to multiply.

For the marginalized youth living in ghettos and favelas who view their options as increasingly limited, gang membership provides a strong sense of belonging and empowerment. Like youth groups and religious organizations, gangs offer structure and solutions for young members of their communities, and the fact that street gangs often function as illicit money-making enterprises adds greatly to their appeal. "The gang is one business that is almost always hiring and may be the only chance many youth have to get a job," Hagedorn writes.

Contemporary gangs tend to be organized like corporations, and many have franchises in different locations. In addition to the emergence of new gangs, established gangs are institutionalizing themselves in cities around the world.

Once gangs become institutionalized, they are almost completely invulnerable to police repression. Institutionalized gang leaders are able to maintain control, keep on top of new developments, and recruit new members even from behind bars. "Rather than prison being a place to send gang members in an attempt to break up the gang, gangs have adapted and have used prison to advance their interests," Hagedorn writes. Gangs have institutionalized themselves in cities from Chicago to Rio de Janeiro, and from Cape Town to Mumbai.

How to Deal with Gangs

The most common public-policy response to gangs is zero tolerance, Hagedorn notes. The average street gang will have a hard time surviving in a gentrified area with a strong police presence. However, this method has not been entirely effective, as the institutionalized gangs simply adapt to increases in police presence and surveillance.

Critics of zero-tolerance policies argue that they penalize entire communities and strengthen young people's attachments to the idealized image of "gangsta" as resistance identity. Such strong-arm approaches, they say, achieve only temporary gains and are destined to backfire in the long run. Hagedorn argues that it is impossible to permanently eliminate gangs or reduce youth violence by using force, so other, more positive and more permanent solutions are necessary.

Hagedorn advocates "bringing gangs and those on society's margins into broader social movements, while demanding they take steps to shed their violent, antisocial habits. This is a difficult task and, for most gangs, may prove impossible." However, he contends that gang members, like the rest of us, have the potential to change for the better. At any rate, he argues, societies have little choice but to try. "We either bring gangs and the underclass into the polity or run the risk of living in a permanent fortress society."

Hagedorn recommends that governments adopt an approach similar to the UN's disarmament, demobilization, and reintegration programs for rehabilitating child soldiers. Such a long-term process would most likely provide education and job skills training, encourage prosocial behavior, and teach former gang members how to reintegrate into the larger community.

Policy makers could also focus on providing better job opportunities and improving education in lower-income communities overall. Prevention is always the best cure. Social programs that provide job training, after-school activities, and recreational leagues have met with success over the years. Gang researchers have seen that increased opportunity as well as a strong support system of family and friends can persuade gang members to leave their thug lives behind.

—Aaron M. Cohen

and individuals must increasingly weigh the opportunities for fast and easy money versus regulation and security.

As competition and opportunities are sought by more players in a larger global market, more creative financial instruments and structured deals set up an environment where payoffs and lack of controls allow fraud and corruption. Without guidelines and a definitive identification of what constitutes punishable criminal activity, new business models will be created that stretch the systems and threaten economic stability, such as the subprime lending debacle.

Super-capitalism will drive a push for new financial instruments and schemes in other areas of corporate fraud, such as

"pumping and dumping" stocks to set deceptive market prices or using Ponzi schemes. Such activities jeopardize not only personal portfolios, but also the stability of the global investment community. In 2006, the FBI investigated 1,165 cases of securities and commodities fraud that amounted to $1.9 billion in restitutions and $62.7 million in seizures.

The growth of unethical business practices that impact free markets will compel international regulatory bodies to define white-collar crime and to establish globally supported tracking systems and venues for prosecution. The challenge is to regulate criminal activities operating in a virtual space of global industries that are becoming more disconnected from national

Global Crime Case: Heroin

The case of heroin ably demonstrates the way in which the networked world of crime crosses international borders, involves a multiplicity of illegality, and presents an ominous picture of a dark future ahead.

Heroin is a derivative from the opium poppy, which is distilled into a potent and highly addictive narcotic. Research published in *The Lancet* (the Journal of the British Medical Association) suggests that heroin is the illegal narcotic that has the highest levels of dependency and physical harm. As a result of this, the drug appears on Schedule I on the Single Convention of Narcotic Drugs.

The principal areas of production for heroin are the "Golden Crescent" (Afghanistan, Pakistan), the "Golden Triangle" (Laos, Vietnam, Myanmar, and Thailand), and Latin America (principally Mexico and Colombia). Global production is currently weighted toward the Golden Crescent, which accounts for an estimated 92% of world production.

Global consumption, however, is skewed toward the developed world. It is difficult to assess the size of the market for heroin in Europe and North America with any great accuracy because, by definition, its illegality makes it unquantifiable. However, the CIA reports that 56% of global seizures occur in Europe and Africa, while only 10% occur in the United States. It is widely held that cocaine is the narcotic of choice in the United States, while Europe displays a preference for heroin.

Heroin tends to be processed locally from the opium poppies at the point of cultivation. It then needs to be transported to the point of consumption, generally using the transport infrastructure of globalization as a means of distribution. The CIA reports that 71% of global seizures take place along land routes. The key land route is the "Balkan Route" that links the Golden Crescent with Europe. This route has two branches—the northern branch that runs north of the Black Sea via Russia, Ukraine, and eastern Europe, and the southern branch that runs south of the Black Sea via Turkey, Bulgaria, Serbia, and Croatia. Along these routes, the transport of heroin acquires another dimension.

In transit, the heroin becomes one of a number of illicit contraband goods being transported from one part of the world to another. Each shipment of heroin may be accompanied by undocumented immigrants, illegal weapons, counterfeit products, and other illicit items. Usually, the illicit goods will accompany licit trade, making their detection difficult for law enforcement agencies.

In this environment, the key profit zone in globalized crime has become in the transit of goods rather than their production or sale to the end user, and the money made there must then be laundered into legitimacy.

The global transmission of funds has grown enormously in recent years. We now live in a world characterized by the absence of exchange controls and where the boundaries of financial institutions do not mirror national boundaries. It is so much easier today for the proceeds of crime to hide in the undergrowth of legitimate financial transactions.

For the heroin trade, this means that the proceeds are repatriated to sources in Afghanistan. There is no doubt that heroin is a key source of revenue to the Taliban, who use this income to purchase weaponry illicitly on the world market. The demise of the Soviet Union brought onto the world market an unprecedented level of weaponry, which has been absorbed into the criminal networks. In turn, the Taliban needs this weaponry to maintain its dominance over the Afghan heroin trade.

This has led to a self-reinforcing trade system that the agencies of law enforcement have found difficult to halt. Efforts have been made to stem the flow of heroin from Afghanistan, to interdict the heroin in transit, and to reduce the outlet points in Europe and North America. There has been some success in each of these areas, but there is also no general shortage of heroin on the streets of Europe and North America.

Despite these trends, we can see hope for progress in three areas.

1. The rising price of oil is raising transport freight costs across the globe. In the longer term, this will lead to fewer goods in transit, making it easier to interdict those illicit goods that are in transit. The balance may tip away from criminal networks and toward law enforcement agencies.
2. The rise of neo-nationalism in the face of resource shortages is likely to make the interdiction of trade goods at the point of entry more acceptable politically. In the face of a perceived threat from external criminal gangs, the delay of goods in port for customs inspection will be much easier, helping the interdiction of heroin in transit.
3. The rising price of wheat globally is undermining the relative financial advantage of opium poppies over wheat as a cash crop in southern Afghanistan. If NATO can protect Afghan farmers so that they can cultivate wheat free from the intervention of the Taliban, then the financial base of the Taliban will be seriously undermined and the global supply of heroin will be significantly reduced.

These three factors provide a ray of hope in the case of heroin addiction in the West, as well as a ray of hope in the war on terror generally and against the Taliban in particular. None of it is due to the actions of the Western governments, but rather represents a self-regulation mechanism in the process of globalization. We could almost say that globalization caused this problem, and globalization may solve it.

—Stephen Aguilar-Millan

jurisdictions. This will require not only international cooperation, but also the sharing of information among law enforcement agencies and the ability to seize assets.

Efforts to deter money laundering and terrorist activities are gaining international cooperation, but going after corporate and securities fraud is another matter. Cooperation in battling these white-collar threats to global financial systems is unlikely until a significant disruption impacts all members of the global free market and until all governments understand that weak systems and corruption impair regional economic development.

Cooperation against Global Crime

One of the flaws in market-based capitalism is that it is open to corrupt influences and encourages undesirable behavior by providing a profit for meeting a demand. As long as there is a demand for narcotics, human servitude, and other illicit goods and services, there will be a market in human misery.

A glimmer of hope may be found in the fact that many of these global criminals desire respectability. They are victims of the system that they exploit, and they are exploited by those operating in the financial world, for whom they provide commissions, fees, and retainers. The point at which dirty money is laundered clean is the point at which those who operate in the world of organized crime wish to enter the mainstream world. This is the Achilles' heel of global organized crime.

Given the global nature of the monetary system that is being used, one would expect an international effort to harmonize the regulation of the global monetary system. By and large, this is happening, but we have not reached a harmonious point just yet, because a wide agreement will entail the sacrifice of some national interests. These national interests are not readily conceded in international negotiations, but progress is being made.

When we look to the future, we can see a greater degree of international cooperation in dealing with globalized crime. Military establishments may offer more support for policing efforts. Modern terrorism has blurred the boundary between war and peace, and modern organized crime has blurred the distinction between law enforcement activities and military operations.

The process of globalization is not yet complete. As an integrated system of trade and finance, it has become very developed. The problems that we currently face with globalization as a process are the result of a system of trade and finance that has developed faster than the regulatory framework in which trade occurs. As we move into the future, we can expect to see the regulatory framework catch up with the new reality of trade and finance. We would hope that this is bad news for organized crime.

STEPHEN AGUILAR-MILLAN is the director of research for *The European Futures Observatory,* 6 Greenways Close, Ipswich, Suffolk IP1 3RB, United Kingdom. E-mail stephena@eufo.org. JOAN E. FOLTZ is a principal of Alsek Research in Chandler, Arizona, a socioeconomic analyst of global development and market behavior and publisher of *Alsek's Not-So-Daily Update.* E-mail jfoltz@cox.net. JOHN JACKSON is a sergeant with the Houston Police Department. E-mail johna.jackson@cityofhouston.net. AMY OBERG is a corporate futurist with the Kimberly-Clark Corporation in Wisconsin. E-mail future_in_sight@yahoo.com.

This article draws from the authors' paper, "The Globalization of Crime," in the World Future Society's 2008 conference volume, *Seeing the Future Through New Eyes* edited by Cynthia G. Wagner. 444 pages. Paperback. $29.95 ($24.95 for members). Order online at www.wfs.org/ wfsbooks.htm.

Causes and Consequences of Wrongful Convictions

Hugo Adam Bedau

While erroneous convictions are found throughout the criminal justice system, the consequences of these errors are especially serious in capital cases. The history of capital punishment—in this country and elsewhere, in the distant past as well as today—is a history of erroneous convictions and executions. The range and variety of irreversible errors in the death penalty system is sobering:

- The defendant was convicted of a murder, rape, or other capital crime that never occurred.
- A capital crime was committed, but the wrong person was tried, convicted, sentenced, and executed.
- The defendant did kill the victim but was insane, mentally retarded, or otherwise not fully responsible.
- The defendant did kill the victim but the killing was in self-defense.
- The defendant did kill the victim but the killing was accidental.
- The defendant did kill the victim but because of incompetent trial counsel or other error he was wrongly convicted of first-degree (capital) murder instead of another type of criminal homicide.
- It is not known whether the defendant was guilty because his guilt and punishment were settled by a lynch mob, not by trial in court.

Every jurisdiction in the United States that has used capital punishment has imposed it on one or more defendants in one or more of these erroneous ways. What is truly amazing is the extent to which advocates of America's current death penalty system have disregarded or otherwise downplayed the significance of these irrevocable errors—as though they were relics of a distant past. Recent events suggest that this tolerance and complacency is wearing thin, however, as legislatures, governors, trial and appellate judges—state and federal—are reeling from the impact of a wide variety of research and scholarly studies identifying wrongful convictions in capital cases.

Without a doubt the most remarkable response to this research so far is also the most recent: the decision this past July by Manhattan federal district court judge Jed S. Rakoff in *United States v. Alan Quinones.* Judge Rakoff ruled that the 1994 federal death penalty statute is unconstitutional because enforcing it poses "an undue risk of executing innocent people." On July 2, 2002, the *New York Times* quoted Harvard's constitutional-law scholar Laurence H. Tribe as saying: "I've been thinking about this issue in a serious way for at least 20 years, and this is the first fresh, new and convincing argument that I've seen." In that same issue, the *Times* editorial page observed that while the decision might be reversed on appeal, "it offers a cogent, powerful argument that all members of Congress—indeed, all Americans—should contemplate."

Scope of the Problem

The issue of wrongful convictions, sentences, and executions in the United States has its terminus ad quem for the present in the release in April 2002 of Arizona death row prisoner Ray Milton Krone, the 100th capital defendant to be released on grounds of innocence in the past 30 years, that is, since the death penalty was re-introduced in the mid-1970s. The terminus a quo for research on this grim subject was the study "Miscarriages of Justice in Potentially Capital Cases" by Michael L. Radelet and me, published in the *Stanford Law Review* in November 1987. That article was the first extensive and documented report on the subject—expanded (with co-author Constance E. Putnam) in our book *In Spite of Innocence* (1992)—covering the entire nation for most of the 20th century.

We co-authors were most impressed with several findings that no prior research had uncovered:

- All but six of America's death penalty jurisdictions had at least one case of wrongful conviction in a capital case.
- The most frequent cause of error was perjury by prosecution witnesses.
- The discovery of error and its rectification was usually not achieved by official participants in the system of criminal justice but by others, in spite of the system.
- In some two dozen cases, reprieve or other form of clemency leading to eventual vindication came just days or even hours before the scheduled execution.
- In all but three dozen of the 350 cases reported in the initial research, the innocence of the convicted defendant was recognized by pardon, indemnity, acquittal or retrial, or some other official action.

Critics typically have ignored these findings and refused to acknowledge the scope of the problem revealed by this research. Instead, they have concentrated on disputing the finding that among the wrongful convictions were two dozen innocent men who had been executed. The critics were quick to respond with various objections, including these three: First, all but one of the innocent-executed cases were pre-*Furman* thus could be dismissed as ancient history, with no relevance to post-*Furman* statutory safeguards. Second, reexamination of several of the cases tended to confirm rather than disconfirm the trial court's verdict of guilty. Third, no government official in the years under study had ever gone on record admitting that he had been (an innocent) party to, or even knew of, a wrongful conviction that ended in the execution of an innocent defendant.

Perhaps the critics will reconsider their confidence that no innocent persons have been executed when they examine the findings in the recent re-investigation by James Acker and his associates of the eight New York cases in our list (one-third of the two dozen at issue). Acker et al., endorse our judgment that all eight were innocent. (See Acker, et al., "No Appeal From the Grave: Innocence, Capital Punishment, and the Lessons of History," in Westervelt and Humphrey, *Wrongly Convicted: Perspectives on Failed Justice* 154–173 (2001).

New Research

Since the work of Radelet, Bedau, and Putnam in 1992, important additional research has been undertaken by several different sets of authors, all of whom have published their results within the past three years. Heading the list by a wide margin is the well named study, *A Broken System: Error Rates in Capital Cases, 1973–1995,* by James S. Liebman, professor of law at Columbia University, and his associates. Part 1 of the Liebman report appeared in the summer of 2000; Part II became available in February 2002. . . . The same consideration applies to the second study, the report and recommendations (of April 2002) to Illinois Governor George Ryan by the special commission he created in March 2000. . . .

At about the same time the Illinois Commission tendered its report, Harvard Law School was host to a conference on "Wrongful Convictions: A Call to Action." The full-day conference was co-sponsored by the Boston law firm of Testa, Hurwitz, and Thibault, and by the New England Innocence Project (an affiliate of the Innocence Project created at Cardozo Law School by Barry Scheck and Peter Neufeld). Although not presenting new research as such and not confined to wrongful convictions in capital cases, the conference proceedings (available on tape from the Criminal Justice Institute, Harvard Law School) amplified printed materials distributed to the participants in a volume of nearly 800 pages, reprinting 56 articles, documents, memoranda, and reports—a virtual omnium gatherum on all aspects of the topic.

Death Penalty

Among the many books on the death penalty published in recent years (I discussed nine of them in my essay-review in *Boston Review* for April/May 2002), only two have much to offer by way of original research that bears on the problem before us,

and neither is confined to death penalty cases. One is *Wrongly Convicted: Perspectives on Failed Justice,* edited by Saundra D. Westervelt and John A. Humphrey (2001). The 14 chapters, each by a different author or authors, are grouped into four parts: the causes of wrongful convictions, the social characteristics of wrongfully convicted prisoners, illustrative case studies, and prospects for the future. The other book is *Actual Innocence: Five Days to Execution, and Other Dispatches from the Wrongly Convicted* (2000, revised 2001), by attorneys Barry Scheck and Peter Neufeld and journalist Jim Dwyer. *Actual Innocence* is largely devoted to narratives of cases where DNA testing came to the rescue, including what the authors seem to believe was the first such case a decade ago (1992) in New York.

These books are particularly interesting due to their broadened scope. Since capital cases represent a small percentage of all criminal convictions, a reasonable inference can be drawn that large numbers of wrongful convictions occur in non-capital cases. Cases involving biological evidence, whether capital or not, are also a small percentage of all criminal cases, so the DNA exonerations examined in *Actual Innocence,* for example, may indicate a similar conclusion. That is, wrongful convictions likely occur in cases without evidence that can be tested as reliably as can biological evidence with DNA technology.

Use of DNA

No doubt the salient factor in the public's interest in the problem of convicting the innocent is the discovery that DNA could be put to forensic uses and provide virtually unassailable evidence for or against the guilt of an accused—at least in those cases (as in rape or felony-murder-rape) where traces of DNA are available and relevant. Evidence of this sort was not available in 1987, but it was by 1994; the case of Kirk Bloodsworth (wrongly convicted of rape-murder in 1983 and released from Maryland's death row a decade later) pioneered the use of DNA results to free a prisoner on death row.

Forensic evidence from DNA testing has also had a powerful impact on courts and legislatures, and it is perhaps the dominant reform in the entire system of criminal justice currently sought by those who appreciate the impact such testing can have on the question of the guilt of the accused. As Scheck and Neufeld observed in their article in the Westervelt and Humphrey book, "Nothing comparable has ever happened in the history of American jurisprudence; indeed nothing like it has happened to any judicial system anywhere."

A Cottage Industry

Recounting stories by or about innocent men released from death row verges on becoming a cottage industry. Two among the many recent additions, not surprisingly, are accounts of Illinois cases. Thomas Frisbie and Randy Garrett, in *Victims of Justice* (1998), tell the story of Alejandro Hernandez and Rolando Cruz, who spent 14 years on death row. David Protess and Rob Warden, in *A Promise of Justice* (1998), tell the story of Dennis Williams (12 years in prison) and Verneal Jimerson (18 years on death row). . . .

In 1987, Bedau and Radelet reported that the most frequent causes of wrongful convictions in capital cases, in descending order of frequency, were: perjury by prosecution witnesses; mistaken eyewitness identification; coerced or otherwise false confession; inadequate consideration of alibi evidence; and suppression by the police or prosecution of exculpatory evidence. The two cases involving the four Illinois defendants mentioned above fall into this pattern. Jimerson was a victim of perjured testimony suborned by the prosecution. William's alibi testimony proved unpersuasive to the jury, and his attorney was incompetent by any reasonable standard. Cruz and his co-defendant were above all victims of perjury by prosecution witnesses, as well as of excessive prosecutorial zeal, erroneous expert testimony, and misleading physical evidence. In short, the causes of error in these cases were the usual ones.

Also in 1987, Bedau and Radelet reported what their data showed to be the most frequent scenarios of vindication, again in descending order of frequent: The defense attorney persists in post-trial efforts to establish his client's innocence; the real culprit confesses; a new witness comes forward; a journalist or other writer exposes the error; a private citizen discovers the error. Cruz and his co-defendant were rescued by the confession of the real murderer; the dogged efforts of a cadre of defense lawyers, and DNA evidence. Verneal Jimerson and his co-defendants were rescued by the detective work of Protess's journalism class at Northwestern University—a perfect illustration of the principle that vindication comes not because of but in spite of the system.

"Legal Lynching"

Thanks to the work of capital defense lawyers—several of whom (Stephan Bright, David Bruck, Bryan Stevenson, Ronald Tabak, Frank Zimring, and especially Anthony Amsterdam) are well known through their lectures and writing—other lawyers and the law-review reading public have been thoroughly educated in the woefully unsatisfactory practices by the defense, the prosecution, and the judiciary in their handling of capital cases at trial and on appeal. This mismanagement, plus the overwhelming evidence that the part of the nation where a death penalty culture is most entrenched is in the southern states of the Old Confederacy, has sparked interest in the connection between yesterday's unlawful lynchings and today's lawful executions. So far, however, to the best of my knowledge the only serious attempt to connect lynching and the death penalty was in passing references by James W. Marquart, Sheldon Ekland-Olson, and Jonathan R. Sorenson, in their monograph, *The Rope, the Chair, and the Needle: Capital Punishment in Texas, 1923–1990* (1994). Nowhere is the connection more provocatively brought to public attention than in the title of the recent book, *Legal Lynching* (2001), by Jesse Jackson, his son, Jesse Jr., and journalist Bruce Shapiro.

Taken strictly, of course, "legal lynching" is an oxymoron, and it is tempting to dismiss the whole idea out of hand as a distorting exaggeration. But to do so would be a grave mistake. First, the mentality that once tolerated—indeed, demanded—lynching a century ago can be seen today in the mentality that tolerates—indeed, demands—continuation of our badly flawed death penalty system. Second, the states that historically were the sites of the most frequent lawless executions—lynchings—are also the states with the greatest frequency of lawful executions today. Third, the complete disregard for due process of law and the rule of law manifest in a lynching survives in the indifference and disrespect for law as the instrument of justice to be found in many (most?) capital cases. Fourth, just as the paradigm lynchings in American history were carried out by white mobs on helpless black men as a populist method of ruthless social control, so the death penalty is to a troubling extent a socially approved practice of white-on-black violence, especially where the crimes involved are black-on-white. Fifth, many of those who opposed lynching in the South relied on the argument that the death penalty could do under color of law what lynching did lawlessly—and the record of abandonment in capital cases of any but the thinnest pretense of due process proved the point. Sixth, in cases where a posse was formed to hunt down an accused with the intention of killing him on the spot, rather than merely taking him into custody, it is virtually impossible to tell whether the killing should be judged murder by a mob or a quasi-legal summary execution.

Finally, just as the defense of lynching a century ago was predicated on states' rights and vigorous resistance to federal interference with local self-government, the attack on federal habeas corpus for state capital defendants takes refuge today, to some extent, in the same hostility to judicial intervention from Washington, D.C. (This is obscured by the Supreme Court's own inconsistent attempts to regulate the nation's death penalty system, which often puts judicial restraint, respect for federalism, and deference to the legislatures ahead of substantive justice under the Bill of Rights.) One way to view the current moratorium movement, insofar as it is supported by those who seek to defend the death penalty, is to see it as the latest nationwide effort to erase the many disturbing parallels between the lynching practices of a century ago and the death penalty practices of our own day.

Reforms

This naturally leads us to inquire about the proposed reforms aimed at reducing the likelihood of convicting the innocent. The subject is too large to address in this essay-review, nor do any of the books and articles under discussion have a monopoly on recommended reforms. Furthermore, the various voices being heard are too many to summarize and evaluate here. Frequently if not unanimously recommended are two reforms: Obtain DNA evidence wherever possible, and exempt the mentally retarded from liability to a death sentence. This latter recommendation in fact became law under the Supreme Court's ruling this past June in *Atkins v. Virginia*.

Liebman and his associates in *A Broken System* confined their 10 reform recommendations to death penalty jurisprudence. Although one of them—abolishing judicial override of the jury's sentencing decision—has become law, thanks to the Supreme Court's ruling this past June in *Ring v. Arizona,* some of their other recommendations may have a longer and rough road to adoption. These include: Requiring proof of guilt "beyond *any* doubt" in a capital case; insulating sentencing and appellate judges who deal with capital cases from "political pressure"; and increasing compensation for capital defense lawyers to provide incentives for "well-qualified lawyers" to do the work.

Mandatory Justice: Eighteen Reforms to the Death Penalty, was released last year by The Constitution Project, part of Georgetown University's Public Policy Institute. Among its recommendations are these four: Adopt a better standard for incompetence of defense counsel than is provided by *Strickland v. Washington;* enact LWOP (life in prison without possibility of parole) as the alternative to the death sentence; conduct proportionality review of all capital convictions and sentences; and treat the jury's "lingering doubt" over the defendant's guilt as a mitigating circumstance in the sentencing phase.

Controlling Evidence

Scheck, Neufeld, and Dwyer offer a list of 40 proposed reforms. Seven of them would restrict the admissibility of eyewitness testimony. Fourteen others are devoted to controlling the evidence tendered by jailhouse snitches. Another 14 would constrain forensic laboratories and the use of their findings. Two of their proposed reforms would be relatively easy to implement; use sequential rather than simultaneous presentation of suspects in police lineups, and videotape all interrogations.

Governor Ryan's Commission on Capital Punishment has produced by far the greatest number of recommendations—no fewer than 85. Nineteen are addressed to police and pre-trial practices; the Commission also joins with Scheck et al. in endorsing videotaping of interrogations and in favoring a sequential lineup. Seven of their recommendations address the role of forensic evidence, and of course they urge wider use of DNA testing. Prosecutorial selection of which homicide cases will be tried as capital cases—one of the most troubling and unregulated areas in capital punishment jurisprudence—is the subject of three proposed reforms.

Ten of the recommendations are aimed at overhauling pre-trial proceedings, including use by the prosecution of testimony by informants in custody ("jailhouse snitches"). They would not bar such testimony; instead, the Commission would require that the defense be fully informed of the prosecution's intention to use such testimony, and that the "uncorroborated testimony" of such a witness "may not be the sole basis for imposition of a death penalty." The Commission agrees with Liebman et al. in favoring "adequate compensation" for trial counsel (although their Recommendation 80 is unfortunately unclear about comparable compensation for defense counsel in post-conviction litigation).

What are we to make of these 150 recommendations (some of which overlap with each other)? Could we imagine a conference devoted to achieving a consensus on reform in which, say, 15 or 20 of these proposals received unanimous endorsement? Could the Supreme Court be persuaded to adopt some if not all of these reforms, just as it has adopted two new rules in *Ring* and *Atkins* this past spring? Or could state legislatures take it upon themselves to introduce some of these reforms, without waiting for the Supreme Court to act? We should have answers to these questions within the next few years.

The Struggle Continues

The Illinois Commission has done its work well and left us with a comprehensive set of model reforms. Taken together with the reforms proposed by Scheck and Liebman and their associates, lawyers, legislators, and the general public have a set of proposals that—if put into practice—would appreciably improve the system in both capital and non-capital cases. Moratorium study commissions in other states could provide re-inforcement on several proposed reforms as well. Yet everything turns on the willingness of legislatures to enact statutes that incorporate reforms. Friends of the death penalty can hardly complain if these reforms narrow the range of death-eligible defendants and increase the economic costs of the entire system, any more than its critics can complain if good-faith adoption of these reforms breathes new life into our current "broken" and deregulated death penalty system.

If the past three decades of struggle over the future of capital punishment in this country have taught us anything, it is this: The appellants in *Gregg v. Georgia* (1976) were right, and the Supreme Court was wrong. The reforms that emerged in the wake of *Furman* (1972) inspired by the Supreme Court's ruling have turned out, to a disturbing extent, to be merely "cosmetic." Astute observers of the system argued even then that it was impossible to design reforms that would be effective in bringing greater fairness into the death penalty system and still serve rational goals of deterrence, incapacitation, and retribution. Whether the death penalty system in this country that would be created if these reforms are enacted will prove to be otherwise cannot be foretold. What can be predicted is that pressure for complete abolition will not vanish or even subside. The struggle over the nation's soul will continue for some time to come.

MR. BEDAU is professor emeritus at Tufts University. From "Causes and Consequences of Wrongful Convictions: An Essay-Review," by Hugo Adam Bedau, *Judicature*. September/October 2002, pages 115–119.

Reforming Juvenile Justice

A century ago, reformers proved that prisons don't help wayward children. Now America is learning that lesson all over again.

BARRY KRISBERG

I n 1899, Illinois and Colorado established a new "Children's Court." The idea was to substitute treatment and care for punishment of delinquent youths. These changes were promoted by child advocates such as the famous social activist Jane Addams and crusading judges like Denver's Ben Lindsey, as well as influential women's organizations and bar associations. Over the next 20 years, the concept of a separate court system for minors spread to most states. Although the new children's court movement lacked adequate resources to fulfill its lofty mission, the intellectual promise was virtually unchallenged for two-thirds of the 20th century.

Several key assumptions lay behind the juvenile-court idea. First, children were not just "small adults," and they needed to be handled differently. Second, there was a need for specially trained legal and correctional professionals to work with minors. Third, placing children in adult prisons and jails made them more antisocial and criminal. And finally, the emerging science of rehabilitation could rescue many of these troubled young people from lives of crime. In the intervening years, a wealth of research has validated each of these premises.

Despite broad support within the academic, legal, and social-work professions, the ideal often failed to live up to its promise. Over time, the juvenile-justice system in many states reverted to the punitive approach it was designed to replace. Though they were often called "training schools," the institutions were juvenile prisons. And the premise that the court, by definition, was acting "in the best interest of the child" left young offenders without the rights guaranteed to adult criminal defendants. There were repeated accounts of abusive practices. The duration of confinement was often unrelated to the severity of the offense. Juvenile hearings were usually secret, with no written transcripts and no right to appeal. Minors were not provided legal counsel, there were no safeguards against self-incrimination, and offenders were denied liberty without the due process of law guaranteed by the U.S. Constitution.

A series of legal challenges culminated in the landmark 1967 Supreme Court decision *In Re Gault.* Writing for the Court, Justice Abe Fortes proclaimed, "Under our Constitution, the condition of being a boy does not justify a kangaroo court." Reviewing the case of 15-year-old Gerald Gault, who was sentenced to six years in an Arizona youth correctional facility for making an obscene phone call, the Court decreed that minors be afforded most of the due-process rights required in adult criminal courts.

Gault signaled a new era of reforms. One was a movement to divert as many youths as possible from the formal court system and to decriminalize "juvenile status offenses" such as truancy, running away, curfew violations, and incorrigibility. The 1970s witnessed widespread efforts to deinstitutionalize or "decarcerate" youngsters, moving them from secure detention centers and training schools to community-based programs that emphasized education and rehabilitation.

The most dramatic example came in 1972 in Massachusetts, where a respected reformer closed all of the state juvenile facilities and started over. Jerome Miller had been recruited to the state Department of Youth Services (DYS) to clean up a range of scandals and abuses. He encountered an intransigent bureaucracy. Corrections officers opposed even such modest reforms as letting youngsters wear street clothing instead of prison uniforms, or not requiring that their heads be completely shaven. Undeterred, Miller decided to close down the state's network of jail-like training schools. As the young inmates of the notorious Lyman School were loaded onto a bus that would take them to dorms at the University of Massachusetts, to be housed temporarily until being reassigned to community programs, one top Miller deputy proclaimed to the shocked guards, "You can have the institutions; we are taking the kids."

The training schools were replaced with a diverse network of small residential programs, typically with 25 children or fewer, located closer to the youths' home communities. A range of non-residential programs included day reporting centers and intensive home-based supervision. The DYS continued to operate about half of the most secure facilities. Private nonprofits were recruited to run the rest, as well as all of the community-based programs.

Although Miller left Massachusetts soon after becoming the department's youth-services commissioner, the Bay State continued to expand and refine the alternatives to the old prison-like training schools and never reopened the large juvenile institutions. Research by Harvard Law School and my organization, the National Council on Crime and Delinquency, showed that the Miller reforms successfully reduced the frequency and severity of new offenses of youth in the new programs compared with the training-school graduates.

As the Massachusetts model spread to many other states, Congress in 1974 created the federal Juvenile Justice and Delinquency Prevention Act, with bipartisan backing. The act established a federal

Office of Juvenile Justice and Delinquency Prevention (OJJDP) to conduct research, provide training, and make grants to states and jurisdictions that voluntarily complied with the act's mandates. The new law required participating states to remove status offenders and dependency cases from secure confinement, and to separate juveniles from adults by "sight and sound" in correctional facilities. In 1980, the act was amended to require that participating states remove minors from jails. Forty-eight states participated.

Miller went on to implement variations of his Massachusetts reforms in Pennsylvania and Illinois. Other states that broadly followed Miller's model included jurisdictions as politically diverse as Utah, Missouri, and Vermont. Often, publicity about abusive conditions in state facilities and lawsuits in federal courts catalyzed these reforms. From 1980 into the 1990s, Colorado, Indiana, Oklahoma, Maryland, Louisiana, Florida, Georgia, Rhode Island, and New Jersey were among states that began closing large, prison-like youth facilities. For a time, it appeared that the Miller reforms would become the "gold standard" for juvenile corrections, as the federal OJJDP provided training and support to jurisdictions seeking to replicate the Massachusetts approach.

> **The much-advertised generation of super-predators never materialized. After 1993, serious juvenile crime began a decade-long decline to historically low levels.**

The Invention of the "Super-Predator"

The rejection in some quarters of a reform model reflects both ideological preconceptions and misinformation about juvenile crime. Rates of serious violent juvenile crime as measured by the National Crime Survey were relatively constant between 1973 and 1989, then briefly rose by more than one-third and peaked in 1993. Some cited demographics, as the children of the baby boomers reached their teenage years. Others pointed to an epidemic of crack cocaine that fueled urban violence, as well as high unemployment and declining economic prospects for low-skilled workers, especially among minority groups. No one really knows for sure. But fear of a violent juvenile crime wave led some to predict a new cohort of "super-predators." Conservative academics such as James Q. Wilson and John DiIulio and a small band of mainstream criminologists such as Alfred Blumstein and James Fox forecast societal disaster. Wilson predicted "30,000 more young muggers, killers, and thieves"; DiIulio in 1990 foresaw another 270,000 violent juveniles by 2010. He warned of a "crime bomb" created by a generation of "fatherless, godless, and jobless [juvenile] super-predators."

The media hyped the story, and many elected officials exploited it. The citizenry was told about a generation of babies, born to "crack-addicted" mothers, who would possess permanent neurological damage, including the inability to feel empathy. The scientific evidence supporting this claim was nonexistent. More than 40 states made it easier to transfer children to adult criminal courts. Educators enacted "zero-tolerance" policies to make it easier to expel youngsters from school, and numerous communities adopted youth curfews. Many jurisdictions turned to metal detectors in public schools, random locker searches, drug tests for athletes, and mandatory school uniforms.

The panic was bipartisan. Every crime bill debated by Congress during the Clinton administration included new federal laws against juvenile crime. Paradoxically, as Attorney General Janet Reno advocated for wider and stronger social safety nets for vulnerable families, President Bill Clinton joined congressional leaders demanding tougher treatment of juvenile felons, including more incarceration in both the adult and youth correctional systems.

However, the much-advertised generation of super-predators never materialized. After 1993, rates of serious juvenile crime began a decade-long decline to historically low levels. And this juvenile crime drop happened before the tougher juvenile penalties were even implemented. The fear-mongering social scientists had based their dire predictions on grossly inaccurate data and faulty reasoning, but the creators of the super-predator myth prevailed in the public-policy arena throughout most of the '90s. As we approached the centennial of the American juvenile court, it looked like the juvenile-justice ideal was dying.

The Ideal of Juvenile Justice Survives

Despite adverse political currents, the juvenile-justice ideal has received a new lease on life thanks to pioneering efforts by states and by foundations, as well as the continuing programmatic influence of the federal approach begun in the 1970s and expanded during the Clinton-Reno era.

One key initiative of the federal OJJDP is known as Balanced and Restorative Justice. This approach, now embraced by many jurisdictions, places a major value on involving victims in the rehabilitative process. By coming to terms with harm done to victims, the youthful offender is also offered a way to restore his or her role in the community.

The second significant federal program is the Justice Department's Comprehensive Strategy for Serious, Violent, and Chronic Juvenile Offenders, first adopted in 1993. The research showed that a very small number of offenders committed most serious juvenile crimes, and that identification and control of these "dangerous few" was key. However, unlike the response to the supposed super-predators, this strategy does not call for an across-the-board crackdown on at-risk youth. A comprehensive body of research assembled by two senior Justice Department juvenile-justice officials, John J. Wilson and James C. Howell, showed that prevention was the most cost-effective response to youth crime, and that strengthening the family and other core institutions was the most important goal for a youth-crime-control strategy.

The proposed comprehensive strategy was adopted by Reno as the official policy position of the Justice Department in all matters relating to juvenile crime, and the program was successfully implemented in more than 50 communities nationwide. The basic idea was to help local leaders build their youth-service systems to provide "the right service, for the right youth, at the right time." This collaborative planning process helped policy-makers and professionals to debunk the myths about juvenile crime and to learn about interventions that were proven, as well as to foster more cooperative activities among multiple agencies. Most important, the effort showed community participants how to effectively respond to juvenile lawbreaking without resorting to mass-incarceration policies.

A third major national reform movement was launched by the Annie E. Casey Foundation in 1992. The goal: to reduce the overuse of juvenile-detention facilities and to redirect funding toward more effective services for at-risk youngsters. The foundation also sought to improve the conditions of confinement for detained youth and to reduce the overrepresentation of minority youths in detention.

The Casey Foundation approach required a multiagency planning process and included the development of improved risk screening, expansion of options for most detained youths, and efforts to expedite the processing of cases. After initial demonstration projects, the foundation has expanded the program to scores of communities. It also offers technical assistance and convenes an annual meeting. At the last such convening, in San Francisco, more than 700 people from across the nation gathered to discuss ways to further reduce unnecessary juvenile detention. The original demonstration project has led to a vibrant national movement, which includes high-quality replication manuals and a documentary, plus academic and professional publications.

These approaches all require collaborations among many sectors of the community. They all employ data and evidence-based practices to guide the reform agenda. Diversity is recognized as vital because one-size-fits-all programs usually fail. Instead, they seek to create a comprehensive continuum of appropriate services. Preventive strategies and early interventions are viewed as far more cost-effective than punitive approaches. All these programs place a great emphasis on involving youth, plus their families and neighbors, in shaping solutions. The core values of the juvenile-justice ideal continue to live. Like the reform impulse of a century ago, the goal is to commit the juvenile-justice system to pursuing the best interests of the child, to strengthening family and community solutions to youth misconduct, and to emphasizing humane and fair treatment of the young.

In spite of the promise embodied in approaches like these, unlawful and brutal practices continue to plague youth correctional facilities in many states. Some jurisdictions are being investigated by the federal government for statutory and constitutional violations of the rights of institutionalized minors. In other locales, advocates for young people are successfully litigating against youth detention and corrections facilities. At the same time, the political hysteria surrounding the super-predator myth appears to be in remission. The chorus is growing to reject approaches such as youth correctional boot camps or "scared straight" programs that use prison visits to try to frighten youngsters away from criminal lives. While some of these dangerous programs continue to exist, many jurisdictions have shut them down. There is growing awareness about the prevalence of mental illness among institutionalized youngsters and the emergence of several initiatives to better meet their health-care needs.

This year's most positive development was the Supreme Court's decision to end the death penalty for those younger than 18 at the time of their offense. But this progress does not minimize the severe problems of the juvenile-justice system. Funding for services for troubled young people in the juvenile-justice and child-welfare systems remains woefully inadequate. Young people still do not have anything resembling adequate legal representation. Too many continue to be banished to the criminal-court system and languish in adult prisons. And racism, sexism, and class biases continue to tarnish the promise of equal justice for all.

The Way Forward

This *American Prospect* special supplement includes reports from places as diverse as California, Texas, New Mexico, Missouri, and Louisiana. All suggest that reform coalitions, often with strange bedfellows, can acknowledge the superiority of the reform approach and change practices that dehumanize young people and fail to reduce juvenile crime. By now the evidence is clear: Small, community-based approaches that stress prevention, education, and restitution rather than prison-like punishment are simply better policy. At the same time, as Ellis Cose recounts, racial disparities remain immense. And as Sam Rosenfeld reports, far too many children who need mental-health services are being dumped into the juvenile-justice system.

Given the overwhelming evidence that reform works, why is there continuing resistance? The answer to this question is complex. First and foremost, since the mid-'60s, crime policy in the United States has been heavily politicized. Democrats and Republicans have competed to position themselves as tough on crime. Being perceived as soft on juvenile offenders is considered a political liability. Second, the media continue to exaggerate the amount of violent crime committed by minors. Isolated stories about vicious crimes that are committed by very young adolescents are widely disseminated and become the grist for talk radio and other media commentary. The simplistic solution has been that tough responses to juvenile crime will deter youthful offenders.

Resistance to proven juvenile-justice models often comes from public-employee unions that fear the loss of jobs as traditional youth correctional facilities are downsized and some funding goes to community-based organizations. Also, severe state and local budget problems have led to a retrenchment in needed services, even as more innovative juvenile-justice models could actually save money. In some locales, organizations purporting to represent families of crime victims have lobbied for tougher penalties for juvenile offenders.

Progressive reforms are often undercut by entrenched biases about the predominantly poor and minority families caught up in the juvenile-justice system. These racial, ethnic, and class prejudices are too often reinforced by media reports that breed fear among the electorate about the "barbarians at the gates." As long as economic and fiscal pressures fuel anxiety over immigrants, the increased competition for jobs, and the deteriorating public-school system, it will be hard to generate compassionate and rational responses for youthful lawbreakers.

Jerome Miller once observed that the history of juvenile justice reflects a pattern of abuse and scandal followed by humanistic changes, but then a return to the previous conditions and bad practices. In a new millennium, one can only hope that proponents of the juvenile-justice ideal can figure out how to end this tragic cycle.

BARRY KRISBERG is president of the National Council on Crime and Delinquency, which is based in Oakland, California.

America Incarcerated
Crime, Punishment, and the Question of Race

GLENN C. LOURY

The early 1990s were the age of drive-by shootings, drug deals gone bad, crack cocaine, and gangsta rap. Between 1960 and 1990, the annual number of murders in New Haven, Connecticut, rose from 6 to 31, the number of rapes from 4 to 168, the number of robberies from 16 to 1,784—all this while the city's population declined by 14 percent. Crime was concentrated in central cities: In 1990 two-fifths of Pennsylvania's violent crimes were committed in Philadelphia, home to one-seventh of the state's population. The subject of crime dominated American domestic-policy debates.

Most observers at the time expected things to get worse. Consulting demographic tables and extrapolating trends, scholars and pundits warned the public to prepare for an onslaught, and for a new kind of criminal—the anomic, vicious, irreligious, amoral juvenile "superpredator." In 1995 one academic commentator predicted a "bloodbath" of juvenile violence in 2005.

And so we prepared. Stoked by fear and political opportunism, but also by the need to address a very real social problem, we threw lots of people in jail, and when the old prisons were filled we built new ones.

But the onslaught never came. Crime rates peaked in 1992 and have dropped sharply since. Even as crime rates fell, however, imprisonment rates continued their upward march. The result, the current American prison system, is a leviathan unmatched in human history.

According to a 2005 report of the International Centre for Prison Studies in London, the United States—with 5 percent of the world's population—houses 25 percent of the world's inmates. Our incarceration rate (714 per 100,000 residents) is almost 40 percent greater than those of our nearest competitors (Bermuda, Belarus, and Russia). Other industrial democracies, even those with significant crime problems of their own, are much less punitive: Our incarceration rate is 6.2 times that of Canada, 7.8 times that of France, and 12.3 times that of Japan. We have a corrections sector that employs more Americans than the combined workforces of General Motors, Ford, and Wal-Mart, the three largest corporate employers in the country, and we are spending some $200 billion annually on law enforcement and corrections at all levels of government, a fourfold increase (in constant dollars) over the past quarter century.

Never before has a supposedly free country denied basic liberty to so many of its citizens. In June 2006 some 2.25 million people were being held in the nearly 5,000 prisons and jails that are scattered across America's urban and rural landscapes. One-third of inmates in state prisons are violent criminals, convicted of homicide, rape, or robbery. The other two-thirds consist mainly of property and drug

> The United States—with 5 percent of the world's population—houses 25 percent of the world's inmates.
>
> Our incarceration rate is 6.2 times that of Canada, 7.8 times that of France, and 12.3 times that of Japan.
>
> A black male resident of the state of California is more likely to go to a state prison than to a state college.

offenders. Inmates are disproportionately drawn from the most disadvantaged parts of society. On average, state inmates have fewer than 11 years of schooling. They are also vastly disproportionately black and brown.

How did it come to this? One argument is that the massive increase in incarceration reflects the success of a rational public policy: Faced with a compelling social problem, we responded by imprisoning people and succeeded in lowering crime rates. This argument is not entirely misguided. Increased incarceration does appear to have reduced crime somewhat. But by how much? Estimates of the share of the 1990s reduction in violent crime that can be attributed to the prison boom range from 5 percent to 25 percent. Whatever the number, analysts of all political stripes now agree that we have long ago entered the zone of diminishing returns. The conservative scholar John DiIulio, who coined the term *superpredator* in the mid-1990s, was by the end of that decade declaring in a *Wall Street Journal* headline that "Two Million Prisoners Are Enough." But there was no political movement for getting America out of the mass-incarceration business. The throttle was stuck.

A more convincing argument is that imprisonment rates have continued to rise while crime rates have fallen because we have become progressively more punitive: not because crime has continued to explode (it hasn't), not because we made smart policy choices, but because we have made a collective decision to increase the rate of punishment.

One simple measure of punitiveness is the likelihood that a person who is arrested will be subsequently incarcerated. Between 1980 and 2001 there was no real change in the chances of being arrested in response to a complaint: The rate was just under 50 percent. But the likelihood that an arrest would result in imprisonment more than doubled, from 13 to 28 percent. And because the amount of time served and the rate of prison admission both increased, the incarceration rate for violent crime almost tripled, despite the decline in the level of violence.

The incarceration rate for nonviolent and drug offenses increased at an even faster pace: Between 1980 and 2001 the number of people incarcerated for nonviolent offenses tripled, and the number of people incarcerated for drug offenses increased by a factor of 11. Indeed, the criminal-justice researcher Alfred Blumstein has argued that none of the growth in incarceration between 1980 and 1996 can be attributed to more crime:

> The growth was entirely attributable to a growth in punitiveness, about equally to growth in prison commitments per arrest (an indication of tougher prosecution or judicial sentencing) and to longer time served (an indication of longer sentences, elimination of parole or later parole release, or greater readiness to recommit parolees to prison for either technical violations or new crimes).

This growth in punitiveness was accompanied by a shift in thinking about the basic purpose of criminal justice. Until the 1970s, the sociologist David Garland argues, the corrections system was commonly seen as a way to prepare offenders to rejoin society. Since then, the focus has shifted from rehabilitation to punishment and stayed there. Felons are no longer persons to be supported, but risks to be dealt with. And the way to deal with the risks is to keep them locked up. As of 2000, 33 states had abolished limited parole (up from 17 in 1980); 24 states had introduced three-strikes laws (up from zero); and 40 states had introduced truth-in-sentencing laws (up from 3). The vast majority of these changes occurred in the 1990s, as crime rates fell.

This new system of punitive ideas is aided by a new relationship between the media, the politicians, and the public. A handful of cases in which a predator does an awful thing to an innocent get excessive media attention and engender public outrage. This attention typically bears no relation to the frequency of the particular type of crime, yet laws—such as three-strikes laws that can give mandatory life sentences to nonviolent drug offenders—and political careers are made on the basis of the public's reaction to media coverage of such crimes.

Despite a sharp national decline in crime, American criminal justice has become crueler and less caring than it has been at any other time in our modern history. Why?

The question has no simple answer, but the racial composition of prisons is a good place to start. The punitive turn in the nation's social policy—intimately connected with public rhetoric about responsibility, dependency, social hygiene, and the reclamation of public order—can be fully grasped only when it is viewed against the backdrop of America's often ugly and violent racial history. There is a reason why our inclination toward forgiveness and the extension of a second chance to those who have violated our behavioral strictures is so stunted, and why our mainstream political discourses are so bereft of self-examination and searching social criticism.

This historical resonance between the stigma of race and the stigma of imprisonment serves to keep alive in our public culture the subordinating social meanings that have always been associated with blackness. Race helps to explain why the United States is exceptional among the democratic industrial societies in the severity and extent of its punitive policy and in the paucity of its social-welfare institutions.

Slavery ended a long time ago, but the institution of chattel slavery and the ideology of racial subordination that accompanied it have cast a long shadow. I speak here of the history of lynching throughout the country; the racially biased policing and judging in the South under Jim Crow and in the cities of the Northeast, Midwest, and West to which blacks migrated after the First and Second World Wars; and the history of racial apartheid that ended only as a matter of law with the civil rights movement. It should come as no surprise that in the post–civil rights era, race, far from being peripheral, has been central to the evolution of American social policy.

The political scientist Vesla Mae Weaver, in a recently completed dissertation, examines policy history, public opinion, and media processes in an attempt to understand the role of race in this historic transformation of criminal justice. She argues—persuasively, I think—that the punitive turn represented a political response to the success of the civil rights movement. Weaver describes a process of "frontlash" in which opponents of the civil rights revolution sought to regain the upper hand by shifting to a new issue. Rather than reacting directly to civil rights developments, and thus continuing to fight a battle they had lost, those opponents (consider George Wallace's campaigns for the presidency, which drew so much support in states like Michigan and Wisconsin) shifted attention to a seemingly race-neutral concern over crime:

> Once the clutch of Jim Crow had loosened, opponents of civil rights shifted the "locus of attack" by injecting crime onto the agenda. Through the process of frontlash, rivals of civil rights progress defined racial discord as criminal and argued that crime legislation would be a panacea to racial unrest. This strategy both imbued crime with race and depoliticized racial struggle, a formula which foreclosed earlier "root causes" alternatives. Fusing anxiety about crime to anxiety over racial change and riots, civil rights and racial disorder—initially defined as a problem of minority disenfranchisement—were defined as a crime problem, which helped shift debate from social reform to punishment.

Of course, this argument (for which Weaver adduces considerable circumstantial evidence) is speculative. But something interesting seems to have been going on in the late 1960s regarding the relationship between attitudes on race and on social policy.

Before 1966 public attitudes on the welfare state and on race varied year to year independently of one another. You could not predict much about a person's attitudes on welfare politics by knowing the person's attitudes about race. After 1966 the attitudes moved in tandem as welfare came to be seen as a race issue. Indeed, the year-to-year correlation between an index measuring liberalism of racial attitudes and attitudes toward the welfare state over the interval 1950 to 1965 was .03. These same two series had a correlation of .68 over the period 1966 to 1996.

The association in the American mind of race with welfare, and the association of race with crime, have been achieved at a common historical moment. Crime-control institutions are part of a larger social-policy complex—they relate to and interact with the labor market, family-welfare efforts, and health and social work activities. Indeed, sociologist Garland argues that the ideological approaches to welfare and crime control have marched rightward to a common beat: "The institutional and cultural changes that have occurred in the crime control field are analogous to those that have occurred in the welfare state more generally." Just as the welfare state came to be seen as a race issue, so too, crime came to be seen as a race issue, and policies have been shaped by this perception.

Consider the tortured racial history of the war on drugs. Blacks were twice as likely as whites to be arrested for a drug offense in 1975 but five times as likely by 1988. Throughout the 1990s, drug-arrest rates remained at historically unprecedented levels. Yet according to the National Household Survey on Drug Abuse, drug use among adults fell from 20 percent in 1979 to 11 percent in 2000. A similar trend occurred among adolescents. In the age groups 12–17 and 18–25, use of marijuana, cocaine, and heroin all peaked in the late 1970s. Thus, a decline in drug use across the board had begun a decade before the draconian antidrug efforts of the 1990s were initiated.

Of course, drug usage rates and drug arrest rates needn't be expected to be identical. Still, we do well to bear in mind that the social problem of illicit drug use is endemic to our whole society. Significantly, throughout the period 1979 to 2000, white high school seniors reported using drugs at a significantly higher rate than black high school seniors. High drug-usage rates in white, middle-class American communities in the early 1980s account for the urgency many citizens felt to mount a national attack on the problem. But how successful has the effort been, and at what cost?

Think of the cost this way: To save middle-class kids from the threat of a drug epidemic—one that might not even have existed by the time that drug incarceration began its rapid increase in the 1980s—we criminalized underclass kids. Arrests went up, but drug prices have fallen sharply over the past 20 years—suggesting that ratcheting up enforcement has not made drugs harder to get on the street. The strategy clearly wasn't keeping drugs away from those who sought them. Not only are prices down, but the data show that drug-related visits to emergency rooms also rose steadily throughout the 1980s and 1990s.

An interesting case in point is New York City. Analyzing arrests by residential neighborhood and police precinct, the criminologist Jeffrey Fagan and his colleagues Valerie West and Jan Holland found that incarceration was highest in the city's poorest neighborhoods, though these were often not the neighborhoods in which crime rates were the highest. Moreover, they discovered a perverse effect of incarceration on crime: Higher incarceration in a given neighborhood in one year seemed to predict higher crime rates in that same neighborhood one year later. This growth and persistence of incarceration over time, the authors concluded, were due primarily to the drug enforcement practices of police and to sentencing laws that require imprisonment for repeat felons. Police scrutiny was more intensive and less forgiving in high-incarceration neighborhoods, and parolees returning to such neighborhoods were more closely monitored. Thus, discretionary police behavior led to a high and increasing rate of repeat prison admissions in the designated neighborhoods, even as crime rates fell.

Fagan, West, and Holland explain the effects of spatially concentrated antidrug-law enforcement in the contemporary American metropolis. Buyers may come from any neighborhood and any social stratum, but the sellers—at least the ones who can be readily found hawking their wares on street corners—come predominantly from the poorest, most nonwhite parts of the city. The police, with arrest quotas to meet, know precisely where to find them. The researchers conclude:

> Incarceration begets more incarceration, and incarceration also begets more crime, which in turn invites more aggressive enforcement, which then re-supplies incarceration. . . . Three mechanisms . . . contribute to and reinforce incarceration in neighborhoods: the declining economic fortunes of former inmates and the effects on neighborhoods where they tend to reside; resource and relationship strains on families of prisoners that weaken the family's ability to supervise children; and voter disenfranchisement that weakens the political economy of neighborhoods.

> One-third of inmates in state prisons are violent criminals, convicted of homicide, rape, or robbery. The other two-thirds consist mainly of property and drug offenders.
>
> Inmates are disproportionately drawn from the most disadvantaged parts of society. On average, state inmates have fewer than 11 years of schooling. They are also vastly disproportionately black and brown.

The effects of imprisonment on people's life chances are profound. For incarcerated black men, hourly wages are 10 percent lower after prison than before. For all incarcerated men, the number of weeks worked per year falls by at least a third after their release.

So consider the nearly 60 percent of black male high school dropouts born in the late 1960s who are imprisoned before their 40th year. While they are locked up, these felons are stigmatized—they are regarded as fit subjects for shaming. Their links to family are disrupted; their opportunities for work are diminished; their voting rights may be permanently revoked. They suffer civic excommunication. Our zeal for social discipline consigns these men to a permanent nether caste. And yet, since these men—whatever their shortcomings—often need to be fathers and lovers and husbands, we are creating a situation in which the children of this nether caste are likely to join a new generation of untouchables. This cycle will continue so long as incarceration is viewed as the primary path to social hygiene.

I have been exploring the issue of causes, of why we took the punitive turn that has resulted in mass incarceration. But even if the racial argument about causes is inconclusive, the racial consequences are clear. To be sure, in the United States, as in any society, public order is maintained by the threat and use of force. We enjoy our good lives only because we are shielded by law and order, which keep the unruly at bay. Yet in this society, to a degree virtually unmatched in any other, those bearing the brunt of order enforcement belong in vastly disproportionate numbers to historically marginalized racial groups. Crime and punishment in America has a color.

In his fine study "Punishment and Inequality in America" (2006), the Princeton University sociologist Bruce Western powerfully describes the scope, nature, and consequences of contemporary imprisonment. He finds that the extent of racial disparity in imprisonment rates is greater than in any other major arena of American social life. At eight to one, the black-to-white ratio of incarceration rates dwarfs the two-to-one ratio of unemployment rates, the three-to-one ratio of nonmarital childbearing, the two-to-one ratio of infant-mortality rates, and the one-to-five ratio of net worth. While 3 out of 200 young whites were incarcerated in 2000, 1 in 9 young blacks were. A black male resident of California is more likely to go to a state prison than to a state college.

The scandalous truth is that the police and penal apparatus are now the primary contact between black American men and the American state. Among black male high school dropouts ages 20 to 40, a third were locked up on any given day in 2000, fewer than 3 percent belonged to a union, and less than one quarter were enrolled in any kind of social program. Coercion is the most salient meaning of government for these young men. Western estimates that nearly 60 percent of black male dropouts born between 1965 and 1969 were sent to prison on a felony conviction at least once before they reached the age of 35.

> We have a corrections sector that employs more Americans than the combined work-forces of General Motors, Ford, and Wal-Mart, and we are spending some $200 billion annually on law enforcement and corrections, a fourfold increase (in constant dollars) over the past quarter century.

One cannot reckon the world-historic American prison buildup over the past 35 years without calculating the enormous costs imposed upon the persons imprisoned, their families, and their communities. (Of course, this has not stopped many social scientists from pronouncing the net benefits of incarceration without doing so.) Deciding on the weight to give to a "thug's" well-being—or to that of his wife or daughter or son—is a question of social morality, not social science. Nor can social science tell us how much additional cost borne by the offending class is justified in order to obtain a given increment of security or peace of mind for the rest of us. These are questions about the nature of the American state and its relationship to its people that transcend the categories of benefits and costs.

Yet the discourse surrounding punishment policy invariably discounts the humanity of the thieves, drug sellers, prostitutes, rapists, and, yes, those whom we put to death. It gives insufficient weight to the welfare, to the humanity, of those who are knitted together with offenders in webs of social and psychic affiliation. What is more, institutional arrangements for dealing with criminal offenders in the United States have evolved to serve expressive as well as instrumental ends. We have wanted to "send a message," and we have done so with a vengeance. In the process, we have created facts. We have answered the question, Who is to blame for the domestic maladies that beset us? We have constructed a national narrative. We have created scapegoats, indulged our need to feel virtuous, and assuaged our fears. We have met the enemy, and the enemy is them.

Incarceration keeps *them* away from *us*. Thus Garland: "The prison is used today as a kind of reservation, a quarantine zone in which purportedly dangerous individuals are segregated in the name of public safety." The boundary between prison and community, Garland continues, is "heavily patrolled and carefully monitored to prevent risks leaking out from one to the other. Those offenders who are released 'into the community' are subject to much tighter control than previously, and frequently find themselves returned to custody for failure to comply with the conditions that continue to restrict their freedom. For many of these parolees and ex-convicts, the 'community' into which they are released is actually a closely monitored terrain, a supervised space lacking much of the liberty that one associates with 'normal life.'"

Deciding how citizens of varied social rank within a common polity ought to relate to one another is a more fundamental consideration than deciding which crime-control policy is most efficient. The question of relationship, of solidarity, of who belongs to the body politic and who deserves exclusion—these are philosophical concerns of the highest order. A decent society will on occasion resist the efficient course of action, for the simple reason that to follow it would be to act as though we were not the people we have determined ourselves to be: a people conceived in liberty and dedicated to the proposition that we all are created equal. Assessing the propriety of creating a racially defined pariah class in the middle of our great cities at the start of the 21st century presents us with just such a case.

My recitation of the brutal facts about punishment in today's America may sound to some like a primal scream at this monstrous social machine that is grinding poor black communities to dust. And I confess that these brutal facts do at times incline me to cry out in despair. But my argument is analytical, not existential. Its principal thesis is this: We law-abiding, middle-class Americans have made decisions about social policy and incarceration, and we benefit from those decisions, and that means from a system of suffering, rooted in state violence, meted out at our request. We had choices and we decided to be more punitive. Our society—the society we have made—creates criminogenic conditions in our sprawling urban ghettos and then acts out rituals of punishment against them as some awful form of human sacrifice.

This situation raises a moral problem that we cannot avoid. We cannot pretend that there are more important problems in our society, or that this circumstance is the necessary solution to more pressing problems—unless we also are prepared to say that we have turned our backs on the ideal of equality for all citizens and abandoned the principles of justice. We ought to ask ourselves two questions: Just what manner of people are we Americans? And in light of this, what are our obligations to our fellow citizens—even those who break our laws?

To address these questions, we need to think about the evaluation of our prison system as a problem in the theory of distributive justice—not the purely procedural idea of ensuring equal treatment before the law and thereafter letting the chips fall where they may, but the rather more demanding ideal of substantive racial justice. The goal is to bring about, through conventional social policy and far-reaching institutional reforms, a situation in which the history of racial oppression is no longer so evident in the disparate life experiences of those who descend from slaves.

I suggest we approach that problem from the perspective of political philosopher John Rawls' theory of justice: first, that we think about justice from an "original position" behind a "veil of ignorance" that obstructs from view our own situation, including our class, race, gender, and talents. We need to ask what rules we would pick if we seriously imagined that we could turn out to be anyone in the society. Second, following Rawls' "difference principle," we should permit inequalities only if they work to improve the circumstances of the least advantaged members of society. But here, the object of moral inquiry is not the distribution among individuals of wealth and income, but instead the distribution of a negative good, punishment, among individuals and, importantly, racial groups.

So put yourself in Rawls' original position and imagine that you could occupy any rank in the social hierarchy. Let me be more concrete: Imagine that you could be born a black American male outcast shuffling between prison and the labor market on his way to an early death to the chorus of *nigger* or *criminal* or *dummy*. Suppose we had to stop thinking of us and them. What social rules would we pick if we actually thought that *they* could be *us*?

I expect that we would still pick some set of punitive institutions to contain bad behavior and protect society. But wouldn't we pick arrangements that respected the humanity of each individual and of those they are connected to through bonds of social and psychic affiliation? If any one of us had a real chance of being one of those faces looking up from the bottom of the well—of being the least among us—then how would we talk publicly about those who break our laws? What would we do with juveniles who go awry, who roam the streets with guns and sometimes commit acts of violence?

What weight would we give to various elements in the deterrence-retribution-incapacitation-rehabilitation calculus, if we thought that calculus could end up being applied to our own children, or to us? How would we apportion blame and affix responsibility for the cultural and social pathologies evident in some quarters of our society if we envisioned that we ourselves might well have been born into the social margins where such pathology flourishes?

If we take these questions as seriously as we should, then we would, I expect, reject a pure ethic of personal responsibility as the basis for distributing punishment. Issues about responsibility are complex, and involve a kind of division of labor—what Rawls called a "social division of responsibility" between "citizens as a collective body" and individuals. When we hold a person responsible for his or her conduct—by establishing laws, investing in their enforcement, and consigning some persons to prisons—we need also to think about whether we have done our share to ensure that each person has a decent set of opportunities for a good life. We need to ask whether we as a society have fulfilled our collective responsibility to ensure fair conditions for each person—for each life that might turn out to be our life.

We would, in short, recognize a kind of social responsibility, even for the wrongful acts freely chosen by individuals. I am not arguing that people commit crimes because they have no choices, and that in this sense the "root causes" of crime are social; individuals always have choices.

My point is that responsibility is a matter of ethics, not social science. Society at large is implicated in an individual's choices because we have acquiesced in—perhaps actively supported, through our taxes and votes, words and deeds—social arrangements that work to our benefit and his detriment, and that shape his consciousness and sense of identity in such a way that the choices he makes, which we may condemn, are nevertheless compelling to him—an entirely understandable response to circumstance. Closed and bounded social structures, like racially homogeneous urban ghettos, create contexts where "pathological" and "dysfunctional" cultural forms emerge; but these forms are neither intrinsic to the people caught in these structures nor independent of the behavior of people who stand outside them.

Thus, a central reality of our time is the fact that there has opened a wide racial gap in the acquisition of cognitive skills, the extent of law-abidingness, the stability of family relations, the attachment to the workforce, and the like. This disparity in human development is rooted in political, economic, social, and cultural factors peculiar to this society and reflective of its unlovely racial history. It is a societal, not communal or personal, achievement.

At the level of the individual case we must, of course, act as if this were not so. There could be no law, no civilization, without the imputation to particular persons of responsibility for their wrongful acts. But the sum of a million cases, each one rightly judged on its merits to be individually fair, may nevertheless constitute a great historic wrong. The state does not only deal with individual cases. It

The racial disparity in imprisonment rates is greater than in any other major arena of American social life. At eight to one, the black-to-white ratio of incarceration rates dwarfs the two-to-one ratio of unemployment rates, the three-to-one ratio of non-marital childbearing, the two-to-one ratio of infant-mortality rates, and the one-to-five ratio of net worth.

also makes policies in the aggregate, and the consequences of these policies are more or less knowable. Who can honestly say—who can look in the mirror and say with a straight face—that we now have laws and policies that we would endorse if we did not know our own situation and genuinely considered the possibility that we might be the least advantaged?

Even if the current racial disparity in punishment in our country gave evidence of no overt racial discrimination—and I view that as a wildly optimistic supposition—it would still be true that powerful forces are at work to perpetuate the consequences of a universally acknowledged wrongful past. This is in the first instance a matter of interpretation—of the narrative overlay that we impose upon the facts.

The tacit association in the American public's imagination of "blackness" with "unworthiness" or "dangerousness" has obscured a fundamental ethical point about responsibility, both collective and individual, and promoted essentialist causal misattributions: When observers are confronted by the facts of racially disparate achievement, racially disproportionate crime rates, and racially unequal school achievement, they will have difficulty identifying with the plight of a group of people whom they (mistakenly) think are simply "reaping what they have sown." Thus, the enormous racial disparity in the imposition of social exclusion, civic excommunication, and lifelong disgrace has come to seem legitimate, even necessary. We fail to see how our failures as a collective body are implicated in this disparity. We shift all the responsibility onto their shoulders, only by irresponsibly—indeed, immorally—denying our own. And yet this entire dynamic has its roots in past unjust acts that were perpetrated on the basis of race.

Given our history, producing a racially defined nether caste through the ostensibly neutral application of law should be profoundly offensive to our ethical sensibilities, to the principles we proudly assert as our own. Mass incarceration has now become a principal vehicle for the reproduction of racial hierarchy in our society. Our country's policy makers need to do something about it. And all of us are ultimately responsible for making sure that they do.

GLENN C. LOURY is a social science professor in the economics department at Brown University and the author of *The Anatomy of Racial Inequality* (Harvard University Press, 2002). Reprinted from *Boston Review* (July/Aug. 2007), a nonpartisan magazine of ideas.

Defeating Terrorism
Is It Possible? Is It Probable?

Marvin J. Cetron

Forecasting International (FI) is in the business of predicting future developments. Therefore, let us begin with a few of the easiest and least welcome predictions that FI has ever made.

- Terrorist events will be more common and bloody in the years ahead than they have been to date. September 11 will prove to have been no more than a taste of things to come.
- Al-Qaeda, often under other names, will grow much larger and more dangerous than the band of fanatics that attacked the Pentagon and the World Trade Center in 2001. This process already is well under way.
- Jihadists, or Muslim extremists, will acquire nuclear weapons within the next 10 years, if they do not possess them already.
- As things stand, the war on terror will drag on for decades, with many tactical successes but little or no strategic benefit. In the long run, this could leave the Western world facing choices even more horrific than the attacks themselves.

The remainder of this article will be devoted to explaining these forecasts and to examining the prospects for changing them. Finding some way to change the obvious direction of the war on terror is the single greatest need that faces not only the United States, but also the rest of the world.

Could 9/11 Have Been Predicted and Prevented?

The terrorist attacks of September 11, 2001, came as a horrifying wake-up call for millions of Americans and their sympathizers around the world. For the first time since the War of 1812, foreign attackers carried out a major assault on the U.S. mainland. For the first time since Pearl Harbor, thousands of Americans were killed without warning.

However, not everyone was entirely surprised by the assault. Every major aspect of the 9/11 attacks had been anticipated in a report called *Terror 2000: The Future Face of Terrorism,* written in 1994. It was the product of a study carried out as part of the Fourth Annual Defense Worldwide Combating Terrorism Conference, sponsored by the Department of Defense's Special Operations and Low-Intensity Conflict branch (SO/LIC) and managed by Peter Probst, then on staff at SO/LIC. Probst was a pioneer in the study of terrorism at DOD and the CIA and, as a private consultant, continues to be a leader in the field. Acting for SO/LIC, Probst contracted with Forecasting International to help manage the conference and to carry out the Terror 2000 study. His contributions to the study itself were so extensive that, had the report been released publicly, Probst would have been listed as co-author.

The common wisdom at the time held that terrorism was quickly becoming obsolete, as rogue states learned that sponsoring terrorist attacks cost far more than any possible benefit was worth. Sponsorship of the Lockerbie bombing had subjected Libya to an air and arms embargo, a ban on some needed oil equipment, and the loss of financial assets. Iraq, long a patron of terrorism, had finally exhausted the world's patience by invading Kuwait and lost a precedent-setting war to a broad coalition of foreign powers led, but by no means dominated, by the United States. With those lessons in mind, no state would be likely to sponsor future terrorist acts, and without that support, terrorism itself would dry up.

The authors of *Terror 2000* saw it differently. Terrorism, they said, would grow more common, not less so. It would not be sponsored by states, but increasingly by Muslim extremists motivated by a bitter hatred of the West in general and America in particular. And it would be designed to cause bloodshed on a level never before seen, even at the cost of the terrorists' own death.

Some specific forecasts anticipated the September 11 attack with almost uncanny accuracy. The participants foresaw the execution of a second, much more successful, attack on the World Trade Center towers; the accomplishment of simultaneous assaults on widely separated targets (also seen in the embassy bombings of 1998); and the deliberate crash of an airplane into the Pentagon. (That last was removed from the report for fear that it would give terrorists a valuable idea they had not already conceived on their own.)

Although the *Terror 2000* report is now more than a decade old, it still offers useful lessons for the present and future war on terror. It is used in the curricula of the National War College, all three service academies, and their counterparts in a number of other countries.

Many of the analyses and recommendations originating in *Terror 2000* have been adopted with little change in later studies of terrorism. The reports of both the Commission on National Security (the Bremer Commission) in 1998 and the National Commission

Futurists Recruited for Terrorism Report

In 2005, Forecasting International teamed with Irene Sanders of the Washington Center for Complexity and Public Policy to identify potential targets of future terrorist events. Like *Terror 2000* (1994), this study involved both subject specialists and general forecasters.

More than 150 very capable participants contributed their expertise to this study. More than 100 professional forecasters filled out the questionnaire during and after a session at the 2005 annual meeting of the World Future Society. More than 50 retired military officers, many of flag rank, also joined in this work, and many had specific experience related to the study of terrorism. So did a number of top executives from the hospitality industry, which has been a frequent target of terrorist attacks. Most valuably of all, the questionnaire also was distributed after our lecture at the 15th Defense World-wide Combating Terrorism Conference, where it was filled out by more than 50 high-ranking military officers currently serving in positions related to counterterrorism.

In all of these groups, a majority provided ideas and insights far beyond the limits of the questions themselves. The forecasters noted how easy it would be for small suicide squads armed with guns, rather than bombs, to attack the crowds at shopping malls, rock concerts, and Washington's many monuments and tourist attractions and pointed out that synagogues, Jewish community centers, the YMCA, and the Israeli embassy all are obvious targets for attack. The retired military careerists foresaw possibilities like random murders of uniformed military officers in the Capitol area and the use of suicide squads to attack military bases or workers arriving at the Pentagon or CIA headquarters. One participant foresaw a possible assault on the then-coming presidential inauguration, with a major strike on the podium and many smaller attacks on crowds throughout Washington.

This work was only a small first step in developing counterterrorist strategies for the future. Yet it is important for what it represents: the beginning of a long and difficult process by which we may avoid the extreme measures considered in this report. This is one effort that absolutely must succeed. The alternative is truly too horrifying to accept.

Top Terrorist Threats: Scenarios Exceeding Impacts of September 11

Forecasting International surveyed military specialists, hospitality industry professionals, and futurists to assess the most-probable and highest-impact terrorist threats.

High-Probability Threats:

- Spread rumors of an impending terrorist attack.
- Attack Saudi oil production.
- Coordinated suicide bombings in Washington, D.C.
- General Internet overload.
- Attribute terrorist attacks in Saudi Arabia to "Zionists."
- Attack commuter trains into New York City or other major city.
- Bomb one or more oil pipelines.
- Take out the vehicle and train tunnels in and out of New York City.

High-Impact Threats:

- Put a suitcase nuclear device at any target.
- Attack the next U.S. presidential inauguration.
- Shoot down *Air Force One*.
- Pack stolen radiological medical waste around conventional explosive and set it off in a populated area (i.e., "dirty bomb").
- Repeat of the 9/11 scenario, attacking major buildings or other significant targets by crashing airliners into them.
- Detonate a tanker full of liquefied natural gas at a terminal in Boston Harbor.
- Nerve gas in the air intakes of large public buildings, such as sports arenas or major office tower.

—Marvin J. Cetron

---

on Terrorism (the Rudman Commission) in 2000 relied heavily on our work. Even the 9/11 Commission used substantial portions of these three studies, including many that first appeared in the *Terror 2000* report.

Despite this, the lessons from *Terror 2000* have yet to be completely absorbed. Many of our recommendations have been implemented only in part, if at all. And some of the thinking that shaped the study—but was not included in the final report—has since emerged as crucial to our understanding of the dangers the United States faces now, and will face in the years to come.

Futurist Community's Contributions

In its day (1994), the *Terror 2000* project was one of the most extensive studies of terrorism ever undertaken. It also was one of the most unusual, due to a combination of resources pioneered by FI.

Like other studies, it involved leading experts in its subject area. Among them were Ambassador Paul Bremer of Kissinger Associates, formerly ambassador-at-large for counterterrorism and more recently administrator of Iraq (2003 to 2004); Brian Jenkins, then with Kroll Associates and now senior vice president at the RAND Corporation; Bruce Hoffman of the RAND Corporation; Paul Wilkinson of the University of St. Andrews in Scotland, a leading adviser in the anti-IRA campaign; Yigal Carmon, counterterrorism adviser to two Israeli prime ministers; and Major General Oleg Kalugin (Retired), who as head of the Soviet KGB foreign counterintelligence directorate had recruited, trained, funded, and managed some of the most dangerous terrorists of the 1970s and 1980s; and of course Peter Probst, who brought his own expertise to the project.

However, it was a second group of advisers that made the study unique. They were professional forecasters. Few had ever considered terrorism before; their expertise was in identifying trends, regardless of subject, and figuring out where they would lead. These included Clement Bezold, president of the Institute for Alternative Futures; Edward Cornish, then president of the World Future Society; Jean Johnson of the National Science Foundation; and Vary Coates, project director for the Congressional Office of Technology Assessment.

The combination of forecasting generalists with terrorism specialists proved to be remarkably productive.

The combination of forecasting generalists with terrorism specialists proved to be remarkably productive. The forecasters provided many ideas that did not fit within the specialists' experience. These included new issues that might inspire terrorism, new methods of attack, potential targets, and many similar items. The specialists in turn kept the forecasters grounded in reality. They accepted some of the forecasters' ideas, rejected some as being too implausible, and elaborated on others, seeing implications that could not be recognized without their knowledge of the subject. A few ideas were rejected by the specialists, but were so strongly supported by the forecasters that they were included in the report despite the objections. The future importance of terrorism by Muslim extremists was one such case.

Terror 2000 was not just a theoretical study. It made specific recommendations for combating the growing threat, from hardening American facilities abroad to improving intelligence collection, particularly human intelligence, and rebuilding the "area studies" think tanks that were abandoned after the end of the Cold War. In retrospect, it seems fair to suggest that al-Qaeda would have found it much more difficult to strike at the United States if these and other suggestions had been implemented.

It was not to be. As the report was nearing completion, the Interagency Group headed by Ambassador Barbara Bodine, then acting coordinator for counterterrorism, objected to its distribution. Bodine feared that a chapter titled "Holy Terror," which forecast dramatic growth in religiously and culturally motivated terrorism by Muslims, would undermine American relationships with the oil-producing countries of the Middle East, and the threat of higher oil prices seemed more immediate and troubling than any possible risk of terrorism. In addition, she believed that little or nothing useful would be accomplished by releasing the report. As Bodine pointed out, in a democracy you can't deal with a crisis until it has become a crisis. In the end, Ambassador Bodine ordered the report shelved, labeled "Unclassified/Government Use Only," and halted its planned distribution to the president, vice president, cabinet members, and members of Congress. The study was remembered only by a few participants who joined in later studies of the terrorist menace.

Today, terrorism is a crisis, but we still are not dealing with it effectively. It is not even clear that we can do so.

Understanding "Holy Terror"

Widespread hostility toward the West will allow al-Qaeda to make a pivotal transition. Today, the terrorists are merely outlaws; they enjoy a base of popular support, but nonetheless remain outside the formal power structure of the Muslim world as it is recognized in other lands. In the next five years, they are likely to become something far more dangerous: legitimate political factions, and even governments, as first Fatah and then Hamas have done in Palestine.

Islam is the second-largest religion in the world today, and probably the fastest growing. There are roughly 1.7 billion Muslims, compared with about 2.1 billion Christians and 900 million Hindus. By 2025, there will be perhaps as many as 2 billion Muslims around the world. In Europe and America, Islam is expanding even faster, thanks in part to immigration and in part to high birthrates. There are about 5 million Muslims in the United States and 1,500 mosques. In France, at the current rate of growth, more than half the population will be Muslim within 20 years.

Islam, we are told, is a religion of peace. Non-Muslims are second class, but they are to be tolerated unless they show themselves to be enemies of Islam. Yet, some aspects of the Muslim world seem difficult to reconcile with claims of tolerance and piety. Consider these statistics, collected by Forecasting International and Battelle:

- One-third of Muslims believe that the 9/11 attacks were justified.
- Two-thirds are unshakably convinced that no Muslims were involved in those events.
- Two-thirds believe that the attacks were carried out by the intelligence services of Britain, the United States, or Israel, and perhaps all three, in an attempt to discredit Muslims.
- These beliefs are held, in roughly those proportions, in every country of the Muslim world, at every socioeconomic and educational level.
- In short, two-thirds of the world's 1.7 billion Muslims, roughly 1 billion people, take it as a matter of faith that the U.S. "war on terror" is no more than a fraud carried out for the purpose of returning them to colonial rule. It did not help that, in the initial phases of the global war on terror, it was referred to as a "Crusade," a word that Muslims have neither forgotten nor forgiven in more than 700 years.

Also significant is the view that, just as there is no god but Allah, and no source of true knowledge but the Koran, there is no valid authority save that of religious leaders. Secular government is illegitimate under God's law, and secular law an oxymoron, inevitably as weak and corrupt as the men who operate it. There is a vast and impassable gulf between secular governments throughout the Muslim world and the people whom they claim to rule. We see it in Pakistan and Iraq, Egypt and Jordan, and even Morocco and Turkey, where decades of secular tradition and rule have not erased the appeal of fundamentalist extremism.

Extremist Muslim attitudes and beliefs create extraordinary volatility when they come into contact with the West. For all their belief in the moral superiority of Islam, many Muslims find the freedom and material prosperity of the West to be enormously seductive. Westerners are hated not for what they do or what they have, but for what they are. The temptation that the West represents—to abandon pious self-denial, to accept freedom and comfort here on Earth and thereby lose Paradise—makes Westerners "enemies of Islam" in a way that no specific action ever could. This is why jihadists no longer seek to change U.S. or Western policies but instead aim simply to destroy these "enemies of Islam."

That implacable hatred takes much of its power from a long history that is every bit as important to Islam as any event in the present day. Time is of little significance to the Muslim worldview. The triumphs of Saladin in the Third Crusades rank alongside the destruction of the World Trade Center, without regard to the centuries that separate them. The pan-Arabism of the Muslim Brotherhood in the 1920s is an obvious extension of the battle to drive infidels from Muslim lands. More recent successes include the bombing of the Marine barracks in Beirut in 1983, the African embassy bombings in 1998, the attack on the U.S.S. Cole, and so endlessly on. Osama bin Laden's jihad is simply the latest expression of an everlasting war against the evils of the West, for the greater glory of Allah.

This is a context in which the terrorist cause can never be lost, much less abandoned. Successes are forever remembered, failures ennobled. It does not matter that Osama now hides in the mountains of Pakistan; he struck a valiant blow against the great Satan. It is not important that Saddam has now been executed; he sent the Americans packing after the first Gulf War and serves as an inspiration to jihadists around the world. Both these heroes will rise again, or live on in Paradise, glorified for all eternity. Through fantasy and repetition and in the light of the eternal battle against evil, losses become gains, defeats become triumphs. And if the terrorist war can never be lost, there is reason to wonder whether the war against it can ever be won.

Forecasts and Recommendations

At Forecasting International, we see three major changes coming in the years ahead that will fundamentally alter both the terrorist threat to the United States and the terms on which the "war" on terror must be fought.

1. The terrorist ranks are growing. In deposing the Taliban regime in Afghanistan and depriving al-Qaeda of a safe haven there, the United States struck a major blow against the terrorist movement as it existed five years ago. Yet by failing to follow up on that success effectively, the nation has squandered much of the benefit that should have been gained from that first step in the counterterrorist battle. And by invading Iraq, the United States has supplied al-Qaeda and its sympathizers with a cause around which to rally their existing forces and recruit new ones. As a result, the terrorist movement is now growing stronger, not weaker.

There is ample evidence to support this assessment. Up to 30,000 foreign fighters are believed to have gravitated toward Iraq, where they are now gaining contacts and experience that will serve them well in future campaigns against Western nations. In this, Iraq is now serving the function that Afghanistan provided in the 1980s. The war in Iraq is building a skilled and disciplined terrorist cadre that will fan out across the world.

Saudi Arabia even has been forced to build a major program aimed at keeping young men from going to Iraq. The Wahhabi in Saudi Arabia are teaching that joining the jihad is the Muslim man's second-greatest duty, behind going to Mecca. After fighting in Iraq, the Muslim men must come back and be available to fight for fundamentalist Islam in Saudi Arabia. Thus are terrorist cells built, independent of al-Qaeda but firmly committed to its goals and methods.

Similar developments are seen elsewhere. The Madrid railway bombings were carried out by a semi-autonomous terrorist cell

based in Morocco, whose members cited the invasion of Iraq as one inspiration for their efforts. In Britain, the London subway bombings in 2005 were the work of a small, independent band of British citizens inspired by al-Qaeda. In France and Australia, authorities have arrested a number of Western converts to Islam, many of whom are believed to have joined al-Qaeda or associated organizations since the invasion of Afghanistan. A report by French intelligence officials estimated between 30,000 and 50,000 such converts, and by implication potential terrorists, in France alone.

It is clear that terrorists have considerable sympathy among Europe's Muslim population. The riots in October and November 2005 affected at least 20 cities in France and touched off lesser violence in Belgium, Denmark, Greece, the Netherlands, Spain, and even Switzerland.

More such events are all but inevitable. Saudi Arabia funds an extensive network of religious schools, from New York to Pakistan. Saudi authorities have admitted that as much as 10% of the curriculum in those schools contains material preaching hatred of other religions and the West. At times, those schools even have coordinated their sermons to deliver consistent anti-Western messages in far-distant locales. In a preliminary study during 2003, Borik Zadeh of the Battelle Institute found that mosques in Ohio, London, Frankfurt, and Paris were delivering virtually identical sermons, the key message of which was an endorsement of global war against the West. In Pakistan, where Saudi Arabia's Wahhabi movement supports thousands of madrassas, the call to jihad is even more enthusiastic. Those schools are recruiting extremists, sending money and fighters to Iraq, and systematically building an extremist cadre that will pursue the battle against the West for generations to come.

They are most dangerous in their target countries: Saudi Arabia, Australia, Europe, and to a lesser extent the United States. Individuals from these countries are absorbing the extremist creed, going to Iraq and learning to fight, and returning to their own countries. France, Denmark, Saudi Arabia, and too many other lands are now home to revolutionaries with all the rights of citizens. Identifying these homegrown, foreign-trained terrorists will be one of the most difficult tasks for antiterrorist forces in the years ahead.

2. Terrorists will gain weapons of mass destruction. The elite among tomorrow's terrorists will have more than plastic explosives with which to make their point. They will have nuclear weapons. Pakistani engineer Abdul Qadeer Khan ensured that when he gave Pakistan what most extremists regard as an "Islamic bomb" and then spread the plans far and wide. If terrorists cannot lay hands on a stolen weapon from the former Soviet Union, they soon may be able to obtain them from either Islamabad or Tehran.

3. Terrorists will rise to power in governments. Rather than obtaining nuclear weapons from a sympathetic government, al-Qaeda or its spin-offs will likely become the government in any of perhaps a dozen countries. Wherever secular government is weak, it might easily be replaced by a much stronger and more virulently anti-American theocracy with leaders drawn straight from the terrorist movement. Candidates for a terrorist takeover include Iran (where the job already is half done), Iraq, Sudan, Syria, Pakistan, Afghanistan, the "stans" of the former Soviet Union, and perhaps the Gulf states.

However, our own choice for "most likely to undergo a religious revolution" is Saudi Arabia, where the royal family has supported the extremist Wahhabi sect for some 200 years. At FI, we will not be surprised if Osama bin Laden returns to his homeland and sets up an Islamist government in Riyadh, with dire consequences for the U.S. economy and for national security.

There is precedent for the transformation from terrorist movement to legitimate government, even among Muslim extremist organizations. In Palestine and other parts of the Middle East, Fatah, Hamas, and Hezbollah provide the kind of social safety net that governments in the region do not. Food, clothing, education, shelter, jobs, and medical assistance all flow from these organizations, bringing them a kind of legitimacy that violent action, however widely admired, never could. This service, combined with the corruption of the Fatah government, was the primary reason Palestinians voted Hamas into power, not the organization's intransigent rejection of Israel's existence.

If the terrorists do manage to gain control of a functional country, the nature of the game changes radically. When terrorists become the government, all terrorism is state sponsored. The budget available to fund terrorist activities grows manifold. The nation's laboratories and scientists become available to develop chemical, biological, and even nuclear weapons for the cause. If the country is Pakistan, where Pervez Musharraf enjoys the support of virtually none of his citizens, nuclear devices already are available. Preventing terrorists from gaining control over those weapons is one of the most pressing necessities now facing the counterterrorist community.

Countering the Terrorist Threats

Unlike any government in the Muslim world, Osama bin Laden already has the allegiance of between 60% and 90% of the people in each country. Equal numbers consider the United States to be a menace intent upon returning the Muslim lands to Western domination. There was a time when that would not have mattered, because most Muslims were so impressed by American wealth and power that the United States seemed invincible. The attacks of September 11 destroyed that useful illusion and told extremists everywhere that the United States could be hurt. U.S. problems in Afghanistan and Iraq have reinforced this lesson. From an antiterrorist perspective, this has probably been the single most dangerous result of the events of the last few years.

As we have seen, the hatred of the West in the Muslim world runs deep. It grows more inflamed with each incident in which terrorists strike effectively at the West. It is further nurtured by the Muslim religious schools sponsored by Saudi Arabia throughout the world. The sight of Osama bin Laden or one of his successors as a head of state could unite the Muslim world in a way that nothing thus far has even approached. It is likely to happen quickly. At FI, we expect to see major changes within the next three to four years.

A nation like the United States might try to expel its Islamic community and wall itself off from Muslim lands, but such measures will not eliminate the danger. For one thing, it wouldn't prevent infiltration of tactical nuclear weapons, which are becoming increasingly portable. Also, for the foreseeable future, the United States will need oil much too badly to cut off all contact with Saudi Arabia, Iraq, and even Iran unless there is no other choice.

Alternatively, the United States could attempt to strike preemptively against the terrorists and their sympathizers. But the number and breadth of targets required to eliminate the terrorist infrastructure and deter its reconstruction could involve so many deaths, and such a horrific level of guilt, that the United States would be unlikely to survive intact. Despite this, FI believes that the Pentagon should plan for this possibility. In case of need, however improbable, the plan must be ready to go with as little notice as possible.

Short of draconian measures, there are a few steps that can be taken to delay the ultimate crisis, perhaps giving enough time to find a permanent and acceptable solution to the problem.

Whatever else American counterterrorism and diplomatic efforts accomplish, the "Muslim bomb" issue—with Pakistan currently possessing nuclear weapons and Iran moving to acquire them—must be addressed. The alternative eventually might be to witness the detonation of an atomic bomb in a major population and financial center.

Nuclear material abandoned around the world must be secured. In 1992, the United States agreed to help Russia secure some 600 metric tons of nuclear material so that it would not fall into the hands of terrorists. A dozen years later, only 135 tons are properly secure, and at least 340 tons remain untouched.

The West also needs to keep track of nuclear scientists in the Muslim world, where jihadist terrorists could gain control. It should not have been possible for Abdul Qadeer Khan to develop key nuclear technologies, let alone to transfer them to Iran unnoticed. Preventing any repetition of this incident is a task for a greatly expanded human intelligence program.

Saudi Arabia must be discouraged from supporting the madrassas and their virulent anti-American, anti-West message. If this cannot be accomplished diplomatically, then other, more stringent methods must be considered.

Some way must be found to keep Iran from producing nuclear weapons. Iran may not be the most certain source of nuclear devices for tomorrow's terrorists, much less the only one, but it is a clearly identifiable threat.

The United States and other target nations must devise more effective, and less intrusive, methods of securing obvious targets against terrorist attack. According to a survey FI carried out among futurists, security specialists, and serving and retired military officers of flag rank, these include schools (as in the hostage-taking at Beslan, Chechnya), churches and synagogues, and shopping malls.

Finally, and most importantly, we need to search for more options. This list of antiterrorist measures is no more than a first attempt to identify the most immediate problem areas and suggest counter measures. None of these efforts will eliminate the terrorist threat. So we need a comprehensive program of research designed to help us better understand the mind-set of jihadists and to identify pressure points that can be used to interrupt the spread of terrorism. The alternatives are too grim to contemplate.

MARVIN J. CETRON is president of Forecasting International Ltd. in Virginia. His e-mail address is glomar@tili.com. The author welcomes feedback on this article, which will also be the topic for a session at the World Future Society's conference WorldFuture 2007: Fostering Hope and Vision for the 21st Century.

Nightmare in Manhattan

If terrorists exploded a nuke in the heart of a big city, how would we cope with the epidemic of radiation sickness that would inevitably follow?

BRUCE GOLDMAN

A truck pulls up in front of New York City's Grand Central Station, one of the most densely crowded spots in the world. It is a typical weekday afternoon, with over half a million people in the immediate area, working, shopping or just passing through. A few moments later the driver makes his delivery: a 10-kiloton atomic explosion.

Almost instantly, an electromagnetic pulse knocks out all electronics within a radius of 4 kilometres. The shock wave levels every building within a half-kilometre, killing everyone inside, and severely damages virtually all buildings for a kilometre in every direction. Detonation temperatures of millions of degrees ignite a firestorm that rapidly engulfs the area, generating winds of 600 kilometres an hour.

Within seconds, the blast, heat and direct exposure to radiation have killed several hundred thousand people. Perhaps they are the lucky ones. What follows is, if anything, even worse.

The explosion scoops out a crater 20 metres across and 10 metres deep, sending thousands of tonnes of highly radioactive debris into the air as a cloud of dust. What goes up must come down, and radioactive detritus starts piling up.

Within the first hour, enough fallout settles to fatally irradiate tens of thousands of people in the immediate area. Even 20 kilometres downwind, the majority of people caught in the path of the plume are exposed to life-threatening levels of radioactivity. Anyone less than 30 kilometres downwind will need to get out or find shelter, fast. For 150 kilometres or more downwind of the blast, dangerous amounts of fallout continue to drizzle down.

This nightmare scenario is one the US government is taking seriously. In the past two years alone, it has committed hundreds of millions of dollars to dealing with the aftermath of an act of urban nuclear terrorism, or a 9/11-style attack on a nuclear plant.

Making a bomb is not as difficult as you might imagine. The "gun-type" atomic weapon akin to the one dropped on Hiroshima is essentially a matter of shooting one piece of highly enriched uranium into another. Princeton University physicist Frank von Hippel, in a *New York Times* interview not long after 9/11, estimated that simply dropping a 45-kilogram lump of weapons-grade uranium onto a second piece of a similar size from a height of about 1.8 metres could produce a blast of 5 to 10 kilotons—that is, the explosive force of 5000 to 10,000 tons of TNT. With enough highly enriched uranium in the world to make hundreds of thousands of such weapons, and frequent reports of nuclear material being stolen from the former Soviet Union, it is far from unthinkable that terrorists could get their hands on enough to make a bomb.

In 2004, a US government-funded working group published an estimate of the number of radiation casualties that would follow a 10-kiloton detonation in a mid-sized city of 2 million, the size of Washington DC (*Annals of Internal Medicine*, vol 140, p 1037). The numbers make for sobering reading: 13,000 killed immediately; 45,000 facing certain death regardless of treatment; 255,000 at risk of dying without hospital treatment; and a further 140,000 in need of observation. Even a 1-kiloton explosion, from a smaller device or an imperfectly executed detonation, would produce perhaps a third to a half that number of radiation casualties, according to group member Jamie Waselenko of the Sarah Cannon Research Institute in Nashville, Tennessee.

It is the quarter of a million lives that could be saved that are exercising the minds of US policymakers. All of those casualties will be suffering from acute radiation syndrome, otherwise known as radiation sickness. All are potential survivors, but at present there would be little that doctors could do for them.

Most of what is known about radiation sickness comes from animal studies and accidents, and from medical records from Hiroshima and Nagasaki. The syndrome is a collection of symptoms that get progressively worse with increasing exposures. The simplest measure of exposure is a unit called a gray—the number of joules of radiation energy absorbed per kilogram of tissue.

Walking Dead

Any exposure above 2 grays or so is deadly serious. People irradiated to this level or higher quickly get sick, then get better again. However, this "latent phase" is only temporary. Some time later, from a few days to a month, they fall ill again, and often die. Not surprisingly, the more radiation you absorb, the more organs are involved, the quicker the immediate symptoms come on and the shorter the latent phase.

The body's most susceptible vital tissue is the bone marrow, specifically the stem cells within it that give rise to new blood cells. These are impaired at doses as low as half a gray and are usually wiped out completely and permanently above 5 grays. When the stem cells die, blood-cell counts—most critically those of neutrophils and platelets—start to drop, eventually plunging to zero after days or weeks. Without neutrophils, the first-responders of the immune system, radiation victims are at high risk of opportunistic infections. Losing platelets is also seriously bad news: without them blood cannot clot, leading to potentially fatal bleeding from even the smallest wound.

Upwards of 5 grays, the gastrointestinal tract is also affected. Radiation kills any rapidly dividing cells, such as the ones lining the intestinal tract. The resulting damage can cause gut bacteria to leak into the bloodstream, where they overwhelm the already compromised immune system and cause septic shock. At exposures above 10 grays, the central nervous system is damaged too, and death is certain, with or without treatment.

The standard treatment for radiation syndrome is "supportive care": blood and platelet transfusions, antimicrobials, fluids, anti-emetics and other "comfort measures". These treatments are better than nothing but are often not enough, and would be extremely difficult to deliver on a mass scale in the aftermath of a nuclear attack. Which means that despite receiving technically survivable doses of radiation, a large proportion of those 255,000 people will die.

The US government is determined to shift the odds in their favour. "What we're aiming to do is to be able to treat every casualty," says Norm Coleman of the National Cancer Institute in Bethesda, Maryland, who has been helping the Department of Health and Human Services plan its response to a nuclear attack.

The government is putting its money where its mouth is. In 2005 it awarded a total of $47 million to several groups of radiation researchers, including $29 million to the newly formed Centers for Medical Countermeasures against Radiation (CMCR). Their mission is to gain a better understanding of the biology of radiation damage, find faster ways of diagnosing radiation exposure levels, and discover better drugs. In July 2004 President Bush signed the Bioshield Act into law, committing $5.6 billion to counter nuclear, biological and chemical threats. And late last year, the government put out a call for companies to develop drugs that preserve and restore neutrophil counts in radiation syndrome, with secondary emphasis on platelets. So far no such drugs have been approved in the US, but there are candidates.

One obvious option is G-CSF (granulocyte colony-stimulating factor), a cytokine that stimulates the bone marrow to pump out new blood cells. Sold by Amgen of Thousand Oaks, California, to treat neutrophil loss caused by cancer therapy, G-CSF works by preventing the death of the bone-marrow precursor cells destined to become neutrophils, and by boosting their rate of proliferation.

G-CSF is not yet licensed for radiation sickness, but it has been used in 28 cases of accidental radiation exposure and boosted neutrophil counts in 25 of them (although many of the patients died anyway). The animal results also look good. In November, Tom MacVittie of the University of Maryland in Baltimore reported that G-CSF, in combination with supportive care, improved survival rates in irradiated dogs. The US government already has large amounts of G-CSF stored in a strategic national stockpile.

Even so, there are serious doubts over G-CSF's suitability for mass administration in the event of a nuclear terror attack. The drug is expensive, up to $400 per dose, and a patient would typically need daily doses for at least two weeks. It can't be left unrefrigerated for more than 24 hours. Worse still, although it has been given to thousands of cancer patients, side effects are common and can be severe, says Waselenko. Another Amgen cytokine, thrombopoietin (TPO), has shown promise in platelet deficiency, but has been ruled out as a radiation countermeasure because it sometimes causes life-threatening side effects.

Doctor's Dilemma

Cytokines' adverse effects present doctors treating radiation syndrome with a dilemma. To save lives you need to treat everyone who might have been exposed, but diagnosing exposures with any real precision takes days, and you don't want to give a drug with potentially serious side effects to people who don't actually need it. One quick-and-dirty sign of serious exposure is nausea and vomiting. The trouble is that almost half of those with dangerous radiation exposure won't vomit, while large numbers of people who are merely traumatised will.

Compounding the problem is the fact that after a detonation, many people will probably be instructed to hunker down in a sheltered spot such as a large building until the fallout has diminished enough to make a dash for it. "These people are going to be several days from even being evaluated," says Waselenko. But you don't have days. G-CSF only works if started within a day or two of irradiation.

So the search is on for better drugs. An ideal radiation countermeasure would be effective, cheap, and easy to make and administer. It would have a long shelf life, minimal side effects if given to someone who turned out not to need it, and would still work even if administered days after exposure. One drug, a steroid called 5-androstenediol or 5-AED, seems to hit most of those targets.

5-AED is cheap, chemically stable and apparently very safe. Developed by Hollis-Eden Pharmaceuticals of La Jolla, California, as an adjunct to chemotherapy, 5-AED was identified as a radioprotectant by Mark Whitnall of the Armed Forces Radiobiology Research Institute (AFRRI) in Bethesda, Maryland, in 1996. It is now being jointly developed as a radiation sickness drug by AFRRI and Hollis-Eden.

Last October, Hollis-Eden announced that in their clinical trial 5-AED significantly increased platelets and neutrophils, without adverse effects, in a group of non-irradiated human volunteers. And in a study led by haematologist Gerard Wagemaker of Erasmus University in Rotterdam, the Netherlands, reported at the annual meeting of the American Society for Hematology in Atlanta, Georgia, in December 2005, 5-AED significantly reduced symptoms in irradiated rhesus monkeys and accelerated the recovery of their neutrophils, platelets, red blood cells and all-important stem cells.

"This steroid exactly mimics the actions of [the platelet-stimulating cytokine] TPO and G-CSF combined—so far, the most effective combination of cytokines for radiation damage to the bone marrow," says Wagemaker.

Although 5-AED is AFRRI's most advanced and, to date, star performer, it's not perfect. Like G-CSF, you need to get it to people quickly: it has yet to be shown effective if used more than a couple of hours after exposure.

Whitnall's team is also looking at other compounds. They have identified some analogues of vitamin E that have mild radioprotective effects in rodents when given prior to irradiation. "At this point we don't really know how they work, though," admits Whitnall. A soybean isoflavone called genistein also appears to provide modest levels of radioprotection, with virtually no side effects. Another very early-stage option is based on stem cells.

Some other drugs are also racking up good results in mice. One agent, a protein isolated from a parasitic microbe, temporarily switches off cells' programmed suicide apparatus, according to Andre Gudkov, chief scientific officer of the agent's developer, Cleveland Biolabs of Cleveland, Ohio. Fewer self-destructing cells seems to translate into higher survival rates for irradiated mice. Another molecule, developed by Proteome Systems of Sydney, Australia, mimics the ability of two closely paired mitochondrial enzymes, superoxide dismutase and catalase, to scavenge for free radicals, and can also keep irradiated mice alive.

The drive to develop radiation countermeasures could have some everyday pay-offs. For one thing, drugs such as 5-AED might allow us to go back to nuclear power with more confidence. And as Wagemaker points out, ageing populations will become increasingly vulnerable to blood disorders, just as the supply of donors will be dropping. "It is expected that the number of platelet infusions that are needed will at least double in 10 years' time," he warns.

No one knows the real odds of a nuclear attack on a big city. Hopefully, the nightmare will never come true, but if it does, at least there may be a stash of lifesaving drugs waiting in the wings.

BRUCE GOLDMAN is a writer based in San Francisco.

UNIT 6

Problems of Population, Environment, Technology, and the Future

Unit Selections

43. **Enough Already,** Paul Ehrlich and Anne Ehrlich
44. **The World's New Numbers,** Martin Walker
45. **Plan B 3.0: Mobilizing to Save Civilization,** Lester R. Brown
46. **The Science of Climate Change,** Anna da Costa
47. **Who's Afraid of Human Enhancement?: A Reason Debate on the Promise, Perils, and Ethics of Human Biotechnology,** Nick Gillespie et al.
48. **The Secret Nuclear War,** Eduardo Goncalves
49. **Update on the State of the Future,** Jerome C. Glenn and Theodore J. Gordon
50. **A User's Guide to the Century,** Jeffrey Sachs
51. **The Rise of the Rest,** Fareed Zakaria

Key Points to Consider

- Why are both population growth and population decline problems?

- What is the current state of the world's environment? How can it be improved?

- What are the greatest threats to the world's environment?

- Are you optimistic or pessimistic about the long-term results of genetic engineering of humans?

- What are the pros and cons about nuclear technology?

- What does your crystal ball say about the future of the world? Which of the assessments of the future that are reviewed in the readings do you find the most plausible?

Student Website
www.mhhe.com/cls

Internet References

Human Rights and Humanitarian Assistance
http://www.etown.edu/vl/humrts.html
The Hunger Project
http://www.thp.org

The previous units have wrestled with many knotty problems within U.S. society. In this unit the focus is on problems of the future, mostly from a worldwide perspective. Any discussion of the future must begin with a look at present population and environmental trends, which are the focus of the first subsection in this unit. The second subsection looks at the problems of new technologies. The final subsection assesses the prospects for the future in very broad terms.

Some scholars are very concerned about the worsening state of the environment, and others are confident that technological developments will solve most of these problems. Since the debate is about the future, neither view can be proved or disproved. Nevertheless, it is important to understand the seriousness of the problems and think about what might be needed to correct them. In the first article the authors present the advantages of a non-growing world population and argue against those who favor population growth so that young people can take care of the increasing numbers of old people. It is true that when our population ages, and the ratio of workers to retirees declines, economic problems mount if nothing changes. But a few manageable changes such as raising the retirement age would take care of the problem. In the next article, Lester Brown catalogs many of the environmental problems that are deteriorating the earth's life support systems. He also identifies potential future problems, such as the crisis in grain prices if much cropland becomes devoted to the production of ethanol for fuel, which is happening as this is being written. The world must make many changes to put it on a sustainable course, and Brown offers his suggestions. The subsequent article by Anna da Costa is just as ominous. She presents the facts and predictions relating to climate change that may be the most important long-term trend affecting mankind. She reviews the expected impacts and the possible steps for addressing the issue.

The next subsection looks at technological problems, specifically biological and nuclear technologies. The first deals with issues that have been explored by DNA research. The beneficial possibilities are enormous; so are the potential dangers and moral questions. For example, society must now decide whether to continue to leave the creation of humans to providence and/or evolution or to genetically engineer our offspring. In the first article in this subsection, several authors debate the issues and options. In the next article, Eduardo Goncalves evaluates another sophisticated technology: nuclear power. It

© U.S. Air Force

can win wars and supply useful electrical energy, but it may have already caused 175 million cancer deaths. Furthermore, the way scientists and governments have acted regarding nuclear energy shows that they cannot always be trusted to pursue the public good in their decisions regarding new technologies.

The final subsection assesses the prospects for the future. The first article, by two prominent futurists, provides a wide range of predictions based on analysis of many trends and current plans. They predict many improvements but also many problems such as massive increases in inequality, frightening environmental problems, weapons of mass destruction (WMD) terrorism, and worldwide plagues from drug-resistant diseases. The next article estimates how the twenty-first century will unfold. Jeffrey Sachs's first concern is how economic and population growth will negatively impact the environment. His next concerns are the problems that new powerful technologies will have. Finally, he is concerned about the conflicts and disturbances that the growing inequalities will produce. The final article outlines another great disturbance to the global arrangements of recent times. America's superpower status has declined in almost every area except the military. In industrial, financial, social, cultural dimensions the world has become multipolar and influenced by many peoples and locations.

Enough Already

In his 1968 classic *The Population Bomb*, Paul Ehrlich warned that we were on the road to disaster. So what has changed to make him and Anne Ehrlich see signs of a brighter future?

PAUL EHRLICH AND ANNE EHRLICH

It has been dubbed the "baby gap," the "birth dearth" and the "demographic slump". Whatever they choose to call it, many politicians and commentators have whipped themselves up into a frenzy about shrinking populations. Across the developed world, governments are using taxpayers' money to encourage women to have more babies. French women get an extra £675-a-month tax break if they have a third child. The Polish government has recently approved a one-off payment of almost £200 for each new baby. Couples in Singapore who have a child before the age of 28 get a £7000 tax break. Meanwhile, Australia's finance minister Peter Costello has gone one step further: as well as instigating a "baby bonus," which now stands at almost £900, in 2004 he also appealed to people's patriotism, urging young women to have one child for themselves, one for their husband, and "one for Australia."

As concern turns to panic, alarmists predict that there will be too few customers to sustain today's levels of consumer spending, too few workers to keep wages low, too few soldiers for national security and a loss of prestige. There are dire warnings that the baby gap will lead to economic stagnation or even collapse. "Populations will age, the customer base will shrink, there will be labor shortages, the tax base will decline, pensions will be cut, retirement ages will increase," writes Ben Wattenberg in his recent book, *Fewer*. Even *Science* highlighted the issue in June in a special report (vol 312, p 1894). "Population losses could bring a raft of negative economic consequences in the industrialized world as well as greater stress on social security and health care systems," the article stated.

But hold on. Unless you are foolish enough to believe that the human population can grow forever, it is obvious that sooner or later we will have to face the consequences of changing age structures. If civilisation is to persist on our finite planet, impending resource shortages and the mounting environmental costs of overpopulation make it imperative that we gradually and humanely reduce our numbers. By how much is

a matter of debate. A decade ago, working with our Stanford University colleague Gretchen Daily, we took a first cut at answering the question: what constitutes an optimal human population? Assuming more or less contemporary aspirations and technological capabilities, highly efficient energy systems and resource use, and a closing of the rich-poor gap, we came up with a figure of around 2 billion—less than a third of today's population. Radical? Certainly. Utopian? Perhaps. Yet 2 billion is the number of people who were alive in the 1930s, and we believe it is an excellent and achievable target to aim for over the long term. The baby gap is the first sign that things are moving in the right direction. Far from being a crisis, it is an opportunity both for nations whose populations are falling and for the planet as a whole.

It is half a century since demographers realised that humanity will not go on growing indefinitely. Based on changes in industrialising nations in the 19th century, they predicted an eventual shift from high birth and death rates to lower birth and death rates worldwide. Better basic sanitation and healthcare, reduced infant mortality and improvements to women's education, status and prospects would combine to decrease birth rates and increase life expectancy. Although on a global scale the population explosion is far from over, this so-called "demographic transition" has now happened in many industrialised societies.

> **"We took a first cut answering the question of what constitutes an optimal human population, and came up with a figure of around 2 billion."**

In a developed country the break-even point for a population comes at around 2.1 children per couple. This is the total fertility rate (TFR) at which the number of births just replaces the parent generation. Such levels were achieved several decades ago in much of Europe, which now has some of the lowest birth rates in the world. TFR stands at 1.28 in Italy and Spain, and just 1.25 in Poland. Europe is not alone, though. Japan's TFR is 1.27 and South Korea's 1.25. Australia and Canada come in at 1.76 and 1.61 respectively. Yet despite such low figures, increasing longevity means that the projected population declines in many of these countries will be less than 10 per cent by 2050. Indeed, countries with relatively high immigration, such as the UK—TFR 1.71—and Australia, are likely to face a significant population increase over the next several decades.

More and Still More

Whatever happened to the population explosion? With all this talk of the "baby gap" you might be forgiven for thinking it is over. In fact, it is still very much happening. Although birth rates have fallen in almost every country over the past few decades, they have not fallen equally fast or far everywhere.

Most countries in Africa, Asia and Latin America have not yet reached replacement reproduction, the level at which each generation gives birth to just enough children to ensure the next generation is no more (or less) numerous. Some are not even close. Demographers project that by 2050 the global population will increase by 2.5 billion to 9 billion, and then continue growing, though at a slackening rate.

In the fastest-growing populations—mainly in sub-Saharan Africa and several Middle Eastern nations—the proportion of people under the age of 15 can be as high as 45 or 50 percent. These are the parents of tomorrow, who quite likely will produce an even larger cohort in the next generation, even if each couple has fewer children than their parents did. It is difficult to predict when reproduction will reach replacement levels in such countries, but it is unlikely to occur in the next few decades. Even when it does, it will take a lifetime—70 years or so—before growth stops. This momentum results from previous higher birth rates that produced ever larger generations of people, who then become parents and grandparents living alongside their children and grandchildren before dying in old age.

Even when a country's fertility falls below replacement level, there is still a lag, although a shorter one, before growth stops and the population slowly begins to shrink. China, for example, has had below-replacement fertility for more than 15 years, yet it may still add another 160 million people—equivalent to the populations of Germany, France and the Netherlands combined—before numbers peak around 2025. Nevertheless, China is one of a handful of developing countries that have already begun to face the problems of an ageing population.

In some other parts of the world, however, numbers are falling rapidly. In Russia and several eastern European nations, fertility rates are similar to the lowest in western Europe, but life expectancies are lower and emigration outweighs immigration. That translates into projected population declines of between 20 and 35 per cent by 2050. Russia's faltering national health system and widespread health problems such as alcoholism, poor nutrition and exposure to toxic pollutants mean that infant mortality is three times as high as in western Europe and the life expectancy for men is just 59 years—20 years lower than in the west. Meanwhile housing shortages, low wages and poor job security all discourage couples from having children. With a TFR of 1.28, the population is shrinking by 700,000 each year.

The US is the exception among developed nations. With a TFR of 2.09 and a high rate of immigration, the population is growing by 1 per cent per year, leading to a projected population increase of 42 per cent by 2050. Interestingly, the population of Mexico, the leading "donor" nation of immigrants to the US, is projected to rise by a more modest 30 per cent by 2050, despite its higher, though falling, TFR of 2.5. Passing the 300 million mark this year, the US has the third largest population in the world after China and India, and is projected to reach 420 million people in 2050, with no end to growth in sight.

Wherever countries are going through the demographic transition, the inevitable consequence of fewer babies born and longer lives is an increase in the average age. Demographers project that by 2050 the number of people in the world over the age of 60 will more than triple from about 600 million now to nearly 1.9 billion—more than 20 per cent of the projected population and as much as 30 to 40 per cent in some countries with dwindling populations.

Coping with this change will doubtless create challenges, but there will also be benefits. Whereas in a developing nation with high birth rates as many as half its citizens may be under the age of 15, in industrialised societies there are typically fewer than 20 per cent. Commentators raising alarms about ageing populations neglect to mention that with fewer children, far less of their society's resources will be needed to support and educate them. In addition, fewer young people means lower crime rates, because crimes—including terrorist acts—are overwhelmingly committed by people aged between 15 and 30. In the US, crime rates fell markedly from about 1990 on—18 years after a big drop in the birth rate. We don't think this is a coincidence.

Other advantages of a non-growing population include less pressure to expand national infrastructure—roads, buildings, housing, schools, hospitals and the like—or to keep creating more jobs. While several European countries perceive labour scarcity in a negative light, it could provide an incentive to increase efficiency and productivity. Globally, of course, there is no shortage of labour. Immigrants augment the workforces of western Europe and the US and, as globalisation proceeds, skilled jobs are being increasingly "outsourced" to developing

Apocalypse Soon?

Much of today's population growth is occurring in rural regions in the developing world, sparking tension both within and between nations as increasing numbers of young people migrate to cities and to wealthier countries looking for a better life. In the US, where large numbers of illegal immigrants enter the country in search of work, opinions on immigration are already sharply divided. Western European nations have tended to accept limited immigration from developing countries as a way to augment their workforce. Here too illegal immigration is increasingly a problem, as thousands of people flee overcrowded labour markets in poor African and Asian countries in search of jobs. In many developing countries, numbers of young working-age people are rising by up to 3 per cent per year.

Dissatisfaction is inevitable where populations of mostly young people face high unemployment, poverty, poor healthcare, limited education, inequity and repressive government. Revolutions and political unrest most often occur in developing nations with growing populations. Unemployed, disaffected young men provide both public support and cannon fodder for terrorism. The majority of terrorists behind 9/11 and attacks in Europe, for instance, have been young adult men. This is also the demographic group responsible for most crime globally.

Expanding populations also create rising demands for food, energy and materials. The strain this puts on ecosystems and resources in developing countries is compounded by demands from industrialised nations keen to exploit everything from timber and tropical fruits to metals and petroleum. Shortages of fresh water are increasingly common, jeopardising food production among many other problems. Rising oil prices may now be signalling the end of cheap energy, which also poses a threat to successful development. At the same time, mounting evidence of global warming makes reducing fossil-fuel use imperative.

If the 5 billion-plus people in developing nations matched the consumption patterns of the 1.2 billion in the industrialised world, at least two more Earths would be needed to support everyone. Politicians and the public seem utterly oblivious to what will be required to maintain crucial ecosystem services and an adequate food supply in the face of rapid climate change and an accelerated loss of biodiversity. The future looks grim, unless patterns of consumption change—with rich nations causing less environmental damage and poor ones consuming more, but adopting the newest, cleanest and most efficient technologies for energy use and production of goods and services.

It seems likely that by 2050 nuclear, biological and chemical weapons of mass destruction will be in the hands of most nations and many subnational groups. Imagine a well-armed world, still split between rich and poor, with unevenly distributed resources and a ravaged environment. Unless we act now, future generations will not have to imagine.

countries, which have large cohorts of young people, many of them well educated. Both processes also contribute to the development of poor countries and help narrow the global rich-poor income gap. As a knock-on effect, this trend will bring increased opportunities for education and jobs, especially for women in developing countries, which is one of the surest ways to lower birth rates.

The indisputable downside of the demographic transition is in the provision of pensions. This has caused growing concern, bordering on panic, in some countries. Such hysteria has even afflicted the US where, despite continued population growth, the post-war "baby boomers" are now beginning to reach retirement age and will be dependent on a smaller proportion of working-age people for their support.

Rather than attempting to turn back the clock and revive population growth as some observers advocate, societies with ageing populations would be better advised to revise their retirement and social security arrangements. After all, people do not become incapacitated after the age of 65. Few older people are dependent in the sense that young children are, and in industrialised countries they are significantly healthier and fitter today than were their counterparts a generation ago. They already make a large, and often undervalued, contribution to society through volunteer programmes working for charitable, civic and public interest organisations.

The experience and expertise of retired people is increasingly being recognised, with many industries and businesses rehiring their retirees at least part-time. The utility industry in the US, for instance, has found that retirement of its ageing workforce will produce key job shortages in the next few years and has begun inaugurating "career-extension and geezer-retention policies". Such policies may require employers to experiment with more flexible working hours and part-time jobs—which will also benefit workers with children. On the other side, social security programmes could save money by establishing more flexible retirement policies for the many people willing and able to continue with paid work beyond the age of 65.

There is no doubt that in the coming decades changing age structures and labour pools will present genuine problems of equity, with consequences for patterns of consumption, employment, migration and the like—all tied to the philosophical question of how we should live our lives. Is it fair to expect 25-year-olds to pay very high taxes to support perfectly healthy 70-year-olds in retirement? Is it reasonable to import a lot of young, cheap labour from poor nations to readjust national age structures? The economic dislocations that rapidly changing age structures can cause must also be considered. These are not, however, insoluble problems. Given their increasingly international nature, they demand open discourse within and between all nations, followed by sustained ameliorative action.

Despite the challenges, we see population shrinkage in industrialised nations as a hugely positive trend. It is, after all, the high-consuming rich in these regions who disproportionately damage humanity's life-support systems, and wield their economic and military power to keep their resource demands satisfied, without regard for the costs to the world's poor and to future generations. The more people there are, the more climate change humanity will face, with a concomitant loss of biodiversity and the crucial ecosystem services it helps provide.

There is no compelling reason to postpone the inevitable end to population growth, and every reason to welcome it. Indeed, the needs of our children and grandchildren for a habitable Earth give us no other realistic choice.

PAUL EHRLICH and his wife ANNE EHRLICH are on the faculty at Stanford University. Their latest book is *One with Nineveh: Politics, consumption, and the human future* (Island Press, 2004).

The World's New Numbers

"Here lies Europe, overwhelmed by Muslim immigrants and emptied of native-born Europeans." That is the obituary some pundits have been writing in recent years. But neither the immigrants nor the Europeans are playing their assigned roles.

MARTIN WALKER

Something dramatic has happened to the world's birthrates. Defying predictions of demographic decline, northern Europeans have started having more babies. Britain and France are now projecting steady population growth through the middle of the century. In North America, the trends are similar. In 2050, according to United Nations projections, it is possible that nearly as many babies will be born in the United States as in China. Indeed, the population of the world's current demographic colossus will be shrinking. And China is but one particularly sharp example of a widespread fall in birthrates that is occurring across most of the developing world, including much of Asia, Latin America, and the Middle East. The one glaring exception to this trend is sub-Saharan Africa, which by the end of this century may be home to one-third of the human race.

The human habit is simply to project current trends into the future. Demographic realities are seldom kind to the predictions that result. The decision to have a child depends on innumerable personal considerations and larger, unaccountable societal factors that are in constant flux. Yet even knowing this, demographers themselves are often flummoxed. Projections of birthrates and population totals are often embarrassingly at odds with eventual reality.

In 1998, the UN's "best guess" for 2050 was that there would be 8.9 billion humans on the planet. Two years later, the figure was revised to 9.3 billion—in effect, adding two Brazils to the world. The number subsequently fell and rose again. Modest changes in birthrates can have bigger consequences over a couple of generations: The recent rise in U.S. and European birthrates is among the developments factored into the UN's latest "middle" projection that world population in 2050 will be just over 9.1 billion.

In a society in which an average woman bears 2.1 children in her lifetime—what's called "replacement-level" fertility—the population remains stable. When demographers make tiny adjustments to estimates of future fertility rates, population projections can fluctuate wildly. Plausible scenarios for the next 40 years show world population shrinking to eight billion or growing to 10.5 billion. A recent UN projection rather daringly assumes a decline of the global fertility rate to 2.02 by 2050, and eventually to 1.85, with total world population starting to decrease by the end of this century.

Despite their many uncertainties, demographic projections have become an essential tool. Governments, international agencies, and private corporations depend on them in planning strategy and making long-term investments. They seek to estimate such things as the number of pensioners, the cost of health care, and the size of the labor force many years into the future. But the detailed statistical work of demographers tends to seep out to the general public in crude form, and sensationalist headlines soon become common wisdom.

Because of this bastardization of knowledge, three deeply misleading assumptions about demographic trends have become lodged in the public mind. The first is that mass migration into Europe, legal and illegal, combined with an eroding native population base, is transforming the ethnic, cultural, and religious identity of the continent. The second assumption, which is related to the first, is that Europe's native population is in steady and serious decline from a falling birthrate, and that the aging population will place intolerable demands on governments to maintain public pension and health systems. The third is that population growth in the developing world will continue at a high rate. Allowing for the uncertainty of all population projections, the most recent data indicate that all of these assumptions are highly questionable and that they are not a reliable basis for serious policy decisions.

In 2007, *The Times* of London reported that in the previous year Muhammad had edged out Thomas as the second most popular name for newborn boys in Britain, trailing only Jack. This development had been masked in the official statistics because the name's many variants—such as Mohammed, Mahmoud, and Muhamed— had all been counted separately. *The Times* compiled all the variants and established that 5,991 Muhammads of one spelling or another were born in 2006, trailing 6,928 Jacks, but ahead of 5,921 Thomases, 5,808 Joshuas, and 5,208 Olivers. *The Times* went on to predict that Muhammad would soon take the top spot.

On the face of it, this seemed to bear out the thesis—something of a rallying cry among anti-immigration activists—that high birthrates among immigrant Muslims presage a fundamental shift in British demography. Similar developments in other European countries, where birthrates among native-born women have long fallen below replacement level, have provoked considerable anxiety about the future of Europe's traditionally Christian culture. Princeton professor emeritus Bernard Lewis, a leading authority on Islamic history, suggested in 2004 that the combination of low

European birthrates and increasing Muslim immigration means that by this century's end, Europe will be "part of the Arabic west, of the Maghreb." If non-Muslims then flee Europe, as Middle East specialist Daniel Pipes predicted in *The New York Sun,* "grand cathedrals will appear as vestiges of a prior civilization—at least until a Saudi-style regime transforms them into mosques or a Taliban-like regime blows them up."

The reality, however, looks rather different from such dire scenarios. Upon closer inspection, it turns out that while Muhammad topped Thomas in 2006, it was something of a Pyrrhic victory: Fewer than two percent of Britain's male babies bore the prophet's name. One fact that gets lost among distractions such as the *Times* story is that the birthrates of Muslim women in Europe—and around the world—have been falling significantly for some time. Data on birthrates among different religious groups in Europe are scarce, but they point in a clear direction. Between 1990 and 2005, for example, the fertility rate in the Netherlands for Moroccan-born women fell from 4.9 to 2.9, and for Turkish-born women from 3.2 to 1.9. In 1970, Turkish-born women in Germany had on average two children more than German-born women. By 1996, the difference had fallen to one child, and it has now dropped to half that number.

These sharp reductions in fertility among Muslim immigrants reflect important cultural shifts, which include universal female education, rising living standards, the inculcation of local mores, and widespread availability of contraception. Broadly speaking, birthrates among immigrants tend to rise or fall to the local statistical norm within two generations.

The decline of Muslim birthrates is a global phenomenon. Most analysts have focused on the remarkably high proportion of people under age 25 in the Arab countries, which has inspired some crude forecasts about what this implies for the future. Yet recent UN data suggest that Arab birthrates are falling fast, and that the number of births among women under the age of 20 is dropping even more sharply. Only two Arab countries still have high fertility rates: Yemen and the Palestinian territories.

In some Muslim countries—Tunisia, the United Arab Emirates, Bahrain, Kuwait, and Lebanon—fertility rates have already fallen to near-European levels. Algeria and Morocco, each with a fertility rate of 2.4, are both dropping fast toward such levels. Turkey is experiencing a similar trend.

Revisions made in the 2008 version of the UN's *World Population Prospects Report* make it clear that this decline is not simply a Middle Eastern phenomenon. The report suggests that in Indonesia, the country with the world's largest Muslim population, the fertility rate for the years 2010–15 will drop to 2.02, a shade below replacement level. The same UN assessment sees declines in Bangladesh (to 2.2) and Malaysia (2.35) in the same period. By 2050, even Pakistan is expected to reach a replacement-level fertility rate.

Iran is experiencing what may be one of the most dramatic demographic shifts in human history. Thirty years ago, after the shah had been driven into exile and the Islamic Republic was being established, the fertility rate was 6.5. By the turn of the century, it had dropped to 2.2. Today, at 1.7, it has collapsed to European levels. The implications are profound for the politics and power games of the Middle East and the Persian Gulf, putting into doubt Iran's dreams of being the regional superpower and altering the tense dynamics between the Sunni and Shiite wings of Islam. Equally important are the implications for the economic future of

Iran, which by mid century may have consumed all of its oil and will confront the challenge of organizing a society with few people of working age and many pensioners.

The falling fertility rates in large segments of the Islamic world have been matched by another significant shift: Across northern and western Europe, women have suddenly started having more babies. Germany's minister for the family, Ursula von der Leyen, announced in February that the country had recorded its second straight year of increased births. Sweden's fertility rate jumped eight percent in 2004 and stayed put. Both Britain and France now project that their populations will rise from the current 60 million each to more than 75 million by mid century. Germany, despite its recent uptick in births, still seems likely to drop to 70 million or less by 2050 and lose its status as Europe's most populous country.

In Britain, the number of births rose in 2007 for the sixth year in a row. Britain's fertility rate has increased from 1.6 to 1.9 in just six years, with a striking contribution from women in their thirties and forties—just the kind of hard-to-predict behavioral change that drives demographers wild. The fertility rate is at its highest level since 1980. The National Health Service has started an emergency recruitment drive to hire more midwives, tempting early retirees from the profession back to work with a bonus of up to $6,000. In Scotland, where births have been increasing by five percent a year, Glasgow's *Herald* has reported "a mini baby boom."

Immigrant mothers account for part of the fertility increase throughout Europe, but only part. And, significantly, many of the immigrants are arrivals from elsewhere in Europe, especially the eastern European countries admitted to the European Union in recent years. Children born to eastern European immigrants accounted for a third of Scotland's "mini baby boom," for example.

In 2007, France's national statistical authority announced that the country had overtaken Ireland to boast the highest birthrate in Europe. In France, the fertility rate has risen from 1.7 in 1993 to 2.1 in 2007, its highest level since before 1980, despite a steady fall in birthrates among women not born in France. France's National Institute of Demographic Studies reports that the immigrant population is responsible for only five percent of the rise in the birthrate.

A similar upturn is under way in the United States, where the fertility rate has climbed to its highest level since 1971, reaching 2.1 in 2006, according to the National Center for Health Statistics. New projections by the Pew Research Center suggest that if current trends continue, the population of the United States will rise from today's total of some 300 million to 438 million in 2050. Eighty-two percent of that increase will be produced by new immigrants and their U.S.-born descendants.

By contrast, the downward population trends for southern and eastern Europe show little sign of reversal. Ukraine, for example, now has a population of 46 million; if maintained, its low fertility rate will whittle its population down by nearly 50 percent by mid-century. The Czech Republic, Italy, and Poland face declines almost as drastic.

In Russia, the effects of declining fertility are amplified by a phenomenon so extreme that it has given rise to an ominous new term—hypermortality. As a result of the rampant spread of maladies such as HIV/AIDS and alcoholism and the deterioration of the Russian health care system, says a 2008 report by the UN Development Program, "mortality in Russia is 3–5 times higher for men and twice as high for women" than in other countries at a comparable stage of development. The report—which echoes earlier findings by demographers such as the Woodrow Wilson Center's Murray Feshbach—predicts that within little more than a decade the working-age population will be shrinking by up to one million people annually. Russia is suffering a demographic decline on a scale that is normally associated with the effects of a major war.

It is important to consider what this means for the future of the Russian economy. Identified by Goldman Sachs as one of the BRIC quartet (along with Brazil, India, and China) of key emerging markets, Russia has been the object of great hopes and considerable investments. But a very large question mark must be placed on the economic prospects of a country whose young male work force looks set to decrease by half.

The Russian future highlights in exaggerated fashion another challenge facing the European countries. Even absent Russia's dire conditions, the social and political implications of an aging population are plain and alarming. At a 2004 conference in Paris, Heikki Oksanen of the European Commission's Directorate-General for Economic and Financial Affairs noted that the European social model of generous welfare states is facing a crisis because the number of retirees is rising while the number of working-age people is declining. "People are aware that there is a problem, but they do not know how serious it is and [what] drastic reforms are necessary," he said.

Oksanen went on to describe the dire implications for European tax systems. A pay-as-you-go pension scheme would take "only" 27 percent of wages if Europeans had replacement-level fertility, retired at age 60, and lived to 78. But if fertility decreased to 1.7 while longevity increased gradually to 83—close to where Europe is now—the tax would rise to 45 percent of the wage bill. Because of its low birthrate, Germany's problem is particularly acute. It currently has about four people of working age for every three dependents. Under one scenario for 2050, those four working-age Germans would be required to support five dependents.

But these sorts of projections don't capture the full picture. There are at least three mitigating factors to be considered, which suggest that the German welfare state and others in Europe might not have to be dismantled wholesale.

The first is that the traditional retirement age of 60 in Italy, France, and Germany is very early indeed, especially considering that life expectancy is approaching 80 and that modern diets and medicine allow many elderly people to continue working well into their seventies. An increase of the retirement age to 65, which is being slowly introduced in France and Germany, would sharply reduce the number of nonworkers who depend on the employed for support, as would more employment for people below the age of 20. A retirement age of 70 in Germany would virtually end the problem, at least until life expectancy rose as high as 90 years.

Second, the work force participation rate in Germany (and much of continental Europe) is relatively low. Not only do Germans retire on the early side, but the generous social welfare system allows others to withdraw from work earlier in life. An increase in employment would boost the revenues flowing into the social security system. For example, only 67 percent of women in Germany were in the work force in 2005, compared with 76 percent in Denmark and 78 percent in Switzerland. (The average rate for the 15 "core" EU states is 64 percent; for the United States, 70 percent.)

David Coleman, a demographer at Oxford University, has suggested that the EU's work force could be increased by nearly a third if both sexes were to match Denmark's participation rates. The EU itself has set a target participation rate of 70 percent for both sexes. Reaching this goal would significantly alleviate the fiscal challenge of maintaining Europe's welfare system, which has been aptly described as "more of a labor-market challenge than a demographic crisis."

The third mitigating factor is that the total dependency ratios of the 21st century are going to look remarkably similar to those of the 1960s. In the United States, the most onerous year for dependency was 1965, when there were 95 dependents for every 100 adults between the ages of 20 and 64. That occurred be cause "dependents" includes people both younger and older than working age. By 2002, there were only 49 dependents for every 100 working-age Americans. By 2025 there are projected to be 80, still well below the peak of 1965. The difference is that while most dependents in the 1960s were young, with their working and saving and contributing lives ahead of them, most of the dependents of 2009 are older, with more dependency still to come. But the point is clear: There is nothing outlandish about having almost as many dependents as working adults.

Population growth on a scale comparable to that which frightened pundits and demographers a generation ago still exists in 30 of the world's least developed countries. Each has a fertility rate of more than five. With a few exceptions—notably, Afghanistan and the Palestinian territories—those countries are located in sub-Saharan Africa. Depending on the future course of birthrates, sub-Saharan Africa's current 800 million people are likely to become 1.7 billion by 2050 and three billion by the end of the century.

One striking implication of this growth is that there will be a great religious revolution, as Africa becomes the home of monotheism. By midcentury, sub-Saharan Africa is likely to be the demographic center of Islam, home to as many Muslims as Asia and to far more than inhabit the Middle East. The non-Arab Muslim countries of Africa—Niger, Mali, Burkina Faso, and Senegal—constitute the one region of the Islamic world where birthrates remain high. In several of these countries, the average woman will have upward of five children in her lifetime.

Christianity will also feel the effects of Africa's growth. By 2025, there will be as many Christians in sub-Saharan Africa—some 640 million—as in South America. By 2050, it is almost certain that most of the world's Christians will live in Africa. As Kenyan scholar John Mbiti writes, "The centers of the church's universality [are] no longer in Geneva, Rome, Athens, Paris, London, New York, but Kinshasa, Buenos Aires, Addis Ababa, and Manila."

But awareness of Africa's religious revolution is usually overshadowed by the fearful possibilities raised by the continent's rapid population growth. By 2050, the national populations are expected to more than double in the Democratic Republic of the Congo and Uganda, reaching 147 million and 91 million, respectively. Smaller countries—such as Liberia, Niger, Mali, Chad, and Burundi—are expected to experience growth of 100 to 200 percent. These are the countries with the weakest state institutions, the least infrastructure, the feeblest economies, and thus the poorest health and education systems. They also face daunting problems of environmental degradation—and the lesson from Darfur and the Rwanda genocide is that disaster can follow when population growth strains local environments so badly that people cannot feed themselves.

The various demographic changes I have described arrived with remarkable speed. At the turn of this century, the conventional wisdom among demographers was that the population of Europe was in precipitous decline, the Islamic world was in the grip of a population explosion, and Africa's population faced devastation by HIV/AIDS. Only a handful of scholars questioned the idea that the Chinese would outnumber all other groups for decades or even centuries to come. In fact, however, the latest UN projections suggest that China's population, now 1.3 billion, will increase slowly through 2030 but may then be reduced to half that number by the end of the century.

Because there are so many assumptions embedded in it, this forecast of the Chinese future could well be wrong. There is one area, however, in which demography relies on hard census data rather than assumptions about the future, and that is in mapping the youth cohort. All of the teenagers who will be alive in 2020 have already been born. So a strong indication of the eventual end of China's dominance of world population statistics is apparent in the fact that there are now 372 million Indians under the age of 15, but only 270 million Chinese. This gap will grow. India seems very likely to become the world's most populous country by 2030 or thereabouts, but only if nothing changes—China maintains its one-child policy and India does not launch the kind of crash program of birth control that Prime Minister Indira Gandhi so controversially attempted in the 1970s.

There is another development that could affect future Indian and Chinese birthrates: the use of sonograms to ascertain the sex of a fetus. Wider availability of this technology has permitted an increase in gender-specific abortions. The official Chinese figures suggest that 118 boys are now being born in China for every 100 girls. As a result, millions of Chinese males may never find a mate with whom to raise a conventional family. The Chinese call such lonely males "bare branches." The social and political implications of having such a large population of unattached men are unclear, but they are not likely to be happy.

Gender imbalances are not limited to China. They are apparent in South Korea, Taiwan, Pakistan, Bangladesh, and increasingly in India, particularly among the Sikhs. Valerie Hudson of Brigham Young University and Andrea den Boer of Britain's University of Kent at Canterbury calculate that there 90 million "missing" women in Asia, 40 million each in China and India, six million in Pakistan, and three million in Bangladesh.

In a recent paper Hudson and den Boer asked, "Will it matter to India and China that by the year 2020, 12 to 15 percent of their young adult males will not be able to 'settle down' because the girls that would have grown up to be their wives were disposed of by their societies instead?" They answered, "The rate of criminal behavior of unmarried men is many times higher than that of married men; marriage is a reliable predictor of a downturn in reckless, antisocial, illegal, and violent behavior by young adult males." Resulting cross-border "bridal raids," rising crime rates, and widespread prostitution may come to define what could be called the geopolitics of sexual frustration.

The state's response to crime and social unrest could prove to be a defining factor for China's political future. The U.S. Central Intelligence Agency asked Hudson to discuss her dramatic suggestion that "in 2020 it may seem to China that it would be worth it to have a very bloody battle in which a lot of their young men could die in some glorious cause." Other specialists are not as alarmed. Military observers point out that China is moving from a conscript army to a leaner, more professional force. And other scholars contend that China's population is now aging so fast that the growing numbers of elderly people may well balance the surge of frustrated young males to produce a calmer and more peaceful nation.

China is also a key site of another striking demographic change: the rapid growth of the global middle class, perhaps the fastest-growing discrete segment of the world's population. While the planet's population is expected to grow by about one billion people by 2020, the global middle class will swell by as many as 1.8 billion, with a third of this number residing in China. The global economic recession will retard but not halt the expansion of the middle class—nobody expected growth without interruption.

The lower the birthrate, the greater the likelihood that a given society is developing—investing in education, accumulating disposable income and savings, and starting to consume at levels comparable to those of the middle classes in developed societies. Absent a shock factor such as war or famine, a society with a falling birthrate tends to be aspirational: Its members seek decent housing, education for their children, provision for health care and retirement and vacations, running water and flush toilets, electricity and appliances such as refrigerators and televisions and computers. As societies clamber up the prosperity chain, they also climb the mobility ladder, seeking bicycles, motor scooters, and eventually cars; they also climb the protein ladder, seeking better, more varied foods and more meat.

This pattern is apparent in China, India, and the Middle East. China's new middle class, defined as those in households with incomes above about $10,000 a year, is now estimated to number between 100 million and 150 million people. Some put the figure in India as high as 200 million. But it is apparent from the urban landscape across the developing world—whether in Mumbai or Shanghai, São Paulo or Moscow, Dubai or Istanbul—that a growing proportion of consumers seek to emulate a Western-international lifestyle, which includes an air-conditioned house with a car in the garage, a private garden, satellite TV, and Internet access, along with the chance to raise a limited number of children, all of whom will have the opportunity to go to college. Whether the biosphere can adapt to such increases in consumption remains a critical question.

Perhaps the most striking fact about the demographic transformation now unfolding is that it is going to make the world look a lot more like Europe. The world is aging in an unprecedented way. A milepost in this process came in 1998, when for the first time the number of people in the developed world over the age of 60 outnumbered those below the age of 15. By 2047, the world as a whole will reach the same point.

The world's median age is 28 today, and it is expected to reach 38 by the middle of the century. In the United States, the median age at that point will be a youngish 41, while it will be over 50 in Japan and 47 in Europe. The United States will be the only Western country to have been in the top 10 largest countries in terms of population size in both 1950 and 2050. Russia, Japan, Germany, Britain, and Italy were all demographic titans in the middle of the 20th century. Today, only Russia and Japan still (barely) make the top 10. They will not stay there long. The world has changed. There is more and faster change to come.

MARTIN WALKER, a senior scholar at the Woodrow Wilson Center, is senior director of A. T. Kearney's Global Business Policy Council.

Article 45

Plan B 3.0: Mobilizing to Save Civilization

LESTER R. BROWN

During the late summer of 2007, the news of accelerating ice melting arrived at a frenetic pace. In early September, the *Guardian* in London reported, "The Arctic ice cap has collapsed at an unprecedented rate this summer, and levels of sea ice in the region now stand at a record low." Experts were "stunned" by the loss of ice, as an area almost twice the size of Britain disappeared in a single week.

Mark Serreze, a veteran Arctic specialist with the U.S. National Snow and Ice Data Center, said: "It's amazing. If you asked me a couple of years ago when the Arctic could lose all of its ice, then I would have said 2100, or 2070 maybe. But now I think that 2030 is a reasonable estimate."

A few days later, the *Guardian,* reporting from a symposium in Ilulissat, Greenland, said that the Greenland ice cap is melting so fast that it is triggering minor earthquakes as pieces of ice weighing several billion tons each break off the ice sheet and slide into the sea. Robert Corell, chairman of the Arctic Climate Impact Assessment, reported that "we have seen a massive acceleration of the speed with which these glaciers are moving into the sea. The ice is moving at 2 meters an hour on a front 5 kilometers [3 miles] long and 1,500 meters deep."

Corell said that when flying over the Ilulissat glacier he had "seen gigantic holes (moulins) in it through which swirling masses of melt water were falling." This melt water lubricates the surface between the glacier and the land below, causing the glacier to flow faster into the sea. Veli Kallio, a Finnish scientist who had been analyzing the earthquakes, said they were new to northwest Greenland and showed the potential for the entire ice sheet to break up and collapse.

Corell noted that the projected rise in sea level during this century of 18–59 centimeters (7–23 inches) by the Intergovernmental Panel on Climate Change was based on data that were two years old. He said that some scientists now believe the increase could be as much as 2 meters.

In late August, a *Reuters* story began with "a thaw of Antarctic ice is outpacing predictions by the U.N. climate panel and could in the worst case drive up world sea levels by 2 meters (6 feet) by 2100, a leading expert said." Chris Rapley, head of the British Antarctic Survey said, "The ice is moving faster both in Greenland and in the Antarctic than the glaciologists had believed would happen."

Several months earlier, scientists had reported that the Gangotri glacier, the principal glacier that feeds the Ganges River, is melting at an accelerating rate and could disappear entirely in a matter of decades. The Ganges would become a seasonal river, flowing only during the monsoon season.

Glaciers on the Tibet-Qinghai Plateau that feed the Yellow and Yangtze rivers are melting at 7 percent a year. Yao Tandong, one of China's leading glaciologists, believes that at this rate, two thirds of these glaciers could disappear by 2060.

These glaciers in the Himalayas and on the Tibet-Qinghai Plateau feed all the major rivers of Asia, including the Indus, Ganges, Mekong, Yangtze, and Yellow Rivers. It is the water from these rivers that irrigates the rice and wheat fields in the region.

We are crossing natural thresholds that we cannot see and violating deadlines that we do not recognize. Nature is the time keeper, but we cannot see the clock. Among the other environmental trends undermining our future are shrinking forests, expanding deserts, falling water tables, collapsing fisheries, disappearing species, and rising temperatures. The temperature increases bring crop-withering heat waves, more-destructive storms, more intense droughts, more forest fires, and, of course, ice melting. . . .

A rise in temperature to the point where the earth's ice sheets and glaciers melt is only one of many environmental tipping points needing our attention. While the earth's temperature is rising, water tables are falling on every continent. Here the challenge is to raise water use efficiency and stabilize population before water shortages become life-threatening.

Population growth, which contributes to all the problems discussed here, has its own tipping point. Scores of countries have developed enough economically to sharply reduce mortality but not yet enough to reduce fertility. As a result, they are caught in the demographic trap—a situation where rapid population growth begets poverty and poverty begets rapid population growth. In this situation, countries eventually tip one way or the other. They either break out of the cycle or they break down.

Over the last few decades, the world has accumulated a growing number of unresolved problems, including those just mentioned. As the stresses from these unresolved problems accumulate, weaker governments are beginning to break down, leading to what are now commonly referred to as failing states.

Failing states are an early sign of a failing civilization. The countries at the top of the lengthening list of failing states are not particularly surprising. They include, for example, Iraq, Sudan, Somalia, Chad, Afghanistan, the Democratic Republic of the

Congo, and Haiti. And the list grows longer each year, raising a disturbing question: How many failing states will it take before civilization itself fails? No one knows the answer, but it is a question we must ask.

A Massive Market Failure

When Nicholas Stern, former chief economist at the World Bank, released his ground-breaking study in late 2006 on the future costs of climate change, he talked about a massive market failure. He was referring to the failure of the market to incorporate the climate change costs of burning fossil fuels. The costs, he said, would be measured in the trillions of dollars. The difference between the market prices for fossil fuels and the prices that also incorporate their environmental costs to society are huge.

The roots of our current dilemma lie in the enormous growth of the human enterprise over the last century. Since 1900, the world economy has expanded 20-fold and world population has increased fourfold. Although there were places in 1900 where local demand exceeded the capacity of natural systems, this was not a global issue. There was some deforestation, but overpumping of water was virtually unheard of, overfishing was rare, and carbon emissions were so low that there was no serious effect on climate. The indirect costs of these early excesses were negligible.

Now with the economy as large as it is, the indirect costs of burning coal—the costs of air pollution, acid rain, devastated ecosystems, and climate change—can exceed the direct costs, those of mining the coal and transporting it to the power plant. As a result of neglecting to account for these indirect costs, the market is undervaluing many goods and services, creating economic distortions.

As economic decisionmakers—whether consumers, corporate planners, government policymakers, or investment bankers—we all depend on the market for information to guide us. In order for markets to work and economic actors to make sound decisions, the markets must give us good information, including the full cost of the products we buy. But the market is giving us bad information, and as a result we are making bad decisions—so bad that they are threatening civilization.

The market is in many ways an incredible institution. It allocates resources with an efficiency that no central planning body can match and it easily balances supply and demand. The market has some fundamental weaknesses, however. It does not incorporate into prices the indirect costs of producing goods. It does not value nature's services properly. And it does not respect the sustainable yield thresholds of natural systems. It also favors the near term over the long term, showing little concern for future generations.

One of the best examples of this massive market failure can be seen in the United States, where the gasoline pump price in mid-2007 was $3 per gallon. But this price reflects only the cost of discovering the oil, pumping it to the surface, refining it into gasoline, and delivering the gas to service stations. It overlooks the costs of climate change as well as the costs of tax subsidies to the oil industry (such as the oil depletion allowance), the burgeoning military costs of protecting access to oil in the politically unstable Middle East, and the health care costs for treating respiratory illnesses from breathing polluted air.

Based on a study by the International Center for Technology Assessment, these costs now total nearly $12 per gallon ($3.17 per liter) of gasoline burned in the United States. If these were added to

the $3 cost of the gasoline itself, motorists would pay $15 a gallon for gas at the pump. In reality, burning gasoline is very costly, but the market tells us it is cheap, thus grossly distorting the structure of the economy. The challenge facing governments is to restructure tax systems by systematically incorporating indirect costs as a tax to make sure the price of products reflects their full costs to society and by offsetting this with a reduction in income taxes.

Another market distortion became abundantly clear in the summer of 1998 when China's Yangtze River valley, home to nearly 400 million people, was wracked by some of the worst flooding in history. The resulting damages of $30 billion exceeded the value of the country's annual rice harvest.

After several weeks of flooding, the government in Beijing announced a ban on tree cutting in the Yangtze River basin. It justified this by noting that trees standing are worth three times as much as trees cut: the flood control services provided by forests were far more valuable than the lumber in the trees. In effect, the market price was off by a factor of three. . . .

Shrinking Forests: The Many Costs

In early December 2004, Philippine President Gloria Macapagal Arroyo "ordered the military and police to crack down on illegal logging, after flash floods and landslides, triggered by rampant deforestation, killed nearly 340 people," according to news reports. Fifteen years earlier, in 1989, the government of Thailand announced a nationwide ban on tree cutting following severe flooding and the heavy loss of life in landslides. And in August 1998, following several weeks of record flooding in the Yangtze River basin and a staggering $30 billion worth of damage, the Chinese government banned all tree cutting in the upper reaches of the basin. Each of these governments had belatedly learned a costly lesson, namely that services provided by forests, such as flood control, may be far more valuable to society than the lumber in those forests.

At the beginning of the twentieth century, the earth's forested area was estimated at 5 billion hectares. Since then it has shrunk to just under 4 billion hectares, with the remaining forests rather evenly divided between tropical and subtropical forests in developing countries and temperate/boreal forests in industrial countries.

Since 1990, the developing world has lost some 13 million hectares of forest a year. This loss of about 3 percent each decade is an area roughly the size of Greece. Meanwhile, the industrial world is actually gaining an estimated 5.6 million hectares of forestland each year, principally from abandoned cropland returning to forests on its own and from the spread of commercial forestry plantations. Thus, net forest loss worldwide exceeds 7 million hectares per year.

Unfortunately, even these official data from the U.N. Food and Agriculture Organization (FAO) do not reflect the gravity of the situation. For example, tropical forests that are clearcut or burned off rarely recover. They simply become wasteland or at best scrub forest, yet they still may be counted as "forest" in official forestry numbers. Plantations, too, count as forest area, yet they also are a far cry from the old-growth forest they sometimes replace.

The World Resources Institute (WRI) reports that of the forests that do remain standing, "the vast majority are no more than small or highly disturbed pieces of the fully functioning ecosystems they once were." Only 40 percent of the world's remaining forest cover can be classified as frontier forest, which WRI defines as "large, intact, natural forest systems relatively undisturbed and big enough to maintain all of their biodiversity, including viable populations of the wide-ranging species associated with each type."

Pressures on forests continue to mount. Use of fire-wood, paper, and lumber is expanding. Of the 3.5 billion cubic meters of wood harvested worldwide in 2005, just over half was used for fuel. In developing countries, fuel-wood accounts for nearly three fourths of the total. . . .

Losing Soil

The thin layer of topsoil that covers the planet's land surface is the foundation of civilization. This soil, typically six inches or so deep, was formed over long stretches of geological time as new soil formation exceeded the natural rate of erosion. As soil accumulated over the eons, it provided a medium in which plants could grow. In turn, plants protect the soil from erosion. Human activity is disrupting this relationship.

Sometime within the last century, soil erosion began to exceed new soil formation over large areas. Now, perhaps a third of all cropland is losing topsoil faster than new soil is forming, reducing the land's inherent productivity. The foundation of civilization is crumbling.

The accelerating soil erosion over the last century can be seen in the dust bowls that form as vegetation is destroyed and wind erosion soars out of control. Among those that stand out are the Dust Bowl in the U.S. Great Plains during the 1930s, the dust bowl in the Soviet Virgin Lands in the 1960s, the huge one that is forming today in northwest China, and the one taking shape in the Sahelian region of Africa. Each of these is associated with a familiar pattern of overgrazing, deforestation, and agricultural expansion onto marginal land, followed by retrenchment as the soil begins to disappear. . . .

From Grassland to Desert

One tenth of the earth's land surface is cropland, but an area four times this size is rangeland—land that is too dry, too steeply sloping, or not fertile enough to sustain crop production. This area—two fifths of the earth's land surface, most of it semiarid—supports the majority of the world's 3.3 billion cattle, sheep, and goats. These livestock are ruminants, animals with complex digestive systems that enable them to digest roughage, converting it into beef, mutton, and milk.

An estimated 200 million people worldwide make their living as pastoralists tending cattle, sheep, and goats. Many countries in Africa depend heavily on their livestock economies for food and employment. The same is true for large populations in the Middle East, Central Asia, Mongolia, and northwest China. Since most land is held in common in these pastoral societies, controlling overgrazing is difficult. . . .

Worldwide, almost half of all grasslands are lightly to moderately degraded and 5 percent are severely degraded. The problem is highly visible throughout Africa, the Middle East, Central Asia, and India, where the growth in livestock numbers tracks that in human numbers. In 1950, 238 million Africans relied on 273 million livestock. By 2006, there were nearly 926 million people

and 738 million livestock. Demands of the livestock industry now often exceed grassland carrying capacity by half or more. . . .

Land degradation from overgrazing is taking a heavy economic toll in lost livestock production. In the early stages of overgrazing, the costs show up in lower land productivity. But as the process continues, it destroys vegetation, leading to erosion and the eventual creation of wasteland and desert. At some point, growth in the livestock population begins to shrink the biologically productive area and thus the earth's capacity to sustain civilization.

Advancing Deserts

Desertification, the process of converting productive land to wasteland through overuse and mismanagement, is unfortunately all too common. Anything that removes protective grass or trees leaves soil vulnerable to wind and water erosion. In the early stages of desertification, the finer particles of soil are removed by the wind, creating the dust storms described earlier. Once the fine particles are removed, then the coarser particles—the sand—are also carried by the wind in localized sand storms.

Large-scale desertification is concentrated in Africa and Asia—two regions that together contain 5 billion of the world's 6.7 billion people. Populations in countries across the north of Africa are being squeezed by the northward advance of the Sahara.

In the vast east-to-west swath of semiarid Africa between the Sahara Desert and the forested regions to the south lies the Sahel, a region where farming and herding overlap. In countries from Senegal and Mauritania in the west to Sudan, Ethiopia, and Somalia in the east, the explosive demands of growing human and livestock numbers are converting land into desert.

Nigeria, Africa's most populous country, is losing 351,000 hectares of rangeland and cropland to desertification each year. While Nigeria's human population was growing from 34 million in 1950 to 145 million in 2006, a fourfold expansion, its livestock population grew from roughly 6 million to 67 million, an 11-fold increase. With the forage needs of Nigeria's 16 million cattle and 51 million sheep and goats exceeding the sustainable yield of grasslands, the northern part of the country is slowly turning to desert. If Nigeria continues toward its projected 289 million people by 2050, the deterioration will only accelerate. . . .

China's desertification may be the worst in the world. Wang Tao, one of China's leading desert scholars, reports that from 1950 to 1975 an average of 1,560 square kilometers of land turned to desert each year. Between 1975 and 1987, this climbed to 2,100 square kilometers a year. From then until the century's end, it jumped to 3,600 square kilometers of land going to desert annually. . . .

In scores of countries, the overgrazing, overplowing, and overcutting that are driving desertification are intensifying as human and livestock populations continue to grow. Stopping the conversion of productive land to desert may now rest on stopping the growth in human and livestock numbers.

Collapsing Fisheries

After World War II, accelerating population growth and steadily rising incomes drove the demand for seafood upward at a record pace. At the same time, advances in fishing technologies, including huge refrigerated processing ships that enabled trawlers to exploit distant oceans, enabled fishers to respond to the growing world demand.

In response, the oceanic fish catch climbed from 19 million tons in 1950 to its historic high of *96 million tons in 2000*. This fivefold growth—more than double that of population during this period—raised the wild seafood supply per person worldwide from 7 kilograms (15.4 pounds) in 1950 to a peak of 17 kilograms in 1988. Since then, it has fallen to 14 kilograms.

As population grows and as modern food marketing systems give more people access to these products, seafood consumption is growing. Indeed, the human appetite for seafood is outgrowing the sustainable yield of oceanic fisheries. Today 75 percent of fisheries are being fished at or beyond their sustainable capacity. As a result, many are in decline and some have collapsed.

While oceanic fisheries face numerous threats, it is over-fishing that directly threatens their survival. Oceanic harvests expanded as new technologies evolved, ranging from sonar for tracking schools of fish to vast driftnets that are collectively long enough to circle the earth many times over.

A 2003 landmark study by a Canadian-German research team published in *Nature* concluded that 90 percent of the large fish in the oceans had disappeared over the last 50 years. Ransom Myers, a fisheries biologist at Canada's Dalhousie University and lead scientist in this study, says: "From giant blue marlin to mighty bluefin tuna, from tropical groupers to Antarctic cod, industrial fishing has scoured the global ocean. There is no blue frontier left."

Myers goes on to say, "Since 1950, with the onset of industrialized fisheries, we have rapidly reduced the resource base to less than 10 percent—not just in some areas, not just for some stocks, but for entire communities of these large fish species from the tropics to the poles." . . .

Overfishing is not the only threat to the world's seafood supply. Some 90 percent of fish residing in the ocean rely on coastal wetlands, mangrove swamps, or rivers as spawning areas. Well over half of the mangrove forests in tropical and subtropical countries have been lost. The disappearance of coastal wetlands in industrial countries is even greater. In Italy, whose coastal wetlands are the nurseries for many Mediterranean fisheries, the loss is a whopping 95 percent.

Damage to coral reefs from higher ocean temperatures and ocean acidification caused by higher atmospheric carbon dioxide levels, as well as damage from pollution and sedimentation, are threatening these breeding grounds for fish in tropical and subtropical waters. Between 2000 and 2004, the worldwide share of destroyed reefs, those that had lost 90 percent of live corals, expanded from 11 percent to 20 percent. The Global Coral Reef Monitoring Network reports that 24 percent of the remaining reefs are at risk of imminent collapse, with another 26 percent facing significant loss in the next few decades, due to mounting human pressures. As the reefs deteriorate, so do the fisheries that depend on them. . . .

The growing worldwide demand for seafood can no longer be satisfied by expanding the oceanic fish catch. If it is to be satisfied, it will be by expanding fish farming. But once fish are put in ponds or cages they have to be fed, most often corn and soybean meal, putting further pressure on land resources.

Disappearing Plants and Animals

The archeological record shows five great extinctions since life began, each representing an evolutionary setback, a wholesale impoverishment of life on earth. The last of these mass extinctions occurred some 65 million years ago, most likely when an asteroid collided with our planet, spewing vast amounts of dust and debris into the atmosphere. The resultant abrupt cooling obliterated the dinosaurs and at least one fifth of all other extant life forms.

We are now in the early stage of the sixth great extinction. Unlike previous extinction events, which were caused by natural phenomena, this one is of human origin. For the first time in the earth's long history, one species has evolved, if that is the right word, to where it can eradicate much of life.

As various life forms disappear, they diminish the services provided by nature, such as pollination, seed dispersal, insect control, and nutrient cycling. This loss of species is weakening the web of life, and if it continues it could tear huge gaps in its fabric, leading to irreversible changes in the earth's ecosystem.

Species of all kinds are threatened by habitat destruction. One of the leading threats to the earth's biodiversity is the loss of tropical rainforests. As we burn off the Amazon rainforest, we are in effect burning one of the great repositories of genetic information. Our descendants may one day view the wholesale burning of this genetic library much as we view the burning of the library in Alexandria in 48 BC.

Habitat alteration from rising temperatures, chemical pollution, or the introduction of exotic species can also decimate both plant and animal species. As the human population grows, the number of species with which we share the planet shrinks. Yet we cannot separate our fate from that of all life on the earth. If the rich diversity of life that we inherited is continually impoverished, eventually we will be impoverished as well.

The share of birds, mammals, and fish that are vulnerable or in immediate danger of extinction is now measured in double digits: 12 percent of the world's nearly 10,000 bird species; 20 percent of the world's 5,416 mammal species; and 39 percent of the fish species analyzed. . . .

In the new world we are entering, protecting the diversity of life on earth is no longer simply a matter of setting aside tracts of land, fencing them off, and calling them parks and preserves. Success in this effort depends also on stabilizing both climate and population.

On the plus side, we now have more information on the state of the earth and the life on it than ever before. While knowledge is not a substitute for action, it is a prerequisite for saving the earth's natural systems—and the civilization that they support.

LESTER R. BROWN founded the Worldwatch Institute in 1974 and launched the Worldwatch Papers, the annual State of the World reports, *WorldWatch* magazine, a second annual entitled *Vital Signs: The Trends That are Shaping Our Future,* and the *Environmental Alert* book series. In May 2001, he founded the Earth Policy Institute. He has authored/ coauthored 50 books.

The Science of Climate Change

The world is warming up. We face ecological, social and economic meltdown, famine, drought, disease and turf wars. For real?

ANNA DA COSTA

For years, scientists have been grappling with climate model after climate model, trying to fully understand the causes, and predict the progression of what has come to be known as global climatic change. In 2001, the Intergovernmental Panel on Climate Change (IPCC) provided irrefutable evidence that the overriding cause of climate change is the human-induced increase of greenhouse gases in our atmosphere. Ever since, as models have increased in their sophistication and complexity, so the true horrors of what climate change holds for our future have been revealed.

What Generates Our Climate?

'Climate', simply described, is the average weather over a certain period of time and space. With recorded surface temperatures today ranging from +58°C to −89°C, Earth's regional climates are highly variable from equator to poles, and across its latitudes. These great variations are brought about by the uneven fail of the Sun's parallel rays across the Earth's curved surface, which heat it more at the equator than at the poles, as well as the lack of physical uniformity of our planet, with land, water and ice distributed non-symmetrically across its surface, each with differing reflective properties.

These two factors influence the way that heat is distributed around the globe, and bring about large-scale movements of air and water, which in turn dictate local patterns of rainfall and nutrient availability. This regional climatic diversity has given rise to a great plethora of life forms, all adapted to their own particular conditions with incredible finesse. There are rainforests, deserts, savannah, coral reefs and mangroves in the tropics; deciduous forests, rich grasslands, chaparral, salt marshes and kelp forests in more temperate climes; taiga, tundra and alpine biomes towards the poles and dizzy heights, and icy wilds at the poles themselves.

Yet Earth's global climate—the average of all its climatic regions—is something quite different. This is far less variable, changing only over a scale of thousands to millions of years. Looking back into Earth's 4.6-billion-year history, it has fluctuated between a 'snowball Earth' and steamy hothouse, with many stages in between, and with these changes there have occurred both great mass extinctions and explosive innovations, shaping life's winding evolutionary path. In this context, modern Man, who finally appeared about 200,000 years ago, has existed but a moment in evolutionary time.

Determined by the relationship between the amount of energy received and lost from its system, Earth's global climate depends on the amount of energy received from the Sun, and the amount of energy trapped at its surface. Although simple in principle, these basic parameters are influenced by a host of factors, which operate on a wide range of temporal and geographical scales, and interact with one another.

The amount of solar energy received by the Earth—the energy input—is affected by fluctuations in solar activity, small variations in Earth's orbit around the Sun (Milankovitch cycles), and any processes that influence the amount of particulate matter in the Earth's atmosphere (which can reduce the amount of solar energy reaching the Earth), such as volcanic activity, asteroid impact or, most recently, flying at high altitudes.

The amount of energy trapped at the Earth's surface is determined by a special property of its atmosphere. The Earth's atmosphere is made up of a number of gases, each with different properties, which are held close to its surface by the forces of gravity. Some, known as the greenhouse gases (GHGs), have a particular structure that enables them to absorb and re-emit heat. These include water vapour (H_2O), carbon dioxide (CO_2), methane (CH_4), nitrous oxide (N_2O), ozone (O_3), and the halocarbons (eg CFCs), and they perform a crucial function in maintaining the Earth's climate by trapping heat at its surface. They all have different strengths; methane, for example, having 23 times the ability to trap heat compared to CO_2, and nitrous oxide 296 times.

The presence of GHGs in the atmosphere is essential to life on Earth, allowing it to maintain an average surface temperature between the boiling and freezing point of water. If they did not exist, the Earth's surface would be 30°C cooler, and similar to the moon.

As the Sun's rays, made up primarily of visible light, reach the Earth's surface, some are absorbed, and some reflected, dependent on what they meet. Those that are absorbed are re-emitted as infra-red radiation (heat). The loosely bound atomic formation of GHG molecules causes them to absorb this reflected heat energy, which they then re-radiate in all directions, where it is likely to be reabsorbed by other GHG molecules. This process of absorption, emission and reabsorption—now known as the Greenhouse Effect—traps heat energy, like a planetary duvet, significantly reducing the amount of heat that is re-radiated out to space. GHGs are kept in a delicate balance in the atmosphere by the natural elemental cycles—for example the carbon and nitrogen cycles—that take place between all living organisms and their environment.

We take it for granted, yet our reliance on a stable climate is fundamental to the structure of our modern society. Our climate has warmed by 0.7°C and already we can see significant changes.

Consequently our climate is mediated not only by numerous physical forces, both external and internal to the Earth, but also by multifaceted life itself. This multitude of interactions is what makes climate science and climate predictions so very complex and so very sensitive.

What is Causing Climate Change?

It is now beyond any reasonable doubt that climate change is happening, it's happening fast, and it is caused by the human input of GHGs into the atmosphere. It is true that the Earth's climate has changed in the past. However, these changes were either slow enough to allow life to move on and adapt to the conditions, or they brought about large-scale extinctions.

The past century has seen a massive shift upwards in average global temperature, to levels not experienced in the previous 650,000 years of Earth's history, and which are almost certainly beyond the evolutionary experience of modern Man. Global temperatures have risen by 0.7°C in the last century, and they are still rising (with a commitment to 1.6°C already, due to a time lag in the effects of GHGs). This temperature rise tightly correlates with increasing concentrations of GHGs in our atmosphere.

Atmospheric levels of CO_2 have been constant, at around 280 parts per million (ppm) for the last 1000 years, but since the dawn of the industrial revolution, in the early 1800s, they have risen by a third, to 380ppm today. CO_2 is not the only GHG that has increased in atmospheric concentration either. Others, particularly methane and nitrous oxide have also increased. Methane emissions currently account for around 15 percent of all GHG emissions, but are predicted to increase to 50 percent by 2100. Thus the warming effect is far greater than that simply produced by CO_2, and is currently equivalent to 430 parts per million (ppm) CO_2e (ie CO_2 equivalent).

By 2030, unless dramatic cuts in emissions have been achieved, parts of Africa will be experiencing a 3°C rise in temperature—the rise that is referred to as the economics of genocide.

This rate of increase is unprecedented during at least the past 20,000 years, according to IPCC scientists, and the present CO_2 concentration has not been exceeded during the past 420,000 years and is likely (66-90 percent chance) not to have been during the past 20 million years.

As was firmly established in the 2001 IPPC report, and is supported by Stern's recent review, this increase in atmospheric GHG concentration is the result of human activity. Crucially, Stern notes that while natural factors (such as orbital variation and solar activity) could have explained some of the early-19th-century trends, we would then have expected a slight cooling over the past 50 years if they were due to natural factors alone, and this strongly contrasts with the observed rise.

It is therefore irrefutable that this buildup of GHGs in our atmosphere is driving global climate change, and that this is due to human activity.

This accumulation of GHGs is primarily driven by the burning of fossil fuels, to serve the ever-growing energy needs of the human population. As the sheer scale of the human enterprise grows, as we continue to industrialise, and the world becomes an ever more global economy, GHG emissions keep on rising. Fossil fuel burning, however, is not the only source of emissions. Deforestation, current farming practices, mining, and poor waste management are also key contributors.

What Are the Implications?

For the past 8,000 years, our planet has been enjoying a remarkably stable climate. This has allowed agriculture to commence, cities to swell, cultures to flourish and hence human civilisation to blossom. Prior to this period of climatic stability, man existed, for the previous 140,000 years, as a hunter-gatherer, unable to settle anywhere for long in a fluctuating and harsh climate. We take it for granted, yet our reliance on a stable climate is fundamental to the structure of our modern society.

Our climate has already warmed by 0.7°C above pre-industrial levels, and even with this seemingly small rise we can see significant changes occurring across the planet. Earth's polar ice caps and land glaciers are melting, which along with the thermal expansion of water has contributed to a sea level rise of 0.2m; worldwide weather patterns are becoming increasingly unpredictable and violent, Hurricane Katrina wreaking havoc in New Orleans in 2005; heatwaves, droughts and flooding are ever more frequent, with the 2003 heatwave in Europe alone claiming an estimated 35,000 lives; and ecosystems are struggling, as the wilting Coral reefs in the Indian and Pacific Oceans serve to remind us. These changes, however, are a mere whisper of what may come if we do not act swiftly and decisively.

At current projections, the IPCC predict atmospheric GHG concentrations to rise to 550-700ppm CO2e by 2050, and 650-1,200ppm by 2100, which will mean a global climatic warming of 2.5°C or more by 2050. It is crucial to note that these rises in temperature won't be uniform, with some regions—primarily the polar regions and mid-latitudes—experiencing far more severe levels of warming. Furthermore, as Stern points out, these figures assume that emissions stay at current levels. As they are currently increasing every year, these are highly conservative estimates.

Yet even with this degree of warming, the impacts will be enormous. Sea levels are expected to rise by more than 0.5 metres, affecting tens to hundreds of millions of people each year.

The water cycle will further intensify, increasing rainfall and flooding in some areas, and droughts and heatwaves in others. Some estimates suggest that these changes, in combination with rising sea levels, will result in 200 million people becoming permanently displaced, and up to four billion people experiencing growing water shortages. Furthermore, melting glaciers will increase flood risk during the wet season, and strongly reduce dry season water supplies to one-sixth of the world's population.

These changes to water supplies, in combination with higher temperatures, will result in declining crop yields, which are likely to leave hundreds of millions, particularly in Africa, without the ability to produce or purchase sufficient food. Meanwhile, continued ocean acidification—a direct result of rising CO_2 levels—will have major effects on marine ecosystems, with possibly adverse consequences on fish stocks, which are already pushed to the brink of collapse by overfishing.

Large-scale losses of biodiversity put the continued functioning of Earth's ecosystems under great threat. Crucially we have neither the technology nor the funds to replace the services they provide.

In terms of human health, not only will there be an increase in worldwide deaths from malnutrition and heat stress; vector-borne diseases, such as malaria and dengue fever, could become more widespread as temperatures rise in the temperate zones.

Already, the number of extreme weather events of all kinds has quintupled since the 1950s, and the frequency of very intense hurricanes and typhoons has doubled since the 1970s. Continued climate change is likely to increase the intensity of storms further. Peak wind speeds of tropical storms are a strongly exponential function of temperature, increasing by 15-20 percent for a 3°C increase in tropical sea surface temperatures. Storms and associated flooding are already the most costly natural disaster today, making up 90 percent of total losses from natural catastrophes in 2005.

However, perhaps the least well known, yet most important, impact of such levels of climatic change, are its effects on our struggling global eco-systems. As the climate changes, we are losing an ever-increasing degree of biodiversity, as species flail under the strains of foreign climates that they are not adapted to weather. One study estimates that with only 2°C of warming, around 15-40 percent of species face extinction, as climate change is occurring too fast for species to adapt.

Apart from being a source of innumerable direct and irreplaceable benefits such as food, medicine, materials, recreation and information, biodiversity both underpins and supports a wealth of life-sustaining processes that are provided by ecosystems across the globe.

The Hadley depictions stare us in the face. The need to reduce emissions while simultaneously conserving the world's rainforests is of paramount importance. We have time only if we act now.

These include the regulation of our global climate and atmosphere, the cycling of nutrients, the purification and retention of fresh water, and the formation and enrichment of soil, to name but a few. These services have been conservatively valued at two times global GDP, the most horrifying market externality yet. Such large-scale losses of biodiversity put the continued functioning of Earth's eco-systems under great threat, diminishing both their resilience and efficiency. Crucially, we have neither the technology nor the funds to replace the services they provide, and, as they become increasingly ragged, Earth becomes ever more vulnerable to change.

Even more disturbing, and so poorly understood that it has been omitted from most climatic models, is the danger of so-called 'positive feedbacks' (or 'non-linear' changes in the climate). Because of the interconnected nature of the climate system, any changes to one aspect ricochet through it and affect many more. These feedbacks can have either a warming or cooling effect on the climate trend. As our climate warms, there is an increasing risk that natural processes could be set in motion that could drive atmospheric GHG concentrations far higher than human activity alone ever would, either by reducing natural absorption of CO_2 or releasing stores of CO_2 and methane.

Weakening the Natural World

These processes include weakening the ability of natural carbon sinks, such as the forests and oceans, to absorb CO_2 from the atmosphere; a reduction of forest biomass through drought, which would release tons of CO_2 into the atmosphere and leave it vulnerable to forest fires (as in Indonesia in a poor *el Niño* year); the thawing of Arctic permafrost and warming of wetlands, which hold (in the form of methane and CO_2) more than double the total cumulative emissions of fossil fuels so far; the release of huge quantities of methane from its cold hydrate stores in the ocean floor; and a reduction in the reflectivity of the polar regions (albedo) as polar ice melts.

Worryingly, there are signs that these changes are already occurring. Substantial thawing of permafrost has begun in some areas, and methane emissions in Northern Siberia have increased by 60 percent since the mid 1970s. The Amazon is suffering the worst drought in more than a century, and the Met Office has warned that by 2030, the total carrying capacity of the biosphere to absorb carbon will have reduced from the current 4 billion tonnes a year, to 2.7 billion.

It is predicted that these climatic feedbacks could drive Earth's climate up by a staggering 10°C by 2100. This would melt the Antarctic and Greenland ice sheets, causing rises of up to 12m in sea levels over centuries or millennia, would slow or stop the North Atlantic Thermohaline Circulation (from which the Gulf Stream arises), throwing a large part of the Northern Hemisphere into Siberian weather conditions and, perhaps most crucially, would spell catastrophe for the various biota across the planet upon which we rely for our oxygen, water, food and materials. In no uncertain terms, such changes would precipitate the sixth mass extinction of life that our planet has witnessed.

> **We, as all life, rely on air, water, food and warmth to survive and without these things our mirage of social constructs will turn to dust. Every irresponsible decision now made amounts to genocide.**

It is a sobering thought that such runaway processes are known to have precipitated mass extinctions in the past. The end-Permian extinction, 251 million years ago, involved a 6°C global temperature rise, thought to have been precipitated by climatic feedbacks following an initial volcanic eruption or meteorite impact. It resulted in a loss of as much as 95 percent of the species on the planet, almost bringing an end to life itself. As Stern notes in his report, a warming of 5°C on a global scale would be far outside the experience of human civilisation and comparable to the difference between temperatures during the last ice age and today.

Scientists have predicted that a rise of more than 2°C is the point at which some of the most dangerous runaway processes could become irreversible. Furthermore, given that climatic predictions are highly conservative, we must err on the side of caution as to what will be safe CO_2 concentrations to reach. As the current atmospheric concentrations of GHGs mean we are already committed to a rise of 1.6°C, global action needs to be rapid, bold and unified.

So What Can Be Done?

Data from 11 separate studies indicates that, stabilising at 450ppm CO_2e, the probability of exceeding a 2°C rise, relative to pre-industrial levels, is 26-78 percent. This probability sharply increases from this point, to 63-99 percent with stabilisation at 550ppm CO_2e.

We have already passed 400ppm CO_2e (we are now at 430ppm CO_2e), and stabilising at 450ppm CO_2e, without overshooting, will require immediate and substantial cuts. Overshooting this level carries many inherent dangers, from which Stern warns it may not be possible to recover. According to Stern, in order to meet this target, global emissions would need to peak in the next 10 years, and then fall at more than 5 percent per year, reaching

70 percent below current levels by 2050. Yet if global citizens are all to be entitled to an equal emissions quota, reaching this level requires cuts of 87 percent for UK citizens. However, emission levels are still rising.

Climate science plainly states that the degree of warming that occurs profoundly affects the impacts we experience. Every small incremental rise in temperature bears the burden of many more deaths and suffering, and carries an ever-increasing threat of further change. Although significant challenges in the process of climate modelling clearly remain, the evidence is strong enough to dictate that any rise above 2°C should be avoided at all costs. Climate change is the greatest threat mankind has ever faced. Every irresponsible decision now made amounts to genocide.

In an evolutionary context, our society and our economy are mere spiders' threads against the blowing gales of the elemental forces. We rely—as does all life—on air, water, food, and warmth to survive; and without these fundamental things, our mirage of social constructs will turn to dust. We are at the mercy of the elements, as we always have been.

Who's Afraid of Human Enhancement?

A Reason Debate on the Promise, Perils, and Ethics of Human Biotechnology

NICK GILLESPIE ET AL.

On August 25 in Washington, D.C., *Reason* staged a debate about "the promise, perils, and ethics of human biotechnology." Moderated by Editor in Chief Nick Gillespie, the panelists included Ronald Bailey, *Reason's* science correspondent and author of *Liberation Biology: The Scientific and Moral Case for the Biotech Revolution;* Eric Cohen, director of the Ethics and Public Policy Center's Biotechnology and American Democracy Program and editor of the group's journal, *The New Atlantis;* and Joel Garreau, a reporter and editor for *The Washington Post* and author of *Radical Evolution: The Promise and Peril of Enhancing Our Minds, Our Bodies, and What It Means To Be Human.* What follows is an edited transcript of the event, which was sponsored by the Donald and Paula Smith Family Foundation and the Institute for Humane Studies. Comments can be sent to letters@Reason.com.

Nick Gillespie: Our purpose tonight is to hash out questions and issues revolving around human enhancement based on technologies that include cloning; stem-cell research; processes to increase longevity, intelligence, and physical abilities; and many other procedures at various stages of development. What was once the province of science fiction—human beings augmented to such a degree that they become "post-human"—is rapidly becoming fact. Indeed, one of our panelists tonight will even argue that within the next century death itself may become optional. These are the sorts of developments that fill some with hope and others with horror.

Our panelists tonight will not agree on very much, but on this basic point I suspect they're in complete agreement: Forget all the talk about Social Security solvency, income tax rates, blue states, red states, even the war in Iraq. The most fundamental social and political issue facing the world today—and tomorrow—is the question of human enhancement.

Ron Bailey will be kicking off our discussion by giving us a quick overview of his feelings about human enhancement.

Ron Bailey: If I could have given my new book a proper 19th-century descriptive title, it might have been *Liberation Biology: The Scientific and Moral Case for the Biotech Revolution, or Why You Should Relax and Enjoy the Brave New World of Immortality, Stem Cells, and Designer Babies.*

Of course, I'm not talking about Aldous Huxley's *Brave New World,* which portrays a society of regimented clones in a world run by top-down controllers, the motto of which is "community, identity, and stability." In fact, the biotech revolution I anticipate is the exact opposite of Huxley's *Brave New World.* Let me illustrate by painting you a short vision of what the biotech revolution could bring by the end of this century.

By 2100 the typical American may attend a family reunion in which five generations are playing together. The great-great-great-grandma is 150 years old, and she will be as vital as she was when she was 30 and as vital as her 30-year-old great-great-grandson, with whom she's playing touch football. After the game, she'll enjoy a plate of salad greens filled with not only a full day's worth of nutrients but the medicines she needs to repair the damage to her aging cells. She'll be able to chat about the academic discipline—maybe economics—that she studied in the 1980s with as much acuity and depth of knowledge and memory as her 50-year-old great-granddaughter who is now studying the same thing.

No one in her extended family will have ever caught a cold. They will be immune from birth to the shocks that human flesh has long been heir to: diabetes, cancer, and Alzheimer's disease. Her granddaughter, who recently suffered an unfortunate transport accident, will be sporting new versions of the arm and lung that got damaged in the wreck, and she'll be playing in that game of touch football with the same skill and energy as anyone else in the family. Infectious diseases that terrified us at the beginning of the 21st century, such as HIV-AIDS and the avian flu, will be horrific historical curiosities for the family to chat about over their plates of super-fat farm-raised salmon, which will be as tasty and nutritious as any fish any human has ever eaten: "Grandma, what was it like when people got colds?" Though few of them will actually think much about it, surrounding them will be a world that is greener and cleaner, one more abundant in natural vegetation and with less of an obvious human footprint than the one we live in now.

Not only will this family enjoy all these benefits, but nearly everyone they work with, socialize with, and meet with will enjoy them as well. It will be a remarkably peaceful and pleasant world. Beyond their health and their wealth, they'll be able to control things such as anti-social tendencies and crippling depression. And they'll manage these problems by individual choice, through new biotech pharmaceuticals and personalized genetic treatments.

This idyllic scenario is more than realistic given the reasonably expected breakthroughs and extensions of our knowledge of human, plant, and animal biology and the mastery of the techniques known collectively as biotechnology. We'll be able to manipulate those biologies to meet human needs and desires.

What is astonishing to me is that an extraordinary transideological coalition of left-wing and right-wing bioconservatives has come together to oppose many of the technological advancements that could make that vision real for the whole of humanity. This coalition of biotech opponents consists of some of our leading intellectuals and policy makers. On the left stand bioethicists such as Daniel Callahan, who founded The Hastings Center, arguably the world's first bioethics think tank; George Annas from Boston University; longtime left-wing activists such as Jeremy Rifkin; and environmentalists such as Bill McKibben. On the right stand Leon Kass, [formerly] the chairman of the President's Council on Bioethics, and his fellow council members Francis Fukuyama and Charles Krauthammer, and also people such as William Kristol, the editor of *The Weekly Standard*.

> **"Forget all the talk about Social Security, income tax rates, blue states, red states, even the war in Iraq. The most fundamental issue facing the world today—and tomorrow—is the questions of human enhancement."**
>
> —Nick Gillespie

Both sides of this coalition abhor efforts to dramatically extend healthy human life spans by decades and even centuries. Both sides oppose creating stem cells derived from cloned embryos that would serve as perfect transplants to replace damaged, diseased, or worn-out body parts, livers, and nerves. Both sides want to outlaw the efforts of parents

to use genetic testing and in vitro fertilization [IVF] and new pharmaceuticals to enhance their children's immune systems, athletic abilities, and intellectual capacities. Both sides of this bioconservative coalition would ban the use of genetically enhanced crops and animals to produce more abundant and more nutritious foods. Astonishingly, they are against heaven. Why? Because they wrongly fear that biotech progress will lead to hell.

In *Liberation Biology,* I thoroughly examine the whole range of bioconservative objections to the biotech revolution. I look forward to addressing them in more detail in the question-and-answer period, but let me note here that the benefits of biotechnology are well-known. The cure of diseases and disabilities for millions of sufferers, the production of more nutritious food with less damage to the natural environment, the enhancement of human physical and intellectual capacities, the retarding of the onset of the ravages of old age—all of these can be easily foreseen.

It is the alleged dangers of biotechnology that are vague, ill-defined, and wholly speculative. While Joel Garreau wonderfully chronicles some of the far-out visions of technological transcendence in *Radical Evolution,* my desires are more modest. All I want to do is dramatically boost people's physical and intellectual capacities, restore the natural environment, and make death optional.

Nick Gillespie: Thank you, Ron. Although I've got to say you've given the opposite side a powerful argument with your vision of a family picnic, especially if you've ever met my cousins. Next up is Eric Cohen.

Eric Cohen: Thanks very much. As a magazine editor, I want to start by simply complimenting Ron's title. I spend a lot of time trying to think of clever titles, which sometimes are the only things people remember about the nice article you publish, and *Liberation Biology* is a very smart title. It's a play, if I understand it correctly, on liberation theology, which is a whole collection of interesting, silly, weird ideas having to do generally with heaven and hell. Ron's title is clever on a couple of levels.

One, it signals that he's breaking from [the concept of heaven and hell]. He's breaking from this whole [religious] mythology, which I suspect in his mind hasn't delivered very much. He's leading us toward the age of flag football with your grandmother and farm-fresh salmon, but he's also signaling that he wants to try to answer some of the same human longings that theology or religion has long answered. So it's an interesting title on that level. I think it's also interesting in [raising the question of] what is it the liberty to do? What is the liberation he's talking about?

It's liberation from all kinds of horrible things in human life—sudden illness, dying children, people who have more ambition than talent, people who have more ideas than time, people who simply don't want to die and want to be a lot more like gods than most human beings are. It's also liberty to do various things, and this brings us to the subject of tonight's panel, which is the question of enhancement.

> "By 2100 the typical American may attend a family reunion in which five generations are playing together. The great-great-grandma is 150 years old, and she will be as vital as her 30-year-old great-great-grandson."
>
> —Ronald Bailey

It seems to me that if you take the word *enhancement* at face value, there simply can't be anything wrong with it, right? *Enhancement* means to make things better, so then [all the things Ron talks about are] great. But the question is whether the things that seem like enhancements really are enhancements. The disquiet that some people have with the biotech revolution is [due to our] worry that in trying to make life better in ways we recognize, we're going to make it worse in ways we can't even imagine. That's the set of problems we face.

I should say most biotech is great. I hope the stocks go up. I hope they cure various diseases or at least develop better treatments for them, but some of the more ambitious and more interesting areas of biotechnology give some of us disquiet.

There are two sides to the disquiet. One has to do with the means that we're going to use to supposedly enhance ourselves and the other has to do with the ends. The conventional worry about enhancement has to do with the quality [of improvements] that the rich are going [to be able to afford]. The wealthy are going to become gene rich and the poor are going to become gene poor, and this is going to worsen the inequalities of life. I'm enough of a free market person to believe that if something works in wealthy societies, eventually most people are going to be able to afford it.

The worries about means are a little different though. Here the stem cell debate is paradigmatic. Everybody wants to cure these horrible diseases. It's an end that all sides of the stem cell debate share. The issue is, should we be destroying human embryos to do it? I think you can make a pretty rigorous, rational, and scientific case that embryos are early human lives and that to use them as mere things would make us a lesser society. The worry here is not about the end we're pursuing but about the means that are used to pursue it.

And let me spend some time asking about those ends. What is it that we're trying to enhance? What are the goals here? I think you can break down four different ways of trying to enhance ourselves—and here I follow the definitive discussion in a report by the President's Council on Bioethics called *Beyond Therapy*. The four ways are superior performance in the various activities of life, better children, long lives or even ageless lives, and happiness. Those are four basic aspirations that are not new, though biotechnology might give us some new ways to pursue them.

If you think it through, there are *Reasons* to at least wonder whether the biotechnologies we're talking about are really going to answer these human longings in any serious way. Obviously everybody's all worked up these days about performance-enhancing drugs in sports, and as Joel tells me, the existing drugs are child's play compared to what's coming. But we have to ask ourselves, is the athlete on steroids a better athlete, a better human athlete? Or has he become more an animal bred for the race? And we might create all kinds of drugs that boost the capacity to, say, remember SAT words. But is that really going to make people smarter, or is it going to narrow their minds in a certain way and make them less able to make the kinds of connections that are essential to real human intelligence and real human wisdom?

The same with the desire for better children. I question whether we would ever be able to design a better child. Can we really make a better musician than Mozart or make a better playwright than Shakespeare? We may be able to make everybody in our wildest dreams as talented as those people, though I doubt it. But there's a deeper issue, which has to do with the nature of the family. It seems to me that parenthood is about not only trying to make your children better but having a welcoming and embracing attitude toward the child that's given to you to raise and given to you to love. I wonder whether embracing full force a kind of designer attitude is really going to make us better parents and better families.

The same with the desire for longevity. There's the worry that we may simply extend debility. It may be that we're going to simply have Alzheimer's disease for 35 years instead of for 10 in the future. I'm not sure that's necessarily progress. In a deeper sense, if we really believed or lived as if we were going to live forever, would we really have the urgency and the aspiration and the ambition to do the things that we do in life? Most of the portraits of immortality that we've seen, or at least many of them, present a less appealing picture than grandma playing flag football. I'm not sure how appealing that is either.

Nick Gillespie: Especially if you're not a Kennedy, right?

Eric Cohen: Right. And let me end with the quintessential aspiration: Everybody wants to be happy. On this much, at least, the ancients and the moderns sort of agreed, although they had different notions of happiness. Will the various interventions in our minds and bodies make us happier? I'm no expert on the future, so we'll have to wait and see, but I think there are real *Reasons* to doubt this. There are *Reasons* to doubt whether our new powers will really make us happy in a genuine human sense. If there were really a pill that simulated love or simulated success or simulated the feeling of playing a great symphony or hitting a great home run, is that really what we aspire to? Simply the simulation? And is there a danger that all these drugs that are supposed to make us happy might just make us more anxious because we're on all these drugs? Everybody's on Prozac, everybody puts a little bit in their coffee, but in fact life still has its hardships and people are still genuinely frustrated and trying to muddle through like most of us do. I wonder whether we'll really be genuinely happy when all the biotech companies promise us happiness in a pill.

These are hard questions. The future's unpredictable, but I think there are at least serious *Reasons* to wonder whether we'll genuinely make ourselves better in all the ways that we hope to by turning to biotech.

Nick Gillespie: Thank you, Eric. I can testify from personal experience, I've already had pills that have made me think I'm as talented as Mozart, but they were not from established pharmaceutical outlets, or FDA-regulated, and I miss them. Joel?

Joel Garreau: Thanks. Eric's journal has made a great impact on me. I'm a paid subscriber to *The New Atlantis,* that's how much I admire his journal. And I've been so dazzled by Ron's work that I've stolen it every chance I've had.

Having been a child of the 1960s, I never anticipated that the most interesting drugs available today [would be] legal and available through prescription. That's the part that really blows my mind. The argument that I make in *Radical Evolution* is that we are at a turning point in history, and there's nothing [that is going to hold that back]. For hundreds of thousands of years, our technologies have been aimed outward at modifying our environment in the fashion of fire, clothes, cities, agriculture, space travel. But now, they are increasingly turned inward at modifying our minds, our memories, our metabolisms, our personalities, our progeny, and possibly our souls. It's not just biotech. It's what I call the GRIN technologies—genetics, robotics, information, and nanotechnology. They are all following a curve of exponential change that is known in the computer industry as Moore's Law. You get regular doublings in capacity every few months.

A doubling is an amazing thing. It means that every few months, every new step is as tall as all of the previous steps combined. The 30 doublings we've had in computer technology since 1959 is an increase of over 400,000 times. We're seeing similar curves in these other technologies, and the significance of this is that it's not going away and it's not science fiction and it's not 100 years from now. It's on our watch, and we have to decide what we're going to do about it in terms of the future of human nature.

This conversation usually gets held in the hall of the technological elite, and the *Reason* I've been typing as

fast as I can is that it's time for the conversation to break out into the mainstream. Only in some kind of a bottom-up way are we going to address these issues. I'm not a big fan of top-down hierarchies, just as a practical matter. And the stuff coming online is going to blow our minds.

For example, I spent the better part of a year at DARPA, the Defense Advanced Research Projects Agency, and the stuff that's in their labs is quite remarkable. Up in Boston, there's a human, Matthew Nagel, who was the first to send an e-mail with his thoughts last summer. He can control a robotic arm with his thoughts. Within three years, these memory drugs that are meant to banish the boomers' "senior moments" are going to be coming on market.

The question that the Educational Testing Service is asking is, what happens if in the very near future you can buy your kids an extra couple of hundred points on their SATs? Think of what parents do now to get their kids into college. Then think of what's happening as these possibilities come online. We're talking about thousands of incremental advances. It's not like we're going to wake up some day and face some big decision. It's one step at a time. How do we handle these advances? And as Ron said, this is really scrambling our politics. Think of how many people love the idea of stem cells who are equally opposed to genetically modified organisms. The distinctions we have now between the left and the right were an Industrial Age reality that is increasingly not part of our future.

It's between the heaven and the hell scenarios that you see the big differences, the optimists vs. the pessimists. On the optimist side, you have the market libertarians and the military right next to some environmentalists and disabled people and even feminists who relish the thought of procreating without men. Then there are the people who fear this: the President's Council on Bioethics hard up against Greenpeace and people who are against the World Bank and Christians who don't believe in Darwin and the Boston Women's Health Collective (which published the feminist classic *Our Bodies, Ourselves*). And Prince Charles. Those are pretty damned strange bedfellows.

The thing about the heaven and the hell scenarios is they basically agree. The heaven scenario says all of these changes are increasing exponentially, and we're going to conquer all the evils of mankind, and it goes straight up and that's terrific. The people who look at the hell scenario also buy this curve of exponential change. But they ask, what happens if this gets into the hands of bumblers or madmen? Their optimistic version of the hell scenario is that we extinguish only the human species in 25 years; the pessimistic version is that we lose all the life on earth. The heaven and hell scenarios are both technodeterminist futures that say technology is moving forward and there's not much we can do about it. Hang on tight. The end. Great summer blockbuster movie, dynamite special effects, not a lot of plot.

The third scenario that I sketch out in *Radical Evolution* is the "prevail" scenario. That's entirely different territory. Prevail [scenarists] don't believe that human history is likely to follow any smooth curves. It's more likely to have hiccups and loops and reverses and belches, as history has in the past. In the prevail scenario, the measure of progress is not how many transistors you can get to talk to each other but how many unpredictable and imaginative humans you can get to talk to each other. The measure of success in prevail is co-evolution. It's child's play to note that if our challenges go up in a curve and if our responses stay flat, we're toast. Stick a fork in us right now. We're done.

But if you get a situation where you can have our responses accelerating as fast as our challenges by bringing humans together in an imaginative way, then you might have a shot. Think of the problems that were facing humanity during the Dark Ages—endless difficulties. Then comes the printing press. All of a sudden you can start collecting and transferring and sharing ideas in a way that had never been possible before. The range of solutions that occurred was beyond the imagination of any one human being or any one country. Global trade, the Enlightenment, the rise of democracy, the rise of science itself.

I'm guardedly hopeful that maybe we're in a period of co-evolution like that now, [where all sorts of new ways of thinking and dealing with things are possible]. Think of 9/11. The fourth airplane never made it to its target. Why? Because the Air Force was quick on the trigger? Uh, no. Because the White House was so smart? Uh, no. What happened was that a bunch of ordinary people like us, empowered by mobile phone technology, figured out, diagnosed, and cured their society's ills in under an hour—and at incredible expense to themselves. That's, I think, an example of co-evolution, and it's a *Reason* why I'm guardedly optimistic about the future.

"I question whether we would ever be able to design a better child. Can we really make a better musician than Mozart or make a better playwright than Shakespeare? I doubt it."

—Eric Cohen

Nick Gillespie: I'll ask each panelist a question before throwing things open to the audience. Ron, tell me one biotechnological development that you actually fear or find troubling.

Ronald Bailey: The possibility of evil people using or creating terrible pathogens and bioterrorism. I'm not at all sure that the current responses that we are trying to develop are going to be successful. The response of our government in developing its new biosecurity system seems geared to shutting down our public knowledge of things, to increasing secrecy. The best way to protect ourselves is to massively support security technologies and hope that they develop so that the defenses that work are widely understood.

Nick Gillespie: Make everything public on some level?

Ronald Bailey: Yes, basically.

Nick Gillespie: Eric, you talk a lot about how "we" have to make decisions about things. That raises what's called the Tonto question: Caught in an ambush, the Lone Ranger turns to his sidekick and says, "Looks like we're surrounded by Indians." And Tonto replies, "Who's we, kemo sabe?" At what level should these decisions be made? I agree these decisions should not be left to "the scientists," but what about the individual's right to choose?

Eric Cohen: A lot of these questions are moral questions and public questions and democratic questions. They're about the kind of society we're going to live in. I think the moral questions presented by the means are easier to deal with in a democratic way. We can have a debate about whether you should kill embryos in order to do research, and we can have an argument about whether we should set limits. I think that's a perfectly legitimate public thing to do. Right now, there are no limits on embryo research. There's not unlimited funding for it, but there are no limits on it at all. Any research scientist in the country can do it.

When you get to the issue of ends, it's a lot more complicated, precisely because these technologies are mixed up with some very desirable things. But in many cases, the means of using them are problematic. There's nothing wrong with developing a pill that you can take to supposedly improve your memory. The question is whether that's actually a good human thing to do. Various people are trying to think about whether you could build a regulatory agency, a kind of hyped-up FDA that dealt with more than just safety issues and dealt with some of the broader issues.

I'm skeptical of the regulatory agency approach. But when it comes to blunt means questions—Should we be engineering children by weeding out the unfit? Should we be using embryos in research?—I think those are questions where there should be a "we." As a society, we should make some collective judgments about the kind of people we want to be.

When you get to some of the more subtle uses of biotech, especially in the enhancement area, then you have smaller levels of "we." Sports teams or leagues are going to set rules about what kinds of drugs are going to be legal in the future. I think these are cultural questions and individual questions. I'm not looking to ban these various drugs. I'm just questioning the wisdom of using many of them and whether they'll actually deliver us the goods we think they will.

Nick Gillespie: Joel, the subtitle of your book mentions "human nature." What is it, and how do we know we're changing it?

Joel Garreau: One of the definitions of human nature that I like the best is that a human is the creature that steals fire from the gods every chance he gets. Or she gets. That's one of the *Reasons* why I don't think these changes are going to go away no matter what country tries to impose some kind of regulatory scheme. This is not just a U.S. question. The superpowers in this regard include India, China, South Korea, and Japan, places that have entirely different ethical and moral takes on what it means to be human than the Judeo-Christian and Western traditions do.

> **"Having been a child of the 1960s, I never anticipated that the most interesting drugs available today [would be] legal and available through prescription. That's the part that really blows my mind."**
>
> —Joel Garreau

In terms of knowing whether we have transcended human nature, I propose the Shakespeare test. Shakespeare knew quite a bit about human nature and he wrote elegantly about it. If you have found somebody who has become so enhanced as to make you wonder whether she's still human, I propose the mental experiment of popping her into your hypothetical time machine and dialing her back to 1605. Present her to Shakespeare and ask him, "What do you think? Is she one of yours? Do you recognize her as human?" I think it would be interesting, for example, if you showed Shakespeare the movie Apollo 13. Once he got past the fact that this was nonfiction and these guys were headed to the moon, he wouldn't have any problem with these guys at all. They're just adventurers who are trying to make it home, like the Greeks of 3,000 years ago.

If you show him the people of the various *Star Trek* series, I don't think he'd have much trouble identifying all of those people as human, although he might stop and scratch his head a little bit about Lt. Comdr. Data [an android]. The guys with the crabs on their foreheads I don't think he'd have any trouble with, but Data, I'd really like to know what kind of take Shakespeare would have on him.

Nick Gillespie: Let's open it up to the audience.

Questioner 1: This is a question for Eric. I agree that we can't know all the effects and impacts of complex changes

of the sorts that we're contemplating here. Neither can Ron. The only test we can use to figure out which of you is right has to be the empirical test. Have something of a free market. Probably some people are going to die at 75 or 80. Some people are going to choose to live to be 150 or 200, and then they're going to look back and say, "Gosh, I wish I'd died at 75." Eric wins.

But if you raise the fear of the future being unpredictable but you don't have any kind of empirical testing of it, you can really stop all progress. You can make that argument against progress in any field that we've ever had progress in, whether it's the use of fossil fuels or computing technology or antibiotics.

Eric Cohen: I think there are some basic principles that allow us to be a decent society. Equality is one. We don't treat other people, even weak, disabled, and vulnerable people, as means to our ends. I think that's a better way to live. If you think that principle through, you can set certain kinds of limits on certain technologies. It may be that if we destroyed as many embryos as we wanted to that we would cure 10 diseases. But I think we can come together and say we wouldn't be a better civilization or society if we did that. It's perfectly legitimate to argue for limits on that sort of thing.

We can say the same about some other technologies, especially those dealing with the beginning of life. Think of pre-implantation genetic screening, where you produce 10 embryos, subject them to all kinds of genetic tests, choose the ones that you think are healthy and promising, and discard the ones that aren't. I think we can set limits on those kinds of things.

I'm not sure that's the right way to govern some of the more subtle self-enhancement technologies. If Ron Bailey, in the privacy of his own home, wants to experiment with memory-enhancing drugs, all the power to him. Maybe he'll write 30 books, and they'll all be great, but I'm frankly very skeptical. I think it's a very superficial and simplistic understanding of human excellence and human intelligence that clings or looks longingly at some of these drugs and believes that they're going to make us smarter and better.

At the end of the day the ways that matter most in being good have to do with character anyway. That's an old-fashioned thing, but I think the people that we most admire are generally people not only of ability but people of character. There's no pill that's going to make us better in that way.

Nick Gillespie: Eric, you raise the question of equality and the ways technology might undercut that. During the past 500 years or so, comprising what's considered the modern era, it seems clear that we've increased human enhancement technologies and the treatment of people as equals. More people have political rights than in the past. There's a greater distribution of goods and opportunities across global society now compared to 50, let alone 500, years ago. If we look at the historical record, it's fair to conclude that technology has not only allowed humans to enhance and augment themselves but has also helped them become more equal.

Eric Cohen: In many ways, technology and progress have served the end of equality. I'm in a kind of weird position, right? I'm arguing both for equality and for excellence in a certain sense. On the one hand, I'm worried that these drugs, to put it bluntly, are going to make us sort of pathetic. I mean, yes, we might hit 900 home runs a season, but frankly some of these athletes are sort of pathetic. They're kind of dependent on their drugs, and they all deny it. [Baltimore Orioles slugger] Rafael Palmeiro wouldn't want to be seen shooting his steroids up in the batter's box because he knows that people would think he's less of an athlete. He's less excellent. He's more like the horses we breed.

Nick Gillespie: Would his wife be upset to learn that he's taking Viagra?

Eric Cohen: I don't know. I'll leave that to them.

Nick Gillespie: Palmeiro is a paid spokesman for Viagra, and he's married. That's why I mentioned it. Does taking Viagra—an enhancement drug—make his marital bed less real, less meaningful?

Eric Cohen: Let me bracket the Viagra question for a minute. There's a worry about these enhancements actually undermining the very excellence that they claim to serve. At the same time, I think there are genuine issues with equality. Yes, equality is much better. From the standpoint of equality, it's a heck of a lot better to live today than it was to live 300 years ago in British society. We are more equal, for the most part, but we also treat people in radically unequal ways, both at the beginning of life and at the end of life. And that's another kind of equality that I think has been compromised. If you take that principle seriously and if you take basic biology seriously, then embryos are embryonic human lives, and we're now talking about using them in research. We already abort children with Down syndrome. Those are ways we're saying these people are not good enough. We're not going to welcome them in our society. We're going to eliminate them, and so from that perspective equality has been hurt. Technology has created a mind-set that has made us more inegalitarian even as it's served the cause of equality. I think both things are happening at once.

Questioner 2: I've got two questions, one for Joel and one for Eric. Joel, you've noted that Asian people have an entirely different way of looking at what it is to be a human being than people in the West do. Can you elaborate on that? Eric, isn't it OK if we just sort of relax and let people live a little longer and make some mistakes?

Joel Garreau: I'm not an expert on Hindu philosophy or Confucianism, but I am interested in the facts on the ground in a lot of these cultures. The Chinese have made no secret of the fact that they want to be dominant in the 2008 Olympics. At the University of Pennsylvania Lee Sweeney has been creating genetically altered Schwarzenegger mice. You ought to see his mice. They've got haunches like steers, and their necks are bigger than their heads, and there isn't a day that goes by that he doesn't get a call from an athlete or a coach who is begging him to use them as a human equivalent of this. Lee thinks that the 2004 Olympics were the last ones without genetically engineered humans.

> **"I wonder who the real futurists are—the Catholics who have 10 kids and oppose embryo research, or the libertarians who have no kids and live to 110 and then get hit by a car?"**
>
> —Eric Cohen

An awful lot of the scientists in India have applauded the restrictions on stem cells in this country because they see our [relatively restrictive government policies] as an opportunity to make the great leap forward past the West in these technologies.

This is not some science fiction future. These are decisions that are happening now. That's why I'm so glad that Eric [and others] are asking the questions they are, because they're really good questions. I'm not crazy about some of the answers, but I'm glad they're asking the questions. I'm also glad that the Europeans are trying this business of using governments to control genetically modified organisms. I doubt that it's going to work on a basic practical level, but I like to see humans taking different approaches [to biotechnology] because we've got a long way to go and a short time to get there.

Eric Cohen: If we all relax, we'd have no panel discussions and get all worked up, and then what would we do in Washington? I'm not sure I have an objection to the pursuit of longevity taken in itself. I'm not sure I'm convinced that it's a great idea either, but I think there we'll just have to kind of wait and see. I would just note anecdotally that a lot of the people I know who are obsessed with longevity are also people who don't have children. One way of thinking about the future is to obsessively try to live longer and think about how we can [improve] the world that we want to inhabit. The other way to think about the future is to think about the world we're going to pass down to those who follow us. I wonder who the real futurists are—the Catholics who have 10 kids and oppose embryo research, or the libertarians who have no kids and live to 110 and then get hit by a car?

And there are ethical questions involved here that mean we can't simply relax. Should we be using nascent human life as a tool to develop therapies [that will let us live longer]?

Ronald Bailey: I've suggested to my wife that we'll have children when we're younger. In any case, with regard to treasuring every embryo, nature certainly doesn't do that; 80 percent of all naturally conceived embryos, as far as we know, are not implanted and never become people or babies or anything else. In fact, the results of IVF are better than those of nature.

Questioner 3: In terms of consenting to genetic treatments, do embryos—or children, for that matter—have the ability to give their consent?

Ronald Bailey: I want to remind everybody in the audience that you did not give consent to be born. In fact, you did not give consent to be born with any of the genes that you have. So any embryos that parents decide to modify stand in exactly the same relation that all previous embryos have stood in.

If you think about what people are apt to do, this isn't really an issue. Would you want the person-to-be to be smarter? Well, yeah, that'd be good. Forty IQ points would be good too. Would they like to have a good immune system? Yeah, they'd like that. What about athletic ability? Yeah, OK. I think you can presume consent for most of the things that parents are going to do for their children because they're not going to try to make them worse. They're going to try to make them better.

From *Reason Magazine* and *Reason.com,* January 2006. Copyright © 2006 by Reason Foundation, 3415 S. Sepulveda Blvd., Suite 400, Los Angeles, CA 90034. www.reason.com

The Secret Nuclear War

Eduardo Goncalves

Hugo Paulino was proud to be a fusilier. He was even prouder to be serving as a UN peacekeeper in Kosovo. It was his chance to help the innocent casualties of war. His parents did not expect him to become one.

Hugo, says his father Luis, died of leukaemia caused by radiation from depleted uranium (DU) shells fired by NATO during the Kosovo war. He was one of hundreds of Portuguese peacekeepers sent to Klina, an area heavily bombed with these munitions. Their patrol detail included the local lorry park, bombed because it had served as a Serb tank reserve, and the Valujak mines, which sheltered Serbian troops.

In their time off, the soldiers bathed in the river and gratefully supplemented their tasteless rations with local fruit and cheeses given to them by thankful nuns from the convent they guarded. Out of curiosity, they would climb inside the destroyed Serbian tanks littering the area.

Hugo arrived back in Portugal from his tour of duty on 12 February 2000, complaining of headaches, nausea and 'flu-like symptoms'. Ten days later, on 22 February, he suffered a major seizure. He was rushed to Lisbon's military hospital, where his condition rapidly deteriorated. On 9 March, he died. He was 21.

The military autopsy, which was kept secret for 10 months, claimed his death was due to septicaemia and 'herpes of the brain'. Not so, says Luis Paulino. 'When he was undergoing tests, a doctor called me over and said he thought it could be from radiation.'

It was only then that Luis learnt about the uranium shells—something his son had never been warned about or given protective clothing against. He contacted doctors and relatives of Belgian and Italian soldiers suspected of having succumbed to radiation poisoning.

'The similarities were extraordinary', he said. 'My son had died from leukemia. That is why the military classified the autopsy report and wanted me to sign over all rights to its release.'

Today, Kosovo is littered with destroyed tanks, and pieces of radioactive shrapnel. NATO forces fired 31,000 depleted uranium shells during the Kosovo campaign, and 10,800 into neighbouring Bosnia. The people NATO set out to protect—and the soldiers it sent out to protect them—are now dying. According to Bosnia's health minister, Boza Ljubic, cancer deaths among civilians have risen to 230 cases per 100,000 last year, up from 152 in 1999. Leukemia cases, he added, had doubled.

Scientists predict that the use of DU in Serbia will lead to more than 10,000 deaths from cancer among local residents, aid workers, and peacekeepers. Belated confessions that plutonium was also used may prompt these estimates to be revised. But while NATO struggles to stave off accusations of a cover-up, the Balkans are merely the newest battlefield in a silent world war that has claimed millions of lives. Most of its victims have died not in war-zones, but in ordinary communities scattered across the globe.

The Hidden Deaths of Newbury

Far away from the war-torn Balkans is Newbury, a prosperous white-collar industrial town in London's commuter belt. On its outskirts is Greenham Common, the former US Air Force station that was one of America's most important strategic bases during the Cold War. The base was closed down after the signing of the INF (Intermediate Nuclear Forces) Treaty by Ronald Reagan and Mikhail Gorbachev. The nuclear threat was over. Or so people thought.

In August 1993, Ann Capewell—who lived just one mile away from the base's former runway—died of acute myeloid leukaemia. She was 16 when she passed away, just 40 days after diagnosis. As they were coming to terms with their sudden loss, her parents—Richard and Elizabeth—were surprised to find a number of other cases of leukaemia in their locality.

The more they looked, the more cases they found. 'Many were just a stone's throw from our front door,' says Richard, 'mainly cases of myeloid leukaemia in young people.' What none of them knew was that they were the victims of a nuclear accident at Greenham Common that had been carefully covered up by successive British and American administrations.

It is believed that the estimated 1,900 nuclear tests conducted during the Cold War released fallout equivalent to 40,000 Hiroshimas in every corner of the globe.

On February 28 1958, a laden B-47 nuclear bomber was awaiting clearance for take-off when it was suddenly engulfed in a huge fireball. Another bomber flying overhead had dropped a full fuel tank just 65 feet away. The plane exploded and burnt uncontrollably for days. As did its deadly payload.

A secret study by scientists at Britain's nearby nuclear bomb laboratory at Aldermaston documented the fallout, but the findings were never disclosed. The report showed how radioactive particles had been 'glued' to the runway surface by fire-fighters attempting to extinguish the blazing bomber—and that these were now being slowly blown into Newbury and over other local communities by aircraft jet blast.

'Virtually all the cases of leukaemias and lymphomas are in a band stretching from Greenham Common into south Newbury,' says Elizabeth. However, the British government continues to deny the cluster's existence, whilst the Americans still insist there was no accident.

Yet this was just one of countless disasters, experiments and officially-sanctioned activities which the nuclear powers have kept a closely-guarded secret. Between them, they have caused a global human death toll which is utterly unprecedented and profoundly shocking.

Broken Arrows

In 1981, the Pentagon publicly released a list of 32 'Broken Arrows'—official military terminology for an accident involving a nuclear weapon. The report gave few details and did not divulge the location of some accidents. It was prepared in response to mounting media pressure about possible accident cover-ups.

But another US government document, this time secret, indicates that the official report may be seriously misleading. It states that 'a total of 1,250 nuclear weapons have been involved in accidents during handling, storage and transportation', a number of which 'resulted in, or had high potential for, plutonium dispersal.'[1]

Washington has never acknowledged the human consequences of even those few accidents it admits to, such as the Thule disaster in Greenland in 1968. When a B-52 bomber crashed at this secret nuclear base, all four bombs detonated, and a cloud of plutonium rose 800 metres in the air, blowing deadly radioactive particles hundreds of miles. The authorities downplayed the possibility of any health risks. But today, many local Eskimos, and their huskies, suffer from cancer, and over 300 people involved in the clean-up operation alone have since died of cancer and mysterious illnesses.

We may never know the true toll from all the bomb accidents, as the nuclear powers classify these disasters not as matters of public interest but of 'national security' instead. Indeed, it is only now that details are beginning to emerge of some accidents at bomb factories and nuclear plants that took place several decades ago.

Soviet Sins

In 1991, Polish film-maker Slawomir Grunberg was invited to a little-known town in Russia's Ural mountains that was once part of a top-secret Soviet nuclear bomb-making complex. What he found was a tragedy of extraordinary dimensions, largely

The Cancer Epidemic

Scientists at St Andrew's University recently found that cells exposed to a dose of just two alpha particles of radiation produced as many cancers as much higher doses of radiation. They concluded that a single alpha particle of radiation could be carcinogenic.

Herman Muller, who has received a Nobel Prize for his work, has shown how the human race's continuous exposure to so-called 'low-level' radiation is causing a gradual reduction in its ability to survive, as successive generations are genetically damaged. The spreading and accumulation of even tiny genetic mutations pass through family lines, provoking allergies, asthma, juvenile diabetes, hypertension, arthritis, high blood cholesterol conditions, and muscular and bone defects.

Dr Chris Busby, who has extensively researched the low-level radiation threat, has made a link between everyday radiation exposure and a range of modern ailments: 'There have been tremendous increases in diseases resulting from the breakdown of the immune system in the last 20 years: diabetes, asthma, AIDS and others which may have an immune-system link, such as MS and ME. A whole spectrum of neurological conditions of unknown origin has developed'.[10]

Around the world, a pattern is emerging. For the first time in modern history, mortality rates among adults between the ages of 15 and 54 are actually increasing, and have been since 1982. In July 1983, the US Center for Birth Defects in Atlanta, Georgia, reported that physical and mental disabilities in the under-17s had doubled—despite a reduction in diseases such as polio, and improved vaccines and medical care.

Defects in new-born babies doubled between the 1950s and 1980s, as did long-term debilitating diseases. The US Environmental Protection Agency adds that 23 per cent of US males were sterile in 1980, compared to 0.5 per cent in 1938.

Above all, cancer is now an epidemic. In 1900, cancer accounted for only 4 percent of deaths in the US. Now it is the second leading cause of premature mortality. Worldwide, the World Health Organisation (WHO) estimates the number of cancers will double in most countries over the next 25 years.

Within a few years, the chances of getting cancer in Britain will be as high as 40 percent—virtually the toss of a coin.

unknown to the outside world, and ignored by post-Cold War leaders.

His film—*Chelyabinsk: The Most Contaminated Spot on the Planet*—tells the story of the disasters at the Soviet Union's first plutonium factory, and the poisoning of hundreds of thousands of people. For years, the complex dumped its nuclear waste—totalling 76 million cubic metres—into the Techa River, the sole water source for scores of local communities that line its banks. According to a local doctor, people received an average radiation dose 57 times higher than that of Chernobyl's inhabitants.

In 1957, there was an explosion at a waste storage facility that blew 2 million curies of radiation into the atmosphere. The kilometre-high cloud drifted over three Soviet provinces, contaminating over 250,000 people living in 217 towns and villages. Only a handful of local inhabitants were ever evacuated.

10 years later, Lake Karachay, also used as a waste dump, began to dry up. The sediment around its shores blew 5 million curies of radioactive dust over 25,000 square kilometres, irradiating 500,000 people. Even today, the lake is so 'hot' that standing on its shore will kill a person within one hour.

Grunberg's film tells of the terrible toll of these disasters on local families, such as that of Idris Sunrasin, whose grandmother, parents and three siblings have died of cancer. Leukaemia cases increased by 41 percent after the plant began operations, and the average life span for women in 1993 was 47, compared to 72 nationally. For men it was just 45.

The Secret Nuclear War

Russia's nuclear industry is commonly regarded as cavalier in regard to health and safety. But the fact is that the nuclear military-industrial complex everywhere has been quite willing to deliberately endanger and sacrifice the lives of innocent civilians to further its ambitions.

The US government, for example, recently admitted its nuclear scientists carried out over 4,000 experiments on live humans between 1944 and 1974. They included feeding radioactive food to disabled children, irradiating prisoners' testicles, and trials on new-born babies and pregnant mothers. Scientists involved with the Manhattan Project injected people with plutonium without telling them. An autopsy of one of the victims reportedly showed that his bones 'looked like Swiss cheese'. At the University of Cincinnati, 88 mainly low-income, black women were subjected to huge doses of radiation in an experiment funded by the military. They suffered acute radiation sickness. Nineteen of them died.

Scientists predict that millions will die in centuries to come from nuclear tests that happened in the 1950s and 1960s.

Details of many experiments still remain shrouded in secrecy, whilst little is known of the more shocking ones to come to light—such as one when a man was injected with what a report described as 'about a lethal dose' of strontium-89.[2]

In Britain too, scientists have experimented with plutonium on new-born babies, ethnic minorities and the disabled. When American colleagues reviewed a British proposal for a joint experiment, they concluded: 'What is the worst thing that can happen to a human being as a result of being a subject? Death.'[3]

They also conducted experiments similar to America's 'Green Run' programme, in which 'dirty' radiation was released over populated areas in the western states of Washington and Oregon

contaminating farmland, crops and water. The 'scrubber' filters in Hanford's nuclear stacks were deliberately switched off first. Scientists, posing as agriculture department officials, found radiation contamination levels on farms hundreds of times above 'safety' levels.

But America's farmers and consumers were not told this, and the British public has never been officially told about experiments on its own soil.

Forty Thousand Hiroshimas

It is believed that the estimated 1,900 nuclear tests conducted during the Cold War released fallout equivalent to 40,000 Hiroshimas in every corner of the globe. Fission products from the Nevada Test site can be detected in the ecosystems of countries as far apart as South Africa, Brazil, and Malaysia. Here, too, ordinary people were guinea pigs in a global nuclear experiment. The public health hazards were known right from the beginning, but concealed from the public. A 1957 US government study predicted that recent American tests had produced an extra 2,000 'genetically defective' babies in the US each year, and up to 35,000 every year around the globe. They continued regardless.

Ernest Sternglass's research shows how, in 1964, between 10,000 and 15,000 children were lost by miscarriage and stillbirth in New York state alone—and that there were some 10 to 15 times this number of fetal deaths across America.[4]

Over the years, the Harwell, Aldermaston and Amersham plants have pumped millions of gallons of llquid contaminated with radioactive waste into the River Thames.

Those who lived closest to the test sites have seen their families decimated. Such as the 100,000 people who were directly downwind of Nevada's fallout. They included the Mormon community of St George in Utah, 100 miles away from 'Ground Zero'—the spot where the bombs were detonated. Cancer used to be virtually unheard of among its population. Mormons do not smoke or drink alcohol or coffee, and live largely off their own homegrown produce.

Mormons are also highly patriotic. They believe government to be 'God-given', and do not protest. The military could afford to wait until the wind was blowing from the test site towards St George before detonating a device. After all, President Eisenhower had said: 'We can afford to sacrifice a few thousand people out there in defence of national security.'[5]

When the leukaemia cases suddenly appeared, doctors—unused to the disease—literally had no idea what it was. A nine-year-old boy, misdiagnosed with diabetes, died after a single shot of insulin. Women who complained of radiation sickness symptoms were told they had 'housewife syndrome'. Many gave birth to terribly deformed babies that became known as 'the sacrifice babies'. Elmer Pickett, the local mortician, had to learn new embalming techniques for the small bodies of wasted children killed by leukaemia. He himself was to lose no fewer than 16 members of his immediate family to cancer.

By the mid-1950s, just a few years after the tests began, St George had a leukaemia rate 2.5 times the national average, whereas before it was virtually non-existent. The total number of radiation deaths are said to have totalled 1,600—in a town with a population of just 5,000.

The military simply lied about the radiation doses people were getting. Former army medic Van Brandon later revealed how his unit kept two sets of radiation readings for test fallout in the area. 'One set was to show that no one received an [elevated] exposure' whilst 'the other set of books showed the actual reading. That set was brought in a locked briefcase every morning.'[6]

Continuous Fallout

The world's population is still being subjected to the continuous fallout of the 170 megatons of long-lived nuclear fission products blasted into the atmosphere and returned daily to earth by wind and rain—slowly poisoning our bodies via the air we breathe, the food we eat, and the water we drink. Scientists predict that millions will die in centuries to come from tests that happened in the 1950s and 1960s.

But whilst atmospheric testing is now banned, over 400 nuclear bomb factories and power plants around the world make 'routine discharges' of nuclear waste into the environment. Thousands of nuclear waste dumping grounds, many of them leaking, are contaminating soil and water every day. The production of America's nuclear weapons arsenal alone has produced 100 million cubic metres of long-lived radioactive waste.

The notorious Hanford plutonium factory—which produced the fissile materials for the Trinity test and Nagasaki bomb—has discharged over 440 billion gallons of contaminated liquid into the surrounding area, contaminating 200 square miles of groundwater, but concealed the dangers from the public. Officials knew as early as the late 1940s that the nearby Columbia River was becoming seriously contaminated and a hazard to local fishermen. They chose to keep information about discharges secret and not to issue warnings.

In Britain, there are 7,000 sites licensed to use nuclear materials, 1,000 of which are allowed to discharge wastes. Three of them, closely involved in Britain's nuclear bomb programme, are located near the River Thames. Over the years, the Harwell, Aldermaston and Amersham plants have pumped millions of gallons of liquid contaminated with radioactive waste into the river.

They did so in the face of opposition from government ministers and officials who said 'the 6 million inhabitants of London derive their drinking water from this source. Any increase in [radio-]activity of the water supply would increase the genetic load on this comparatively large group.'[7] One government minister even wrote of his fears that the dumping 'would produce between 10 and 300 severely abnormal individuals per generation'.

Public relations officers at Harwell themselves added: 'the potential sufferers are 8 million in number, including both Houses of Parliament, Fleet Street and Whitehall'. These discharges continue to this day.

Study after study has uncovered 'clusters' of cancers and high rates of other unusual illnesses near nuclear plants, including deformities and Down Syndrome. Exposure to radiation among Sellafield's workers, in northwest England, has been linked to a greater risk of fathering a stillborn child and leukaemia among off-spring. Reports also suggest a higher risk of babies developing spina bifida in the womb.

Although the plant denies any link, even official MAFF studies have shown high levels of contamination in locally-grown fruit and vegetables, as well as wild animals. The pollution from Sellafield alone is such that it has coated the shores of the whole of Britain—from Wales to Scotland, and even Hartlepool in north-eastern England. A nationwide study organised by Harwell found that Sellafield 'is a source of plutonium contamination in the wider population of the British Isles'.[8]

> **Study after study has uncovered 'clusters' of cancers and high rates of other illnesses near nuclear plants, including deformities and Down Syndrome. Exposure to radiation among Sellafield's workers, in NW England, has been linked to a greater risk of fathering a stillborn child and leukaemia among off-spring.**

Those who live nearest the plant face the greatest threat. A study of autopsy tissue by the National Radiological Protection Board (NRPB) found high plutonium levels in the lungs of local Cumbrians—350 per cent higher than people in other parts of the country. 'Cancer clusters' have been found around nuclear plants across the globe—from France to Taiwan, Germany to Canada. A joint White House/US Department of Energy investigation recently found a high incidence of 22 different kinds of cancer at 14 different US nuclear weapons facilities around the country.

Meanwhile, a Greenpeace USA study of the toxicity of the Mississippi river showed that from 1968–83 there were 66,000 radiation deaths in the counties lining its banks—more than the number of Americans who died during the Vietnam war.

Don't Blame Us

Despite the growing catalogue of tragedy, the nuclear establishment has consistently tried to deny responsibility. It claims that only high doses of radiation—such as those experienced by the victims of the Hiroshima and Nagasaki bombs—are dangerous, though even here they have misrepresented the data. They say that the everyday doses from nuclear plant discharges, bomb factories and transportation of radioactive materials are 'insignificant', and that accidents are virtually impossible.

The truth, however, is that the real number and seriousness of accidents has never been disclosed, and that the damage from fallout has been covered up. The nuclear establishment now grudgingly (and belatedly) accepts that there is no such thing as a safe dose of radiation, however 'low', yet the poisonous discharges continue. When those within the nuclear establishment try to speak out, they are harassed, intimidated—and even threatened.

John Gofman, former head of Lawrence Livermore's biomedical unit, who helped produce the world's first plutonium for the bomb, was for years at the heart of the nuclear complex. He recalls painfully the time he was called to give evidence before a Congressional inquiry set up to defuse mounting concern over radiation's dangers.

'Chet Holifield and Craig Hosmer of the Joint Committee (on Atomic Energy) came in and turned to me and said: "Just what the hell do you think you two are doing, getting all those little old ladies in tennis shoes up in arms about our atomic energy program? There are people like you who have tried to hurt the Atomic Energy Commission program before. We got them, and we'll get you." '[9]

Gofman was eventually forced out of his job. But the facts of his research—and that of many other scientists—speak for themselves.

The Final Reckoning

But could radiation really be to blame for these deaths? Are the health costs really that great? The latest research suggests they are.

It is only very recently that clues have surfaced as to the massive destructive power of radiation in terms of human health. The accident at Chernobyl will kill an estimated half a million people worldwide from cancer, and perhaps more. 90 per cent of children in the neighbouring former Soviet republic of Belarus are contaminated for life—the poisoning of an entire country's gene pool.

Ernest Sternglass calculates that, at the height of nuclear testing, there were as many as 3 million foetal deaths, spontaneous abortions and stillbirths in the US alone. In addition, 375,000 babies died in their first year of life from radiation-linked diseases.[11]

Rosalie Bertell, author of the classic book *No Immediate Danger*, now revised and re-released, has attempted to piece together a global casualty list from the nuclear establishment's own data. The figures she has come up with are chilling—but entirely plausible.

Using the official 'radiation risk' estimates published in 1991 by the International Commission on Radiological Protection (ICRP), and the total radiation exposure data to the global population calculated by the UN Scientific Committee on the Effects of Atomic Radiation (UNSCEAR) in 1993, she has come up with a terrifying tally:

- 358 million cancers from nuclear bomb production and testing
- 9.7 million cancers from bomb and plant accidents

The Final Reckoning

How many deaths is the nuclear industry responsible for? The following calculations of numbers of cancers caused by radiation are the latest and most accurate:*
from nuclear bomb production and testing: 385 million
from bomb and plant accidents: 9.7 million
from the 'routine discharges' of nuclear power plants (5 million of them among populations living nearby): 6.6 million
likely number of total cancer fatalities worldwide: 175 million
[Added to this number are 235 million genetically damaged and diseased people, and 588 million children born with diseases such as brain damage, mental disabilities, spina bifida, genital deformities, and childhood cancers.]

*Calculated by Rosalie Bertell, using the official 'radiation risk' estimates published in 1991 by the International Commission on Radiological Protection (ICRP), and the total radiation exposure data to the global population calculated by the UN Scientific Committee on the Effects of Atomic Radiation (UNSCEAR) in 1993.

- 6.6 million cancers from the 'routine discharges' of nuclear power plants (5 million of them among populations living nearby).
- As many as 175 million of these cancers could be fatal.

Added to this number are no fewer than 235 million genetically damaged and diseased people, and a staggering 588 million children born with what are called 'teratogenic effects'—diseases such as brain damage, mental disabilities, spina bifida, genital deformities, and childhood cancers.

Furthermore, says Bertell, we should include the problem of nonfatal cancers and of other damage which is debilitating but not counted for insurance and liability purposes'[12]—such as the 500 million babies lost as stillbirths because they were exposed to radiation whilst still in the womb, but are not counted as 'official' radiation victims.

It is what the nuclear holocaust peace campaigners always warned of if war between the old superpowers broke out, yet it has already happened and with barely a shot being fired. Its toll is greater than that of all the wars in history put together, yet noone is counted as among the war dead.

It is the nuclear holocaust that peace campaigners always warned of if war between the old superpowers broke out, yet it has already happened and with barely a shot being fired.

Its virtually infinite killing and maiming power leads Rosalie Bertell to demand that we learn a new language to express a terrifying possibility: 'The concept of species annihilation means a relatively swift, deliberately induced end to history, culture, science, biological reproduction and memory. It is the ultimate human rejection of the gift of life, an act which requires a new word to describe it: omnicide'.[13]

Notes

1. 'Report of the safety criteria for plutonium-bearing weapons—summary', US Department of Energy, February 14, 1973, document RS5640/1035.

2. Strontium metabolism meeting, Atomic Energy Division–Division of Biology and Medicine, January 17, 1954.

3. memorandum to Bart Gledhill, chairman, Human Subjects Committee. LLNL, from Larry Anderson, LLNL, February 21, 1989.

4. see 'Secret Fallout, Low-Level Radiation from Hiroshima to Three-Mile Island'. Ernest Sternglass, McGraw-Hill, New York, 1981.

5. see 'American Ground Zero; The Secret Nuclear War', Carole Gallagher, MIT Press. Boston, 1993.

6. Washington Post, February 24, 1994.

7. see PRO files AB 6/1379 and AB 6/2453 and 3584.

8. 'Variations in the concentration of plutonium, strontium-90 and total alpha-emitters in human teeth', RG. O'Donnell et al, Sd. Tot. Env, 201 (1997) 235–243.

9. interview with Gofman, DOE/OHRE Oral History Project, December 1994, pp 49–50 of official transcripts.

10. 'Wings of Death—nuclear pollution and human health', Dr. Chris Busby, Green Audit, Wales, 1995

11. see 'Secret Fallout, Low-Level Radiation from Hiroshima to Three-Mile Island', Ernest Sternglass, McGraw-Hill, New York, 1981.

12. from 'No Immediate Danger—Prognosis for a Radioactive Earth', Dr Rosalie Bertell. Women's Press. London 1985 (revised 2001)

13. pers. Comm. 4 February 2001

Further Readings

'No Immediate Danger—Prognosis for a Radioactive Earth', Dr Rosalie Bertell, Women's Press, London (revised 2001)

'Deadly Deceit—low-level radiation, high-level cover-up', Dr. Jay Gould and Benjamin A. Goldman, Four Walls Eight Windows, New York, 1991

'Wings of Death—nuclear pollution and human health', Dr. Chris Busby, Green Audit, Wales, 1995

'American Ground Zero: The Secret Nuclear War', Carole Gallagher, MIT Press, Boston, 1993

'Radioactive Heaven and Earth—the health effects of nuclear weapons testing in, on, and above the earth', a report of the IPPNW International Commission, Zed Books, 1991 'Secret Fallout. Low-Level Radiation from Hiroshima to Three-Mile Island', Ernest Sternglass, McGraw-Hill, New York, 1981

'Clouds of Deceit—the deadly legacy of Britain's bomb tests', Joan Smith, Faber and Faber, London, 1985

'Nuclear Wastelands', Arjun Makhijani et al (eds), MIT Press, Boston, 1995 'Radiation and Human Health', Dr. John W. Gofman, Sierra Book Club, San Francisco, 1981

'The Greenpeace Book of the Nuclear Age—The Hidden History, the Human Cost', John May, Victor Gollancz, 1989

'The Unsinkable Aircraft Carrier—American military power in Britain', Duncan Campbell, Michael Joseph, London 1984

EDUARDO GONCALVES is a freelance journalist and environmental researcher. He is author of tile reports *Broken Arrow—Greenham Common's Secret Nuclear Accident* and *Nuclear Guinea Pigs—British Human Radiation Experiments,* published by CND (UK), and was researcher to the film *The Dragon that Slew St George.* He is currently writing a book about the hidden history of the nuclear age.

Update on the State of the Future

JEROME C. GLENN AND THEODORE J. GORDON

I s the future getting better or worse? According to the latest edition of State of the Future, global prospects for improving the overall health, wealth, and sustainability of humanity are improving, but slowly.

The picture painted by the report gives much cause for hope. The world has grown to 6.5 billion people, 1 billion of whom are connected by the Internet, and the annual economy is approaching $60 trillion. However, there is also much cause for concern. The great paradox of our age is that, while more and more people enjoy the benefits of technological and economic growth, increasing numbers of people are poor, unhealthy, and lack access to education. In the years ahead, globalization will present humanity with both challenges and opportunities as increased connectivity highlights our strengths and our shortcomings as a global community.

A race is under way between the increasing proliferation of threats and our growing ability to improve humanity's condition. Understanding the nature of this race entails looking at the contradictory forces at work in our world. Here is a brief assessment of those forces, along with possible strategies for positive resolution.

World Trade: Engine of Opportunity and Disparity

Explosive economic growth over the previous decades has led to dramatic increases in life expectancy, literacy, and access to safe drinking water and sanitation, as well as to decreases in infant mortality for the vast majority of the world. At the same time, the ratio of the total income of people in the top 5% to those in the bottom 5% has grown from 6 to 1 in 1980 to more than 200 to 1 now. That ratio is not sustainable.

Unfortunately, economic disparities could grow unless a global partnership emerges between the rich and the poor, using the strength of free markets with rules based on global ethics. That, in turn, could trigger increased migration of the poor to rich areas and result in a range of complex conflicts and humanitarian disasters.

With their high technology and low wages, China and India will become giants of world trade. This should force the developing world to rethink its trade-led economic growth strategies. China alone could produce 25% of all manufactured goods in the world by 2025.

Environmental Sustainability

The Millennium Ecosystem Assessment found that 60% of our life-support systems are gone or in danger of collapse. A collaboration of 1,360 experts from 95 countries produced a global inventory of the state of the Earth's ecosystems. According to their assessment, degradation could grow worse by 2050 as another 2.6 billion people are added to the Earth. Current absorption capacity of carbon by oceans and forests is about 3 to 3.5 billion tons per year. Yet, 7 billion tons are added to the atmosphere annually, which could increase to 14 billion tons per year if current trends continue—eventually leading to greenhouse effects beyond the ability of humans to control. Events like the 2004 Asian tsunami and the Millennium Ecosystem Assessment's pronouncement are helping the world to realize that environmental security deserves greater attention.

At the same time, economic growth (often achieved at the expense of environmental security) is also sorely needed. A measure of the degree to which developing nations need growth can be seen in the increase in development aid from wealthier nations to economically struggling ones over recent years. Official development assistance to cash-strapped nations increased to $78.6 billion in 2004, the highest level ever.

Until Africa shifts from being primarily an exporter of raw materials to a more scientifically oriented culture, it has no chance of closing its economic gap with the developed world.

Organizations like the World Bank and the United Nations Development Program (UNDP) have long relied on economic development indicators, but integrated sustainable development indicators (to measure world progress toward sustainability) are recent inventions. Our ability to measure sustainable economic development has improved. As part of the multilateral Environment and Security Initiative, international organizations such as UNDP and NATO have begun to offer expertise and resources to promote environmental security in addition to economic security.

The Central European Node of the Millennium Project has created a Sustainable Development Index composed of seven major subject areas, 14 indicators (two for each major area), and 64 variables (various numbers of variables for individual indicators). This index was calculated for 179 countries to express their state of development and progress toward sustainable development. It allows a mapping of sustainable development as well as comparison among different countries.

The countries rated as most sustainable were Sweden, Finland, and Switzerland, while those rated as least sustainable were Afghanistan, Somalia, and Burundi. Other sustainable development indicators include the Environmental Sustainability Index, the Dashboard of Sustainability, the Ecological Footprint Calculator, the Living Planet Index, and the Well-Being Index.

The concepts of environmental diplomacy and human security are gaining recognition in both military and diplomatic circles. Our research showed a noticeable increase in the number of articles, formal studies, and conferences related to environmental security during the past year. The environment is becoming recognized as being on a par with cultural and ethnic issues in security analysis. Advances in satellites, sensors, and the Internet are making it possible to monitor environmental situations more effectively.

Development Goals: Moving Ahead or Lagging Behind?

It seems that the UN Millennium Development Goal of cutting poverty in half between 2000 and 2015 may well be met on a global basis—but not in Africa and some parts of Asia. The dynamics of urbanization have facilitated many important improvements to the human condition. In other words, urbanization, once thought a problem, is now seen as part of the solution to poverty, ignorance, disease, and malnutrition.

Hunger and water scarcity will worsen unless more serious and intelligent investments are made. Water supply has to be increased, not simply redistributed. Despite improved access to safe drinking water and better sanitation during the last decade, 1.1 billion people still do not have access to safe drinking water and 2.6 billion people—half the population in developing countries—lack adequate sanitation.

Global Information Culture

Nearly 15% of the world is connected to the Internet, and the majority of the world's population may be connected within 15 years, making cyberspace an unprecedented medium for civilization. This new distribution of the means of production in the knowledge economy is cutting through old hierarchical controls in politics, economics, and finance. It is becoming a self-organizing mechanism that could lead to dramatic increases in humanity's ability to invent its future. Millions share ideas and feelings with strangers around the world, increasing global understanding. Google and other search engines have made the world's knowledge available to previously isolated populations. This will provide a more even playing field for the future knowledge economy.

The advent of the "24-7 always on" globalized world of ubiquitous computing implies that we will be making many more decisions per day and constantly changing our own and others' schedules and priorities. Information overload will make it increasingly difficult to separate the noise from the signal of what is important to know in order to make good decisions.

Civilization is also becoming increasingly vulnerable to cyber-terrorism, power outages, information pollution (misinformation, pornography, junk e-mail, and media violence), and virus attacks.

As the integration of cell phones, video, and the Internet grows, prices for this technology will fall. This will accelerate globalization and allow swarms of people to quickly form and disband, coordinate actions, and share information ranging from stock market tips to bold new contagious ideas (meme epidemics).

In a sad and ironic twist, despite the expansion of communications technology and, as a result, the power of individuals to speak freely, in 2004 only 17% of the world's people lived in countries that enjoyed a free press.

Medicine Is Becoming Cheaper as Some Illnesses Spread

Many of the world's most devastating illnesses will become less expensive to treat. However, increasing threats from new and reemerging diseases and from drug-resistant microorganisms have attracted the concern of the World Health Organization. Malaria, tuberculosis, and AIDS were expected to kill more than 6 million people in 2005. There were 4.9 million new HIV/AIDS cases in 2004, while more than 3.1 million people died of AIDS—200,000 more than the previous year. The current spread of HIV in eastern Europe and Asia implies that the number of AIDS patients in these areas may eventually dwarf the AIDS population in Africa. As human encroachment on the natural environment continues, increased interspecies contacts could lead to the spread to humans of infectious diseases known previously only in wild animals.

Peace and Security

The United Nations has defined terrorism as "actions already proscribed by existing conventions; any action constitutes terrorism if it is intended to cause death or serious bodily harm to civilians or noncombatants with the purpose of intimidating a population or compelling a government or an international organization to do or abstain from doing any act." This agreement should lead to greater international cooperation.

While prospects for security in places like Kashmir have improved, the horrors in Sudan, the Congo, Iraq, and Israeli-Palestinian areas continue, as do nuclear uncertainties with Iran and North Korea. The world has yet to agree about when it is right to use force to intervene in the affairs of a country that is significantly endangering its own or other peoples. Conventional military force has little effect in combating the asymmetrical and intrastate warfare as the boundaries between war, civil unrest, terrorism, and crime become increasingly blurred. Although Yasser Arafat's death has restarted the Middle East peace process, internal Islamist political reforms have been evolving quietly for the past several years that could lead either to new negotiations or negotiation setbacks as ideological hardliners insert themselves into the negotiation process.

Because weapons of mass destruction may be available to individuals over the next generation, the welfare of anyone should be the concern of everyone. Such platitudes are not new, but the consequences of their failure will be quite different in the future when one person can be massively destructive.

Technology Is Accelerating, Along with Demand for Energy

Most people still do not appreciate how fast science and technology will change over the next 25 years and would be surprised to learn about recent breakthroughs. For example, several years ago light was stopped by a yttrium-silica crystal and then released; it has also been slowed in gas and then accelerated. Adult stem cells have been regressed to embryo-like flexibility to grow replacement tissue. In experiments, humans with small computer chips implanted in their brains have been able to perform limited computer functions via thought. To help the world cope with the acceleration of change, it may be necessary to create an international science and technology organization to arrange the world's science and technology knowledge as well as to examine the potential consequences of various technological breakthroughs.

The factors that caused the acceleration of science and technology innovation are themselves accelerating, hence, the acceleration of scientific and technological accomplishments over the past 25 years will appear slow compared with the rate of change in the next 25. Since technology is growing so rapidly along several fronts, the possibility of it growing beyond human control must now be taken seriously.

In contrast, running this technology will require energy. World energy demand is forecast to increase by 60% from 2002 to 2030 and to require about $568 billion in new investments every year to meet that demand. Oil production is declining among the majority of producers. Meanwhile, in 2003 the Texas Transportation Institute found that U.S. traffic jams alone wasted 2.3 billion gallons of gasoline, adding greenhouse gases and hastening the day when the oil wells run dry.

Technology has the power to resolve this issue if governments and people develop the will to use it toward that end. The time has come for an Apollo-like program to increase the world's supply of nonpolluting energy.

Nanotechnology: Growing Possibility and Peril

Nanotechnology will provide an extraordinary range of benefits for humanity, but as with any advance, it is wise to forecast problems in order to avoid them. Little is known about the environmental and health risks of manufactured nanomaterials. For example, artificial blood cells (respirocytes) that dramatically enhance human performance could cause overheating of the body and bio-breakdowns. Disposal of highly efficient batteries that use nanomaterials could affect ecosystems and human health.

Since the military is a major force in nanotechnology research and development, it can play a key role in understanding and managing nanotechnology risks. As a result, the Millennium Project put together an expert Delphi panel to identify and rate important forms of nanotechnology-related environmental pollution, to look at health hazards that could result from any military and/or terrorist activities, and to suggest military research that might reduce these problems.

Other Key Issue Areas

Military expenditures in 2005 were expected to reach $1 trillion. At the same time, annual income for organized crime has passed $2 trillion. It is time for an international campaign to develop a global consensus for action against transnational organized crime, which is increasingly interfering with governments' ability to act. Weapons of mass destruction are still stockpiled and form a threat that has yet to be addressed realistically.

The global population is expanding, retracting and aging. The world population has grown by 4 billion people since 1950 and may grow another 2.6 billion by 2050 before it begins to fall. According to the UN's lower forecasts (which have proven to be more accurate), world population could fall to 5.5 billion by 2100—an astonishing 1 billion fewer people than are alive today. This assumes that there will be no major life extension breakthroughs by then. In any case, civilization will have to adapt to a world in which older people form the majority.

The world is slowly beginning to realize that improving the political and economic status of women is one of the most cost-effective ways to address various global challenges. Despite this, women, on average, are still paid 18% less than are men. Male violence toward women results in more casualties than does war.

The Challenge for Tomorrow's Leaders and Managers

The combination of economic growth and technological innovation has made it possible for 3 to 4 billion people to have relatively good health and living conditions. However, unless our financial, economic, environmental, and social behavior are improved along with our industrial technologies, that could change very quickly.

Few leaders have been trained in the theory and practice of decision making, and few know how advanced decision-support software could help them. We know the world is increasingly complex and that the most serious challenges are global in nature, yet we are unpracticed at improving and deploying Internet-based management tools and concepts. Formalized training in ethics and decision making for policy makers could result in a significant improvement in the quality of global decisions.

The heartening news is that global ethical standards are emerging from a variety of sources, such as the International Organization for Standardization (ISO), corporate ethics indexes, interreligious dialogues, UN treaties, the Olympic

Committee, the International Criminal Court, various NGOs, Internet blogs, and the international news media. Ethical decision making in a global context should be informed by an understanding of the key challenges facing our world, as well as of their interconnectedness. The establishment of the eight UN Millennium Development Goals was a giant step in this direction.

The next should be the creation of global transinstitutions for water, energy, AIDS, education, and so on. Current institutional structures are not getting the job done. In addition to the moral imperative and social benefits of addressing these goals and challenges, there is also great wealth to be made resolving these issues on behalf of grateful populations. However, making this a reality will require future-oriented politicians, which in turn will require a better educated public to elect more future-minded leaders globally.

Meeting the Future's Challenges

Although many people criticize globalization's potential cultural impacts, it is increasingly clear that cultural change is necessary to address global challenges. Simply put, the development of genuine democracy requires cultural change, as does preventing AIDS, promoting sustainable development, ending violence against women, ending ethnic violence, etc. The tools of globalization, such as the Internet and global trade, should be used to help cultures adapt in a way that preserves their unique contributions to humanity while improving the human condition. These tools can help policy makers, leaders, and educators who fight against hopeless despair, blind confidence, and ignorant indifference—attitudes that too often have blocked efforts to improve the prospects for humanity.

Future synergies among nanotechnology, biotechnology, information technology, and cognitive science could dramatically increase the availability of food, energy, and water.

Connecting people and information will increase collective intelligence and create value and efficiency while lowering costs. Yet a previous and troubling finding from the Millennium Project remains unresolved. It is increasingly clear that humanity has the resources to address global challenges, but how much wisdom, goodwill, and intelligence humanity will focus on these challenges is anyone's guess.

Just as it would be difficult for the human body to work if the neurons, muscles, bones, and so on were not properly connected, so, too, is it difficult for the world to work if people, ideas, resources, and challenges are not seen in a single context. The initial global infrastructure to manage globalization is being built through such mechanisms as the ISO, the World Trade Organization's rules of trade, and Internet protocols.

The moment-by-moment connectivity among ideas, people, resources, and challenges in order to create optimal solutions, however, is yet to be developed. A worldwide race to connect everything not yet connected is just beginning. Wise institutions and organizations will make great wealth by completing the links among systems by which civilizations function and flourish.

JEROME C. GLENN has been the executive director of the American Council for the United Nations University (AC/UNU) since 1988. E-mail: jglenn@igc.org. **THEODORE J. GORDON** has served as a space scientist in the Apollo program. He is the founder of The Futures Group and was a co-founder of the Institute for the Future. E-mail: Tedjgordon@att.net.

Glenn and Gordon have been codirectors of the Millennium Project of the AC/UNU since 1996. This article draws from *2005 State of the Future* (AC/UNU, 2005) which is available from the Futurist Bookshelf, www.wfs.org/bkshelf.htm. The Millennium Project's address is The Millennium Project, American Council for the United Nations University, 4421 Garrison St., N.W., Washington, D.C. 20016. Fax 202-686-5170; Web site www.stateofthefuture.org.

A User's Guide to the Century

JEFFREY D. SACHS

The "new world order" of the twenty-first century holds the promise of shared prosperity . . . and also the risk of global conflict. This is the paradox of our time. The scale of human society—in population, level of economic production and resource use, and global reach of production networks—gives rise to enormous hopes and equally momentous challenges. Old models of statecraft and economics won't suffice. Solutions to our generation's challenges will require an unprecedented degree of global cooperation, though the need for such cooperation is still poorly perceived and highly contested by political elites and intellectuals in the United States and elsewhere.

Our world is characterized by three dominant patterns: rapid technological diffusion, which creates strong tendencies toward technological and economic convergence among major regions of the world; extensive environmental threats resulting from the unprecedented scale of global economic activity and population; and vast current inequalities of income and power, both between and within countries, resulting from highly diverse patterns of demography, regional endowments of natural resources, and vulnerabilities to natural and societal disruptions. These characteristics hold the possibilities of rapid and equalizing economic growth, but also of regional and global instability and conflict.

The era of modern economic growth is two centuries old. For the first one hundred years, this was a strong *divergence* in economic growth, meaning a widening gap in production and income between the richest regions and the rest of the world. The dramatic divergence of per capita output, industrial production and living standards during the nineteenth century between the North Atlantic (that is, Western Europe and the United States) and the rest of the world was accentuated by several factors. The combination of first-mover industrialization, access to extensive coal deposits, early development of market-based institutions, military dominance resulting from vast industrial power, and then colonial dominance over Africa and Asia all contributed to a century of *economic divergence,* in which the North Atlantic greatly expanded its technological lead (and also military advantage) vis-à-vis the rest of the world. The apogee of "Western" relative dominance was roughly the year 1910. Until the start of World War I, this economic and technological dominance was nearly overpowering.

The period 1910–1950 marked a transition from global economic divergence to economic convergence. Most importantly, of course, was Europe's self-inflicted disaster of two world wars and an intervening Great Depression, which dramatically weakened Europe and proved to be the downfall of the continent's vast overseas empires. Below the surface, longer-term forces of convergence were also stirring. These deeper forces included the global spread of literacy, Western science, the modern technologies of transport and communications, and the political ideas of self-determination and economic development as core national objectives.

Since 1950, we have entered into an era of global convergence, in which much of the non-Western world is gradually catching up, technologically, economically, geopolitically and militarily. The North Atlantic is losing its uniquely dominant position in the world economy. The technological and economic catching-up, most notable of course in Asia, is facilitated by several factors—the spread of national sovereignty following European colonialism; vastly improved transport and communications technologies; the spread of infectious-disease control, mass literacy and public education; the dissemination of global scientific and engineering knowledge; and the broad adoption of a valid "catch-up model" of economic development based on technology imports within a mixed public-private system. The system was modeled heavily on the state-led market development of Japan, the only non-Western country to succeed in achieving modern industrialization during the nineteenth century. Japan's economic development following the Meiji Restoration in 1868 can indeed be viewed as the invention of "catch-up growth."

The modern age of convergence, begun with Japan's rapid rebuilding after World War II, was extended in the 1950s and 1960s by the rise of Korea, Taiwan, Hong Kong and Singapore, all built on an export-led growth model using U.S. and Japanese technologies and institutions. Convergent economic growth then spread through Southeast Asia (notably Indonesia, Malaysia and Thailand) in the 1970s and 1980s, again supported by Japanese and U.S. technologies, and Japanese aid and development concepts. The convergence patterns were greatly expanded with the initiation of rapid market-based growth in China after 1978 (which imitated strategies in East and Southeast Asia) and then India in the 1980s (and especially after market-based reforms initiated in 1991). In the early twenty-first century, both Brazil and Mexico are similarly experiencing rapid technological catch-up.

In economic terms, the share of global income in the North Atlantic is now declining quickly as the emerging economies of Asia, the Middle East and Latin America grow rapidly. This is, of course, especially true when output and income are measured in purchasing-power-adjusted terms, thereby adding weight to the share of the emerging economies. By 2050, Asia will be home to more than half of global production, up from around 20 percent as of 1970. In geopolitical terms, the unipolar world of the North Atlantic is over. China, India, Brazil and other regional powers now fundamentally constrain the actions of the United States and Western Europe. This shift to multipolarity in geopolitics is bound to accelerate in the coming decades.

Modern economic growth did not end humans' dependence on their physical environment, contrary to the false impressions sometimes given by modern urban life. Our food still comes from farms, not from supermarkets and bakeries. Our crops still demand land and water, not simply microwaves and gas grills. Our industrial prowess has been built mainly on fossil fuels (first coal, then oil and natural gas), not merely on cleverness and efficiency. Our food production demands enormous inputs of energy and water, not only high-yield seeds. The bottom line is that the growth of the world economy has meant a roughly commensurate growth in human impacts on the physical world, not an escape from such impacts. These anthropogenic impacts are now so significant, and indeed threatening to the sustainable well-being of humans and other species, that Nobel Laureate Paul Crutzen (a codiscoverer of the human-induced loss of stratospheric ozone) has termed our age the Anthropocene, meaning the geological epoch when human activity dominates or deranges the earth's major biogeophysical fluxes (including the carbon, nitrogen and water cycles, among others).

The world economy is now characterized by 6.7 billion people—roughly ten times more than in 1750—producing output at a rate of roughly $10,000 per person per year in purchasing-power-adjusted prices. The resulting $67 trillion annual output (in approximate terms, as precision here should not be pretended) is at least one hundredfold larger than at the start of the industrial era. The human extent of natural-resource use is unprecedented—indeed utterly unrecognizable—in historical perspective, and is now dangerous to long-term well-being. While the typical economist's lighthearted gloss is that Malthusian resource pessimism was utterly and fully debunked generations ago—overcome by human ingenuity and technical know-how—it is more correct to say that the unprecedented level of global human output has been achieved not by overcoming resource constraints, but by an unprecedented appropriation of the earth's natural resources.

In fact, the current rate of resource use, if technologies remain constant, is literally unsustainable. Current fossil-fuel use would lead to the imminent peak of oil and gas production within years or decades, and of conventional coal deposits within decades or a century or two. We would see dangerous human impacts on the global climate system, and hence regional climates in all parts of the world, through greenhouse-gas emissions. The appropriation of up to half of the earth's photosynthetic potential, at the cost of other species, would occur. There would be massive deforestation and land degradation as a result of the increasing spatial range and the intensification of farming and pasture use; massive appropriation of freshwater resources, through depletion of fossil aquifers, diversion of rivers, melting of glaciers, drainage of wetlands, destruction of mangroves and estuaries, and other processes. And, an introduction of invasive species, pests and pathogens through a variety of human-induced changes.

The mistaken belief that we've overcome "similar" resource constraints in the past is no proof that global society will do it again, or at least do it successfully without massive economic and social upheavals, especially in view of the fact that our earlier "solutions" were rarely based on resource-saving technologies. Indeed, most earlier "solutions" to resource constraints typically involved new ways to "mine" the natural environment, not to conserve it. This time around, human societies will have to shift from resource-using technologies to resource-saving technologies. Some of the needed technologies are already known but often not widely used, while others will still have to be developed, demonstrated and diffused on a global scale.

Human pressures on the earth's ecological systems are bound to increase markedly in the years ahead. The global economy has been growing between 3 and 5 percent per year, meaning the economy will take fourteen to twenty-three years to double. Thus, the intense environmental and resource pressures now occurring will increase markedly and in short order. The catch-up growth of the largest emerging markets—Brazil, China and India, with around 40 percent of the world's population—is based squarely on the adoption and diffusion of resource-intensive technologies, such as coal-fired power plants and standard internal-combustion-engine vehicles.

The age of convergence offers the realistic possibility of ending extreme poverty and narrowing the vast inequalities within and between countries. The catching-up of China and India, for example, is rapidly reducing the national poverty rates in both countries. Other regions will also experience rapid declines in poverty rates. Yet the actual record of poverty reduction and trends in inequality leave major gaps in success. There are many parts of the planet where the numbers, and sometimes even proportions, of people in extreme poverty are rising rather than falling. Even more generally, the gaps between the rich and poor within nations seem to be widening markedly in most parts of the world.

Significant regions of the world—including sub-Saharan Africa, Central Asia, and parts of the Andean and Central American highlands—have experienced increasing poverty during the past generation. These places left behind by global economic growth tend to display some common infirmities. For example: long distances from major global trade routes, landlocked populations, heavy burdens of tropical diseases, great vulnerabilities to natural hazards (such as earthquakes, tropical storms and the like), lack of nonbiomass energy resources, lack of low-cost access to irrigation, difficult topography (e.g., high elevations and steep slopes), widespread illiteracy and a rapid growth of population due to consistently high fertility rates.

These conditions tend to perpetuate extreme poverty, and often lead to a vicious circle in which poverty contributes to further environmental degradation, persistence of high fertility rates, and social conflicts and violence, which in turn perpetuate or intensify the extreme poverty. These vicious circles (or "poverty traps") can be broken, but to succeed often requires external financial and technological assistance. Assistance like building infrastructure raises productivity and thereby controls the interlocking problems of transport costs, disease, illiteracy, vulnerability to hazards and high fertility. Without the external assistance, a continuing downward spiral becomes much more likely. The adverse consequences can then include war, the spread of epidemic diseases, displaced populations and mass illegal migration. On top of this can be the spread of illicit activities (drug trafficking, smuggling, kidnapping and piracy) and continued serious environmental degradation with large-scale poaching, land degradation and rampant deforestation, to name a few.

The global forces of demographic change, economic convergence and global production systems are also apparently contributing to rising inequalities within societies. Technological advances favor educated workers and leave uneducated workers behind. The entry of China and India into the global trading and production system, similarly, has pushed down the relative wages of unskilled workers in all parts of the world. Geography has played a key role, favoring those regions and parts of countries which are most easily incorporated into global production systems and which are well endowed with energy, fertile land, water and climate conducive to food production. Rapid population growth in rural and poverty-stricken regions (sub-Saharan Africa) has dramatically lowered well-being in these places. In general, urban dwellers have done better than rural dwellers in the past twenty years in almost all parts of the world.

Even relatively homogenous societies are facing major challenges of social stability as a result of massive changes in demographic patterns and economic trends across ethnic, linguistic and religious communities. By 2050, roughly half of the U.S. population will be "white, non-Hispanic," down from around 80 percent as of 1950. This trend reflects both the differential fertility rates across different subpopulations as well as the continued rapid in-migration of Hispanics into the United States. Such large demographic changes can potentially create major fissures in society, especially when there have been long histories of intercommunal strife and suspicion.

The new world order is therefore crisis prone. The existence of rapidly emerging regional powers, including Brazil, China and India, can potentially give rise to conflicts with the United States and Europe.

The combination of rapid technological diffusion and therefore convergent economic growth, coupled with the natural-resource constraints of the Anthropocene, could trigger regional-scale or global-scale tensions and conflicts. China's rapid economic growth could turn into a strenuous, even hot, competition with the United States over increasingly scarce hydrocarbons in the Middle East, Africa and Central Asia. Conflicts over water flow in major and already-contested watersheds (among India, Bangladesh and Pakistan; China and Southeast Asia; Turkey, Israel, Iraq and Jordan; the countries of the Nile basin; and many others) could erupt into regional conflicts. Disagreements over management of the global commons—including ocean fisheries, greenhouse gases, the Arctic's newly accessible resources, species extinctions and much more—could also be grounds for conflict.

The continuation of extreme poverty, and the adverse spillovers from laggard regions, could trigger mass violence. Local conflicts can draw in major powers, which then threaten expanded wars—as in Afghanistan, Somalia and Sudan. When poverty is combined with rapid population growth and major environmental shocks (such as prolonged droughts in the Sahel and the Horn of Africa) there is a distinct likelihood of mass population movements, such as large-scale illegal migrations of populations escaping hunger and destitution. Such movements in the past have contributed to local violence, as in South Africa of late, and even to war, as in Darfur.

These intersecting challenges of our crowded world, multipolarity, unprecedented demographic and environmental stresses, and the growing inequalities both within and between countries, can trigger spirals of conflict and instability—disease, migration, state failure and more—and yet are generally overlooked by the broad public and even by many, if not most, foreign-policy analysts. The instability of the Horn of Africa, the Middle East and Central Asia has been viewed wrongly by many in the U.S. public and foreign-policy community mainly as the battleground over Islamic extremism and fundamentalism, with little reflection on the fact that the extremism and fundamentalism is often secondary to illiteracy, youth unemployment, poverty, indignation, economic hopelessness and hunger, rather than religion per se. The swath of "Islamic" extremist violence across the African Sahel, Horn of Africa, and into the Middle East and Central Asia lies in the world's major dryland region, characterized by massive demographic, environmental and economic crises.

The security institutions—such as ministries of defense—of the major powers are trained to see these crises through a military lens, and to look for military responses, rather than see the underlying demographic, environmental and economic drivers—and the corresponding developmental options to address them. Genuine global security in the next quarter century will depend on the ability of governments to understand the true interconnected nature of these crises, and to master the scientific and technological knowledge needed to find solutions.

In the United States, I propose a new Department for International Sustainable Development, which would oversee U.S. foreign assistance and initiatives related to sustainable development in low-income countries, including water, food production, disease control and climate-change adaptation and mitigation.

I propose five major guideposts for a more-functional foreign policy in the coming years. First, we will need, on a global scale, to develop and diffuse new sustainable technologies so that the global economy can continue to support broad-based economic growth. If we remain stuck with our current technologies, the world will face a zero-sum struggle for increasingly scarce resources across competing regions. The new sustainable technologies will not arise from market forces alone. All major technological advances, such as the introduction of large-scale solar or nuclear power, will require massive public-sector investments (in basic science, demonstration projects, diffusion of proven technologies and regulatory framework) alongside the R&D of private markets. These public investments will be global-scale, internationally cooperative efforts.

Free-market ideologues who are convinced that technologies emerge from market forces alone should think again. They might compare the successful government-led promotion of nuclear power in France with the failure of the private-sector-led nuclear-power industry in the United States, which failed because of a collapse in U.S. public confidence in the safety of the technology. Similarly, they can examine the highly successful public-private partnerships linking the public-sector National Institutes of Health with the private-sector pharmaceutical industry, or the public-sector investments that underpinned the start-up of computer and Internet technologies.

Second, we will need to address the still-rapid rise of the world's population, heavily centered in the world's poorest countries. Sub-Saharan Africa is on a trajectory that will expand its population from around 800 million to 1.8 billion by 2050, according to the medium-fertility forecast of the United Nations Population Division. Yet that extent of population increase, an added 1 billion people, resulting from Africa's very high fertility rates, would actually be a grave threat to Africa's economy, political stability and environment, and would inevitably spill over adversely into the rest of the world. Rapid and voluntary fertility reduction in Africa is possible, if girls can be encouraged to stay in school through the secondary level; if family planning and contraception are made widely available; if child mortality is reduced (giving confidence to parents to reduce fertility rates); and if women are economically empowered.

Third, the world will need to address critical failings in the management of the global commons, most importantly, by restricting greenhouse-gas emissions, protecting the oceans and biodiversity, and managing transnational water resources sustainably at the regional level. Of course several global treaties have committed the world's nations to do just this, but these treaties have yet to be implemented. Three treaties of overriding importance are the UN Framework Convention on Climate Change, the UN Convention on Biological Diversity and the UN Convention to Combat Desertification. If these treaties are honored, the global commons can be sustainably managed.

Fourth, we will need to take seriously the risks of impoverished "failed states," to themselves, to their neighborhoods and to the world. The poorest and least-stable countries are rife with risks to peace and avoidable human tragedies like the 10 million children each year who die tragically and unnecessarily before their fifth birthday, largely the result of extreme poverty. Darfur, the Horn of Africa, Yemen, Afghanistan, Pakistan, Sri Lanka and elsewhere are places trapped in vicious cycles of extreme violence and poverty. These poverty-conflict traps can be broken, most importantly if the donors of the G-8, the oil-rich states in the Middle East, and the new donors in Latin America and Asia will pool their efforts to ensure the success of the Millennium Development Goals in today's impoverished and fragile regions.

Fifth, and finally, we require a new analytical framework for addressing our generation's challenges, and a new governmental machinery to apply that framework. Traditional problems of statecraft—the balance of power, alliances, arms control and credible deterrence—certainly will continue to play a role, but we need to move beyond these traditional concepts to face the challenges of sustainable development ahead. Will our era be a time of wondrous advances, based on our unprecedented scientific and technological know-how, or will we succumb to a nightmare of spreading violence and conflict? We face world-shaping choices. Our global challenges are unique to our generation, in scale and character. Vision, leadership and global cooperation will be our most important resources for ensuring our future well-being.

JEFFREY D. SACHS is the director of the Earth Institute at Columbia University and author of *Common Wealth: Economics for a Crowded Planet* (Penguin, 2008).

The Rise of the Rest

It's true China is booming, Russia is growing more assertive, terrorism is a threat. But if America is losing the ability to dictate to this new world, it has not lost the ability to lead.

Fareed Zakaria

Americans are glum at the moment. No, I mean really glum. In April, a new poll revealed that 81 percent of the American people believe that the country is on the "wrong track." In the 25 years that pollsters have asked this question, last month's response was by far the most negative. Other polls, asking similar questions, found levels of gloom that were even more alarming, often at 30- and 40-year highs. There are reasons to be pessimistic—a financial panic and looming recession, a seemingly endless war in Iraq, and the ongoing threat of terrorism. But the facts on the ground—unemployment numbers, foreclosure rates, deaths from terror attacks—are simply not dire enough to explain the present atmosphere of malaise.

American anxiety springs from something much deeper, a sense that large and disruptive forces are coursing through the world. In almost every industry, in every aspect of life, it feels like the patterns of the past are being scrambled. "Whirl is king, having driven out Zeus," wrote Aristophanes 2,400 years ago. And—for the first time in living memory—the United States does not seem to be leading the charge. Americans see that a new world is coming into being, but fear it is one being shaped in distant lands and by foreign people.

Look around. The world's tallest building is in Taipei, and will soon be in Dubai. Its largest publicly traded company is in Beijing. Its biggest refinery is being constructed in India. Its largest passenger airplane is built in Europe. The largest investment fund on the planet is in Abu Dhabi; the biggest movie industry is Bollywood, not Hollywood. Once quintessentially American icons have been usurped by the natives. The largest Ferris wheel is in Singapore. The largest casino is in Macao, which overtook Las Vegas in gambling revenues last year. America no longer dominates even its favorite sport, shopping. The Mall of America in Minnesota once boasted that it was the largest shopping mall in the world. Today it wouldn't make the top ten. In the most recent rankings, only two of the world's ten richest people are American. These lists are arbitrary and a bit silly, but consider that only ten years ago, the United States would have serenely topped almost every one of these categories.

These factoids reflect a seismic shift in power and attitudes. It is one that I sense when I travel around the world. In America,

we are still debating the nature and extent of anti-Americanism. One side says that the problem is real and worrying and that we must woo the world back. The other says this is the inevitable price of power and that many of these countries are envious—and vaguely French—so we can safely ignore their griping. But while we argue over why they hate us, "they" have moved on, and are now far more interested in other, more dynamic parts of the globe. The world has shifted from anti-Americanism to *post*-Americanism.

I. The End of Pax Americana

During the 1980s, when I would visit India—where I grew up—most Indians were fascinated by the United States. Their interest, I have to confess, was not in the important power players in Washington or the great intellectuals in Cambridge.

People would often ask me about . . . Donald Trump. He was the very symbol of the United States—brassy, rich, and modern. He symbolized the feeling that if you wanted to find the biggest and largest anything, you had to look to America. Today, outside of entertainment figures, there is no comparable interest in American personalities. If you wonder why, read India's newspapers or watch its television. There are dozens of Indian businessmen who are now wealthier than the Donald. Indians are obsessed by their own vulgar real estate billionaires. And that newfound interest in *their own* story is being replicated across much of the world.

How much? Well, consider this fact. In 2006 and 2007, 124 countries grew their economies at over 4 percent a year. That includes more than 30 countries in Africa. Over the last two decades, lands outside the industrialized West have been growing at rates that were once unthinkable. While there have been booms and busts, the overall trend has been unambiguously upward. Antoine van Agtmael, the fund manager who coined the term "emerging markets," has identified the 25 companies most likely to be the world's next great multinationals. His list includes four companies each from Brazil, Mexico, South Korea, and Taiwan; three from India, two from China, and one each from Argentina, Chile, Malaysia, and South Africa. This is something much broader than the much-ballyhooed rise of China or even Asia. It is the rise of the rest—the rest of the world.

We are living through the third great power shift in modern history. The first was the rise of the Western world, around the 15th century. It produced the world as we know it now—science and technology, commerce and capitalism, the industrial and agricultural revolutions. It also led to the prolonged political dominance of the nations of the Western world. The second shift, which took place in the closing years of the 19th century, was the rise of the United States. Once it industrialized, it soon became the most powerful nation in the world, stronger than any likely combination of other nations. For the last 20 years, America's superpower status in every realm has been largely unchallenged—something that's never happened before in history, at least since the Roman Empire dominated the known world 2,000 years ago. During this Pax Americana, the global economy has accelerated dramatically. And that expansion is the driver behind the third great power shift of the modern age—the rise of the rest.

At the military and political level, we still live in a unipolar world. But along every other dimension—industrial, financial, social, cultural—the distribution of power is shifting, moving away from American dominance. In terms of war and peace, economics and business, ideas and art, this will produce a landscape that is quite different from the one we have lived in until now—one defined and directed from many places and by many peoples.

The post-American world is naturally an unsettling prospect for Americans, but it should not be. This will not be a world defined by the decline of America but rather the rise of everyone else. It is the result of a series of positive trends that have been progressing over the last 20 years, trends that have created an international climate of unprecedented peace and prosperity.

I know. That's not the world that people perceive. We are told that we live in dark, dangerous times. Terrorism, rogue states, nuclear proliferation, financial panics, recession, outsourcing, and illegal immigrants all loom large in the national discourse. Al Qaeda, Iran, North Korea, China, Russia are all threats in some way or another. But just how violent is today's world, really?

A team of scholars at the University of Maryland has been tracking deaths caused by organized violence. Their data show that wars of all kinds have been declining since the mid-1980s and that we are now at the lowest levels of global violence since the 1950s. Deaths from terrorism are reported to have risen in recent years. But on closer examination, 80 percent of those casualties come from Afghanistan and Iraq, which are really war zones with ongoing insurgencies—and the overall numbers remain small. Looking at the evidence, Harvard's polymath professor Steven Pinker has ventured to speculate that we are probably living "in the most peaceful time of our species' existence."

Why does it not feel that way? Why do we think we live in scary times? Part of the problem is that as violence has been ebbing, information has been exploding. The last 20 years have produced an information revolution that brings us news and, most crucially, images from around the world all the time. The immediacy of the images and the intensity of the 24-hour news cycle combine to produce constant hype. Every weather disturbance is the "storm of the decade." Every bomb that explodes is BREAKING NEWS. Because the information revolution is so new, we—reporters, writers, readers, viewers—are all just now figuring out how to put everything in context.

We didn't watch daily footage of the two million people who died in Indochina in the 1970s, or the million who perished in the sands of the Iran-Iraq war ten years later. We saw little of the civil war in the Congo in the 1990s, where millions died. But today any bomb that goes off, any rocket that is fired, any death that results, is documented by someone, somewhere and ricochets instantly across the world. Add to this terrorist attacks, which are random and brutal. "That could have been me," you think. Actually, your chances of being killed in a terrorist attack are tiny—for an American, smaller than drowning in your bathtub. But it doesn't feel like that.

The threats we face are real. Islamic jihadists are a nasty bunch—they do want to attack civilians everywhere. But it is increasingly clear that militants and suicide bombers make up a tiny portion of the world's 1.3 billion Muslims. They can do real damage, especially if they get their hands on nuclear weapons. But the combined efforts of the world's governments have effectively put them on the run and continue to track them and their money. Jihad persists, but the jihadists have had to scatter, work in small local cells, and use simple and undetectable weapons. They have not been able to hit big, symbolic targets, especially ones involving Americans. So they blow up bombs in cafés, marketplaces, and subway stations. The problem is that in doing so, they kill locals and alienate ordinary Muslims. Look at the polls. Support for violence of any kind has dropped dramatically over the last five years in all Muslim countries.

Militant groups have reconstituted in certain areas where they exploit a particular local issue or have support from a local ethnic group or sect, most worryingly in Pakistan and Afghanistan where Islamic radicalism has become associated with Pashtun identity politics. But as a result, these groups are becoming more local and less global. Al Qaeda in Iraq, for example, has turned into a group that is more anti-Shiite than anti-American. The bottom line is this: since 9/11, Al Qaeda Central, the gang run by Osama bin Laden, has not been able to launch a single major terror attack in the West or any Arab country—its original targets. They used to do terrorism, now they make videotapes. Of course one day they will get lucky again, but that they have been stymied for almost seven years points out that in this battle between governments and terror groups, the former need not despair.

Some point to the dangers posed by countries like Iran. These rogue states present real problems, but look at them in context. The American economy is 68 times the size of Iran's. Its military budget is 110 times that of the mullahs. Were Iran to attain a nuclear capacity, it would complicate the geopolitics of the Middle East. But none of the problems we face compare with the dangers posed by a rising Germany in the first half of the 20th century or an expansionist Soviet Union in the second half. Those were great global powers bent on world domination.

If this is 1938, as some neoconservatives tell us, then Iran is Romania, not Germany.

Others paint a dark picture of a world in which dictators are on the march. China and Russia and assorted other oil potentates are surging. We must draw the battle lines now, they warn, and engage in a great Manichean struggle that will define the next century. Some of John McCain's rhetoric has suggested that he adheres to this dire, dyspeptic view. But before we all sign on for a new Cold War, let's take a deep breath and gain some perspective. Today's rising great powers are relatively benign by historical measure. In the past, when countries grew rich they've wanted to become great military powers, overturn the existing order, and create their own empires or spheres of influence. But since the rise of Japan and Germany in the 1960s and 1970s, none have done this, choosing instead to get rich within the existing international order. China and India are clearly moving in this direction. Even Russia, the most aggressive and revanchist great power today, has done little that compares with past aggressors. The fact that for the first time in history, the United States can contest Russian influence in Ukraine—a country 4,800 miles away from Washington that Russia has dominated or ruled for 350 years—tells us something about the balance of power between the West and Russia.

Compare Russia and China with where they were 35 years ago. At the time both (particularly Russia) were great power threats, actively conspiring against the United States, arming guerrilla movement across the globe, funding insurgencies and civil wars, blocking every American plan in the United Nations. Now they are more integrated into the global economy and society than at any point in at least 100 years. They occupy an uncomfortable gray zone, neither friends nor foes, cooperating with the United States and the West on some issues, obstructing others. But how large is their potential for trouble? Russia's military spending is $35 billion, or 1/20th of the Pentagon's. China has about 20 nuclear missiles that can reach the United States. We have 830 missiles, most with multiple warheads, that can reach China. Who should be worried about whom? Other rising autocracies like Saudi Arabia and the Gulf states are close U.S. allies that shelter under America's military protection, buy its weapons, invest in its companies, and follow many of its diktats. With Iran's ambitions growing in the region, these countries are likely to become even closer allies, unless America gratuitously alienates them.

II. The Good News

In July 2006, I spoke with a senior member of the Israeli government, a few days after Israel's war with Hezbollah had ended. He was genuinely worried about his country's physical security. Hezbollah's rockets had reached farther into Israel than people had believed possible. The military response had clearly been ineffectual: Hezbollah launched as many rockets on the last day of the war as on the first. Then I asked him about the economy— the area in which he worked. His response was striking. "That's puzzled all of us," he said. "The stock market was higher on the last day of the war than on the first! The same with the shekel." The government was spooked, but the market wasn't.

Or consider the Iraq War, which has produced deep, lasting chaos and dysfunction in that country. Over two million refugees have crowded into neighboring lands. That would seem to be the kind of political crisis guaranteed to spill over. But as I've traveled in the Middle East over the last few years, I've been struck by how little Iraq's troubles have destabilized the region. Everywhere you go, people angrily denounce American foreign policy. But most Middle Eastern countries are booming. Iraq's neighbors—Turkey, Jordan, and Saudi Arabia—are enjoying unprecedented prosperity. The Gulf states are busy modernizing their economies and societies, asking the Louvre, New York University, and Cornell Medical School to set up remote branches in the desert. There's little evidence of chaos, instability, and rampant Islamic fundamentalism.

The underlying reality across the globe is of enormous vitality. For the first time ever, most countries around the world are practicing sensible economics. Consider inflation. Over the past 20 years hyperinflation, a problem that used to bedevil large swaths of the world from Turkey to Brazil to Indonesia, has largely vanished, tamed by successful fiscal and monetary policies. The results are clear and stunning. The share of people living on $1 a day has plummeted from 40 percent in 1981 to 18 percent in 2004 and is estimated to drop to 12 percent by 2015. Poverty is falling in countries that house 80 percent of the world's population. There remains real poverty in the world—most worryingly in 50 basket-case countries that contain 1 billion people—but the overall trend has never been more encouraging. The global economy has more than doubled in size over the last 15 years and is now approaching $54 trillion! Global trade has grown by 133 percent in the same period. The expansion of the global economic pie has been so large, with so many countries participating, that it has become the dominating force of the current era. Wars, terrorism, and civil strife cause disruptions temporarily but eventually they are overwhelmed by the waves of globalization. These circumstances may not last, but it is worth understanding what the world has looked like for the past few decades.

III. A New Nationalism

Of course, global growth is also responsible for some of the biggest problems in the world right now. It has produced tons of money—what businesspeople call liquidity—that moves around the world. The combination of low inflation and lots of cash has meant low interest rates, which in turn have made people act greedily and/or stupidly. So we have witnessed over the last two decades a series of bubbles—in East Asian countries, technology stocks, housing, subprime mortgages, and emerging market equities. Growth also explains one of the signature events of our times—soaring commodity prices. $100 oil is just the tip of the barrel. Almost all commodities are at 200-year highs. Food, only a few decades ago in danger of price collapse, is now in the midst of a scary rise. None of this is due to dramatic fall-offs in supply. It is demand, growing global demand, that is fueling these prices. The effect of more and more people eating, drinking, washing, driving, and consuming will have seismic effects on the global system. These may be high-quality problems, but they are deep problems nonetheless.

The most immediate effect of global growth is the appearance of new economic powerhouses on the scene. It is an accident of history that for the last several centuries, the richest countries in the world have all been very small in terms of population. Denmark has 5.5 million people, the Netherlands has 16.6 million. The United States is the biggest of the bunch and has dominated the advanced industrial world. But the real giants—China, India, Brazil—have been sleeping, unable or unwilling to join the world of functioning economies. Now they are on the move and naturally, given their size, they will have a large footprint on the map of the future. Even if people in these countries remain relatively poor, as nations their total wealth will be massive. Or to put it another way, any number, no matter how small, when multiplied by 2.5 billion becomes a very big number. (2.5 billion is the population of China plus India.)

The rise of China and India is really just the most obvious manifestation of a rising world. In dozens of big countries, one can see the same set of forces at work—a growing economy, a resurgent society, a vibrant culture, and a rising sense of national pride. That pride can morph into something uglier. For me, this was vividly illustrated a few years ago when I was chatting with a young Chinese executive in an Internet café in Shanghai. He wore Western clothes, spoke fluent English, and was immersed in global pop culture. He was a product of globalization and spoke its language of bridge building and cosmopolitan values. At least, he did so until we began talking about Taiwan, Japan, and even the United States. (We did not discuss Tibet, but I'm sure had we done so, I could have added it to this list.) His responses were filled with passion, bellicosity, and intolerance. I felt as if I were in Germany in 1910, speaking to a young German professional, who would have been equally modern and yet also a staunch nationalist.

As economic fortunes rise, so inevitably does nationalism. Imagine that your country has been poor and marginal for centuries. Finally, things turn around and it becomes a symbol of economic progress and success. You would be proud, and anxious that your people win recognition and respect throughout the world.

In many countries such nationalism arises from a pent-up frustration over having to accept an entirely Western, or American, narrative of world history—one in which they are miscast or remain bit players. Russians have long chafed over the manner in which Western countries remember World War II. The American narrative is one in which the United States and Britain heroically defeat the forces of fascism. The Normandy landings are the climactic highpoint of the war—the beginning of the end. The Russians point out, however, that in fact the entire Western front was a sideshow. Three quarters of all German forces were engaged on the Eastern front fighting Russian troops, and Germany suffered 70 percent of its casualties there. The Eastern front involved more land combat than all other theaters of World War II put together.

Such divergent national perspectives always existed. But today, thanks to the information revolution, they are amplified, echoed, and disseminated. Where once there were only the narratives laid out by *The New York Times, Time, Newsweek,* the BBC, and CNN, there are now dozens of indigenous networks and channels—from Al Jazeera to New Delhi's NDTV to Latin America's Telesur. The result is that the "rest" are now dissecting the assumptions and narratives of the West and providing alternative views. A young Chinese diplomat told me in 2006, "When you tell us that we support a dictatorship in Sudan to have access to its oil, what I want to say is, 'And how is that different from your support of a medieval monarchy in Saudi Arabia?' We see the hypocrisy, we just don't say anything—yet."

The fact that newly rising nations are more strongly asserting their ideas and interests is inevitable in a post-American world. This raises a conundrum—how to get a world of many actors to work together. The traditional mechanisms of international cooperation are fraying. The U.N. Security Council has as its permanent members the victors of a war that ended more than 60 years ago. The G8 does not include China, India or Brazil—the three fastest-growing large economies in the world—and yet claims to represent the movers and shakers of the world economy. By tradition, the IMF is always headed by a European and the World Bank by an American. This "tradition," like the segregated customs of an old country club, might be charming to an insider. But to the majority who live outside the West, it seems bigoted. Our challenge is this: Whether the problem is a trade dispute or a human rights tragedy like Darfur or climate change, the only solutions that will work are those involving many nations. But arriving at solutions when more countries and more non-governmental players are feeling empowered will be harder than ever.

IV. The Next American Century

Many look at the vitality of this emerging world and conclude that the United States has had its day. "Globalization is striking back," Gabor Steingart, an editor at Germany's leading news magazine, *Der Spiegel,* writes in a best-selling book. As others prosper, he argues, the United States has lost key industries, its people have stopped saving money, and its government has become increasingly indebted to Asian central banks. The current financial crisis has only given greater force to such fears.

But take a step back. Over the last 20 years, globalization has been gaining depth and breadth. America has benefited massively from these trends. It has enjoyed unusually robust growth, low unemployment and inflation, and received hundreds of billions of dollars in investment. These are not signs of economic collapse. Its companies have entered new countries and industries with great success, using global supply chains and technology to stay in the vanguard of efficiency. U.S. exports and manufacturing have actually held their ground and services have boomed.

The United States is currently ranked as the globe's most competitive economy by the World Economic Forum. It remains dominant in many industries of the future like nanotechnology, biotechnology, and dozens of smaller high-tech fields. Its universities are the finest in the world, making up 8 of the top ten and 37 of the top fifty, according to a prominent ranking produced by Shanghai Jiao Tong University. A few years ago the National Science Foundation put out a scary and much-discussed statistic. In 2004, the group said, 950,000 engineers graduated from China and India, while only 70,000 graduated from the

United States. But those numbers are wildly off the mark. If you exclude the car mechanics and repairmen—who are all counted as engineers in Chinese and Indian statistics—the numbers look quite different. Per capita, it turns out, the United States trains more engineers than either of the Asian giants.

But America's hidden secret is that most of these engineers are immigrants. Foreign students and immigrants account for almost 50 percent of all science researchers in the country. In 2006 they received 40 percent of all PhDs. By 2010, 75 percent of all science PhDs in this country will be awarded to foreign students. When these graduates settle in the country, they create economic opportunity. Half of all Silicon Valley start-ups have one founder who is an immigrant or first generation American. The potential for a new burst of American productivity depends not on our education system or R&D spending, but on our immigration policies. If these people are allowed and encouraged to stay, then innovation will happen here. If they leave, they'll take it with them.

More broadly, this is America's great—and potentially insurmountable—strength. It remains the most open, flexible society in the world, able to absorb other people, cultures, ideas, goods, and services. The country thrives on the hunger and energy of poor immigrants. Faced with the new technologies of foreign companies, or growing markets overseas, it adapts and adjusts. When you compare this dynamism with the closed and hierarchical nations that were once superpowers, you sense that the United States is different and may not fall into the trap of becoming rich, and fat, and lazy.

American society can adapt to this new world. But can the American government? Washington has gotten used to a world in which all roads led to its doorstep. America has rarely had to worry about benchmarking to the rest of the world—it was always so far ahead. But the natives have gotten good at capitalism and the gap is narrowing. Look at the rise of London. It's now the world's leading financial center—less because of things that the United States did badly than those London did well, like improving regulation and becoming friendlier to foreign capital. Or take the U.S. health care system, which has become a huge liability for American companies. U.S. carmakers now employ more people in Ontario, Canada, than Michigan because in Canada their health care costs are lower. Twenty years ago, the United States had the lowest corporate taxes in the world. Today they are the second-highest. It's not that ours went up. Those of others went down.

American parochialism is particularly evident in foreign policy. Economically, as other countries grow, for the most part

the pie expands and everyone wins. But geopolitics is a struggle for influence: as other nations become more active internationally, they will seek greater freedom of action. This necessarily means that America's unimpeded influence will decline. But if the world that's being created has more power centers, nearly all are invested in order, stability and progress. Rather than narrowly obsessing about our own short-term interests and interest groups, our chief priority should be to bring these rising forces into the global system, to integrate them so that they in turn broaden and deepen global economic, political, and cultural ties. If China, India, Russia, Brazil all feel that they have a stake in the existing global order, there will be less danger of war, depression, panics, and breakdowns. There will be lots of problems, crisis, and tensions, but they will occur against a backdrop of systemic stability. This benefits them but also us. It's the ultimate win-win.

To bring others into this world, the United States needs to make its own commitment to the system clear. So far, America has been able to have it both ways. It is the global rule-maker but doesn't always play by the rules. And forget about standards created by others. Only three countries in the world don't use the metric system—Liberia, Myanmar, and the United States. For America to continue to lead the world, we will have to first join it.

Americans—particularly the American government—have not really understood the rise of the rest. This is one of the most thrilling stories in history. Billions of people are escaping from abject poverty. The world will be enriched and ennobled as they become consumers, producers, inventors, thinkers, dreamers, and doers. This is all happening because of American ideas and actions. For 60 years, the United States has pushed countries to open their markets, free up their politics, and embrace trade and technology. American diplomats, businessmen, and intellectuals have urged people in distant lands to be unafraid of change, to join the advanced world, to learn the secrets of our success. Yet just as they are beginning to do so, we are losing faith in such ideas. We have become suspicious of trade, openness, immigration, and investment because now it's not Americans going abroad but foreigners coming to America. Just as the world is opening up, we are closing down.

Generations from now, when historians write about these times, they might note that by the turn of the 21st century, the United States had succeeded in its great, historical mission—globalizing the world. We don't want them to write that along the way, we forgot to globalize ourselves.

Test-Your-Knowledge Form

We encourage you to photocopy and use this page as a tool to assess how the articles in *Annual Editions* expand on the information in your textbook. By reflecting on the articles you will gain enhanced text information. You can also access this useful form on a product's book support website at *http://www.mhhe.com/cls*.

NAME: DATE:

_____

TITLE AND NUMBER OF ARTICLE:

_____

BRIEFLY STATE THE MAIN IDEA OF THIS ARTICLE:

_____

LIST THREE IMPORTANT FACTS THAT THE AUTHOR USES TO SUPPORT THE MAIN IDEA:

_____

WHAT INFORMATION OR IDEAS DISCUSSED IN THIS ARTICLE ARE ALSO DISCUSSED IN YOUR TEXTBOOK OR OTHER READINGS THAT YOU HAVE DONE? LIST THE TEXTBOOK CHAPTERS AND PAGE NUMBERS:

_____

LIST ANY EXAMPLES OF BIAS OR FAULTY REASONING THAT YOU FOUND IN THE ARTICLE:

_____

LIST ANY NEW TERMS/CONCEPTS THAT WERE DISCUSSED IN THE ARTICLE, AND WRITE A SHORT DEFINITION:

We Want Your Advice

ANNUAL EDITIONS revisions depend on two major opinion sources: one is our Advisory Board, listed in the front of this volume, which works with us in scanning the thousands of articles published in the public press each year; the other is you—the person actually using the book. Please help us and the users of the next edition by completing the prepaid article rating form on this page and returning it to us. Thank you for your help!

ANNUAL EDITIONS: Social Problems 10/11

ARTICLE RATING FORM

Here is an opportunity for you to have direct input into the next revision of this volume.
We would like you to rate each of the articles listed below, using the following scale:

1. **Excellent: should definitely be retained**
2. **Above average: should probably be retained**
3. **Below average: should probably be deleted**
4. **Poor: should definitely be deleted**

Your ratings will play a vital part in the next revision.
Please mail this prepaid form to us as soon as possible.
Thanks for your help!

RATING	ARTICLE	RATING	ARTICLE
	1. Social Problems: Definitions, Theories, and Analysis		28. Good Parents, Bad Results
	2. The Fragmentation of Social Life: Some Critical Societal Concerns for the New Millennium		29. Overworked, Time Poor, and Abandoned by Uncle Sam: Why Don't American Parents Protest?
	3. Spent		30. Peer Marriage
	4. Who Rules America?: Power, Politics, and Social Change		31. Against School: How Public Education Cripples Our Kids, and Why
	5. Inside the Hidden World of Earmarks		32. Can the Center Find a Solution That Will Hold?: The High School Experience: Proposals for Improvement
	6. Foresight for Government		
	7. A Smarter Planet		
	8. Reversal of Fortune		33. Fixing Hospitals
	9. Born to Buy: Interview with Juliet Schor		34. The Medical Mafia
	10. Why Aren't U.S. Cities Burning?		35. Fighting Crime: An Economist's View
	11. Who We Are Now		36. The Aggregate Burden of Crime
	12. The Invisible Ones		37. The Globalization of Crime
	13. How Stratification Works: The American Stratification System		38. Causes and Consequences of Wrongful Convictions
	14. Goodbye, Horatio Alger: Moving up Economically Is Now Impossible for Many, If Not Most, Americans		39. Reforming Juvenile Justice
			40. America Incarcerated: Crime, Punishment, and the Question of Race
	15. The Myth of the "Culture of Poverty"		41. Defeating Terrorism: Is It Possible? Is It Probable?
	16. Can Extreme Poverty Be Eliminated?		42. Nightmare in Manhattan
	17. A Work in Progress		43. Enough Already
	18. Brave New Welfare		44. The World's New Numbers
	19. Inequalities That Endure?: Racial Ideology, American Politics, and the Peculiar Role of the Social Sciences		45. Plan B 3.0: Mobilizing to Save Civilization
			46. The Science of Climate Change
	20. Why We Hate		47. Who's Afraid of Human Enhancement?: A Reason Debate on the Promise, Perils, and Ethics of Human Biotechnology
	21. American Dreamers		
	22. Great Expectations		
	23. Human Rights, Sex Trafficking, and Prostitution		48. The Secret Nuclear War
	24. Answers to Questions about Marriage Equality		49. Update on the State of the Future
	25. (Rethinking) Gender		50. A User's Guide to the Century
	26. The Frayed Knot		51. The Rise of the Rest
	27. The Opt-Out Myth		

**NO POSTAGE
NECESSARY
IF MAILED
IN THE
UNITED STATES**

BUSINESS REPLY MAIL
FIRST CLASS MAIL PERMIT NO. 551 DUBUQUE IA

POSTAGE WILL BE PAID BY ADDRESSEE

McGraw-Hill Contemporary Learning Series
501 BELL STREET
DUBUQUE, IA 52001

ABOUT YOU

Name   Date

Are you a teacher? ❑ A student? ❑
Your school's name

Department

Address   City   State   Zip

School telephone #

YOUR COMMENTS ARE IMPORTANT TO US!

Please fill in the following information:
For which course did you use this book?

Did you use a text with this ANNUAL EDITION? ❑ yes ❑ no
What was the title of the text?

What are your general reactions to the Annual Editions concept?

Have you read any pertinent articles recently that you think should be included in the next edition? Explain.

Are there any articles that you feel should be replaced in the next edition? Why?

Are there any World Wide Websites that you feel should be included in the next edition? Please annotate.

May we contact you for editorial input? ❑ yes ❑ no
May we quote your comments? ❑ yes ❑ no